Ninth
Edition

CONTEMPORARY LOGISTICS

Paul R. Murphy, Jr.
John Carroll University

Donald F. Wood
San Francisco State University

PEARSON

Prentice
Hall

UPPER SADDLE RIVER, NEW JERSEY 07458

Library of Congress Cataloging-in-Publication Data

Murphy, Paul Regis.
    Contemporary logistics / Paul R. Murphy, Donald F. Wood. — 9th ed.
        p. cm.
Includes index.
    ISBN-13: 978-0-13-156207-3
    ISBN-10: 0-13-156207-X
    1. Physical distribution of goods. 2. Business logistics. I. Wood, Donald F., 1935-
II. Title.
    HF5415.6.J6 2008
    658.5—dc22   2007018606

Editor-in-Chief: David Parker
Product Development Manager: Ashley Santora
Project Manager, Editorial: Keri Molinari
Editorial Assistant: Christine Ietto
Marketing Manager: Jodi Bassett
Marketing Assistant: Ian Gold
Project Manager, Production: Renata Butera
Permissions Project Manager: Charles Morris
Senior Operations Supervisor: Arnold Vila
Operations Specialist: Michelle Klein
Creative Director Central Design: Jayne Conte
Cover Design: Bruce Kenselaar
Cover Illustration/Photo: Getty Images, Inc.
Composition: Pine Tree Composition, Inc.
Full-Service Project Management: John Shannon
Printer/Binder: Courier Westford
Typeface: 10/12 Times Ten Roman

Credits and acknowledgments borrowed from other sources and reproduced, with permission, in this textbook appear on appropriate page within the text.

Pearson Education Ltd.
Pearson Education Singapore, Pte. Ltd
Pearson Education, Canada, Ltd
Pearson Education–Japan

Pearson Education Australia PTY, Limited
Pearson Education North Asia Ltd
Pearson Educación de Mexico, S.A. de C.V.
Pearson Education Malaysia, Pte. Ltd

10 9 8 7 6 5 4 3 2 1
ISBN 0-13-156207-X
ISBN 978-0-13-156207-3

Contents

CHAPTER 2   THE SUPPLY CHAIN MANAGEMENT CONCEPT   32

CHAPTER 3   LOGISTICS AND INFORMATION TECHNOLOGY   57

CONTEMPORARY LOGISTICS

CHAPTER 14   ORGANIZING AND ANALYZING LOGISTICS SYSTEMS   360

Preface

This edition of *Contemporary Logistics* reflects a global landscape far different from when the previous edition appeared in 2004. Today's organizations operate in an environment that continues to be influenced by the terrorist attacks on the United States in 2001, an almost dizzying pace of technological advancement, and globalization of commerce that might have been unthinkable as recently as 25 years ago. Although these and other events present both challenges and opportunities for logistics managers, the logistics discipline still remains fun, exciting, and dynamic—characteristics that are reflected in our revision.

The reader will find additions, deletions, and modifications of content that reflect reviewer comments, student comments, and the authors' workplace, consulting, and research experiences. One of the most prominent changes in the ninth edition is that it contains 14 chapters, down from 15 chapters in the eighth edition. In addition, several chapters in the ninth edition are noticeably different from the eighth edition. Chapter 4 has a new title, "Demand Management, Order Management, and Customer Service," and begins with a discussion of demand management and demand forecasting, material that is new to this edition.

Chapters 6 and 7, which focus on transportation-related issues, have also been extensively modified in the present edition. Both have new titles ("Transportation" for chapter 6 and "Transportation Management" for chapter 7), and chapter 6 now takes a more "traditional" (i.e., mode-by-mode) approach to the relevant subject matter. Chapter 11, now called "Procurement," is substantially changed in the ninth edition, and a notable addition to chapter 11 is a section on Investment Recovery. Part III of the book is now titled "Organizing, Analyzing, and Controlling Logistics Systems" and now consists of two chapters, rather than the three chapters in the eighth edition. Chapter 14, now titled "Organizing and Analyzing Logistics Systems," has added a section that focuses on organizing logistics within the firm.

Another notable feature of the ninth edition is that the list of Key Terms at the beginning of each chapter has been expanded, and each key term is now defined in the Glossary, which contains more than 300 terms, up from approximately 250 terms in the previous edition. Moreover, the vast majority of the end-of-chapter Suggested Readings in the ninth edition have been published since 2000. One feature that continues in the ninth edition is cartoons, which highlight the humorous aspects of logistics and supply chain management.

The current edition of *Contemporary Logistics* has been prepared by Paul Murphy, and he welcomes your comments and suggestions at drmurphy@jcu.edu. Paul gratefully acknowledges the substantial contributions that the late Donald F. Wood, James C. Johnson, and Daniel L. Wardlow made to earlier editions.

Acknowledgments

Thanks go out to the following individuals, whose help and support made possible the writing of this and previous editions: Glen Adams, Standard Oil Company; Fred Altstadt, Four-phase System; Scott A. Ames, Logistics Associates; Folger Athearn, Jr., Athearn & Company; Can Atli; Donald W. Baldra, Schering Corporation; Charles L. Ballard, Hudson Valley Community College; Carl Bankard, York College of Pennsylvania; James H. Barnes, University of Georgia; Tayfun Tugberk Bekiroglu; Warren Blanding, Marketing Publications, Inc.; James F. Briody, Fairchild Camera and Instrument Company; Hank Bulwinkel, Towson State University; Frank Burinsky; W. R. Callister, Del Monte Corporation; Neil D. Chaitin, Challenge Equipment Corporation; W. M. Cheatham, Specialty Brands; Carolyn Coggins; Bill Cunningham, Memphis State University; Bob J. Davis, Western Illinois University; Patricia J. Daugherty, University of Oklahoma; Rick Dawe, Fritz Logistics Institute; George Derugin; Gary Dicer, University of Tennessee; John R. Doggett, *Warehousing Review*; W. R. Donham, Cambridge Plan International; A. J. Faria, University of Windsor; Joseph Garfall; Donald C. Garland, Zellerbach Paper; Navneet Gill; Stanley Groover, Towson State University; Carl Guelzo, Towson State University; Mark Haight, University of Wisconsin Center at Barron County; Jay Hamerslag, Hamerslag Equipment Company; Gerald Hampton; Lowell Hedrick, Phillips Petroleum Company; Weldon G. Helmus, Hewlett-Packard; Lynn Hill, Heublein, Inc.; Stephen G. Hill, Dole Packaged Foods Company; Stanley J. Hille, University of Missouri at Columbia; Donald Horton, American Warehousemen's Association; Rufus C. Jefferson; Creed Jenkins, Consolidated Distribution Services; J. M. Johnson, Johnson & Johnson; J. Richard Jones, Memphis State University; Robert E. Jones, F. E. Warren Air Force Base; Henry M. Karel, Shelby State Community College; R. L. Kemmer, GTE Service Corporation; Bob Kingston, Kaiser Permanente Medical Care Program; David Kupferman; Tibi Lacatus, Sertapak; C. John Langley Jr., University of Tennessee; Art LaPlant, Schlage Lock Company; Joseph R. Larsen, CIBA Pharmaceutical Company; Sean Laughlin; Ron Lennon, Towson State University; Douglas Long; Harry Loomer, University of Wisconsin Center at Barron County; Christopher Low; Irving C. MacDonald; Ernest Y. Maitland, British Columbia Institute of Technology; Don Marsh, United Airlines Maintenance Operations; Darwyn Mass, Rocky Mountain Motor Tariff Bureau; Frank McDonald; Michael McGinnis, University of South Alabama; Chinnubbie McIntosh, Warren Petroleum Company; Jim Meneley, American Honda Motor Company; Henry Metzner, University of Missouri–Rolla; Edward J. Meyers, Pacific Gas & Electric Company; Donald D. Mickel, Sacramento Army Depot; Lowell S. Miller; Rory K. Miller, California Maritime Academy; Joseph F. Moffatt, University of Southwestern Louisiana; Paul R. Neff, Boeing Company; Donald P. Nelson, National Distribution Agency; David Norton, Nabisco; Thomas Paczkowski, Cayuga Community College; Taeho Park, San Jose State University; Donald Pefaur, Trammell Crow Distribution Corporation; Ray Perin, Perin Company; Andru M. Peters, Andros, Inc.; Robert R. Piper; Lee Plummer, North Carolina State

University; Ira Pollack; Ruby Remley, Cabrini College; Richard L. Rickenbacher, Safeway Stores; Dale S. Rogers, University of Nevada, Reno; Frank R. Scheer, University of Tennessee; Karl Schober; Skip Sherwood, California State University at Fresno; Charles S. Shuken, Metropolitan Warehouse Company; Melvin Silvester; David A. Smith, State University of New York at Buffalo; Jerome V. Smith, Consolidated Freightways; Michael Smith, Christian Brothers University; R. Neil Southern, University of Memphis; F. J. Spellman; Jack M. Starling, North Texas State University; Joseph J. Stefanic, Agrico Chemical Company; Wendell M. Stewart, Kearney Management Consultants; Stephen Stover; T. M. Tipton, USCO Services, Inc.; Teddy N. Toklas, Oakland Naval Supply Center; Lee Totten, Western New England College; Frances Tucker, Syracuse University; Roy Dale Voorhees, Iowa State University; Peter F. Walstad; Bill Walton, Pacific American Warehousing & Trucking Company; Boyd L. Warnick, Utah Technical College; Mary Margaret Weber, Missouri Western State College; Marcus A. Weiss-Madsen; Terry C. Whiteside, Montana State Department of Agriculture; Lynn Williams, Logisticon; Kenneth C. Williamson, James Madison University; Warren Winstead, George Washington University; Doreen Wood; Suzan C. Woods, Logisticon; Jean Woodruff, Western New England College; Ronald S. Yaros; Mark Zborowski; James Ziola, Consolidated Freightways; and Howard Zysman, Morada Distribution, Inc.

At Pine Tree Composition, Paul extends thanks to John Shannon, while at Prentice Hall, Paul extends thanks to Renata Butera, Christine Ietto, and Keri Molinari.

Paul R. Murphy, Jr.
University Heights, Ohio

PART I

OVERVIEW OF LOGISTICS

Part 1 sets the stage for this text by introducing the many dimensions of the complex and dynamic subject of logistics and its role within supply chain management. The first three chapters of *Contemporary Logistics* serve as the structural foundation on which the remainder of the text is built.

Chapter 1 discusses logistics concepts and examines the reasons for their recent growth in importance in business firms. It covers the economic impacts of logistics and marketing terms. It also introduces the concept of marketing channels and tells about the ownership channel, the negotiations channel, the promotions channel, the financing channel, and the logistics channel.

Chapter 2 looks at the supply chain management concept, which links one's suppliers' suppliers and one's customers' customers. Also covered is logistics outsourcing, or 3PL (third-party logistics).

Chapter 3 provides an overview of the general types of information management systems that are applicable across each business function, and it provides examples of how these general types of information systems are specifically applied in logistics management. The remainder of Chapter 3 covers selected opportunities and challenges associated with emerging information technologies.

1

LOGISTICS AND THE SUPPLY CHAIN

Special logistics staffs handle the movement of items and displays for trade shows and special events. This sleek Mercedes racer is being loaded aboard a KLM Boeing 747.

Photo © KLM–Royal Dutch Airlines Photo Archives. Reproduced with permission.

Key Terms

- Channel intermediaries
- Cost trade-offs
- Economic utility
- FOB destination pricing
- FOB origin pricing
- Form utility
- Freight absorption
- Inbound logistics
- Landed costs
- Logistics
- Mass logistics
- Materials management
- Phantom freight
- Place utility
- Possession utility
- Postponement
- Power retailer
- Reverse logistics
- Stock-keeping units (SKUs)
- Stockouts
- Systems approach
- Tailored logistics
- Time utility
- Total cost approach

Learning Objectives

- To learn the definition of logistics
- To understand the economic importance of logistics
- To learn of recent events and their influences on logistics practices
- To gain an understanding of logistics practices within a firm
- To learn different pricing policies
- To know about logistics careers

ECONOMIC IMPACTS OF LOGISTICS

At this point, you may have limited awareness of, and knowledge about, logistics—the subject matter of this textbook. However, if that is the case, you're really not very different from lots of other people who inhabit this planet, and it might come as a surprise to you that logistics tends to have significant economic impacts. From a macroeconomic perspective, Table 1-1 summarizes U.S. logistics costs in relation to gross domestic product (GDP) for five-year time periods between 1960 and 2005. Note that logistics as a percentage of GDP has declined from approximately 15 percent in 1960 to less than 10 percent in 2005 and that annual aggregate logistics costs now approach $1.2 trillion. Although absolute and relative logistics costs in relation to GDP vary from country to country (logistics expenditures in China are estimated to be about 19 percent),[1] logistics is most definitely an important component in any country's economy.

Continuing with a macro perspective, logistics can also play an important role in a nation's economic growth and development. Hannigan and Mangan pointed out that logistics, particularly improvements in transportation efficiency, played a key role in the explosive growth of Ireland's economy in the mid- and late-1990s (they had a GDP increase of 62 percent in this period). According to Hannigan and Mangan, future growth of Ireland's economy will not be

---

[1]Paul Page, "The China Effect," *Traffic World,* May, 8, 2006, 19–21.

TABLE 1-1	The Cost of the Business Logistics System in Relation to Gross Domestic Product (GDP)				
	In $ Billion				
Year	*Inventory Carrying Costs*	*Transportation Costs*	*Administrative Costs*	*Total U.S. Logistics Cost*	*Logistics As a Percentage of GDP*
1960	31	44	3	78	14.7
1965	38	64	4	106	14.7
1970	56	91	6	153	14.7
1975	97	116	9	222	13.5
1980	220	214	17	451	16.1
1985	227	274	20	521	12.4
1990	283	351	25	659	11.4
1995	302	441	30	773	10.4
2000	377	590	39	1,006	10.1
2005	393	744	46	1,183	9.5

Sources: Rosalyn Wilson and Robert Delaney, Twelfth Annual *State of Logistics Report,* 2001; Rosalyn Wilson, Seventeenth Annual *State of Logistics Report,* 2006.

possible without improvements to its logistical capabilities.[2] In a similar fashion, both the Chinese government and the private sector recognize that as China's labor cost advantage shifts to other countries, logistics efficiency becomes an essential component to fueling an economy that has been expanding at between 8 and 10 percent per year.[3]

Apart from the previous examples of macro-level economic impacts, the economic impacts of logistics can affect individual consumers such as you. These impacts can be illustrated through the concept of **economic utility,** which is the value or usefulness of a product in fulfilling customer needs or wants. The four general types of economic utility are possession, form, time, and place. Logistics clearly contributes to time and place utilities.

Possession utility refers to the value or usefulness that comes from a customer being able to take possession of a product. Possession utility can be influenced by the payment terms associated with a product. Credit and debit cards, for example, facilitate possession utility by allowing the customer to purchase products without having to produce cash or a cash equivalent. Likewise, automotive leases allow customers to take possession of a more desirable model than would be possible with conventional automotive loans.

Form utility refers to a product's being in a form that (1) can be used by the customer and (2) is of value to the customer. Although form utility has generally been associated with production and manufacturing, logistics can also contribute to form utility. For example, to achieve production economies (i.e., lower cost per unit), a soft-drink company may produce thousands of cases of a certain type of soft drink (e.g., diet cola). You're not likely to purchase diet cola by the thousands of cases (unless you're having a really big social event!) but rather in smaller lot sizes, such as a six- or twelve-pack. Through *allocation,* which will be discussed more fully in

---

[2]Kevin Hannigan and John Mangan, "The Role of Logistics and Supply Chain Management in Determining the Competitiveness of a Peripheral Economy," *Irish Marketing Review* 14, no. 1 (2001): 35–42.
[3]Peter Tirschwell, "In China, Full Speed Ahead," *Journal of Commerce,* April 17, 2006, 38.

Chapter 2, logistics can break the thousands of cases of diet cola into the smaller quantities that are desired by customers.

Place utility refers to having products available *where* they are needed by customers; products are moved from points of lesser value to points of greater value. Continuing with the diet cola example, place utility is increased by moving the soda from a point of lesser value (e.g., stored in a warehouse) to a point of greater value (e.g., on a supermarket shelf).

Closely related to place utility is **time utility,** which refers to having products available *when* they are needed by customers. It's important to recognize that different products have different sensitivities to time; three-day late delivery of perishable items likely has more serious consequences than three-day late delivery of nonperishable items.

Note that simultaneous achievement of possession, form, place, and time utility goes a long way toward facilitating—but not guaranteeing—customer satisfaction. Consider the experience of a former student who used an online service to order Valentine's Day flowers for his out-of-state girlfriend. The online service facilitated possession utility by allowing for a secured payment by credit card. A healthy arrangement of the correct bouquet (form utility) arrived at the girlfriend's residence on Valentine's Day (place and time utility). The problem: The greeting card that accompanied the flowers had a wrong name for the girlfriend (but the right name for the boyfriend)!

LOGISTICS: WHAT IT IS

Now that you have a better understanding of the economic impacts of logistics, it's important to define what logistics is. Since approximately 1980, tremendous—and rapid—change has occurred in the business logistics field. One consequence of this rapid change is that business logistics has been referred to by a number of different terms, each having slightly different meanings. In recent years, some of the terms used to refer to business logistics have included (but are not limited to) the following:

- Business logistics
- Distribution
- Industrial distribution
- Logistics
- Logistics management
- Materials management
- Physical distribution
- Supply chain management

In essence, each of these terms is associated with managing the flows of goods and information from a point of origin to a point of consumption.

Although the aforementioned terms are similar, they aren't the same; from a managerial perspective, this poses a potential problem of comparing apples to oranges as opposed to comparing apples to apples or oranges to oranges. For example, suppose that one organization defines logistics to include two activities—transportation and inventory management—whereas a second organization defines logistics to include three activities—transportation, inventory management, and warehousing. It seems reasonable that the second organization's total cost of logistics would be higher than the first organization's (because the second organization's logistics encompasses more activities). However, it would be a mistake to conclude that, because of the higher total costs, the second organization is less effective or efficient with respect to logistics because the two organizations have different definitions of logistics.

In an effort to avoid potential misunderstanding about the meaning of **logistics,** this book adopts the current definition promulgated by the Council of Supply Chain Management Professionals (CSCMP), one of the world's most prominent organizations for logistics professionals. According to the CSCMP, "Logistics is that part of Supply Chain Management that plans, implements, and controls the efficient, effective forward and reverse flow and storage of goods, services, and related information between the point of origin and the point of consumption in order to meet customers' requirements."[4]

Let's analyze this definition in closer detail. First, logistics is part of supply chain management. We'll talk about supply chains and supply chain management in greater detail in Chapter 2, but the key point for now is that logistics is part of a bigger picture in the sense that the supply chain focuses on coordination among business functions (such as marketing, production, and finance) within and across organizations. The fact that logistics is explicitly recognized as part of supply chain management means that logistics can affect how well (or how poorly) an individual firm—and its associated supply chain(s)—can achieve goals and objectives.

The CSCMP definition also indicates that logistics "plans, implements, and controls." Of particular importance is the word *and,* which suggests that logistics should be involved in all three activities—planning, implementing, controlling—and not just one or two. Some suggest, however, that logistics is more involved in the implementation than in the planning of certain logistical policies.[5]

Note that the CSCMP definition also refers to "efficient and effective forward and reverse flows and storage." Broadly speaking, effectiveness can be thought of as, "How well does a company do what they say they're going to do?" For example, if a company promises that all orders will be shipped within 24 hours of receipt, what percentage of orders are actually shipped within 24 hours of receipt? In contrast, efficiency can be thought of as how well (or poorly) company resources are used to achieve what a company promises it can do. For instance, some companies use premium or expedited transportation services—which cost more money—to cover for shortcomings in other parts of its logistics system.

With respect to forward and reverse flows and storage, logistics has traditionally focused on forward flows and storage, that is, those directed *toward* the point of consumption. Increasingly, however, the logistics discipline has recognized the importance of reverse flows and storage **(reverse logistics),** that is, those that *originate* at the point of consumption. Although the majority of the discussion in this book focuses on forward logistics, the relevance and importance of reverse logistics continues to grow as more companies recognize its tactical and strategic implications.[6] Reverse logistics is also likely to gain attention in the future as more companies recognize it as an opportunity for competitive advantage.[7]

The CSCMP definition also indicates that logistics involves the flow and storage of "goods, services, and related information." Indeed, in the contemporary business environment, logistics is as much about the flow and storage of information as it is about the flow and storage of

---

[4]*www.cscmp.org.*

[5]Paul R. Murphy, Richard F. Poist, and Charles D. Braunschwieg, "Role and Relevance of Logistics to Corporate Environmentalism: An Empirical Assessment," *International Journal of Physical Distribution and Logistics Management* 25, no. 2 (1995): 5–19; Paul R. Murphy and Richard F. Poist, "Socially Responsible Logistics: An Exploratory Study," *Transportation Journal* 41, no. 4 (2002): 23–35.

[6]Dale S. Rogers and Ronald Tibben-Lembke, "An Examination of Reverse Logistics Practices," *Journal of Business Logistics* 22, no. 2 (2001): 129–148.

[7]James Stock, Thomas Speh, and Herbert Shear, "Many Happy (Product) Returns," *Harvard Business Review* 80, no. 7 (2002): 16–17.

goods. The importance of information in contemporary logistics is captured by Fred Smith, CEO and chairman of FedEx (a leading logistics service provider), who believes that "information about the package is as important as the package itself."[8]

Finally, the CSCMP definition indicates that the purpose of logistics is "to meet customer requirements." This is important for several reasons, with one being that logistics strategies and activities should be based on customer wants and needs, rather than the wants, needs, and capabilities of other parties. Although a customer focus might seem like the proverbial no-brainer, one implication of such a focus is that companies actually have to communicate with their customers to learn about their needs and wants. It suffices to say that, even today, some companies continue to be hesitant about communicating with their customers.

A second reason for the importance of meeting customer requirements is the notion that because different customers have different logistical needs and wants, a one-size-fits-all logistics approach **(mass logistics)**—in which every customer gets the same type and levels of logistics service—will result in some customers being overserved while others are underserved. Rather, companies should consider **tailored logistics** approaches, in which groups of customers with similar logistical needs and wants are provided with logistics service appropriate to these needs and wants.[9]

The principles in this textbook are generally applicable not only to for-profit organizations but also to the workings of governmental and nonprofit entities. For instance, from a governmental perspective, logistics is quite germane to the armed forces, which shouldn't be surprising, given that logistics was first associated with the military. Moreover, the Asian earthquake and tsunami in late 2004 provides an excellent example of the relevance of logistics to nonprofit organizations. In a relatively short time period, a variety of humanitarian organizations, with the help of private-sector companies, were able to deliver relief supplies such as food and medicine to the region and distribute them to the affected population.[10]

THE INCREASED IMPORTANCE OF LOGISTICS

The formal study of business logistics, and predecessor concepts such as traffic management and physical distribution, has existed since the second half of the twentieth century. Quite frankly, from approximately 1950 to 1980, limited appreciation was shown for the importance of the logistics discipline. Since 1980, however, increasing recognition has been given to the topic, and several key reasons are discussed next.

A Reduction in Economic Regulation

During the 1970s and the 1980s, widespread reductions in economic regulation (commonly referred to as *deregulation*) relaxed government control of carriers' rates and fares, entry and exit, mergers and acquisitions, and more. These controls were particularly onerous in the U.S. transportation industry in the sense that price competition was essentially nonexistent, and customers were pretty much forced to accept whatever service the carriers chose to provide. This meant that logistics managers had relatively little control over one of the most important cost components in a logistics system (see Table 1-1).

---

[8]Jonathan Reiskin, "Carriers Invest in Web Sites, Software, Networks," *Transport Topics,* May 8, 2006, 10.

[9]Joseph B. Fuller, James O'Conor, and Richard Rawlinson, "Tailored Logistics: The Next Advantage," *Harvard Business Review* 71, no. 3 (1993): 87–98.

[10]Stephen Tierney, "Industry Responds in Time of Need," *Supply Chain Europe,* February 2005, 22.

Reductions in economic regulation in the U.S. airfreight, railroad, and trucking industries allowed individual carriers flexibility in pricing and service. This flexibility was important to logistics for several reasons. First, it provided companies with the ability to implement the tailored logistics approach discussed earlier, in the sense that companies could specify different service levels, and prices could be adjusted accordingly. Second, the increased pricing flexibility allowed large buyers of transportation services to reduce their transportation costs by leveraging large amounts of freight with a limited number of carriers.

Although the preceding discussion has focused on lessened economic regulation in the United States, it appears that deregulation has had similar effects in other countries. For example, lessened economic regulation of transportation has been identified as a primary reason for a reduction in the cost of freight transportation in Ireland.[11] Likewise, privatization of water ports has been found to improve their operational efficiency.[12]

Changes in Consumer Behavior

A common business adage suggests that "change is the only constant." Although changes in consumer behavior are commonly the purview of the psychology and marketing disciplines, such changes have important logistical implications as well. Several examples of changes in consumer behavior (market demassification, changing family roles, and rising customer expectations) and their possible logistical implications are discussed next.

The concept of *market demassification* suggests that, in contrast to mass markets, an ever-increasing number of market segments has distinct preferences. One way to address market demassification is through mass customization, which refers to the ability of a company to deliver highly customized products and services that are designed to meet the needs and wants of individual segments or customers. In mass customization, one size does not fit all needs, and this means that logistics systems must be flexible rather than rigid. To this end, logistics service providers such as FedEx and UPS offer a variety of delivery options to prospective customers. For example, next-day service—which used to mean delivery sometime during the next business day—can now be purchased in terms of delivery by the end of the next business day, delivery by midafternoon of the next business day, delivery by midmorning of the next business day, and delivery by early morning of the next business day. As a general rule, the earlier the delivery time, the more expensive the transportation cost.

In terms of *changing family roles,* fifty years ago less than 30 percent of U.S. adult women were in the workforce; today, by contrast, approximately 60 percent are in the working world.[13] One consequence from this has been an increasing emphasis on the convenience associated with a family's shopping experiences. This convenience is manifested in various ways to include extended store hours, home delivery of purchased items, and ready-to-eat–ready-to-cook foods. Each of these has logistics-related implications. With extended store hours—some stores are now open 24 hours—retailers must address issues such as the optimal delivery times for replenishment trucks and when to replenish merchandise. Although home delivery certainly adds to the purchaser's convenience, one challenge is the coordination of delivery times with the

---

[11]Hannigan and Mangan, 2001.

[12]Jose Tongzen and Wu Heng, "Port Privatization, Efficiency, and Competitiveness: Some Empirical Evidence from Container Ports (Terminals)," *Transportation Research—Part A* 39, no. 5 (2005): 405–424.

[13]Philip Kotler and Gary Armstrong, *Marketing Principles,* 11th ed. (Upper Saddle River, NJ: Prentice Hall, 2006), Chapter 1.

purchaser's ability to receive the item(s). Finally, the growth in ready-to-eat–ready-to-cook foods means that some food processors have added high-volume cooking systems at their production facilities. In addition, ready-to-eat–ready-to-cook foods have different packaging requirements, such as reusable bags.[14]

As for *rising customer expectations*, it should come as no surprise that customer expectations tend to increase through time, which means that a satisfactory level of performance in the past might not be considered as so today. Consider that a made-to-order, direct-to-consumer personal computer was unheard of as recently as 25 years ago. Today this concept, pioneered by Dell Computer, has become ubiquitous in the personal computer industry and has profoundly changed distribution channels and supply chains in the sense that make-to-order has much different production and inventory requirements than does make-to-stock. Moreover, Dell was able to produce made-to-order, direct-to-customer computers in a very short period of time, and its time-compressed, high-customization model has raised consumer expectations in other industries as well. For example, one company is focusing on build-to-order automobiles that will be *produced and delivered* to customers within 14 days of ordering.[15]

Technological Advances

Prior to the start of every academic year, Beloit College (Wisconsin) releases an annual survey concerning what members of the incoming freshmen class know about the year of their birth. If you were born in the mid-1980s or later, you may not remember a world without personal computers or digital cameras. In addition, you probably haven't used (and may have never seen, except in pictures) a self-correcting electric typewriter. We're not trying to take a stroll down memory lane. Rather, our point is that tremendous technological advances—in the course of your lifetime—have had profound influences for business management and, by extension, for business logistics.

From a logistical perspective, some of the most important technological advances have involved computer hardware and software in the sense that management of logistics involves a tremendous amount of data. The sheer magnitude of these data makes manual analysis a difficult and time-consuming process; technological advances in computer hardware, software, and capacity have allowed logisticians to make faster, more informed, and more accurate decisions with respect to customer service, transportation, inventory management, and other logistics activities.

The Internet—virtually unknown and unused until the mid-1990s—has also proved to be a powerful tool for improving logistical effectiveness and efficiency. Although Internet applications can be used for many logistical activities, research suggests the heaviest use of the Internet involves purchasing or procurement and transportation. Typical purchasing-related Internet applications include checking vendor price quotes and vendor negotiations, whereas claims management and pickup and delivery are common transportation uses.[16] With respect to pickup and delivery, for example, UPS drivers now carry wireless handheld computers that instantaneously warn if a mistake (such as picking up an incorrect shipment) is about to occur. UPS estimates that this system is saving over 75,000 miles of travel per day to correct pickup and delivery errors.[17]

---

[14]L. Patrick, "Cooked Products Ring the Register," *High-Volume Cooking,* March 2006, 12–13.

[15]Ken Cottrill, "Custom Built," *Traffic World,* July 22, 2002, 13–14.

[16]Richard A. Lancioni, Michael A. Smith, and Hope J. Schau, "Strategic Internet Application Trends in Supply Chain Management," *Industrial Marketing Management* 32, no. 3 (2003): 211–217.

[17]Reiskin, 2006.

The Growing Power of Retailers

Another influence on logistics involves the emergence of **"power retailers"** such as Wal-Mart, Home Depot, and Best Buy that often wield greater power than the companies that supply them. Power retailers, which can be found in various retail formats (e.g., mass merchandisers, category killers), are characterized by large market share and low prices. Furthermore, power retailers are often the largest customers for some of their suppliers; for example, Wal-Mart accounts for over 15 percent of Procter & Gamble's annual sales.[18]

Many power retailers explicitly recognize superior logistics as an essential component of their corporate strategies, and because of this, their logistical practices are often viewed as a barometer for emerging logistics trends. In the 1990s, for example, Wal-Mart and Warner-Lambert were the first two companies to explore collaborative planning, forecasting, and replenishment (CPFR), a practice in which trading partners share planning and forecasting data to better match up supply and demand. Since then, there have been hundreds of successful (e.g., increased sales, reduced inventory levels) CPFR initiatives, although to be fair, not all CPFR initiatives have been successful. Power retailers have also been logistical trendsetters with respect to focusing on improved inventory turnover (the number of times inventory sells in one year). This emphasis on inventory turnover forces suppliers to be more efficient in the sense that they should focus on providing those products that will be bought by consumers, as opposed to supplying slower-moving products that sit on store shelves for extended periods of time. In fact, some Wal-Mart suppliers will not introduce new products into the commercial marketplace without input from Wal-Mart during the new product development process.

Globalization of Trade

Although countries have traded with each other for thousands of years, globalization's impact is greater today than ever before. Consider that world trade expanded from approximately $7.6 trillion to approximately $12.6 trillion between 2001 and 2005, which represents an increase of over 65 percent.[19] World trade is projected to continue its meteoric increase in the coming years, even in the face of record energy prices and geopolitical uncertainties.

Although many factors, such as rising standards of living and multicountry trade alliances, have contributed to the growth of global trade, it's safe to say that logistics has played a key role, too. Having said this, one should recognize that international logistics is much more challenging and costly than domestic logistics. With respect to challenges, the geographic distances between buyers and sellers are often greater (which may translate into longer transit times), and monitoring logistics processes is sometimes complicated by differences in business practices, culture, and language. As for costs, the greater geographic distances tend to result in higher transportation costs, and documentation requirements can be quite costly as well.[20]

THE SYSTEMS AND TOTAL COST APPROACHES TO LOGISTICS

Logistics is a classic example of the systems approach to business problems. From a companywide perspective, the **systems approach** indicates that a company's objectives can be realized by recognizing the mutual interdependence of the major functional areas of the firm, such as marketing,

---

[18]Jagmohan Raju and Z. John Zhang, "Channel Coordination in the Presence of a Dominant Retailer," *Management Science* 24, no. 2 (2005): 254–262.

[19]"World Economic Outlook," *www.imf.org.*

[20]Donald F. Wood, Anthony P. Barone, Paul R. Murphy, and Daniel L. Wardlow, *International Logistics,* 2nd ed. (New York: AMACOM, 2002).

production, finance, and logistics. One implication of the systems approach is that the goals and objectives of the major functional areas should be compatible with the company's goals and objectives. This means that *one logistics system does not fit all companies* because goals and objectives vary from one firm to another.

A second implication is that decisions made by one functional area should consider the potential implications on other functional areas. For example, implementation of the marketing concept, which focuses on satisfying customer needs and wants, has resulted in a marked increase of the number of **stock-keeping units (SKUs)** or line items of inventory (each different type or package size of a good is a different SKU) offered for sale by many companies. From a logistics perspective, the proliferation of SKUs means (1) more items to identify, (2) more items to store, and (3) more items to track.

Just as the major functional areas of a firm should recognize their interdependence, so too should the various activities that comprise the logistics function (what we'll call *intrafunctional logistics*). The logistics manager should balance each logistics activity to ensure that none is stressed to the point where it becomes detrimental to others.

This can be illustrated by referring to Figure 1-1, which indicates that business logistics is made up of **inbound logistics** (movement and storage of materials into a firm), **materials management**

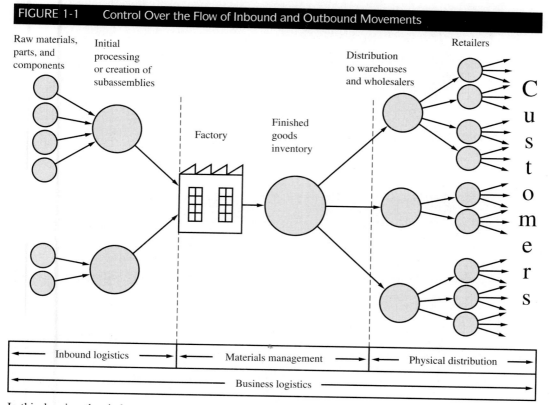

FIGURE 1-1   Control Over the Flow of Inbound and Outbound Movements

In this drawing, the circles represent buildings where inventories are stored, and the lines with arrows represent movement performed by carriers, a stop-and-start process. Current thought deals more with flows, possibly in different volumes and at different speeds, but without the inventory standing still. The supply chain extends to both the left and right of this diagram and includes the suppliers' suppliers and the customers' customers.

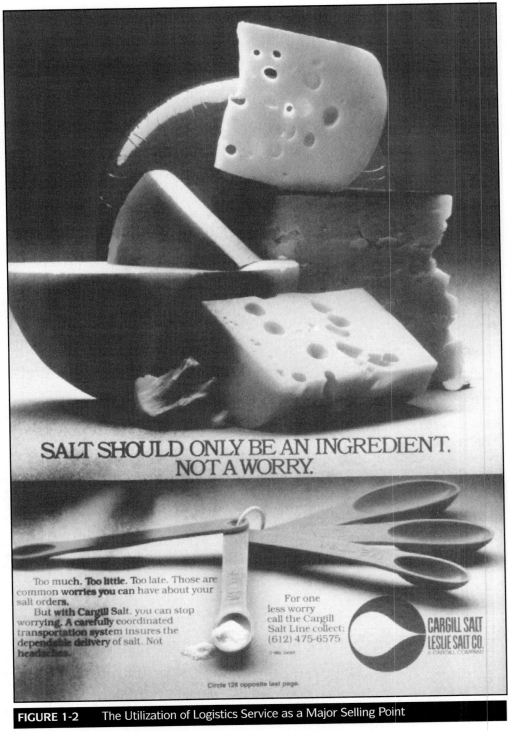

FIGURE 1-2　The Utilization of Logistics Service as a Major Selling Point

Reproduced with permission of Cargill, Incorporated.

(movement and storage of materials and components within a firm), and **physical distribution** (storage of finished product and movement to the customer). Intrafunctional logistics attempts to coordinate inbound logistics, materials management, and physical distribution in a cost-efficient manner that supports an organization's customer service objectives. Figure 1-2, an advertisement for Cargill salt, shows how a company can differentiate a commodity product (salt) by stressing a dependable logistics system.

Inbound logistics, materials management, and physical distribution can be coordinated in many ways. One way is by using the same truck to deliver materials and component parts and to pick up finished goods. Although this may appear to be little more than common sense—and *common sense is one of the keys to being an effective logistics manager*—consider the case of the company that used the same trucking company to deliver materials and parts to one of its production plants as well as to take finished products from the facility. Unfortunately, one truck would arrive early in the morning to deliver the materials and components, and another truck would arrive in the late afternoon to pick up the finished products. How could this happen? Quite simply: The inbound logistics group and the outbound logistics group were unaware that they were using the same trucking company—the two groups never communicated!

Logistics managers use the **total cost approach** to coordinate inbound logistics, materials management, and physical distribution in a cost-efficient manner. This approach is built on the premise that all relevant activities in moving and storing products should be considered as a whole (i.e., their total cost), not individually. Use of the total cost approach requires an understanding of **cost trade-offs;** in other words, changes to one logistics activity cause some costs to increase and others to decrease.

The key to the total cost approach is that all relevant cost items are considered simultaneously when making a decision. The objective is to find the approach with the lowest total cost that supports an organization's customer service requirements. For example, a decision to use expedited transportation translates into higher transportation costs. At the same time, expedited transportation allows a company to reduce its inventory carrying costs and may also reduce the cost of failing to serve particular customers.[21] Although a company's transportation costs increase when utilizing expedited transportation, the costs of other logistics activities decrease; as a result, the total costs of logistics activities decrease—without negatively affecting customer service.

When used in the logistics decision-making process, the total cost concept approach forms what is commonly called the *total logistics concept*. This concept is unique not because of the activities performed, but because of the integration of all activities into a unified whole that seeks to minimize distribution costs in a manner that supports an organization's customer service objectives. The total logistics concept can be extended to include a firm's suppliers and customers, such as in supply chain management, which will be covered in Chapter 2.

LOGISTICAL RELATIONSHIPS WITHIN THE FIRM

From a companywide perspective, the system and total cost approaches to logistics require an understanding of logistics and its relationships with other functional areas. A later chapter is devoted specifically to purchasing, so our discussion here focuses on logistical relationships with finance, marketing, and production.

---

[21]Peter Bradley, "Speed Curbs Inventory," *Logistics Management,* November 2001, 45–47.

Finance

The logistics department regularly interfaces with the finance area, in part because logistical decisions are only as good as the quality of cost data with which they are working. The finance staff, which is concerned with predicting future cash flows, is dependent on logistics for information concerning the status of finished products that are somewhere between the end of the firm's production line and the purchaser's receiving dock.

The finance staff is often charged with the responsibility of allocating the firm's limited funds to projects desired by the various operating departments. As such, the finance department is often instrumental in approving capital budgeting decisions that affect logistics, such as the acquisition of materials handling equipment (e.g., forklifts) and packaging equipment (e.g., a shrink-wrap machine). In such situations, finance personnel may decide between purchasing or leasing the relevant equipment, assuming they have approved the decision to acquire it.

Inventory is another area of interest for finance managers, in part because in financial terms inventory is recorded as an asset; all assets of a firm must be paid for by either short-term (hopefully) or long-term financing. One aspect of concern with respect to inventory is its valuation; should inventory be valued in terms of LIFO (last in, first out) or FIFO (first in, first out)? A second concern is that finance often measures inventory in terms of its cost or value in dollars, whereas logistics tends to measure inventory in terms of units.

A third inventory-related concern involves the concept of *inventory float,* which refers to the cash flow associated with holding inventory.[22] In general terms, the inventory costs are for the time period from when one pays a vendor until the time one collects from the customer for the same goods. Unfortunately, there can be a mismatch between inventory turnover (how many times products sell during a time period) and its associated cash flows; suppose, for example, that the inventory turnover is four weeks whereas the lag between paying vendors and collecting from customers is six weeks.

Marketing

Contemporary marketing places a heavy emphasis on customer satisfaction, and logistics strategies can facilitate customer satisfaction through reducing the cost of products, which can translate into lower prices as well as bringing a broader variety of choices closer to where the customer wishes to buy or use the product. Logistics strategies offer a unique way for a company to differentiate itself among competitors, and logistics now offers an important route for many firms to create marketing superiority.

As such, outbound logistics can be a positive (or negative) marketing asset, with key relationships between outbound logistics and the four primary components of the marketing mix. The following discussion about logistics and marketing focuses on the marketing mix, sometimes referred to as the *four Ps* of marketing (place, price, product, and promotion).

Place Decisions

One important marketing concern is place. Decisions regarding place involve two types of networks: logistics and the marketing channel (which is discussed in greater detail later in this chapter). Logistics decisions concern the most effective way to move and store the product from where it is produced to where it is sold. An effective logistics system can provide positive support by enabling the firm to attract and utilize what it considers to be the most productive

---

[22]Joseph Cavinato, "What Does Your Inventory Really Cost?" *Distribution,* March 1988, 68–72.

channel and supply chain members. Frequently, the channel members are in a position to pick and choose which manufacturer's products they wish to merchandise. If a manufacturer is not consistently able to provide a certain product at the right time, in the right quantities, and in an undamaged condition, the channel members may end their relationship with the supplier or cease active promotion of the supplier's product.

From a marketing perspective, place decisions may also involve new strategies for reaching new customers. An increasingly popular strategy in the retailing industry involves a concept known as *co-branding,* which refers to one location where customers can purchase products from two or more name-brand retailers. Yum! Brands, for example, is the parent company of A&W All American Food, KFC, Long John Silver's, Pizza Hut, and Taco Bell, and you may have eaten at a site where either two or three of these brands are available. From a marketing perspective, co-branding can (1) offer potential customers convenience (satisfying multiple needs in one place), (2) increase customer spending per transaction, and (3) boost brand awareness.[23] Logistical challenges with co-branding include the costs and timing of product delivery. Yum! has addressed these issues by scheduling one delivery per location, which requires co-loading trailers with products for all five chains.

Price Decisions

It is good business sense, and common sense, to recognize that a firm cannot be profitable and grow—in fact, it can be doomed—if it does not control its logistics costs. Obviously, the price of a product must cover relevant production, marketing, distribution, and general administrative costs, and firms with serious waste in their logistics systems will be faced with several choices, none of which is particularly attractive. One choice would be to pass on the higher logistics costs to customers, thus increasing product price. A second option would be to keep price the same but reduce product quality or quantity, which might result in customer defections. Alternatively, a firm could absorb the higher costs, which would cause a decrease in product contribution margins.

Because transportation costs can account for up to 50 percent of a product's total logistics costs,[24] transportation cost factors become important in determining the method used to quote the firm's selling price. A firm can control its transportation costs by using one of several pricing methods, the two most common being **FOB origin** and **FOB destination** (delivered) **pricing systems**. An FOB origin price does not include any transportation costs to the purchaser. With this type of pricing, the purchaser is responsible for the selection of the transportation mode(s) and carrier(s) because the buyer assumes the expense of the transportation from a factory or warehouse. This system of pricing is easy for the seller to administer and always yields the same net return from each sale.

Marketers don't necessarily like FOB origin pricing because it is extremely difficult to adopt uniform retail prices on a regional or national basis. Because each purchaser is a different distance from a factory or warehouse, their **landed costs**—the price of the product at the source plus transportation costs to its destination—are different. Because purchasers tend to have a predetermined margin based on total landed costs, the end result is that each purchaser ends up with a different retail price.

---

[23]Rhonda Bauer, "Co-branding: Growing Family or Family Feud?" *Franchising World,* May–June 2002, 22–23.
[24]Scott Swenseth and Michael Godfrey, "Incorporating Transportation Costs into Inventory Replenishment Decisions," *International Journal of Production Economics* 77, no. 2 (2002): 113–130.

In an FOB destination system, the seller quotes the purchaser a price that includes both the price of the product and the transportation cost to the purchaser's receiving dock, and the seller has the prerogative to select the mode(s) and carrier(s) to deliver the product. An average amount of transportation cost is added to the cost of each product, with the idea being that the average transportation cost reflects the cost of shipping the goods to a point that is the average distance from the seller's place of business. Note that with FOB destination, each purchaser ends up with the same landed cost.

Under FOB destination pricing, buyers located relatively close to the seller's point (closer than average) pay more than their share of freight charges, which is called **phantom freight.** The opposite situation occurs when the buyer actually pays lower freight charges than the seller incurs in shipping the product, which is known as **freight absorption.** Phantom freight and freight absorption are illustrated in Figure 1-3 for shipments originating in Omaha.

Marketers find FOB destination pricing attractive for several reasons. The first is that it enables a company to expand the geographic area to which its product is sold because distant customers in a region do not pay the full costs of transportation. Second, because each purchaser has the same landed costs, it is much easier for a company to apply a uniform retail price on a regional or national basis. Third, product distribution is managed by the seller, who can control the logistics network, making it function in a manner that is most beneficial to the firm's overall objectives.

There are also several drawbacks to FOB destination pricing. As pointed out previously, the seller is responsible for product distribution, which means that it is the seller's responsibility to understand the various distribution activities and the trade-offs among them. This understanding cannot be learned in a short period of time. A second drawback is that this pricing system essentially discriminates based on a company's location; in essence, those firms located closer to the seller subsidize the transportation costs of those firms located further from the seller. Some sellers, to avoid alienating these customers, will allow them to order FOB origin if they so desire.

An important consideration with both FOB origin and destination pricing involves the terms of sale, or when the freight charges are paid. *Freight prepaid* refers to a situation in which the applicable charges are paid at the time a shipment is tendered to a carrier, whereas *freight collect* refers to charges being paid at the time of shipment delivery.[25] As such, there are three payment options for FOB origin and three for FOB destination:

- *FOB origin, freight collect:* The buyer pays freight charges and owns the goods in transit. This is the most common FOB origin term.
- *FOB origin, freight prepaid:* The seller pays the freight charges, but the buyer owns the goods in transit.
- *FOB origin, freight prepaid and charged back:* The seller pays the freight charges in advance but bills the buyer for them. The buyer owns the goods in transit.
- *FOB destination, freight prepaid:* The seller pays the freight charges and also owns the goods in transit. This is what is generally referred to as *FOB destination pricing.*
- *FOB destination, freight collect:* The buyer pays the freight charges when the goods arrive, and the seller owns the goods while they are in transit.
- *FOB destination, freight prepaid and charged back:* The seller owns the goods in transit, prepays the freight charges, and bills the buyer for the freight charges.

---

[25]Ira Breskin, "More Retailers Go 'Freight Collect' on Inbound Shipments," *Logistics Management,* May 2004, 22–24.

National Single-Zone Pricing

Every customer in the United States pays $11 per unit.

Multiple-Zone Pricing

There are three zones: The midwestern zone, paying $10.00 per unit, and the East Coast and West Coast zones, paying $11.95 per unit.

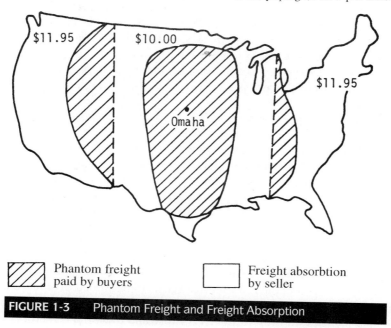

| | Phantom freight paid by buyers | | Freight absorbtion by seller |

FIGURE 1-3 Phantom Freight and Freight Absorption

Logistics managers play an important role in product pricing. They are expected to know the costs of providing various levels of customer service and therefore must be consulted to determine the trade-offs between costs and customer service. Because many distribution costs produce per unit savings when larger volumes are handled, the logistics manager can also help formulate the firm's quantity discount pricing policies.

Product Decisions

A number of potential interfaces are possible in terms of product decisions between marketing and logistics. For example, as noted earlier, the marked increase in product offerings—which allows for more customer choice—creates logistical challenges in terms of identification, storage, and tracking.

Another product interface between marketing and logistics involves the amount of particular SKUs to hold. Marketers often prefer to carry higher quantities of particular items because this reduces the likelihood of **stockouts** (being out of an item at the same time there is demand for it). From a logistics perspective, higher quantities of inventory (1) necessitate additional storage space and (2) increase inventory carrying costs.

Product design, which is often the purview of marketers, can also have important implications for logistical effectiveness and efficiency. For example, long-necked glass beverage containers might be more distinctive than aluminum cans; however, from a logistics perspective, long-necked bottles take up more space and are more likely to be damaged than aluminum cans.

Promotion Decisions

Many promotional decisions require close coordination between marketing and logistics. One important situation concerns the availability of highly advertised products, particularly when a company is running pricing campaigns that lower the price of certain items. Few things are more damaging to a firm's goodwill than being stocked out of items that are heavily promoted in a sales campaign. In addition, in some instances imbalances of product supply and demand can be viewed as *bait and switch tactics*—that is, enticing customers with the promises of a low-priced product, only to find that it is unavailable, but that a higher-priced substitute product is readily available.

Once a decision is made to introduce a new product, the logistics staff assumes responsibility for having the product in place on the scheduled release date—not earlier, not later. In certain industries, such as music, motion pictures, and books, the ease of technological piracy has added to the complexity of having a product in place on the scheduled release date. For example, in an effort to lessen potential piracy with the November 2001 U.S. release of the *Harry Potter and the Sorcerer's Stone* motion picture, the distributors divided each print of the film into two separate shipments "so that no single shipment contained the entire version of the film."[26]

Production

Perhaps the most common interface between production and logistics involves the length of production runs. In many cases, the production people favor long production runs of individual products because this allows the relevant fixed costs to be spread over more units, thus resulting in a lower production cost per unit. Long production runs generate large amounts of inventory, and it is often a logistics staff responsibility to store and track the inventory. Another consideration with long production runs is that sometimes excessive inventory for particular products

---

[26]David Biederman, "Logistics Wizards Deliver," *Traffic World,* November 26, 2001, 8.

occurs because of limited (or no) demand for them. At a minimum, these products (sometimes referred to as *dead stock*) add to a company's inventory carrying costs and also take up space that could be used to store other products. A situation is known to have occurred in which fork-lift drivers would periodically move dead stock of about 150 refrigerators from one warehouse area to another, just to ensure that the refrigerators did not sit in the same place for an extended period of time!

Increasing utilization of the **postponement** concept (the delay of value-added activities such as assembly, production, and packaging until the latest possible time[27]) also influences the inter-face between production and logistics. More specifically, some value-added activities (e.g., case packing, case labeling) that were traditionally performed at a production plant are now per-formed in warehousing facilities. As a result, warehousing facilities may need to add new types of equipment and be configured differently to allow specific value-added activities to take place.[28]

MARKETING CHANNELS

Another concept that is useful to studying the marketing relationships between and among firms is to look at marketing channels. The marketing channels concept describes the institu-tional setting by which goods and services move forward. One takes a broad look at existing transactions and how the markets in which they are carried out were formed. Marketing is a series of processes performed by a coordinated group of firms that facilitate exchange.

> Marketing channels can be viewed as sets of interdependent organizations involved in the process of making a product or service available for use or consumption. From the outset, it should be recognized that not only do marketing channels satisfy demand by supplying goods and services at the right place, quantity, quality, and price, but they also stimulate demand through promotional activities of the units (e.g., retailers, manu-facturers' representatives, sales offices, and wholesalers) constituting them. Therefore, the channel should be viewed as an orchestrated network that creates value for the consumer through the generation of form, possession, time, and place utilities.[29]

The principal, traditional actors in the marketing channel are the manufacturer, the whole-saler, and the retailer. Each in turn assumes ownership of the inventory of goods. Each also assumes risks associated with temporary inventory ownership. The channel members in this arrangement, carrying out this task, can also be referred to as the *ownership channel*. The same or related parties also get together in other channel arrangements, and these channels are called the *negotiations channel,* the *financing channel,* the *promotions channel,* and the *logistics channel.* The logistics channel handles the physical flow of product, which is the principal topic of this book. All channels and channel activities can be graphed as networks.

Information is also freely carried up and down, back and forth, and between channels. One of the functions of the channel system is to give each actor sufficient information to make a cor-rect, rational decision. Information availability is important to a channel's functioning: Channels will fail if some of the actors feel that necessary information is lacking. Although

---

[27]John J. Coyle, Edward J. Bardi, and C. John Langley, *The Management of Business Logistics: A Supply Chain Perspective,* 7th ed. (Mason, OH: South-Western, 2003).

[28]"Taking the Hit-or-Miss Out of Make-to-Order," *Modern Materials Handling,* Mid-May 1999, 14–16.

[29]Louis W. Stern and Adel I. El-Ansary, *Marketing Channels,* 4th ed. (Upper Saddle River, NJ: Prentice Hall, 1992), 1.

information flows in both directions, there is some bias in that most channel members are usually more concerned about buyers' needs than sellers' needs. New products, for example, are developed with customers in mind. Selling is carried out more aggressively and is considered more glamorous than procurement. Of course, one channel member's sale is another channel member's purchase.

It is safe to assume that over 99 percent of the decisions made within channels are for repeat purchases (also called *rebuys*); hence, many of the transactions are not strictly new but are either exact repeats or repeats with minor modifications from whatever was done yesterday or last week. There is also a stock of goodwill included in many transactions. People prefer doing business with people they like. This is especially true today, with the emphasis on collaboration and partnerships, rather than adversarial relationships, between buyers and sellers.

Established channels tend to operate with the same channel members over time. Only a few participants are in the action for the first time; when they join a channel, they must establish their credibility and learn that channel's rules of the game. Let us look more closely at how the three traditional parties—the manufacturer, the wholesaler, and the retailer—interact in each of the five mentioned channels.

The *ownership channel* covers movement of the title to the goods. The goods themselves might not be physically present or even exist. If a good is in great demand, one might have to buy it before it is produced, such as a commissioned piece of art or a scarce new consumer product. Sometimes, a product will not be made until there are sufficient financial commitments, which is often the case with new models of airline aircraft. The party owning the good almost always has the right to trade or sell it and bears the risks and costs associated with having it in inventory. Also, while owning the good, one can use it as collateral for a loan, although this may place some restrictions on its use or movement.

The *negotiations channel* is the one in which buy and sell agreements are reached. This could include transactions face-to-face or by telephone, e-mail, electronic data interchange, or almost any other form of communication. In many situations, no actual negotiations take place; the price for the product is stated, and one either buys at that price or does not. In some trades, auctions are used; in others, highly structured, organized trading takes place, such as markets for some commodities. One part of the negotiations covers how activities in the other channels are to be handled. For example, each buying party will specify the point and time of delivery and the point and time of payment. Even packaging design may be negotiated. (An old Henry Ford story is that suppliers of some parts were directed to ship in wooden crates built of good lumber and to very exacting specifications. It turned out that the empty crates were then partially disassembled and became floorboards in Ford Model Ts.)

The *financing channel* handles payments for goods. More importantly, it handles the company's credit. The multiple participants in the channel have different financial strengths, and often one must help another to keep the entire channel alive. For example, a newly opened retail store may have some of its goods placed on consignment, meaning that the wholesaler, not the store, owns them. The retailer will reimburse the wholesaler only for goods sold; the wholesaler bears nearly all the financial risks. Sometimes, in an effort to develop what it believes is a necessary new product line, a wholesaler will assist the manufacturer by putting up cash in advance along with an order. Alternatively, the wholesaler will place a large, firm order, and the manufacturer can take that order to a bank and use it as a basis for receiving a loan. The logistics channel is often designed so that a payment must be received to trigger the release of the order or part of the order. Credit is important to all parties in the channel, who frequently receive or extend it, and credit becomes an integral part of the negotiations. If bills are not paid when due or if credit is overextended, collection becomes a financing channel function.

The *promotions channel* is concerned with promoting a new or an existing product. This is probably most closely related to the financing channel because monetary allowances are often part of the promotion effort. However, the promotion channel and the logistics channel are linked in several ways. First, there may be special advertising materials, such as coupon books, floor advertising posters, or displays, which must be distributed with the promoted product. Second, some of the cartons or consumer packs may have special labeling, and their placement at retailers must coincide with other promotional efforts. Third, because logistics personnel handle order processing, they have instantaneous records of actual sales, which indicate the initial success of the promotional efforts.

As mentioned previously, the *logistics channel*, its components, and its functioning are the main topics of this book. The most significant contribution that the logistics channel makes to the overall channel process is the *sorting function*. This function involves rearranging the assortment of products as they flow through the channels toward the customer, taking large blocks of single products and rearranging them into quantities, assortments, and varieties that consumers prefer. The sorting function bridges "the discrepancy between the assortment of goods and services generated by the producer and the assortment demanded by the consumer. The discrepancy results from the fact that manufacturers typically produce a large quantity of a limited variety of goods, whereas consumers usually desire only a limited quantity of a wide variety of goods."[30] The sorting function has four steps, and these are important to understanding the concept of goods flowing through the logistics channel (and the supply chain):

- *Sorting out* is sorting a heterogeneous supply of products into stocks that are homogeneous.
- *Accumulating* is bringing together similar stocks from different sources.
- *Allocating* is breaking a homogeneous supply into smaller lots.
- *Assorting* is building up assortments of goods for resale, usually to retail customers.

These steps take place between the manufacturer and the consumer, which means that they are performed by the wholesaler, the retailer, or specialist intermediaries. In addition to the major actors or primary participants in a logistics channel, many less-well-known actors play minor but essential roles. They are called **facilitators** or **channel intermediaries.** Intermediaries make the entire system function better. They spring up and flourish in areas where communications and other interactions between major parties are not well meshed. In international transactions, for example, translators may be an important intermediary. Intermediaries also function in areas needing orderly routines, such as order processing, and in searching, for example, when customers are looking for products or producers are looking for customers. Intermediaries fill niches, they are very well focused, and they serve as buffers. Usually, they do not take an ownership position in the products or goods being handled.

The five channels discussed previously show where intermediaries function and fit. They are used only when needed, and most channel actors know when to rely on them. For example, in the ownership channel, the most common intermediary is the bank or finance company, which may assume temporary or partial ownership of goods as part of an ongoing transaction. Often, this is a condition for the extension of credit. Banks routinely loan funds to all parties in a channel, making it possible for goods to be manufactured, marketed, and sold.

Brokers, or intermediaries between a buyer and a seller, are associated with the negotiation channel. When one contracts with a trucker to carry a truckload of freight, one often uses

---

[30]Stern and El-Ansary, *Marketing Channels,* 6.

a broker. One reason brokers are used in this situation is that the individual trucker believes that his or her time is more profitably spent driving, rather than being on the phone trying to negotiate for the next load. It is easier for the trucker to let the broker find the load and then give the broker 10 to 15 percent off the top.

Intermediaries in the financing field are again often banks, who supply the credit necessary for a deal to be finalized. Sometimes insurance is also a requirement in the agreement, so insurance companies may also serve as intermediaries. Sometimes accountants are called in to verify certain information. For big-ticket items, such as ships or houses, the buyer almost always borrows money to finance part of the purchase. Providers of financing are intermediaries, as are those who bring together buyers, sellers, and sources of credit.

The promotions channel has intermediaries that aid with promotions, such as firms that design, build, and transport product exhibits for display at trade shows. Advertising agencies can handle the preparation and media placement of advertising materials, and firms often use public relations agencies to represent them to the news media. Some companies choose to outsource their personal selling functions by hiring an intermediary to provide them with a contract sales force. These promotion efforts handled by intermediaries must be coordinated with the firm's overall marketing communication activities.

The logistics channel has many intermediaries, and many are mentioned in this book. The most common is the freight forwarder, whose function is to assemble small shipments into larger shipments and then tender them in truckload or railcarload quantities to truck lines or to railroads. In international logistics, intermediaries abound; more than a hundred different types could be listed. One example of specialization is cargo surveyors, who specialize in coffee, devoting their careers to examining and arbitrating damage claims involving shipments of coffee beans.

ACTIVITIES IN THE LOGISTICAL CHANNEL

To successfully apply the systems and total cost approaches to logistics, it is essential to understand the various logistics activities. Keep in mind that because one logistics system does not fit all companies, the number of activities in a logistics system can vary from company to company. Activities that are considered to be logistics related include, but are not limited to, the following:

Customer service	Demand forecasting
Facility location decisions	Industrial packaging
Inventory management	Materials handling
Order management	Parts and service support
Production scheduling	Procurement
Returned products	Salvage and scrap disposal
Transportation management	Warehousing management

Customer Service

There can be many definitions of customer service, such as "keeping existing customers happy." Customer service involves making sure that the right person receives the right product at the right place at the right time in the right condition and at the right cost. Customer service is discussed in greater detail in Chapter 4.

Demand Forecasting

Demand forecasting refers to efforts to estimate product demand in a future time period. The growing popularity of the supply chain concept has prompted increasing collaboration among supply chain partners with respect to demand forecasting. Such collaboration can enhance efficiency by reducing overall inventory levels in a supply chain. We discuss demand forecasting in Chapter 4.

Facility Location Decisions

It's often said that the success of a retail store depends on three factors: location, location, and location. It can also be said that the success of a particular logistics system is dependent on the location of the relevant warehousing and production facilities. Facility location decisions are increasingly important as the configuration of logistics systems is altered due to the impacts of multinational trade agreements. Facility location decisions are covered in Chapter 8.

Industrial Packaging

Packaging can have both a marketing (consumer packaging) and logistical (industrial packaging) dimension. Industrial (protective) packaging refers to packaging that prepares a product for storage and transit (e.g., boxes, crates), and industrial packaging has important interfaces with the materials handling and warehousing activities. As such, Chapter 5 discusses industrial packaging in conjunction with materials handling.

Inventory Management

Inventory refers to stocks of goods that are maintained for a variety of purposes, such as for resale to others, as well as to support manufacturing or assembling processes. When managing inventory, logisticians need to simultaneously consider three relevant costs—the cost of carrying (holding) product, the cost of ordering product, and the cost of being out of stock. Chapter 9 provides further discussion concerning inventory management.

Materials Handling

Materials handling refers to the short-distance movement of products within the confines of a facility (e.g., plant, warehouse). Because materials handling tends to add costs (e.g., labor costs, product loss, and product damage) rather than value to logistics systems, managers pursue cost-efficiency objectives such as minimizing the number of handlings and moving the product in a straight line whenever possible. Materials handling considerations are presented in Chapter 5.

Order Management

Order management refers to management of the activities that take place between the time a customer places an order and the time it is received by the customer. As such, order management is a logistics activity with a high degree of visibility to customers; order management is discussed in Chapter 4 (as is customer service).

Parts and Service Support

Parts and service support refers to after-sale support for products in the form of repair parts, regularly scheduled service, emergency service, and so on. These activities can be especially important for distributors of industrial products, and relevant considerations include the number and location of repair part facilities, order management, and transportation.[31] Discussions of parts and service support appear in several chapters.

Production Scheduling

Production scheduling refers to determining how much to produce and when to produce it. As noted previously, a key interface between production and logistics involves the quantity to be produced, with increasing tension between make-to-stock (generally involving large production lots) and make-to-order (generally involving small production lots) philosophies. Production scheduling is discussed in several chapters.

Procurement

Procurement refers to the raw materials, component parts, and supplies bought from outside organizations to support a company's operations.[32] Procurement's direct link to outside organizations means that its strategic importance has increased as the supply chain management philosophy has become more popular. Procurement is discussed in more detail in Chapter 11.

Returned Products

Products can be returned for various reasons, such as product recalls, product damage, lack of demand, and customer dissatisfaction. The logistical challenges associated with returned products can be complicated by the fact that returned products often move in small quantities and may move outside forward distribution channels. This topic is examined in Chapter 13.

Salvage and Scrap Disposal

Salvage refers to "equipment that has served its useful life but still has value as a source for parts," whereas scrap refers to "commodities that are deemed worthless to the user and are only valuable to the extent they can be recycled."[33] Salvage and scrap disposal are prominent reverse logistics activities and are discussed in Chapter 11.

Transportation Management

Transportation can be defined as the actual physical movement of goods or people from one place to another, whereas transportation management (traffic management) refers to the management of transportation activities by a particular organization. As pointed out earlier, transportation can account for up to 50 percent of a firm's total logistics costs and thus represents the most costly logistics activity in many organizations. The transportation system is discussed in Chapter 6, and transportation management is discussed in Chapter 7.

Warehousing Management

Warehousing refers to places where inventory can be stored for a particular period of time. As noted previously, important changes have occurred with respect to warehousing's role in contemporary logistics and supply chain systems. Warehousing is discussed in Chapter 10.

---

[31]Lisa H. Harrington, "Win Big with Strategic 3PL Relationships," *Transportation & Distribution,* October 1999 118–126.

[32]Donald J. Bowersox, David J. Closs, and M. Bixby Cooper, *Supply Chain Logistics Management* (Boston: McGraw-Hill Irwin, 2002).

[33]Glossary of Public Purchasing and Warehouse Inventory Terms, *fcn.state.fla.us/fcn/centers/purchase/standardmanual/glossary.htm.*

LOGISTICS CAREERS

The logistics manager has a highly complex and challenging position, in part because the logistician needs to be both a generalist and specialist. As a generalist, the logistician must understand the relationship between logistics and other corporate functions, both within and outside the firm. As a specialist, the logistician must understand the relationships between various logistics activities and must have some technical knowledge of the various activities.

In recent years, the job market for logisticians has been strong at both the undergraduate and MBA levels. Logistics-related jobs include, but are not limited to, logistics analyst, consultant, customer service manager, logistics engineer, purchasing manager, transportation manager, and warehouse operations manager.[34] Unlike twenty to thirty years ago, career paths in logistics can lead to the executive suite; indeed, the current CEO of Wal-Mart began his Wal-Mart career in the logistics area. Compensation levels for entry-level positions requiring an undergraduate degree in logistics range from the mid-$30K to the lower $50K level. Moreover, the median compensation for senior-level logisticians was approximately $230,000 in 2004.[35]

Because of the growing importance of logistics, a number of professional organizations are dedicated to advancing the professional knowledge of their members. The rationale for these professional associations is that the state of the art is changing so rapidly that professionals must educate and reeducate themselves on a regular basis. Some of the more prominent professional logistics organizations are summarized in the appendix to this chapter.

Summary

This chapter introduced the topic of logistics, which the CSCMP defines as "that part of Supply Chain Management that plans, implements, and controls the efficient, effective forward and reverse flow and storage of goods, services, and related information between the point of origin and the point of consumption in order to meet customers' requirements."

The economic impacts of logistics were discussed along with reasons for the increased importance of logistics since 1980. Systems and total cost approaches to logistics were discussed, as were logistical relationships within a firm, with a particular focus on various interfaces between marketing and logistics. A brief description of a number of logistics activities was presented, and the chapter concluded with a brief look at logistics careers.

Questions for Discussion and Review

1. Did it surprise you that logistics can be such an important component in a country's economic system? Why or why not?
2. Distinguish between possession, form, time, and place utility.
3. How does logistics contribute to time and place utility?
4. How can a particular logistics system be effective but not efficient?
5. Explain the significance of the fact that the purpose of logistics is to meet customer requirements.
6. Explain how an understanding of logistics management could be relevant to your favorite charitable organization.
7. Discuss three reasons for why logistics has become more important since 1980.
8. Which reason for the increased importance of logistics do you believe is most important? Why?

---

[34]*www.cscmp.org.*

[35]Bernard LaLonde and James Ginter, "The Ohio State University 2004 Survey of Career Patterns in Logistics," retrieved from *www.cscmp.org.*

9. What are some practical implications of the idea that one logistics system does not fit all companies?
10. Distinguish between inbound logistics, materials management, and physical distribution.
11. What is the systems approach to problem solving? How is this concept applicable to logistics management?
12. Explain what is meant by the total cost approach to logistics.
13. Define what is meant by a cost trade-off. Do you believe that this concept is workable? Why or why not?
14. What are several areas in which finance and logistics might interface?
15. Briefly discuss each of the four basic aspects of the marketing mix and how each interfaces with the logistics function. In your opinion, which component of the marketing mix represents the most important interface with logistics? Why?
16. Why do marketers tend to prefer FOB destination pricing rather than FOB origin pricing?
17. What are several ways in which logistics and production might interface?
18. Briefly discuss the ownership, negotiations, financing, promotions, and logistics channels.
19. Discuss five activities that might be part of a company's logistics department.
20. Logistics managers must be both generalists and specialists. Why is this true? Does this help to explain why there tends to be an imbalance in the supply of, and demand for, logistics managers?

Suggested Readings

Bowersox, Donald J., David J. Closs, and Theodore P. Stank. "Ten Mega-trends That Will Revolutionize Supply Chain Logistics." *Journal of Business Logistics* 21, no. 2 (2000): 1–16.

Gammelgaard, Britta, and Paul D. Larson. "Logistics Skills and Competencies for Supply Chain Management." *Journal of Business Logistics* 22, no. 2 (2001): 27–50.

Giminez, Christina, and Eva Ventura. "Logistics-Production, Logistics-Marketing and External Integration: Their Impact on Performance." *International Journal of Operations and Production Management* 25, no. 1 (2005): 20–38.

Knemeyer, A. Michael, and Paul R. Murphy. "Logistics Internships: Employer and Student Perspectives." *International Journal of Physical Distribution & Logistics Management* 32, no. 2 (2002): 135–152.

Lewis, Ira. "Logistics and Electronic Commerce: An Interorganizational Systems Perspective." *Transportation Journal* 40, no. 4 (2000): 5–13.

Lowe, David. *Dictionary of Transport and Logistics.* London: Kogon Page, 2002.

Mentzer, John T., Soonhong Min, and Michelle L. Bobbitt, "Toward a Unified Theory of Logistics." *International Journal of Physical Distribution & Logistics Management* 34, no. 8 (2004): 606–627.

Mollenkopf, Diane, Antony Gibson, and Lucie Ozanne. "The Integration of Marketing and Logistics Functions: An Examination of New Zealand Firms." *Journal of Business Logistics* 21, no. 2 (2000): 89–112.

Rutner, Stephen M., and Stanley E. Fawcett. "The State of Supply Chain Education." *Supply Chain Management Review* 9, no. 6 (2005): 55–60.

Stock, James R. "Marketing Myopia Revisited: Lessons for Logistics." *International Journal of Physical Distribution & Logistics Management* 32, no. 1 (2002): 12–21.

C A S E S

CASE 1-1   SUDSY SOAP, INC.

Frank Johnson was outbound logistics manager for Sudsy Soap, Inc. He had held the job for the past five years and had just about every distribution function well under control. His task was made easier because shipping patterns and volumes were unchanging routines. The firm's management boasted that it had a steady share in "a stable market," although a few stockholders grumbled that Sudsy Soap had a declining share in a growing market.

The Sudsy Soap plant was in Akron, Ohio. It routinely produced 100,000 48-ounce cartons of powdered dish soap each week. Each carton measured about half a cubic foot, and each working day, 15 to 20 railcar loads were loaded and shipped to various food chain warehouses and to a few large grocery brokers. Johnson worked with the marketing staff to establish prices, so nearly all soap was purchased in railcar-load lots. Shipments less than a full carload did not occur very often.

Buyers relied on dependable deliveries, and the average length of time it took for a carton of soap to leave the Sudsy production line and reach a retailer's shelf was 19 days. The best time was 6 days (to chains distributing in Ohio), and the longest time was 43 days (to retailers in Alaska and Hawaii).

Sudsy Soap's CEO was worried about the stockholders' criticism regarding Sudsy's lack of growth, so he hired a new sales manager, E. Gerard Beever (nicknamed "Eager" since his college days at a Big Ten university). Beever had a one-year contract and knew he must produce. He needed a gimmick.

At his university fraternity reunion, he ran into one of his old fraternity roommates, who was now sales manager for an imported line of kitchen dishes manufactured in China and distributed by a firm headquartered in Hong Kong. The product quality was good, but competition was intense. It was difficult to get even a toehold in the kitchen dinnerware market. Beever and his contact shared a common plight: They were responsible for increasing market shares for products with very little differentiation from competitors' products. They both wished they could help each other, but they could not. The reunion ended and each went home.

The next week, Beever was surprised to receive an e-mail message from his old roommate:

We propose a tie-in promotion between Sudsy Soap and our dishes. We will supply at no cost to you 100,000 each 12-inch dinner plates, 7-inch pie plates, 9-inch bread and butter plates, coffee cups, and saucers. Each week you must have a different piece in each package, starting with dinner plates in week 1, pie plates in week 2, and so on through the end of week 5. Recommend this be done weeks of October 3, October 10, October 17, October 24, and October 31 of this year. Timing important because national advertising linked to new television show we are sponsoring. We will give buyers of five packages of Sudsy Soap, purchased five weeks in a row, one free place setting of our dishes. Enough of your customers will want to complete table settings that they will buy more place settings from our retailers. Timing crucial. Advise immediately.

Beever was pleased to receive the offer but realized a lot of questions had to be answered before he could recommend that the offer be accepted. He forwarded the message to Johnson with an added note:

Note attached message offering tie-in with dishes. Dishes are of good quality. What additional information do we need from dish distributor, and what additional information do you need before we know whether to recommend acceptance? Advise ASAP. Thanks. ■

QUESTIONS

1. Assume that you are Frank Johnson's assistant, and he asks you to look into various scheduling problems that might occur. List and discuss them.
2. What packaging problems, if any, might there be?
3. Many firms selling consumer goods are concerned with problems of product liability. Does the dish offer present any such problems? If so, what are they? Can they be accommodated?
4. Should the exterior of the Sudsy Soap package be altered to show what dish it contains? If so, who should pay for the extra costs?
5. Assume that you are another one of Johnson's assistants and your principal responsibility is managing the inventories of all the firm's inputs, finished products, packages, and outbound inventories. What additional work will the dish proposal cause for you?
6. You are Beever. Your staff has voiced many objections to the dish tie-in proposal, but you believe that much of the problem is your staff's reluctance to try anything innovative. Draft a message to the dish company that, although not accepting their proposal, attempts to clarify points that may be subject to misinterpretation and also takes into account some of your staff's legitimate concerns.

CASE 1-2   KIDDIELAND AND THE SUPER GYM

KiddieLand is a retailer of toys located in the Midwest. Corporate headquarters is in Chicago, and its 70 stores are located in Minnesota, Wisconsin, Michigan, Illinois, Indiana, Ohio, Iowa, and Kentucky. One distribution center is located in Columbus (for Kentucky, Indiana, Michigan, and Ohio) and one in Chicago (for Illinois, Iowa, Minnesota, and Wisconsin).

KiddieLand markets a full range of toys, electronic games, computers, and play sets. Emphasis is on a full line of brand-name products together with selected items sold under the KiddieLand brand. KiddieLand's primary competitors include various regional discount chains. The keys to KiddieLand's success have been a comprehensive product line, aggressive pricing, and self-service.

Donald Hurst is KiddieLand's logistics manager. He is responsible for managing both distribution centers, for traffic management, and for inventory control. Don's primary mission is to make sure all stores are in stock at all times without maintaining excessive levels of inventory.

One morning in late January, while Don was reviewing the new year's merchandising plan, he discovered that starting in March, KiddieLand would begin promoting the Super Gym Outdoor Children's Exercise Center. Don was particularly interested that the new set would sell for $715. In addition, the Super Gym is packaged in three boxes weighing a total of 450 pounds. "Holy cow!" thought Don. "The largest set we have sold to date retails for $159 and weighs only 125 pounds."

"There must be some mistake," thought Don as he walked down the hall to the office of Olga Olsen, KiddieLand's buyer for play sets. Olga was new on her job and was unusually stressed because both of her assistant buyers had just resigned to seek employment on the West Coast.

As soon as Olga saw Don, she exclaimed, "Don, my friend, I have been meaning to talk to you." Don knew right then that his worst fears were confirmed.

The next morning Don and Olga met with Randy Smith, Don's traffic manager; A. J. Toth, general manager for KiddieLand's eight Chicago stores; and Sharon Rabiega, Don's assistant for distribution services. Because the previous year had been unusually profitable, everyone was in a good mood because this year's bonus was 50 percent larger than last year's.

Nevertheless, A. J. got to the point: "You mean to tell me that we expect somebody to stuff a spouse, three kids, a dog, and 450 pounds of Super Gym in a small sedan and not have a conniption?"

Randy chimed in, "Besides, we can't drop ship Super Gyms from the manufacturer to the consumer's address because Super Gym ships only in quantities of 10 or more."

Olga was now worried. "We can't back out of the Super Gym now," she moaned. "I have already committed KiddieLand for 400 sets, and the spring–summer play set promotion went to press last week. Besides, I am depending on the Super Gym to make my gross margin figures."

"What about SUVs?" asked Toth. "They make up half the vehicles in our parking lots. Will the three packages fit inside them?"

By now the scope of the problem had become apparent to everyone at the meeting. At 3 P.M. Don summarized the alternatives discussed:

1. Purchase a two-wheeled trailer for each store.
2. Find a local trucking company that can haul the Super Gym from the KiddieLand store to the customer.
3. Stock the Super Gym at the two distribution centers and have the truck that makes delivery runs to the retail stores also make home deliveries.
4. Charge for delivery if the customer cannot get the Super Gym home.
5. Negotiate with the Super Gym manufacturer to ship directly to the customer.

When the meeting adjourned, everyone agreed to meet the following Monday to discuss the alternatives. On Thursday morning a record-breaking blizzard hit Chicago; everyone went home early. KiddieLand headquarters was closed on Friday because of the blizzard. By Wednesday, the same group met again.

Don started the meeting. "Okay," Don began, "let's review our options. Sharon, what did you find out about buying trailers for each store?"

"Well," Sharon began, "the best deal I can find is $1,800 per trailer for 70 trailers, plus $250 per store for an adequate selection of bumper hitches, and an additional $50 per year per store for licensing and insurance. Unfortunately, bumpers on the newest autos cannot accommodate trailer hitches."

"Oh, no," moaned Olga, "we only expect to sell 5.7 sets per store. That means $368 per Super Gym for delivery," she continued as she punched her calculator, "and $147 in lost gross margin!"

Next, Randy Smith summarized the second option. "So far we can get delivery within 25 miles of most of our stores for $38.21 per set. Actually," Randy continued, "$38.21 is for delivery 25 miles from the store. The rate would be a little less for under 25 miles and about $1.50 per mile beyond 25 miles."

A. J. Toth chimed in, "According to our marketing research, 85 percent of our customers drive less than 25 minutes to the store, so a flat fee of $40 for delivery would probably be okay."

Randy continued, "Most delivery companies we talked to will deliver twice weekly but not daily."

Sharon continued, "The motor carrier that handles shipments from our distribution centers is a consolidator. He said that squeezing an 18-wheeler into some subdivisions wouldn't make sense. Every time they try, they knock down a couple of mailboxes and leave truck tracks in some homeowner's lawn."

Olga added, "I talked to Super Gym about shipping direct to the customer's address, and they said forget it. Whenever they have tried that," Olga continued, "the customer gets two of one box and none of another."

"Well, Olga," Don interrupted, "can we charge the customer for delivery?"

Olga thought a minute. "Well, we have never done that before, but then we have never sold a 450-pound item before. It sounds like," Olga continued, "our choice is to either absorb $40 per set or charge the customer for delivery."

"That means $16,000 for delivery," she added.

"One more thing," Don said. "If we charge for shipping, we must include that in the copy for the spring–summer brochure."

Olga smiled. "We can make a minor insert in the copy if we decide to charge for delivery. However," she continued, "any changes will have to be made to the page proofs—and page proofs are due back to the printer next Monday." ∎

QUESTIONS

1. List and discuss the advantages and disadvantages of purchasing a two-wheeled trailer for each store to use for delivering Super Gyms.
2. List and discuss the advantages and disadvantages of having local trucking companies deliver the Super Gym from the retail stores to the customers.
3. List and discuss the advantages and disadvantages of stocking Super Gyms at the distribution centers, and then having the truck that makes deliveries from the distribution center to the retail stores also make deliveries of Super Gyms to individual customers.
4. List and discuss the advantages and disadvantages of charging customers for home delivery if they are unable to carry home the Super Gym.
5. Which alternative would you prefer? Why?
6. Draft a brief statement (catalog copy) to be inserted in the firm's spring–summer brochure that clearly explains to potential customers the policy you recommended in question 5.
7. In the first meeting, A. J. asked about SUVs, but there was no further mention of them. How would you follow up on his query?

A P P E N D I X   1

LOGISTICS PROFESSIONAL ORGANIZATIONS

APICS—The Association for Operations Management *(www.apics.org)*

APICS "builds operations management excellence in individuals and enterprises through superior education and training, internationally recognized certifications, comprehensive resources, and a worldwide network of accomplished industry professionals." APICS offers three certification programs: Certified in Integrated Resource Management (CIRM), Certified in Production and Inventory Management (CPIM), and Certified Supply Chain Professional (CSCP).

American Society of Transportation and Logistics (AST&L) *(www.astl.org)*

AST&L was founded by industry leaders "to ensure a high level of professionalism and promote continuing education in the field of transportation and logistics." It offers one certification program, Certified in Transportation and Logistics (CTL), and has added a new entry-level designation, Professional Designation in Logistics and Supply Chain Management (PLS).

Council of Supply Chain Management Professionals *(www.cscmp.org)*

Formerly known as the Council of Logistics Management, the CSCMP is a nonprofit professional organization "that helps supply chain managers connect and collaborate . . . and become more effective professionals."

Delta Nu Alpha (DNA) *(www.deltanualpha.org)*

DNA is an "international organization of professional men and women in all areas and at all levels of transportation and logistics." Its primary focus is on education.

International Society of Logistics (SOLE) *(www.sole.org)*

The International Society of Logistics, formerly the Society of Logistics Engineers, is a "non-profit international professional society composed of individuals organized to enhance the art and science of logistics technology, education and management." It has one certification program: Certified Professional Logistician (CPL).

Supply Chain & Logistics Canada (SCL) *(www.sclcanada.org)*

SCL is a "non-profit organization of business professionals interested in improving their logistics and supply chain management skills through a comprehensive program of education, research and networking opportunities."

The Chartered Institute of Logistics and Transport in the UK—CILT (UK) *(www.ciltuk.org)*

CILT (UK) "is the professional body for transport, logistics and integrated supply-chain management."

Warehousing Education and Research Council (WERC) *(www.werc.org)*

WERC is a "professional organization focused exclusively on warehousing management, providing practical, how-to-information to help members grow professionally as they improve warehouse and company performance."

2

THE SUPPLY CHAIN MANAGEMENT CONCEPT

Enhance productivity with spring-loaded latches on doors and walls for fast set-up, knock-down, and interior access.

- <u>First</u> with drop doors in the walls for quick, easy product access.
- <u>First</u> with a long side wall door to deliver secure, rigid stacking.
- <u>First</u> with solid, one-piece base for handling any load up to 2,000 lbs.

Easy collapse and wall protection with Buckhorn's unique, non-sequential folding pattern.

Prevent fork spearing and extend container life with steel corner hit plates.

Key Terms

- Agile supply chain
- Bullwhip effect
- Contract logistics
- Data mining
- Fast supply chain
- Fourth-party logistics (lead logistics provider)
- GSCF model
- Partnerships
- Perfect order
- SCOR model
- Supply chain
- Supply chain collaboration
- Supply chain management
- Third-party logistics (logistics outsourcing)

Learning Objectives

- To learn about supply chains and their management
- To understand differences between transactional and relational exchanges
- To realize the importance of leveraging technology
- To appreciate barriers to supply chain management

As pointed out in Chapter 1, contemporary thinking views logistics as part of supply chain management, and there are many examples of the importance of logistics to supply chain management. Research on underperforming supply chains, defined as those exhibiting poor service, unproductive assets, or high variable operating costs, suggests that logistical considerations can be crucial to improving substandard supply chain performance. For example, one example of poor service, damaged shipments, might be caused by shoddy materials handling practices. Poor inventory turnover, an example of unproductive assets, can be addressed by consolidating stocking points and eliminating slow-moving items. Finally, high transportation costs, one example of high operating costs, call for an examination of modal or carrier selection policies as well as of transportation routing decisions.[1]

This chapter provides an overview of **supply chain management (SCM),** and we will begin with a discussion of its evolution. Indeed, supply chain management is a relatively new concept in the sense that it was rarely mentioned in either the academic or practitioner literature prior to 1990. According to Professor Mentzer and colleagues, "the supply chain concept originated in the logistics literature, and logistics has continued to have a significant impact on the SCM concept."[2] More specifically, a dominant logistical philosophy throughout the 1980s and into the early 1990s involved the integration of logistics with other functions in an organization in an effort to achieve the enterprise's overall success.[3] The early to mid-1990s witnessed a growing recognition that there could be value in coordinating the various business functions not only within organizations but *across* organizations as well—what can be referred to as a supply chain management philosophy.

---

[1]Foster Pinley and Chap Kistler, "Fixing an Underperforming Supply Chain," *Supply Chain Management Review* 9, no. 8 (2005): 46–52.

[2]John T. Mentzer et al., "Defining Supply Chain Management," *Journal of Business Logistics* 22, no. 2 (2001): 1–25.

[3]Richard F. Poist, "Evolution of Conceptual Approaches to Designing Business Logistics Systems," *Transportation Journal* 25, no. 1 (1986): 55–64.

Since the early to mid-1990s a growing body of literature has focused on supply chains and supply chain management, and this literature has resulted in a number of definitions for both concepts. As was the case when defining logistics, it's important to have a common understanding of what is meant by *supply chain* and *supply chain management.*

A **supply chain** "encompasses all activities associated with the flow and transformation of goods from the raw material stage (extraction), through to the end user, as well as the associated information flows."[4] Figure 2-1 presents illustrations of several types of supply chains, and it's important to note several key points. First, supply chains are not a new concept in that organizations traditionally have been dependent on suppliers, and organizations traditionally have served customers. For example, Procter & Gamble (P&G), a prominent multinational company that produces consumer products, needed raw materials to make soap, as well as customers for the soap, when it was founded in 1837; today, P&G still needs raw materials to make soap—as well as customers for the soap.

Figure 2-1 also points out that some supply chains can be much more complex (in terms of the number of participating parties) than others, and coordinating complex supply chains is likely to be more difficult than doing so for less-complex supply chains. Moreover, complex supply chains may include "specialist" companies, such as third-party logistics providers, to facilitate coordination among various supply chain parties. Note also that customers are an integral component in supply chains, regardless of their complexity.

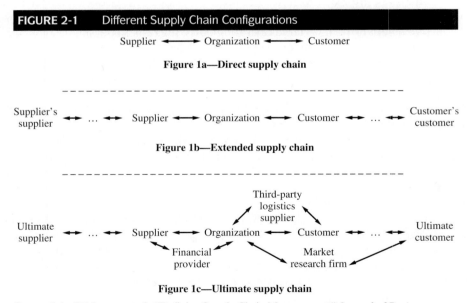

FIGURE 2-1   Different Supply Chain Configurations

Supplier ⟷ Organization ⟷ Customer

Figure 1a—Direct supply chain

Supplier's supplier ⟷ ... ⟷ Supplier ⟷ Organization ⟷ Customer ⟷ ... ⟷ Customer's customer

Figure 1b—Extended supply chain

Ultimate supplier ⟷ ... ⟷ Supplier ⟷ Organization ⟷ Customer ⟷ ... ⟷ Ultimate customer

Third-party logistics supplier
Financial provider
Market research firm

Figure 1c—Ultimate supply chain

Source: John T. Mentzer et al., "Defining Supply Chain Management," *Journal of Business Logistics* 22, no. 2 (2001): 1–25.

---

[4]Robert B. Handfield and Ernest L. Nichols, Jr., *Introduction to Supply Chain Management* (Upper Saddle River, NJ: Prentice Hall, 1999).

According to the Council of Supply Chain Management Professionals (CSCMP),

> Supply Chain Management encompasses the planning and management of all activities involved in sourcing and procurement, conversion, and all Logistics Management activities. Importantly, it also includes coordination and collaboration with channel partners, which can be suppliers, intermediaries, third-party service providers, and customers. In essence, Supply Chain Management integrates supply and demand management within and across companies.[5]

Moreover, although nearly any organization can be part of a supply chain(s), SCM "requires overt management efforts by the organizations within the supply chain."[6]

Successful supply chain management requires companies to adopt an enterprise-to-enterprise point of view, which can cause organizations to accept practices and adopt behaviors that haven't traditionally been associated with buyer–seller interactions (as will be seen in the following section). Moreover, successful supply chain management requires companies to apply the systems approach (previously mentioned in Chapter 1) across all organizations in the supply chain. When applied to supply chains, the systems approach suggests that companies must recognize the interdependencies of major functional areas within, across, and between firms. In turn, the goals and objectives of individual supply chain participants should be compatible with the goals and objectives of other participants in the supply chain. For example, a company that is committed to a high level of customer service might be out of place in a supply chain comprised of companies whose primary goal is cost containment.

Although a number of supply chain management frameworks have been developed, two of the more prominent are the **SCOR (Supply-Chain Operations Reference)** and **GSCF (Global Supply Chain Forum)** models. Their prominence is due to the fact that both identify processes in such a way that the processes can actually be implemented, and thus evaluated, by organizations; both models are also supported by major corporations.[7] Both models are briefly described next.

The SCOR model identifies five key processes—*Plan, Source, Make, Deliver, Return*—associated with supply chain management (see Figure 2-2). Moreover, closer analysis of the five key processes, and their definitions, indicates the important role of logistics in supply chain management. It can be argued that logistics has some involvement in both sourcing and making; for example, with respect to making, recall the discussion in Chapter 1 about the concept of postponement resulting in value-added activities being performed in warehousing facilities. Alternatively, logistics can be heavily involved in delivering and returning; the definition of delivery specifically mentions the key logistics components of order management, transportation management, and distribution management.

Eight relevant processes are identified in the GSCF model (see Figure 2-3)—*customer relationship management, customer service management, demand management, order fulfillment, manufacturing flow management, supplier relationship management, product development and commercialization,* and *returns management.* As is the case in the SCOR model, logistics also plays an important role in the supply chain processes in the GSCF model. For example, logistical

---

[5]*www.cscmp.org.*

[6]Mentzer et al., "Defining Supply Chain Management."

[7]Douglas M. Lambert, Sebastian J. Garcia-Dastugue, and Keely L. Croxton, "An Evaluation of Process-Oriented Supply Chain Management Frameworks," *Journal of Business Logistics* 26, no. 1 (2005): 25–51.

SCOR Process	Definitions
Plan	Processes that balance aggregate demand and supply to develop a course of action which best meets sourcing, production, and delivery requirements
Source	Processes that procure goods and services to meet planned or actual demand
Make	Processes that transform product to a finished state to meet planned or actual demand
Deliver	Processes that provide finished goods and services to meet planned or actual demand, typically including order management, transportation management, and distribution management
Return	Processes associated with returning or receiving returned products for any reason. These processes extend into post-delivery customer support

FIGURE 2-2   Five Processes in the Supply Chain Operations Reference (SCOR) Model

Source: SCOR Model, Version 5.0, Pittsburgh: Supply Chain Council, Inc.

considerations such as on-time pickup and delivery might be part of the customer service management process, whereas logistics can contribute to supplier relationship management in terms of inbound material flow. Moreover, reverse logistics is a key logistical consideration for the returns management process.[8]

KEY ATTRIBUTES OF SUPPLY CHAIN MANAGEMENT

A number of key attributes are associated with supply chain management, including customer power, a long-term orientation, leveraging technology, enhanced communication across organizations, inventory control, and interorganizational collaboration. Although each of these is discussed in the following paragraphs as discrete entities, interdependencies exist among them. For example, advances in technology could facilitate enhanced communication across organizations, whereas a long-term orientation could facilitate interorganizational collaboration.

Customer Power
You're probably familiar with the adage that "information is power." In recent years, the customer has gained tremendous power over buying decisions, in large part because of greater access to information.[9] This access, largely fueled by the Internet, allows the

---

[8]Douglas M. Lambert, "The Eight Essential Supply Chain Management Processes," *Supply Chain Management Review* 8, no. 6 (2004): 18–26.

[9]Glen. L. Urban, "Customer Advocacy: A New Era in Marketing," *Journal of Public Policy and Marketing* 24, no. 1 (2005): 155–159.

GSCF Process	Definitions
Customer Relationship Management	Provides the structure for how relationships with customers are developed and maintained
Customer Service Management	Represents the company's face to customer
Demand Management	Balances customer requirements with supply chain capabilities
Order Fulfillment	Encompasses all activities necessary to define customer requirements, design a network, and enable a firm to a meet customer requests while minimizing total delivered cost
Manufacturing Flow Management	Includes all activities necessary to obtain, implement, and manage manufacturing flexibility in the supply chain and to move products through the plants
Supplier Relationship Management	Provides the structure for how relationships with suppliers are developed and maintained
Product Development and Commercialization	Provides the structure for working with customers and suppliers to develop products and bring them to market
Returns Management	Manages activities associated with returns, reverse logistics, "gatekeeping," and return avoidance within the firm and across key members of the supply chain

FIGURE 2-3 Eight Processes in the Global Supply Chain Forum (GSCF) Model

Source: Douglas M. Lambert, "The Eight Essential Supply Chain Management Processes," *Supply Chain Management Review*, September 2004, 18–26.

consumer to become highly knoweledgable about an individual organization and its products—as well as also becoming highly knowledgeable about competing organizations and their products.

This increased power of customers has important implications for the design and management of supply chains. For example, because customer needs and wants change relatively quickly, supply chains should be fast and agile, rather than slow and inflexible. A **fast supply chain** emphasizes a speed and time component, whereas an **agile supply chain** focuses on an organization's ability to respond to changes in demand with respect to volume and variety.[10] Failure to be fast and agile can result in decreased market share, reduced profitability, lower stock price, or dissatisfied customers for supply chain participants.

Furthermore, the customer power concept suggests that traditional factory-driven, push supply chains should be replaced by customer-centric, pull-oriented ones. And where traditional supply chains use metrics (measures) such as labor costs and freight costs, customer-centric

---

[10]Martin Christopher, "The Agile Supply Chain," *Industrial Marketing Management* 29, no. 1 (2000): 37–44.

supply chains are concerned with **perfect orders** (i.e., *simultaneous* achievement of relevant customer metrics such as on-time delivery and correct order quantity) and total supply chain management cost.[11]

Long-Term Orientation

Well-run supply chains improve the long-term performance of the individual companies and the supply chain as a whole. This emphasis on long-term performance suggests that supply chains should employ a long-term as opposed to a short-term orientation with the various participants—suppliers, customers, intermediaries, and facilitators. Importantly, a long-term orientation tends to be predicated on *relational exchanges*, whereas a short-term orientation tends to focus on *transactional exchanges*. For relational exchanges to be effective, a transactional "What's in it for me?" philosophy needs to be replaced by a relational "What's in it for us?" philosophy. Relational exchanges tend to be characterized by a far different set of attributes than are transactional exchanges, including—but not limited to—trust, commitment, dependence, investment, and shared benefits.[12]

At a minimum, relational exchange may result in individual supply chain participants having to rethink (and rework) their approaches to other supply chain participants. Commitment, for example, suggests that supply chain participants recognize the importance of maintaining the relationship that has been established, as opposed to regularly changing participants to take advantage of short-term bargains. Moreover, relational exchanges—and by extension, supply chain management—cannot be successful without information sharing among various participants. However, this is much more easily said than accomplished, in part because the previously mentioned business adage, "Information is power," can make supply parties somewhat hesitant to share information, lest they jeopardize their competitive advantages or expose organizational shortcomings.

Partnerships, which can be loosely described as positive, long-term relationships between supply chain participants, are part and parcel of a relational exchange. Key characteristics of supply chain partnerships include, but are not limited to, high interdependence among supply chain participants, shared information, compatible goals, mutual trust, and buying decisions based on value as opposed to cost or price. Recent research has empirically demonstrated favorable relationships between supply chain partnerships and performance-related outcomes such as cost reduction, improved profits, and revenue growth.[13]

Leveraging Technology

It is argued that technology has been at the center of changes taking place that affect the supply chain, and that two key factors—computing power and the Internet—have sparked much of this change.[14] With respect to the former, supply chains can be complex entities consisting of multiple organizations, processes, and requirements. As such, attempts at mathematically modeling supply chains to maximize shareholder wealth or minimize costs (1) were not very practical prior to the advent of computers and (2) took a great deal of time, even after computers

---

[11]Kevin O'Marah, "The Leaders' Edge: Driven by Demand," *Supply Chain Management Review*, Vol. 9, No. 4, 2005, pp. 30-36.

[12]Robert M. Morgan and Shelby D. Hunt, "The Commitment–Trust Theory of Organizational Commitment," *Journal of Marketing,* Vol. 58, No. 3, 1994, pp. 20–38.

[13]Rachel Duffy and Andrew Fearne, "The Impact of Supply Chain Partnerships on Supplier Performance," *International Journal of Logistics Management* 15, no. 1 (2004): 57–71.

[14]Barbara Rosenbaum, "The Technology-Enabled Supply Chain Network," *Industrial Management* 43, no. 6 (2001): 6–10.

were introduced. However, the introduction and continued development of the computer chip now allows for fast, low-cost mathematical solutions to complex supply chain issues.

Business futurists Joseph Pine and James Gilmore have referred to the Internet as "the greatest force of commodization known to man, for both goods and services."[15] With respect to supply chains, the Internet can facilitate efficiency and effectiveness by providing opportunities for supply chains to simultaneously improve customer service and reduce their logistics costs.[16]

It's important to recognize that the Internet has important implications for both business-to-consumer links and business-to-business links within supply chains. (These implications are more fully discussed in later chapters.) For now, it suffices to say that the Internet can allow one supply chain party to have virtually instantaneous visibility to the same data as other parties in the supply chain. Such instantaneous visibility offers the opportunity for supply chains to become more proactive and less reactive, which can translate into lower inventories and improved profitability throughout the supply chain.[17]

Enhanced Communication across Organizations

Because supply chains depend on huge quantities of real-time information, it is essential that this information can be seamlessly transmitted across organizations. For example, retail point-of-sale information can be transmitted directly to suppliers and translated into orders for replenishment of product. Alternately, vendors may allow customers to query vendor inventory records to determine what products are in stock and where the stocks are located. The enhanced communication across organizations is dependent on both technological capabilities and a willingness to share information (part of a long-term orientation). Figure 2-4 shows a handheld computer with radio-frequency connections used to communicate some real-time inventory information regarding a truck and its contents.

Inventory Control

Another attribute of supply chain management involves various activities that can be lumped under the inventory-control rubric. For example, supply chain management attempts to achieve a smoother and better-controlled flow of inventory with fewer expensive inventory "lumps" along the way. In this situation, the focus is on reducing the so-called **bullwhip effect,** which is characterized by variability in demand orders among supply chain participants—the end result of which is inventory *lumps*.[18] In short, one aspect of inventory control in supply chain management is to move from a pattern of stops and starts to a continuous flow.

A second aspect of inventory control in supply chain management involves a reduction in the amount of inventory in the supply chain, or what one scholar has termed a *JAZ (just about zero)* approach.[19] Inventory can be reduced in a number of ways, such as smaller, more frequent orders; the use of premium transportation; demand-pull, as opposed to supply-push, replenishment; and the elimination or consolidation of slower-moving product, among others. However,

---

[15]B. Joseph Pine and James H. Gilmore, *The Experience Economy* (Boston: Harvard Business School Press, 1999).

[16]George Gecowets and Michael J. Bauer, "The e-ffect of the Internet on Supply Chain & Logistics," *World Trade* 13, no. 9 (2000): 71–80.

[17]Rosenbaum, "The Technology-Enabled Supply Chain Network."

[18]Hau L. Lee, V. Padmanabhan, and Seungin Whang, "The Bullwhip Effect in Supply Chains," *Sloan Management Review* 38, no. 3 (1997): 93–102.

[19]Richard W. Oliver, "The End of Inventory?" *The Journal of Business Strategy* 20, no. 1 (1999): 8–11.

FIGURE 2-4 Information Supplied by the Truck Driver Is Recorded and Then Transmitted by the Small Computer

Source: Photo courtesy of the Telxon Corporation.

prominent supply chain disruptions in the early part of the twenty-first century—terrorist attacks (such as September 11, 2001), natural disasters (such as hurricanes and earthquakes), and health pandemics (such as sudden acute respiratory syndrome [SARS] and avian flu) have caused some supply chains to reassess their emphasis on inventory reduction.

Interorganizational Collaboration

Because a primary objective of supply chain management is to optimize the performance of the supply chain as a whole, rather than optimizing the performance of individual organizations, collaboration among supply chain participants is essential. Collaboration within an organization (internal collaboration) can sometimes be problematic, so how can an organization successfully collaborate with other supply chain participants (external collaboration)?

A great deal has been written about supply chain collaboration in recent years, and a review of what's been written might leave the reader confused in the sense that some writings indicate that supply chain collaboration is currently more wishful thinking than practical reality, that few organizations engage in collaboration, and those that do haven't experienced much improvement in performance. Alternatively, other writings indicate that supply chain collaboration is widely applied, and participating organizations experience noticeable performance-related improvements. One reason for the widely divergent views of supply chain collaboration is that there are myriad definitions of it. For our purposes, **supply chain collaboration** will be defined as "cooperative, supply chain relationships—formal or informal—between manufacturing companies and their suppliers, business partners or customers, developed to enhance the overall business performance of both sides."[20]

In addition, some writers believe that supply chain collaboration is strategic in nature (a "narrower" view), whereas others view collaboration as ranging from transactional to strategic behaviors (a "broader" view). We'll take the broader view, which suggests that supply chain collaboration can be classified as transactional, tactical information sharing, or strategic in nature (summarized in Figure 2-5). According to this rubric, although transactional and tactical information sharing are currently the most prevalent types of collaboration, strategic collaborations are increasing and offer the best opportunity for improving supply chain performance.[21]

BARRIERS TO SUPPLY CHAIN MANAGEMENT

Although supply chain management may sound attractive from a conceptual perspective, a number of barriers can block its effective implementation, and these are discussed in the following paragraphs.

FIGURE 2-5	Levels of Supply Chain Collaboration	
Relationship Type	**Definition**	**Examples of Data Exchanged**
Transactional	Integrate and automate the flow of information to align with product flow	Purchase orders; invoices
Tactical information sharing	Share information before or after a purchase is made	Order status; product prices
Strategic	Joint buyer/seller processes, decision-making and measurement (often proprietary)	Forecasts; fulfillment processes

Source: John Matchette and Andy Seikel, "How to Win Friends and Influence Supply Chain Partners," *Logistics Today,* December 2004, 41.

---

[20]John Matchette and Andy Seikel, "How to Win Friends and Influence Supply Chain Partners," *Logistics Today,* December 2004, 40–42.
[21]Ibid.

Regulatory and Political Considerations

Several decades ago, many of the supply chain arrangements in use today would have been considered illegal under certain regulatory statutes. In the United States, for example, cross-business coordination was fostered by the passage of the National Cooperative Research and Development Act of 1984. Long-term commitments, which are one of the bedrocks of supply chain management, may stifle competition to the extent that they make it more difficult for others to enter particular markets. Although the overall global climate for business has shifted toward allowing more cooperation among firms, it still would be wise to seek sound legal advice before entering into future supply chain arrangements.

Political considerations such as war and governmental stability can also act as a barrier to supply chain management. With respect to war, the early years of the twenty-first century have witnessed ongoing tensions in the Middle East, ongoing tensions between Pakistan and India (both with nuclear weapon capabilities), and a war in Iraq, as well as civil and political unrest in various parts of Africa. These political uncertainties might cause some organizations to shy away from joining or developing supply chains that rely on companies located in warring countries. Governmental stability is also a key consideration, because supply chain management is so dependent on interorganizational coordination. Governmental policies that either discourage such coordination or discourage doing business with certain countries would obviously have a negative impact on supply chain efficiency.

Lack of Top Management Commitment

Top management commitment is regularly cited as an important component when individual companies attempt to initiate and implement new initiatives, programs, and products. Because of supply chain management's interorganizational focus, top management commitment is absolutely essential if supply chain efforts are to have any chance of success. Top management has the ability to allocate the necessary resources for supply chain endeavors and the power to structure, or restructure, corporate incentive policies to focus on achieving organizational and interorganizational (as opposed to functional) objectives.

Unfortunately, recent research presents a "mixed bag" of sorts with respect to top management commitment to supply chain management. More specifically, although senior management tends to be aware of supply chain management, actual senior management commitment to SCM occurs in only one of every three organizations.[22] Top management may be hesitant to fully commit to supply chain management because it is uncomfortable with (or does not understand) one or more of its underpinnings. For example, some companies may be uncomfortable with the concept of customer power in supply chains. Alternatively, other companies may be hesitant to enter into long-term relationships because such relationships might be perceived as limiting their operational flexibility.

Reluctance to Share, or Use, Relevant Information

One tenet of supply chain management is that well-run supply chains are characterized by information sharing among their participants. Nevertheless, some organizations are reluctant to share information, particularly information that might be considered proprietary in nature. However, this reluctance can contribute to supply chain problems because members may be

---

[22]Stanley E. Fawcett, Jeffrey A. Ogden, Gregory M. Magnan, and M. Bixby Cooper, "Organizational Commitment and Governance for Supply Chain Success," *International Journal of Physical Distribution & Logistics Management* 36, no. 1 (2006): 22–35.

making decisions based on erroneous data or assumptions. For example, one cause of the bullwhip effect is asymmetrical information among supply chain participants.

Furthermore, advances in computer hardware and software now permit copious amounts of information to be processed and analyzed relatively quickly. To this end, **data mining,** a technique that looks for patterns and relationships in relevant data, allows companies to lend order and meaning to their data. For example, frequent shopper cards, such as those offered by grocery chains, offer the opportunity to develop highly detailed profiles of individual customers. Some companies, however, are reluctant to fully utilize the information that comes from this data; they believe that the highly detailed data that can be provided by the cards—what was purchased, when it was purchased, where it was purchased, how it was purchased—potentially violate the customer's right to privacy.

Incompatible Information Systems

Twenty years ago, a major barrier to interorganizational collaboration was incompatible computer hardware; today, by contrast, software compatibility is likely the more pressing issue. A key software question involves the decision between a single integrator approach and a best-of-breed approach. In a single integrator approach, all relevant software applications (e.g., inventory management, transportation management, warehouse management) are provided by a single vendor (and might be part of one applications suite, similar to Microsoft Office). One advantage to the single integrator approach is that there should be coordination across the various applications.[23]

Alternatively, a best-of-breed approach chooses the best application for a particular function, so that an organization could have transportation management software from one company and warehouse management software from another company.[24] However, best-of-breed solutions often require additional software packages to coordinate these different applications—and these integrations don't always proceed smoothly. One well-known example of a not-so-smooth integartion involved Hershey Foods' effort to integrate several specialized supply chain software packages. The growing pains of this integration included unfilled candy orders for Halloween and Christmas, longer delivery times, increased inventory levels, and upset customers.[25]

Incompatible Corporate Cultures

Because supply chain management emphasizes a long-term orientation and partnerships between various participants, it is important that the participants be comfortable with the companies they will be working with. In a broad sense, corporate culture refers to "how we do things around here" and reflects an organization's vision, values, and strategic plans. It's important to recognize that compatible corporate cultures don't require all organizations to be the same. Rather, organizations should identify potential differences that could negatively affect supply chain effectiveness and efficiency. For example, an organization with a participative management style might not mesh very well with an organization that has an autocratic management style.[26]

---

[23]Joel D. Wisner, G. Keong Leong, and Keah-Choon Tan, *Principles of Supply Chain Management: A Balanced Approach* (Mason, OH: South-Western Publishing, 2005), Chapter 7.

[24]Ibid.

[25]Craig Stedman, "Failed ERP Gamble Haunts Hershey," *Computerworld,* November 1, 1999, 1–2.

[26]Douglas M. Lambert and A. Michael Knemeyer, "We're in This Together," *Harvard Business Review* 82, no. 12 (2004) 114–122.

All manifestations of corporate culture may provide important clues about the ability of companies to work together. For instance, one of the more notable supply chain failures in recent years involved the dissolution of the relationship between Office Max and Ryder Integrated Logistics. Although a number of reasons explain why this relationship didn't succeed, the two companies had quite different dress codes. Indeed, a Ryder manager told one of the authors that it was clear from the first face-to-face meeting that the companies were going to have difficulty working together—in large part because of their vastly different dress codes!

Globalization

Although much of the discussion so far has focused on domestic supply chains, one should recognize that supply chains are becoming increasingly global in nature. Reasons for the increased globalization of supply chains include lower-priced materials and labor, the global perspective of companies in a supply chain, and the development of global competition, among others.[27] Supply chain integration can be challenging in a domestic setting, but integration challenges are even greater in global supply chains due to cultural, economic, technological, political, spatial, and logistical differences.

Global supply chains translate into both longer and more unpredictable lead times (time from when an order is placed until it is received) for shipments, which increases the chance that customer demand might not be fulfilled, due to a potential out-of-stock situation. In addition, recent research indicates that glitches are routine occurrences in global supply chains; causes include, but are not limited to, documentation errors, packaging errors, routing errors, incomplete shipments, and failure to follow order guidelines. These and other global supply chain glitches drive up supply chain costs and potentially jeopardize customer satisfaction.[28]

SUPPLY CHAIN MANAGEMENT AND INTEGRATION

An individual firm can be involved in multiple supply chains at the same time, and it's important to recognize that expectations and required knowledge can vary across supply chains. For example, food manufacturers may sell to grocery chains, institutional buyers, specialty firms (which might position the food items as gifts), and industrial users (which might use the product as an ingredient in another product that they manufacture). It seems reasonable to assume that the packaging expectations of specialty firms might be more demanding than those of industrial users.

Supply chains are integrated by having various parties enter into and carry out long-term mutually beneficial agreements. These agreements are known by several names, to include *partnerships, strategic alliances, third-party arrangements,* and *contract logistics.* Whatever they are called, these agreements should be designed to reward all participants when collaborative ventures are successful, and they should also provide incentives for all parties to work toward success. In a similar fashion, the participants should share the consequences when cooperative ventures are less successful than desired.

When an organization enters into a long-term agreement with a source or customer, the organization must keep in mind how this arrangement could affect the rest of the supply

---

[27]Pedro Reyes, Mahesh S. Raisinghani, and Manoj Singh, "Global Supply Chain Management in the Telecommunications Industry: The Role of Information Technology in Integration of Supply Chain Entities," *Journal of Global Information Technology Management* 5, no. 2 (2002): 48–67.

[28]Beth Enslow, "Best Practices in Global Trade Management Stress Speed and Flexibility," *World Trade*, January 2006, 36–40.

chain. Ideally, all participants in the supply chain will meet at one time and work out whatever agreements are necessary to ensure that the entire supply chain functions in the most desirable manner.

To integrate a particular supply chain, the various organizations must recognize the shortcomings of the present system and examine channel arrangements as they currently exist and as they might be. All this is done within the framework of the organization's overall strategy, as well as any logistics strategies necessary to support the goals and objectives of the firm's top management.

Broadly speaking, organizations can pursue three primary methods when attempting to integrate their supply chains. One method is through *vertical integration,* where one organization owns multiple participants in the supply chain; indeed, the Ford Motor Company of the 1920s owned forests and steel mills and exercised tight control over its dealers. The most common examples of vertical integration today are some lines of paint and automotive tires. It's important to recognize that regulations (often in the form of state laws) may limit the degree of vertical integration that will be permitted in particular industries.

A second possible method of supply chain coordination involves the use of *formal contracts* among various participants. One of the more popular uses of contracts is franchising, which attempts to combine the benefits of tight integration of some functions along with the ability to be very flexible while performing other functions. From a supply chain perspective, a franchiser may exert contractual influence over what products are purchased by a franchisee, acceptable vendors (suppliers) of these products, and the distribution of the product to the franchisee. For example, distribution for some McDonald's franchisees in the United States (e.g., food, beverage, and store supplies) is provided by the Martin-Brower Company.

A third method of supply chain coordination involves *informal agreements* among the various organizations to pursue common goals and objectives, with control being exerted by the largest organization in the supply chain. Although this method offers supply chain participants flexibility in the sense that organizations can exit unprofitable or unproductive arrangements quickly and with relative ease, organizations should be aware of potential shortcomings. For one, the controlling organization may be so powerful that the supply chain becomes more like a dictatorship than a partnership. Moreover, the same flexibility that allows for exiting unprofitable or unproductive arrangements also allows parties the ability to switch supply chains when presented with what appears to be a better deal.

Third-Party Logistics

In Figure 2-1, we saw that the ultimate supply chain contains several types of organizations (e.g., financial provider, third-party logistics supplier, market research firm), which exist to facilitate coordination among various supply chain participants. Because this is a logistics textbook, the most relevant facilitator for our purposes is the third-party logistics supplier, so it is especially relevant to examine its impact on logistics and supply chains.

Third-party logistics, also called **logistics outsourcing** or **contract logistics,** continues to be one of the most misunderstood terms in logistics and supply chain management. As we have seen with other supply chain concepts (e.g., collaboration, supply chain management), there is no commonly accepted definition of third-party logistics (3PL). Some definitions, for instance, take a "broad" perspective by suggesting that any logistics activity not performed in house is representative of third-party logistics. Other definitions, in contrast, emphasize that 3PL arrangements involve a long-term perspective between buyer and seller and that the parties have a relationship, as opposed to transactional, perspective.

Regardless of whether one takes a broad or narrow perspective, the general idea behind third-party logistics is that one company (say, a manufacturer) allows a specialist company to provide it with one or more logistics functions (e.g., warehousing, outbound transportation). Some well-known 3PL providers include Exel Logistics, FedEx Supply Chain Services, Kuehne and Nagle, Schenker Logistics, and UPS Supply Chain Solutions. A great deal of consolidation has occurred among 3PL providers in recent years (e.g., Deutsche Post acquired Exel, UPS Supply Chain Solutions acquired Menlo Logistics, among others), and this consolidation is expected to continue into the future. Although these consolidations could provide customers a broader range of supply chain services, consolidation could also lead to fewer competitive options.[29]

What we'll call *contemporary* third-party logistics began to emerge in the second half of the 1980s, and several factors distinguish contemporary 3PL from previous incarnations. First, this system tends to have formal contracts between providers and users that are at least one year (typically three to five years) in duration. Contemporary 3PL also tends to be characterized by a relational (as opposed to a transactional) focus, a focus on mutual benefits, and the availability of customized (as opposed to standardized) offerings.[30] Thus, a contemporary 3PL provider views its customer as a party with whom it is going to have a long-term, as opposed to short-term, relationship. In addition, 3PL providers and users actively seek out policies and practices, such as cost reduction, that can benefit both parties. Finally, the nature and scope of customized offerings can be specified in the relevant contract, and they often require both parties to make specific investments to fulfill the relationship.

Contemporary third-party logistics has shown tremendous growth over the past 15 years. In the early 1990s, U.S. expenditures for 3PL services were approximately $10 billion, whereas in 2005 these expenditures exceeded $100 billion, and some sources suggest that U.S. 3PL expenditures should grow by at least 10 percent per year through 2010. And although contemporary 3PL has generally been associated with Western Europe and North America, there are indications that third-party logistics will become increasingly important in other parts of the world, such as Eastern Europe and Asia.

3PL customers can demand a number of different activities, with some of the most common involving inbound and outbound transportation, carrier negotiation and contracting, and freight consolidation.[31] Moreover, some 3PL providers have begun to offer so-called supplemental services—such as final product assembly, product installation, and product repair, among others—that are beyond their traditional offerings. As noted in Chapter 1, these supplemental 3PL services can blur traditional distinctions among supply chain participants (e.g., product assembly has generally been performed by the manufacturing group). Importantly, however, this blurring of distinctions may actually facilitate supply chain integration, in that there is less emphasis on functional issues and more emphasis on cross-functional processes.[32]

The decision to use 3PL services can be driven by strategic considerations, in the sense that an organization believes that one or more aspects of its supply chain(s) need to be transformed.

---

[29]Jeff Berman, "Recent Deals Drive Logistics Industry Consolidation," *Logistics Management*, January 2006, 14–16.

[30]J. M. Africk and C. S. Calkins, "Does Asset Ownership Mean Better Service?" *Transportation and Distribution* 35, no. 5 (1994): 49–61.

[31]A. Michael Knemeyer, Thomas M. Corsi, and Paul R. Murphy, "Logistics Outsourcing Relationships: Customer Perspectives," *Journal of Business Logistics* 24, no. 1 (2003): 77–109.

[32]Remko I. van Hoek, "The Contribution of Performance Measurement to the Expansion of Third-Party Logistics Alliances in the Supply Chain," *International Journal of Operations & Production Management* 21, no. 1/2 (2001): 15–29.

Alternatively, the decision to use 3PL services could be more tactical in nature; an organization might have an inefficient distribution network, an inability to control internal costs, a costly or inflexible workforce, outdated warehousing facilities, or outdated information systems. Whether strategic or tactical in nature, the use of 3PL services is driven by recognition that an organization does not have sufficient internal capabilities to address the issue, or issues, in question.[33]

Although logistics outsourcing has the potential to improve both the effectiveness and efficiency of supply chains, 3PL arrangements can easily result in failure (i.e., an inability for one party to provide what is expected by the other party). One common cause of 3PL failure is unreasonable and unrealistic expectations, generally from the user's perspective; for example, it might be unrealistic (and unreasonable) for a customer to expect a 3PL provider to cut the user's annual transportation expenditures by 50 percent. Another cause of failure in 3PL arrangements involves a lack of flexibility. Regardless of how thoroughly the provider and customer have prepared for a 3PL arrangement, unexpected issues and challenges are bound to arise. Has the arrangement been structured so that unexpected occurrences can be dealt with in a timely and satisfactory manner?[34]

One measure of the pervasiveness of outsourcing in supply chain management can be seen in the evolution of **fourth-party logistics (4PL)**, or the **lead logistics provider (LLP),** concept, which emerged in the mid-1990s. Because 4PL/LLP is still relatively young, there is disagreement as to what it should be called as well as how it should be defined. With respect to the former, lead logistics provider appears to be emerging as the moniker of choice, but some providers, such as UPS Supply Chain Services, don't use either term to describe their services. And although an exact definition is elusive, for our purposes 4PL/LLP will refer to a company whose primary purpose is to ensure that various 3PLs are working toward the relevant supply chain goals and objectives. Whatever one calls it, by one estimate, 4PL/LLP currently accounts for approximately 20 percent of total logistics outsourcing expenditures, and revenues are projected to continue growing in the future.[35]

The 4PL/LLP concept appears to be well suited for large organizations with global supply chains such as General Motors, Ford, Merck, and Carrefour. Vector SCM, a joint venture between General Motors (GM) and Con-way, Inc. (formerly CNF, Inc.), is perhaps the quintessential 4PL/LLP. Vector SCM was initially established to manage and integrate GM's supply chain for inbound materials and finished goods and is also in charge of GM's logistics expenditures, which are approximately $6 billion per year.[36]

Supply Chain Software

It has been pointed out on several occasions that the interorganizational coordination of activities, functions, and processes is a daunting task. A large part of the challenge of interorganizational coordination involves the tremendous amount of information to be transmitted across, and be available to, supply chain participants. To this end, supply chain software packages have been developed to address the data and informational needs of supply chain participants, and these packages run the gamut in terms of costs and problem-solving capabilities.

---

[33]Brooks Bentz, "So You Think You Want to Outsource?" *Logistics Today*, May 2006, 24–27.

[34]James A. Tompkins, "The Business Imperative of Outsourcing," *Industrial Management*, January/February 2006, 8–12.

[35]David Biederman, "Inside the Supply Chain: Fourth-Party Logistics," *The Journal of Commerce*, June 6, 2005, 28–31.

[36]Ibid.

Software costs can range from $0 (e.g., *www.freightquote.com*) to tens of millions of dollars (e.g., enterprise resource planning installations). With respect to problem-solving capabilities, some software packages focus on specific functional areas, such as inventory management, reverse logistics, transportation management, or warehousing mangement. Other software packages focus on specific supply chain processes, such as collaborative planning, forecasting and replenishment (CPFR), customer relationship management (CRM), or supplier relationship management (SRM). Still other packages attempt to simultaneously optimize supply chain processes across organizations. Regardless of which type of software package is chosen, it's important to keep in mind that many are developed for general applications, and buyers may need to modify the packages to address their specific needs, thus adding to the costs of the software.

The supply chain software market has been characterized by a great deal of consolidation in recent years, spurred in part by major enterprise resource planning (ERP) vendors such as SAP and Oracle. Although ERP vendors began to add logistics-related modules to their newer edition ERP programs (such as Sap R/3), these logistics-related modules haven't been as strong as best-of-breed applications. To address this shortcoming, Oracle has acquired two highly regarded supply chain software vendors, Retek (inventory management) and G-Log (transportation management), since 2004; these acquisitions allow Oracle to offer potential customers a software suite consisting of an ERP package along with inventory management and transportation management.[37]

Summary

This chapter focused on the supply chain concept and began by defining supply chain and supply chain management. Supply chains consist of a number of different parties and include the end customer; supply chain management requires companies to adopt an enterprise-to-enterprise point of view.

The chapter also discussed key attributes of supply chain management, such as customer power, a long-term orientation, and leveraging technology. Various barriers to supply chain management, such as lack of top management commitment and reluctance to share, or use, relevant data, were also presented. We also looked at integration in supply chain management with a particular emphasis on third-party logistics and supply chain software.

Questions for Discussion and Review

1. Discuss the differences between a supply chain and supply chain management.
2. Discuss the SCOR and GSCF models of supply chain management.
3. What are four key attributes of supply chain management?
4. Why do contemporary supply chains need to be fast and agile?
5. What is the difference between relational and transactional exchanges? Which is more relevant for supply chain management? Why?
6. This chapter suggests that technology has been at the center of changes taking place that affect the supply chain. Do you agree or disagree? Why?
7. Discuss the impact of the Internet on supply chain management.
8. Discuss some of the ways that inventory can be reduced in the supply chain.
9. Do you agree or disagree that supply chain collaboration can be classified as transactional, tactical information sharing, or strategic in nature? Why?
10. How might regulatory and political conditions act as barriers to supply chain management?

---

[37]William Hoffman, "Supply Chain Version 2.0," *Traffic World*, October 3, 2005, 19.

11. Why is top management commitment necessary for successful supply chain management?
12. Some companies are hesitant to use frequent shopper cards because the data provided could violate the customer's privacy. Do you agree or disagree? Why?
13. Discuss the best of breed and single integrator approaches.
14. Do you think corporate cultures are relevant for supply chain management? Why or why not?
15. Why is supply chain integration so difficult in global supply chains?
16. Discuss the three primary methods that organizations can use to integrate their supply chains.
17. Discuss the factors that distinguish contemporary third-party logistics from earlier types of third-party logistics.
18. What are some reasons for using third-party logistics services? What are some reasons that third-party logistics arrangements aren't always successful?
19. Do you agree or disagree with the sentiment that fourth-party logistics companies (lead logistics providers) merely add unnecessary cost and few service improvements to supply chains? Why?
20. Discuss the various types of supply chain software.

Suggested Readings

Bagchi, Prabir K., and Tage Skjoett-Larsen. "Supply Chain Integration: A European Survey." *International Journal of Logistics Management* 16, no. 2 (2005): 275–290.

Christopher, Martin, and Hau Lee. "Mitigating Supply Chain Risk Through Improved Confidence." *International Journal of Physical Distribution & Logistics Management* 34, no. 5 (2004): 388–396.

Cooper, Martha C., Douglas M. Lambert, and Janus D. Pagh. "Supply Chain Management: More Than a New Name for Logistics." *International Journal of Logistics Management* 8, no. 1 (1997): 1–14.

Ellram, Lisa M., Wendy L. Tate, and Corey Billington. "Understanding and Managing the Services Supply Chain." *Journal of Supply Chain Management: A Global Review of Purchasing & Supply* 40, no. 4 (2004): 17–32.

Gibson, Brian J., John T. Mentzer, and Robert L. Cook. "Supply Chain Management: The Pursuit of a Consensus Definition." *Journal of Business Logistics* 26, no. 2 (2005): 17–25.

Fawcett, Stanley E., Jeffrey A. Ogden, Gregory M. Magnan, and M. Bixby Cooper. "Organizational Commitment and Governance for Supply Chain Success." *International Journal of Physical Distribution & Logistics Management* 36, no. 1 (2006): 22–35.

Fawcett, Stanley E., Lisa M. Ellram, and Jeffrey A. Ogden. *Supply Chain Management: From Vision to Implementation* (Upper Saddle River, NJ: Prentice Hall, 2007).

Larson, Paul D., Peter Carr, and Kewal S. Dhariwal. "SCM Involving Small versus Large Suppliers: Relational Exchange and Electronic Communication Media." *Journal of Supply Chain Management: A Global Review of Purchasing & Supply* 41, no. 1 (2005): 18–29.

Lieb, Robert C. "The 3PL Industry: Where It's Been, Where It's Going." *Supply Chain Management Review* 9, no. 6 (2005): 20–27.

Reeve, James M., and Mandyam M. Srinivasan. "Which Supply Chain Design Is Right for YOU?" *Supply Chain Management Review* 9, no. 4 (2005): 50–57.

Sengupta, Sumantra. "The Top 10 Supply Chain Mistakes." *Supply Chain Management Review* 8, no. 5 (2004): 42–49.

Simatupang, Togar M., and Ramaswami Sridharan. "The Collaboration Index: A Measure for Supply Chain Collaboration." *International Journal of Physical Distribution & Logistics Management* 35, no. 1 (2005): 44–62.

Wisner, Joel D., G. Keong Leong, and Keah-Choon Tan. *Principles of Supply Chain Management: A Balanced Approach* (Mason, OH: South-Western Publishing, 2005).

CASES

CASE 2-1   JOHNSON TOY COMPANY

Located in Biloxi, Mississippi, the Johnson Toy Company is celebrating its seventy-fifth year of business. Amy Johnson, who is president, and Lori Johnson, who is vice president, are sisters and are the third generation of their family to be involved in the toy business. The firm manufactures and sells toys throughout the United States. The toy business is very seasonal, with the majority of sales occurring before Christmas. A smaller peak occurs in the late spring–early summer period, when sales of outdoor items are good.

The firm relies on several basic designs of toys—which have low profit margins but are steady sellers—and on new designs of unconventional toys, whose introduction is always risky but promises high profits if the item becomes popular. The firm advertises regularly on Saturday morning television shows for children.

Late last year, just before Christmas, the Johnson Toy Company introduced Jungle Jim the Jogger doll, modeled after a popular television show. Sales skyrocketed, and every retailer's stock of Jungle Jim the Jogger dolls was sold out in mid-December; the Johnson Company could have sold several million more units if they had been available before Christmas. Based on the sales success of this doll, Amy and Lori made commitments to manufacture 10 million Jungle Jim the Jogger dolls this year and to introduce a wide line of accessory items, which they hoped every doll owner would also want to have. Production was well underway, and many retailers were happy to accept dolls in January and February because they were still a fast-selling item, even though the toy business itself was sluggish during these months.

Unfortunately, in the aftermath of a Valentine's Day party in Hollywood, the television actor who portrayed Jungle Jim the Jogger became involved in a widely publicized sexual misadventure, the details of which shocked and disgusted many readers and TV viewers, and we would be embarrassed to describe them. Ratings of the television series plummeted, and within a month it had been dropped from the air. On March 1, the Johnson Company had canceled further production of the Jungle Jim the Jogger dolls, although it had to pay penalties to some of its suppliers because of the cancellation. The company had little choice because it was obvious that sales had stopped.

On April 1, a gloomy group assembled in the Johnson Company conference room. Besides Amy and Lori, those present included Carolyn Coggins, the firm's sales manager; Cheryl Guridi, the logistics manager; Greg Sullivan, the controller; and Kevin Vidal, the plant engineer. Coggins had just reported that she believed there were between 1.5 million and 2 million Jungle Jim the Jogger dolls in retail stores, and Sullivan had indicated there were 2,567,112 complete units in various public warehouses in Biloxi. Vidal said that he was still trying to count all the unassembled component parts, adding that one problem was that they were still being received from suppliers, despite the cancellation.

Amy said, "Let's wait a few weeks to get a complete count of all the dolls and all the unassembled component parts. Lori, I'm naming you to work with Carolyn and Kevin to develop recommendations as to how we can recycle the Jungle Jim item into something we can sell. Given the numbers involved, I'm willing to turn out some innocuous doll and sell it for a little more than the cost of recycling because we can't take a complete loss on all these damned Jungle Jim dolls! Greg says we have nearly 2.6 million of them to play with, so let's think of something."

"Your 2.6-million figure may be low," said Coggins. "Don't forget that there may be nearly 2 million in the hands of the dealers and that they will return them."

"Return them?" questioned Amy. "They're not defective. That's the only reason we accept returns. The retailers made a poor choice. It's the same as if they ordered sleds and then had a winter with no snow. We are no more responsible for Jungle Jim's sex life than they are!"

Cheryl Guridi spoke up: "You may be underestimating the problem, Amy. One of our policies is to accept the dealer's word as to what is defective, and right now there are a lot of dealers out there claiming defects in the Jungle Jim dolls. One reason that Kevin can't get an accurate count is that returned dolls are showing up on our receiving dock and getting mixed up with our in-stock inventory."

"How can that happen?" asked Amy, angrily. "We're not paying the freight, also, are we?"

"So far, no," responded Guridi. "The retailers are paying the freight just to get rid of them."

"We've received several bills in which the retailer has deducted the costs of the Jungle Jim dolls and of the freight for shipping them back from what he owes us," said Sullivan. "That was one item I wanted to raise while we were together."

"We can't allow that!" exclaimed Amy.

"Don't be so sure," responded Sullivan. "The account in question has paid every bill he's owed us on time for 40 years. Do you want *me* to tell him we won't reimburse him?"

"This is worse than I imagined," said Amy. "Just what are our return policies, Lori?"

"Well, until today, I thought we had only two," said Lori. "One for our small accounts involves having our salespeople inspect the merchandise when they make a sales call. They can pick it up and give the retailer credit off the next order."

"Sometimes they pick up more than defective merchandise," added Coggins. "Often, they'll take the slow movers out of the retailer's hands. We have to do that as a sales tool."

"That's not quite right," interjected Vidal. "Sometimes, the returned items are just plain shopworn—scratched, dented, and damaged. That makes it hard for us because we have to inspect every item and decide whether it can be put back into stock. When we think a particular salesperson is accepting too many shopworn items, we tell Carolyn, although it's not clear to me that the message reaches the salespeople in the field."

"I wish I had an easy solution," said Coggins. "We used to let our salespeople give credit for defects and then destroy everything out in the field. Unfortunately, some abused the system and resold the toys to discount stores. At least now we can see everything we're buying back. I agree we are stuck with some shopworn items, but our salespeople are out there to sell, and nothing would ruin a big sale quicker than for our salespeople to start arguing with the retailer, on an item-by-item basis, as to whether something being returned happens to be shopworn."

"Is there a limit to what a salesperson is permitted to allow a retailer to return?" asked Amy.

"Well, not until now," responded Coggins. "But with this Jungle Jim snafu we can expect the issue to occur. In fact, I have several phone queries on my desk concerning this. I thought I'd wait until after this meeting to return them."

"Well, I think we'd better establish limits—right now," said Amy.

"Be careful," said Lori. "When I was out with the salespeople last year, I gathered the impression that some were able to write bigger orders by implying that we'd take the unsold merchandise back, if need be. If we assume that risk, the retailer is willing to take more of our merchandise."

"Are there no limits to this policy?" asked Amy.

"Informal ones," was Coggins's response. "It depends on the salesperson and the account. I don't think there is much abuse, although there is some."

"How do the goods get back to us under these circumstances?" asked Amy.

"The salespeople either keep them and shuffle them about to other customers, or—if it's a real loser—they ask us what to do," replied Coggins.

"Greg," said Amy, "do our records reflect these returns and transfers?"

"Oh, fairly well," was his response. "We lose track of individual items and quantities, but if the salesperson is honest—and I think ours are—we can follow the dollar amount of the return to the salesperson's inventory, to another retailer, or back here to us. We do not have good controls on the actual items that are allowed for returns. Kevin and I have difficulty in reconciling the value of returned items that wind up back here. Carolyn's records say they're okay for resale, and Kevin says they're too badly damaged."

"I insist on the reconciliation before we allow the goods back into our working inventory," said Guridi. "That way I know exactly what I have here, ready to ship."

"You know, I'm finding out more information about inventories and returns than I thought existed," said Amy.

"Too many trips to Paris, dearest," said Lori, and the others all suppressed smiles.

Amy decided to ignore Lori's remark, and she looked at Guridi and asked, "Are you satisfied with your control over inventories, Cheryl?"

"I have no problem with the ones here in Biloxi," was Guridi's response, "but I have an awful time with the inventories of return items that salespeople carry about with them, waiting to place them with another retailer. I'm not always certain they're getting us top dollar, and each salesperson knows only his or her own territory. When Carolyn and I are trying to monitor the sales of some new item, we never know whether it's bombing in some areas and riding around in salespeople's cars as they try to sell it again."

"Have you now described our returns policy, such as it is?" asked Amy, looking at everybody in the room.

"No," was the response murmured by all. Sullivan spoke: "For large accounts we deduct a straight 2 percent off wholesale selling price to cover defectives, and then we never want to hear about the defectives from these accounts at all."

"That sounds like a better policy," said Amy. "How well is it working?"

"Up until Jungle Jim jogged where he shouldn't, it worked fine. Now a number of large accounts are pleading 'special circumstances' or threatening to sue if we don't take back the dolls."

"They have no grounds for suit," declared Amy.

"You're right," said Coggins, "but several of their buyers are refusing to see our sales staff until the matter is resolved. I just heard about this yesterday and meant to bring it up in today's meeting. I consider this very serious."

"Damn it!" shouted Amy, pounding the table with her fist. "I hope that damned jogger dies of jungle rot! We're going to lose money this year, and now you're all telling me how the return policy works, or doesn't work, as the case may be! Why can't we just have a policy of all sales being final and telling retailers that if there is an honest defect they should send the goods back here to us in good old Biloxi?"

"Most of the small accounts know nothing about shipping," responded Vidal. "They don't know how to pack, they don't know how to prepare shipping documents, and they can't choose the right carriers. You ought to see the hodgepodge of shipments we receive from them. In more cases than not, they pay more in shipping charges than the products are worth to us. I'd rather see them destroyed in the field."

Sullivan spoke up. "I'd object to that. We would need some pretty tight controls to make certain the goods were actually destroyed. What if they are truly defective, but improperly disposed of, then fall into the hands of children who play with them and the defect causes an injury? Our name may still be on the product, and the child's parents will no doubt claim the item was purchased from one of our retailers. Will we be liable? Why can't we have everything come back here? We have enough volume of some returned items that we could think in terms of recycling parts."

Vidal responded, "Recycling is a theoretical solution to such a problem, but only in rare instances will it pay. In most instances the volume is too small and the cost of taking toys apart is usually very high. However, the Jungle Jim product involves such a large volume that it is prudent and reasonable to think up another product that utilizes many of the parts. It would even pay to modify some machines for disassembling the Jungle Jim doll."

"As I listen to this discussion," said Lori, "one fact becomes obvious: We will never have very good knowledge about volume or patterns of returns until it's too late. That's their very nature."

Guridi asked, "Could we have field representatives who do nothing but deal with this problem? The retailers would be told to hang onto the defectives until our claims reps arrive."

Coggins replied, "That would be expensive, because most retailers have little storage space for anything and would expect our claims rep to be there immediately. Besides, it might undermine our selling efforts if retailers could no longer use returns to negotiate with as they talked about new orders."

"That may be," interjected Amy, "but we cannot continue having each salesperson tailoring a return policy for each retailer. That's why we're in such a mess with the jogger doll. We have to get our return policy established, made more uniform, and enforced. We cannot go through another fiasco like Jungle Jim the Jogger for a long time. We're going to lose money this year, no matter what, and I have already told Kevin that there will be virtually no money available for retooling for next year's new products." ∎

QUESTIONS

1. From the standpoint of an individual concerned with accounting controls, discuss and evaluate Johnson Toy Company's present policies for handling returned items.
2. Answer question 1, but from the standpoint of an individual interested in marketing.
3. Propose a policy for handling returns that should be adopted by the Johnson Toy Company. Be certain to list circumstances under which exceptions would be allowed. Should it apply to the Jungle Jim dolls?
4. Should this policy, if adopted, be printed and distributed to all of the retailers who handle Johnson Toy Company products? Why or why not? If it should not be distributed to them, who should receive copies?
5. Assume that it is decided to prepare a statement on returns to be distributed to all retailers and that it should be less than a single double-spaced page. Prepare such a statement.
6. On the basis of the policy in your answer to question 3, develop instructions for the Johnson Toy Company distribution and accounting departments with respect to their roles and procedures in the handling of returns.
7. Assume that you are Cheryl Guridi, the firm's logistics manager. Do you think that the returns policy favored by the logistics manager would differ from what would be best for the firm? Why or why not?
8. Until the policy you recommend in your answer to question 3 takes effect, how would you handle the immediate problem of retailers wanting to return unsold Jungle Jim the Jogger dolls?

CASE 2-2   WYOMO GROCERY BUYERS' COOPERATIVE

Located in Billings, Montana, the Wyomo Grocery Buyers' Cooperative served the dry grocery and produce needs of about 150 area food stores from Great Falls to Butte in the northwest and from Casper to Cheyenne in the southeast. All dry groceries were shipped out of a 20,000-square-foot warehouse in Billings, built by the co-op in 1968. Produce was handled out of the Billings warehouse and small, rented warehouses in Cheyenne and Great Falls. At these warehouses, the co-op bagged some bulk products, such as potatoes, onions, and oranges, into 5-, 10-, and 20-pound bags carrying the co-op label. The warehouses also stocked items used by the stores, such as butcher paper, cash-register tape, plastic produce bags, and various sizes of brown bags.

The co-op had its own fleet of 15 tractors and 19 trailers that operated out of Billings, as well as 6 straight trucks with refrigerated bodies, with 2 each working out of Billings, Cheyenne, and Great Falls. Dry grocery deliveries were made once or twice a week, and produce deliveries were handled separately and were made two or three times a week, depending on each store's volume. Both dry grocery and produce trucks traveled approximately the same routes each week, and goods for both large and small stores were carried aboard the same truck. Stores were responsible for placing orders with the co-op, although a co-op representative would call on a weekly basis, and one of her or his functions was to help some store operators complete their order forms.

The co-op was owned by member grocery stores and run by a board of directors elected by the member stores. The directors hired the general manager, Peter Bright. Directors were elected with member stores having at least one vote. Stores with larger sales volumes got more votes, although their additional votes were not proportional to their additional sales. (This was because several years ago smaller stores realized they could lose their power, so they capped the additional votes a larger store could be given.)

Goods were being sold to members on the basis of cost to the co-op plus 23 percent to cover warehousing and transportation from the warehouses to the members' retail stores. Each year the co-op's revenues exceeded costs by a small margin; 20 percent of this excess was returned to the members in direct proportion to their purchases from the co-op, and the remainder was considered capital and reinvested in the co-op. The co-op's level of business was not growing. Its members were losing sales to chain food stores and chain discount department stores, which were moving into the region.

A continual problem facing the board of directors was the political split between small and large stores belonging to the co-op. Small grocery stores stocked only 1,000 to 2,000 different items or lines of merchandise (stock-keeping units or SKUs) carried by the co-op, whereas larger members needed to carry 6,000 to 8,000 SKUs to compete with the chains. The latter group of co-op members consisted of the more aggressive merchants, most of whom felt that the co-op should forget about its small members and instead help them battle the chains. From time to time they threatened to form their own co-op.

At issue was a long-standing controversy that was debated at every quarterly meeting of the co-op's directors. Indeed, it had been a problem since the 1950s, when tissue manufacturers started manufacturing toilet paper and facial tissues in colors in addition to white. Later they introduced floral patterns for facial tissue and, more recently, started packaging in a variety of designer dispenser boxes. The tissue manufacturers did this to capture more shelf space in retailers' stores. For example, if only white tissue were sold, it could be displayed on a shelf and occupy only 12 inches of shelf space (measured along the front). If white, pink, yellow, blue, and green tissue were all to be displayed, each would require its own 12 inches of shelf space, so a total of 60 inches of shelf space would be needed. The same held for toilet paper (and many other products).

From the co-op's standpoint, five colors of tissue multiplied the warehouse workload because each color of tissue was handled as a separate product or SKU. Each required a line on order forms, each required its own slot in warehouses, and each had to be picked separately. However, total volume of tissue handled remained the same. The volume that was once white was now merely spread over five colors. From the co-op's warehousing standpoint, the only result had been to raise handling costs as a percentage of sales volume.

The co-op's small-store members, who continued to carry only white tissue and toilet paper, thought that it was unfair for the co-op to raise its handling charges because some of its large-store members now wanted to carry five colors of tissue. Large-store members retorted that they had to carry this variety if they were to compete successfully with the chains.

The main warehouse, built in 1968, had now reached its capacity. Actually, it was over capacity. It was built and engineered to carry 7,000 to 7,500 SKUs, but it was now carrying just over 8,000. Some items were doubled up in slots or left in aisles or at one of the receiving docks, but these practices were causing operational difficulties and driving up costs.

At the directors' quarterly meeting, a proposal was made to raise the co-op's charges to its members from 23 to 27 percent to generate more funds for capital investment. Money was needed for a new 32,000-square-foot warehouse in Billings that could handle up to 10,500 SKUs.

At the meeting, Seth Hardy, a long-time director, who operated a small store at Absarokee, Montana, and who generally spoke for the small-store members, said, "Our warehouse now handles over 8,000 different items. We're told that we need a new one, costing God-knows-what so we can handle 10,000 to 11,000 different items. It's the tissue issue all over again. The manufacturers want to make the same thing in 10 colors and want 10 times the shelf space and 10 separate bins in our warehouse!"

"Big stores see things differently," said Peter Bright, the co-op's general manager. "Manufacturers are so anxious to get shelf space for new products that they'll even bribe a store owner to give them space on a shelf. They call it a 'stocking allowance.'"

"That hasn't happened to me," retorted Hardy. "Is it because my store is too small or that I look too honest?"

"Probably both," was Bright's reply.

"How's the bribe paid?" asked Chris Jones, a director who owned a large store.

"I'm not sure that I should know the answer to that," said Bright, "but I've been told that if they're dealing with the store owner they offer several free cases of other items in their product line that the store is already carrying. If they're dealing with a salaried manager, they may slip him or her some cash, or so I've been told."

"Maybe we can get them to bribe us to stock their goods in our warehouse," commented Jones.

Hardy gave Jones an angry look and then snapped, "We're straying from the topic. Our business as a co-op is not increasing. Therefore, I make the following motion: Resolved, that to keep the number of different items our warehouse handles limited to 8,000, all Wyomo buyers be limited to a certain number of SKUs, with the total assigned to all buyers totaling 8,000. If a buyer wants to add a SKU, he or she will have to drop another." ■

QUESTIONS

1. Co-op members presently pay for goods "on the basis of cost to the co-op plus 23 percent to cover warehousing and transportation from the warehouses to the members' retail stores." Is this a fair way to cover warehousing costs? Can you think of a better way? If so, describe it.

2. Answer the problem posed in question 1 with respect to transportation costs.

3. Toward the end of the case, Bright described how some manufacturers pay bribes to get shelf space in retail stores. Should retailers accept such bribes? Why or why not?

4. The case says, "Stores were responsible for placing orders with the co-op, although a co-op representative would call on a weekly basis, and one of her or his functions was to help some store operators complete their order forms." Is this a function that the co-op should be performing? Why or why not?

5. The case mentions that some of the larger stores that belonged to the co-op sometimes threatened to form their own co-op. Assume that you are hired by some of them to study the feasibility of such a move. List the various topics that you would include in your study.

6. How would you vote on Hardy's motion? Why?

7. Would it make a difference whether you represented a large or small store? Why?

8. Are there other strategies that the co-op might pursue to overcome this problem? If so, describe them.

3

LOGISTICS
AND INFORMATION
TECHNOLOGY

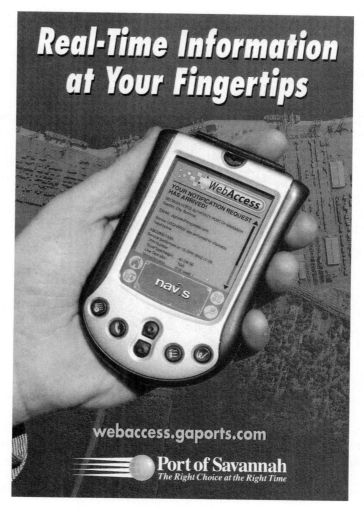

An example of information technology in logistics

Key Terms

- Application-specific software
- Artificial intelligence (AI)
- Communication system
- Data
- Decision support system (DSS)
- Electronic commerce
- Electronic data interchange (EDI)
- Enterprise resource planning (ERP) system
- Global positioning systems (GPS)
- Information
- Logistics information system (LIS)
- Office automation system
- On-demand software
- Radio-frequency identification (RFID)
- Simulation
- Transaction processing system (TPS)
- Voice-based order picking
- Wireless communication

Learning Objectives

- To appreciate the importance of effective and efficient utilization of information for logistics management
- To learn about general types of information systems and their logistical applications
- To understand key differences between the logistics of online shopping and the logistics of traditional shopping

The logistics discipline has been through many changes since the first edition of this book was published in the mid-1970s. The first edition, for example, primarily focused on physical distribution management, and the corresponding definition emphasized the *movement and storage of goods*. The current edition of this book, by contrast, is focused on logistics and its role in supply chain management. Moreover, the corresponding definition of logistics (see Chapter 1) mentions the *flows and storage of goods, services, and related information*.

The effective and efficient utilization of information can be quite beneficial to logistics and supply chain management, and four of the more prominent benefits include the following:

- Greater knowledge and visibility across the supply chain, which makes it possible to replace inventory with information
- Greater awareness of customer demand via point-of-sale data, which can help improve planning and reduce variability in the supply chain
- Better coordination of manufacturing, marketing, and distribution through enterprise resource planning (ERP) tools
- More streamlined order processing and reduced lead times enabled by coordinated logistics information systems[1]

In short, the effective and efficient use of information allows organizations to simultaneously reduce their costs and improve customer satisfaction in the sense that organizations stock the inventory that will be demanded by customers. For example, several U.S.-based grocery chains have carefully studied Hispanic consumers and learned that they place greater emphasis on fresh produce than do other ethnic groups. As such, grocery stores located in heavily Hispanic areas often stock more fresh produce than do grocery stores located in other areas.

Before proceeding further, it's important to distinguish between **data** and **information:** "data are simply facts—recorded measures of certain phenomena—whereas information is a body of

---

[1]Stephen M. Rutner, Brian J. Gibson, Kate L. Vitasek, and Craig G. Gustin, "Is Technology Filling the Information Gap?" *Supply Chain Management Review,* March/April 2001, 58–63.

facts in a format suitable for decision making."[2] Advances in technological hardware and software now allow contemporary logisticians access to abundant amounts of data in relatively short periods of time. Contemporary logisticians and supply chain managers must first determine which data are relevant for their purposes. Next the data need to be organized and analyzed; once analyzed, managers should make the appropriate decision or decisions. In the contemporary business environment, these actions must be completed in as short a time period as possible.

The first part of this chapter will provide an overview of general types of information management systems that are applicable across each business function. In addition, examples of how these general types of information systems might be specifically applied in logistics management are provided. The remainder of the chapter focuses on selected opportunities and challenges that are associated with new technologies such as electronic commerce.

GENERAL TYPES OF INFORMATION MANAGEMENT SYSTEMS

Professor Steven Alter has identified six different types of information systems that are applicable to every business function.[3] These six categories, summarized in Figure 3-1, form the basis of the discussion in this section.

Office Automation System

Office automation systems provide effective ways to process personal and organizational business data, to perform calculations, and to create documents.[4] Included in office automation systems are general software packages—word processing, spreadsheet, presentation, and database management applications—that most of you probably learned in an introductory computer class.

The most relevant general software package for logisticians is the spreadsheet. Whereas early spreadsheet programs for personal computers were little more than speedy calculators, today's spreadsheets have a multitude of capabilities that allow managers to solve a variety of business problems relatively quickly and inexpensively.

Indeed, logistics spreadsheet applications into the early 1990s tended to reflect the rather limited capabilities of the existing software packages. For example, representative topics included economic order quantity (EOQ) calculations, warehouse sizing, transportation modal and carrier decisions, production planning, and center of gravity location decisions, among others.[5] As we moved through the 1990s, increased spreadsheet capabilities allowed organizations to analyze issues that had traditionally been solved by specially designed computer programs. In this vein, the classic issue of transportation cost minimization—transporting products from multiple sources to multiple destinations, at a minimum transportation cost—could be analyzed using spreadsheet software.[6] More recently, spreadsheets have been used to determine the optimal number of warehouse locations for key customers of a regional chemical distributor.[7]

---

[2]William G. Zikmund and Michael d'Amico, *Marketing,* 7th ed. (Cincinnati, OH: South-Western, 2001), p. 125.

[3]The framework in this section is adapted from S. Alter, *Information Systems,* 4th ed. (Upper Saddle River, NJ: Prentice Hall, 2002).

[4]Steven Alter, *Information Systems,* 4th ed. (Upper Saddle River, NJ: Prentice Hall, 2002), p. 191.

[5]John E. Tyworth and William L. Grenoble, "Spreadsheet Modeling in Logistics: Advancing Today's Educational Tools," *Journal of Business Logistics* 12, no. 1 (1991): 1–25.

[6]Brian J. Parker and David J. Caine, "Minimizing Transportation Costs: An Efficient and Effective Approach for the Spreadsheet User," *Transport Logistics* 1, no. 2 (1997): 129–137.

[7]Charles A. Watts, "Using a Personal Computer to Solve a Warehouse Location/Consolidation Problem," *Production and Inventory Management Journal* 41, no. 4 (2000): 23–28.

System type	Logistics examples
Office automation system: provides effective ways to process personal and organizational business data, to perform calculations, and to create documents	Spreadsheet applications to calculate optimal order quantities, facility location, transport cost minimization, among others
Communication system: helps people work together by interacting and sharing information in many different forms	Virtual meetings via computer technology Voice-based order picking
Transaction processing system (TPS): collects and stores information about transactions; controls some aspects of transactions	Electronic data interchange Automatic identification technologies such as bar codes Point-of-sale systems
Management information system (MIS) and executive information system (EIS): converts TPS data into information for monitoring performance and managing an organization; provides executives information in a readily accessible format	Logistics information system
Decision support system (DSS): helps people make decisions by providing information, models, or analysis tools	Simulation Application-specific software such as warehouse management systems Data mining
Enterprise system: creates and maintains consistent data processing methods and an integrated database across multiple business functions	Logistics modules of enterprise resource planning systems

FIGURE 3-1   General Types of Information Management Systems

Source: Taken from Steven Alter, *Information Systems,* 4th ed. (Upper Saddle River, NJ: Prentice Hall, 2002), p. 191.

Communication System

Communication systems help various stakeholders—employees, suppliers, customers—work together by interacting and sharing information in many different forms.[8] From a logistical perspective, the importance of well-defined and well-executed communication systems was highlighted by the events of September 11, 2001, especially for companies that use or provide airfreight services. Because of the total shutdown of the U.S. aviation system for several days following the terrorist attacks, many air shipments were diverted onto trucks, thus delaying many deliveries. As such, airfreight providers such as FedEx worked feverishly to inform customers when their shipments would be arriving.[9]

Many advances in telecommunication technology—such as fax machines, personal computers, electronic mail, cellular phones, and personal digital assistants (PDAs), among others—have occurred since the first edition of this book was published about 30 years ago. As recently as the 1990s, some of these technologies were considered workplace "luxuries." Today, by contrast, many

---

[8]Alter, *Information Systems*, Chapter 5.
[9]Kristen S. Krause, "FedEx's 9–11 Response," *Traffic World,* September 9, 2002, 12–13.

of these technologies are essential for enabling the contemporary logistician to perform in the workplace.

Electronic data interchange, or EDI (to be discussed in the next section), was viewed by many experts as the measuring stick for logistics information technology in the 1990s. By contrast, **wireless communication** has emerged as the measuring stick during the first decade of the twenty-first century.[10] For our purposes, wireless communication refers to communication without cables and cords and includes infrared, microwave, and radio transmissions, among others.

Although wireless communication has many logistical applications, we'll take a look at two of the more popular types, namely, global positioning systems and voice-based order picking. **Global positioning systems,** or GPS, refer to a network of satellites that transmits signals that pinpoint the exact location of an object. Global positioning systems have become quite valuable to the transportation component of logistics in that, at a minimum, GPS allows carriers to keep track of their vehicles. GPS systems provide customer service benefits in the sense that carriers' customers can have real-time visibility in terms of shipment locations, which can be very helpful if a shipment needs to be diverted or rerouted. At the same time, GPS systems benefit carriers by providing data on vehicle speeds (assuming greater importance as fuel costs continue to increase) as well as driver behavior. A sometimes ancillary benefit is that GPS systems can be helpful in locating lost or stolen transportation equipment.

Voice-based order picking refers to the use of speech to guide order-picking activities. Early voice-based picking systems were characterized by high adoption costs, poor voice quality, and systems that were easily disrupted by other noises. Contemporary voice-based systems, by contrast, are less costly, are more powerful, have better voice quality, and are less cumbersome for workers to use. Companies that have adopted newer-generation voice-based technology have reported increased productivity and higher pick accuracy.[11]

Continuing advances in hardware and software have resulted in dramatic cost reductions for wireless communication, and one implication is that the technology is no longer limited to those companies with the deepest financial resources. Moreover, hardware and software cost reductions have shortened the relevant investment payback period; GPS systems often pay for themselves within one year,[12] whereas the payback period for voice-based order picking systems is less than six months in some cases.[13]

Transaction Processing System (TPS)

A **transaction processing system** collects and stores information about transactions and may also control some aspects of transactions. The primary objective of a TPS is the efficient processing of transactions, and to this end, organizations can choose to do batch or real-time processing.[14] With batch processing, data are collected and stored for processing at a later time, with the later time perhaps being based on schedule (e.g., process every six hours) or volume (e.g., process once twenty-five transactions have accumulated) considerations. Real-time processing, not surprisingly, means that transactions are processed as they are received. Although batch processing might be somewhat out of step with the contemporary emphasis on speed and time reduction, it can be quite effective when real-time processing is not necessary. Moreover, in comparison with real-time systems, batch processing tends to be less costly and easier for employees to learn.

---

[10]Roger Morton, "Working Without a Wire," *Logistics Today*, February 2005, 29–33.

[11]Roger Morton, "Wireless in the Warehouse," *Logistics Today*, May 2006, 44–45.

[12]Leonard Klie, "The Value of Information," *Frozen Food Age*, January 2006, 26.

[13]Leonard Klie, "Warehouses Are Going Mobile," *Food Logistics*, March 15, 2005, 37–38.

[14]Alter, *Information Systems*, Chapter 5.

A prominent example of a logistics-related TPS is **electronic data interchange (EDI),** the computer-to-computer transmission of business data in a structured format. Because EDI provides for the seamless transmission of data across companies (assuming technological compatibility), it can facilitate the integration of, and coordination between, supply chain participants. Thus, firms with strong EDI links to both suppliers and customers might have a substantial advantage over supply chain arrangements without such implementations. Common uses of EDI include invoicing, purchase orders, pricing, advanced shipment notices, electronic funds transfer, and bill payment.

EDI has a number of benefits, including reductions in document preparation and processing time, inventory carrying costs, personnel costs, information float, shipping errors, returned goods, lead times, order cycle times, and ordering costs. In addition, EDI may lead to increases in cash flow, billing accuracy, productivity, and customer satisfaction. Potential drawbacks to EDI include a lack of awareness of its benefits, high setup costs, lack of standard formats, and incompatibility of computer hardware and software.

These drawbacks, the dramatic rise of the Internet, and the development of XML (extensible markup language, a fast, flexible text format that facilitates data exchange via the Internet) have resulted in speculation that EDI is an endangered technology and unlikely to be relevant to logistics and supply chain management in the future. In reality, EDI has increased in popularity during the early years of the twenty-first century; key EDI users such as Wal-Mart and J.C. Penney either continue to add new EDI partners or increase the number of EDI transactions.[15] Moreover, the Internet appears to act as a complement to, rather than substitute for, EDI. For example, Owens Corning, a manufacturer of glass fiber and building materials, utilizes EDI with its transportation carriers. At the same time, these carriers are expected to regularly monitor their performance metrics by accessing Owens Corning's Carrier Web Portal.[16]

Automatic identification technologies, another type of logistics-related TPS, include optical character recognition (which can read letters, words, and numbers), machine vision (which can scan, inspect, and interpret what it views), voice-data entry (which can record and interpret a human voice), radio-frequency identification (which can be used where there is no line of sight between scanner and label), and magnetic strips.

Automatic identification systems are an essential component in point-of-sale (POS) systems. Operationally, POS systems involve scanning Universal Product Code (UPC) labels, either by passing the product over an optical scanner or recording it with a handheld scanner. The UPC is read and recorded into a database that supplies information such as the product's price, applicable taxes, whether food stamps can be used, and so on. The specific price of each product and its description are also flashed on a monitor screen positioned near the counter. When all the products have been recorded, the customer receives verification that lists the products purchased, the price of each article, and the total bill.

Ultimately, the idea behind POS systems is to provide data to guide and enhance managerial decision making, as illustrated by the variety of ways that POS data can be used in the restaurant industry. One restaurant with multiple dining areas, for example, uses POS data to identify potential no-shows by analyzing customers who have reserved tables in the same evening for two (or more) of the dining areas. Another restaurant implemented a POS system that resulted in a substantial improvement in order fulfillment; the POS system virtually eliminated the largest cause of mistakes: handwritten orders.[17]

---

[15]Carol Sliwa "EDI: Alive and Well After All These Years," *Computerworld*, June 14, 2004, 1, 51.

[16]Aaron Huff, "Talk This Way," *Commercial Carrier Journal*, March 2006, 78–84.

[17]Margaret Sheridan, "Touch Control," *Restaurants & Institutions,* October 15, 2000, 94–97.

Bar code scanners currently remain the most popular automatic identification system in use. They work to integrate suppliers and customers along the supply chain because all parties read the same labels; in addition, the transfer of goods between parties can be recorded by simple electronic means. Traditionally, laser scanners have been used to read bar codes. The scanners record inventory data and may be directly attached to a computer that uses the data to adjust inventory records and track product movement.

There has been a great deal of recent interest in **radio-frequency identification (RFID)** technology, due in part to RFID compliance initiatives championed by the U.S. Department of Defense and Wal-Mart. Although RFID is presently a $2 billion industry on a global basis, it is projected to grow dramatically in the coming years, exceeding a $25 billion industry by 2015.[18] Conceptually, RFID involves the use of radio frequency to identify objects that have been implanted with an RFID tag. Compared to bar codes, RFID (1) does not require clear line of sight between an object and RFID hardware, (2) can store much larger quantities of data, and (3) offers both read and write capabilities. Potential RFID benefits include inventory reductions, fewer stockouts, labor cost reductions, and the ability to capture tremendous amounts of customer-related data.

One increasingly prominent drawback to RFID involves privacy concerns, such as the inappropriate use of the technology. For example, a major retailer embedded RFID chips into a particular line of cosmetic products, and consumers who selected this product from the store shelf were videobeamed, via webcam, to the manufacturer's headquarters![19] Another drawback to more widespread RFID adoption involves the costs of installing RFID-related hardware and software, particularly the cost of RFID tags, which at the time of publication ranged between 15 and 25 cents apiece (down from approximately 50 cents apiece in 2002) for read-only tags. Some suggest that widespread adoption of RFID will only occur when the price for read-only tags drops below five cents apiece.[20]

Management Information System (MIS) and Executive Information System (EIS)

These systems convert TPS data into information for monitoring performance and managing an organization, with the objective of providing managers and executives with the information they really need.[21] To this end, a **logistics information system** (LIS) can be defined as "the people, equipment, and procedures to gather, sort, analyze, evaluate, and distribute needed, timely, and accurate information to logistics decision makers."[22]

As shown in Figure 3-2, an LIS begins with a logistics manager requesting information and ends with the manager receiving regular and customized reports. For logistics managers to receive *needed* information, it's important that they be fairly specific when submitting requests. For example, a logistics manager who wants information about a specific warehouse or distribution center needs to request information on, say, "the Chicago warehouse," rather than information on "corporate warehouses."

Timely information would appear to be incumbent on the effectiveness and efficiency of a company's particular LIS, and timely information can encompass several dimensions. On the one

---

[18]Rajhu Das, "RFID Market to Reach 7.26 Billion in 2008," *Adhesives & Sealants*, May 2006, 32–34.

[19]Tom Andel, "Big Brother in Aisle Five?" *Paperboard Packaging*, February 2006, 4.

[20]Ibid.

[21]Alter, *Information Systems*, Chapter 5.

[22]Adapted from a definition of marketing information system provided by Gary Armstrong and Philip Kotler in *Marketing: An Introduction,* 7th ed. (Upper Saddle River, NJ: Prentice Hall, 2005), Chapter 4.

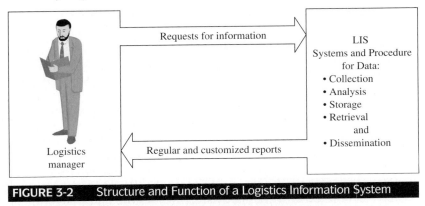

FIGURE 3-2   Structure and Function of a Logistics Information System

Source: Adapted from Michael Etzel, Bruce Walker, and William Stanton, *Marketing,* 14th ed. (New York: McGraw-Hill Irwin, 2007), p. 172.

hand, *timely* can refer to the up-to-date status of information, which can be influenced by a company's collection and analysis procedures. Information collection should emphasize both internal and external sources; unfortunately, internal sources of logistics information are not always as plentiful as desired. Indeed, research into the business value attributable to logistics discovered that "logistics measurement is happening much less frequently than one might imagine."[23] External sources focus on information from outside the company and include information about customers, competitors, and suppliers, along with information about economic, technological, political, legal, and sociocultural environments.

With respect to information analyses, the POS systems described in the previous section are excellent for collecting data—but the data also must be analyzed to be of any value to managers. Consider the following quote from a restaurant consultant: "When restaurants come to us with financial problems, the first thing I ask to see is the data. When they show me a year's worth of numbers, *many times no one has really looked at it* (authors' emphasis)."[24] The following section on decision support systems provides more about information analyses.

Timely also can refer to how quickly managers receive the information requested; this is affected by each company's retrieval and dissemination procedures. A manager's ability to quickly receive information can be influenced by computer hardware and software, and faster and more powerful microchips have helped to reduce retrieval and dissemination times. In a similar vein, timely dissemination of information has been facilitated by advances in personal digital assistants and cell phones. Alternatively, retrieval and dissemination can be slowed by hardware and software glitches, including power outages, system crashes, and computer viruses.

Accurate information may also reflect the effectiveness and efficiency of a company's logistics information system. As such, an LIS must be concerned with the nature and quality of the relevant data; for instance, although the Internet can provide access to tremendous amounts of external information at a very low cost, the validity of some Internet information is suspect. Keep in mind the *GIGO*—garbage in/garbage out—principle: Information that is erroneous, misrepresented, or unclear will likely result in poor decisions by logisticians.

---

[23]James S. Keebler, Karl B. Manrodt, David A. Durtsche, and D. Michael Ledyard, *Keeping Score: Measuring the Business Value of Logistics in the Supply Chain* (Oak Brook, IL: Council of Logistics Management, 1999), Chapter 2.
[24]Margaret Sheridan, "Touch Control," *Restaurants & Institutions*, October 15, 2000, 94–97.

Decision Support Systems (DSS)

Decision support systems help managers make decisions by providing information, models, or analysis tools,[25] and they can be widely applied and used by logisticians. Specific uses of DSS in logistics include, but are not limited to, vehicle routing issues, the selection of public warehouses, and the choice between less-than-truckload and full-truckload shipments. Several of the more prominent logistics-related DSS techniques are discussed in the following paragraphs.

Simulation involves a computer model that is a series of mathematical relationships, often expressed as a series of linear equations. Simulation reliability is achieved by making the model as akin to the real world as possible. Such factors as transport mode availability, transportation costs, location of vendors, warehouse locations, customer locations, customer service requirements, and plant locations must all be accurately reflected in the model.

The primary advantage of simulation is that it enables the firm to test the feasibility of proposed changes at relatively little expense. In addition, it prevents firms from experiencing the public embarrassment of making a major change in their logistics system that might result in a deterioration of customer service levels or an increase in total operating expense.

Many logistics system simulation models exist, and they differ according to mathematical approach, computer capacity needed, and amount of data input. Many of the programs have as their initial focus the improvement of customer service. A second focus is to integrate inbound and outbound logistics functions. Although simulation can be a powerful analytic tool, a poorly constructed simulation involving bad data or inaccurate assumptions about the relationships among variables can deliver suboptimal or unworkable solutions to logistics problems. Insights gleaned from simulation experts provide a list of what not to do:

1. Performing a simulation without a clear definition of the objectives
2. Believing that the model itself can compensate for poor data collection
3. Lacking an understanding of statistical processes
4. Failing to do order profiling
5. Ignoring the effects of randomness
6. Incorporating randomness inappropriately
7. Failing to consider downtime
8. Making illogical assumptions
9. Failing to question the results
10. Failing to recognize that simulation is a study tool[26]

Simulation is an important tool, and as Figure 3-3 illustrates, very little business behavior cannot be simulated.

Artificial intelligence (AI) "is a branch of computer science that studies the computational requirements for tasks such as perception, reasoning, and learning, and develops systems to perform those tasks."[27] AI is a highly sophisticated use of the computer in which it can be programmed to "think" as a trained, skilled human would in specific situations, and AI encompasses a number of different areas such as expert systems, fuzzy logic, and neural networks. Anyone who is familiar with computers knows they can be programmed to respond to different questions, often by asking more definitive questions. In theory, one needs to know the questions to ask, when and how to ask them, and also the various relationships among all possible answers—a difficult but not impossible task.

---

[25]Alter, *Information Systems*, Chapter 5.

[26]Karen A. Field, "Data Quality Can Make or Break a Simulation," *Modern Materials Handling,* January 1997, 57.

[27]David B. Leake, "Artificial Intelligence," in *Van Nostrand Scientific Encyclopedia,* 9th ed. (New York: Wiley, 2002).

*"It can't actually think, but when it makes a mistake,
it can put the blame on some other computer."*

FIGURE 3-3   Computers Can Simulate Many Forms of Business Behavior

Source: Reproduced by permission of the artist and the Masters Agency.

Seminal AI research in logistics involved the development of AI systems for managing certain parts inventories of the U.S. Air Force.[28] This research utilized eight human experts to develop and critique a long list of decision rules that a computer model had to follow to answer questions regarding inventory stocking levels. The magnitude of the task is illustrated by the fact that the final expert system that was devised contained nearly 450 separate decision rules. One of the more popular recent applications of AI in logistics is focused on selected issues with highway traffic, to include predicting urban traffic flows and managing traffic congestion.

A third type of DSS is what can be broadly labeled as **application-specific software,** which has been developed to help managers deal with specific logistics functions or activities. This software can focus on either planning or operational (execution) capabilities and includes, but is not limited to, supply chain management (SCM) software, transportation management systems (TMS), and warehouse management systems (WMS).[29] As was pointed out in Chapter 2, there has been a great deal of consolidation among supply chain software providers in recent

---

[28]Mary K. Allen, *The Development of an Artificial Intelligence System for Inventory Management Using Multiple Experts* (Oak Brook, IL: The Council of Logistics Management, 1986).

[29]Sunil Chopra and Peter Meindl, *Supply Chain Management: Strategy, Planning, and Operation* (Upper Saddle River, NJ: Prentice Hall, 2001), Chapter 12.

years. Nevertheless, the supply chain software market is expected to show annual growth rates of approximately 9 percent through the end of the first decade of the twenty-first century.

Data mining (previously mentioned in Chapter 2), which can be defined as "the application of mathematical tools to large bodies of data in order to extract correlations and rules,"[30] is a DSS technique that has grown in popularity in recent years. Data mining utilizes sophisticated quantitative techniques to find "hidden" patterns in large volumes of data; these patterns allow managers to improve their decision-making abilities as well as enhance their organization's competitive advantage. Although data mining has been characterized as a "fishing expedition" of sorts—in the sense of applying sophisticated quantitative techniques merely to find relationships, whether meaningful or not—data mining, in reality, should follow a well-defined methodology.[31]

Efficient data mining is dependent on data warehouses, that is, a central repository for all the relevant data collected by an organization. Wal-Mart, which is acknowledged to have one of world's foremost data warehouses, and its vendors make extensive use of data mining to improve supply chain effectiveness and efficiency. For example, data mining has allowed Wal-Mart to discover that when hurricanes are projected to hit the state of Florida, demand dramatically increases for two products, beer and Kellogg's Pop Tarts (a toasted pastry product)! So, when a hurricane is projected to hit Florida, Wal-Mart makes sure that additional stocks of beer and Pop Tarts are available in its stores there.

Enterprise System

Enterprise systems, the final general type of information management system to be discussed, create and maintain consistent data processing methods and an integrated database across multiple business functions.[32] The most prominent example of enterprise systems is probably **enterprise resource planning (ERP)** systems, which "integrate the internal operations of an enterprise with a common software platform and centralized database."[33] In theory, ERP systems (such as those offered by Oracle and SAP) allow all prospective users access to a single database when making decisions. The attractiveness of ERP systems comes from their potential for lower costs (such as inventory reductions), as well as increased productivity and increased customer satisfaction.

Although contemporary ERP systems encompass a firmwide perspective, their origins can be traced back to logistics and manufacturing in the form of inventory control and materials requirement planning programs.[34] Unlike these earlier programs, today's ERP systems (conceptually, at least) provide an opportunity for all functional areas within a firm to access and analyze a common database—which might not have been previously possible because (1) certain data was proprietary to a particular functional area and (2) of insufficient or slow computing capabilities.

One of the most frequently mentioned shortcomings of ERP systems involves the costs of installation. It's common knowledge that ERP software is relatively expensive; however, the software is only one part of ERP implementation costs. For example, the vast amounts of data necessary for ERP systems may necessitate new or upgraded computer hardware. Other hidden or frequently overlooked costs of ERP implementation include employee training, data conversion

[30]Sam Joseph and Daniel Scuka, "AI," *Japan Inc.*, November 2001, 20–28.

[31]Michael S. Garver, "Try New Data-Mining Techniques," *Marketing News*, September 16, 2002, 31–33.

[32]Alter, *Information Systems*, Chapter 5.

[33]Joel D. Wisner, G. Keong Leong, and Keah-Choon Tan, *Principles of Supply Chain Management: A Balanced Approach* (Mason, OH: South-Western, 2005), p. 192.

[34]Kuldeep Kumar and Jos van Hillegersberg, "ERP Experiences and Evolution," *Communications of the ACM* 43, no. 4 (2000): 23–26.

(converting existing data into a usable and consistent format), integrating and testing a new system, maintenance costs, and consultant fees. Indeed, consultant fees can quickly ratchet up ERP implementation costs; there are suggestions that consultant fees may be three times more costly than the software itself.[35] When all relevant costs are factored in, ERP installation costs can easily reach into the tens of millions of dollars, and installation costs in the hundreds of millions of dollars are not out of the question.

A second shortcoming is that implementation of ERP systems can be a very time-consuming process. Indeed, many of the hidden costs of ERP implementation mentioned in the previous paragraph are the result of hidden time associated with ERP implementation. For instance, employee training, data conversion, and integrating and testing the new system all require time beyond the installation of the ERP software itself. A general rule of thumb is that actual time to implement ERP systems may range from two to four times longer than the time period specified by the ERP vendor.

Given the preceding discussion on time and implementation costs, it is not surprising that some ERP installations do not go as smoothly as desired, and research has discovered several key differentiators between organizations with successful and unsuccessful ERP installations. More specifically, the successful organizations are much more likely than their unsuccessful counterparts to (1) recognize that ERP is more than just a software program, requiring a sea change in way companies operate and (2) have unqualified top management support.[36]

Although less-than-successful ERP installations can generate higher-than-anticipated costs or lower-than-anticipated revenues, ERP glitches often have a logistical component to them. For example, ERP implementation problems at a leading manufacturer of home medical products caused the company to lower its revenue estimates for several time periods. From a logistical perspective, the ERP-related problems meant that the company missed shipment deadlines, could not respond to customer inquiries, and had limited if any information about order status. The order-related problems, in turn, resulted in a higher-than-normal level of returns associated with incorrect orders, and the missed shipment deadlines caused the company to spend more money for expedited transportation.[37]

ELECTRONIC COMMERCE AND LOGISTICS

Electronic commerce (e-commerce) has been defined as "any form of economic activity that can be conducted via electronic connections."[38] Although electronic connections can include phone and telegraph lines, electronic communications are most commonly associated with computer-to-computer connections, such as EDI and the Internet. This section focuses on electronic commerce via the Internet, in part because the tremendous growth of online shopping in recent years shows little sign of slowing down, with indications that online sales could account for approximately 10 percent of all retail sales by 2010. In addition, effective and efficient logistics management is viewed as a key success factor for online shopping.[39]

---

[35]Bob Violino, "Will a New Planning System Bust You?" *Baseline*, June 2005, 88.

[36]Vidyarana B. Gargeya and Cyndee Brady, "Success and Failure Factors of Adopting SAP in ERP System Implementation," *Business Process Management Journal* 11, no. 5 (2005): 501–506.

[37]Marc L. Songini, "Faulty ERP App Results in Shortfall for Medical Firm," *Computerworld*, January 2, 2006, 8.

[38]R. T. Wigand, "Electronic Commerce: Definition, Theory, and Context," *The Information Society* 13, no. 1 (1997) 1–16.

[39]Alberto Grando and Marco Gosso, "Avoiding the E-Commerce Trap," *EBF* (Summer 2004) 48–51.

The Internet offers the potential for both cost reduction and service improvement across and within logistics function, and research suggests that transportation and order management are the two logistics functions exhibiting the highest amount of Internet usage. Within transportation, the Internet can be used to monitor the on-time performance of carriers and to monitor claims; the Internet's use within order management includes customer order placement and providing customer price quotes.[40] These are just a few of the ways in which the Internet can be used for transportation and order management. Numerous examples also demonstrate how the Internet can be utilized in other logistics functions.

Managing the various logistics functions has been profoundly influenced by the Internet. For example, **on-demand software,** or "software that users access on a per-use basis instead of software they own or license for installation,"[41] has experienced meteoric growth since the beginning of the twenty-first century. Logistics-related applications for on-demand software include collaborative forecasting, inventory optimization, and transportation management, among others. Transportation management systems appear particularly amenable to on-demand software, with on-demand adoptions currently approaching 50 percent of all TMS purchases.[42]

One reason for on-demand's popularity is that its pay-per-use formula allows customers to avoid high capital investment costs, which speeds up return on investment for the software. In addition, because on-demand involves operational as opposed to capital expenditures, it becomes a viable option for many companies that could not afford to purchase, install, and maintain application-specific software such as transportation management systems and warehousing management systems. Other advantages to on-demand include faster and less-costly installation, a smaller information technology staff, and regular upgrades and updates from the software provider.[43]

Although on-demand software appears to be quite attractive, particularly from a financial perspective, it has several potential drawbacks. For example, the regular software upgrades and updates mentioned earlier can sometimes be *too numerous* and *too frequent,* and customers can struggle to keep up with them. Moreover, on-demand software allows for a limited amount of customization, meaning that customers need to fit what they're doing to what the software can achieve.[44] And, because the Internet is the primary transaction medium for on-demand software, security issues such as data protection have been identified as a key concern. However, it appears that a number of on-demand customers have been slow to include security considerations as part of the on-demand decision process.[45]

The Internet has also profoundly influenced channel design by allowing companies to offer an alternate distribution channel (or alternate distribution channels) to already existing channels. In some cases, this alternate channel is direct (i.e., no intermediaries between the producer and final customer) in nature because the final customer orders directly from the producer rather than through an intermediary. The removal of intermediaries between producer and consumer—called disintermediation—can clearly affect the design of logistics systems in the sense that there could be changes in both the number and location of fixed facilities such as warehouses and distribution centers.

---

[40]Richard A. Lancioni, Michael F. Smith, and Terence A. Oliva, "The Role of the Internet in Supply Chain Management," *Industrial Marketing Management* 29 (January 2000): 45–56.

[41]David Hannon, "On-Demand Brings Spend Control to the Masses," *Purchasing,* March 2, 2006, 40–42.

[42]Bridget McCrea, "On-Demand Is on the Rise," *Logistics Management,* March 2006, 47–50.

[43]John Fontana, "What's Behind On-Demand's Software Rise," *Network World,* December 12, 2005, 1, 14.

[44]Hannon, "On-Demand Brings Spend Control."

[45]Paul F. Roberts and Dennis Fisher, "Insecurity on Demand," *eWeek,* February 6, 2006, 21–26.

It should be noted that there are logistical similarities between online retailing and in-store retailing. For example, many logistical functions and activities—such as transportation, warehousing, materials handling, and order management—occur in both. Likewise, both may use the same type of equipment and materials, such as bar coding and warehouse management systems.

Alternatively, powerful differences exist between online and in-store retailing with respect to the execution of logistics functions and activities. For example, the orders associated with online shopping tend to be more plentiful and in much smaller quantities than those associated with in-store retailing. As such, online retailing requires an order management system capable of handling high volumes of orders, and it's also essential that the information management system be capable of correctly transmitting each order so that it can be filled in a timely fashion.

In addition, because of smaller order quantities, online shopping is characterized by open-case, rather than full-case, picking; open-case picking is facilitated by materials handling equipment, such as totes and push carts. Moreover, open-case picking necessitates that products be slotted (placed) in locations that facilitate picking effectiveness and efficiency. Not surprisingly, e-fulfillment's smaller order quantities have important packaging implications as well, in the sense that companies need containers—small cartons, envelopes, bags—that are well suited to holding small quantities of product.[46] Some companies that engage in both online and in-store retailing choose to outsource online's pick-and-pack activities because they are so different than for in-store retailing.[47]

Two other key logistical considerations for online retailing involve transportation and returned orders. The smaller order quantities occasioned by online retailing tend to favor transport companies with extensive delivery networks and expertise in parcel shipments. This, in turn, suggests that outbound shipments tend to be picked up at a loading dock by small-capacity vehicles, such as delivery vans. Moreover, many online retailers are challenged by "last-mile" considerations (those related to delivering product to the customer) such as congestion, frequent stops, and return trips if the customer is not available to accept the delivery.

Although returned orders are an issue in all types of retailing, the return rates associated with online shopping tend to be much higher than with other types of retailing; one estimate suggests 10 percent return rates for traditional forms of retailing, compared to approximately 30 percent for online purchases.[48] Because many of these returns are from individual customers, not businesses or organizations, online retailers should attempt to make the return process as painless as possible. As such, when online customers receive their orders, they might also receive information on how to return the order and a return label, as well as a return container such as an envelope or bag. A relatively smooth and painless returns process not only improves return effectiveness and efficiency, but can also be an effective way of building and maintaining customer loyalty.[49]

Furthermore, it's important to note that a "one size fits all" logistics strategy is not likely to facilitate the effectiveness and efficiency of online shopping. Rather, a variety of logistics strategies might need to be applied, and it's important to recognize the potential trade-offs associated with the different strategies. For example, one way of addressing the last-mile issue of customer unavailability would be to install some type of receptacle (e.g., a drop box) for the product at the customer's residence. However, these receptacles might not be feasible for large items (such as a refrigerator), for perishable items (such as certain types of food), or for

---

[46]Norm Saenz, Jr., "Picking the Best Practices for E-fulfillment," *IIE Solutions* 33, no. 3 (2001): 37–40.

[47]William Hoffman, "One-Click Shopping," *Journal of Commerce*, February 20, 2006, 22–23.

[48]Saenz, "Picking the Best Practices."

[49]Tim Parry, "Many Happy Returns?" *Multichannel Merchant*, February 2006, 37.

extremely valuable items (such as jewelry). The challenges of implementing the appropriate logistics strategy, or strategies, for online shopping are exacerbated by the fact that (1) a particular customer may require vastly different levels of service depending on the product ordered and (2) a particular product may require vastly different levels of service depending on the customer ordering it.[50]

Summary

This chapter discussed key issues of logistics and information technology. Six general types of information management systems were examined, with a particular emphasis on relevant logistical applications. Topics discussed include EDI, automatic identification technologies, artificial intelligence, data mining, and enterprise resource planning systems, among others. Emerging information management issues, such as wireless communication and radio-frequency identification, were highlighted.

The chapter concluded with a discussion of electronic commerce and logistics. On-demand software was examined, and there was a discussion of the similarities and differences between online and in-store retailing.

Questions for Discussion and Review

1. In what ways can information be helpful in logistics and supply chain management?
2. Discuss how your favorite store substitutes information for inventory.
3. Name the six general types of information management systems, and give one logistics application for each one that you've named.
4. Do you view the spreadsheet as the most relevant general software package for logisticians? Why or why not?
5. How can communication systems facilitate logistics management in the aftermath of situations such as terrorist attacks and natural disasters?
6. What advances in telecommunications technology do you view as being most beneficial to logistics management? Why?
7. Discuss how wireless communications can improve logistical effectiveness and efficiency.
8. Discuss the benefits and drawbacks of EDI.
9. Do you believe that EDI is a viable technology for contemporary logistics management? Support your answer.
10. Discuss the relationship between automatic identification technologies and point-of-sale systems.
11. Why are some companies hesitant to adopt RFID technology?
12. Discuss the importance of timely and accurate information to a logistics information system.
13. The chapter listed ten logistics simulation what not to do's. Which two do you think are most important? Why?
14. What kind of uses does artificial intelligence have for logistics?
15. What is data mining? How might it be used in logistics?
16. Discuss advantages and disadvantages of enterprise resource planning systems.
17. How might unsuccessful ERP implementations lead to logistical shortcomings?
18. Refer back to the logistical activities listed in Chapter 1; pick two that you're interested in and research how they have been influenced by the Internet. Are you surprised by your findings? Why or why not?
19. Discuss the advantages and disadvantages of on-demand software.
20. From a logistical perspective, what are some of the differences between online and in-store retailing?

---

[50]Grando and Gosso, "Avoiding the E-Commerce Trap."

Suggested Readings

Angeles, Rebecca, and Ravi Nath. "Partner Congruence in Electronic Data Interchange (EDI)-Enabled Relationships." *Journal of Business Logistics* 22, no. 2 (2001): 109–127.

Auramo, Jaana, Jouni Kauremaa, and Kari Tanskanen. "Benefits of IT in Supply Chain Management: An Exploratory Study of Progressive Companies." *International Journal of Physical Distribution & Logistics Management* 35, no. 2 (2005): 82–100.

Green, Forrest B. "Managing the Unmanageable: Integrating the Supply Chain with New Developments in Software." *Supply Chain Management: An International Journal* 6, no. 5 (2001): 208–211.

Hill, Craig A., and Gary D. Scudder. "The Use of Electronic Data Interchange for Supply Chain Coordination in the Food Industry." *Journal of Operations Management* 20 (2002): 375–387.

Jones, Mary C., and Randall Young. "ERP Usage in Practice: An Empirical Investigation." *Information Resources Management Journal* 19, no. 1 (2006): 23–42.

Lancioni, Richard A., Michael F. Smith, and Terence A. Oliva. "The Role of the Internet in Supply Chain Management." *Industrial Marketing Management* 29 (2000): 45–56.

Lai, Kee-Hung, E. W. T. Ngai, and T. C. E. Cheng. "Information Technology Adoption in Hong Kong's Logistics Industry." *Transportation Journal* 44, no. 4 (2005): 1–9.

Maltz, Arnold, Elliot Rabinovich, and Rajiv Sinha. "Logistics: The Key to e-Retail Success." *Supply Chain Management Review* 8, no. 3 (2004): 56–63.

Mei, Zeiliang, and John Dinwoodie. "Electronic Shipping Documentation in China's International Supply Chains." *Supply Chain Management: An International Journal* 10, no. 3 (2005): 198–205.

Min, Hokey. "The Applications of Warehouse Management Systems: An Exploratory Study." *International Journal of Logistics: Research & Applications* 9, no. 2 (2006): 111–126.

Murphy-Hoye, Mary, Hau L. Lee, and James B. Rice, Jr. "A Real-World Look at RFID." *Supply Chain Management Review* 9, no. 5 (2005): 18–26.

Rutner, Stephen M., Brian J. Gibson, Kate L. Vitasek, and Craig M. Gustin. "Is Technology Filling the Information Gap?" *Supply Chain Management Review* 5, no. 2 (2001): 58–64.

Sanders, Nada R., and Robert Premus. "IT Applications in Supply Chain Organizations: A Link Between Competitive Priorities and Organizational Benefits." *Journal of Business Logistics* 23, no. 1 (2002): 65–83.

Sedlak, Patrick S. "The Second Wave of E-Fulfillment." *Supply Chain Management Review* 5, no. 3 (2001): 82–88.

Van Hoek, Remko. "E-supply Chains—Virtually Non-Existing." *Supply Chain Management* 6, no. 1 (2001): 21–28.

Williams, Lisa R., Terry L. Esper, and John Ozment. "The Electronic Supply Chain: Its Impact on the Current and Future Structure of Strategic Alliances, Partnerships, and Logistics Leadership." *International Journal of Physical Distribution & Logistics Management* 32, no. 8 (2002): 703–719.

C A S E S

CASE 3-1   SPORTS CAR CARE

Tayfun Bekiroglu, living in Santa Barbara, is a dot-com millionaire with a car collection consisting of 20 vintage sports cars. He wants to show five of these cars at the Pebble Beach Concours d'Elegance. Recently he realized that five of his cars needed both repair and repainting, although some needed total repainting, while others needed only some touch-up work. He had his own shop with two bays, one for repairs and one for painting. Painting and repainting would occur after the repairs.

Tayfun wants to have his cars repaired and repainted within 30 working days. Each of the cars' repair and repaint times are indicated in Exhibit 3-A.

Use a Gantt chart and the following approach to answer the case questions. Information about Gantt charts can be found on the Internet, as well as in operations management textbooks. Use this approach to figure out the order of the cars that are going to be taken in for repairing and repainting. The cars needing the least amount of repair time should be taken first, whereas the cars with the least amount of paint/repaint time should be taken last. Once you find the car with the least amount of repair time, you put that car in first place and set the order for the remaining cars. The same applies to the car with the least amount of repaint time. You find the car with the least amount of repaint time, put it in last place, and deal with the remaining cars.

Therefore, you start from the beginning and from the end of the order and finish the order in the middle. At the middle, you may need to do some slight reshuffling. The next step is to draw the Gantt chart (Exhibit 3-B) according to the order you determined. Then, according to the Gantt chart that you draw, you should be able to determine the total time that is going to be consumed in the body shop. ∎

EXHIBIT 3-A

Cars	Repair (days)	Paint (days)
(P) Porsche 911 Carrera 2	5	2
(F) Ferrari Testarossa	1	6
(A) Audi S8	9	7
(L) Lamborghini Diablo	3	8
(B) Bentley Continental GT	10	4

EXHIBIT 3-B

```
CARS
                                              -------- : repair
                                              xxxxx  : paint
Ferrari  |  ---xxxxxxxxxx
Lamb.    |     -------     xxxxxxxxx
Audi     |        ----------------  xxxxxxx
Bentley  |                 ----------------xxxxx
Porsche  |                          ----------xxxxx

         DDDDDDDDDDDDDDDDDDDDDDDDDDDDDDDDD
              time (each D = one day)
```

QUESTIONS

1. If Tayfun had a sixth car to repair/repaint, could he fit it inside the 30 working days limit? If so, how long could the repairs and paint/repaint take?
2. Somewhat to his embarrassment, Tayfun suddenly learned that only cars built in the United States were to be shown at Pebble Beach. Luckily, he had some in his stable, though they also would need some repairs and painting/repainting. Following are the five U.S.-built cars with their required times for repair and paint/repaint.

Determine the order of the U.S. cars that are going to be taken into repair and repaint.
3. Draw a Gantt chart of the given work processes.
4. Calculate the total least amount of processing time for the work processes.
5. If Tayfun had a sixth U.S. car to repair/repaint, could he fit it inside the 30 working days limit? If so how long could the repairs and paint/repaint take?

Cars	Repair (days)	Paint (days)
(Q) Qvale	4	3
(F) Ford Shelby	2	7
(O) Olds Toronado	8	6
(C) Corvette	1	7
(D) Dodge Viper	9	5

CASE 3-2 JUST-IN-TIME IN KALAMAZOO

Jim Ballenger was president of a medium-size firm that manufactured mini motor homes in Kalamazoo, Michigan. The firm had expanded from a local Midwest market to a national one, including Southern California and New England. As markets had expanded, so too had sources of supply for the company, with major suppliers located in Southern California, the Pacific Northwest, and Michigan. The decision to found the company in Michigan had been made for two reasons: Jim's former associates in the auto industry were there, and the largest single component of the mini—the truck or van chassis on which the rest of the vehicle is built—was purchased from one of the U.S. light-truck makers.

Like others in the field, Jim's company actually manufactured very few of its components. Virtually the entire product was assembled from components purchased from outside vendors. There was, however, a well-defined order in which

the components could most efficiently be installed in the vehicle. Recently, it had become clear to Jim that transportation and inventory costs were a relatively large portion of his component parts expenses and that they might be ripe for a substantial reduction. He had been hearing about just-in-time (JIT) systems. According to some notes he had taken at a professional meeting, the JIT production system was developed by the Toyota Motor Company more than 50 years ago. It involves an approach to inventory that, in turn, forces a complementary approach to production, quality control, supplier relations, and distributor relationships. The major tenets of JIT can be summarized as follows:

1. Inventory in itself is wasteful and should be minimized.
2. Minimum replenishment quantity is maintained for both manufactured and purchased parts.

3. Minimum inventory of semifinished goods should be maintained—in this case, partially completed motor homes.

4. Deliveries of inputs should be frequent and small.

5. The time needed to set up production lines should be reduced to the absolute minimum.

6. Suppliers should be treated as part of the production team. This means that the vendor makes every effort to provide outstanding service and quality and that there is usually a much longer-lasting relationship with a smaller number of suppliers than is common in the United States.

7. The objective of the production system is zero defects.

8. The finished product should be delivered on a very short lead time.

To the U.S. inventory planner, vice president of logistics, and production planner, an operation run on the preceding principles raised a number of disturbing prospects. Jim Ballenger was very aware of the costs that might arise if a JIT production system were to be established. From the materials management standpoint, the idea of deliberately planning many small shipments rather than a few large ones appeared to ensure higher freight bills, especially from more distant suppliers, for which freight rates would make the most difference.

With regard to competition among suppliers, Jim often had the opportunity, in the volatile mini-motor-home market, to buy out parts and component supplies from manufacturers that were going out of business. Those components could be obtained at a substantial savings, with the requirement that inventory in the particular parts be temporarily increased or that purchases from existing vendors be temporarily curtailed. Perhaps the greatest question raised by JIT, however, had to do with the probability of much more erratic production as a result of tight supplies of components. Both with suppliers' products and with his own, Jim operated with the (generally tacit) assumption that there would be some defective components purchased and that there

would likely be something wrong with his product when it first came off the assembly line. For this reason, the Kalamazoo minis were extensively tested (Their advertising said, "We hope you'll never do what we do to your Kalamazoo mini."), as were the components prior to installation. To the extent that only a few of a particular type of component were on hand, the interruption in the production schedule would be that much greater. It might entail expensive rush orders for replacement components or equally expensive downtime for the entire plant.

Jim was also concerned about his relationship with his suppliers, as compared, say, to a large auto manufacturer. In the mini-motor-home business, generally the manufacturers are small and the component makers are large. In this situation, it was somewhat more difficult to see the idea of the supplier as a part of the production team, in the sense that the supplier would be expected to make a special effort in either quality control or delivery flexibility on behalf of one of its almost miniscule accounts.

Despite these concerns, Jim was painfully aware that he was using a public warehouse near his plant that usually contained between $500,000 and $1,000,000 in inventory, on which he paid more than 1.5 percent per month for the borrowed funds used to buy it, as well as expenses relating to the use of the warehouse itself. In addition, his firm was now producing so many different models (one with a bath, one with a shower only) and using so many different appliances (various types of radio, three varieties of refrigerator, and so forth) that the costs of a safety stock for each component were going up every day.

As an aid to making his decision on whether to try a JIT orientation at his plant, Jim's executive assistant, Kathy Williams, drew up a table that summarized the anticipated impacts of a JIT system (see Exhibit 3-C). The figures are based on random samples of inventory items. The major component of any mini motor home—the chassis—would always be purchased on a one-at-a-time basis from Ford, Chevrolet, Dodge, or International. With rare

EXHIBIT 3-C   10 Percent Random Sample of Component Inventory

Item	Current System					Using JIT		
	Distance from vendor (in miles)	*Average number of units used each week*	*Current lot size purchased*	*Unit cost*	*Average freight cost per unit*	*JIT lot size*	*Unit cost*	*Average freight cost per unit (surface)*
Gas range	1,145	10	200	$100	$20	10	$105	$22
Toilet	606	10	240	80	18	10	100	18
Pump	26	56	125	16	3	7	15	4
Refrigerator (large)	22	6	120	110	20	6	113	25
Refrigerator (small)	22	7	15	95	15	1	85	15
Foam cushion	490	675	1,500	8	2	75	7	3
DVD Player (type D)	1,800	9	24	136	11	3	130	26
Dome lights	3	824	1,720	2	0	36	4	0
Awning brackets	48	540	1,200	4	1	60	5	1
Insect screens	159	570	1,240	7	1	50	7	2

Note: The plant operates 52 weeks per year and produces 10 mini motor homes per week.

exceptions, it would always be available on demand. It would be delivered through the local dealer. If the dealer did not have one in stock, one could easily be obtained from another area dealership.

Exhibit 3-C is a representative 10 percent sample of Ballenger's components inventory. It covers weekly use of each item, the current lot size purchased, and so on. Before figuring the total costs under the present and JIT systems, two additional facts must be noted. First, Ballenger's inventory carrying costs are assumed to be 20 percent per year on the average investment in inventory on hand, including its acquisition and transportation costs.

Second, under the current system, the number of units of each type of component kept in stock is calculated as follows: For those items purchased from vendors more than 500 miles away, a safety stock representing four weeks of use is maintained. For items from vendors between 100 and 500 miles away, a safety stock representing two weeks of use is maintained. For items from closer sources, a safety stock representing one week of use is maintained. In addition to safety stocks, the average inventory of any item is the current lot size purchased, divided by 2.

If you are familiar with Excel or other spreadsheet software, you might try using it here, although it is not necessary. ∎

QUESTIONS

1. What is the total annual cost of maintaining the components inventory under the present system?
2. What would be the total annual cost of maintaining the components inventory under the JIT system (assuming no safety stocks)?
3. Should Ballenger take into account any other costs or benefits from the JIT system? If so, what are they?
4. If the JIT system is adopted, are there safety stocks of any item that should be maintained? If so, which ones and how much?
5. If the JIT system is adopted, what changes, if any, should occur in the relationships between Ballenger's firm and his suppliers of components? Discuss.
6. Assume that Ballenger has switched to the JIT system and that he receives a surprise phone call from a competitor who is going out of business. The competitor wants to sell Ballenger 7,000 dome lights of the type listed in Exhibit 3-C. Should Ballenger buy them? If so, at what price?
7. Carrying costs are 20 percent. Is there a level of carrying costs at which both Ballenger's present system and a JIT system have similar costs? If so, what is it?

PART II

ELEMENTS OF LOGISTICS SYSTEMS

Part II presents a detailed examination of several elements of logistics systems and is written with an emphasis on outbound movements. Chapter 4 looks at demand management, order management, and customer service. Demand management involves managing customer demand through the supply chain, whereas order management deals with incoming orders, and customer service deals with keeping existing customers happy. Protective packaging and materials handling are covered in Chapter 5; both are related to a product's physical movement.

Two chapters are devoted to transportation because it often represents the highest-cost logistics activity in a company. Chapter 6 provides an overview of transportation modes and intermediaries, and Chapter 7 covers the management of transportation activities.

The topic of Chapter 8 is selecting the site for a production or distribution center. Inventory management, possibly the key to successful logistics management, is handled in Chapter 9. Inventories are kept in warehouses and distribution centers, which is the subject of Chapter 10. Chapter 11 looks at the procurement function.

Chapter 12, the last chapter in this section, deals with international logistics, although certain other aspects of this topic are touched on in other chapters. International logistics management is a rapidly growing field.

CHAPTER 4

DEMAND MANAGEMENT, ORDER MANAGEMENT, AND CUSTOMER SERVICE

Some shipments and some customers require extra attention. This aircraft fuselage, being loaded aboard an Atlantic Container Line Ro/Ro vessel, was being shipped by Boeing to the Paris Air Show.
Source: Atlantic Container Line.

Key Terms

- Benchmarking
- Cause-and-effect (associative) forecasting
- Collaborative planning, forecasting and replenishment (CPFR)
- Customer satisfaction
- Customer service
- Demand management
- Judgmental forecasting
- Make-to-order
- Make-to-stock
- Order cycle

- Order delivery
- Order fill rate
- Order management
- Order picking and assembly
- Order processing
- Order transmittal
- Order triage
- Pick-to-light technology
- Service recovery
- Time series forecasting
- Transit time

Learning Objectives

- To understand demand forecasting's role in logistics management
- To understand the order cycle and its role in logistics management
- To understand the dimensions of customer service
- To examine the establishment of customer service objectives
- To describe the measurement and control of customer service

This chapter discusses two key issues: (1) how an organization determines what the customer wants and (2) how an organization facilitates the customer getting what is wanted. We will analyze these issues in terms of demand management (how an organization determines what the customer wants) along with order management and customer service (how an organization facilitates the customer getting what is wanted). Demand management is important because effective and efficient supply chains have learned to match both supply and demand; failure to do so can result in oversupply (more supply than demand) or undersupply (less supply than demand) of products. Oversupply likely means higher than desired inventory costs, whereas undersupply can mean a dissatisfied—or even lost—customer.

Order management and customer service begin where demand management ends. The ability to determine that the customer wants, say, a black shovel, is nice, but is the customer able to communicate this desire to an organization? Once the customer's desire for a black shovel is communicated to an organization, is the organization able to fulfill this desire? Although these might seem like basic, commonsense questions, reality may be quite different. Indeed, one lesson learned in the early years of online retailing was that many companies were quite good at understanding and stimulating customer demand as well as receiving orders associated with the demand. Unfortunately, some of these companies were far less adept at processing these orders; orders arrived late (if they arrived at all), arrived incomplete, and arrived with incorrect product(s). Not surprisingly, these fulfillment shortcomings caused a great deal of customer dissatisfaction, which explains why some early online retailers (e.g., etoys.com) are no longer in business.

DEMAND MANAGEMENT

Demand management can be defined as "the creation across the supply chain and its markets of a coordinated flow of demand."[1] A key component in demand management is demand (sales) forecasting, which refers to an effort to project future demand. Without question demand forecasting is helpful in **make-to-stock** situations (when finished goods are produced prior to receiving a customer order). However, demand forecasting can also be helpful in **make-to-order** situations (when finished goods are produced after receiving a customer order). Make-to-order situations generally involve some combination of standard and custom components, and forecasting could be quite helpful in projecting the standard components needed. For example, although Dell Corporation might not be able to forecast the exact configuration of each order for computers that it receives, Dell might be able to forecast the percentage of orders for desktop and laptop computers (i.e., standard components).

Entire books are devoted to demand forecasting; space limitations prevent a comprehensive discussion of the topic in this text. Rather, we will offer an overview of demand forecasting so the reader can understand forecasting's role in determining what the customer wants.

Demand Forecasting Models[2]

The three basic types of forecasting models are (1) **judgmental,** (2) **time series,** and (3) **cause and effect.** Judgmental forecasting involves using judgment or intuition and is preferred in situations where there is limited or no historical data, such as with a new product introduction. Judgment forecasting techniques include surveys and the analog technique, among others. With survey forecasting, questionnaires (surveys) are used to learn about customer preferences and intentions. A strong understanding of survey design and population sampling methodologies is necessary in survey forecasting, and you should recognize that customer intentions don't always translate into actual behavior. Analog forecasting involves determining an analog (similar item) to the item being forecast and then using the analog's demand history as a basis for the relevant forecast. A key challenge is selecting the appropriate analog to use.

An underlying assumption of time series forecasting is that future demand is solely dependent on past demand. For example, if this year's sales were 7 percent higher than last year's sales, a time series forecast for next year's sales would be this year's sales plus 7 percent. Time series forecasting techniques include, but are not limited to, simple moving averages and weighted moving averages. The simple moving average is calculated by summing the demand across different time periods and then dividing by the number of time periods. Because each time period is assigned the same importance (weight), the simple moving average may not adequately reflect recent upturns or downturns in demand. To address this shortcoming, the weighted moving average technique assigns greater importance (weight) to the more recent data. The differences in forecasted demand between the simple and weighted moving averages can be seen in the example in Table 4-1.

Cause-and-effect (also referred to as associative) forecasting assumes that one or more factors are related to demand and that the relationship between cause and effect can be used to estimate future demand. In many countries, for example, there tends to be an inverse relationship

---

[1] John T. Mentzer, "A Telling Fortune," *Industrial Engineer,* April 2006, 42–47.

[2] The discussion of demand forecasting models is drawn from Chaman L. Jain, "Benchmarking Forecasting Models," *Journal of Business Forecasting* 24, no. 4 (2005/2006): 9–10, 12 as well as Joel D. Wisner, G. Keong Leong, and Keah-Choon Tan, *Principles of Supply Chain Management: A Balanced Approach* (Mason, OH: South-Western Publishing, 2005), Chapter 5.

TABLE 4-1 Forecast Example Using the Simple and Weighted Moving Average Techniques

Time period (1)	Demand (2)	Simple moving Average Weighting Factor (3)	Projected Demand (4; = 2×3)	Weighted Moving Average Weighting Factor (5)	Projected Demand (6; = 2×5)
Last month	250	.25	62.5	.40	100
Two months ago	230	.25	57.5	.30	69
Three months ago	200	.25	50	.20	40
Four months ago	180	.25	45	.10	18
Forecast			**215**		**227**

between the level of interest rates and the consumers' ability to buy a house (e.g., as interest rates increase, housing sales tend to decrease). Examples of cause-and-effect forecasting include simple and multiple regression; in simple regression, demand is dependent on only one variable, whereas in multiple regression, demand is dependent on two or more variables.

Demand Forecasting Issues

It's important to recognize that the selection of a forecasting technique (or techniques) depends on a variety of factors, such as the situation at hand, forecasting costs in terms of time and money, and the accuracy of various forecasting techniques. With respect to the situation at hand, as pointed out earlier, judgmental forecasting is appropriate where there is little or no historical data available. For instance, Apple Corporation's initial sales estimates for the iPod (a portable digital audio player), which was introduced in 2001, were based on judgment and intuition—the iPod was not only a new product, but a somewhat revolutionary product as well. Managers should also understand time and monetary costs associated with each particular forecasting technique. Survey research, for example, can require quite a bit of both money and time, depending on the media (i.e., mail, telephone, electronic, in-person) used to collect and analyze the data.

Forecasting accuracy refers to the relationship between actual and forecasted demand, and accuracy can be affected by various considerations. One of the challenges with the analog technique is selecting the appropriate analog, because an inappropriate selection will reduce forecast accuracy. For instance, when a movie studio releases a sequel to a previously successful motion picture, a forecasting analog based on the initial release will likely generate a different estimate than a forecasting analog based on the performance patterns of sequels to other movies—and one analog will be more accurate than the other. Forecast accuracy can have important logistical implications, as illustrated at Ventura Foods, where improved forecasting has allowed a reduction in transportation costs because fewer shipments need to be expedited—and expedited transportation can cost two and one-half times as much as regular transportation.[3]

Up to this point, we have treated demand forecasting as a discrete entity in the sense that each supply chain member generates its own demand forecasts. You may recall that Chapter 1 briefly mentioned the **CPFR (collaborative planning, forecasting, and replenishment)** concept, where supply chain partners share planning and forecasting data to better match up supply and

---

[3]Brian Albright, "Ventura Foods Improves Demand Forecasts," *Frontline Solutions,* July/August 2005, 36.

demand. Conceptually, CPFR suggests that supply chain partners will be working from a collectively agreed-to single forecast number as opposed to each member working off its own forecast projection. Successful CPFR implementations, involving firms such as Wal-Mart, Tesco, and Procter & Gamble, have resulted in 20 to 30 percent improvements in forecasting accuracy as well 20 to 30 percent reductions in order cycle times.[4] Although these are impressive results, you should recognize that (1) not all CPFR initiatives have been successful and (2) there can be significant challenges associated with getting supply chain partners to share the relevant data needed to develop the forecast(s).

We'll conclude our discussion of demand forecasting with a brief look at forecasting that is done via computer software. Computer software forecasting dates back over 30 years, and there has been tremendous advancement in its breadth and computational power—forecasts that might have taken minutes or hours on a mainframe computer can now be generated in a matter of seconds or minutes on a personal computer. And although it would seem as if this advancement would contribute to improved forecasts, software-based forecasting continues to be plagued by some of the issues (inappropriate technique for the situation at hand, costs, forecast error) discussed earlier in this section. For example, Microsoft's Excel spreadsheet is currently the most heavily used software for business forecasting, in part because it is relatively easy to learn and its low cost. However, because Excel's statistical procedures are considered to be unreliable, relatively unsophisticated and out of date, its forecasts can contain a great deal of error. Alternatively, multimillion-dollar software packages that are solely devoted to demand forecasting have also been problematic on occasion because of difficulty in understanding how to use them.[5] It's important to keep in mind that no software package—regardless of its sophistication and cost—is capable of totally eliminating forecast errors.

ORDER MANAGEMENT

Order management refers to management of the various activities associated with the **order cycle;** the order cycle (which can also be referred to as replenishment cycle or lead time) refers to the time from when a customer places an order to when the goods are received. The order cycle can be subdivided into four aspects, or stages: order transmittal, order processing, order picking and assembly, and order delivery, each of which will be discussed more fully later.

There is a key link between order management and demand forecasting, in that a firm does not simply wait for orders to arrive to learn what's happening. Forecasts are made of sales and of the inventories that must be stocked so that the firm can fill orders in a satisfactory manner. There is also a key link between order management and customer service because many organizations analyze customer service standards in terms of the four stages of the order cycle.

When the four stages of the order cycle are carefully run and skillfully coordinated, impressive gains in performance can be realized. Because order cycle lengths continue to get shorter, a lack of cooperation across the order cycle stages can create delays and serve as a competitive disadvantage in part because longer order cycles necessitate buyers to hold increased levels of inventory.

---

[4]Ron Ireland, "ABC of Collaborative Planning Forecasting and Replenishment," *The Journal of Business Forecasting* 24, no. 2 (2005), 3–4, 10.

[5]Michael Gilliland and Michael Leonard, "Forecasting Software—The Past and Future," *The Journal of Business Forecasting* 25, no. 1 (2006): 33–36.

Before proceeding to a discussion of the four order cycle stages, several points should be made. First, the order cycle should be analyzed not only in terms of total cycle time but in cycle time variability (reliability) as well. Just as longer order cycles necessitate increased levels of inventory, so, too, does greater cycle time variability require additional levels of inventory (regardless of cycle time length). It's important to understand that each stage of the order cycle can be characterized by variability, and in some cases the variability can be quite pronounced. Consider the U.S. railroad that analyzed transit times on one of its origin–destination pairs that was located approximately 400 miles apart. The railroad discovered an average transit time of eight days, with a minimum of three days and a maximum of *28 days*, and the railroad's customers coped with the erratic transit times by holding additional inventory to avoid out-of-stock situations.[6]

A second consideration is that order management has been profoundly affected by advances in information systems. For example, one of this book's authors worked in the U.S. trucking industry in the early 1980s, and if a customer telephoned to learn about a shipment's status, a very manual—and, unfortunately, a time-consuming (at a minimum, the phone call had to be answered) and not always successful—shipment tracking process was initiated. Today, by contrast, that same customer doesn't have to place a phone call; in many cases, she/he can simply log on to a particular carrier's Web site to learn about a shipment's status.

A third consideration is that order management and the order cycle are vitally important to the perfect order concept that has emerged as a key logistics and supply chain metric in recent years. Although there are various definitions of a perfect order, the definitions focus on a common theme, namely, *simultaneously achieving relevant customer metrics*, however those metrics might be defined (e.g., order delivered to the right person, at the right time, in the correct quantity, among others). We don't mean to be negative but rather realistic in pointing out that each stage of the order cycle offers plentiful opportunities for error—and thus failure to achieve a perfect order. We'll offer select examples of potential errors when discussing the four components of the order cycle.

Order Transmittal

Order transmittal refers to the time from when the customer places an order until the seller receives the order. In general, there are five possible ways to transmit orders: in person, by mail, by telephone, by facsimile (fax) machine, and electronically. Figure 4-1 shows an example of a form that could be used for either mail or fax orders, and Figure 4-2 shows an example of an online order form.

Each method of order transmittal has advantages and disadvantages, and each performs differently with respect to the cost of ordering, the time to order, the potential for order errors, and ordering convenience. For example, in-person orders greatly reduce the potential for order errors, if for no other reason that the order can be physically inspected prior to being accepted. However, in-person ordering isn't always convenient (or practical) in situations where the supplier is geographically distant. Although ordering by mail might be more convenient than in-person ordering, mail is considered to be a relatively slow form of order transmittal, and there are occasions when the order never reaches the intended destination (lost in the mail). Ordering by telephone can be fast and convenient, but order errors generally aren't detected until the order is delivered. Many of us have placed a telephone order for home

---

[6]Judy A. Perry, "Who's Watching the Numbers That Count?" *Railway Age*, May 2005, 10.

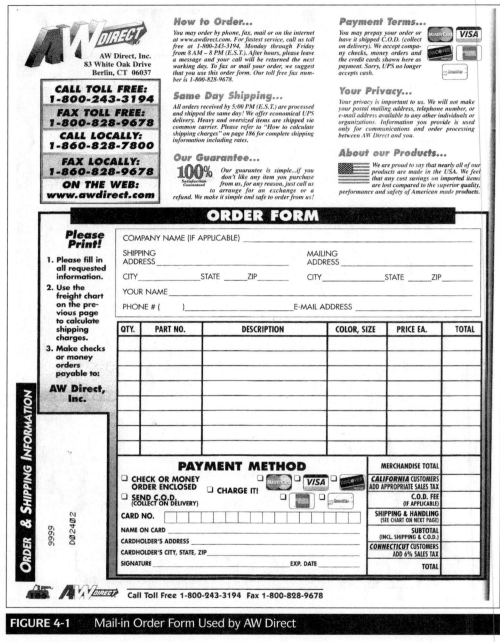

FIGURE 4-1   Mail-in Order Form Used by AW Direct

Source: AW Direct, Inc.

Shipping Information   https://order.store.yahoo.com/cgi-bin/s...9d8d1e188d83481ec0c7145c68978cb87859a4a

▓ OnlineMuseumShop

For FedEx shipments, your order must be submitted by 11 a.m. ET for next-day delivery.

If ordered items are to be shipped FedEx and one of these items is on backorder, the backordered item(s) will be sent seperately at an additional FedEx shipping charge. Please check to see if your order contains items on backorder.

FedEx shipping cannot be applied to Canada or oversea addresses.

Questions about an item? Call our customer service department 8 a.m. to 5 p.m. ET at 1-800-227-5597.

If you are submitting a message for your gift, please limit it to 60 characters in length. Thank you.

1. Review your order from Museum of Fine Arts, Boston - Online Gift Shop

Item	Options	Unit Price	Quantity	Subtotal
Wallets	MFA Signature Gift Presentation?: No Description: Edward Hopper Notecard Wallet	13.95	1	13.95
	Subtotal for Museum of Fine Arts, Boston - Online Gift Shop			13.95

Shipping and tax may be added to your order. For terms, see the Info page.

2. Enter the Coupon Code
If you have a coupon that can be redeemed from Museum of Fine Arts, Boston - Online Gift Shop, please enter the offer code in the box below.

Coupon Code: [   ] *(optional)*

3. Choose the shipping address

First Name: [   ]   Last Name: [   ]
Address: [   ]
[   ]

City: [   ]   State: [   ]
Zip: [   ]   Phone: [   ]
Country: [US United States ▼]

4. Specify gift options for your order
Include this message with my gift:

5. Choose shipping options for Museum of Fine Arts, Boston - Online Gift Shop

Standard Shipping [▼]

[Cancel] [Continue]

FIGURE 4-2   Order Form Used by the Online Gift Shop of the Museum of Fine Arts, Boston

Source: Museum of Fine Arts, Boston Catalog.

delivery of a large, one topping pizza—only to be delivered a small, one topping pizza with the incorrect topping!

Both facsimile and electronic ordering are techniques that have emerged over the past 25 years, and both have had immense impacts on the order transmittal process. The fax can be fast, convenient, and unlike the telephone provides hard copy documentation of an order. However, the seller's fax machine can be cluttered with junk (unwanted) faxes, and the quality of the fax transmission can result in hard-to-read orders—which increases the chances of order errors in the form of incorrect product or incorrect quantity. Electronic ordering, which includes EDI and the Internet, can be fast, convenient, and accurate, particularly those orders involving scanners and bar codes. A major concern with ordering via the Internet is the security of the data being transmitted; indeed, there are estimates that the costs associated with the theft of data from Internet transactions now exceed $350,000 *per incident*![7]

Order Processing

Order processing refers to the time from when the seller receives an order until an appropriate location (such as a warehouse) is authorized to fill the order. Advances in technology have allowed most firms to computerize many aspects of their order processing systems. For instance, order forms, whether printed or in computer format, are designed so that the use of computers by both the customer and the vendor is facilitated. Similarly, the billing of customers is increasingly done through computerized and electronic networks.

Figure 4-3, which presents an order processing flowchart, highlights that there are many distinct order processing activities. Typical order processing activities include checking an order for completeness and accuracy, checking the buyer's ability to purchase, entering the order into the system, crediting a salesperson with a sale, recording the transaction, determining inventory location, and arranging for outbound transportation. Although some of the activities must be performed sequentially (e.g., an order can't be transported until a company knows from which location(s) it will be filled), some might be performed simultaneously (e.g., crediting a salesperson with a sale and recording the transaction). Note that one way to reduce order cycle time is to identify activities that can be performed simultaneously (and then perform the relevant activities simultaneously, rather than sequentially).

An understanding of the various order processing activities is only a first step, however. Companies differ in their approaches to managing order processing and its activities, and these different approaches can have important implications on order cycle effectiveness and efficiency as well as on customer satisfaction. We'll highlight different managerial approaches by discussing three order processing activities, order receipt, order triage, and the location(s) used to fill an order, in the following paragraphs.

With respect to order receipt, Figure 4-3 indicates that incoming orders are divided into categories, one for EDI orders that are allowed to bypass checking for completeness and accuracy and one category for all other orders. It could be argued that all orders, regardless of transmission method, should be checked for completeness and accuracy; incomplete or inaccurate orders can negatively affect customer satisfaction and increase costs in the sense of addressing order irregularities. However, checking all orders for completeness and accuracy adds costs and time to the order cycle. Alternatively, companies might structure the order receipt function to reflect historical trends on order completeness and accuracy. Under this scenario, order transmission methods that consistently exhibit superior completeness and accuracy would bypass the order check activity.

---

[7]Scott Roberston, "Hacker Heaven," *American Metal Market*, May 1, 2006, 4–5.

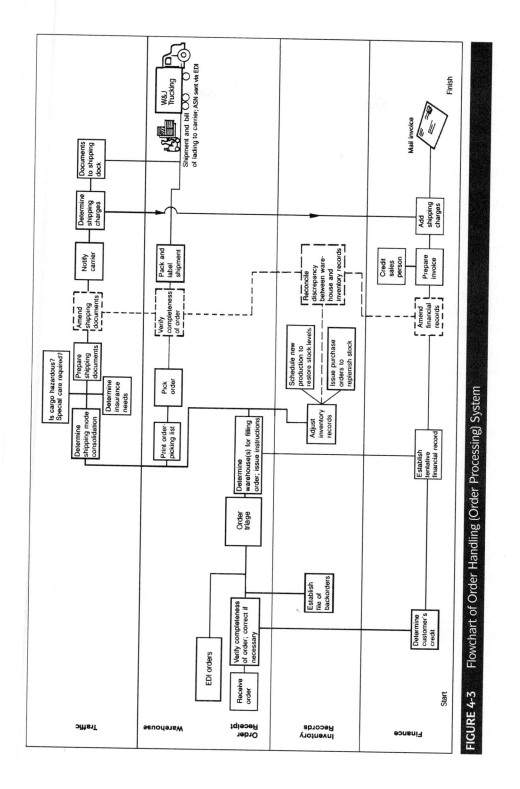

FIGURE 4-3 Flowchart of Order Handling (Order Processing) System

Figure 4-3 also contains an order triage activity. The triage concept is often associated with the medical field and refers to classifying patients in terms of the severity of their illness or malady, and the classification allows doctors to prioritize which patients should be attended to before others. Similarly, **order triage** refers to classifying orders according to preestablished guidelines so that a company can prioritize how orders should be filled. However, not all companies prioritize orders, and those that do must decide the attribute(s) used to prioritize (e.g., first in, first served; customer longevity; customer sales). Although there is no one right attribute to use for order prioritization, you should recognize that the chosen attribute(s) are likely to delight one set of customers (those that exhibit the chosen attribute) and disappoint other customers.

Another key order processing decision (see Figure 4-3) involves determining the location(s) from which an order is to be filled. As was the case with order triage, companies should have clear, consistently applied rules to help in making this decision, but there are companies that decide which facility to use on an order-by-order basis—which can lead to inconsistent order cycle time and cost. A commonsense approach would be to fill an order from the facility location that is closest to the customer, with the idea that this should generate lower transportation costs as well as a shorter order cycle time. Alternatively, an order could be filled from the facility location that currently has the largest amount of requested product; this likely would increase both order cycle time and transportation cost, but could help the seller by reducing excess inventory at a particular location.

Order Picking and Assembly

Order picking and assembly is the next stage of the order management process, and it includes all activities from when an appropriate location (such as a warehouse) is authorized to fill the order until goods are loaded aboard an outbound carrier. Although order picking and assembly is sometimes overlooked because neither activity is very glamorous, order picking and assembly often represents the best opportunity to improve the effectiveness and efficiency of an order cycle; order picking and assembly can account for up to two-thirds of a facility's operating cost and time.[8]

Importantly, the effectiveness and efficiency of order picking and assembly can often be improved without large expenditures. For example, one suggestion involves "shadowing" existing order pickers to learn about their routines and the challenges they face, such as items that aren't where they should be, aisle congestion, or talkative coworkers. Another suggestion is to analyze order pickers' travel time, in part because travel time accounts for between 60 and 80 percent of total pick time. Moreover, travel time can be reduced through better slotting (placement) of products in the relevant facility.[9] For example, a company might place its most heavily demanded items in a fairly central and easily accessible location as opposed to a more remote and less-accessible location.

Order picking and assembly has been greatly affected by advances in technology such as handheld scanners, radio-frequency identification (RFID), and voice-based order picking. Another order picking technique that has grown in popularity in recent years is **pick-to-light technology,** in which orders to be picked are identified by lights placed on shelves or racks. One advantage to pick-to-light technology is that the worker simply follows the lights from pick to pick, as opposed to the worker having to figure out an optimal picking path. Advances in picking technology, such as pick to light, generally result in higher pick rates and fewer picking errors, along with reduced training time and reduced levels of employee turnover.[10]

---

[8]Susan Lacefield, "Ten Tips for Faster Picking," *Logistics Management,* July 2005, 71–76.
[9]Ibid.
[10]Karen Berman, "Best Picks," *Multichannel Merchant,* August 2005, 53–54.

After orders have been picked, the assembled orders are checked to ensure that they were accurately picked. If there is a stockout on a particular item, the information is sent back to the order handling department so that original documents can be adjusted. A packing list is enclosed with each outgoing order, indicating what items were picked and the initials of the individuals who prepared the order for shipment. The consignee will check the packing list on receipt of the order and verify that all items are present.

Order Delivery

The final phase of the order cycle is **order delivery,** which refers to the time from when a transportation carrier picks up the shipment until it is received by the customer. A key metric associated with order delivery is **transit time,** or the elapsed time from when the order is picked up until it is received by the customer. Not surprisingly, there have been many changes to the order delivery process in recent years, and several of these changes will be highlighted in the following paragraphs. An underlying theme of these changes involves delivery options that represent the customer's increasing power in business transactions.

For example, carriers historically provided a limited number of options in terms of transit time alternatives, and shippers thus had to incorporate the rather inflexible transit times into calculations of the length of an order cycle. However, as pointed out in Chapter 1, some transportation service providers now offer prospective shippers a diverse menu of transit time options. For example, during 2006 the FedEx Corporation purchased Watkins Motor Lines, a long-haul trucking company. This purchase will allow FedEx, through its various corporate subsidiaries, to offer prospective customers transportation alternatives that range from same-day to four-day service.

Another key change is that more and more shippers are emphasizing both the elapsed transit time as well as transit time reliability (variability); recall that increases in order cycle variability translate into higher inventory levels. To this end, more buyers are utilizing delivery appointments that contain delivery windows, or the time span within which an order must arrive. Although some delivery windows are one hour in length, other windows are as narrow as 15 minutes. So, if a carrier has a 9:00 A.M. delivery appointment with a 15-minute delivery window, it must arrive no later than 9:15 A.M. Oftentimes, failure to meet the relevant delivery window means that the carrier must wait for the next open delivery time—which might not be until the end of the day.

A third important change associated with order delivery involves transportation carriers revamping their operations to provide faster transit times to customers. For example, 500 miles traditionally served as the maximum range for overnight service in the trucking industry. In recent years, by contrast, the maximum range for overnight service by truck has been pushed to between 600 and 700 miles. This expanded coverage is important because many shippers are hesitant to pay for premium transportation service such as that provided by expedited carriers and airlines.[11]

CUSTOMER SERVICE

Customers are important to organizations, and organizations that view customers as a "nuisance" may not last very long in today's highly competitive business environment. Moreover, a frequently cited business metric is that it costs approximately five times as much to develop a new customer as it does to retain an existing one. Regardless of the exact figure, it's easier for

---

[11]John D. Boyd, "Getting Grounded," *Traffic World,* April 3, 2006, 18–21.

an organization to keep an existing customer than it is to acquire new customers. To this end, **customer service** strives to keep customers happy and creates in the customer's mind the perception of an organization that is easy to do business with.

Customer service can be an excellent competitive weapon and is more difficult for competitors to imitate than other marketing mix variables such as price and promotion. Nordstrom's (a high-end retailer) has a long-standing reputation for excellent customer service, and this customer focus often leads Nordstrom's to do things that competitors cannot or will not match. For example, one of the authors was shopping at a local Nordstrom's and found a belt that he liked, but the store didn't have the correct size in stock. Several days later, the author received a call from a Nordstrom's salesperson indicating that the desired belt was available for purchase at the local store. The salesperson had located the belt at another Nordstrom's and had the belt expedited—via *air freight*—to the local store. With a retail value of approximately $45, it's likely that the particular Nordstrom's lost money on this purchase. It's a reasonable assumption, however, that few other retailers would copy Nordstrom's behavior in servicing the customer.

Customer service is sometimes used interchangeably with **customer satisfaction,** but the two concepts are not synonymous; rather, customer service can be a component of customer satisfaction. Customer satisfaction compares a customer's actual experience with the expected experience, and if the actual experience equals or exceeds the expected experience, then a customer would be satisfied. Conversely, if the actual experience does not measure up to the expected experience, then a customer would be dissatisfied. Customer service can influence both the expected and actual experience and hence influence customer satisfaction. Although many examples could be used to illustrate this point, consider that toll-free telephone numbers are a common customer service option provided by many organizations. Those without toll-free numbers could cause customer dissatisfaction because of the *customer's expectation* that this is a service that should be offered by all organizations. (Note that we haven't even discussed the customer's reason(s) for telephoning an organization.)

Macroenvironmental changes, such as globalization and advances in technology, are causing organizations and individuals to demand higher levels of customer service. As was pointed out in an earlier chapter, customer expectations continue to increase over time; if the associated performance (service) levels fail to keep up, then customer dissatisfaction is a likely outcome. In addition, as emphasized in this chapter, reliable service enables a firm to maintain a lower level of inventory, especially of safety stocks, which produces lower inventory holding costs. Third, in an increasingly automated and computerized world, the relationships between customers and vendors can become dehumanized. This situation is both frustrating and inefficient from the customer's viewpoint. The firm that can offer a high level of customer service, especially on a personal basis, will find that it has a powerful sales advantage in the marketplace.

Furthermore, the increased use of vendor quality-control programs necessitates higher levels of customer service. In recent years, many firms, especially retailers and wholesalers, have become more inventory conscious. This emphasis has resulted in computer-assisted analysis to identify vendors who consistently give either good or bad levels of service. In the past, with manual systems, repeated and serious customer service errors occurred before a vendor's activities were singled out for corrective action. Today, these factors are automatically programmed into computers, and companies are able to closely monitor the quality of service they receive from each vendor.

We've talked at some length about customer service, but we've yet to offer a formal definition of it. Keeping in mind that there are myriad customer service definitions, for our purposes customer service will be defined as "the ability of logistics management to satisfy users in terms of time, dependability, communication, and convenience."[12] Let's take a closer look at each of these four dimensions of customer service.

Time

Clearly, the order cycle is a major component of the time dimension of customer service. At the risk of sounding redundant, businesses today are looking to reduce order cycle times—longer cycle times translate into higher inventory requirements.

Dependability

Dependability refers to the reliability of the service encounter and consists of three elements, namely, consistent order cycles, safe delivery, and complete delivery.[13] Our earlier discussion of the order cycle highlighted the importance of consistency (reliability/dependability)—inconsistent order cycles necessitate higher inventory requirements. And although order cycle time is important, an increasing number of companies are trading off order cycle speed for order cycle consistency. More specifically, these companies are willing to accept a slower order cycle so long as it exhibits a high level of consistency.

Safe delivery brings loss and damage considerations into play. Product can be lost or damaged for a multitude of reasons, but they are rather immaterial to a customer—a lost or damaged product can cause a variety of negative ramifications for a customer, such as out-of-stock situations. **Order fill rate,** or the percentage of orders that can be completely and immediately filled from existing stock, is one way of measuring the completeness of delivery. As is the case with loss and damage, incomplete deliveries result in negative customer ramifications, such as out-of-stock situations.

It is unlikely that loss and damage can ever be totally eliminated; because orders are picked and assembled, they are handled—and every time product is handled provides opportunities for loss and damage. However, the seller may be able to minimize the number of times an order is handled, perhaps by redesigning the order pick process. And, even if an organization has highly accurate demand forecasting, it's also unlikely that it will be able to achieve a 100 percent fill rate (i.e., all incoming orders are filled completely). Consider the situation of the McDonald's restaurant where two people walked in and placed a take-out order for 142 Egg McMuffins! Although the restaurant was successfully able to fill this order (but not before ensuring that the two customers could pay for it), the inventory needed to fill it meant that a lot of other orders for Egg McMuffins went unfilled, at least until the next scheduled delivery of foodstuffs.

Communication

Effective communication should be a two-way exchange between seller and customer, with the goal of keeping both parties informed. Moreover, effective communication requires that the correct parties be involved in the process; if a customer has a logistics-related question, then the customer should be communicating with someone with logistics expertise. Moreover, customer service can be enhanced if *complete information* is exchanged between the participants; a delivery address can be helpful, but outstanding characteristics of the delivery address would be even more helpful, as illustrated by the case of the transportation company that was responsi-

---

[12]Roger A. Kerin, Steven W. Hartley, and William Rudelius, *Marketing: The Core* (Boston: McGraw-Hill/Irwin, 2004), p. 297.
[13]Ibid.

ble for delivering a $750,000 shipment of computer racks. What the transportation company didn't find out—until it actually made the delivery—was that the customer was located on the 17th floor of an office building in the central business district of a major city. Because neither the transportation company nor the office building had the appropriate equipment to facilitate the shipment's handling, the delivery was delayed until the proper equipment could be located and brought to the building.[14]

Two-way communication between seller and customer has certainly benefited from technological advances such as cell phones, personal digital assistants, and the Internet. These technological advances allow for less costly and more frequent contacts between the two parties. Having said this, technology such as text messaging and the Internet can depersonalize the communication process, which is why periodic telephone interaction and even face-to-face contact between seller and customer are recommended.[15] (You should recognize that personal communication is an essential part of conducting business in many cultures.)

Convenience

The convenience component of customer service focuses on the ease of doing business with a seller. Having said this, different customers may have different perceptions of the "ease of doing business" concept. For example, for a college student the "ease of doing business" with a bank might mean access to automatic teller machines, whereas for a small business owner it might mean bank tellers who specifically focus on commercial deposits and withdrawals. As such, sellers should have an understanding of their customer segments and how each segment views the "ease of doing business."

Moreover, from the seller's perspective, certain costs may be associated with convenience; for example, there may be a charge for pizza that's delivered to your residence (or "free delivery areas" might be very small in geographic coverage). As a result, sellers must assess the extent to which their customers are willing to pay for convenience. In recent years many airlines have discovered that allowing customers to arrange their own travel via the Internet is quite cost effective for the airlines in that the costs of processing an electronic ticket are approximately $1 compared to $10 for processing a paper ticket. As a result, customers who arrange their travel by telephoning an airline's customer service agent may now be charged a fee for talking to the service agent (a service that for many years was "free" to the customer).

ESTABLISHING CUSTOMER SERVICE OBJECTIVES

Because customer service standards can significantly affect a firm's overall sales success, establishing goals and objectives is an important senior management decision. Distribution is closely related to customer service, so the outbound logistics department plays an important role in the establishment of customer service goals and objectives. Some companies distinguish goals from objectives when establishing customer service standards. Goals tend to be broad, generalized statements regarding the overall results that the firm is attempting to achieve. Unfortunately, some firms' statements of customer service goals are couched in platitudes lacking specific objectives specifying how the goals are to be achieved. This is a serious problem because if the customer service objectives or standards are not stated in specific terms, they may be ignored or be too vague to provide any real guidance to operating personnel.

---

[14]John Paul Quinn, "How to Avoid Communication Breakdowns," *Logistics Management*, April 2006, 37–41.
[15]Ibid.

Objectives, the means by which goals are to be achieved, state certain minimum requirements and are more specific than goals. Objectives should be specific, measurable, achievable, and cost effective; the latter two are extremely important because relatively small increases in the overall level of customer service objectives can substantially increase the costs of maintaining the increased level of customer service. In other words, although it might be possible to achieve a particular objective, to do so might be cost prohibitive. Consider, for example, an objective to reduce order picking errors from 5 to 2 percent within a 12-month time period. Let's assume that this objective is specific and measurable. Although 12 months might be a reasonable time period in which to achieve the 3 percent reduction in order pick errors, what will it cost to achieve this reduction? Will the company be forced to hire additional personnel to check the picked orders? Will the current order picking process need to be restructured, perhaps through the addition of new technology? Can the company afford new people or new technology? If so, is the somewhat marginal improvement in customer service worth the additional costs?

A central element in establishing customer service goals and objectives is determining the customer's viewpoint. This means asking customers for their insights about customer service. What services would the customer like to receive that presently aren't available from the seller? What services do customers view as the most important? How well does the seller currently provide what the customer wants? What could be improved?

Because customer service is a competitive tool, it's also important to learn how the customer evaluates the service levels of competing sellers. Many companies evaluate their service performance through **benchmarking** (comparison of an organization's performance to the performance of other organizations), and well-run organizations benchmark not only against competitors but against best-in-class organizations as well. The benchmarking should not only involve numerical comparisons of relevant metrics (e.g., fill rates) but should also learn about the processes associated with the metrics (e.g., how a best-in-class organization achieves its fill rates).

The nature of the product also affects the level of the customer service that should be offered. Substitutability, which refers to the number of products from which a firm's customers can choose to meet their needs, is one aspect. If a firm has a near monopoly on an important product (i.e., few substitutes are available), a high level of customer service is not required because a customer who needs the product will buy it under any reasonable customer service standard. However, if many products can perform the same task, then customer service standards become important from a competitive marketing point of view.

Another product-related consideration when establishing customer service goals and objectives is where the product is in its product life cycle. A product just being introduced needs a different kind of service support than one that is in a mature or declining market stage. When introducing a new product, companies want to make sure that there is sufficient supply of it to meet potential customer demand, and so companies might use expedited transportation to protect against out-of-stock situations. It is far less likely that the same company would use expedited transportation to guard against an out-of-stock situation with a product in the decline phase of the product life cycle.

Establishing minimum acceptable order sizes is an ever-increasing customer service problem because many customers want to order smaller quantities at more frequent intervals. Orders of decreasing size make diminishing (and eventually negative) contributions to profits. In any particular marketing situation, detailed analysis is needed regarding both why small orders are placed and the possible reactions of existing customers to a new policy that requires either a larger minimum order size or a surcharge on small orders to offset losses. Some retail stores, for example, require a specified level of spending before customers are allowed to pay with credit cards.

MEASURING AND CONTROLLING CUSTOMER SERVICE

Grandiose statements and platitudes regarding a firm's level of customer service represent little more than rhetoric unless the customer service standards to support them are actually implemented. To accomplish this, a systematic program of measurement and control is required. The ability to measure is the ability to control, and *you can't manage what you can't measure.* Control is the process of taking corrective action when measurements indicate that the goals and objectives of customer service are not being achieved. Measurement by itself is merely wasted time and effort if no action is taken based on the feedback received. The actions taken after deficiencies have been identified can lead to an effective and efficient customer service program.

Several key issues are associated with measurement, one of which involves determining the data sources to be used. Ideally, an organization might want to collect measurement data from both internal and external sources. With respect to internal sources, an organization might audit credit memos, which are the documents that must be issued to correct errors in shipping and billing. Comparing them with the volume of error-free activity gives a measure of relative activity accuracy in performance. External measurement data can be collected from actual customers, as illustrated in Figures 4-4 and 4-5. Figure 4-4 shows a relatively short form used by a company located in Northern Spain to learn the data and time of product delivery. The form in Figure 4-5 is a bit more detailed and asks customers about mistakes in quantities received as well as whether the correct product was shipped, along with other issues.

FIGURE 4-4	Form Used By a Spanish Firm for Surveying the Time Element of Delivery Service.

⊘ temper

CONTROL DEL TIEMPO DE TRANSPORTE

*Estimado cliente: estamos intentado reducir al mínimo el tiempo de transporte de nuestro almacén al suyo. Le agradeceríamos mucho si nos indica el día y la hora aproximada en que recibió este material y **nos pasa este documento por fax.***

Albarán nº

RECIBIDO EL DIA   /   /   **HORA APROXIMADA**   :

COMENTARIOS

Número de fax GRATUITO: 900 121 875

¡ MUCHAS GRACIAS POR SU AYUDA !

The customer is asked to provide the invoice number, note the date that the order was received, and fax it (toll-free) to the shipper.
Source: SFT Group.

CALIDAD DEL SERVICIO DE ALMACÉN

Estimado cliente,

Con objeto de seguir mejorando nuestro servicio, le rogamos conteste a este breve cuestionario y nos lo envíe a nuestro **fax GRATUITO 900 121 875**, *o por correo, a la atención de la Srta. Rosa Pereda, si desea asegurar la confidencialidad (en algunos envíos por fax consta el nombre de la empresa).*

- ¿ Hay equivocaciones en las cantidades de los materiales que les suministramos ?

Muchas veces .... ☐
A menudo .... ☐
Algunas veces .... ☐
Casi nunca .... ☐
Nunca lo tuvimos .... ☐

OBSERVACIONES Y CONSEJOS:

_____
_____
_____

- ¿ Hay equivocaciones en las referencias de los materiales (servir un tipo por otro)?

Muchas veces .... ☐
A menudo .... ☐
Algunas veces .... ☐
Casi nunca .... ☐
Nunca lo tuvimos .... ☐

OBSERVACIONES Y CONSEJOS:

_____
_____
_____

- El embalaje, ¿ es el correcto y los materiales llegan bien o no es correcto y los productos llegan dañados ?

Mal muchas veces .... ☐
Mal a veces .... ☐
Normal .... ☐
Bueno (mejor que la media) ..... ☐
Muy bueno .... ☐

OBSERVACIONES Y CONSEJOS:

_____
_____
_____

- El paquete exteriormente y el albarán interior, ¿ recogen toda la información que Vd. necesita ?

Información mala .... ☐
Información normal .... ☐
Información buena .... ☐

OBSERVACIONES Y CONSEJOS:

_____
_____
_____

FIGURE 4-5   Form Used By a Firm Located in Northern Spain to Query Customers About Several Service Elements

Question 1 asks about mistakes in quantities shipped. Question 2 asks whether correct goods were shipped. Question 3 asks about the adequacy of packaging, and question 4 is about labeling. The completed form can be returned by toll-free fax.

TABLE 4-2	Select customer service measures
Customer Service Dimension	**Measure**
Time	Order cycle time
	Inquiry response time
Dependability	Perfect order
	On-time delivery
Communication	Customer complaints
	Order status information
Convenience	Returns process
	Response to emergency situations

A second key issue associated with customer service measurement is determining what factors to measure. Some firms choose those aspects of customer service that are the easiest to measure, which isn't necessarily a good idea because aspects that are difficult to measure may provide better insights into customer likes and dislikes. Some firms choose those aspects of customer service that they believe are most important, which isn't necessarily a good idea either because these aspects might be relatively unimportant from the customer's perspective.

Because so many potential customer service measurements exist, it's not possible to provide a simple list that would be applicable across the board. Nevertheless, the metrics that are chosen should be relevant and important from the customer's perspective. Moreover, the measure should be consistent with the four dimensions of customer service—time, dependability, convenience, and convenience—discussed earlier. Table 4-2 provides representative customer service measures for each of these four dimensions.

Moreover, although customer service must be measured if it is to be managed, organizations should resist the tendency to "measure everything that moves." Excessive measurement can strain an organization because it requires the collection of tremendous amounts of data, and once collected, the data must be analyzed. This can result in "analysis paralysis," or the idea that so much time is required for analysis that there's little if any time left to make decisions based on the data. Rather, organizations should utilize a limited number of meaningful and relevant metrics. 3M Corporation, for example, utilizes approximately 15 items to measure its customer service.

Service Failure and Service Recovery

We will conclude our discussion of customer service with a look at service failure and service recovery. Regardless of how well run an organization is, some situations will occur where its actual performance does not meet the customer's expected performance (i.e., a service failure). Service failure has emerged as a prominent business issue in recent years, in part because organizations have learned that customers can easily become disaffected. For example, some sources suggest that nearly two-thirds of customers who experience a problem with *purchases of less than $5* won't do business with that company again.[16] Service failure and service recovery are particularly relevant to the order cycle; for example, order entry might be less convenient than desired by customers, whereas late or erratic deliveries can play havoc with customer supply chains.

---

[16]John Tschohl, "Turning Service into Opportunities," *TWICE: This Week in Consumer Electronics*, March 27, 2006, 78.

Given that service failures are inevitable, organizations will be faced with service recovery decisions. For our purposes, **service recovery** will refer to a process for returning a customer to a state of satisfaction after a service or product has failed to live up to expectations. Although service recovery often generates significant out-of-pocket costs, well-run organizations recognize that good (or excellent) service recovery can actually result in *increased* customer loyalty. Indeed, satisfactory service recovery tends to increase a customer's willingness to recommend the offending organization; unsatisfactory service recovery magnifies the initial failure.[17]

There is no set formula for service recovery, in part because each service failure is unique in its impact on a particular customer. Having said this, there are general guidelines for dealing with service recovery, and it's important to recognize that these guidelines may not only assuage the customer but may also result in an organization improving its operations. For example, one recovery guideline is fair treatment for customers.[18] In the logistics discipline, one example of fair treatment involves service guarantees by transportation companies; if a shipment misses various delivery parameters (e.g., on time, undamaged), then customers can receive a full refund (or aren't billed for the transportation). Besides reducing customer risk, many transportation companies that have implemented service guarantees have improved relevant aspects of their performance such as on-time delivery, which has meant a decrease in the amount of payouts for deficient service.

Summary

Demand management deals with determining what customers want, and a key component involves demand forecasting. The chapter discussed basic demand forecasting models along with select forecasting issues such as cost and accuracy.

Also discussed were order management and the order cycle. The order cycle, the period of time from when the order is placed until it is received, can be subdivided into four distinct stages, and the order cycle, as well as each stage in it, was discussed.

Customer service strives to keep customers happy, and the four dimensions of customer service were discussed. The chapter also looked at the establishment of customer service objectives as well as the measurement and control of customer service. The chapter concluded with a discussion of service failure and recovery.

Questions For Discussion And Review

1. What is the relationship between demand management, order management, and customer service?
2. Discuss the three basic demand forecasting models.
3. List and discuss several demand forecasting issues.
4. Is computer software a panacea for demand forecasting? Why or why not?
5. Define and describe the order cycle. Why is it considered an important aspect of customer service?
6. What are some causes of order cycle variability? What are the consequences of order cycle variability?
7. Define the perfect order concept. What is its relevance to the order cycle?
8. List the various methods of order transmittal and discuss relevant characteristics of each.
9. Define order triage and explain how it can affect order processing.
10. What is pick-to-light technology, and how can it improve order picking?
11. Discuss the order delivery stage of the order cycle.
12. How can customer service act as a competitive weapon?

---

[17]Leonard L. Berry and Jonathan A. Leighton, "Restoring Customer Confidence," *MHS* 24, no. 1 (2004): 15–19.
[18]Ibid.

13. Distinguish between customer service and customer satisfaction.
14. Why are organizations and customers demanding higher levels of customer service?
15. List and discuss the three elements of the dependability dimension of customer service.
16. What are some advantages and disadvantages to technological advances designed to facilitate buyer–seller communications?
17. Distinguish between customer service goals and objectives.
18. How do characteristics such as substitutability and product life cycle stage influence the development of customer service goals and objectives?
19. Should organizations use a limited, or extensive, number of customer service measures? Support your position.
20. What is meant by service recovery? How is it relevant to logistics?

Suggested Readings

Brewer, Peter C., and Thomas W. Speh. "Using the Balanced Scorecard to Measure Supply Chain Performance." *Journal of Business Logistics* 21, no. 1 (2001): 75–93.

Croxton, Keely L. "The Order Fulfillment Process." *International Journal of Logistics Management* 14, no. 1 (2003): 19–32.

Gardner, Chris, Cheryl Harrity, and Kate Vitasek. "A Better Way to Benchmark." *Supply Chain Management Review* 9, no. 3 (2005): 20–28.

Lambert, Douglas M., and Terrance L. Pohlen. "Supply Chain Metrics." *International Journal of Logistics Management* 12, no. 1 (2001): 1–19.

Maltz, Arnold, Eliot Rabinovich, and Rajiv Sinha. "Order Management for Profit on the Internet." *Business Horizons* 48, no. 2 (2005): 113–123.

McCarthy, Teresa M., and Susan L. Golicic. "Implementing Collaborative Forecasting to Improve Supply Chain Performance." *International Journal of Physical Distribution & Logistics Management* 32, no. 6 (2002): 431–454.

Mentzer, John T., and Mark A. Moon. "Understanding Demand." *Supply Chain Management Review* 8, no. 4 (2004): 38–45.

Morash, Edward A. "Supply Chain Strategies, Capabilities, and Performance." *Transportation Journal* 41, no. 1 (2001): 37–54.

Novack, Robert A., and Douglas J. Thomas. "The Challenges of Implementing the Perfect Order Concept." *Transportation Journal* 43, no. 1 (2004): 5–16.

Taylor, John C., Stanley E. Fawcett, and George C. Jackson. "Catalog Retailer In-Stock Performance: An Assessment of Customer Service Levels." *Journal of Business Logistics* 25, no. 2 (2004): 119–137.

Towill, Denis, and Martin Christopher. "The Supply Chain Strategy Conundrum: To be Lean or Agile or To be Lean and Agile?" *International Journal of Logistics: Research & Applications* 5, no. 3 (2002): 299–309.

Vitasek, Kate, and Karl B. Manrodt. "Finding Best Practices in Your Own Backyard." *Supply Chain Management Review* 9, no. 1 (2005): 54–58.

CASES

CASE 4-1   CHEEZY WHEEZY

Starting as a small retail store in New Glarus, Wisconsin, the Cheezy Wheezy firm had slowly grown into a chain of nine retail shops located in southern Wisconsin and northern Illinois. In recent years, nearly all its competitors had begun issuing catalogs, widely distributed in late October, advertising gift packages of cheeses, jams, jellies, and other fancy food items. Henry Wilson, son of the firm's founder, had convinced his father that Cheezy Wheezy should also issue a catalog.

It was then March, and the last snows were melting. Henry Wilson had called his third staff meeting in as many weeks to discuss the catalog project. Present were Henry (whose title was vice president); Susan Moore, the sales manager; Jeff Bell, the inventory manager; and Robert Walker, the traffic manager. Also present was Robert Caldwell, from a Milwaukee-based ad agency that was handling many aspects of the catalog project.

Moore and Caldwell had just finished describing the catalog's tentative design and the allocation of catalog pages to various product lines. Caldwell then said, "We are to the point where we must design the order form, which will be stapled inside the center pages. It will be a single 8 1/2-by-11-inch sheet. The customer will remove it from the catalog, complete it, fold it into the envelope shape, lick the gummed lines, and mail it in. The order form will be on one side of the sheet. On the other will be the instructions for folding and Cheezy Wheezy's mailing address in New Glarus; the remainder of the space will be ads for some impulse items. Right now we're thinking of a Santa Claus–shaped figure molded out of cheese."

"Enough of that," said Wilson, "this group isn't here to discuss Santa dolls. We're here to design the order form. We may also have to talk a little about selling terms. Susan?"

Responding to her cue, Moore said, "Our biggest problem is how to handle the transportation and shipping costs. We've studied all our competitors' catalogs. Some absorb the costs into the product's price, some charge by weight of the order, some charge by money value of order, and some ship COD."

"How important are shipping costs, Susan?" asked Bell.

"Plenty," was her response. "They run $2 to $3 for a 1- or 2-pound package. If you take a pound of cheese that we sell in our retail stores for $2, here are our costs if it goes by catalog: cost of goods, $1; order management, 50 cents; overhead, including inventory carrying costs, 50 cents; packaging for shipment, 50 cents; and transportation costs to any point in the United States ranging between $1.75 and $3.20. If, however, we're dealing with bigger shipments, the relative costs vary."

"I'm not following you," said Wilson.

"It's like this," responded Moore. "The wholesale cost of cheese to us is the same per pound, no matter how much is sold. Order-processing costs are approximately the same for each order we'll be receiving by mail. Overhead and inventory carrying costs are always present but may be allocated in a variety of ways. Packaging costs are also about the same per order. They go up only a few cents as we move to larger cartons. Transportation costs are hard to describe because of their tapers. Right now our whole catalog project is bogged down with the problem of transportation cost tapers."

"Tapers?" said Wilson, turning to Walker. "You've never told me about tapers before. It sounds like some kind of animal."

"That's tapir, t-a-p-i-r," said Walker. "We're talking about tapers, t-a-p-e-r-s."

"Oh," said Wilson. "What are they?"

"When one ships small packages of cheese," said Walker, "rates are based on two factors, the weight being shipped and the distance. As weight or distance increases or both—the rates go up but not as quickly. This is called the *tapering principle*. To ship 2 pounds of cheese from New Glarus to St. Louis costs $2.40; 3 pounds cost $3.30; 5 pounds cost $4.60; and so on. One hundred pounds—no, 50 pounds is a better example because some of the parcel services we'll be using won't take 100 pounds—50 pounds would cost $21. There's also a distance taper. The 2-pound shipment that costs $2.40 to St. Louis is $3.40 to Denver and $4.15 to Los Angeles."

"Can't we use the average transportation costs?" asked Bell. "That's what we do with inventory carrying costs."

"Won't work," said Caldwell. "You'll be overpriced for small, short-distance shipments and will lose sales. For heavy long shipments, you'll be underpriced and will make so many sales that you might soon go belly up."

Wilson shuddered and inquired, "Does that mean we charge by weight and by distance?"

Moore answered, "It's not that easy. In the cheese business, people buy by the pound, but shipping weights—which include packaging—are actually more. A customer who orders 3 pounds of cheese is in fact receiving 3 pounds of cheese plus 6 ounces of packaging materials. I wish we could sell a pound of cheese that consisted of 14 ounces of cheese and 2 ounces of packing material, but that would be illegal at worst, and of questionable ethics, at best."

"We have the same problems with distance," added Walker. "We're trying to sell in 50 states, but who knows how far they are from New Glarus? We could have tables and maps in the catalog, but they take up valuable selling space. Also, if it looks too complex, we may just turn off some potential customers before they complete their orders."

"Some of our clients have another problem," added Caldwell, "and that is split orders. The customer will want 10 pounds of cheese, but it will be five 2-pound packages sent to five different locations. That has an impact on both packaging and transportation costs."

"So, what do we do?" asked Wilson. ∎

QUESTIONS

1. Assume that Cheezy Wheezy goes into the catalog order business. What policy should it adopt for handling stockouts—that is, what should the company do when it receives mail orders that it cannot completely fill because one or more of the desired items are out of stock?

2. Some mail customers will complain that the items Cheezy Wheezy shipped never arrived. What policy should Cheezy Wheezy adopt to deal with this?

3. Should the order form, which will be stapled into the center of the catalog and will be addressed to Cheezy Wheezy, be of the postage-paid type, which means that Cheezy Wheezy will pay the first-class postage rate plus a few cents on each envelope delivered to it, or should the customer be expected to add a first-class stamp to the order before he or she mails it? Discuss.

4. Cheezy Wheezy's headquarters are in New Glarus, but the company also operates in southern Wisconsin and northern Illinois. Is New Glarus the best address to use for receiving mail orders for cheese? Might there be advantages,

perhaps, in having the mail addressed to a more major city—say, Madison, Milwaukee, or Chicago? Discuss.

5. From the facts that have been presented in the case, how would you handle the matter of charging for the *packaging* costs of each shipment? Why?

6. How would you handle the matter of charging for the *transportation* costs of each shipment? Why?

7. Taking your answers to questions 5 and 6, write out, in either text or tabular form, the explanation of shipping charges that your catalog customers will read. (*Note:* As used here, *shipping* includes both packaging and transportation.)

8. On a single 8 1/2-by-11-inch sheet of paper, design a catalog order form for use by Cheezy Wheezy.

9. Contemplate a simple Web site for Cheezy Wheezy to sell its products within the United States. How, if at all, would the order form used in its Web site differ from an order form printed and mailed as part of a catalog? Would any sales or shipping policies be changed? Discuss.

CASE 4-2   HANDY ANDY, INC.

Handy Andy, Inc., produced garbage/trash compactors at a factory in St. Louis, Missouri, and sold them throughout the United States. Nearly all sales were in large urban areas where trash-collection costs were high.

The basic unit was about 3 feet high, 2 feet deep, and 1 1/2 feet wide. A deluxe model had the same dimensions but contained more features. Because most of the sales represented units to be placed in existing kitchens, a wide variety of colors and trims were manufactured, providing an exterior that would match almost any kitchen decor. The standard model came in five colors with three different trims for a total of 15 different combinations. The deluxe model came in eight colors and four different trims for a total of 32 different combinations. Retail prices were set by the dealer, with prices for the standard model ranging between $310 and $350 and for the deluxe model between $390 and $450. Sales in an area were usually slow until trash collectors, faced with rising landfill costs, raised their rates per can of refuse picked up.

Because of the sporadic sales patterns and the wide number of colors and trims available, retailers usually stocked only a display unit or two. They had available an expensively printed brochure that included paint chips so buyers could select the color and finish they wanted. When the retailer completed the sale, he or she would take the order and promise delivery and installation within a given number of days. In each major city, there was one major Handy Andy dealer (factory distributor). Each dealer maintained a complete stock of all styles and trims of the Handy Andy compactors. (Handy Andy, Inc., insisted that these factory distributors stock at least five units each of the 47 different styles available.) The general agreement between the factory distributors and Handy Andy was that the factory distributor would deliver and install the compactor within five days after the distributor who had made the sale informed the factory distributor. For the delivery and installation, the factory distributor received 9 percent of the unit's wholesale price, half paid by distributor who had made the sale and half paid by Handy Andy as a credit against future orders.

José Ortega worked in Handy Andy's distribution department in the St. Louis headquarters. He currently was working on a project to determine whether the compactor's warranty should be extended from one year to two years. The units were well built, and there had been almost no warranty work requested in the first year of each model's life. Because Handy Andy would have no records of work performed after the one-year period had expired, Ortega was randomly contacting buyers, using long-distance phones. Their names and phone numbers came from postcards they had mailed in to register the warranty at time of purchase (see Exhibit 4-A). The phrase at the bottom of the card referring to Handy Andy's records was to keep the buyer from waiting for a problem to occur and then mailing in the card. Whether this statement was necessary was unknown because so few defects had been reported. Ortega was in the process of contacting 500 purchasers who had owned the compactors for between one year and four years (when they had first been introduced) to determine whether the compactors had required repairs and, if so, the extent and cost of the repairs. In talking to purchasers, Ortega was impressed by the fact that there were remarkably few complaints involving the durability of the compactors.

Another type of complaint did arise, however, one that Ortega had difficulty understanding until he heard many buyers, usually from the same few cities, tell an almost identical story. It appeared that in these cities the factory distributor would contact individuals who had purchased Handy Andy compactors from other, smaller dealers and would attempt to have them cancel the original order. The factory distributor told the buyer that the model originally requested was out of stock

MAIL WITHIN FIVE DAYS OF INSTALLATION!

Serial Number _____
(8-digit number under the switch)
Purchased from:
Dealer's name _____

City _____

Date of purchase _____/_____/200_____
                        MONTH   DAY

Your
name _____

Address _____

City _____State_____ZIP_____

This card requires no postage. Just fill out and drop in any mailbox. Your warranty is good for one year from the date of purchase, as determined by our records. Contact your dealer first if you have questions.

HANDY ANDY, INC.
St. Louis, MO 63129

EXHIBIT 4-A   Return Postcard

but that a better model could be supplied for the same price. The factory distributors also indicated that the buyers would receive better service if they bought from them because, they claimed, they provided service for all Handy Andy models sold in their area. In addition, the factory distributors in these few cities indicated that they, not Handy Andy, Inc., stood behind the one-year warranty.

Ortega realized that he was uncovering a larger problem than he had been assigned to explore. He chatted briefly with his supervisor, who told him to revise the format of his interview to include a few more questions concerning the installation. She also told him to begin calling individuals who had owned compactors for less than a year. Ortega did this, and the only new information he uncovered was that the factory distributors in almost all cities did a better job of installing compactors that they had sold than they did those sold by smaller dealers. The delivery was faster (in terms of elapsed time since sale), more time was spent explaining to the customer how the compactor worked, and phone calls were made to the customer 3 days and 10 days after installation to make certain that the customer had no additional questions concerning the compactor's operation. When a compactor that had been sold by a smaller dealer was delivered, it was frequently left in the middle of the kitchen with scarcely a word exchanged between the customer and the installation personnel.

Ortega had another meeting scheduled with his supervisor. As he entered her office, he was surprised to see Handy Andy's vice president of marketing also sitting in the office. Ortega's supervisor asked him to tell the vice president the results of his interviews.

The marketing vice president asked Ortega, "Do you think this pattern exists in all markets?"

"No," was Ortega's reply. "I'd say it was a problem in Jacksonville, Baltimore, Cleveland, Louisville, Denver, and San Diego. It may be a problem in Dallas and New Orleans. My sample wasn't very well structured in a metropolitan market sense; you will recall that it was a nationwide sample that was trying to look at repairs." ■

QUESTIONS

1. Is this a customer service problem? Why or why not?
2. Marketing channels are the arrangement of intermediaries (wholesalers, retailers, and the like) that the firm uses to achieve its marketing objectives. Is the problem discussed in Handy Andy's marketing channels? Why or why not?
3. Logistics channels handle the physical flow of goods or services. Is the problem discussed in Handy Andy's logistics channel? Why or why not?
4. It appears that the factory distributors are exploiting the smaller dealers. Yet from what we can tell, Handy Andy in St. Louis has heard no complaints from the smaller dealers. Why wouldn't they complain?
5. What should Handy Andy's marketing vice president do? Why?
6. Redesign the warranty postcard, staying within the same dimensions, and include questions or statements that will make it easier for Handy Andy headquarters to detect whether installation practices of the type discussed in this case occur.
7. In the case is the statement, "The factory distributors in these few cities indicated that they, not Handy Andy, Inc., stood behind the one-year warranty." Is this a problem for Handy Andy? Why or why not?
8. Assume that the situation described in question 7 is a problem. How should the firm deal with it?

5

PROTECTIVE PACKAGING AND MATERIALS HANDLING

This shipment required extra attention. These container cranes, built in Shanghai, were being delivered to the Port of Oakland. The Golden Gate Bridge is in the background. The time selected for passing under the bridge was at low tide, and vehicular traffic on the bridge was halted briefly to reduce the weight pushing down on the deck of the bridge.

Photo courtesy Port of Oakland. ©Robert Campbell, 2002.

Key Terms

- Building-blocks concept
- Closed-loop systems
- Container
- Cube out
- Ergonomics
- Materials handling
- Package testing
- Packaging
- Pallet (skid)

- Part-to-picker system
- Picker-to-part system
- Shrink-wrap
- Slip sheet
- Unitization
- Unit loads
- Unit load devices
- Weighing out

Learning Objectives

- To know how product features and characteristics affect packaging and materials handling
- To identify the functions performed by packaging
- To appreciate select issues that affect packaging and package choice
- To analyze the utilization of unit loads in materials handling
- To identify materials handling principles and materials handling equipment

This chapter deals with the physical handling of products, with a particular emphasis on packaging and materials handling. Each product has unique physical properties that, along with the normally accepted volumes or quantities in which it is traded or moved, determine how and when the product is packaged. A product may move in bulk from the manufacturer to a wholesaler, where the product may be placed into some type of container (e.g., barrel, box, or crate) prior to further distribution.

In turn, packaging attributes strongly influence materials handling concerns; nonpackaged products necessitate different handling than do packaged products. For example, bulk items (i.e., free flowing or loose) can be handled by pumps, shovels, or conveyor devices. Nonbulk materials can be placed in various types of containers and can be handled by such conveyances as carts, cranes, dollies, and forklifts.

PRODUCT CHARACTERISTICS

Various product characteristics can influence packaging and materials handling considerations. One is the product's physical characteristics; substances exist in three forms—solid, liquid, gas—and each form has specific packaging requirements. For instance, metal cylinders are one method for the packaging of gases, whereas metal pails can be used for the packaging of liquids. Another physical characteristic is the product's ability to withstand the elements; coal piles can be exposed to rain, whereas salt piles cannot. In a similar vein, some products can be exposed to freezing conditions, but others cannot. Product density (weight per volume) is yet another physical characteristic that can affect packaging considerations.

The physical characteristics of some goods change while they are moving in the logistics channel. Fresh fruits and vegetables are the best-known examples. Even after they are picked, they continue to give off gases and moisture and to generate heat—a process known as *respiration*. Fruits and vegetables are harvested before they are ripe so they will reach the retail stores as they ripen. Ripening processes can be delayed through the use of lower temperatures or application of gases.

Products such as fresh produce, meats, fish, and baker's yeast are referred to as *perishables*. They require special packaging, loading, storage, and monitoring as they are moved from source to customer. The growth in popularity of washed, cut lettuce sold in plastic bags is an example of how packaging can benefit several members of the supply chain. The lettuce grower benefits because smaller, misshaped heads can be used, not merely the eye-pleasing, "perfect" heads. Both the retailer and the customer benefit because the shelf life is much longer for bagged lettuce than for head lettuce (bagged lettuce also carries a higher markup than does head lettuce).

Tropical fish are carried in plastic bags with enough water to cover them, but no more than necessary, to keep weight down. The area in the bag above the water is filled with oxygen. Sometimes tranquilizers are added to water to keep fish calm. The bag is sealed and placed in a plastic foam cooler, similar to a picnic cooler, which is then placed inside a cardboard box. Fish must be transported within 36 hours, although the time can be extended if oxygen is added to the bags.

In addition to physical characteristics, products also possess chemical characteristics that affect the manner in which they should be handled. Certain pairs of products are incompatible. For example, commodities that are sensitive to ethylene, such as mangoes, bananas, and broccoli, should never be held for more than a few hours in the same area as products that emit ethylene, such as apples, avocados, and cantaloupes.

The various properties of goods must also be made known to consumers to help them make the correct buying decision and care for the product properly. Figure 5-1 is a portion of a fabric care label that goes on Levi's jeans sold in Japan. Figure 5-2 is used for marking lumber. The (a) position is for the trademark of the accrediting agent, such as the National Hardwood Lumber Association or the Pacific Lumber Inspection Bureau; (b) identifies the specific mill; (c) indicates whether lumber is heat-treated; and (d) is for the country of origin, which is necessary if the lumber is exported. Interest has grown in having an additional symbol that indicates

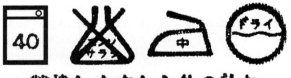

染しますから他の物と
分けて洗って下さい。

品　質　表　示

綿　　100%

リーバイ・ストラウス　ジャパンK.K.

米　国　製

FIGURE 5-1   Portion of Fabric Care Label for Levis Jeans Sold in Japan

From left to right the pictures say, Wash at 40° centigrade, use no chlorine bleach, iron at the medium temperature setting; the jeans can be dry cleaned. The text below the label gives the fabric content, the nation of origin, and the name *Levi Strauss.*
Source: Courtesy of Levi Strauss Japan K.K.

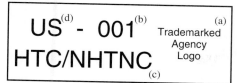

FIGURE 5-2   Lumber Markings

Source: American Lumber Standard Committee, Inc.

the wood used for packing was free of insects. Nations in various parts of the world are concerned that untreated wood and wood materials used in packing carries a wide variety of unwanted insects.

Hazardous Cargo

Under certain conditions, almost any material can possess hazardous qualities. Flour dust can explode, and grain in elevators can self-ignite and burn. Special care is needed to handle these and many other substances. Governmental regulations address the movements of hazardous materials, which are often classified into seven categories: explosives, compressed gases, flammable liquids, oxidizers, poisons, radioactive materials, and corrosive materials.

The specific requirements differ for each hazardous commodity, but all of them involve labeling, packaging and repackaging, placing warnings on shipping documents, and notifying carriers in advance. A common requirement on transferring flammable materials is that the vehicle and the receiving or discharging device both be electrically grounded. Care must be taken to properly clean tanks, pumps, hoses, and cleaning apparatus to avoid contamination of the next cargo that is handled. Legislation passed after the Exxon *Valdez* oil spill requires petroleum carriers and tank farms to have in place extensive response plans for dealing with possible spills. As part of their response plan, these companies make extensive commitments to have available equipment and trained personnel to deal with spills. Many belong to industry cooperatives, meaning that they expect to help, and be helped by, each other. Some large cleanup contractors can also be relied on to help.

All levels of governments issue numerous regulations, with differences between domestic and international shipments. Effective on October 1, 1994, the United States adopted for domestic use the global hazardous materials packaging and labeling regulations developed through the United Nations. However, these regulations are not used in all nations. At the local level, prohibitions sometimes apply to the use of certain tunnels or bridges during specified hours by trucks carrying explosives or other dangerous cargo. Some major U.S. cities, including Washington, D.C., and Boston, are attempting to pass legislation that would force trucks and railroads to route hazardous shipments away from highly populated areas. (Not surprisingly, such legislation is opposed by those living in the less-populated areas that would be subjected to the rerouted hazardous shipments.)

Shipping documents must also indicate whether the cargo is of hazardous nature, and sometimes additional documentation is required. Packages, containers, trailers, and railcars carrying hazardous materials must carry distinct signs, or placards, identifying the hazard.

PACKAGING

Packaging can be thought of in terms of the **building-blocks concept,** where a very small unit is placed into a slightly larger unit, which then might be placed into a larger unit, and so on. Consider the various bags, cans, cartons, jars, and so on that the customer sees on the shelves of a grocery store. These units were likely unpacked from some larger container, such as a crate or box, and these crates or boxes might have been delivered to the store on a unit load (which will be discussed later in the chapter).

The building-blocks hierarchy is important to remember because each of the different building blocks is inside another, and their total effect should be to protect the product. They function in a complementary sense. When the consumer-size package is very solid, the larger packaging elements require less-sturdy packaging materials because the smaller packages are themselves sturdy. Alternatively, when the smallest package isn't very solid (e.g., the retail packaging for lightbulbs), the larger packaging elements will require very sturdy packaging materials and/or careful arrangement of the smallest product to minimize damage.

Packaging, which refers to materials used for the containment, protection, handling, delivery, and presentation of goods,[1] serves three general functions: to promote, to protect, and to identify (label) the relevant product. It's important to understand that these functions can sometimes come into conflict. For example, although from a retailing standpoint it may be desirable to have an attractive promotional message on the outside of each box, when these boxes are in a warehouse, the same message might make it easier for a thief to determine quickly which boxes contain the most valuable items. Using an alternative identification scheme, such as code numbers on the outside of the box, will likely reduce opportunities for theft (the would-be thief will have to open boxes to see what is inside them).

Promotional Functions of Packaging

Although packaging is thought to be primarily protective, it may also contain features with a sales orientation. With the growth of mass merchandising and a corresponding reduction in the number of salespeople, for many products customers can examine only the printing and pictures on closed cartons before making their choices. Some merchants build displays using box or case lots of goods to create the impression that they have made an extra-large purchase of a certain item, presumably at a lower price per unit that is then being passed on to the consumer. In this instance, it would be appropriate to display some advertising on the outside of the box.

Figure 5-3 illustrates another issue involving sales and protective packaging. The razor-blade container, shown at the bottom, is quite small. Because razor blades are often displayed next to chain-store checkout stands, from a marketing standpoint it is useful to display them on a rack. However, to reduce the problem of shoplifting, it is necessary to mount the blades on a stiff card that is larger than most people's pockets. The net effect of these two steps is to increase the cube, or volume, of each razor-blade package by over 700 percent. Other small products, such as camera film, batteries, and compact discs, must also be placed in large packages to reduce shoplifting.

Protective Functions of Packaging

A protective package should perform the following functions:

1. Enclose the materials, both to protect them and protect other items from them.
2. Restrain them from undesired movements within the container when the container is in transit.
3. Separate the contents to prevent undesired contact, such as through the use of corrugated fiberboard partitions used in the shipment of glassware.
4. Cushion the contents from outside vibrations and shocks.

---

[1] *Logistics Dictionary*, www.tntfreight.com.

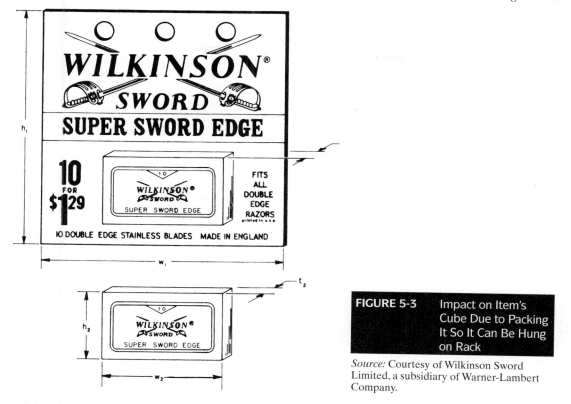

FIGURE 5-3 Impact on Item's Cube Due to Packing It So It Can Be Hung on Rack

Source: Courtesy of Wilkinson Sword Limited, a subsidiary of Warner-Lambert Company.

5. Support the weight of identical containers that will be stacked above it as part of the building-blocks concept. This could mean that in some situations, stacks in a warehouse are up to 20 feet high.

6. Position the contents to provide maximum protection for them. If one were packaging combined sets of wastebaskets and lamp shades, the package would be designed so that the lamp shades were protected by the wastebaskets.

7. Provide for fairly uniform weight distribution within the package, because most equipment for the automatic handling of packages is designed for packages whose weight is evenly distributed. Also, individuals handling packages manually assume that the weight inside is evenly distributed.

8. Provide enough exterior surface area so that identification and shipping labels can be applied, along with specific instructions such as "This Side Up" or "Keep Refrigerated." Today, this would also mean providing a uniform location for the application of bar codes. Handling symbols, such as a picture of an umbrella meaning "Keep Dry," might also be used.

9. Be tamperproof to the extent that evidence of tampering can be noticed (mainly at the retail level of packaging for some foods and drugs).

10. Be safe in the sense that the package itself (both in conjunction with the product carried and after it has been unpacked) presents no hazards to consumers or to others.

Figure 5-4 shows a checklist prepared by the Fibre Box Association, indicating the range of considerations that go into package choice. Firms that sell packaging material are helpful sources of information to potential users. Often, they provide technical advice.

checklist for box users

The corrugated box contains and protects your product, but it can also serve many functions which aid in packing, storage, distribution, marketing and sales. This checklist is a guide to the information you'll want to supply to your box maker. He can then offer suggestions and recommendations to utilize every value-added advantage that corrugated can offer.

YOUR PRODUCT

	yes	no
1. Have you given your box maker a description of your product and its use, the exact dimensions, weight and physical characteristics?	☐	☐
2. Is the product likely to settle or shift?	☐	☐
3. Is it perishable, fragile, or hazardous in any way?	☐	☐
4. Will it need extra protection against vibration, impact, moisture, air, heat or cold?	☐	☐
5. Will it be shipped fully assembled?	☐	☐
6. Will more than one unit be packed in a box?	☐	☐
7. Will accessories, parts or literature be included with the product?	☐	☐
8. Have you provided your box maker with a complete sample of your product as it will be packed?	☐	☐

YOUR PACKING OPERATION

	yes	no
1. Is your box inventory adequately geared to re-order lead time?	☐	☐
2. Is your box inventory arranged to efficiently feed your packing lines?	☐	☐
3. Is your inventory of boxes properly stored?	☐	☐
4. Will you be setting up the boxes on automatic equipment? (If so, what type? Size? Method of closure?)	☐	☐
5. Will your product be packed automatically? (If so, with what type of equipment?)	☐	☐
6. If more than one unit or part goes into each box, have you determined the sequence?	☐	☐
7. Will inner packing—shells, liners, pads, partitions—be inserted by hand?	☐	☐
8. Is your closure system—tape, stiches, glue—compatible with the box, packing line speed, customer needs and recycling considerations?	☐	☐
9. Will the box be imprinted or labeled?	☐	☐
10. Will a master pack be used for a multiple of boxes to maintain cleanliness or appearance?	☐	☐

YOUR STORAGE

	yes	no
1. Have you determined the gross weight of the filled box?	☐	☐
2. Does the product itself help support weight in stacking?	☐	☐
3. Will the bottom box have to support the full weight in warehouse stacking?	☐	☐
4. Will boxes be handled by lift trucks which use clamps, finger lifts or special attachments?	☐	☐
5. Will filled boxes be palletized? (The size of pallet and pallet pattern may justify a change in box design or dimensions, if only to reduce or eliminate overhang.)	☐	☐
6. Would a change in box style or size make more efficient use of warehouse space?	☐	☐
7. Will filled boxes be subject to unusual conditions during storage—high humidity, extreme temperatures, etc.?	☐	☐
8. Is the product likely to be stored outdoors at any time during its distribution?	☐	☐
9. Would color coding simplify identification of various packed products?	☐	☐

YOUR SHIPPING

	yes	no
1. Have you reviewed the appropriate rules of the transportation service you intend to use (rail, truck, air, parcel post, etc.)?	☐	☐
2. Is your container authorized for shipment of your product?	☐	☐
3. If the package is not authorized, have you requested appropriate test shipment authorization from the carrier?	☐	☐
4. Does your product require any special caution or warning label or legend for shipment?	☐	☐
5. Have you determined the actual inside dimensions of the transportation vehicle so that you can establish how your filled boxes will be stacked or braced?	☐	☐

YOUR CUSTOMER

	yes	no
1. Does your customer have any special receiving, storage or handling requirements that will affect box design?	☐	☐
2. Will the box be used as part of a mass display?	☐	☐
3. Is the box intended as a display-shipper?	☐	☐
4. Will it contain a separate product display?	☐	☐
5. Will it be used as a carry-home package, requiring a carrying device?	☐	☐
6. Does it need an easy-opening feature?	☐	☐
7. Can surface design, symbols or colors relate to promotional materials or to other products of the same corporate family?	☐	☐
8. Should instructions or opening precautions be printed on the box?	☐	☐
9. Can the box be made to better sell your product?	☐	☐

FIGURE 5-4   Checklist for Box Users

Source: Copyright permission granted from the Fibre Box Association

Carriers' tariffs and classifications influence (if not control) the type of packaging and packing methods that must be used. In freight classification documents, the type of packaging is specified. The commodity is listed, followed by a comma and then by a phrase—such as "in machine-pressed bales," "in barrels," "in bales compressed in more than 18 lb. per square foot," "folded flat, in packages," "celluloid covered, in boxes," "SU" (setup), or "KD" (knocked down—or disassembled and packed so that it occupies two-thirds or less of the volume it would occupy in its setup state). The carriers established these different classifications for two main reasons. First, packaging specifications determined by product density encourage shippers to tender loads in densities that make the best use of the equipment's weight and volume capabilities. IKEA, the Swedish-based home furnishings chain, designs many of its products so that they can be shipped in a dense form. Such products are often displayed unassembled in retail stores, and customers realize that they can easily take them home in their autos.

Second, carrier specifications for protective packaging reduce the likelihood of damage to products while they are being carried; this, in turn, reduces the amount of loss and damage claims placed against the carrier. Figure 5-5 shows the type of label (the "box maker's certificate," or BMC) that motor carriers and railroads require on fiber boxes used for shipping freight. It is the fiber box manufacturer's assurance to the motor carriers and railroads that the boxes will be sturdy enough to meet their handling specifications. Note that a number of measures are used. For example, the size limit shown, 75 inches, means that the material should not be used in a package where the total length, width, and height, when added together, exceed 75 inches.

It is difficult to know exactly how much carrier tariffs and classifications control shippers' packaging. Responsibility for damage in transit is one issue subject to carrier–shipper contract negotiation; if the carrier remains liable, the carrier specifies the level of packaging protection to be used. If the shipper assumes responsibility, the shipper may choose the type of packaging to use. Carrier deregulation has allowed corrugated packaging manufacturers and their customers to innovate with performance outside the traditional carrier packaging rules. As specific

FIGURE 5-5   Boxmaker's Guarantee

Source: Courtesy of the American Trucking Association.

contract rates are negotiated between individual carriers and shippers, packaging requirements may, of course, be one element of negotiation.

Airlines, express delivery companies, and the U.S. Postal Service also have packaging requirements, although they are somewhat less detailed than those used by rail and motor common carriers. With respect to international shipments, The International Air Transport Association regulates the packaging of air shipments, and limited packaging requirements apply to ocean shipments. However, exporters nearly always buy additional insurance coverage for their export shipments, and the type of packing influences the insurance rates.

Labeling

Packaging is usually done at the end of the assembly line, so package labeling also occurs there because using this location avoids accumulating an inventory of preprinted packages. This is also a key point for control because this is where there is an exact measure of what comes off the assembly line. As the packaged goods are moved from the end of the assembly line, they become stocks of finished goods and become the responsibility of the firm's outbound logistics system. Near the point where product packaging occurs, it is necessary to maintain a complete inventory of all the packages, packing materials, and labels that will be used.

Once the material being packaged is placed into the box and the cover is closed, the contents are hidden. At this point, it becomes necessary to label the box. Whether words or code numbers are used depends on the nature of the product and its vulnerability to pilferage. Retroflective labels that can be read by optical scanners may also be applied. Batch numbers are frequently assigned to food and drug products, so they may be more easily traced in case of a product recall. Figure 5-6 shows a small sampling of labels that can be purchased for individual placement on cartons or pallets.

Bar codes are widely used in labeling, and they are read by scanners, or sensors; Figure 5-7 shows a bar-code laser scanner. Scanners often do more than signal the presence of a container or part. They also give the computer as much information as it needs about that part to maintain accurate production and inventory records and to determine the routing of that part from one workstation to another. Leading firms are moving away from the one-dimensional bar code to a code with two dimensions, which can hold considerably more information in a small space.

Not all labels are visible to the naked eye; some are tiny chips that are embedded into the product and can be read using various electronic devices. These RFID (radio frequency identification) labels allow information contained in the chips to be updated as they move through the supply chain. As their price drops, their use will increase; more widespread RFID adoption should allow companies to cut costs, waste, and theft.[2]

Many regulations govern the labeling of packaging, including the labeling of weight, specific contents, and instructions for use. Today, much of this information must also be placed outside the larger cartons as well, because some retail outlets sell in carton lots, and the buyer does not see the consumer package until he or she reaches home. In an increasingly global economy, it is important to recognize that labeling regulations differ from country to country. As a general rule, labeling requirements and enforcement tend to be more stringent in economically developed countries than in economically developing ones.

Moreover, labeling requirements within a particular country can differ from state to state (or province to province). In the United States the liquor (alcoholic beverage) industry is

---

[2]Nic Fildes, "Tag That Stores Detailed Data May Cut Costs, Waste, and Theft," *Wall Street Journal*, March 19, 2003, B4A.

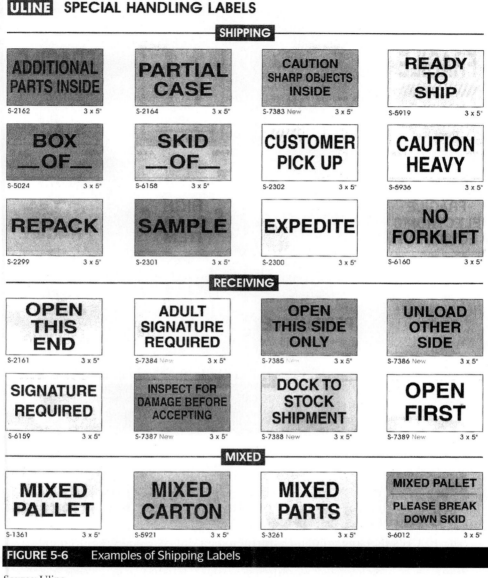

FIGURE 5-6   Examples of Shipping Labels

Source: Uline.

heavily regulated, and states have liquor control boards that are responsible for regulating liquor-related activities within state borders. For example, the Pennsylvania Liquor Control Board (PLCB) mandates that the following information be on all cases of products received in any of our warehouses:

- UPC [Universal Product Code] (barcode and readable)
- The PLCB/State item number

FIGURE 5-7   A Handheld Laser Scanner Scanning Labels on a Pallet Load of Product Sitting in a Warehouse Rack

Source: Courtesy of PSC Inc.

- A brief description of the product (including name, size and vintage or proof)
- The Shipping Container Code (SCC) (barcode and readable must appear on two adjacent sides, see "Label Placement" for details)[3]

The PLCB's labeling guidelines further spell out case code requirements and specifications (e.g., the size of identification numbers), SCC label requirements and specifications (e.g., only fourteen-digit SCCs are currently acceptable), label placement (e.g., the SCC label must be placed 1 1/4 inches (plus or minus 1/8 inch) from the container's bottom), packaging information (e.g., the ability to withstand transport, handling, and stacking), and shipping instructions (e.g., loads should be placed on slip sheets whenever possible). Note the specificity of these guidelines, and consider how easy it might be to make an error. Failure to comply with these labeling guidelines subjects the offending organization to surcharges, administrative fees, or penalty charges.[4]

---

[3]*www.lcb.state.pa.us.*
[4]*Ibid.*

Package Testing and Monitoring

To properly design a protective package system requires three important kinds of information: the severity of the distribution environment, the fragility of the product to be protected, and the performance characteristics of various cushion materials. When new products or new packaging techniques are about to be introduced, it is sometimes advisable to have the packages pretested. Various packaging material manufacturers and trade organizations provide free **package testing.** Independent testing laboratories can also be used. The packages are subject to tests that attempt to duplicate all the expected various shipping hazards: vibrations, dropping, horizontal impacts, compression (having too much weight loaded on top), overexposure to extreme temperatures or moisture, and rough handling. Figure 5-8 shows the side of a corrugated container that failed a compression test.

In addition to the testing of new products or new packages, shippers should keep detailed records on all loss and damage claims. Statistical tests can be applied to the data to determine whether the damage pattern is randomly distributed. If it is not, efforts are made toward providing

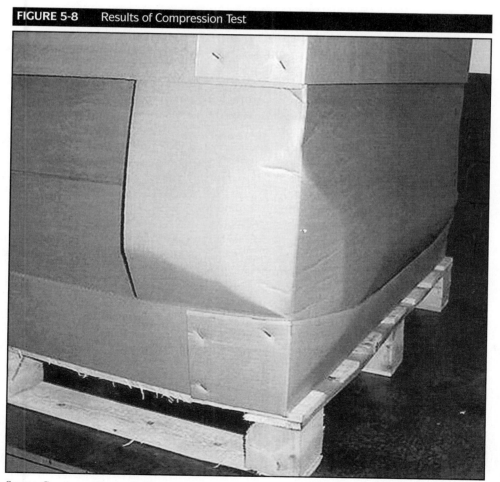

FIGURE 5-8   Results of Compression Test

Source: Courtesy of Sertapak Group.

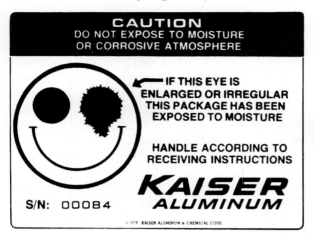

FIGURE 5-9   Kaiser Aluminum's Moisture-Alert Label

When the product is shipped, both eyes are normal; that is, they look like the eye on the left. The figure shows how the label looks after the product is exposed to moisture. The receiver is to record the conditions of the label in the shipping document.

additional protection for areas in the package that are overly vulnerable. Carriers also have provisions that allow shippers to follow special rules while testing new packaging materials. UPS customers ship sample parcels to various UPS district offices, and UPS employees at those sites then report back with comments about how well the packaging withstood the UPS trip.

Related to package testing is actual monitoring of the environment the package must pass through. This is done by enclosing recording devices within cartons of the product that are shipped. The measuring devices may be very simple, such as hospital-like thermometers that record only temperature extremes and springs that are set to snap only if a specified number of g's (a measure of force) are exceeded. Kaiser Aluminum, which was troubled with problems of water-stain damage, devised the small sticker with the happy face shown in Figure 5-9. Above the happy face's smile are two eyes, but one of the eyes is printed in a special ink that dissolves when it comes into contact with moisture. If the receiver of the shipment notices that the eye is distorted, he or she can assume that the shipment has been exposed to moisture and should be inspected for damage. More sophisticated devices record a series of variables over time, such as temperature, humidity, and acceleration force and duration (in several directions). Acceleration force and duration are usually recorded along three different axes, making it possible to calculate the precise direction from which the force originated.

Sophisticated monitors are expensive, but they may be necessary to solve a problem of recurrent in-transit damage. Less-complicated devices are used to record temperatures and may or may not be used as the basis for a damage claim against a carrier. They may be used aboard a shipper's own equipment to ensure quality control. A frozen food distributor wants to be certain that its product has not thawed and been refrozen in transit. Large shipments of apples are accompanied by a mechanical temperature recorder, which provides the receiver with a greater workable knowledge of each load, such as information on temperature variation that may affect the speed at which the receiver should handle and merchandise the apples.

Environmental Protection
Public concern for environmental protection has had an impact on packaging and materials handling practices. Many materials used in packaging can be recycled. Use of disposable packing materials is often viewed as wasteful, and it is becoming increasingly expensive as costs increase for dumping in landfill sites.

Dust and vapors produced during bulk-cargo transfer operations are also being scrutinized more closely by public agencies. Coal dust can be blown for several miles from a large coal pile. In port areas, bulk materials that were once stored outside are now in enclosed structures. For products still left outside, elaborate vacuum systems are used to capture the dust created by handling, and ditches around the facility capture rainwater runoff so that it can be run through filters. Some states require handlers of petroleum products, including retail gasoline stations, to install vapor recovery systems. For liquids with vapor-escape problems, the transfer processes are redesigned so that tanks and other receptacles are loaded from the bottom rather than the top.

The environmental protection movement has had a profound impact on the packaging industry on a worldwide basis. One of the most noteworthy examples is Germany's Packaging Ordinance that was enacted in the early 1990s. This legislation attempted to address Germany's solid waste problem by requiring manufacturers to take back and either reuse or recycle post-consumer packaging. Similar legislation was adopted by the European Union in the mid-1990s.

Although the use of plastic for packaging has grown dramatically over the past quarter century—plastic tends to be cheaper, more versatile, and more consumer friendly than paper—plastic leaves a great deal to be desired from an environmental perspective. One of plastic's most frequently cited shortcomings is the length of time it takes to biodegrade, which can be up to *several hundred years*. Moreover, the manufacture of plastic products is dependent on petroleum, which is a diminishing natural resource (and an extremely costly resource in recent years). A third environmental concern with plastic packaging involves litter, and sometimes this litter has unintended ecological consequences. For example, plastic litter in the Pacific Ocean off the California coast is estimated to kill 100,000 marine animals a year either from ingestion or strangulation.[5]

A key problem facing those trying to choose packaging materials is that each nation's (and, for that matter, each state's or province's) regulations can differ in terms of acceptable packaging. One reason that regulations differ is that different entities view environmental problems differently and enact regulations that address the issues of current concern to them. For instance, the California example cited in the previous paragraph prompted legislation aimed at reducing plastic packaging due to litter-related as well as ecological considerations. Other plastic-related legislation, by contrast, is aimed at reducing the amount of packaging material that ends up in landfills.

Firms can adopt one or more of the following environmentally friendly packaging strategies. One is to reduce the amount of packing materials used, but this is tempered by the fact that, as pointed out earlier, transportation carriers have a great deal of influence on packaging specifications for goods they are transporting. Possible suggestions to reduce the amount of packing materials include the use of just one material, which should improve recyclability, as well as changing a product or format to minimize packaging waste.[6]

A second packaging strategy is to use environmentally friendly packaging materials. For example, Aveda is a cosmetics company that takes pride in its environmental consciousness, particularly with respect to product packaging. Between 2000 and 2004, Aveda was able to raise the use of postconsumer recycled content in its shampoo bottles from 45 to 80 percent, with some product lines reporting 100 percent postconsumer recycled content.[7] And, even though

---

[5]Steve Toloken, "California Cracking Down on Plastic Litter," *Plastic News,* September 26, 2005, 9.
[6]Trish Lorenz, "No More Pass the Parcel," *Design Week,* April 14, 2005, 9.
[7]Danielle Sacks, "It's Easy Being Green," *Fast Company,* August 2004, 50–51.

plastic isn't the most environmentally friendly product, some plastics are more environmentally friendly than others. Polyvinyl chloride (PVC), commonly referred to as vinyl, is an extremely unfriendly plastic because it produces dioxin, a highly carcinogenic (cancer-causing) chemical.

A third strategy is to use reusable containers, such as refillable glass beverage bottles. This cannot be done for all products, because problems arise when goods in reused containers are contaminated by traces of whatever product had been carried earlier. As an example, dressed poultry (that is, the removal of blood and feathers after slaughter) often carries salmonella organisms (which are killed in cooking), and the organisms survive in the wooden crates used by the poultry processor and then may spread to vegetables if they are transported later in the same crate. As a result, the U.S. Food and Drug Administration (FDA) issued an order restricting the reuse of such containers to avoid food contamination. A number of companies currently utilize returnable containers of some type in their operations. Pep Boys, an automotive parts retailer, utilizes plastic totes for approximately 60 percent of the stock-keeping units that are shipped from its distribution centers to its retail stores. Moreover, the totes are designed so that they nest inside one another, which improves space utilization when the totes are returned from stores to the distribution centers.[8]

The fourth strategy is to retain or support services that collect used packaging and recycle it. Figure 5-10 shows a pallet shredder used to reduce wooden pallets and crating to pieces of wood averaging 50 square inches in plane area. This reduces the cubic volume of the scrap by about 75 percent, making it easier to ship and to process. The fourth strategy is well suited for companies that receive large quantities of packaged products; if sufficient units of waste material can be collected, it is easier to process for reuse. Some recycling companies specialize in plastic bottles, wooden pallets, cardboard cartons, aluminum cans, and glass bottles, among others.

Note that both the third and fourth strategies add a returned packaging loop to the supply chain and are examples of **closed-loop systems,** or those that consider the return flow of products, their reuse, and the marketing and distribution of recovered products.

Metric System

The United States, along with Liberia and Myanmar (formerly Burma), are the only three countries in the world that do not currently use the metric system of measurement. Although this lack of uniformity might have been a relatively minor nuisance 30 years ago, economic globalization has led to increasing pressure on U.S. exporters to market their products overseas in metric units. Indeed, some importing nations levy fines against products that are not sold in metric measurements. More and more products are being packaged and sold in metric units, with the nonmetric equivalents printed in smaller type. For example, residents of the United States used to be able to purchase soft drinks in 16-ounce containers. Today, by contrast, the 16-ounce beverage container has been replaced by the .5-liter (approximately 16.9 ounces) beverage container.

One U.S. industry that has prominently embraced the metric system is the liquor-producing industry. This industry's conversion to the metric system, which began in the 1970s, illustrates several of the potential challenges that might stand in the way of the United States formally adopting the metric system. As pointed out earlier in the chapter, the liquor industry is heavily regulated in the United States, and one example of this regulation is the high taxes that are applied to alcoholic beverages. These taxes became an issue in converting to the metric system because they were drawn up to be applicable to half pints, pints, quarts, and other English units of measure, as

---

[8]Connie Robbins Gentry, "If It's Not Broke, Reuse It," *Chain Store Age,* February 2004, 52–53.

| **FIGURE 5-10** | A Pallet Shredder Designed to Reduce the Cubic Volume of Wooden Pallets and Crating So That They Cost Less to Transport |

Source: Courtesy of Blower Application Company, Inc.

opposed to half liters and liters. Moreover, the liquor industry's adoption of the metric system also caused some short-term packaging issues because the cartons that were used for transporting and storing quart bottles were in some cases just a bit too small to hold one-liter bottles.

UNIT LOADS IN MATERIALS HANDLING

As mentioned earlier in this chapter, the packaging of materials is based on the building-blocks concept of putting products in containers that will provide efficient yet manageable units. This section discusses unit loads, an extension of the building-blocks concept to very large quantities. The basic unit in unit loading is the **pallet** or **skid** (a small platform (made of plastic, steel, or wood) on which goods are placed for handling by mechanical means). Unit loading involves the securing of one or more boxes to a pallet or skid so that the boxes can be handled by mechanical means, such as a forklift. The boxes or other containers secured to a pallet are known as a **unit load.** The term **unitization** is used to describe this kind of handling.

The unit load offers several advantages, one of which is additional protection to the cargo because the cartons are secured to the pallet by straps, shrink-wrapping, or some other bonding device. This provides a sturdier building block. A second unit load advantage is that pilferage is discouraged because it is difficult to remove a single package or its contents. Also, a pallet can be stacked so that the cartons containing the more valuable or more fragile items are on the inside of the unit load. The major advantage of the unit load is that it enables mechanical devices to be substituted for manual labor. Many machines have been devised that can quickly build up or tear down a pallet load of materials. Robots can be used when more sophisticated integrated movements are needed for loading or unloading pallets. An example of robot-assisted palletizing and depalletizing exists in the printing industry, in which bundles of printed pages must be stacked in a specified order.

The unit load does have its limitations, however. It represents a larger quantity of an item than a single box—often 30 to 50 times as much. Therefore, it is of limited value to shippers or consignees who deal in small quantities. And, although one unit load advantage is that mechanical devices can be substituted for manual labor, these mechanical devices cost money to purchase or lease. Manual pallet jacks (trucks) can range in price from $350 to $3,000 dollars, whereas forklifts can range in price from $15,000 to $30,000. Moreover, routine maintenance (another expense) should be performed on forklifts to keep them in optimal operating condition.

Yet another drawback to the unit load is the lack of standardization in terms of pallet sizes. Although the International Standards Organization (ISO) has established six international pallet size standards—four in metric units, two in English units—literally hundreds of different pallet sizes are used by companies in the United States. If these shipments are exported from the United States, they must be repalletized, which means an increase in manual labor, and thus a diminution in potential advantages to the unit load concept.[9]

Lift trucks are the common workhorse used around warehouses to move pallets. They come in many designs. Figure 5-11 shows a lift truck used for picking stock in warehouses; in this model, the operator rides with the load rather than at ground level. This truck is also battery powered, which is common for lift trucks used inside buildings. Batteries are recharged at night.

The discussion in this chapter thus far has emphasized the building of loads from small blocks into large blocks. However, the reverse is also true; that is, the large units or blocks must be broken down into their smaller component blocks, with the very smallest unit being the single item that the retail customer carries home. Figure 5-12 illustrates this by showing a high-rise warehouse four tiers high. At the right, a lift truck places full unit loads into a gravity-flow rack system. As they are used, the pallets move to the left, where order pickers break down the unit loads into single boxes. This also results in a FIFO inventory retrieval system (i.e., the first item in is also the first item out).

The Unit Load Platform

An important issue with respect to unit loading concerns the platform (basic unit) on which to place the unit load. As mentioned before, the pallet is generally viewed as the basic unit in unit loading. In the United States, the wooden pallet has long been the backbone of the unit load in the sense that the vast majority (between 80 and 90 percent) of pallets in use were made of wood. One reason for the long-standing popularity of wooden pallets is that they were thought of as free, or costless, for many years. Even though wooden pallets are no longer viewed as free (new wooden pallets cost between $8 and $10), they are relatively inexpensive compared to plastic pallets, which range in cost from $10 to $80, and steel pallets, which range in cost from $25 to over $200.

---

[9]"Marshall White on the State of Pallets," *Modern Materials Handling,* March 2006, 53–58.

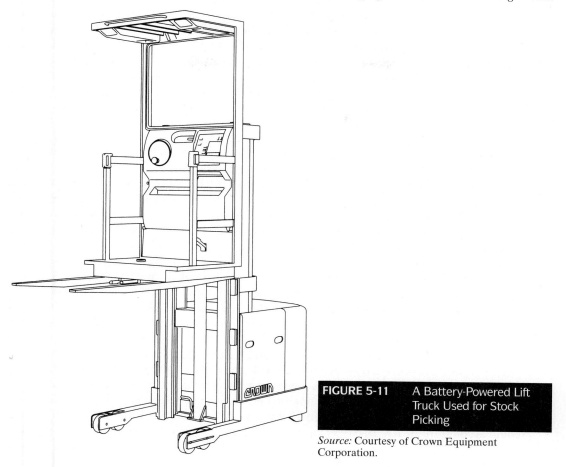

FIGURE 5-11   A Battery-Powered Lift Truck Used for Stock Picking

Source: Courtesy of Crown Equipment Corporation.

FIGURE 5-12   A Warehouse Where Unit Loads Are Broken Down into Boxes

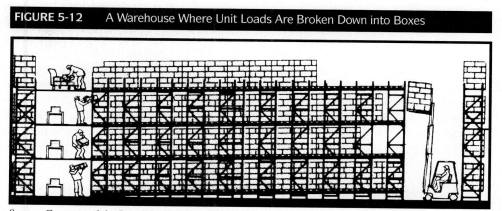

Source: Courtesy of the Interlake Corporation.

Each pallet material has its strengths and weaknesses, with price being a major drawback to both plastic and steel pallets. One potential advantage to plastic and steel is their longevity relative to wood. For example, although wood pallets might last only one use, some companies view wood's life span as between two and three years.[10] Plastic pallets, by contrast, last at least five years, and life spans of over 10 years are not uncommon,[11] whereas steel pallets can last for over 20 years. Another shortcoming of wood pallets is that they can break and splinter, which could pose safety dangers to workers and also necessitates pallet repairs (assuming the pallet is salvageable). Both plastic and steel pallets are unlikely to break and splinter, thus improving worker safety and resulting in minimal repair costs.

Yet a further disadvantage of wood pallets is that their weight relative to plastic and steel, with a typical 48-inch-by-40-inch wood pallet weighing approximately 50 pounds. Fifty pounds is a significant weight in many logistics systems because it represents the approximate weight at which there is a noticeable increase in injuries, particularly back injuries, from manual handling. Furthermore, wood and plastic are much more flammable than is steel. Although you might not think of fires as being a logistical issue, consider that there are an estimated 2,500 warehouse fires annually in the United Kingdom.

Although pallets are a popular unit load platform, one disadvantage (regardless of material) is its height (approximately six inches), meaning that a pallet may occupy as much space as a layer of cases of canned soft drinks. When goods are loaded aboard pallets into railcars, trailers, or containers, the space occupied by the pallet is unproductive. One alternative to the pallet is a **slip sheet,** a flat sheet of either fiberboard material or plastic, which is placed under the unit load. **Shrink-wrap** (plastic wrapping that when heated shrinks in size to form a cover over the product) or banding straps are used to attach the unit load to the slip sheet. Until the early part of the twenty-first century, one major drawback was high product damage rates due to the fragility of the slip sheets. However, advances in technology have created stronger plastics that can be used for slip sheets and produced a corresponding decrease in damage rates. These improved damage rates and the low costs for slip sheets ($.90 to $1.50) relative to pallets suggest that slip sheets could account for nearly 30 percent of product shipments (up from 10 percent) by 2010.[12]

BEYOND THE UNIT LOAD

The next step in the building-blocks process is to stow the unit-load pallets into a waiting truck trailer, railcar, or container van. Figure 5-13 shows a computer printout from load-planning software; it suggests how to load a container with different sizes of cartons and tells where the loads for several customers should be loaded. The software recognizes, for example, that some cartons cannot be laid on their sides or cannot have other cartons placed on top of them. The software also takes into account the load's center of gravity and the allowable weights on axles. When planning for refrigerated loads, the software will also take into account the need for air spaces.

Slight clearances must be maintained between pallets to allow for the loading and unloading processes. Bracing or inflatable dunnage bags are used to fill narrow empty spaces. When inflated, they fill the void space and function as both a cushion and a brace. Figure 5-14 shows inflated dunnage bags. A problem involved with any bracing or cushioning device is that the load is subjected to forces from all directions. Even when cargoes are properly braced, various

---

[10]"Pallets Keep Distribution Cooking," *Modern Materials Handling,* October 2000, 101.

[11]A. John Geis, "7 Ways to Cut Materials Handling Costs," *Paperboard Packaging,* August 2005, 10s–13s.

[12]Leonard Klie, "Slipping into the Future," *Food Logistics,* May 2004, 38–40.

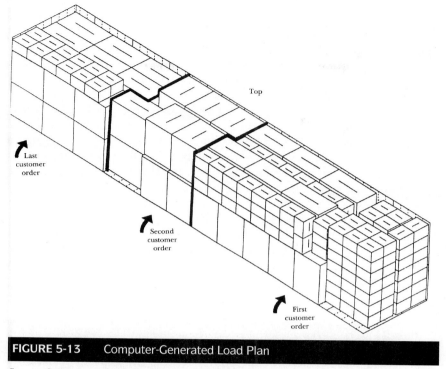

FIGURE 5-13   Computer-Generated Load Plan

Source: Courtesy of TOPS Engineering Corp.

forces such as vibration, pitch, and roll can still cause damage: Continued vibrations may loosen screws on machinery or cause the contents of some bags or packages to settle, changing the type of support they give to the materials packed above them. For products that present this problem, special preloading vibrators are used to cause the load to settle immediately.

Some goods are so heavy that they utilize the railcar's, trailer's, or container's weight capacity without filling its cubic capacity (a situation called **weighing out**). These loads, such as heavy machinery, must be carefully braced, and the weight must be distributed as evenly as possible. In highway trailers, for example, it is dangerous to have one side loaded more heavily than the other. In addition, the load should be distributed evenly over the axles.

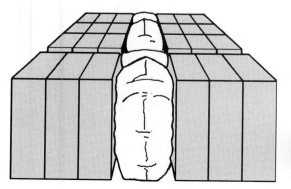

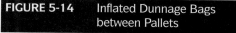

FIGURE 5-14   Inflated Dunnage Bags
between Pallets

Source: Courtesy of Sea-Land Service Inc.

MATERIALS HANDLING

Materials flow through the supply chain, and how they are handled physically is the subject of **materials handling,** which deals with the short-distance movement of the material between two or more points. This short-distance movement distinguishes materials handling from transportation (which will be discussed in Chapters 6 and 7). Mechanical devices are often used in the materials handling process.

Nearly all products that are packaged—often in consumer-size boxes, bottles, or cans—are handled by the building-block concept of packaging that has been described previously. A particularly important type of equipment in this building-block concept is the **container,** which can be defined as "a uniform, sealed reusable metal 'box' in which goods are shipped."[13] Because the container is interchangeable among rail, truck, and water carriers, containers can be used in intermodal applications and provide the advantages offered by each of several modes. Containers are generally 8 feet wide, 8 feet high, and 20, 28, 35, 40, or more feet long. Both ocean carriers and railroads have developed methods of handling two or more containers at one time, thereby reducing the number of individual lifting and storage moves. Most containers are dry-cargo boxes, although some are insulated and come with temperature-controlling devices. Still others contain one large tank; still others are flatbed. Figure 5-15 shows several different types of containers.

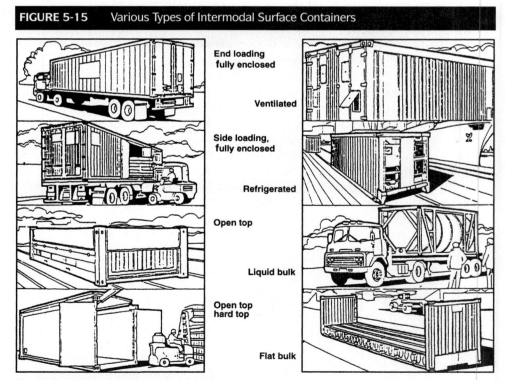

FIGURE 5-15   Various Types of Intermodal Surface Containers

End loading
fully enclosed

Ventilated

Side loading,
fully enclosed

Refrigerated

Open top

Liquid bulk

Open top
hard top

Flat bulk

Source: Ports of the World, 14th edition, CIGNA Property & Casualty Companies.

---

[13]Derived from *www.amx.usda.gov/tmd/export/glossary.htm.*

Air freight containers, often referred to as **unit load devices (ULDs),** are constructed of light-weight metals and come in different sizes. Unlike the containers in Figure 5-15, air freight ULDs have somewhat irregular shapes, dictated by the contours of the fuselage into which they must fit.

The other way that products, especially large quantities of products, are handled is in *bulk*. Bulk materials are in loose rather than in packaged form and are handled by pumps, shovel devices, conveyor belts (Figure 5-16), or the mere force of gravity. The decision must be made as to where in the supply chain the bulk materials should be placed into smaller containers for further

FIGURE 5-16	Imported Raw Sugar Moving along and up a Conveyor Belt in Galveston, Texas

Source: Courtesy of the Port of Galveston.

sale or shipment. Sometimes, bagged and bulk quantities of the same material are part of the same shipment. In vessels, bagged rice is placed on top of bulk rice to provide load stability.

Bulk cargoes have various handling characteristics, one of which is *density*. Consider three different bulk materials, namely, iron ore, coal, and grain. The Great Lakes steamer *Richard J. Reiss* uses only two-thirds of its cubic capacity when carrying iron ore, yet the 15,800 tons of ore lower the vessel to its maximum allowable draft of 24 feet, 8 inches. Alternatively, when loaded with coal, the vessel **cubes out**; that is, the cubic capacity is filled before reaching its weight capacity, and the vessel is lowered to only 20 feet, 6 inches. Grain loads are even lighter; the *Richard J. Reiss* draft when full of grain is slightly less than 20 feet.[14]

A material's *angle of repose* is the size of angle that would be formed by the side of a conical stack of that material. The greater the angle, the higher the pile of materials that can be placed on a specific land area. Anthracite coal has an angle of repose of approximately 27 degrees, whereas for iron ore the angle is 35 degrees. This means more cubic yards of ore can be stockpiled on a given site and that the ore can be carried on a slightly steeper, narrower conveyor belt.

Bulk liquids also have unique handling characteristics. Resistance to flow is measured as viscosity, which can be lowered by increasing the temperature of a liquid. Molasses, cooking oils, and many petroleum products are heated before an attempt is made to pump them.

Gases have unique handling properties, although most of them are handled within completely enclosed pipeline systems. An exception is liquefied natural gas, or LNG, which is cooled and compressed into liquid form that is 1/630 of its volume in gaseous state. In its liquefied, highly pressurized state, it is transported by oceangoing vessels in special tanks.

The handling process itself may change the characteristics (or quality) of the product. Rice grains cannot fall far without being broken. This influences the design of loading and unloading facilities so that the grains of rice never drop more than a few feet at any one time. When sugar is handled, a dust is formed because of abrasion between sugar crystals. This dust is also sugar, but it is in much finer form and has different sensitivities to moisture. The dust must be separated from the rest of the sugar, or the quality of the final bakery product in which the sugar is used will be affected.

An ideal equipment configuration for one bulk cargo may not be able to handle another. Another consideration is the size of particle of the cargo in question; costs are involved in pulverizing to a uniform size so it can be handled by pneumatic or slurry devices.

Materials Handling Principles

As a supply chain is linked together, one of the concerns of those involved with logistics is the physical transfer of the product from one party to another: How will it be handled? In what form will it be? In what quantities? What kind of equipment is needed to handle or to store it? Materials handling processes generally receive little public attention. An exception to this was the new luggage-handling system at the Denver airport, which was initially so defective that it delayed the airport's opening by many months.

The College–Industry Council on Material Handling Education, which is sponsored by the Material Handling Institute, has developed a list of 10 materials handling principles. The principles are more important when laying out the intended design or when troubleshooting to learn why a system is not performing well. The Material Handling Institute suggests that these principles, which are listed following, are "the key to greater productivity, customer service, and profitability."[15]

---

[14]Correspondence from the Reiss Steamship Company to the authors.

[15]This quotation, the ten material handling principles, and their descriptions come from "The Ten Principles of Material Handling," *www.mhia.org.*

1. The *planning principle.* All material handling should be the result of a deliberate plan where the needs, performance, objectives and functional specification of the proposed methods are completely defined at the outset.
2. The *standardization principle.* Material handling methods, equipment, controls, and software should be standardized within the limits of achieving overall performance objectives and without sacrificing needed flexibility, modularity, and throughput.
3. The *work principle.* Material handling work should be minimized without sacrificing productivity or the level of service required of the operation.
4. The *ergonomic principle.* **Ergonomics** refers to the science that seeks to adapt work or working conditions to suit the abilities of the worker. With this principle, human capabilities and limitations must be recognized and respected in the design of material handling tasks and equipment to ensure safe and effective operations.
5. The *unit load principle.* Unit loads shall be appropriately sized and configured in a way that achieves the material flow and inventory objectives at each stage in the supply chain.
6. The *space utilization principle.* Effective and efficient use must be made of all available space.
7. The *system principle.* Material movement and storage activities should be fully integrated to form a coordinated, operational system that spans receiving, inspection, storage, production, assembly, packaging, unitizing, order selection, shipping, transportation, and the handling of returns.
8. The *automation principle.* Material handling operations should be mechanized or automated where feasible to improve operational efficiency, increase responsiveness, and improve consistency and predictability.
9. The *environmental principle.* Environmental impact and energy consumption should be considered as a criteria when designing or selecting alternative equipment and material handling systems.
10. The *life cycle cost principle.* A thorough economic analysis should account for the entire life cycle of all material handling equipment and resulting systems.

These 10 principles are accompanied by varying numbers of key points to consider when implementing the principles. With respect to the *planning principle,* for example, one key point is that the material handling plan should be in line with the strategic objectives of the organization. In a similar fashion, the *work principle* reminds us of a lesson that many of us learned in geometry class: The shortest distance between two points is a straight line. One key point associated with the *environmental principle* reinforces our earlier discussion in the sense that material handling and packaging products should be chosen with reusability or biodegradability in mind.[16]

Materials Handling Equipment

A comprehensive discussion of materials handling equipment is beyond the scope of this text. Having said this, it's important to recognize that decisions about materials handling equipment can affect the effectiveness, efficiency, and safety of logistics systems. Although forklifts, for example, facilitate the effective and efficient handling of unit loads, forklifts can be dangerous; in the United States over *1,000 warehouse employees* died from forklift-related incidents between 1980 and 2004.[17]

---

[16]*Ibid.*

[17]Lisa H. Harrington, "The Safety Zone," *Inbound Logistics,* May 2006, 44–54.

Moreover, it is important that the materials handling equipment be aligned with an organization's objectives, customers, and products. This seems to be common sense, but the authors are aware of a consumer products company that redesigned one of its storage facilities with the primary purpose to be state of the art in terms of materials handling equipment. Less than a year later, the storage facility had to be redesigned because the state-of-the-art materials handling equipment was inconsistent with the types of products sold by the company as well as with its customers' ordering requirements.

Materials handling equipment can be divided into two categories—storage equipment and handling equipment. Examples of storage equipment include shelves, racks, and bins, whereas examples of handling equipment include conveyor systems, lift trucks, carts, and cranes. Although storage and handling equipment are very different, the choice of one influences the choice of the other. For example, the use of racks allows for narrow aisles, but narrow aisles require specialized handling equipment capable of moving both vertically and horizontally.

Materials handling equipment can also be categorized in terms of whether they are labor intensive, mechanized, or automated. True automation, such as automatic guided vehicles (AGVs), refers to an absence of human intervention, whereas mechanization refers to equipment that complements, rather than replaces, human contact (e.g., forklift).[18] A key trade-off among labor, mechanization, and automation involves the relevant volumes; because automation is a very high fixed cost option, sufficient volume is needed to make it cost effective. It has been suggested that automation becomes economically viable only when a facility handles at least 50,000 cartons a day.[19]

Decisions as to materials handling equipment can also be influenced by an organization's order picking and assembly system. In **picker-to-part systems,** an order picker goes to where a product is located, such as with a forklift, whereas in **part-to picker systems,** the pick location is brought to the picker, such as with carousels. These two systems involve trade-offs between travel time; recall that travel time accounts for between 60 and 80 percent of total order picking time.

Summary

As this chapter demonstrates, many considerations must be taken into account as one chooses packaging, such as the product's physical characteristics. Packages have multiple functions, such as sales and protection, and a sturdy package contributes to a product's solid image. Some products are hazardous to either the environment or to persons handling them, and they require special packaging and attention. Transportation carriers often specify the packaging that must be used. Concerns about recycling and environmental protection also affect the choice of packaging materials.

Retail packages are placed into cartons, which are often loaded onto pallets to form unit loads. These unit loads may then be placed into transport vehicles.

All materials have their unique handling and storage characteristics, and materials handling refers to the short-distance movement of these materials between two or more points. A series of materials handling principles can improve the effectiveness and efficiency of logistics systems. Materials handling equipment can be categorized as serving either storage or handling purposes, and this equipment should be aligned with an organization's objectives, customers, and products.

---

[18]Mary Aichlmayr, "Making a Case for Automation," *Transportation & Distribution*, June 2001, 85–90.
[19]*Ibid.*

Questions for Discussion and Review

1. How do product characteristics influence packaging and materials handling considerations?
2. Discuss some of the packaging requirements associated with hazardous cargo.
3. What is the building-blocks concept? How is it applied to the handling of packaged goods?
4. The chapter describes approximately 10 functions that a protective package should accomplish. Does every package have to accomplish every function? Explain.
5. Discuss the relationship between the level of protective packaging used relative to the packaging requirement of transportation carriers.
6. Discuss the role of labeling in logistics management.
7. Why is it important to recognize that labeling requirements may differ from country to country?
8. Describe some of the devices that are used to monitor conditions during the journey that a shipment makes.
9. What are some environmental disadvantages to plastic packaging?
10. What environmentally friendly packaging strategies might a firm adopt?
11. What information is needed to design a protective package properly?
12. What are some potential advantages to the unit load?
13. Discuss the disadvantages of the unit load.
14. What trade-offs exist between wood, plastic, and steel pallets?
15. Is the slip sheet currently a viable alternative to the pallet? Why or why not?
16. What issues does the logistics manager face once unit loads have been placed onto a transportation vehicle?
17. Discuss the various handling characteristics associated with bulk cargoes.
18. Describe two materials handling principles. Which of the two do you believe is more important? Why?
19. Why is it important that materials handling be aligned with an organization's objectives, customers, and products?
20. Does your hometown have mandatory recycling requirements? If so, what kinds of products must be recycled?

Suggested Readings

Dempsey, Patrick G., and Wayne S. Maynard. "Manual Materials Handling." *Professional Safety* 50, no. 5 (2005): 20–25.

Denis, D., M. St.-Vincent, D. Imbeau, and R. Trudeau. "Stock Management Influence on Manual Materials Handling in Two Warehouse Superstores." *International Journal of Industrial Ergonomics* 36, no. 3 (2006): 191–201.

Drickhamer, David. "AGVS: Pick Up and Deliver." *Material Handling Management* (August 2005): 16–18.

Gonzalez-Torre, Pilar L., B. Adenso-Diaz, and Hakim Artiba. "Environmental and Reverse Logistics Policies in European Bottling and Packaging Firms." *International Journal of Production Economics* 88, no. 1 (2004): 95–104.

Jahne, Marianne. "Packages and Physical Distribution: Implications for Integration and Standardization." *International Journal of Physical Distribution & Logistics Management* 34, no. 2 (2004): 123–139.

Jung, Myung-Chul, Joel M. Haight, and Andris Freivalds. "Pushing and Pulling Carts and Two-Wheeled Hand Trucks." *International Journal of Industrial Ergonomics* 35, no. 1 (2005): 79–89.

Klevas, Jenny. "Organization of Packaging Resources at a Product-Developing Company." *International Journal of Physical Distribution & Logistics Management* 35, no. 2 (2005): 116–131.

Mathisson-Ojmertz, Birgitta and Mats I. Johansson. "Influences of Process Location on Materials Handling: Cases from the Automotive Industry." *International Journal of Logistics: Research & Applications* 3, no. 1 (2000): 25–39.

Mollenkopf, Diane, David Closs, Diana Twede, Sangjin Lee, and Gary Burgess. "Assessing the Viability of Reusable Packaging: A Relative Cost Approach." *Journal of Business Logistics* 26, no. 1 (2005): 169–197.

White, Marshall S., and Peter Hamner. "Pallets Move the World." *Forest Products Journal* 55, no. 3 (2005): 8–16.

CASE

CASE 5-1   LET THERE BE LIGHT LAMP SHADE COMPANY

Started in Madison, Wisconsin, after the student unrest of the 1960s had died down, the Let There Be Light Lamp Shade Company served an upscale local market for many years. It designed and built custom lamp shades and lamp globes. In the mid-1980s, some architects who had once studied under Frank Lloyd Wright in nearby Spring Green were commissioned to design several large public buildings in Asia. A total of 5,400 identical lights were to be installed, and the Let There Be Light Lamp Shade Company wished to bid on the work. Terms of sale would include delivery to the foreign port where the buyer would take possession.

Transportation costs would be a hurdle. In the initial design, the shades were cylinders that were 11 inches high and 11 inches in diameter and were packed into boxes that were 12 by 12 by 12 inches. (We refer to these shades as style A.) The packages cost 60 cents each and weighed 1 pound each. The shades cost $4 each to manufacture. They weighed 9 pounds each and 10 pounds packaged.

They would be shipped to the Port of Oakland. The land rate to Oakland was $1,000 per 40-foot container, without regard to weight, although the weight of the load could not exceed 44,000 pounds per loaded container because of highway weight restrictions. The interior dimensions of the intermodal container were 8 feet wide by 8.5 feet high by 40 feet long.

Ocean rates from Oakland to the overseas port were $22 per ton (2,000 pounds), except that the ocean conference used a measurement

ton that indicated that for bulky loads every 40 cubic feet would equal 1 ton for rate-making purposes. (That is, a shipment weighing, say, 130 pounds and occupying 80 cubic feet would cost as though it weighed 4,000 pounds.) Insurance costs were 2 percent of the value of the shipment ready to be loaded aboard ship in Oakland. (This is calculated as all of the company's costs up to this point.)

Because of the large size of the order, Let There Be Light Lamp Shade Company realized that it could custom design a shade that, rather than being a cylinder, would be shaped like a cone. The advantage to that was that the shades could be nested. Some padding would be required between the shades, but the nested shades would also help protect each other. However, cutting out material for conical shapes results in waste, so production costs would be higher. Two alternative cone-shaped designs were proposed (referred to as styles B and C).

Style B cost $5 per shade to manufacture and could be shipped nested in packages of six. The package dimensions were 12 by 12 by 48 inches, and when holding six shades, a package weighed 62 pounds. Each package cost $2, and this included padding between the shades.

Style C cost $6 per shade to make and could be shipped nested in packages of 10. The package dimensions were 12 by 12 by 50 inches, and when holding 10 shades, a package weighed 101 pounds. Each package cost $3, including padding between the individual shades. ■

QUESTIONS

1. How many style A shades can be loaded into an intermodal container?
2. How many style B shades can be loaded into an intermodal container?
3. How many style C shades can be loaded into an intermodal container?
4. What are the total costs of delivering the style A shades to the port of importation?
5. What are the total costs of delivering the style B shades to the port of importation?
6. What are the total costs of delivering the style C shades to the port of importation?
7. Which style would you recommend? Why?

Products characteristics Q
mode of transport Q

CHAPTER

6 | TRANSPORTATION

The equipment available for shipping products has changed. The top photograph shows a tank car from 1865, built by placing two wooden tubs on a flat car. The bottom photograph shows a tank car as it is used today. The sign in the center of the car includes a toll-free telephone number for product emergencies.
Photos courtesy of Union Tank Car Company.

Key Terms

- Accessorial service
- Barge
- Broker
- Common carrier
- Consignee
- Contract carrier
- Department of Transportation
- Dimensional (dim) weight
- Excess capacity
- Exempt carrier
- Freight forwarder
- Intermodal transportation

- Line-haul
- Parcel carriers
- Piggyback transportation
- Private carrier
- Rail gauge
- Shippers' associations
- Slurry systems
- Surface Transportation Board
- TEU
- Terminal
- Ton miles
- Transportation

Learning Objectives

- To learn about the five modes of transportation
- To understand trade-offs between the five modes
- To realize the role of freight forwarders and other transportation specialists
- To learn about different types of regulation and their influence on transportation
- To understand the legal classification of carriers
- To appreciate that different countries have different transportation infrastructures as well as different approaches to regulation

Transportation, which can be defined as the actual, physical movement of goods and people between two points, is pivotal to the successful operation of any supply chain because it carries the goods, literally, as they move along the chain. Transportation influences, or is influenced by, many logistics activities to include

1. Transportation costs are directly affected by the location of the firm's plants, warehouses, vendors, retail locations, and customers.
2. Inventory requirements are influenced by the mode of transport used. High-speed, high-priced transportation systems require smaller amounts of inventories in a logistics system, whereas slower, less-expensive transportation requires larger amounts of systemwide inventory.
3. The transport mode selected influences the packaging required, and carrier classification rules dictate package choice.
4. The type of carrier used dictates a manufacturing plant's materials handling equipment, such as loading and unloading equipment and the design of the receiving and shipping docks.
5. An order-management methodology that encourages maximum consolidation of shipments between common points enables a company to give larger shipments to its carriers and take advantage of volume discounts.
6. Customer service goals influence the type and quality of carrier and carrier service selected by the seller.

This chapter begins with a brief look at the transportation infrastructure in various countries throughout the world, and this is followed by a thorough discussion of the five different types, or modes, of transportation: air, motor carrier (truck), pipeline, rail, and water (these are listed in alphabetical order). The chapter also discusses intermodal transportation and transportation specialists and concludes with an examination of transportation regulation and the legal classification of carriers.

In keeping with past practice in this and other basic logistics texts, the discussion of transportation will primarily be presented from the perspective of the United States and will primarily focus on domestic (within the U.S.) transportation. Having said this, readers should recognize that an individual country's topology, economy, infrastructure, and other macroenvironmental factors could result in a different transportation system than that found in the United States. Moreover, the globalization of the world's economy means that an increasing number of shipments are being transported between multiple countries (international transportation), a topic that will be discussed in Chapter 12.

And because readers of this text increasingly reside outside of the United States, it might be helpful to present a brief comparison of the transportation infrastructure that exists in several different countries. This infrastructure data, which appear in Table 6-1, indicate wide disparities in the various infrastructures; at a minimum, a lack of infrastructure makes it difficult to use that mode in domestic (within-country) transportation.

The relevant infrastructure statistic for air transportation in Table 6-1 is the number of paved runways over 3,047 meters (approximately 10,000 feet). This length is significant because a 10,000-foot runway is generally viewed as adequate for accommodating the largest existing wide-body aircraft (although the 10,000-foot benchmark will probably have to increase once the Airbus A-380 jetliner begins operations), and wide-body aircraft are essential to long-haul international movements. According to Table 6-1, the United States by far has the most airports with paved runways of at least 10,000 feet, an indication that the United States is well positioned to

TABLE 6-1   Infrastructure Statistics in Several Countries

	Brazil	China	India	United Kingdom	United States
Air[a]	8	54	17	8	191
Highway (paved)	94,871 km	1,447,682 km	2,411,001 km	387,674 km	4,164,964 km
Pipeline (oil)	5,212 km	14,478 km	5,613 km	6,420 km	244,620 km
Broad gauge (1.676 meters) rail	4,907 km		45,718 km	460 km	
Standard gauge (1.435 meters) rail	194 km	71,898 km		16,814 km	227,736 km
Narrow gauge (1.000 meter) rail	23,915 km		14,406 km		
Water (inland)	50,000 km	123,964 km	14,500 km	3,200 km	41,009 km
Comparative area	Slightly smaller than the U.S.	Slightly smaller than the U.S.	Slightly more than 1/3 the U.S.	Slightly smaller than the U.S. state of Oregon	

[a] Number of paved runways over 3,047 meters (approximately 10,000 feet)

Source: The World Factbook, www.cia.gov, 2006.

participate in long-haul international movements. One indication of China's economic growth is their 54 10,000-foot runways, a number that is likely to increase over the next 10 years.

The infrastructure statistics for highway, pipeline, rail, and water, presented in kilometers (1 kilometer is equivalent to approximately .62 miles), provide some interesting findings. For example, although Brazil and China are approximately the same geographic size, China currently has about 15 times more paved highway kilometers than Brazil. The data also indicate that oil pipelines are much more prevalent in the United States, and that China has much more extensive inland waterways, relative to the four other countries listed in Table 6-1.

The information on **rail gauge** (the distance between the inner sides of two parallel rail tracks) is intriguing. Both China and the United States use only one size—standard—rail gauge (1.435 meters) in their rail infrastructure. Brazil, by contrast, uses broad gauge (1.676 meters), standard gauge, *and* narrow gauge (1.000 meter) in its rail infrastructure, whereas India uses both broad gauge and narrow gauge rail. Although the United Kingdom predominately uses standard gauge rail, a small portion of its rail system consists of broad gauge rail. The data on rail gauge are important because nonuniform rail gauge within a country, or between neighboring countries (such as China and India), means that shipments moving by rail will need to be transferred from one vehicle to another, which adds to both delivery time and costs.

TRANSPORTATION MODES

Each of the five modes of transportation exists because of certain attributes that provide one or more advantages over the other modes of transportation. The attractiveness of a particular mode depends on the following attributes[1]:

- Cost (price that a carrier charges to transport a shipment)
- Speed (elapsed transit time from pickup to delivery)
- Reliability (consistency of delivery)
- Capability (amount of different types of product that can be transported)
- Capacity (volume that can be carried at one time)
- Flexibility (ability to deliver the product to the customer)

It is important to recognize that public policy can affect a mode's performance on these attributes. Railroads, for example, were the dominant mode, as measured by **ton miles** (the number of tons multiplied by the number of miles transported) and revenues, in the United States from the nineteenth century through the middle part of the twentieth century. However, the development of the U.S. Interstate Highway System allowed motor carriers to improve their speed, reliability, and flexibility, and although railroads still have the largest share of ton miles, motor carriers now account for the majority of freight revenues. From a public policy perspective, construction costs of the Interstate Highway System were primarily paid for by the U.S. government (90 percent), with the remaining construction costs paid for by state governments. This funding by both the federal and state governments is significant because U.S. railroads have been responsible for the construction costs of their track systems, whereas rail construction costs in other nations are often covered by the national government. As such, the U.S. railroads have a substantial cost disadvantage relative to motor carriers, and this cost disadvantage must be captured in railroad pricing practices.

---

[1]Drawn from David J. Bloomberg, Stephen LeMay, and Joe B. Hanna, *Logistics* (Upper Saddle River, NJ: Prentice Hall, 2002), Chapter 7.

AIRFREIGHT

When one thinks of air transportation, one immediately thinks of speed, particularly on the **line-haul** (terminal-to-terminal movement of freight or passengers); today's jet aircraft are capable of traveling between 500 and 600 miles per hour, a speed that far exceeds any other form of transportation. Indeed, air is generally the fastest mode of transportation for shipments exceeding 600 miles (recall that some trucking companies now offer overnight service of between 600 and 700 miles).

However, air transportation is a quite expensive form of transportation, and the line-haul cost of airfreight service is regarded as its primary disadvantage; many companies simply cannot afford to have their shipments travel by air. Moreover, because most shippers and **consignees** (receivers of freight) are not located at an airport, this requires transportation from the shipper to the origin airport as well as from the destination airport to the consignee. This **accessorial service** (transportation service that is supplemental to the line-haul) adds to both transportation costs and transit time and also increases the number of times a shipment is handled (thus increasing handling costs and the opportunities for loss and damage).

Unlike other forms of transportation, the great majority of airfreight is carried in the freight compartments of passenger airplanes (so called belly freight). This belly freight limits the capacity available for air shipments and is particularly problematic with respect to narrow-body (single-aisle) aircraft. A narrow-body Boeing 737-800, for example, can carry approximately 10 tons of belly freight, whereas a wide-body Boeing 777-200 can carry approximately 60 tons of belly freight.[2] However, wide-body aircraft devoted to all-cargo service have impressive carrying capacity; an all-cargo Boeing 747 can carry about 100 tons (see Figure 6-1). Likewise, the freighter version of the world's largest commercial jetliner, the Airbus A-380, has projected cargo capacity of nearly 150 tons.

The cost, speed, and capacity attributes mean that, for the most part, airfreight is best suited to high-value, lower-volume products that are of a perishable nature or otherwise require urgent or time-specific delivery. Airfreight rates discourage bulky cargo and use **dimensional weight** (also called dim weight), which considers a shipment's density (the amount of space occupied in relation to actual weight) to determine a shipment's billable weight.[3] Examples of products that move by air include:

FIGURE 6-1   Air Freight Capabilities

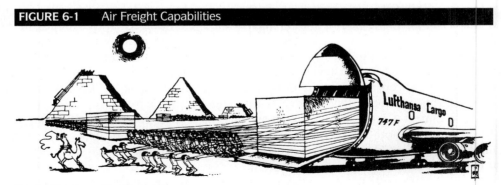

Source: Courtesy of Lufthansa Cargo.

---

[2]Data derived from Continental Airlines' cargo division, *www.cocargo.com.*
[3]*www.ups.com.*

- Wearing apparel
- Electronic or electrical equipment, such as computers, televisions, and DVD players
- Printed matter
- Machinery and parts
- Cut flowers and nursery stock
- Auto parts and accessories
- Fruits and vegetables
- Metal products
- Photographic equipment, parts, and film

The reliability of airfreight is somewhat problematic. On the one hand, air's tremendous speed relative to the other modes offers the potential to "make up lost time" that isn't possible with the other modes. Alternatively, because so much airfreight is belly freight, the increasing congestion and resultant delays associated with air passenger transportation mean congestion and delays for airfreight. Moreover, weather conditions such as fog, snow, and thunderstorms can have an adverse effect on the reliability of airfreight transportation. Indeed, Federal Express located its first (and still primary) hub in Memphis, Tennessee, in part because Memphis rarely experiences foggy conditions.

MOTOR CARRIERS

The backbone of the U.S. highway system is the Interstate Highway System (its formal name is the National System of Interstate and Defense Highways), which was approved by federal legislation in 1956. This nearly 47,000-mile, high-speed, limited-access highway system has had a profound impact on economic development in the United States over the past 50 years. From a logistics perspective, many companies began to locate manufacturing, assembly, and distribution facilities in close proximity to interstate highways. Indeed, part of Wal-Mart's success has been attributed to its ability to recognize the logistical opportunities of the interstate system before competitors did. Likewise, close proximity to one or more interstate highways has been a major determinant in the location of manufacturing facilities for non-U.S. automakers such as BMW, Honda, and Toyota.[4]

The most important business user of the highway system is the motor carrier (trucking) industry. One way of classifying motor carriers is according to whether they carry less-than-truckload (**LTL**) or truckload (**TL**) traffic. LTL shipments range from about 150 to 10,000 pounds; they are often too big to be handled manually, yet they do not fill a truck. Trucks that carry LTL freight have space for and plan to carry shipments of many other customers simultaneously. Unlike TL carriers, LTL carriers operate through a system of **terminals** (a facility where freight is shifted between vehicles), and from each terminal small trucks go out to customers, delivering and picking up shipments. These shipments are then taken to a terminal, where they are loaded aboard line-haul trucks, which are driven to a terminal near the freight's destination. The goods are unloaded from the line-haul carrier, move through the terminal, and are loaded aboard a small truck for local delivery. Prominent LTL carriers include Yellow Freight, Roadway, FedEx Freight, and ABF Freight System.

TL carriers focus on shipments of greater than 10,000 pounds, and although the exact weight depends on the product, it is close to the amount that would physically fill a truck trailer. For glassware, this might be 18,000 pounds; for canned goods, it might be 40,000 pounds.

---

[4]"Roads to Somewhere," *The Economist*, June 24, 2006, 36–38.

Although TL traffic may involve only one customer, it is possible that large shipments (greater than 10,000 pounds) from several customers can be consolidated into a truckload shipment. Whereas LTL shipments are routed through terminals, TL shipments tend to move directly from the shipper's location to the consignee's location. Prominent TL carriers include Schneider National, J.B. Hunt, Swift Transportation, and Werner Enterprises.

Although LTL companies tend to be limited in the type of freight that they haul—primarily dry freight such as apparel, books, greeting cards, among others—TL companies can carry a plethora of freight types. These include, but are not limited to, dry freight, foodstuffs, refrigerated products, liquid products, animals and livestock, automobiles, and steel. Overall, although motor carriers have the ability to haul many different kinds of freight, their capacity is limited by highway weight and size (width, length) restrictions. For example, motor carriers using the Interstate Highway System are limited to a maximum gross vehicle weight of 80,000 pounds. With respect to size considerations, truck trailers can be a maximum of 102 inches wide; the maximum length for tractor–trailer combinations varies from state to state. You should recognize that some countries do not have size and weight restrictions for motor carriers.

Although U.S. motor carriers can travel wherever there are roads, their length of haul is mitigated by several factors, such as speed limits and hours-of-service (HOS) rules. HOS rules have been the subject of near constant legislation in the United States since the beginning of the twenty-first century, and rather than trying to articulate the relevant rules, suffice it to say that—unlike automobile drivers—motor carriers are limited in terms of the number of hours that can be driven in a 24-hour period, as well as the number of hours that can be driven in a one-week period. Both HOS and highways speed limits have long been justified on the basis of safety concerns, and some states have followed a two-tier speed limit policy in which the maximum speed for motor carriers is lower than for noncommercial vehicles. Nevertheless, several U.S. states (e.g., Texas) have raised their maximum speed limit in recent years, and others have eliminated the lower maximum speed limit that was applied to truckers, actions that potentially increase motor carriers' length of haul. Readers should recognize some countries may not have hours of service rules for motor carrier operators or speed limits (such as portions of the German Autobahn).

Without question, the primary advantage for motor carriers is flexibility, or the ability to deliver the product to the customer (or where the customer has relatively easy access to it). For example, if you bought this textbook at your university's bookstore, this book was delivered there by some type of motor carrier, perhaps an LTL carrier. If you bought this textbook from an online site, then it was most likely delivered to your residence by a truck, perhaps a small package truck. Indeed, a longtime slogan of the American Trucking Associations (a trade group that represents motor carrier interests) was, "If you have it, it moved by truck."

As was the case with airfreight, weather considerations also affect the reliability of motor carrier delivery, and relevant weather considerations include fog, snow, flooding, and high winds (which can affect bridge crossings). The reliability of motor carrier service is also affected by highway congestion, which is caused by increased travel demand, weather, roadway incidents (e.g., disabled vehicle, accident), and construction. This congestion tends to be most severe in major metropolitan areas and is not likely to be alleviated by additional highway construction. Rather, technology-based approaches, such as intelligent transportation systems and computer routing software that factors in congestion, are being used to deal with road congestion.

Although the cost of motor carrier service is lower than for airfreight, motor carriers tend to be more costly than the remaining modes of transportation. Moreover, there can be significant cost variation depending on the type of motor carrier service that is purchased. Expedited trucking, such as provided by Panther Transportation and FedEx Custom Critical, tends to have the highest cost per *hundredweight* (100 pounds), whereas truckload transportation tends to have the lowest cost per hundredweight. These cost variations highlight the importance of understanding the trade-offs between logistical activities that were discussed in Chapter 1. For example, suppose an organization manufactures 8,000 pounds of crayons per day. The company could have one 8,000-pound LTL shipment each day, or the company could accumulate five days of crayons into one 40,000-pound TL shipment. This would be done to take advantage of the lower TL rate per hundredweight; however, to receive the lower TL rate, the company will need to hold inventory, thus increasing inventory and storage costs.

PIPELINES

Pipelines are a unique mode of transportation because it is the only one without vehicles, and this is significant for several reasons. First, there is no need for vehicle operators, an important consideration given that vehicle operators in some modes, such as airplane pilots and ship captains, can achieve annual compensation in excess of $100,000. In addition, vehicle operators sometimes engage in work stoppages (e.g., strikes) and can be the cause of accidents. The lack of vehicles also means that pipeline transportation is one way; other modes have two-way transportation, a fronthaul and a backhaul. The backhaul is often a significant source of **excess capacity**, or unused available space.

Pipelines' lack of vehicles means that it is the most reliable form of transportation in part because there aren't vehicle-related disruptions (such as accidents), and pipelines are virtually unaffected by adverse weather conditions. Having said this, pipelines tend to be the slowest form of transportation; the lack of vehicles means that the relevant product needs to be forced through the pipeline, often by pumping stations. The slow speed for pipelines is significant because this increases overall transit times and thus necessitates additional inventory in the logistics system.

From a capability perspective, pipelines are quite limited in the sense that products must be liquid, liquefiable, or gaseous in nature. Indeed, pipelines are probably best known for transporting petroleum products, and petroleum pipelines are characterized as either crude oil or product pipelines. *Gathering lines,* which are 6 inches or smaller in diameter, start at each well and carry crude oil to concentration points. *Trunk lines* carry crude oil from gathering-line concentration points to the oil refineries. Their diameter varies from 3 to 48 inches; 8- to 10-inch pipe is the most common size. Product pipelines carry products such as gasoline or aviation fuel from the refineries to tank farms (storage tanks) located nearer to customers. These products are stored at the tank farms and then delivered to customers by truck or by rail, an indication that pipelines have limited delivery flexibility.

Slurry systems allow bulk commodities to become liquefiable by grinding the solid material to a certain particle size, mixing it with a liquid to form a fluid muddy substance, pumping that substance through a pipeline, and then decanting the liquid and removing it, leaving the solid material. Although water is the most common liquid used in slurry systems, other liquids, such as methanol, can be used. The Black Mesa pipeline, which transports pulverized coal from northern Arizona to an electric-generating station, is probably the best-known slurry pipeline currently in operation; other slurry pipelines in current operation transport phosphate, limestone, copper concentrate, and iron concentrate.[5]

---

[5]*www.blackmesapipeline.com.*

Although pipelines tend to have limited capabilities with respect to the products that can be transported, pipelines are capable of transporting very large product volumes. For example, the 48-inch Trans-Alaska pipeline, which is 789 miles long, has a discharge capacity of two million barrels of oil per day. Moreover, pipelines are quite costly to construct and thus have high fixed costs; however, because these fixed costs can be spread over rather large capacities, pipelines offer their users a relatively low cost per unit.

RAILROADS

Although approximately 550 freight railroads operate in the United States, over 90 percent of the rail industry's revenues and ton-miles are accounted for by the seven Class I (2004 revenues of at least $289.4 million) freight railroads.[6] Moreover, the U.S. railroad industry is dominated by four freight carriers, the Burlington Northern (BN), CSX, Norfolk Southern (NS), and Union Pacific (UP); the BN and UP pretty much dominate west of the Mississippi River, whereas CSX and NS have a similar position east of the Mississippi River. This level of market concentration and domination isn't found in the other modes, and from a practical perspective it can create limited service and pricing options for potential customers.

One possible manifestation of limited service options might be seen in the railroads' rather uneven reliability in recent years. Like other modes with vehicles, railroad reliability is affected by weather conditions, and in recent years the western railroads have dealt with severe mudslides that have damaged and destroyed many miles of track. Weather factors notwithstanding, uneven service performance in recent years by the four major U.S. freight carriers has caused the **Surface Transportation Board (STB),** a government agency with responsibility for regulating railroad pricing and service issues, to require Class I railroads to annually submit their fall planning strategies in an effort to avoid potential large-scale service disruptions from insufficient or inadequate equipment.

U.S. freight railroads present an intriguing paradox in the sense that they are not either the "best" or "worst" on any of the six attributes (capability, capacity, cost, flexibility, reliability, speed) that we're using as a basis of comparison for the five transport modes. For example, although freight railroads have the potential to transport many different kinds of products (capability), they have tended to focus on lower-value, high-volume shipments of bulk-type commodities such as coal, chemicals, farm products, and nonmetallic minerals. Having said this, the growth of intermodal transportation (which will be more fully discussed later in the chapter) has given railroads access to manufactured and packaged products, which tend to be higher value. Overall, railroads are superior to air, motor, and pipeline, but inferior to water, in terms of their ability to transport different kinds of products. In a similar fashion, rails possess less flexibility (ability to deliver the product to the customer) than motor carriers, unless the customer is located on a rail line or has a rail siding (a track that runs from a main line to a particular facility). However, rails generally have greater flexibility than air, water, and pipeline.

In terms of the volume that can be carried at any one time (capacity), rails are superior to air and motor, but not as good as pipeline or water. Boxcars (used to carry general freight), hopper cars (used to carry products like coal and minerals), and tank cars (used for liquid or liquefiable products) have usable carrying capacities of approximately 100 tons. Although this dwarfs the capacity of a typical truck trailer, consider that the carrying capacity of one **barge** (flatboard boat used to transport heavy products) is about 1,500 tons.

---

[6]*www.aar.org.*

Freight railroads are also right in the middle of the five modes when it comes to cost (price that a carrier charges to transport a shipment) and speed (elapsed transit time from pickup to delivery) considerations. Although railroads are less expensive than air and motor, they are more expensive than pipeline and water. Alternatively, railroads are faster than both pipeline and water, but slower than air and truck.

WATER

Freight moves by water on the Great Lakes, using vessels called lake freighters (lakers), as well as on inland waterways, using barges. Waterborne commerce also moves via oceangoing vessels between the mainland states (Lower 48) and Alaska, Hawaii, and Puerto Rico. Our discussion will focus on the inland waterways, primarily rivers, which are dredged to a depth of nine feet—the minimum depth required for most barges. Although minimum dredging depths might appear to be a rather mundane topic, it is actually quite important in the sense that inland water transportation is somewhat unreliable due to weather-related conditions such as drought and icing.

Drought creates problems because when water levels drop below acceptable levels, barges are forced to reduce their loads, or barge traffic might be halted altogether, situations that require alternate means of transportation. During 2006, for example, drought conditions effectively shut down the Missouri River, and asphalt shipments that normally moved by barge were shifted to tanker trucks.[7] Icing is a problem in northern states such as Minnesota and Wisconsin; the ice closes the rivers and prevents year-round operation. Because of this, customers can stockpile inventories in the fall to last through winter months or can use alternate methods of transportation.

Flooding is another weather-related consideration that can affect the reliability of inland water transportation. Whereas there isn't sufficient water in drought situations, with flooding there is too much water. The disruptions from flooding tend to be of a shorter duration than those associated with drought, but any disruption negatively affects transportation reliability. However, not all of the unreliability associated with inland water transportation is weather related. More specifically, the waterways' *lock* system (a lock raises or lowers barges so they can meet the river's level as they move upstream or downstream) also contributes to transport unreliability. Many locks on the U.S. inland waterway system are quite old, and because of this, malfunctions occasionally occur. Moreover, some of the older locks are too small to accommodate the length of today's tows (combination of towboat and barges), meaning that the tow must be broken and put through the lock in several parts.

Inland water transportation in the United States is also characterized by slow average speeds of approximately six miles per hour. It should be noted that transit times will be affected by the direction of travel; upstream movements that go against the prevailing current will be slower than downstream movements. In addition, inland waterways can be circuitous in nature, which can add to transit time. And, as previously pointed out, transit times may be extended because of lock-related considerations.

Yet another drawback to inland water transportation is inflexibility in the sense that it can only operate where there are appropriate waterways; moreover, users of inland water transportation need to be located on or near commercial waterways. Some U.S. rivers are not used for commercial purposes, such as the Snake River, which runs through Wyoming, Idaho, and Washington.

---

[7]"Missouri River Closed to Barges," *AWO Letter*, July 21, 2006, 6.

Turning now to more positive attributes, inland water transportation is relatively inexpensive to users. At one time inland water transportation was considered to be the least expensive form of transportation, but fuel taxes that were imposed on inland water transportation in the 1980s permitted pipelines to become the least expensive mode. Nevertheless, inland water transportation is quite inexpensive when compared to rail and motor carrier transportation. As a general guideline, on a ton-mile basis, rail costs are approximately twice as high as inland water carriers, whereas truck costs are approximately 20 times higher than inland water carriers.

Although inland water carriers tend to focus on lower-value bulk commodities that can be handled by mechanical means such as pumps, scoops, and conveyors, many different kinds of products can be carried. The predominant commodity moved by barge is petroleum and petroleum-related products, followed by coal. Other products that move extensively in the inland waterway system include grain and grain products, industrial chemicals, and forestry products. And, of the modes with vehicles, inland water carriers offer the greatest capacity, or volume that can be carried at one time. For example, one barge has the capacity of approximately 15 rail cars and 60 tractor–trailer combinations.[8]

INTERMODAL TRANSPORTATION

We have discussed each mode as if they act in isolation from the other modes, but in an increasingly global economy, multiple modes are used to transport a shipment from its origin to its destination. Intermodal transportation occurs when two or more modes work closely together in an attempt to utilize the advantages of each mode while at the same time minimizing their disadvantages. For example, a company might use **piggyback transportation,** that is, either truck trailer-on-flatcar or container-on-flatcar, to take advantage of rail's low transportation costs on the line-haul along with truck's ability to provide door-to-door service. For our purposes, **intermodal transportation** refers to transportation when using a container or other equipment that can be transferred from the vehicle of one mode to the vehicle of another mode without the contents being reloaded or disturbed.[9] Figure 6-2 shows a drawing of a RoadRailer vehicle, which conceptually facilitates intermodal transportation because the vehicle can operate on both highways and railways.

The container is regarded as the key development in intermodal transportation over the past 30 years. A container is a box that can range between 10 and 53 feet long, and containers can be moved seamlessly between water, rail, and truck. Most containers are made of steel and are general purpose in nature, meaning that they can carry any type of freight. Specialized intermodal containers are also available that carry tanks for holding liquids or gases as well containers that hold insulated or refrigerated cargo. As pointed out in Chapter 5, containers are moved by mechanical devices such as container cranes, and companies need only handle a container and not the freight inside it—thus providing a dramatic reduction in freight handling costs.

Although containers can range between 10 and 53 feet in length, a commonly used metric is **TEU,** which stands for 20-foot equivalent unit; volumes of intermodal traffic are commonly expressed as so many TEUs, meaning they would fill that many 20-foot containers. Water

---

[8]*www.americanwaterways.org.*

[9]This definition comes from Barton Jennings and Mary C. Holcomb, "Beyond Containerization: The Broader Concept of Intermodalism," *Transportation Journal* 35, no. 3 (1995): 5–13.

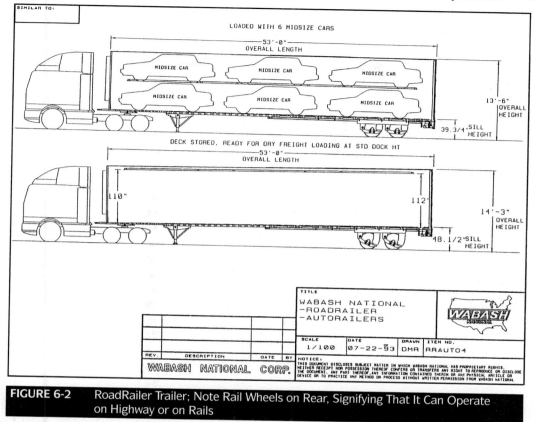

FIGURE 6-2 RoadRailer Trailer; Note Rail Wheels on Rear, Signifying That It Can Operate on Highway or on Rails

Source: Courtesy of RoadRailer Division, Wabash National Corp.

ports, for example, are often ranked in terms of the number of TEUs that are handled in a particular period of time. Likewise, containerships are measured by the number of TEUs that can be carried, and containership capacity continues to increase over time. Indeed, 8,000 TEU containerships—considered unthinkable as recently as 15 years ago—are in operation today, and there are suggestions that 12,000 TEU containerships could be operational within the next 10 years.

Not only did the container revolutionize freight handling, it also spurred cooperation between various modes to develop more effective and efficient transport offerings, such as *land bridge* services. Rather than all water service between two ports, land bridge services involve the use of surface transportation—usually rail transportation—between the origin and destination port. Consider, for example, a shipment of pineapples from Hawaii to Europe. Rather than the shipment going by water from Hawaii through the Panama Canal and then on to Europe, under land bridge service, the pineapples would move by containership from Hawaii to a U.S. West Coast water port. From this port, the containers of pineapple could be placed on railcars and shipped across the United States to an East Coast port, where the containers would be loaded onto a vessel for continuation of the shipment to Europe. Although the land bridge adds to total transportation costs, the primary advantage to land bridge service is the reduction in total transit time from the origin to destination port.

TRANSPORTATION SPECIALISTS

In addition to the five basic modes and intermodal transportation, a number of different transportation specialists can provide value-added services to prospective customers. We'll discuss several transportation specialists in the paragraphs that follow. **Freight forwarders** are not modes, but from the shipper's viewpoint, they are analogous to other carriers. There are two types of domestic freight forwarders—surface and air—and they can best be thought of as consolidators of freight.

Both surface and air carriers give volume discounts to customers shipping large quantities of freight at one time. For example, the LTL rate from city A to city B might be $5 per 100 pounds for shipments less than 20,000 pounds, whereas the TL rate might be $2 per 100 pounds when shipments of 20,000 pounds or more are tendered. Truckload rates are lower than LTL rates for three reasons: (1) the shipper loads the goods, and the consignee unloads the trailer; (2) the load goes directly from shipper to consignee without passing through terminals; and (3) paperwork, billing, and other administrative costs are little more for a 25,000-pound shipment than they would be for a 250-pound shipment.

The freight forwarder exists by offering a service to shippers that must use LTL rates because they do not generate enough volume to use TL rates. Without the freight forwarder, the shipper has to use the $5 LTL rate. The freight forwarder, however, offers the same transportation service for a rate between the LTL and TL rate—say, $4. This is possible because the freight forwarder consolidates all the small shipments it has and gives them to the carrier (a trucker in this case) and hence qualifies for the $2 TL rate. The freight forwarder typically offers pickup and delivery service but does not perform the line-haul service. This is done by motor carriers or railroads (in terms of intermodal service).

Some forwarders specialize in certain cargoes. A common example is in the garment industry, in which many small garment firms send large numbers of a few garments each to retail shops in most large cities. The garment forwarders use special containers in which the garments are on hangers and thus ready for display on arrival. Another specialized forwarder relocates house pets. The firm handles health inspection prior to shipment, arranges for cages and quarantines (if required), books flights, and handles all documentation.

The air forwarding industry works with the air carriers. The forwarders consolidate shipments and tender them in containers that are ready for aircraft loading. This results in significant ground-handling savings for the airlines. Therefore, airlines encourage forwarder traffic because it results in an agreeable division of labor: The forwarders provide the retailing function and deal with each individual shipper and consignee, and the airline concentrates on wholesaling, moving the forwarders' loaded containers among major cities.

Shippers' associations perform basically the same function as surface and air freight forwarders, except that they do not operate as profit-making organizations. Shippers' associations are membership cooperatives where membership can be based on different considerations, such as shipping a particular commodity or commodities, belonging to a particular industry, or being located in a particular area. Although shippers' associations tend to be thought of as providing a large number of transportation-related services for its members (full-service associations), some shippers' associations are primarily focused on achieving the lowest rates for their members ("rate negotiator" associations). The main benefit of shippers' associations, whether they are full service or rate negotiators, is transportation cost savings for its members.[10]

---

[10]Information from the Web site of the American Institute for Shippers' Associations, *www.shippers.org.*

Brokers are another type of transportation specialist; they are companies that look to match a shipper's freight with a carrier to transport it. Brokers look to secure the best transportation rate and service package available for shippers, while attempting to ensure that carriers operate as close as possible to maximum capacity. Brokers can handle both LTL and TL shipments; those handling LTL shipments consolidate them and then turn them over to motor carriers, freight forwarders, or shippers' associations. With respect to TL shipments, brokers will retain a particular carrier and receive a portion of the transportation charges as compensation.

In some cases, *third-party logistics companies* are involved in arranging transportation services. They try to find clients with complementary transportation needs so that equipment utilization can be increased, which should reduce transportation costs to the respective clients. As an example, Exel Logistics was able to persuade Chrysler and Ford to share space on trucks that were delivering repair parts to both Chrysler and Ford dealerships in a particular geographic area. Exel was able to show both Chrysler and Ford that dedicated equipment (that is, equipment carrying only Chrysler or only Ford parts) led to additional equipment, additional shipments, and excess capacity for each party—thus increasing the costs of distributing the repair parts.

Much of the discussion up to this point has assumed that we are dealing with shipments that weigh at least several hundred pounds. We'll conclude our discussion of transportation specialists by looking at **parcel carriers**, companies that specialize in transporting parcels, which are often referred to as packages that weigh up to 150 pounds. Parcel shippers have a variety of potential options available to them, one of which is Parcel Post, a service of the U.S. Postal Service that was specifically established to send packages through the mail system. Parcel Post has definite size and weight limitations (approximately 70 pounds), with transportation charges based on weight and distance. In most cases, a parcel must be carried to the post office, but it will be delivered to the receiver.

Another option for parcel shippers is United Parcel Service (UPS), which financially dwarfs any other transportation company in the United States (2006 revenue from package deliveries of approximately $40 billion). UPS was able to attract customers in its early years because it offered certain services, such as automatic daily pickups, multiple delivery attempts, and the return of undeliverable packages, that were not available from competitors such as Parcel Post—and UPS was able to offer this service at rates that were competitive with Parcel Post. Unlike the Parcel Post, UPS rates include both pickup and delivery, and today it offers a range of services via several modes of transport, to include truck, rail, and air.

Whereas UPS started as a package delivery company that emphasized line-haul movement by truck and in the 1980s expanded into air transportation, Federal Express (now FedEx Express) started as a package delivery company that emphasized service by air transportation and expanded into line-haul movement by truck (FedEx Ground). Both UPS and FedEx now offer package shippers service options that include same-day service involving air transportation, next-day service involving air or truck, and second-day service involving air or truck, among others. The weight limitations for UPS and FedEx range from 70 pounds to 150 pounds, depending on the type of service purchased.

Package services are also available from Greyhound Lines (called Greyhound Package Express), which is the primary intercity bus company in the United States. As is the case with UPS and FedEx, several service options are available for package delivery, such as same-day service (which generally uses a courier company) and standard service (where the packages travel in special compartments on the bus). Packages that are sent via Greyhound Package Express are limited to a maximum weight of 100 pounds.[11]

---

[11]*www.greyhoundlines.com.*

TRANSPORTATION REGULATION

The five modes of transportation have been influenced, and continue to be influenced, by various types of regulation by federal, state, and local governments. You may not be aware, for example, that in the United States commercial airline pilots must retire on reaching 60 years of age (although there is an effort to increase this mandatory retirement to 65 years of age). Likewise, you might not be aware that there are very specific guidelines for the placement of lighting on truck trailers. The existence of these and other regulations have implications not only for transportation companies, but also for users of transportation companies because regulations can affect the effectiveness and efficiency of a user's logistics system. Indeed, regulation costs money—regulations need to be codified, and there are government agencies (regulatory bodies) to enforce the regulations.

Our discussion in this section will focus on federal regulation of transportation in the United States, and we will look at environmental, safety, and economic regulation. However, before proceeding with this discussion, readers should recognize that the level and degree of transportation regulation varies from country to country. For example, many of the world's more industrialized economies have instituted fairly stringent regulations with respect to vehicle emissions (air pollution) from trucks and rail engines. In lesser economically developed countries, emissions regulations are much less stringent—if they exist at all. We're not here to judge the appropriateness (inappropriateness) of transportation regulation in individual countries; rather, logisticians need to understand the relevant transportation regulations of the countries in which they conduct business as well as the cost and service ramifications of these regulations.

Environmental Regulation

The Environmental Protection Agency (EPA), a U.S. federal regulatory agency that was established to protect human health and the environment, influences transportation in a number of different ways. A major transportation-related concern of the EPA involves water, noise, and air pollution. With respect to noise pollution, noise standards promulgated by the EPA meant that commercial airlines had to equip their fleet with quieter engines. In terms of air pollution, the EPA has mandated that beginning in 2007 heavy-duty truck engines must meet stringent emissions standards. These standards will require truckers to use ultra-low-sulfur diesel fuel—which isn't readily available and is noticeably more expensive (perhaps 60 cents a gallon higher) than traditional diesel fuel.

The EPA is also quite concerned with resource conservation, and this is particularly germane in that transportation accounts for approximately two-thirds of the petroleum consumption in the United States. As such, improved fuel efficiency and reduced consumption of petroleum have become important issues for many transportation companies. For example, we mentioned in an earlier chapter how technological advances are helping UPS to improve its fleet's fuel efficiency, and the Web sites for both UPS and FedEx prominently highlight their involvement with alternative energy sources, such as propane and electricity.[12]

Safety Regulation

The U.S. **Department of Transportation** (DOT) is the federal government body with primary responsibility for transportation safety regulation. Although the DOT's safety responsibilities encompass all five modes of transportation, safety regulation of inland water carriers is primarily the responsibility of the U.S. Coast Guard, which is now part of the U.S. Department of Homeland

---

[12]*www.ups.com; www.fedex.com.*

Security. The key government safety agency for each mode, and an example of safety-related issues, will be discussed next.

The Federal Aviation Administration (FAA) has primary responsibility for air transportation safety and strives to improve the safety and efficiency of aviation. For example, FAA data indicate that, on an annual basis, approximately 20 percent of all air transportation accidents are weather related.[13] The Federal Motor Carrier Safety Administration (FMCSA), a relatively new government agency, started operations in January 2000 and is primarily focused on large trucks and buses. A recent FMCSA report on accidents involving large trucks indicated that driver behavior was much more likely than weather, road conditions, or equipment factors to cause these accidents.[14] The Federal Railroad Administration (FRA) has primary responsibility for safety in the U.S. railroad industry and employs over 400 safety inspectors who investigate operating practices, track and structures, and signal and train control issues, among others.[15]

Another relatively new transportation safety agency is the Pipeline and Hazardous Materials Safety Administration (PHSMA), which was created in late 2004. Like other transportation safety agencies, the PHMSA collects data on relevant accidents, such as those involving liquid pipelines, and classifies the accidents according to cause, damage, and fatalities or injuries.[16] Finally, the U.S. Coast Guard (USCG), which has primary responsibility for safety issues with inland waterways, has been involved with a public–private partnership with the American Waterways Organization (a trade association) to improve tugboat, towboat, and barge safety. This partnership has resulted in a dramatic decrease in the severity of accidents as well as a noticeable decline in the number of crew fatalities.[17]

Economic Regulation

Economic regulation in transportation refers to control over business practices and activities such as entry and exit, pricing, service, accounting and financial issues, and mergers and acquisitions. Federal economic regulation of transportation, which began in the 1870s, was justified because of transportation's economic and social importance as well as a belief that transportation companies would not act in the public's best interest without economic regulation.[18] Economic regulation resulted in the creation of two key economic regulatory bodies, the Interstate Commerce Commission (ICC), with authority over rail, motor, inland water, and oil pipelines, and the Civil Aeronautics Board (CAB), with authority over air transportation.

Beginning in the late 1970s, various sectors of the transportation industry experienced a reduction in economic regulation, and in 1985 the CAB went out of existence. In addition to further reduction in economic regulation, the ICC Termination Act of 1995 eliminated the ICC and transferred the remaining economic regulatory functions to the Surface Transportation Board (STB), which is part of the Department of Transportation. Although the STB has primary responsibility for resolving railroad rate and service disputes and reviewing potential rail mergers, it continues to have some jurisdiction over motor carriers, domestic water transportation, and the rates and services of pipelines that are not regulated by the Federal Energy Regulatory Commission.[19]

---

[13]*www.faa.dot.gov.*

[14]*www.fmcsa.dot.gov.*

[15]*www.fra.dot.gov.*

[16]*www.phmsa.dot.gov.*

[17]*www.americanwaterways.org.*

[18]Donald V. Harper, *Transportation in America,* 2nd ed. (Englewood Cliffs, NJ: Prentice Hall, 1982), Chapter 19.

[19]*www.stb.dot.gov.*

From a logistics perspective, economic deregulation of transportation is important because it allowed transportation companies much greater freedom with respect to pricing and service options—two attributes that are at the heart of the tailored logistics concept that was presented in Chapter 1. In addition, the economic deregulation that occurred in the United States has been the catalyst for economic deregulation in Canada and some European nations.[20]

LEGAL CLASSIFICATION OF CARRIERS

Although there has been a dramatic reduction in economic regulation since the late 1970s, the legal classification of carriers continues to be relevant. More specifically, transportation carriers are classified as either for hire or private, and for-hire carriers can be further subdivided into common, contract, and exempt carriers. The legal classification of carriers is important because of the varying levels of economic regulation that are applicable to the different carriers (for example, common carriers have more extensive economic regulation than contract carriers). However, all carriers, regardless of their degree of economic regulation, must comply with the relevant environmental and safety regulations.

The key factor that separates a **common carrier** from other forms of transportation is that the common carrier has agreed to serve the general public. To ensure that the general public is adequately serviced, common carriers assumed four specific obligations: to serve, to deliver, to charge reasonable rates, and to avoid discrimination in pricing and service. The service obligation means that common carriers are supposed to serve all customers who request service, so long as the commodity and origin/destination are within a carrier's scope of service. For example, a motor carrier that specializes in dry van, general freight service would not be expected to transport a shipment of liquid chemicals. Even though a company might not want to carry certain types of freight, its undesirability (see Figure 6-3) is not a legitimate reason to avoid the obligation to serve.

The obligation to deliver requires that a carrier provide timely pickup and delivery as well as ensuring that the delivered shipment is in the same condition as the picked up shipment (i.e., the avoidance of lost or damaged freight). The obligation to charge reasonable rates has long been viewed as offering protection for both carriers and users; the idea of reasonable rates guards against rates so low that carriers are unable or unwilling to carry freight, and it guards against rates so high that users are unwilling or unable to tender freight to carriers. The obligation to avoid discrimination in pricing and service suggests that similarly situated customers (e.g., customers that ship the same product, customers that ship to the same origin and destination point) should receive identical treatment. One of the key provisions of the ICC Termination Act of 1995 was the elimination of the reasonable rate obligation (hence also the obligation to avoid discrimination in pricing and service) for many types of motor carriers.

A **contract carrier** offers a specialized service to customers on a contractual basis, and the contract specifies the compensation to be received, the services to be provided, and the type of equipment to be used, among others. Unlike the common carrier, the contract carrier is under no obligation to render services to the general public and only has to serve customers with whom it has contracts. Moreover, the contract carrier is under no obligation to treat its customers on an equal basis. Because each contract can be tailored to the specifications of individual customers, contract carriage is viewed as offering many of the advantages of private transportation (such as control over service) while avoiding many of the disadvantages of private transportation (e.g., the hiring of drivers, owning equipment).

---

[20]John J. Coyle, Edward J. Bardi, and Robert A. Novack, *Transportation,* 6th ed. (Mason, OH: South-Western, 2006).

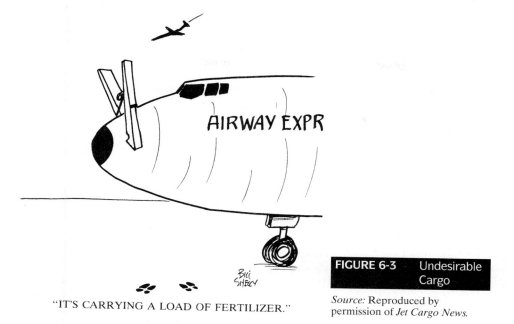

"IT'S CARRYING A LOAD OF FERTILIZER."

FIGURE 6-3   Undesirable Cargo

Source: Reproduced by permission of *Jet Cargo News.*

Exempt carriers are for-hire carriers that have been exempted from economic regulation through provisions in various pieces of legislation; the appropriate rates and services must be negotiated directly between the carrier and user. For example, the Transportation Act of 1940, which brought domestic water carriers under economic regulation, exempted liquid bulk commodities from economic regulation, as well as dry-bulk commodities, so long as no more than three dry-bulk commodities were moved in a particular tow.[21] In a similar fashion, the Motor Carrier Act of 1935, which brought motor carriers under economic regulation, exempted unprocessed agricultural commodities from economic regulation; the Motor Carrier Act of 1980, which lessened economic regulation for motor carriers, exempted agricultural seeds and plants from regulation.[22]

Private carriers, which are exempt from any economic regulation, are companies whose primary business is other than transportation and provide their own transportation service by operating trucks, railcars, barges, ships, or airplanes. Private transportation is most prevalent in the trucking industry, accounting for over 50 percent of the U.S. highway mileage for trucks.[23] Prominent private truckers in the United States include Wal-Mart, ExxonMobil, Kraft Foods, and Frito-Lay, among others.

Operational control is a key advantage to private transportation. For example, shipments can move at a time convenient for the company, as opposed to a time that might be convenient for a carrier. Private transportation may also be a cost-effective form of transportation, particularly in situations where the company can find backhaul traffic; revenue from the backhaul can be used to offset costs on both the backhaul and fronthaul.

[21]Harper, *Transportation in America.*

[22]Ibid.

[23]*www.nptc.org.*

Although private transportation can be a cost-effective form of transportation, a key disadvantage is that it can be quite costly, in part because of the capital expenditures that are necessary to own or lease the relevant vehicles. Moreover, managerial costs are often ignored or underestimated; transportation managers assume that, along with their many other responsibilities, they will also supervise the private transportation operation. Later, when it is discovered that all but the smallest private fleets each require a full-time manager (to supervise vehicle scheduling, maintenance, labor relations, and so on), the firm is faced with a large, unanticipated expense.

Summary

Transportation, the actual, physical movement of goods and people between two points, is pivotal to the success of any logistics or supply chain operation. We began with a comparison of transportation infrastructures in several different countries and found dramatic infrastructural differences across the countries. This comparison is important in the sense that a manager in one country should understand that transportation capabilities in other countries may be different from those in the manager's home country.

The chapter presented a discussion of the five modes of transportation in terms of each mode's capability, capacity, cost, flexibility, reliability, and speed. This mode-by-mode discussion was followed by a look at intermodal transportation. The roles that can be played by transportation specialists such as freight forwarders and brokers were also examined.

Environmental regulation, safety regulation, and economic regulation can have a tremendous influence on the various modes, and the level of regulation is not uniform across or within modes. The chapter concluded with a look at the four legal classifications of carriers—common, contract, exempt, and private.

Questions For Discussion And Review

1. Why is transportation important to a firm's supply chain operations?
2. Why is it important to know about the characteristics of a country's transportation infrastructure?
3. List some products that frequently move by airfreight. Why do you think that airfreight was selected as the mode to use?
4. How do truckload operations differ from less-than-truckload operations?
5. How do speed limits and hours-of-service rules potentially affect motor carrier service?
6. What are advantages and disadvantages to a pipeline's lack of vehicles?
7. What are pipeline slurry systems? How do they function?
8. Discuss the drawbacks to rail transportation.
9. How do weather conditions influence the reliability of inland water carriers?
10. Discuss the positive attributes of inland water transportation.
11. What is a land bridge service? How might it be applied?
12. What are freight forwarders? How do they function? What services do they perform?
13. What is a shippers' association?
14. Why do truckload rates tend to be lower than less-than-truckload rates?
15. Discuss the various options that are available to parcel shippers.
16. List several environmental regulations and describe their impact on transportation.
17. Pick three modes of transportation, name the federal agency responsible for safety regulation for each of the modes you've picked, and provide a safety-related issue for each mode.
18. Define what is meant by economic regulation. Why is transportation economic deregulation important?
19. How does a common carrier differ from a contract carrier?
20. Discuss advantages and disadvantages to private transportation.

Suggested Readings

Allen, W. Bruce, Michael Sussman, and Drew Miller. "Regional and Short Line Railroads in the United States." *Transportation Quarterly* 56, no. 4 (2002): 77–113.

Coyle, John J., Edward J. Bardi, and Robert A. Novack. *Transportation.* 6th ed. Mason, OH: South-Western, 2006.

Evers, Philip. T., and Carol J. Johnson. "Performance Perceptions, Satisfaction, and Intention: The Intermodal Shipper's Perspective." *Transportation Journal* 40, no. 2 (2000): 27–39.

Hull, Bradley Z. "Oil Pipeline Markets and Operations." *Journal of the Transportation Research Forum* 44, no. 2 (2005): 111–127.

Hurst, D. Michael. "Surface Transportation's Regulatory Roller Coaster." *Journal of Transportation Law, Logistics and Policy* 73, no. 2 (2006): 180–219.

Johnson, James C., Diane J. McClure, Kenneth C. Schneider, and Donald F. Wood. "Short-Line Railroad Managers: Their Incomes, Joys, and Frustrations." *Journal of Transportation Law, Logistics and Policy* (Spring 2002): 260–279.

Levinson, Mark. *The Box: How the Shipping Container Made the World Smaller and the World Economy Bigger.* Princeton, NJ: Princeton University Press, 2006.

McBride, Michael F. "Railroads May Not Refuse to Carry Dangerous Commodities." *Journal of Transportation Law, Logistics and Policy* 69, no. 4 (2002): 391–397.

Mejza, Michael C., Richard E. Barnard, Thomas M. Corsi, and Thomas Keane. "Driver Management Practices of Motor Carriers with High Compliance and Safety Performance." *Transportation Journal* 42, no. 4 (2003): 16–29.

Moore, Robert S., Stephen LeMay, Melissa L. Moore, Pearson Lidell, Brian Kinard, and David McMillen. "An Investigation of Motorists' Perceptions of Trucks on the Highways." *Transportation Journal* 44, no. 1 (2005): 20–32.

Ohnell, Sofia, and Johan Woxenius. "An Industry Analysis of Express Freight from a European Railway Perspective." *International Journal of Physical Distribution & Logistics Management* 33, no. 8 (2003): 735–751.

Rockey, Craig F. "Progress and Promise of Rail Intermodal." *Journal of Transportation Law, Logistics and Policy* 71, no. 2 (2004): 197–211.

Young, Richard R., Peter F. Swan, and Richard H. Burn. "Private Railcar Fleet Operations: The Problem of Excessive Customer Holding Time in the Chemicals and Plastics Industries." *Transportation Journal* 42, no. 1 (2002): 51–59.

CASE

CASE 6-1   BOONE SHOE COMPANY

This case shows how a carrier's transportation charges were determined using printed tariff documents, in the precomputer era. It begins with an example and then turns into a problem with questions.

Assume that an archaeology museum wants to move 30,000 pounds of bones from Sioux Falls, South Dakota, to Hannibal, Missouri. It wants to use railroads because this shipment is in no particular hurry. To establish the rating

(class), it is necessary first to find the commodity in the Uniform Freight Classification (UFC) index. Exhibit 6-A contains the page from the index that contains human bones. Note that the letters *noibn* follow "human bones." The letters stand for "not otherwise indexed by name." We are referred to item number 13350. Exhibit 6-B is the page in the UFC that contains item number 13350. This tariff also specifies how the human bones are to be packaged for presentation

UNIFORM FREIGHT CLASSIFICATION 7

INDEX TO ARTICLES

STCC No.	Article	Item	STCC No.	Article	Item
	Hulls,Concluded:			Huskers,Concluded:	
20 914 45	Cottonseed,mixed with meal 37130		35 225 23	Corn,and fodder shredders, combined,ot hand,	
20 914 25	Cottonseed,not ground . . .31250,131270			SU 3370,14050	
20 939 46	Fleaseed (psyllium). 33800,80090		34 236 79	Corn,hand	
34 412 15	Launch,steel 11690			(husking gloves) 36260	
37 329 12	Launch,wooden,in the white,		35 225 60	Corn,noibn,ot hand,	
	KD. 11490			KD 3360,14050	
37 329 13	Launch,wooden,in the white,		35 225 59	Corn,noibn,ot hand,SU,	
	SU. 11490			on wheels. 3360,14050	
20 939 55	Nut,noibn. 86140			Green corn. 62530	
20 418 30	Oat. 47110		35 227 30	Husking gloves,corn	
20 999 25	Peanut,crushed or ground 37530		34 236 79	(corn huskers) 36260	
20 939 20	Peanut,not crushed nor ground. . . 37540			Husking pins. 36500	
20 939 46	Psyllium seed (fleaseed) . . 33800,80090		34 236 80	Husks,corn (shucks) 37350	
20 449 15	Rice,ground and rice bran,		01 199 30	Hydrants,or sections 29520	
	feed. 37580		33 219 16	Hydrastis canadensis (golden seal)	
20 449 20	Rice,ground,feed 37590		28 311 51	roots,ground or powdered . . 33590,33800	
20 449 25	Rice,unground (rice chaff),			Hydrastis canadensis (golden seal) roots,	
	feed 37600		01 915 31	not ground nor powdered. . . 33620,33800	
09 131 55	Shrimp . . . . δ			Hydraulic accumulators,mining,	
20 923 16	Soybean,ground 37640			ore milling or smelting. 63480	
20 923 17	Soybean,not ground 37640		32 411 15	Hydraulic cement. 21680,177130	
20 939 56	Sunflower seed 83440		35 999 16	Hydraulic cylinders,ot rotary,steel 60780	
20 939 27	Tung nut 52790		35 691 45	Hydraulic rams. 161240,64890	
20 939 64	Velvet bean,ground 95550		35 329 10	Hydraulic rotary swivels,oil,	
20 939 66	Velvet bean,not ground 95560			water or gas well. 72070	
28 311 21	Human blood,liquid,frozen or		29 912 10	Hydraulic system fluid,ot,	
	chilled.. 11355			petroleum. 14690	
39 998 21	Human bones,noibn. 13350			Hydraulic wheel presses 166800	
39 994 10	Human hair 48320		34 434 38	Hydro-pneumatic tanks,copper,	
39 994 20	Human hair goods,noibn. 48390			cylindrical closed at both ends. . 89040	
39 994 15	Human hair samples,mounted on		34 434 40	Hydro-pneumatic tanks,silicon	
	cardboard 48360			bronze,cylindrical,closed at	
40 291 47	Human hair waste,not stumps nor			both ends. 89050	
	combed hair 95490		34 434 42	Hydro-pneumatic tanks,steel,14	
	Humidifiers:			gauge or thicker,cylindrical,	
41 111 10	Air and blowers or fans combined,			closed at both ends. 89060	
	mounted on freight			Hydrobarometers 32990	
	automobile. 73400		38 213 15	Hydrocarbon gas,noibn 45630	
35 857 20	Air and blowers or fans combined,		28 139 92	Hydrocarbon recovery systems. . . . δ	
	noibn. 130740,58510		35 599 78	Hydrochloric (muriatic)	
35 857 45	Air bakers',cast iron. . .58610,158720		28 194 50	acid 2340,33800	
37 142 12	Coolers and filters,air,			Hydrocyanic acid. 2260	
	automobile,non-electric 8125		28 194 34	Hydrofluoric and sulphuric acid,	
34 336 49	Hot air house heating		28 194 42	mixed. 2280,33800	
	furnace,automatic 12700		28 194 38	Hydrofluoric acid 2270,33800	
34 299 30	Humidors,ot display. 52800		40 251 65	Hydrofluoric acid waste,	
14 917 15	Humus 27320			aqueous. . . . . δ	
33 992 50	Hungarian nails,noibn,brass,		28 194 46	Hydrofluosilicic acid 2290,33800	
	bronze or copper. 149771,50810		28 139 20	Hydrogen bromide,anhydrous,	
33 152 25	Hungarian nails,noibn,steel,with			liquefied. 45410	
	ot steel or zinc		28 139 22	Hydrogen chloride,anhydrous,	
	heads 149781,50820			liquefied. 45420	
33 152 30	Hungarian nails,noibn,steel,		28 199 31	Hydrogen dioxide 24020,33800	
	with steel heads. 149781,50830		28 134 60	Hydrogen gas. 45640	
33 152 35	Hungarian nails,noibn,steel,		28 199 31	Hydrogen peroxide 24020,33800	
	with zinc heads 149781,50840		28 139 46	Hydrogen sulphide 45650	
	Hurdles,track,steel with		20 469 10	Hydrol (corn,sorghum grain	
	wooden cross bars,			or wheat sugar final	
	noibn. 7580			molasses). 37360	
	Hurdles,track steel with		38 219 14	Hydrometers 33000	
	wooden cross bars,uprights		28 186 20	Hydroxy acetic acid 2300,33800	
	folded to base,or SU nstd,		40 251 62	Hydroxy aldehydes,waste,	
	in nests of five or			containing not less than	
	more. 7580			40% water. 96090	
22 995 73	Hurds,hemp or ramie. 52810		28 612 20	Hypernic extracts,dry 35860	
35 225 29	Huskers and pickers combined,		28 612 21	Hypernic extracts,liquid or	
	corn. 3390,14050			paste. 35870	
35 225 61	Huskers and shellers,combined,		40 291 57	Hypo-mud,photo silver 95720	
	corn,ot hand. 3380,14050				
	Huskers:				
35 225 24	Corn and fodder shredders,				
	combined,ot hand,KD 3370,14050				

EXHIBIT 6-A   Index Page from Freight Classification

to the carrier. (This is important for all products: The classification dictates how products must be packaged.) On the right-hand edge of Exhibit 6-B are the appropriate ratings, or classes. The first rating of 200 is the less-than-carload (LCL) rating. (*LCL* stands for "less-than-carload" and dates to the time when railroads carried small shipments of mixed freight weighing,

say, a few hundred or thousand pounds each.) Then, Exhibit 6-B states that if 20,000 or more pounds are tendered to the carrier, the carload (CL) rating is 100. Because this shipment involves 30,000 pounds, the CL rating of 100 will be used. The next requirement is to determine the rate bases number. Exhibit 6-C illustrates a typical tariff page containing this information. The

UNIFORM FREIGHT CLASSIFICATION 7

13250–13470

Item	ARTICLES	Less Carload Ratings	Carload Minimum (Pounds)	Carload Ratings
	BOILERS, FURNACES, RADIATORS, STOVES, RELATED ARTICLES OR PARTS NAMED (Subject to Item 11960)—Concluded: Group No. 1			
13250	Coal hods (scuttles) or vases, steel; cookers or steamers, stock feed, noibn; furnaces, house heating, hot air, with or without equipment of air conditioning apparatus or thermostats; griddles, kettles, pots, skillets or spiders, sheet steel; holloware, cast iron, as described in Item 49880; house heating furnace casing parts; sugar or syrup evaporator kettles, iron; stove or range cabinets, closets or high shelves, steel; stove or range ovens; stove or range parts, iron or steel, other than castings, noibn; stove pipe drums or drum ovens; stove pipe or elbows, sheet iron, steel or tin plate, side seams closed; stove pipe thimbles, sheet or sheet iron or steel or tin plate, side seams closed; stove or range reservoirs or reservoir attachments; tee joints and draft regulators combined, stove pipe.			
13260	Group No. 2 Air registers, noibn, including air louvres, iron or steel; andirons, iron; ash scrapers; heating furnace pipe or elbows, sheet iron, steel or tin plate; house heating furnace castings, tin plate; burners, gas, for coal, oil or wood stoves, see Note 58, Item 13271; oil burning outfits for brooders or coal or wood stoves; pans, baking, dripping or frying, sheet steel; fire pokers, iron; sad irons, with or without stands, other than self-heating; stove boards, iron or metal clad wood or fibreboard; stove cover lifters, iron; stove or range castings, iron; stove pipe, sheet iron, steel or tin plate, side seams not closed, nested; dampers, noibn, iron; stove pipe thimbles, cast iron or plate or sheet iron or tin plate, side seams not closed, nested; stove shovels, sheet steel; water heaters, noibn			
13261	Note 52.—Weight of articles in Group 2, Item 13260, must not exceed 50% of weight upon which charges are assessed.			
13265	Mixed CL of two or more of the following articles, viz.: Stoves or ranges, iron or steel; dampers, noibn, iron; electric logs, see Note 54, Item 13266; fireplace grates or grate baskets, with or without heating units; fireplace grate parts, noibn; gas logs; heaters, gas, with or without clay radiants; andirons (fire dogs); fenders or fireplace guards or screens, brass, see Note 54, Item 13266; fenders or fireplace guards or screens, iron or steel, plain or brass coated or plated, or with brass trimming; fireplace sets (shovels and tongs), with or without hearth brushes, holders or pokers, brass or brass and iron combined, see Note 54, Item 13266; fireplace sets (shovels and tongs), with or without hearth brushes, holders or pokers, iron; lighters, fire, brass or iron, see Note 54, Item 13266; or wood holders or racks, fireplace, see Note 54, Item 13266		24,000R	45
13266	Note 54.—Aggregate weight of articles subject to this note must not exceed 50% of weight upon which charges are assessed.			
13267	Note 56.—Section 2 of Rule 34 is not applicable.			
13270	Superheaters, other than locomotive: SU, loose or in packages	70	24,000R	40
13271	KD, or superheater parts, KD, loose or in packages	65	24,000R	40
	Note 58.—Ratings apply only on burners for converting coal, oil or wood stoves into gas stoves.			
13272	Note 60.—Weight of articles subject to this note shall not exceed 10% of weight upon which charges are assessed.			
13280	Tanks, oil stove, sheet steel, 26 gauge or thicker, capacity not exceeding 5 gallons, in boxes or crates	110	16,000R	60
13281	Note 66.—Ratings also apply on stoves or ranges designed for separate permanent installation of oven and surface cooking units.			
13282	Note 68.—CL ratings will include iron or steel garbage or offal incinerators, not exceeding 25% of the weight upon which freight charges are assessed.			
13295	Bolster rolls for beds, couches or lounges, fibreboard with plywood ends and reinforcing ribs, upholstered, in Package 9F	150	10,000R	100
13300	Bolster rolls for beds, couches or lounges, noibn, in boxes or crates	200	10,000R	100
13310	Bone, charred filtering (animal charcoal), other than spent, in bags or barrels	70	36,000	35
13320	Bone, charred filtering (animal charcoal), spent, in bags	50	40,000	20
13330	Bone, charred filtering, synthetic, in bags or barrels	70	36,000	35
13340	Bone ash, in bags, barrels or boxes	55	36,000	30
13350	Bones, human, noibn, prepaid, in barrels or boxes	200	20,000R	100
13360	Bones, noibn, ground or not ground, LCL, in bags or barrels, or in barrels with cloth tops; CL, loose or in packages	50	40,000	22½
13370	Book ends, moulded wood or plaster, in boxes	85	24,000R	55
13380	Book stacks, library, consisting of iron brackets, floor framing, stairs, railings, standards, and shelves, in packages; also CL, loose	70	36,000	40
13390	Boot or shoe arch supports or arch support insoles, in boxes	100	20,000R	70
13400	Boot or shoe forms or trees, in barrels or boxes	85	20,000R	55
13410	**BOOTS, SHOES, OR BOOT OR SHOE FINDINGS:**			
13420	Boot or shoe findings, noibn, in bales, barrels or boxes, or in barrels with cloth tops	100	16,000R	70
13430	Boots or shoes, noibn, see Note 1, item 13431, in boxes; in trunks in crates; in salesmen's sample trunks, locked; in Packages 277 or 1197; also in straight CL in Package 1126	100	24,000R	70
13431	Note 1.—Ratings also apply on Huaraches (Mexican leather sandals) in bamboo baskets or hampers, tops securely closed.			
13440	Boots or shoes, old, used, leather, having value other than for reclamation of raw materials, prepaid, see Note 2, Item 13441, in packages; also CL, loose	85	36,000	50
13441	Note 2.—Old used shoes rebuilt or repaired, will be rated as shoes, noibn.			
13450	Boots or shoes, plastic, rubber or rubber and canvas, felt or wool combined, in bales or boxes	100	15,000R	70
13460	Boots or shoes, wooden or leather with wooden soles, in packages	92½	24,000R	65
13470	Box toe boards, in packages; also CL, loose	70	36,000	35

EXHIBIT 6-B   Page Showing Classification of Articles

appropriate rate bases number between Sioux Falls, South Dakota, and Hannibal, Missouri, is 448. Finally, it is necessary to establish the specific rate per hundred pounds. Exhibit 6-D contains a tariff page that uses the rating (class) and rate bases number to determine the rate, which is $3.07 in this example. The total charge can now be determined using this formula:

Rate (per hundred pounds) TIMES weight (in hundred-pound units) = charge
or $3.07 \times 300 = \$921$

Freight Tariff No. W-1000

APPLICATION OF RATE BASES

BETWEEN (See Item 100)

RATE BASES APPLICABLE

AND (See Item 100)	Greeley Centre, Neb.	Green Bay, Wis.	Greenbush, Minn.	Grenville, S.D.	Grinnell, Iowa	Grover, Colo.	Hallock, Minn.	Hannaford, N.D.	Hannibal, Mo.	Harvard, Ill.	Hawarden, Iowa	Haxtun, Colo.	Hays, Kan.	Hazen, N.D.	Herington, Kan.	Hermanville, Mich.	Hermosa, S.D.	Herrick, S.D.	Hettinger, N.D.	Hibbing, Minn.
Rugby .... N.D.	716	716	233	340	680	944	202	128	855	768	465	914	939	306	824	687	609	714	461	372
Rulo .... Neb.	240	619	712	627	237	546	718	621	251	477	244	438	318	699	179	715	619	347	669	636
Russell .... Kan.	335	844	919	834	479	474	925	828	457	606	451	482	27	906	121	941	695	506	875	868
St. Cloud .... Minn.	489	350	262	223	317	828	287	241	495	401	250	737	712	433	596	367	558	487	461	193
St. Francis .... Kan.	309	918	935	850	568	502	941	844	620	809	467	363	363	922	332	985	646	487	892	884
St. Ignace .... Mich.	937	256	681	735	619	1277	713	722	659	392	713	1186	1098	914	959	166	1064	935	966	477
St. James .... Minn.	358	380	430	345	220	697	436	363	408	388	133	607	581	488	465	414	498	356	457	314
St. Joseph .... Mo.	284	579	737	652	213	587	743	646	207	437	269	479	293	724	154	676	657	383	694	614
St. Louis .... Mo.	583	458	854	812	305	890	880	833	⊕	498	545	783	561	983	414	553	940	652	952	719
Sabetha .... Kan.	223	640	740	655	273	524	747	649	267	498	272	414	277	727	155	736	604	349	697	666
Sabula .... Iowa	492	246	639	597	146	832	665	618	⊕	⊕	364	741	625	792	486	343	756	572	762	504
Sac City .... Iowa	250	464	545	460	143	589	552	472	317	362	115	499	462	561	347	540	510	302	530	442
Salem .... S.D.	330	539	456	359	313	670	442	304	488	512	76	579	553	383	438	572	340	328	352	437
Salina .... Kan.	258	767	842	757	402	526	848	751	380	619	374	405	104	829	44	864	618	429	798	791
Salisbury .... Mo.	412	515	778	734	201	720	804	757	91	362	383	612	393	838	253	611	771	497	808	649
Sanborn .... Minn.	376	407	396	311	238	715	402	329	427	415	151	625	599	454	483	430	470	374	423	325
Sanish .... N.D.	793	817	368	428	768	962	336	247	942	871	543	933	1016	227	901	815	628	791	447	506
Sargent .... Neb.	102	750	766	681	408	475	773	675	530	641	298	389	406	754	308	816	538	314	723	716
Sauk Centre .... Minn.	517	392	234	181	359	857	254	199	537	443	279	766	740	391	625	409	546	515	419	228
Sault Ste Marie .... Mich.	955	273	685	739	664	1294	717	726	708	452	730	1203	1144	918	1004	184	1082	953	984	481
Sawyer .... Kan.	405	872	987	903	522	656	994	897	480	719	520	552	210	975	158	968	765	576	944	923
Schley .... Minn.	648	427	146	276	476	988	178	258	654	518	409	897	871	450	756	399	670	646	522	82
Scott City .... Kan.	461	959	1044	959	594	437	1051	953	572	811	576	486	244	1032	228	1055	726	632	1001	993
Scottsbluff .... Neb.	365	980	897	804	638	175	883	746	729	871	529	145	565	765	467	1046	222	544	735	946
Sedalia .... Colo.	490	1105	1095	1001	762	130	1081	943	832	996	554	180	361	963	505	1171	420	669	932	1071
Sedalia .... Mo	413	568	831	787	254	709	857	792	144	415	415	603	371	870	224	664	794	529	840	702
Seney .... Mich.	891	210	605	660	601	1231	637	646	644	388	667	1140	1080	838	941	120	1012	889	906	401
Severy .... Kan.	375	757	920	835	410	643	926	829	364	605	452	522	231	907	114	854	735	521	877	811
Sharon Springs ..... Kan.	355	965	982	897	608	317	988	891	623	851	514	366	140	969	287	1031	606	534	938	931
Shawano .... Wis.	690	38	553	544	403	1030	585	570	447	190	498	939	882	505	741	107	860	721	763	351
Shawnee .... Wyo.	479	1023	864	771	731	165	850	677	843	948	539	259	612	732	581	1056	190	575	702	940
Sheboygan .... Wis.	700	63	613	604	356	1040	645	631	397	129	522	949	835	817	696	159	905	745	822	411
Sheldon .... Ill.	653	275	802	760	304	986	828	781	⊕	⊕	533	881	717	962	578	372	925	738	931	601
Sheldon .... Iowa	267	471	464	379	216	607	471	392	395	415	43	516	490	480	375	505	429	265	449	404
Shenandoah .... Iowa	218	571	657	572	189	547	663	566	268	429	189	441	383	644	243	556	577	303	614	562
Sheridan Lake ...... Colo.	536	1034	1120	1035	669	361	1126	1029	647	886	652	411	319	1107	303	1131	651	707	1077	1069
Sidney .... Neb.	328	943	908	815	601	102	894	757	691	834	492	73	504	909	429	1009	233	507	746	909
Simpson (Johnson Co.) .... Ill.	733	552	995	953	446	1040	1021	974	⊕	⊕	686	933	711	1123	564	649	1081	818	1093	835
Sioux City .... Iowa	211	527	512	427	236	550	518	421	398	453	44	459	434	499	318	561	444	209	468	461
Sioux Falls .... S.D.	299	499	437	340	273	639	444	337	448	473	46	548	522	422	407	533	380	297	392	397
Sisseton .... S.D.	537	503	318	193	439	831	304	230	627	552	284	786	760	385	645	521	496	535	354	370
Smithboro .... Ill.	625	432	858	816	309	932	884	837	⊕	⊕	549	825	604	987	464	528	944	710	956	711
South Beloit .... Ill.	588	150	634	592	242	928	660	613	⊕	⊕	433	837	721	805	581	247	819	653	802	434
Sparta .... Ill.	637	490	908	866	359	944	934	887	⊕	⊕	599	837	607	1036	460	587	994	722	1006	769
Spencer .... Iowa	303	443	500	415	180	643	507	428	359	379	79	552	527	516	411	486	465	302	486	386
Spooner .... Wis.	570	253	353	379	379	909	385	394	510	328	345	818	786	586	659	247	697	568	599	149
Springfield .... Ill.	580	369	794	752	261	894	820	773	⊕	⊕	501	786	584	938	445	466	895	695	908	642
Stafford .... Kan.	360	841	942	858	479	568	949	852	449	688	475	507	165	930	113	937	720	531	899	880
Stanley .... N.D.	795	804	348	419	759	1023	317	214	934	856	544	993	1018	315	903	799	688	793	535	486
Stapleton .... Neb.	212	827	843	759	485	423	850	753	575	718	376	365	411	831	313	893	519	391	800	973
Sterling .... Colo.	343	958	948	855	616	106	934	796	707	849	507	33	460	816	443	1024	273	522	785	924
Stiles Jct. .... Wis.	722	28	576	575	419	1061	607	602	463	207	530	971	899	788	759	75	892	753	794	371
Stockton .... Kan.	271	838	867	782	481	539	874	776	477	707	399	418	217	854	247	819	630	442	824	817
Strasburg .... Colo.	477	1086	1003	1015	730	144	1094	957	779	973	635	194	299	977	443	1153	434	656	946	1053
Stratton .... Neb.	256	866	883	798	516	275	889	792	586	757	415	202	329	870	298	932	442	435	839	832
Streator .... Ill.	583	297	732	690	231	916	758	711	⊕	⊕	460	811	648	888	503	370	852	668	858	556
Streeter .... N.D.	582	630	304	241	547	810	290	134	721	687	332	780	805	257	690	648	475	580	327	411
Studley .... Kan.	330	923	956	871	558	388	963	865	536	775	488	398	157	944	200	1006	677	409	913	906
Sturgeon Bay .... Wis.	762	58	630	821	449	1102	662	648	492	236	570	1011	928	834	788	154	934	793	839	428
Sublette .... Kan.	479	971	1062	977	606	473	1069	971	580	819	340	523	261	1049	240	1067	763	650	1019	1007

⊕ For rates refer to I. F. A. Tariff No. I-1002. I. C. C. No. 757, R. G. Raasch, Agent.

EXHIBIT 6-C Tariff Page Showing Point-to-Point Rate Bases

"Red" Boone founded the Boone Shoe Company in St. Joseph, Missouri, during the 1930s. Red started to make moccasins for friends who had always admired the ones he had made for himself. Over time, the reputation of Boone shoes spread, and Red expanded his product line and hired additional employees. The real growth of the company took place during World War II. In 1942, almost as a joke, Red submitted a bid to the War Department to produce 100,000 pairs of combat boots. Much to his surprise, the contract was accepted, probably because Red

Tariff W-1000

CLASS RATES IN CENTS PER 100 POUNDS

RATE BASIS NUMBERS	400	300	250	200	175	150	125	110	100	97½	95	92½	90	87½	85	82½	80	77½	75	73½	72½	70	67½	66
5	328	246	205	164	144	123	103	90	82	80	78	76	74	72	70	68	66	64	62	60	59	57	55	54
10	356	267	223	178	156	134	111	98	89	87	85	82	80	78	76	73	71	69	67	65	65	62	60	59
15	384	288	240	192	168	144	120	106	96	94	91	89	86	84	82	79	77	74	72	71	70	67	65	63
20	408	306	255	204	179	153	128	112	102	99	97	94	92	89	87	84	82	79	77	75	74	71	69	67
25	420	315	263	210	184	158	131	116	105	102	100	97	95	92	89	87	84	81	79	77	76	74	71	69
30	448	336	280	224	196	168	140	123	112	109	106	104	101	98	95	92	90	87	84	82	81	78	76	74
35	460	345	288	230	201	173	144	127	115	112	109	106	104	101	98	95	92	89	86	85	83	81	78	76
40	480	360	300	240	210	180	150	132	120	117	114	111	108	105	102	99	96	93	90	88	87	84	81	79
45	492	369	308	246	215	185	154	135	123	120	117	114	111	108	105	102	99	95	92	90	89	86	83	81
50	504	378	315	252	221	189	158	139	126	123	120	117	113	110	107	104	101	98	95	93	91	88	85	83
55	524	393	328	262	229	197	164	144	131	128	124	121	118	115	111	108	105	102	98	96	95	92	88	86
60	536	402	335	268	235	201	168	147	134	131	127	124	121	117	114	111	107	104	101	98	97	94	90	88
65	556	417	348	278	243	209	174	153	139	136	132	129	125	122	118	115	111	108	104	102	101	97	94	92
70	564	423	353	282	247	212	176	155	141	137	134	130	127	123	120	116	113	109	106	104	102	99	95	93
75	572	429	358	286	250	215	179	157	143	139	136	132	129	125	122	118	114	111	107	105	104	100	97	94
80	588	441	368	294	257	221	184	162	147	143	140	136	132	129	125	121	118	114	110	108	107	103	99	97
85	600	450	375	300	263	225	188	165	150	146	143	139	135	131	128	124	120	116	113	110	109	105	101	99
90	616	462	385	308	270	231	193	169	154	150	146	142	139	135	131	127	123	119	116	113	112	108	104	102
95	624	468	390	312	273	234	195	172	156	152	148	144	140	137	133	129	125	121	117	115	113	109	105	103
100	636	477	398	318	278	239	199	175	159	155	151	147	143	139	135	131	127	123	119	117	115	111	107	105
110	656	492	410	328	287	246	205	180	164	160	156	152	148	144	139	135	131	127	123	121	119	115	111	108
120	676	507	423	338	296	254	211	186	169	165	161	156	152	148	144	139	135	131	127	124	123	118	114	112
130	700	525	438	350	306	263	219	193	175	171	166	162	158	153	149	144	140	136	131	129	127	123	118	116
140	720	540	450	360	315	270	225	198	180	176	171	167	162	158	153	149	144	140	135	132	131	127	123	119
150	740	555	463	370	324	278	231	204	185	180	176	171	167	162	157	153	148	143	139	134	134	130	125	122
160	756	567	473	378	331	284	236	208	189	184	180	175	170	165	161	156	151	146	142	139	137	132	128	125
170	784	588	490	392	343	294	245	216	196	191	186	181	176	172	167	162	157	152	147	144	142	137	132	129
180	796	597	498	398	348	299	249	219	199	194	189	184	179	174	169	164	159	154	149	146	144	139	134	131
190	812	609	508	406	355	305	254	223	203	198	193	188	183	178	173	167	162	157	152	149	147	142	137	134
200	828	621	518	414	362	311	259	228	207	202	197	191	186	181	176	171	166	160	155	152	150	145	140	137
210	852	639	533	426	373	320	266	234	213	208	202	197	192	186	181	176	170	165	160	157	154	149	144	141
220	868	651	543	434	380	326	271	239	217	212	206	201	195	190	184	179	174	168	163	159	157	152	146	143
230	884	663	553	442	387	332	276	243	221	215	210	204	199	193	188	182	177	171	166	162	160	155	149	146
240	900	675	563	450	394	338	281	248	225	219	214	208	203	197	191	186	180	174	169	165	163	158	152	149
250	940	705	588	470	411	353	294	259	235	229	223	217	212	206	200	194	188	182	176	173	170	165	159	155
280	964	723	603	482	422	362	301	265	241	235	229	223	217	211	205	199	193	187	181	177	175	169	163	159
300	996	747	623	498	436	374	311	274	249	243	237	230	224	218	212	205	199	193	187	183	181	174	168	164
320	1032	774	645	516	452	387	323	284	258	252	245	239	232	226	219	213	206	200	194	190	187	181	174	170
340	1060	795	663	530	464	398	331	292	265	258	252	245	239	232	225	219	212	205	199	195	192	186	179	175
360	1092	819	683	546	478	410	341	300	273	266	259	253	246	239	232	225	218	212	205	201	198	191	184	180
380	1116	837	698	558	488	419	349	307	279	272	265	258	251	244	237	230	223	216	209	205	202	195	188	184
400	1148	861	718	574	502	431	359	316	287	280	273	265	258	251	244	237	230	222	215	211	208	201	194	189
420	1180	885	738	590	516	443	369	325	295	288	280	273	266	258	251	243	236	229	221	217	214	207	199	193
440	1204	903	753	602	527	452	376	331	301	293	286	278	271	263	256	248	241	233	226	221	218	211	203	199
460	1228	921	768	614	537	461	384	338	307	299	292	284	276	269	261	253	246	238	230	226	223	215	207	203
480	1260	945	788	630	551	473	394	347	315	307	299	291	284	276	268	260	252	244	236	232	228	221	213	208
500	1288	966	805	644	564	483	403	354	322	314	306	298	290	282	274	266	258	250	242	237	233	225	217	213
520	1308	981	818	654	572	491	409	360	327	319	311	302	294	286	278	270	262	253	245	240	237	229	221	216
540	1344	1008	840	672	588	504	420	370	336	328	319	311	302	294	286	278	270	260	252	247	244	235	227	222
560	1368	1026	855	684	599	513	428	376	342	333	325	316	308	299	291	282	274	265	257	251	248	239	231	226
580	1396	1047	873	698	611	524	436	384	349	340	332	323	314	305	297	288	279	270	262	257	253	244	236	230
600	1420	1065	888	710	621	533	444	391	355	346	337	328	320	311	302	293	284	275	266	261	257	249	240	234
620	1448	1086	905	724	634	543	453	398	362	353	344	335	326	317	308	299	290	281	272	266	262	253	244	239
640	1476	1107	923	738	646	554	461	406	369	360	351	341	332	323	314	304	295	286	277	271	268	258	249	244
660	1508	1131	943	754	660	566	471	415	377	368	358	349	339	330	320	311	302	292	283	277	273	264	254	249
680	1532	1149	958	766	670	575	479	421	383	373	364	354	345	335	326	316	306	297	287	282	278	268	259	253
700	1560	1170	975	780	683	585	488	429	390	380	371	361	351	341	332	322	312	302	293	287	283	273	263	257
720	1592	1194	995	796	697	597	498	438	398	388	378	368	358	348	338	328	318	308	299	293	289	279	269	263
740	1616	1212	1010	808	707	606	505	444	404	394	384	374	364	354	343	333	323	313	303	297	293	283	273	267
760	1640	1230	1025	820	718	615	513	451	410	400	390	379	369	359	349	338	328	318	308	301	297	287	277	271
780	1672	1254	1045	832	732	627	523	460	418	408	397	387	376	366	355	345	334	324	314	307	303	293	282	276
800	1700	1275	1063	850	744	638	531	468	425	414	404	393	383	372	361	351	340	329	319	312	308	298	287	281
825	1724	1293	1078	862	754	647	539	474	431	420	409	399	388	377	366	356	345	333	323	317	312	302	291	284
850	1756	1317	1098	878	768	659	549	483	439	428	417	406	395	384	373	362	351	340	329	323	318	307	296	290
875	1784	1338	1115	892	781	669	558	491	446	435	424	413	401	390	379	368	357	346	335	328	323	312	301	294
900	1812	1359	1133	906	793	680	566	498	453	442	430	419	408	396	385	374	362	351	340	333	328	317	306	299
925	1840	1380	1150	920	805	690	575	506	460	449	437	426	414	403	391	380	368	357	345	338	334	322	311	304

EXHIBIT 6-D   Tariff Page Showing Application of Rate Bases to Charges

In this table interpolation is not used. Instead, if you cannot find the exact number in the left-hand column, use the next higher printed value.

noted in the bid that a sufficient noncombat labor force (females and retirees) to produce boots existed in the area.

The main production input, leather, was easily obtained at the nearby Kansas City stockyards. After the war, the Boone Company expanded its production of civilian shoes and related products and also continued to supply the military with all types of leather footwear. Red Boone's son, Barry, was in charge of all marketing and distribution activities.

Larry Gitman functioned as the firm's warehouse, purchasing, and traffic manager. After two years as a management trainee with a large motor carrier, Larry had accepted the position at Boone Shoe Company. Because of the firm's steady annual growth rate of 15 percent, Barry Boone had authorized Larry to hire an assistant.

Steve Knapp, just out of high school, was working part time from 1:00 to 6:00 P.M. and also attending the local community college. Steve had progressed so rapidly that Larry felt comfortable taking a three-week vacation, his first extended vacation in some years.

During Larry's vacation, Steve assumed Larry's responsibilities. As Steve sat in his office, the intercom buzzed, and Barry asked Steve to pick up line 3 and take part in the conversation. The call was from Tom Cook, Boone's salesman for Minnesota and Wisconsin. Tom stated, "I'm calling from the buying office of Lawson Department Stores in Green Bay. Although they're currently overstocked in shoes, they are interested in buying a sizable quantity of our Light Stride arch-support insoles. They plan on giving them away with their shoes in order to stimulate shoe sales. They want to buy FOB destination. I need to know in the next few minutes the cost of sending 17,000 pounds of the arch supports from St. Joseph to Green Bay."

Steve asked, "Will they accept a rail shipment?"

Tom replied, "The buyer said he expected the shipment to come via rail."

Barry came on the line and asked, "Steve, can you look up this info for Tom?"

Steve said, "No problem. I'll call you back with the answer in 15 minutes or less." ■

QUESTIONS

1. Assume there are no commodity or exception rates in effect for this shipment. Using Exhibits 6-B, 6-C, and 6-D, calculate the applicable charge.
2. Steve remembered that he had heard Larry speak of shipping "wind." This involved paying the CL minimum weight in order to receive the CL rate, even if the shipment actually weighed less than the carload minimum weight. Should this technique be used for the shipment? Why or why not?
3. The buyer will pay on receipt of the shipment, which is valued at $21,000 plus any transportation charges. Boone Shoe Company borrows money from the bank regularly on an open line of credit and is currently paying interest on its debt at the rate of 15 percent per year. If rail LCL service is used, delivery time to Green Bay will be about 10 days. If rail CL service is used, delivery time will be six days. What is the additional advantage to Boone Shoe Company if it chooses to use CL service?

4. (This is a continuation of question 3.) Boone Shoe Company also owns several large trucks, although Steve is uncertain whether they are available for immediate use. He knows that they could make the delivery to Green Bay in two days. He checks the highway distance from St. Joseph to Green Bay and finds that it is 588 miles. Larry had once told Steve that it cost the company 85 cents per mile to operate its highway trucks. Do you think that a truck should be used if it is available? Why?
5. (This is a continuation of questions 2 and 3.) Another alternative is to make the shipment by rail from Boone's St. Louis warehouse. Rail delivery time will be four days. What price should Tom Cook be told to quote to Lawson's?
6. Boone Shoe Company often sells large quantities—from 10,000 up to 30,000 pounds—of arch-support insoles on an FOB-delivered basis. After referring to Exhibit 6-B, do you think there is a minimum weight (in this 10,000- to 30,000-pound range) that customers should be encouraged to order? If so, what is it?

CHAPTER
7
TRANSPORTATION MANAGEMENT

A train carrying intermodal containers in the Pacific Northwest. Each bloc consists of five joined, articulated cars, each carrying two containers.
Source: Don Wilson, Port of Seattle.

Key Terms

- Amodal shipper
- Bill of lading
- Class rate system
- Commodity rate
- Demurrage
- Density
- Detention
- Diversion
- Documentation
- Expediting

- Freight bill
- Freight claims
- Hazardous material
- Reconsignment
- Routing
- Routing guide
- Stowability
- Tracing
- Transportation management
- Weight break

Learning Objectives

- To learn about contemporary transportation management
- To understand how rates are determined
- To learn about modal and carrier selection
- To distinguish among various transportation documents
- To understand select activities associated with making and receiving shipments

The transportation manager's job is much different today than when the first edition of this text was published in the late 1970s, in part because of globalization and changes in regulation. With respect to globalization, consider that in the late 1970s, the People's Republic of China (China) had just begun to emerge from the Cultural Revolution, a movement that had severely restricted the country's economic development. Today, by contrast, China has the second-largest economy in the world (based on gross domestic product) and is a key source of manufactured products for many countries. The transportation requirements associated with a shipment of, say, toys from Shanghai, China, to Des Moines, Iowa, are noticeably different than those for a shipment of toys from Cleveland, Ohio, to Des Moines.

As for changes in regulation, Chapter 6 pointed out that a reduction of economic regulation began in the late 1970s and with it came greater options in terms of both pricing and service. These pricing and service options have meant that transportation managers have morphed from a reactive to a proactive focus; rather than simply accepting the available pricing and service packages that were established by regulation (reactive), today's transportation manager can play an active role (proactive) in blending the appropriate pricing and service packages for an organization.

For our purposes, **transportation management** will refer to the buying and controlling of transportation services by either a shipper or consignee.[1] Today more than ever before, organizations are concerned about transportation management because transportation represents a major expense item. In general terms, freight transportation accounts for approximately 6 percent of U.S. gross domestic product. Moreover, transportation is the most costly logistics activity for many organizations, and as pointed out in Chapter 6, transportation is pivotal to the successful operation of any supply chain.

---

[1]John J. Coyle, Edward J. Bardi, and Robert A. Novack, *Transportation,* 6th ed. (Mason, OH: South-Western, 2006).

Similar to Chapter 6, the discussion in this chapter will be approached from the perspective of the transportation manager in the United States. Again, it's important for readers to understand that a particular country's transportation system, along with the degree of government involvement in transportation, will influence the nature of transportation management in that country.

Although the majority of this chapter will focus on several of the transportation manager's key responsibilities, it should be pointed out that transportation managers are also involved with many other operations of the firm. They can assist marketing by quoting freight rates for salespeople, suggesting quantity discounts that can be based on transportation savings, and selecting carriers and routes for reliable delivery of products. Transportation managers can help manufacturing by advising on packaging and materials handling and making certain that an adequate supply of transportation is available when it is needed. Transportation managers can aid the outbound shipping process by providing simplified shipping or routing guides, drawing up transportation documents, and encouraging shipment consolidations. Finally, they can help purchasing by advising about methods to control the costs and quality of inbound deliveries and by tracing and expediting lost or delayed shipments of important inputs.

RATE (PRICING) CONSIDERATIONS

Rate Determination

Studies have indicated that transportation managers can spend up to one-third of their time dealing with rate (pricing) considerations.[2] At one time, all rates appeared in tariffs (a book that contained published freight rates), and it wasn't uncommon to have to refer to multiple tariffs to find the applicable rate. Although most rates today are negotiated between shippers and carriers, many of these negotiated rates are based on long-standing freight rate determination practices. More specifically, transportation rates are based on three primary factors—product, weight, and distance—which will be discussed next:

- Relationships between *different products,* in terms of their handling characteristics, for example, the difference between carrying 2,000 pounds of ballpoint pens and 2,000 pounds of live chickens
- Relationships between shipments of *different weights,* for example, shipments of 10 pounds each versus shipments of 1,000 pounds each versus shipments of 100,000 pounds each
- Relationships between *different distances* the products are carried, for example, from Boston, Massachusetts, to Albany, New York, versus from Atlanta, Georgia, to Spokane, Washington

Rate making has to define all three relations in numeric form and then has to devise methods of tying those numbers into a rate of so many cents per hundredweight (cwt) for a specific haul. The three relationships just mentioned are of continual importance to the transportation manager because if they can be altered, the total transportation charges will be altered.

One approach to rate making is to determine one specific rate for every possible combination of product, weight, and distance—in other words, a **commodity rate.** Although a commodity rate is very good for dealing with demand-specific situations, the number of commodity rates quickly becomes overwhelming (and potentially counterproductive) when you consider how many different products, weights, and distances exist. For example, because there are over 30,000 "important" shipping and receiving points in the United States, in the commodity rate

---

[2]Donald F. Wood and Richard S. Nelson, "Industrial Transportation Management: What's New?" *Transportation Journal* 39, no. 2 (1999): 26–30.

system there would need to be separate rates for all possible combinations of shipping and receiving points—a number that is in the trillions of trillions![3]

When you consider that the transportation rate structure dates to the time of economic regulation in the late 1800s—a time when "office automation" *might* have meant a manual typewriter—it becomes clear that the transportation community needed a way to simplify rate determination. This was accomplished through the **class rate system,** which simplified each of the three primary rate factors—product, weight, and distance. One widely used system for simplifying the number of products is the National Motor Freight Classification (NMFC), which has 18 separate ratings, or classes, from 500 to 35[4]; the higher the rating, the greater the relative charge for transporting the commodity. Classification numbers are very important because they are code words that describe cargo in a manner that carriers and shippers understand, and classification descriptions also specify the packaging that must be used and that carriers require. Figure 7-1 shows a page of the National Motor Freight Classification; note the detail. *NOI* stands for "not otherwise indexed by number" (i.e., one cannot find a definition that fits more closely). Packages are referred to by number; they are described in great detail in the classification document.

Four factors are used to determine a product's freight classification, namely, *density, stowability, ease of handling,* and *liability to damage and theft.* **Density,** which refers to how heavy a product is in relation to its size, is viewed as the primary factor for setting a product's classification, in part because of the opportunity costs associated with it. That is, a product with low density (i.e., low weight per cubic foot), such as foam rubber, can easily fill a vehicle's usable capacity (cubing out) before the reaching the maximum weight (weighing out). As a result, low-density products are assigned a higher classification; for example, at the time of this book's publication, products with densities of less than one pound per cubic foot are assigned to Class 500.[5]

Stowability refers to how easy the commodity is to pack into a load, and possible considerations involve the commodity's ability to be loaded with hazardous materials and ability to load freight on top of the commodity. Ease or difficulty of handling refers to challenges to handling that might be presented by a commodity's size, weight, and so on. Finally, the liability for loss and damage considers, among others, a commodity's propensity to damage other freight, its perishability, and its value.[6]

Just as the freight classification is used to simplify the number of commodities, distances are simplified in terms of a rate basis number; higher rate basis numbers reflect greater distances between two points. Increasingly, computers can make these calculations utilizing the zip codes of the shipment's origin and destination. With the commodity rating and the rate bases number, the specific rate per hundred pounds can be located in another tariff. This tariff simplifies with respect to weight in the sense that rates for different weight groups (e.g., less than 500 pounds; 500–999 pounds; 1,000–1,999 pounds) will be presented; the rate for shipments weighing less than 500 pounds will be higher than that for shipments between 500–999 pounds, and so on.

Finally, to establish the specific cost of moving commodity A between city B and city C, one must use the following formula:

Weight (in hundred-pound units) × rate (per hundred pounds) = transportation charge

By way of illustration, suppose that a 450-pound shipment is assigned a rate of $40.00 per hundredweight. The applicable transportation charges would be $180 (4.5 hundredweights times $40.00 per hundredweight).

---

[3]Coyle, Bardi, and Novack, *Transportation.*
[4]*www.nmfta.org.*
[5]Ibid.
[6]Ibid.

ITEM	ARTICLES	CLASS
86700	**GLASS:** subject to item 86500	
	Glass, flat, see Note, item 86736, NOI:	
86720	Bent, NOI, in boxes or crates:	
Sub 1	220 united inches or less; when in shipments weighing less than 30,000 pounds, see Note, item 86512 .	
Sub 2	Exceeding 220 united inches but not exceeding 15 feet in length nor 9 feet in breadth; when in shipments weighing less than 24,000 pounds, see Note, item 86512	85
Sub 3	Exceeding 15 feet in length or 9 feet in breadth; when in shipments weighing less than 24,000 pounds, see Note, item 86512	100
86730	Not bent, see Note, item 86731, in boxes, crates or Packages 195, 198, 235, 785, 2008, 2025, 2147, 2149, 2160, 2239, 2245, 2281 or 2497; when in shipments weighing less than 40,000 pounds, see Note, item 86512:	250
Sub 1	220 united inches or less, see Note, item 86737	65
Sub 2	Exceeding 220 united inches but not exceeding 15 feet in length nor 9 feet in breadth	100
Sub 3	Exceeding 15 feet in length or 9 feet in breadth	200
86731	NOTE—Flat glass, not bent, may also be cut to size, edges beveled or ground, or holes cut or drilled.	
86736	NOTE—The term 'flat' applies to glass known as sheet, plate, polished prism, rolled, window or float glass, whether or not polished, laminated, colored, opalescent, opaque, chipped, decorated, wired, etched, figured, acid dipped, ground, sandblasted, metalized (sprayed with atomized metal while glass is hot) or tempered, but not when silvered for mirrors, nor flashed, nor framed or leaded (set in or framed by lead or other metal).	
86737	NOTE—Provisions will also apply on shipments weighing 40,000 pounds or more when glass is shipped on its flat surface in wooden boxes on pallets.	
86750	**Glass,** leaded, see Note, item 86752; when in shipments weighing less than 24,000 pounds, see Note, item 86512:	
Sub 1	With landscape, pictorial or religious designs, packed in boxes	200
Sub 2	With curved, angled or straight line patterns, or with designs other than landscape, pictorial or religious, in boxes	100
86752	NOTE—The term 'leaded glass' means glass either colored or clear, set in lead or in other metal.	
86770	**Glass,** microscopical slide or cover, see Note, item 86771, in boxes; when in shipments weighing less than 36,000 pounds, see Note, item 86512	70
86771	NOTE—Does not apply on microscope slides or slide cover glasses. Applies only on the glass from which these articles are manufactured.	
86830	**Glass,** rolled, overlaid with aluminum strips with metal terminals attached, in boxes or crates; when in shipments weighing less than 30,000 pounds, see Note, item 86512	77.5
86840	**Glass,** rolled, overlaid with aluminum strips, NOI, in boxes or crates; when in shipments weighing less than 36,000 pounds, see Note, item 86512	70
86900	**Glass,** silvered for mirrors, not framed, nor backed nor equipped with hangers or fastening devices:	
Sub 1	Shock (window glass, silvered), in boxes, see Note, item 86902; when in shipments weighing less than 30,000 pounds, see Note, item 86512	85
Sub 2	Other than shock glass, in packages shown:	
Sub 3	Bent; when in shipments weighing less than 24,000 pounds, see Note, item 86512:	
Sub 4	Not exceeding 15 feet in length nor 9 feet in breadth, in boxes	100
Sub 5	Exceeding 15 feet in length or 9 feet in breadth, in boxes	250
Sub 6	Not bent, see Package 785:	
Sub 7	120 united inches or less, in boxes, crates or Packages 198 or 235; when in shipments weighing less than 30,000 pounds, see Note, item 86512	70
Sub 8	Exceeding 120 united inches but not exceeding 15 feet in length or 9 feet in breadth; when in shipments weighing less than 40,000 pounds, see Note, item 86512	100
Sub 9	Exceeding 15 feet in length or 9 feet in breadth, in boxes or crates; when in shipments weighing less than 40,000 pounds, see Note, item 86512	200
86902	NOTE—Glass, silvered for mirrors, which has been framed or backed, or equipped with hangers or fastening devices, is subject to the classes for mirrors, NOI.	
86940	**Glass,** window, other than plate, with metal edging other than sash or frames, in boxes; when in shipments weighing less than 30,000 pounds, see Note, item 86512	77.5
86960	**Glazing Units,** glass, not in sash, see Note, item 86966, in boxes, crates or Packages 2149 or 2281; when in shipments weighing less than 30,000 pounds, see Note, item 86512	70
86966	NOTE—Applies on units consisting of sheets of glass separated by air or vacuum, sealed at all edges with same or other materials.	
87100	**Glass Factory Flattening Stones, Floats, Gathering Rings or Pot Rings or Glasshouse Pots,** clay; in boxes, crates, drums or on skids; or loose when weighing each 2,500 pounds or more packed in packing material and securely braced	85
87500	**GLASSWARE GROUP:** Articles consist of Glassware or Glass Articles, see Note, item 87512, as described in items subject to this grouping.	
87512	NOTE—All articles of glassware which are plated, mounted or trimmed with gold or silver will be subject to the provisions provided for glassware, gold or silver deposit, gold or silver mounted or gold or silver trimmed.	
87520	**Ampoules (Ampuls),** in boxes, drums or Package 2362	100
87540	**Aquariums or Terrariums,** capacity over ½ gallon, see Note, item 87552, in boxes, crates or drums:	
Sub 1	Each in individual fibre box, two or more smaller sizes nested within one larger.	85
Sub 2	NOI	150
87550	**Aquariums or Terrariums,** NOI, capacity ½ gallon or less, see Note, item 87552, in boxes, crates or drums	100
87552	NOTE—Applies only on aquariums or terrariums constructed with metal or plastic frames.	
87560	**Aquariums or Terrariums,** glass, with plastic frames, disassembled into panels, in boxes	70
87570	**Ballotini (Decorative Glass Globules),** in boxes.	85
87590	**Balls,** lightning rod, in boxes or drums.	85

FIGURE 7-1 Page from National Motor Freight Classification

Source: Reprinted from the National Motor Freight Classification © ATA 2002

A commodity's freight classification is established by the National Classification Committee, which consists of up to 100 carriers representing all 50 U.S. states, the District of Columbia, Canada, and Mexico. There is often a natural tension between shippers and carriers with respect to a product's classification; shippers tend to prefer a lower classification number (which translates into a lower rate), whereas carriers tend to prefer a higher classification number. Transportation managers can appeal a commodity's classification, and Figure 7-2 shows an excerpt from the National Motor Freight Classification Committee's hearing docket concerning a proposal to adopt new classifications for spark plugs. The present classification is described first in the figure, and then the proposal is shown. Figure 7-3 shows an applicant's completed worksheet for submission to the classification committee.

FIGURE 7-2   Motor Carrier Classification Docket Proposal for Changing the Classification of Spark Plugs

---

PROPOSED

PRESENT CLASSIFICATION: (Show specific NMFC item number and description under which commodity is now being classified.)

ITEM NO.	DESCRIPTION	LTL	TL	MW
	PRESENT			
177080	**Spark Plugs,** NOI, in boxes:			
Sub 1	Card mounted, blister packed or skin packed	100	55	24
Sub 2	Other than card mounted, blister packed or skin packed	85	45	30

PROPOSED AMENDMENTS: (Show description, classes and MW exactly as you propose them to be established in the Classification.)

ITEM NO.	DESCRIPTION	LTL	TL	MW
	PROPOSED			
177080	**Spark Plugs,** NOI, in boxes:			
Sub 1	Card mounted, blister packed or skin packed	100	55	24
Sub 2	Other than card mounted, blister packed or skin packed :			
>Sub 3	Density less than 30 pounds per cubic foot; or actual value exceeding $6.00 per pound; or where no density or value is shown at time of shipment	85	45	30
>Sub 4	Density in pounds per cubic foot of 30 or greater, and actual value not exceeding $6.00 per pound, see Note, item NEW	70	37.5	36
NEW	NOTE -- Shipper must certify on shipping orders and bills of lading at time of shipment that density is 30 pounds or greater per cubic foot and that the actual value per pound does not exceed $6.00.			

JUSTIFICATION: Due to the density, value per pound and ease of handling of the involved commodities, the proposed changes are warranted.

_____

_____

If you have any questions regarding the proper execution of these forms or require technical assistance please contact our staff at (703) 838-1869.

Source: Permission to reproduce this material has been granted by the National Motor Freight Traffic Association, Inc.

TRANSPORTATION CHARACTERISTICS

I. **DENSITY:** (Please base your calculations on the exterior dimensions and the shipping weight of the commodity as packaged for shipment.)

Model	Description of Package	Length	Width	Height	Weight	Density*
Spark	packaged individually,	38"	38"	42"	1280 #	36.5
plugs	then packaged into cartons					
(boxed)	of 10, then packaged into					
	cartons of 100. Shipped					
	in master cartons on skids.					

*To determine the density (pounds per cubic foot), multiply the three dimensions of the article as packed for shipment. If the result is in cubic inches, divide by 1728 to convert to cubic feet. Then divide the weight by the cubic feet. To determine the cubic feet of space occupied by a drum, pail, or other cylindrical container, square the greatest diameter and multiply that result by the height or length. If the package is of irregular shape, use the greatest dimensions, including all projections.

II. **LIABILITY**

1) Claim value per package (Please match the models with those reported under **DENSITY**)

Model	Description of Package	Weight	Dollar Amount	Value Per Pound
Spark	packaged individually,	1280 #	$7200	$5.63
plugs	then packaged into cartons			
(boxed)	of 10, then packaged into			
	cartons of 100. Shipped			
	in master cartons on skids.			

2) Does the commodity require temperature control?   NO

3) Is the commodity subject to U.S. Department of Transportation Regulations governing hazardous materials? Yes ___ No XX If yes, what HMT commodity description and label are required?

4) Does commodity have protruding edges?   NO

5) Is commodity liquid NO dry NO paste NO

FIGURE 7-3   Worksheet for Motor Carrier Classification Docket Proposal for Changing the Classification of Spark Plugs

Source: Permission to reproduce this material has been granted by the National Motor Freight Traffic Association, Inc.

Note that Figure 7-2 contains the notations "LTL," "TL," and "MW," and each has a number underneath it. If we look at the first listing in Figure 7-2, Item 177080 Sub 1, we see the number 100 associated with LTL, the number 55 associated with TL, and the number 24 associated with MW. This indicates that the product is Class 100 for less-than-truckload (LTL) shipments and Class 55 for truckload (TL) shipments. "MW" stands for minimum weight, and the "24" indicates that the truckload rate can be applied at a shipment weight of 24,000 pounds.

The fact that the LTL classification number is higher than the TL classification number means that the LTL rate will be higher than the corresponding TL rate. When combined with a minimum weight requirement, this suggests that it is possible to reduce transportation costs by sending an LTL shipment as if it met the minimum requirement for a truckload rate. This illustrates the **weight break** concept, that is, the shipment size that equates transportation charges for different rates and weight groups. Although typically applied to the LTL and TL trade-off, the weight break concept can be applied whenever rates differ by volume and a minimum weight is specified for the higher volume classification.

The formula for calculating the weight break is as follows:

Higher volume rate × minimum weight = lower volume rate × weight break

Suppose, for example, that the LTL rate is $1.25 per cwt (hundredweight), the TL rate is $.80 per cwt, and the TL minimum is 25,000 pounds. The weight break is

$$\$.80 \text{ per cwt} \times 250 \text{ cwt} = \$1.25 \text{ per cwt} \times \text{weight break}$$
$$\$200 = \$1.25 \text{ per cwt} \times \text{weight break}$$
$$160 \text{ cwt} = \text{weight break}$$

In other words, the transportation costs ($200) for the LTL and TL rates are equal at 160 cwt, or 16,000 pounds. As such, if the actual shipment weight is less than 16,000 pounds, then the LTL rate should be applied, while shipments weighing between 16,000 and 24,999 pounds should be sent at the TL weight of 25,000 pounds.

Although the freight classification system might appear to be arcane and ill-suited to today's highly computerized world, over 1,100 motor carriers, ranging from nationwide truckers to local delivery companies, currently use the National Motor Freight Classification. Moreover, even though today's transportation pricing system is much different than existed under economic regulation, the NMFC can provide a starting point for price negotiations between carriers and shippers.[7]

The changes in economic regulation discussed in Chapter 6 have had a profound impact on rate determination. Tariff requirements have been greatly relaxed, if not eliminated altogether; as a result, carriers, users, and transportation specialists can exchange pricing data via electronic means, including electronic data interchange (EDI) and e-mail. In many cases, transportation rates are now available on carrier Web sites, and they all work about the same way: One enters in the origin and destination zip codes, the weight and classification of each shipment, any supplemental services needed (these include inside delivery and advanced notification, among others), and whatever discount the carrier has awarded the shipper. After entering the appropriate information, the user receives an estimate of the transportation costs for the shipments in question.

---

[7]Ibid.

TABLE 7-1	Representative Rate and Service Items in the Carrier—Shipper Negotiation Process	
Adjustment to rates	Arbitration	Articles and commodities covered
Audit rights	Basis for charges	Billing procedures
Carrier equipment and drivers	Carrier insurance	Carrier notification requirements
Detention time	Duration of agreement	Estimated transportation volume
How loss and damage claims are handled	Lead times	Pallet loading
Proof of delivery		
	Renegotiation and reopening of contract	Schedule of rates and charges
Termination of agreement	Transportation service level	Waiver of terms

Rate and Service Negotiations

As pointed out earlier in the chapter, the contemporary transportation manager is much less constrained by rate and service regulations and thus has the opportunity to assume a proactive role in rate and service negotiations. Today's transportation manager can craft rate and service packages that best meet an organization's logistical needs, and these rate and service packages can conceivably vary from product to product, location to location, or customer to customer.

The rate and service flexibility afforded by economic deregulation allows transportation managers to take advantage of trade-offs between price and service. For example, two-day delivery of product should be cheaper than next-day delivery of product. These price and service trade-offs are limited only by the transportation manager's creativity and ingenuity. Consider the following two examples from the railroad industry. In one case, the shipping organization agreed to pay the railroad a premium for each railcar that was delivered on a precise, previously agreed on schedule. In the second case, an organization agreed to ship six million pounds of intermodal freight each year between Houston and Chicago. The shipper agreed to pay the railroad an additional $75 per trailer when at least 90 percent of the trailers completed the rail movement within 96 hours. Although these two examples illustrate situations where monetary premiums were paid for meeting predetermined service standards, the rate and service negotiations can also include *monetary penalties* for failure to achieve predetermined service standards.

It is not possible to present a comprehensive list of all possible rate and service items that might by negotiated by shippers and carriers. However, Table 7-1 contains a representative list of items that might be used in the negotiation process.

MODAL AND CARRIER SELECTION

Transportation managers have long been responsible for both modal and carrier selection, and research suggests that this activity accounts for between 10 and 15 percent of the transportation manager's time.[8] Conceptually, modal and carrier selection is a two-step process where the transportation manager first determines the appropriate mode, or modes, to use and then selects a particular carrier, or carriers, within the chosen mode(s). At a minimum, an understanding of the modal characteristics presented in Chapter 6 would be helpful in the modal selection process.

---

[8]Wood and Nelson, "Industrial Transportation Management."

Unfortunately, the carrier selection procedure appears to be less straightforward than that for modal selection, in part because although there are but five modes, there may be (1) a number of different types of carriers and (2) a plethora of individual carriers within the individual modes. For example, recent research involving truckload motor carriers found "action and follow-up on service complaints" to be the most important selection factor for intermodal shippers, compared to the ninth most important factor among tank truck shippers.[9]

Carrier selection is also less straightforward due to a lack of agreement on the number of relevant factors that might be used in carrier selection. For example, the number of carrier selection factors evaluated in academic research studies has ranged from less than 10 to over 150. As was the case with rate and service negotiation, it's not possible to provide a comprehensive of all possible factors that might be used in the carrier selection decision. Table 7-2 contains a list of 20 characteristics that were evaluated in a recent carrier selection study.

Modal and carrier selection has become even murkier since the mid-1990s with the rise in what we'll call the **amodal shipper.** An amodal shipper refers to a transportation manager who purchases a prespecified level of transportation service (e.g., two-day delivery for a particular price) and is indifferent to the mode(s) and/or carrier(s) used to provide the actual transportation service. Indeed, research by a leading transportation research firm indicates that shippers are exhibiting more interest in transportation metrics such as transit time and transit time dependability than in transportation modes. One reason for the growth of amodalism is that non-asset-based third-party logistics companies have the ability to develop multimodal solutions to a client's transportation problems.[10] Amodalism is also aided by companies such as UPS and FedEx that own companies that provide different types of transportation services (e.g., air, expedited, LTL, parcel).

TABLE 7-2 Possible Carrier Selection Characteristics	
Characteristic	*Characteristic*
Consistent dependable transit times	Billing accuracy
Competitive pricing	Action and follow-up on service complaints
Communication of service disruptions	Equipment availability
Knowledge and problem-solving skills of contact personnel	Quality of drivers
General reputation for quality and integrity	Financial stability
Proactive monitoring of delivery appointments	Ability to provide expedited service
Ability to handle all transportation needs	Satellite tracing and communications
Traditional EDI capabilities	Internet tracking
Internet POD	Ability to implement fuel surcharge
Internet freight posting services	Internet pricing

Source: John L. Kent and Carlo D. Smith, "Carrier Selection Criteria: Differences Among Truckload Motor Carrier Offerings," *Journal of Transportation Management* 16, no. 2 (2005): 48–59.

---

[9]John L. Kent and Carlo D. Smith, "Carrier Selection Criteria: Differences Among Truckload Motor Carriers, *Journal of Transportation Management* 16, no. 2 (2005): 48–59.

[10]"Transport Buying Shifts from Mode to Metrics," *Transportation and Distribution*, January 2006, 34–35.

DOCUMENTATION

You might recall that the definition of logistics presented in Chapter 1 refers to the *management of information*. The documents associated with transportation shipments, or **documentation,** are one important source of logistics information. Transportation documentation serves both a practical function (e.g., what, where, and how much is being transported) as well as potentially providing legal recourse if something goes awry. Our discussion here will focus on the documents associated with domestic shipments; the documentation for international shipments is presented in Chapter 12.

The transportation department is responsible for completing all the documents needed to transport the firm's products. Today, many carriers provide software that enables the shipper to use computers to generate all the commonly used documents. Some shippers also have their own order processing software that is capable of generating transportation documents.

Bill of Lading

The most important single transportation document is the bill of lading, which is the basic operating document in the industry. The **bill of lading** functions as a delivery receipt when products are tendered to carriers. On receipt of the freight, the carrier signs the bill of lading and gives the original to the shipper. The signed original of the bill of lading is the shipper's legal proof that the carrier received the freight. The bill of lading is a binding contract, specifying the duties and obligations of both carrier and shipper. The bill of lading contract for surface carriers is basically standardized by law and greatly simplifies the transportation manager's job because it specifies exactly the duties of the shipper and carrier.

There are two types of bills of lading: the straight bill of lading and the order bill of lading. On a *straight bill of lading,* which is printed on white paper, the name of the consignee is stated in the appropriate place, and the carrier is under a strict legal obligation to deliver the freight to the named consignee and to no one else. Ownership of the goods is neither stated nor implied. On the *order bill of lading,* which is printed on yellow paper, the name of the consignee is not specified. For example, assume that a lumber company in Seattle has loaded a boxcar of plywood that it has not yet sold. It would use an order bill and tender the shipment to the Burlington Northern Railroad, which would start the car moving toward Chicago. Once a buyer for the plywood is found, the shipper would send the original copy of the order bill by mail to a bank near the buyer and would also tell the buyer which bank had possession of the order bill. The buyer would go to the bank and pay for the plywood, and the bank would give the original copy to the buyer. The buyer would take it to the railroad, and the railroad would deliver the carload of plywood. Order bills can also be used when faced with slow-paying customers because the order bill guarantees that the customer must pay for the products prior to receipt.

An additional classification for bills of lading is the specific form: long, short, or preprinted. The *long-form bill of lading,* which may be either an order or straight bill, contains the standard information on the face of the bill (see Figure 7-4), and on the reverse side it contains the entire contract between carrier and shipper. The reverse side is printed in extremely small print. Because of the difficulty of reading the long-form contract and the printing costs of including the contract on all bills, in 1949 the railroads and motor carriers adopted the short-form bill of lading. The short form has the following statement on its face: "Every service to be performed hereunder shall be subject to all the terms and conditions of the Uniform Domestic Straight Bill of Lading."

Another kind of bill of lading—which may be long, short, order, or straight—is preprinted. In theory, the bill of lading is prepared and issued by the carrier. In fact, however, most shippers buy their bills of lading and then have them preprinted with a list of the products they regularly

UNIFORM FREIGHT CLASSIFICATION 7

(Uniform Domestic Straight Bill of Lading, adopted by Carriers in Official and Western Classification
territories, March 15, 1922, as amended August 1, 1930, and June 15, 1941.)

UNIFORM STRAIGHT BILL OF LADING

Original—Not Negotiable

Shipper's No............

(To be Printed on "White" Paper)

Agent's No.............

Company

RECEIVED, subject to the classifications and tariffs in effect on the date of the issue of this Bill of Lading,

at.., 19...

from..

the property described below, in apparent good order, except as noted (contents and condition of contents of packages unknown), marked, consigned, and destined as indicated below, which said company (the word company being understood throughout this contract as meaning any person or corporation in possession of the property under the contract) agrees to carry to its usual place of delivery at said destination, if on its own road or its own water line, otherwise to deliver to another carrier on the route to said destination. It is mutually agreed, as to each carrier of all or any of said property over all or any portion of said route to destination, and as to each party at any time interested in all or any of said property, that every service to be performed hereunder shall be subject to all the conditions not prohibited by law, whether printed or written, herein contained, including the conditions on back hereof, which are hereby agreed to by the shipper and accepted for himself and his assigns.

(Mail or street address of consignee—For purposes of notification only.)

Consigned to..

Destination..State of.......................County of..................

Route...

Delivering Carrier.....................................Car Initial......................Car No...........

No. Pack- ages	Description of Articles, Special Marks, and Exceptions	*Weight (Subject to Correction)	Class or Rate	Check Column	Subject to Section 7 of conditions, if this shipment is to be delivered to the consignee without recourse on the consignor, the consignor shall sign the following statement:
					The carrier shall not make delivery of this shipment without payment of freight and all other lawful charges.
					(Signature of consignor.)
					If charges are to be prepaid, write or stamp here, "To be Prepaid."
					....
					Received $.............. to apply in prepayment of the charges on the property described hereon.
					Agent or Cashier.
					Per................. (The signature here acknowledges only the amount prepaid.)

*If the shipment moves between two ports by a carrier by water, the law requires that the bill of lading shall state whether it is "carrier's or shipper's weight."

Note.—Where the rate is dependent on value, shippers are required to state specifically in writing the agreed or declared value of the property.

The agreed or declared value of the property is hereby specifically stated by the shipper to be not exceeding

....................................per..................

Charges advanced:

$....................

....................................Shipper.   ....Agent.

Per.......................   Per.......................

Permanent postoffice address of shipper..

FIGURE 7-4   A Long-Form Bill of Lading

ship. Figure 7-5 illustrates a *preprinted short-form bill of lading.* Shippers go to the expense of buying and printing their own bills because, in practice, they frequently prepare them prior to calling the carrier. The preparation is part of their computerized order management procedures. The preprinted bill can be prepared more rapidly and with less chance of error. The shipper can insert the correct classification rather than letting the carrier determine it.

NAME OF CARRIER

STRAIGHT BILL OF LADING — SHORT FORM — Original — Not Negotiable

RECEIVED, subject to the classifications and tariffs in effect on the date of the issue of this Bill of Lading,

the property described below, in apparent good order, except as noted (contents and condition of contents of packages unknown), marked, consigned, and destined as indicated below, which said carrier (the word carrier being understood throughout this contract as meaning any person or corporation in possession of the property under the contract) agrees to carry to its usual place of delivery at said destination. If on its route, otherwise to deliver to another carrier on the route to said destination. It is mutually agreed, as to each carrier of all or any of said property over all or any portion of said route to destination, and as to each party at any time interested in all or any of said property, that every service to be performed hereunder shall be subject to all the terms and conditions of the Uniform Domestic Straight Bill of Lading set forth (1) in Official, Southern, Western and Illinois Freight Classifications in effect on the date hereof, if this is a rail or rail-water shipment, or (2) in the applicable motor carrier classification or tariff if this is a motor carrier shipment.

Shipper hereby certifies that he is familiar with all the terms and conditions of the said bill of lading set forth in the classification or tariff which governs the transportation of this shipment, and the said terms and conditions are hereby agreed to by the shipper and accepted for himself and his assigns.

FROM KILSBY - TUBESUPPLY   At TULSA, OKLA.   DATE   19

CARRIER'S NO.

SHIPPER'S NO.

CONSIGNED TO

(Mail or street address of consignee—For purposes of notification only.)

DESTINATION   STATE   COUNTY

DELIVERY ADDRESS

(To be filled in only when shipper desires and governing tariffs provide for delivery thereof.)

ROUTE   DELIVERING CARRIER   VEHICLE OR CAR INITIAL & NO.

No. Packages	KIND OF PACKAGE, DESCRIPTION OF ARTICLES, SPECIAL MARKS AND EXCEPTIONS		*Weight (Sub. to Corr.)	Class or Rate	Ck. Col.	FOB POINT
BOXES	PIPE OR TUBING WROUGHT STEEL, N.O.I.	☐ 20 GA. AND THINNER HEAVIER THAN ☐ 20 GA.				
TUBES	PIPE OR TUBING WROUGHT STEEL, N.O.I.	☐ 20 GA. AND THINNER HEAVIER THAN ☐ 20 GA.				
PCS	PIPE OR TUBING WROUGHT STEEL, N.O.I.	☐ 20 GA. AND THINNER HEAVIER THAN ☐ 20 GA.				
BDLES	PIPE OR TUBING WROUGHT STEEL, N.O.I.	☐ 20 GA. AND THINNER HEAVIER THAN ☐ 20 GA.				
BOXES	PIPE OR TUBING ALUMINUM	☐ 2" DIA. AND UNDER OVER ☐ 2" DIA.				
TUBES	PIPE OR TUBING ALUMINUM	☐ 2" DIA. AND UNDER OVER ☐ 2" DIA.				
PCS	PIPE OR TUBING ALUMINUM	☐ 2" DIA. AND UNDER OVER ☐ 2" DIA.				
BDLES	PIPE OR TUBING ALUMINUM	☐ 2" DIA. AND UNDER OVER ☐ 2" DIA.				

Subject to Section 7 of Conditions of applicable bill of lading. If this shipment is to be delivered to the consignee without recourse on the consignor, the consignor shall sign the following statement:
The carrier shall not make delivery of this shipment without payment of freight and all other lawful charges.

KILSBY - TUBESUPPLY

(Signature of Consignor)
If charges are to be prepaid, write or stamp here, "To be prepaid."

Rec'd $ ___ to apply in prepayment of the charges on the property described hereon.

Agent or Cashier
Per ___
(The signature here acknowledges only the amount prepaid.)

Charges Advanced $

"Shipper's imprint in lieu of stamp; not a part of bill of lading approved by the Interstate Commerce Commission."

The Fibre Boxes used for this shipment conform to the specifications set forth in the box maker's certificate thereon, and all other requirements of Rule 41 of the Consolidated Freight Classification.

C.O.D.

☐ **PACKING LIST**

☐ SMALL SHIPMENT SERVICE REQUESTED
PREPAID/RELEASED VALUE NOT EXCEEDING 50¢ LB.   SIGNED BY

CUST. P.O. #

KILSBY - TUBESUPPLY   SHIPPER, PER _____

Permanent Post Office Address of Shipper

1819 NO. GARNETT ROAD
TULSA, OKLA. 74116

AGENT, PER _____

1

FIGURE 7-5   A Preprinted Short-Form Bill of Lading

A few shippers are adopting their own bills of lading, which carriers may be reluctant to accept because the carriers may be subject to new liabilities specified in the documents. Carriers are advised to supply drivers with stickers to place on the bills of lading indicating that their signature means only that they have picked up the freight.

Freight Bill

Another basic document that the transportation manager must be familiar with is the **freight bill,** which is an invoice submitted by the carrier requesting to be paid. Often, the transportation manager must approve each freight bill before it is paid, and carriers must be paid within a specific number of working days. In an attempt to meet these time limits, many transportation managers now participate in automated *freight bill-paying services*. Once the transportation manager initiates the program with the payment service, the carriers submit their freight bills

ATLAS TRAFFIC CONSULTANTS CORP.
FREIGHT AUDITING SERVICE
18-42 COLLEGE POINT BLVD., FLUSHING, N. Y. 11356 • (212) 461-0555

CARRIER CODE	CARRIER'S O/C NO.	CLAIM DATE	ATLAS CLAIM NUMBER
XYZR		1/07/93	0454799W

CLIENT NAME NO. 3096200 — XYZ CHEMICAL CO. *

TARIFF AUTHORITY
SWL TARIFF NO. 3355F ITEM 4455H
CLASS'N ITEM SUB CLASS

CARRIER
ABC RAILROAD CO.
1 PACIFIC PLAZA
LOS ANGELES, CA 94110
OVERCHARGE CLAIM DEPARTMENT

SUP 358-CINN INTERMEDIATE TO ANDERSON IND - ROUTE 130260 NO 138170 AS AUTHORIZED IN NOTE 2

ENCLOSURES:
1 ☐ FREIGHT BILL
☐ B/L
☐ SUPPORTING STATEMENT

F.B. NO.	DATE	ORIGIN / DESTINATION / DESCRIPTION AS SHOWN BY YOUR BILL	AS CHARGED WEIGHT	AS CHARGED RATE	AS CHARGED CHARGES	AS SUGGESTED WEIGHT	AS SUGGESTED RATE	AS SUGGESTED CHARGES
868569	5/16/92	ELDON TX CINN OH T/C ISOCYANATE	190000	486	9,234.00	165150	312	5,152.68
			TOTALS *	* *	9234.00			5152.68

OUR AUDIT INDICATES ERROR IN CHARGES AS STATED. KINDLY ARRANGE FOR PROMPT SETTLEMENT PAYABLE TO OUR CLIENT NAMED ABOVE. MAILING VOUCHER AND CORRESPONDENCE TO **ATLAS TRAFFIC CONSULTANTS CORP.** *DUE OUR CLIENT $ 4081.3

ATLAS TRAFFIC CONSULTANTS CORP. HEREBY AGREES TO PROTECT THE CARRIER WITH WHOM THIS CLAIM IS FILED BY REASON OF SETTLEMENT WITHOUT SURRENDER OF THE ORIGINAL PAID FREIGHT BILL AND WE UNEQUIVOCALLY GUARANTEE REIMBURSEMENT. J B Silverman, President

* PLEASE AMEND IF IN ERROR ADD 6% INTEREST.

CARRIER COPY

FIGURE 7-6 An Overcharge Claim Form

Source: Courtesy of Atlas Traffic Consultants Corporation, Flushing, NY.

directly to the service. The payment service treats the freight bills as checks drawn on the shipper's freight account and then pays the carriers.

One continuing issue with freight bills involves companies being charged too much (overcharges) for transportation services. To detect current errors that result in overcharges and to correct these errors in the future, shippers conduct *internal audits* (work is performed by employees of the company) of their freight bills. Some shippers also conduct *external audits* (work is performed by an independent third party) of their freight bills. Figure 7-6 is an example of a form used by a freight-bill auditor to request that a common carrier reimburse the auditor (on behalf of the auditor's client) for the carrier's overcharges.

Freight Claims

Another key documentation issue involves **freight claims,** which refers to a document that notifies a carrier of wrong or defective deliveries, delays, or other delivery shortcomings.[11] Filing claims against carriers is a routine matter, and many carriers post filing instructions and/or sample claim forms on their Web sites. The following instructions are representative of freight claims instructions: "Claims must be in writing; the claim must be supported by the original freight bill,

[11] *Logistics Dictionary,* 2005, accessed at *www.tntfreight.com.*

the original bill of lading, and the original invoice for the goods being shipped; filing of claims should take place as soon as possible after the occurrence, and must be filed within nine months of the delivery date to meet the bill of lading contract requirements."[12] Note that there are time limitations—nine months from the delivery date—within which the claim must be filed.

Although many freight claims are settled using this process, on some occasions shippers and carriers disagree in terms of claim settlement. The Transportation Arbitration Board (TAB) was formed by shippers and carriers as a means of settling claim disputes. When a carrier and shipper (or consignee) agree to submit their case to TAB, they both pay a fee. The shipper (consignee) prepares the claim file, including a written statement explaining why it is believed that the claim should be paid. This is sent to the carrier, which adds its file and contentions to the claim file. The claim file is then returned to the claimant, who has a final opportunity to offer a rebuttal brief, with a copy of the rebuttal going to the carrier. The claimant then sends the entire file to TAB, where a decision is made.

One of the most difficult and challenging aspects of claim work is the determination of the exact dollar amount of the damage. The law states that the common carrier is responsible for the full actual loss sustained by the shipper or consignee. How can this figure be determined? A common rule of thumb is the following: The basic thought underlying the federal statutes that define the liability and prescribe the measure of damages in cases of this kind is that the owner shall be made whole by receiving the proper money equivalent for what has actually [been] lost; or, in other words to restore [the owner] to the position he or she would have occupied, had the carrier performed its contract.[13]

A key factor in determining the value of the full actual loss is the word *earned*. Assume that a retailer owned the products shipped via a common carrier and that they were damaged beyond repair. The question arises, "Should the retailer recover the wholesale price or the retail price?" If the products destroyed were going into a general inventory replacement stock, the retailer would recover the wholesale price plus freight costs (if they had been paid) because the retail price has not been earned. Assume, instead, that a product is ordered especially for a customer. When the product arrives, it is damaged, and the retailer's customer states that he or she will wait no longer and cancels the order. In this situation, the retailer is entitled to the retail price because the profit would have been earned if the carrier had properly performed its service.

Another difficult area for shippers and carriers alike involves *concealed loss or damage*. If a shipment arrives in damaged condition, and the damage is detected before the consignee accepts the goods, the issue is not whether the carrier is liable but the dollar amount of the claim that the carrier must pay. However, concealed loss and damage cases are more difficult to handle because the exterior package does not appear to be damaged or tampered with. At a later date, the consignee opens the package and finds that the product is damaged or missing. As can be appreciated, carriers are reluctant to pay concealed loss and damage claims for two reasons. If the package came through the shipment with no exterior damage, then there is a strong possibility that the product was improperly protected on the inside. If this is the case, the carrier is exempted from liability because improper packaging is the fault of the shipper. Second, the possibility exists that the consignee's employees broke or stole the products.

Since deregulation, the volume of claims activity has dropped because, during the negotiation process, the shipper may agree to hold the carrier less liable for claims in return for lower

---

[12]*www.bullocks-express.com.*
[13]*Atlantic Coast Line Ry. Co. v. Roe*, 118 So. 155.

transportation charges. In addition, the transportation deregulation acts have reduced carrier liability. The Staggers Act of 1980, which lessened railroad economic regulation, and the Motor Carrier Act of 1980, which pertained to trucks, permitted railroads and motor carriers, respectively, to establish released value rates (wherein the shipper agrees that a commodity is worth no more than so many dollars per hundred pounds in case a claim is filed, in return for a lower rate).

MAKING AND RECEIVING SHIPMENTS

Another key area of decision making in transportation management involves making and receiving shipments, which refers to tactical planning and control of shipments along with supervision of freight loading and unloading.[14] A number of activities are associated with making and receiving shipments, and we'll discuss some of them in the paragraphs that follow.

Consolidating Small Shipments

Small shipments, often defined as those that weigh more than 150 pounds and less than 500 pounds, represent one of the most challenging situations faced by the transportation manager. As mentioned in Chapter 6, the nature of transportation costs is that it costs less on a per-pound basis to ship a larger quantity because certain costs (fixed, administrative, or terminal) are the same per shipment. When the shipment is larger, such costs can be allocated over a larger weight. The transportation manager faces the decision of whether and when to consolidate large numbers of small shipments into small numbers of large shipments. Some shipment consolidation activities are shown in Figure 7-7.

Smaller shipments are problematic for several reasons. From a carrier perspective, there may be reluctance to accept small shipments because they tend to require a high degree of manual labor, thus increasing labor costs. In addition, there is a belief by some carriers that they lose money on small shipments because the revenues from them don't sufficiently reflect cost considerations. From a transportation manager's perspective, a large number of small shipments means that there needs to be an information system capable of keeping track of each shipment's status; as a general rule, it's easier to keep track of, say, one shipment of 10 units than to keep track of 10 shipments of one unit. However, it could take some time to accumulate 10 units, and the increased time could result in poorer service to the final customer. Moreover, although a 10-unit shipment might yield transportation cost savings, there would be inventory cost considerations in the sense that it's more costly to hold 10 units than to hold 1 unit.

Potential solutions for consolidating small shipments involve consolidation across time or place.[15] Continuing with the 10-unit example from the previous paragraph, and supposing that 2 units are available for shipment each day, consolidation across time could be accomplished through volume guidelines (e.g., minimum shipment of 8 units, which would mean a shipment on the fourth day) or time guidelines (e.g., ship every third day, in which case the shipment volume would be 6 units). In consolidation across place, the transportation manager looks to build volume with shipments going to a similar destination or similar destinations, and this often involves looking outside one's firm. Transportation specialists such as freight forwarders, shippers' associations, and transportation brokers (each of which were discussed in Chapter 6) can be helpful in achieving consolidation across place.

---

[14]John E. Tyworth, Joseph L. Cavinato, and C. John Langley, *Traffic Management: Planning, Operations, and Control* (Prospect Heights, IL: Waveland Press, 1991).

[15]Ibid.

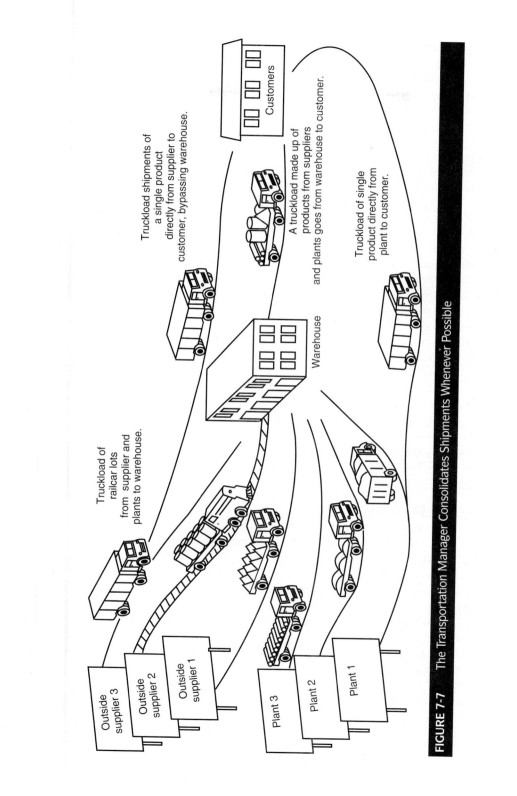

Outside supplier 3

Outside supplier 2

Outside supplier 1

Plant 3

Plant 2

Plant 1

Truckload of railcar lots from supplier and plants to warehouse.

Warehouse

Truckload shipments of a single product directly from supplier to customer, bypassing warehouse.

A truckload made up of products from suppliers and plants goes from warehouse to customer.

Truckload of single product directly from plant to customer.

Customers

FIGURE 7-7 The Transportation Manager Consolidates Shipments Whenever Possible

Demurrage and Detention

Demurrage is a penalty payment made by the shipper or consignee to a railroad for keeping a railcar beyond the time when it should be released back to the carrier. Demurrage is also collected by inland water carriers if their barges are kept by the shipper or consignee for a longer period than allowed. Pipelines are involved with demurrage if oil stored in tanks at destination is not removed within specified time limits. **Detention** is basically the same concept as demurrage, except that it usually refers to the trucking industry. Users of containers owned by the airlines are subject to similar charges. With both demurrage and detention, carriers are concerned that their equipment is idle and unproductive—a less-than-optimal situation for a revenue-generating asset. From the shipper or consignee perspective, idle transportation vehicles such as a rail car or truck trailer can act as temporary (and potentially inexpensive) warehousing.

Both demurrage and detention operate on a "free-time" principle; that is, shippers or consignees are permitted a specified amount of time to load or unload freight before monetary penalties are levied. Many carriers currently offer averaging agreements, where an accounting system of debits and credits is established, for demurrage and detention. A credit is received every time the shipper or consignee releases a piece of equipment early, and a debit is recorded each time a piece of equipment is surrendered to a carrier late. These averaging agreements are typically one month in duration, and at the end of a month, credits and debits are totaled, and the particular demurrage account is settled. As a general rule, credits are not allowed to be carried over from one month to another.

Since deregulation, individual carriers have had much greater freedom with respect to demurrage and detention policies, and because of this, it is difficult to generalize with respect to free time policies and penalty payments. For example, as of mid-2007, the Union Pacific Railroad was transitioning away from free time policies, whereas the CSX Railroad provided 24 hours of free time for loading and 48 hours of free time for unloading railcars. The Union Pacific's penalty payments for demurrage violations were $75 per car, regardless of car type, whereas the CSX was charging $90 per day per car, except in case of refrigerated units, where the charge was $150 per day per car.[16]

Diversion and Reconsignment

Diversion occurs when the shipper notifies the carrier, prior to the shipment's arrival in the destination city, of a change in destination. **Reconsignment** is similar to diversion, but it occurs after the shipment has arrived in the destination city. Diversion has long been associated with the lumber industry; in a typical scenario, lumber would be harvested in the Northwest United States, loaded on a railcar, and then sent to Chicago—prior to an actual buyer being identified. Once a buyer for the lumber was identified, the shipment would then be diverted to the appropriate destination. Diversion can also be used for perishable products such as fruits and vegetables.

Although we present diversion and reconsignment as two separate concepts, the two terms are sometimes used interchangeably. The distinction, or lack thereof, between the two concepts may be reflected in the monetary charges for the service(s). For example, the Union Pacific Railroad views diversion and reconsignment as two distinct concepts and charges $315 for diversion (excluding lumber) and $100 for reconsignment (excluding lumber). Alternatively,

---

[16]Information derived from *www.uprr.com* and *www.csx.com*.

the BNSF Railroad uses the two concepts interchangeably; even so, the BNSF differentiates with respect to monetary charges based on whether the request is filed electronically ($200) or by fax ($400).[17]

Routing

Routing can be defined as the process of determining how a shipment will be moved between consignor and consignee or between place of acceptance by the carrier and place of delivery to the consignee.[18] One example of routing is a **routing guide,** which provides guidance in terms of a preferred list of carriers for shipments moving between two points. For example, Owens and Minor, a distributor of medical and surgical supplies to hospitals, has divided the United States into five regions, with a list of four preferred carriers for each of the 25 possible origin and destination combinations (e.g., origin in region 1, destination in region 2; origin in region 5, destination in region 3; and so on). Not only do Owens and Minor specify preferred carriers for each origin and destination combination, but it also specifies the ordering of the carriers (most preferred, second most preferred, etc.) for each combination.[19]

An increasingly important routing issue involves the transportation of hazardous materials. A **hazardous material** is defined in the Hazardous Materials Transportation Act of 1974 as "a substance or material in a quantity and form which may pose an unreasonable risk to health and safety or property when transported in commerce." Hazardous materials are very common and include some everyday household items. The potential danger involved in the transportation of hazardous materials has been recognized for some time; the federal government began regulating its transport in 1838, and since then hundreds of changes have been made to federal statutes dealing with the transportation of hazardous materials. In addition, U.S. regulations have been modified to resemble more closely those issued by the United Nations regarding international movements of dangerous goods. Today, an organization is required to know, track, and record the location of all hazardous materials that it owns, controls, or are being generated. Originating shippers' documents must include a phone number that will be answered 24 hours a day.

Transportation managers working for firms that handle hazardous materials have several important responsibilities. While the hazardous materials are under the managers' control, they must see that the materials are moved safely. Federal requirements prescribe the training of personnel to handle the materials, the packaging of the product, the marking and labeling of the packages, the placarding of the vehicles that transport the materials, and the information required on shipping documents. The colors, symbols, and numbers of the diamond-shaped placards seen on truck trailers, containers, and railcars identify the hazardous properties of the products being carried. Figure 7-8 shows a container designed specifically for carrying drums of hazardous materials; should one rupture, it would drain into a sump.

The routing of hazardous materials has become a particularly contentious issue since the terrorist attacks of September 11, 2001. As mentioned earlier in the text, a number of large U.S. metropolitan areas are seeking bans on railroad movement of hazardous materials through major cities. These proposed bans have the potential to create major transportation

---

[17]Information derived from *www.uprr.com* and *www.bnsf.com.*
[18]*Logistics Dictionary,* 2005.
[19]*www.owens-minor.com/locations/routeguide.asp.*

FIGURE 7-8 Specialized Container with Sump to Capture Hazardous Waste Leaks from Barrels

Source: Safety Storage, Inc.

problems in the sense that railroads have a common carrier obligation to transport hazardous materials. If these shipments are prohibited from moving through major cities, they will be rerouted through other, less-populated areas—but it's not likely that these areas will be happy with this situation. Moreover, rerouting will add to transit times and transport costs, and the railroads' costs of hauling hazardous materials have increased dramatically in recent years because of higher insurance premiums associated with transporting hazardous materials.[20]

---

[20]R.G. Edmonson, "Not in My Backyard," *Journal of Commerce,* July 24, 2006, 34–36.

Tracing and Expediting

Tracing refers to determining a shipment's location during the course of its move, and the ability to trace shipments directly affects **expediting,** which involves the need to rapidly move a shipment to its final destination. Today many transportation carriers have information systems that provide real-time information about shipment status, and this information is widely available to customers through the Internet, thus making it fast and easy to trace shipments. Moreover, where expediting historically involved shipments by air transportation, in recent years expediting has seen an increasing use of motor carriers. We know from Chapter 6 that motor carriers are less expensive than air transportation, and because expedited motor carriers can often dedicate one truck to one shipment, expedited shipment by motor carriage can provide *faster and more reliable* service than expedited shipments involving air transportation.[21]

TRANSPORTATION MANAGEMENT SYSTEMS

Contemporary transportation managers are increasingly utilizing transportation management systems (TMS), or computerized software packages, to help them manage many of the activities that we've discussed in this chapter. A number of different TMS programs are available to choose from, and installation costs range from approximately $50,000 to several million dollars, depending on a package's capabilities and the scope of implementation.[22] With respect to package capabilities, Table 7-3 presents a representative list of 15 tasks that might be performed by a TMS package. Although several TMS packages currently perform all 15 functions, several other packages also currently perform only one function. Because of the many different TMS options that are available to a transportation manager, it's important that an organization utilizes a TMS package that best suits its needs, as opposed to one from a "name" provider or one that offers many unneeded options.

TABLE 7-3	Transportation Management Systems Task Capabilities	
Task Capability		**Task Capability**
Asset tracking		Carrier selection
Claims management		Driver management
Freight payment		Load planning
Load tendering		Order or shipment visibility
Package delivery verification		Package pickup tracking
Pickup scheduling		Rating
Real-time route reporting		Route optimization
Shipment consolidation		

Source: "Transportation Management Systems Solution Selector," *Logistics Today,* September 2004, 76–80.

---

[21] Aaron Kapp, "Advantage Ground," *Air Cargo World,* August 2005, 26–30.

[22] Bridget McCrea, "How to Navigate the TMS Landscape," *Logistics Management,* February 2006, 45–47.

TRANSPORTATION SERVICE QUALITY

We'll conclude this chapter with a look at transportation service quality. Chapter 4 pointed out that macroenvironmental changes, such as globalization and advances in technology, have caused organizations to demand higher levels of service quality, and this is particularly true for transportation services. For example, the combination of real-time information systems and global positioning systems now allows for virtually instantaneously tracking of a shipment. In addition, this tracking information can be directly provided to the transportation manager at her or his computer (or personal digital assistant) — as opposed to the "old days," where the transportation manager had to contact the carrier for information about a shipment.

As pointed out earlier, economic deregulation allowed for both price and service competition among carriers, and this resulted in the need for organizations to measure their carriers' performance. To this end, some transportation managers developed performance scorecards that contained a list of relevant attributes (perhaps the same attributes used to select carriers) and an evaluation of each carrier on every attribute. The performance scorecard could be used as a diagnostic tool; if an individual carrier's performance is rated as lower than, say, 70, then the carrier might be put on probation for a certain time period. If performance does not show satisfactory improvement during the probationary period, then the carrier might be fired.

There are also more "positive" manifestations of transportation service quality. A number of organizations now officially recognize (e.g., a press release, an awards recognition dinner, a plaque) transportation carriers that provide superior service. In addition, some of the logistics trade publications annually recognize transportation service excellence. For example, *Logistics Management* annually conducts its "Quest for Quality," in which users of transportation services are asked to rate transportation companies on five dimensions: on-time performance, value, customer service, information technology, and equipment and operations. Individual carriers receive a "Quest for Quality" award when their overall rating on the five dimensions exceeds their industry average, and many of these carriers prominently feature this award on their Web sites.

Summary

This chapter covered transportation management, which refers to the buying or selling of transportation services by a shipper or consignee. Since economic deregulation, a firm's transportation manager has had a great deal of flexibility in dealing with carriers. The transportation manager has many specific duties, one of the most important of which is rate determination. The transportation manager is also responsible for modal and carrier selection, and an emerging trend involves a focus on transportation metrics as opposed to transportation mode.

Documentation is another responsibility of the transportation manager, and the chapter discussed key documents such as the bill of lading, freight bills, and freight claims. Another key area of decision making in transportation management is making and receiving shipments, which includes activities such as shipment consolidation, demurrage, and detention, among others. The chapter concluded by looking at transportation management systems and transportation service quality.

Questions For Discussion And Review

1. How is the transportation manager's job different today than when the first edition of this book was published in the late 1970s?
2. Discuss how transportation managers could be involved with other operations of the firm.
3. Briefly explain the class rate system.

4. Discuss the four factors used in determining a product's freight classification.
5. Explain the weight break concept.
6. Discuss how a transportation manager might take advantage of the trade-offs between price and service.
7. Why is the carrier selection process less straightforward than the modal selection process?
8. Define what is meant by an amodal shipper, and discuss the factors that have contributed to its growth.
9. The bill of lading is the single most important document in transportation. Discuss some of the basic functions it performs.
10. Distinguish between the straight bill of lading and the order bill of lading.
11. What is a freight bill? Why should each freight bill be audited?
12. What is the basic rule of thumb regarding the determination of the full actual loss sustained by the shipper or consignee in a loss or damage claim situation?
13. Discuss the basic issues, conflicts, and problems involved in concealed loss and damage claims.
14. Explain why smaller shipments are challenging to transportation managers.
15. Discuss the basic idea of demurrage and detention and how averaging agreements can be helpful in this area.
16. Distinguish between diversion and reconsignment.
17. Explain how a routing guide might be used by a transportation manager.
18. What challenges might occur if rail movements of hazardous materials are banned from going through major cities?
19. Distinguish between tracing and expediting. Why are motor carriers being used to a greater extent in expediting?
20. What is a carrier performance scorecard? How might it be used by transportation managers?

Suggested Readings

Ampuja, Jack and Ray Pucci. "Inbound Freight: Often a MISSED Opportunity." *Supply Chain Management Review* 6, no. 2 (2002): 50–57.

Clair, Lee A., and Steven D. Fox. "Time to Simplify Trucking Tariffs." *Supply Chain Management Review.* 8, no. 3 (2004): 36–42.

Holcomb, Mary Collins, and Karl B. Manrodt. "The Shippers' Perspective: Transportation and Logistics Trends and Issues." *Transportation Journal* 40, no. 1 (2000): 15–25.

Min, Hokey. "Outsourcing Freight Bill Auditing and Payment Services." *International Journal of Logistics: Research & Applications* 5, no. 2 (2002): 197–211.

Keller, Scott B. "Driver Relationships with Customers and Driver Turnover: Key Mediating Variables Affecting Driver Performance in the Field." *Journal of Business Logistics* 23, no. 1 (2002): 39–64.

Kent, John L., and Carlo D. Smith. "Carrier Selection Criteria: Differences among Truckload Motor Carrier Offerings." *Journal of Transportation Management* 16, no. 2 (2005): 48–59.

Poli, Patricia M., and Carl A. Scheraga. "A Balanced Scorecard Framework to Assessing LTL Motor Carrier Quality Performance." *Transportation Quarterly* 57, no. 3 (2003): 105–130.

Premeaux, Shane R. "Motor Carrier Selection Criteria: Perceptual Differences between Shippers and Motor Carriers." *Transportation Journal* 42, no. 2 (2002): 28–38.

Wagner, William B., and Robb Frankel. "Quality Carriers: Critical Link in Supply Chain Relationship Development." *International Journal of Logistics: Research and Applications* 3, no. 3 (2000): 245–257.

Wood, Donald F., and Richard S. Nelson. "Industrial Transportation Management: What's New?" *Transportation Journal* 39, no. 2 (1999): 26–30.

C A S E S

CASE 7-1 CHIPPY POTATO CHIP COMPANY

Located in Reno, Nevada, since 1947, the Chippy Potato Chip Company manufactured potato chips and distributed them within a 100-mile radius of Reno. It used its own trucks for delivery in the Reno, Carson City, and Lake Tahoe areas and common carrier trucking for all other outgoing shipments. All of its motor carrier shipments were on an LTL basis. The applicable motor carrier freight rating, or classification, for LTL potato chips was 200. This classification was high, although potato chips are often given as textbook examples of bulky freight that will cause a truck to cube out. Even after much of the motor carrier industry was deregulated, Chippy had difficulty finding contract truckers interested in negotiating specific contract rates. This was because potato chips—as a result of their bulk—were not a desirable cargo from the truckers' point of view.

The potato chips were packed in bags containing 8 ounces of chips. Twenty-four 8-ounce bags were packed in cartons that were 12 inches by 12 inches by 36 inches. The packed carton weighed 14 pounds. The 8-ounce bags of chips

wholesaled FOB plant for 40 cents each and retailed at 59 cents.

Recently the Chippy firm acquired rights to produce a new type of chip, made from powdered potatoes, yielding chips of identical shape that could be packed in tubular containers. A 5-ounce paper tube of chips would wholesale (FOB plant) at 40 cents and retail for 59 cents. The new chips were much less bulky: Twenty-four 5-ounce containers could be packed in a carton measuring one cubic foot. The filled carton weighed 10 pounds. (The difference between the weight of chips and that of cartons is due to packaging materials. The carrier is paid on the basis of carton weight.)

Chippy management believed that because the new chips were less bulky, the LTL classification of 200 was too high. Management decided to ask the motor carrier classification bureau for a new, lower classification. (Motor carrier rates for a movement are the classification multiplied by a distance factor. If the classification were lowered, the rate would be lowered proportionally for all shipments.) ∎

QUESTIONS

1. If you worked for Chippy, what new classification would you ask for? Give your reasons.
2. Classifications are based on both cost and value of service. From the carrier's standpoint, how has cost of service changed?
3. Given the existing LTL classification of 200, how has value of service to the customer changed?
4. The new tubular containers are much sturdier. If you worked for Chippy, how—if at all—would you argue that this factor influences classification?
5. You work for the motor carrier classification bureau and notice that the relationship between

the weight of potato chips and the weight of packaging has changed. How, if at all, should this influence changes in the product's classification?

6. One of Chippy's own trucks, used for local deliveries, has two axles and an enclosed body measuring (inside) 7 feet by 8 feet by 20 feet and is limited by law to carrying a load of no more than 8,000 pounds. Because the truck is not supposed to be overloaded, what combinations, expressed in terms of cartons of both new- and old-style chips can it legally carry? (*Hint:* Use a piece of graph paper.)

CASE 7-2 NÜRNBERG AUGSBURG MASCHINENWERKE (N.A.M.)

The Nürnberg Augsburg Maschinenwerke, one of Germany's most successful manufacturing companies, enjoys a long tradition. It dates from 1748, when the St. Antony Iron Mill opened in Oberhausen (located in the heart of the Ruhrgebiet industrial region) during the beginning years of German industrialization. The owners soon founded additional iron and coal mills, then established the firm as Gute Hoffungshuette (GHH). Shortly following, in Augsburg and Nürnberg, several companies joined together to form Nürnberg Augsburg Maschinenwerke (N.A.M.). These two firms, GHH and N.A.M., would ultimately merge in the early twentieth century. In the interim, N.A.M. had distinguished itself through the work of Rudolf Diesel, who invented his famous engine and then brought it to N.A.M. late in the nineteenth century. The diesel engine competed with the internal combustion engine in early automotive design and today powers heavy trucks, turbines, railroad engines, and ships. Based on this success, N.A.M. swiftly expanded manufacturing operations and distribution across the globe, only to have its foreign operations compromised by international politics on two occasions. First, N.A.M. lost most of its foreign property in the wake of World War I, a setback that, among other adjustments, encouraged its merger with GHH in 1920. Second, N.A.M. lost all of its foreign property again after World War II and had to rebuild and restructure much of its domestic operation as well. In 1955, the company opened a truck unit in Munich, which would later become the new company headquarters.

By 2003 the company had reclaimed its preeminence as a global player in heavy truck and bus design, engineering, and manufacturing, as well as in print technology, rocket, and energy science. It had reestablished both its plants and sales offices across the globe. It is one of the largest diesel engine makers in the world. Karl

Huber was the N.A.M. regional vice president of sales for South America. He supervised a team of local sales representatives in the countries of that continent, plus a small group of people in the Munich headquarters.

On August 15, Huber received an e-mail from Leopold Escabar in Caracas, who had just returned from an important meeting with local authorities in charge of redesigning the local public transportation systems for the Brazilian cities of São Paulo and Rio de Janeiro. Escabar had attended the meeting along with salespeople from competing truck and bus companies. Escabar gave Huber some good news and some bad news. Escabar had been told N.A.M. was favored to receive an order for 224 N.A.M. class #4-G two-section articulated buses (or "accordion" buses, as Escabar liked to call them), with the possibility of securing a contract for an additional 568 buses. To win the business, however, N.A.M. would have to meet cost and timing guarantees.

The customers first required that N.A.M. must match or beat the total price per unit, including shipping, that N.A.M. had received for a shipment of 233 buses to the transit district of Buenos Aires, 6 months earlier. That price was (Eurodollar) 124,500 per bus. Huber had built in a small extra profit margin on the Buenos Aires deal, so he felt confident that to meet their pricing demand he could shave profit a little, if necessary, in this case.

The second guarantee, however, was more worrisome: The Brazilian authorities were feeling political heat because they were badly behind schedule in implementing their transportation plan and needed proof to show the public that their new programs were underway. So they had made this offer to N.A.M. on strict condition that the company could ensure delivery of the first 25 buses to Santos, the port that serves São Paulo, by November 15 (only 3 months away). If N.A.M.

delivered this initial 90-day order on time, the company would receive a contract for the remaining 199 vehicles to be delivered in full within the following 15 months. The follow-on order for 568 more vehicles was, essentially, contingent on meeting terms of the initial contract to the letter, with regard to the 224 buses. All buses were to be delivered to Santos, a principal Brazilian port.

Huber whistled softly to himself as he read Escabar's e-mail. This would be a major order. In a single stroke, it could move him ahead of his regional sales targets for several quarters to come. Huber immediately sent back an e-mail, instructing Escabar to tentatively accept the offer, assuring the local authorities that they'd have their 25 buses in 90 days and the rest within 18 months. N.A.M. would formally agree to the proposal within 5 working days. Then he scratched his head and tried to figure out how. Huber had 4 days before the next managing director's meeting, at which time he would present the project and, with the vice president for production, propose a plan to accomplish it. Huber lunged for the phone and, scarcely glancing at the number pad, his fingers automatically dialed 4823.

Dieter Berndsen, the production V.P., listened as his old friend Huber described the opportunity, jotting down notes as he went. He explained to Huber that the factory in Munich was already producing to its limits, and the two other German facilities were also facing a backlog of orders through the fourth quarter. So Berndsen offered two immediate possibilities. First, he considered wait listing a 40-bus order from the Thai military at the Munich plant. He said he was reluctant to do this, however, because the Thais had ordered several product modifications, and the Munich line had been already set up to handle them. Second, Berndsen suggested sending the new Brazil order to N.A.M.'s Prague facility. Prague was the smallest of all the European plants and had the oldest, slowest assembly lines, but they were just finishing up manufacture of an order of #4-G's and, due to a recent order cancellation, would now be working at

only 70 percent capacity through year-end. Within 8 weeks, figured Berndsen, Prague could easily handle the order for Brazil's first 25 buses.

Huber eagerly agreed, as Berndsen decided to recommend Prague for this assignment. The problem was that this facility could not produce fast enough to fulfill more than 20 percent of the rest of the contract (for the 224 buses), which meant that he would have to coordinate production and delivery on the rest of this order from other plants. Sighing audibly over the phone line, Berndsen said, "Thanks a lot for the new headache, Hubie. Let me mull this one over for a bit before I call you back. But don't worry, we'll make your deadline—and you will make your bonus. Just remember to cut me in for a piece."

Huber chuckled, thanked him, and hung up.

Berndsen decided to split the full order (224 buses) among the factories in Prague and the much larger plant in Munich. To finalize both scheduling and pricing, he now needed to estimate the time it would take to fulfill the order, as well as the cost of transportation. He was inclined to use the Deutsche Bundesbahn to transport the buses by train to the North Sea port of Bremerhaven, but he wasn't sure that this was the best solution for each of the plants involved.

Berndsen's immediate problem was the first shipment of buses, which would be ready to leave Prague on October 15. Berndsen asked Marcus Weiss, his supply-chain analyst, to create a worksheet that would show all costs and times required to get the buses from the Prague factory to the port of Bremerhaven, and he also asked Weiss to identify viable alternatives. (Europe possesses an extensive network of rivers and channels that connect together its network of commercial waterways. Barges represent alternatives to the road and railroad. The European Green movement continually asked shippers to use the water routes and, occasionally, would attempt to publicly embarrass shippers who used trucks rather than water.) Consequently, the Prague plant sometimes transported buses on barges via the Elbe, north to Hamburg. The German plants occasionally

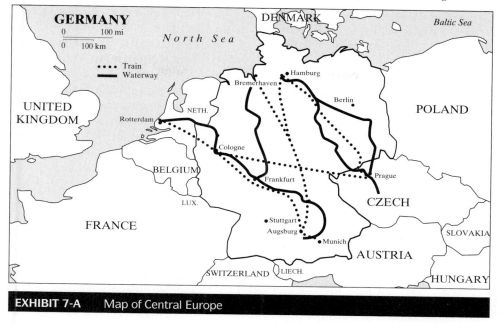

GERMANY

0   100 mi
0   100 km

●●●● Train
▬▬▬ Waterway

North Sea

DENMARK   Baltic Sea

Hamburg

Bremerhaven

Berlin

POLAND

UNITED
KINGDOM

Rotterdam

NETH.

Cologne

BELGIUM

Frankfurt

Prague

CZECH

LUX.

FRANCE

Stuttgart
Augsburg

Munich

SLOVAKIA

AUSTRIA

SWITZERLAND   LIECH.

HUNGARY

EXHIBIT 7-A   Map of Central Europe

shipped north to Bremerhaven or Hamburg, via a network of industrial waterways, or westward, over the River Rhein, to the port of Rotterdam in the Netherlands. (See Exhibit 7-A.)

Following is some of the information Weiss assembled for Berndsen:

- By train, the geographic distances between plants and ports were as follows: Prague to Hamburg 490K, Prague to Rotterdam 640K.
- N.A.M. would need 3 days to get the buses from the factories in Prague to the port of Bremerhaven or Hamburg by train and 4 or 5 days to reach Rotterdam. The advantage of Rotterdam comes, however, in the shipping time from there to Santos, which saves a day versus Bremerhaven or Hamburg, and ocean shipping charges are 5 percent less.
- The Czech railway could transport the load to the border with Germany, where the Deutsche Bundesbahn would take over the flatcars, which carry two buses each. The Bundesbahn quotes a price of € 1,643 per flatcar from Prague to

Hamburg, which includes the service by its Czech partner. If rail were used from Prague to Rotterdam, the cost per flatcar would be € 1,943. In either port, it costs another € 45 per bus to have it unloaded and driven to alongside the vessel. The vessel line can load and pack 20 buses per day, charging € 25 per bus and up to 30 buses with overtime charges. The overtime charges would amount to an additional € 15 per bus (for buses 21, 22, and so on). All charges per bus included detaching the two halves.

- Using the waterways instead of trains to reach the Hamburg port from Prague would decrease the transportation cost by 48 per bus. Waterway transportation would increase the transport time necessary by 3 days to Hamburg.
- For transoceanic shipping on any of these routes, N.A.M. works with Hapag-Lloyd AG. Hapag-Lloyd is able to offer a cheap and flexible commodity cost, through its alliance with NYK, P&O Nedlloyd, MISC, and OOCL, for the ocean transport of the buses. One vessel could carry up to

125 buses as deck cargo, but they would have to be disassembled at their accordion junctions and then reassembled again at their destination.

- The cost per bus (in shipments of 20 buses or more) from Bremerhaven or Hamburg to Santos is quoted at € 6,000, and the trip requires 18 days. Hapag-Lloyd indicates that deck space is available for the initial shipment of 25 buses on vessels departing Hamburg on October 24, October 27, October 31, and November 3. Hapag-Lloyd also has space on vessels leaving from Rotterdam to Santos on October 23, October 28, and November 2.
- Handling (unloading) in Santos is estimated to cost another € 94 per bus, and this includes reattaching the two halves.
- The interest for N.A.M.'s line of credit is 10 percent. ■

QUESTIONS

1. Assume that you are Weiss. How many viable alternatives do you have to consider regarding the initial shipment of 25 buses?
2. Which of the routing alternatives would you recommend to meet the initial 90-day deadline for the 25-bus shipment? Train or waterway? To which port(s)? What would it cost?
3. What additional information would be helpful for answering question 2?
4. How important, in fact, are the transport costs for the initial shipment of 25 buses?
5. What kinds of customer service support must be provided for this initial shipment of 25 buses? Who is responsible?
6. The Brazilian buyer wants the buses delivered at Santos. Weiss looks up the International Chamber of Commerce's year 2000 Incoterms and finds two categories of "delivered" at a receiving port:

   - *DES (Delivered Ex Ship)*. In this type of transaction, the seller must pay all the costs and bear all the risk of transport up to the foreign port of unloading but not including the cost or risk of unloading the cargo from the ship.
   - *DEQ (Delivered Ex Quay)*. This is the same as DES, except that the terms provide for the seller to pay the costs of unloading the cargo from the vessel and the cost of import clearance.

   How should he choose? Why?
7. Would you make the same routing recommendation for the second, larger (199 buses) component of the order, after the initial 90-day deadline is met? Why or why not?
8. How important, if at all, is it for N.A.M. to ship via water to show its support of the Green movement's desires?

8

DISTRIBUTION CENTER, WAREHOUSE, AND PLANT LOCATION

When large tonnages of raw materials are involved, a site that is adjacent to water transport routes is often used. This site is in Chicago, and stockpiles of materials, conveyor equipment, and a self-unloading Great Lakes vessel are all visible.

Photo courtesy of KCBX Terminals Co., Chicago, IL.

Key Terms

- Brownfields
- Center-of-gravity approach
- Empowerment zone
- Expatriate workers
- Facility closing
- Facility location
- Facility relocation
- Free trade zone
- Grid system
- Intermodal competition
- Intramodal competition
- Inventory tax
- Maquiladoras
- Pure materials
- Quality-of-life considerations
- Right-to-work laws
- Supplier parks
- Sweatshops
- Weight-gaining products
- Weight-losing products

Learning Objectives

- To examine the screening or focusing concept of plant or warehouse location
- To explain the general process of determining the optimum number of facilities
- To describe the major factors that influence facility location
- To examine a site's specialized location characteristics
- To explain systems to determine the location that minimizes transportation costs
- To learn about facility relocation and facility closing

Facility location is a logistics/supply chain activity that has evolved from a tactical decision to one of tremendous strategic importance in numerous organizations. In particular, this chapter discusses **facility location,** which refers to choosing the locations for distribution centers, warehouses, and production facilities to facilitate logistical effectiveness and efficiency. To this end, this chapter will examine general and specialized influences on facility location, describe several elementary techniques for choosing general locations, and conclude with an examination of facility relocation and facility closing.

The major factors influencing locational decisions are markets and resource availability; most facilities are located near one or the other. Labor and transport services are two other key factors in facility location. Labor is of special significance because it can be considered as both a market (in the sense of demand for products) and a resource (in terms of human resources to staff a particular facility). The transportation system makes other resource factors mobile and allows a firm to combine factors of production that originate great distances apart.

Advances in technology and communications have had considerable influence on locational decisions in recent years. Consider the experience of Westflex Pipe Manufacturing, which has corporate headquarters in California. Because 40 percent of its sales are to customers located east of the Rocky Mountains, Westflex decided to add a production facility in closer proximity to these customers. How did Westflex choose the location of this facility? It used the Internet to gather relevant data that narrowed the choice to a few locations, and Westflex ultimately located the new production plant in Nebraska. The Internet allowed Westflex to collect the data inexpensively and relatively quickly.[1]

---

[1]Lance Yoder, "How the Internet Impacts the Site Selection Process," *Expansion Management* 16, no. 9 (2000): 10.

For many years, facility location relied on a cost versus value trade-off, in the sense that firms were looking for the most value at the least cost. Since the late 1980s, however, a third dimension has been added to facility location, namely, time considerations. As a result, facility location decisions increasingly seek to balance cost, value, and time considerations; firms are seeking the most value at the least cost in the least elapsed amount of time.[2]

The location decision process involves several layers of screening or focus, with each step becoming a more detailed analysis of a smaller number of areas or sites. The initial focus is on the region, the delineation of which can vary depending on whether a company has a multinational or domestic focus. Thus, a multinational company might initially focus on a region of the world, such as Western Europe, the Pacific Rim, or North America. By contrast, a domestic focus might target a state (province/territory) or group of states (provinces/territories).

The next focus is more precise; it usually involves a selection of the area(s) in which the facility will be located, as illustrated in Figure 8-1 from a brochure describing a site in the Manchester–Liverpool area of England. Once this has been determined, a detailed examination of various locations within the selected area is appropriate. Figure 8-2 shows a map of a specific site along the Little Calumet River, between Chicago, Illinois, and Hammond, Indiana.

MORE FOR DISTRIBUTION

Location and access to Britain, Ireland and Europe are the reasons why . . .

Sanyo
Fiat
Woolworth
Safeway
Nestle
Marks & Spencer
Rowntree-Mackintosh
Goodyear
Dresser
Koehring
Bostitch
Travenol
Becton-Dickinson
Anixter
Snap-on-Tools
Avdel
Compair
Inmac
Allied Breweries
Schweppes

are serving their customers in Britain and Europe through the Warrington-Runcorn centered motorways, railways, seaports and airport complex of Manchester-Liverpool.

Freehold Sites - Ready Space - Custom Premises

For information please contact The Estates Department Warrington & Runcorn Development Corporation P.O. Box 49 Warrington England WA1 2LF ■ Telephone (0925) 51144 ■ Telex 627225

Warrington & Runcorn Development Corporation

WARRINGTON & RUNCORN DEVELOPMENT CORPORATION P.O. BOX 49, WARRINGTON, ENGLAND WA1 2LF

FIGURE 8-1 Advertisement Showing a Site's Location as an Advantage in Reaching British and Continental European Markets

Source: Warrington and Runcorn Development Corporation, England.

---

[2] George Stalk Jr. and Thomas M. Hout, *Competing Against Time* (New York: Free Press, 1990).

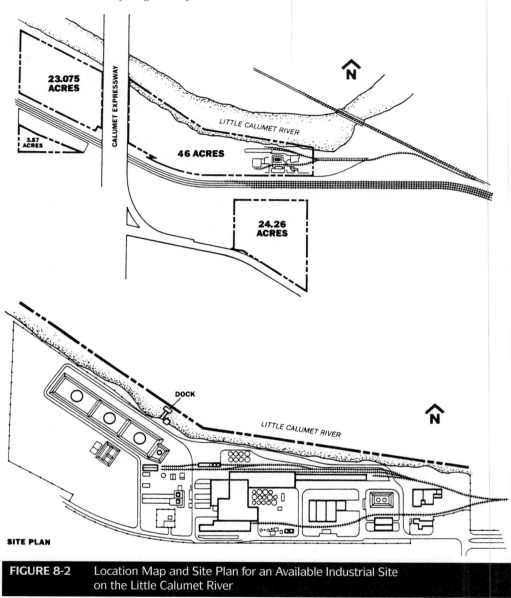

FIGURE 8-2   Location Map and Site Plan for an Available Industrial Site on the Little Calumet River

Source: Courtesy of Donald F. Schroud of Hiffman Shaffer Anderson, Inc.

This detailed examination should include a physical inspection of the location as well as a thorough analysis of relevant zoning and regulatory considerations. Failure to do so can result in costly—and potentially embarrassing—mistakes, as illustrated by the unfortunate experience of a major supermarket chain. The company picked a site for a new grocery store, received the appropriate construction permits, built the store, hired relevant personnel, and stocked the store with products. Several days before the store's grand opening, the parent company was threatened with legal action by a competing supermarket that had a store located across the street from the new store. The legal action referred to the relevant zoning laws—which had not been checked prior to beginning construction—that prohibited any new grocery store from being built within a one-mile radius of the existing grocery store! As a result, the supermarket chain had to cancel its grand opening, close the brand-new store, transfer the products to other stores, and lay off many of the newly hired personnel.[3]

DETERMINING THE NUMBER OF FACILITIES

An early, albeit overlooked, step in the facility location decision should involve determining the total number of facilities that a firm should operate. That is, rather than asking the question, "Where should we locate a new facility?" organizations should be thinking about the optimal number of facilities in their system. Although an additional facility may indeed be required, the general trend in recent years has been for companies to reduce the number of facilities in their distribution networks.

Few firms start business on one day and have a need for large-scale production and distribution the next day. Rather, distribution and production facilities tend to be added one at a time, as needed. The need for additional distribution and production facilities often arises when an organization's service performance from existing facilities drops below "acceptable" levels. Retailers, for example, might add a distribution center when some of its stores can no longer consistently be supplied within two days by existing facilities.

Most analytical procedures for determining the number of facilities are computerized because of the vast number of permutations involved, as well as the complementary relationships between current facilities in a distribution network. Analyzing, for example, whether an organization with 250 stores and five distribution centers should add or remove one distribution center is challenging enough in and of itself. Factoring in that each distribution center is designed to serve a specific number of retail locations—and serve as a backup to one or more of the other distribution centers—makes the decision even more complex. Furthermore, conducting sensitivity analysis on varying levels of customer service could result in an entirely different series of ideal facility locations, depending on the level of customer service that is expected.

Fortunately, a number of software packages exist to help organizations determine both the number and location of facilities in their logistics networks. Chicago Consulting, for example, annually develops a list entitled, "The 10 Best Warehouse Networks," which lists those available for serving the U.S. population, and in 2006 Chicago Consulting debuted a list of "The 10 Best Chinese Warehouse Networks" for serving mainland China (see Figure 8-3). Although these lists are limited in the sense that they only look at one component in location (how long it takes to get from a particular city—or cities—to the majority of the country's population), the network is valuable in showing how altering the number of facilities affects transit time to the particular population. With respect to China, for example, going from two to five warehouses allows a company to save nearly one day of lead time to the Chinese population. By contrast, moving from five to ten warehouses saves a bit less than one-half day in lead time.[4]

---

[3]Example drawn from one author's personal experience.
[4]*www.chicago-consulting.com.*

THE 10 BEST CHINESE WAREHOUSE NETWORKS
Networks with the Lowest Possible "Time-to-the-Chinese Population"

Number of Warehouses	Average Distance to the Chinese Population (Miles)	Average Transit Lead-Time to the Chinese Population (Days)	Best Warehouse Locations		
ONE	504	3.38	XINYANG		
TWO	377	2.55	LIANYUAN	FEICHENG	
THREE	309	2.15	PINGXIANG	JINAN	ZIYANG
FOUR	265	1.87	PINGXIANG CHANGCHUN	JINING	ZIYANG
FIVE	228	1.65	SHAOGUAN CHANGCHUN	HANDAN NANJING	ZIYANG
SIX	207	1.53	SHAOGUAN CHANGCHUN	HANDAN NANJING	NEIJIANG URUMQI
SEVEN	184	1.42	GUANGZHOU CHANGCHUN HONGHU	HANDAN JINGJIANG	NEIJIANG URUMQI
EIGHT	168	1.31	GUANGZHOU CHANGCHUN HONGHU	LIAOCHENG YIXING BAOJI	YIBIN URUMQI
NINE	154	1.24	BEILIU CHANGCHUN YUEYANG	LIAOCHENG LIYANG BAOJI	YIBIN URUMQI ZHANGZHOU
TEN	141	1.20	BEILIU CHANGCHUN YUEYANG TIANJIN	KAIFENG YIXING BAOJI	YIBIN URUMQI ZHANGZHOU

The 10 Best Chinese Warehouse Networks have been developed based on the lowest possible transit lead-times to "customers" represented by the Chinese population. For example, Xinyang provides the lowest possible lead-time for one warehouse. Any other place will increase transit lead-time to the Chinese population. Similarly putting any three warehouses in any locations other than Pingxiang, Jinan or Ziyang will cause the transit lead-time to be higher than 2.15 days.

© Chicago Consulting
8 South Michigan Avenue, Chicago, IL 60603
(312) 346-5080, www.chicago-consulting.com

Chicago Consulting ❮❯

FIGURE 8-3   Chicago Consulting's 10 Best Chinese Warehouse Networks

Source: Courtesy of Terry Harris, Managing Partner of Chicago Consulting.

GENERAL FACTORS INFLUENCING FACILITY LOCATION

Tangible products are the combination of raw materials, component parts, and labor—with the mixture varying from product to product—made for sale in various markets. Thus, raw materials, component parts, labor, and markets all influence where to locate a manufacturing, processing, or assembly facility. Warehouses, distribution centers, and cross-docking facilities exist to facilitate the distribution of products. Their locations are in turn influenced by the locations of plants whose products they handle and the markets they serve.

The discussion that follows covers the location of manufacturing, processing, assembly, and distribution facilities along the supply chain. The relative importance of each factor varies with the type of facility, the product being handled, its volume, and the geographic locations being considered. Although much of the discussion deals with single facilities, the decision process often involves a combination of facilities, in which case one must take into account the relationships among them.

Natural Resources

The materials used to make a product must be extracted directly from the ground or sea (as in the case of mining or fishing) or indirectly (as in the case of farm products). In some instances, these resources may be located great distances from the point where the materials or their products will be consumed. For materials that lose no weight in processing, known as **pure materials,** the processing point can be anywhere near the raw material source and the market.

However, if the materials must be processed at some point between where they are gathered and where they are needed, their weight-losing or weight-gaining characteristics become important for facility location. If the materials lose considerable weight in processing, known as **weight-losing products,** then the processing point should be near the point where they are mined or harvested, largely to avoid the payment of unnecessary transportation charges. If the raw materials gain weight in processing, known as **weight-gaining products,** then the processing point should be close to the market. Sugar derived from sugar beets provides an example of a weight-losing product (a yield of roughly 1 pound of sugar from 6 pounds of sugar beets), whereas bottled soft drinks are an example of a weight-gaining product.

In addition to its use for bottling, water (of one type or another) is a requirement for the location of many facilities. For some industrial processes, water is used for cooling, and in some climates it is possible to use naturally flowing water for air conditioning during warm months. Some processing operations require water both for cleaning purposes and as a medium for carrying away waste. Water is also necessary for fire protection, and the fire insurance premiums charged depend on the availability of some type of water supply.

Historically, the relationship between natural resources and facility location revolved around how the natural resources would be incorporated into products making their way toward consumers. Over the past quarter century, however, discussion of natural resources and facility location has increasingly factored in environmental considerations of one type or another. One set of considerations involves the various types of pollution, namely, air, noise, and water. Another environmental consideration involves the conservation of natural resources—and not necessarily the natural resources used in production processes. For example, a U.S.-based electronics association has urged its members to boycott tantalum (a metallic element) that originates in the Congo because the tantalum is being mined from a nature and wildlife preserve.[5]

---

[5]George Leopold, "Boycott Is Urged on Tantalum from Congo," *Electronic Engineering Times,* April 23, 2001, 42.

Moreover, developing nations often face an interesting dilemma with respect to facility location—especially manufacturing plants—and environmental considerations. By limiting the number and scope of environmental regulations associated with manufacturing facilities, developing countries can speed their economic growth and thus help raise their standard of living. Doing so, however, greatly increases the likelihood of damaging, perhaps irreversibly, a country's natural resources, not to mention creating potential health-related problems for its citizens.[6]

Regarding real estate, distribution and production facilities may require large parcels of land to facilitate effective and efficient operations. An example of land requirements for a particular type of facility is a 250,000-square-foot distribution center that could require at least 50 acres of land. In general, real estate tends to be more plentiful and less costly in more rural locations—locations that might not have adequate transportation or labor resources. Some companies, particularly those needing large-capacity facilities, view the availability and costs of real estate as important a locational determinant as transportation and labor considerations.[7]

Population Characteristics—Market for Goods

Population can be viewed as both a market for goods and a potential source of labor. Customer considerations, particularly as they affect customer service, play a key role in where consumer goods companies tend to locate their distribution facilities. In fact, the popular press is replete with stories involving distribution facilities being located in a particular area so that companies can better serve their current and potential customers.

Planners for consumer products pay extremely close attention to various attributes of current and potential consumers. Not only are changes in population size of interest to planners, but so are changes in the characteristics of the population—particularly as those characteristics influence purchasing habits. With respect to population size, one reason that China and India are potentially attractive to consumer products marketers is that these two countries account for approximately one-third of the world's population. As for population characteristics, longer life spans can increase the demand for health-related products such as prescription medications.

In an effort to learn more about population size and characteristics, many countries conduct a detailed study, or census, typically once every 10 years or so. Although census methodologies and the type of information collected often vary across countries, the resulting data can provide valuable insights for distribution planners in terms of where populations are growing and at what rates. For instance, although a 2005 update to the 2000 U.S. Census projected a 10 percent increase in total population between 2000 and 2010, the population growth is unlikely to be uniform across the various states. Population is the Northeast, for example, is expected to grow at approximately 4 percent, compared to a 14 percent projected growth in the West.[8]

Population Characteristics—Labor

Labor is a primary concern in selecting a site for manufacturing, processing, assembly, and distribution. Organizations can be concerned with a number of labor-related characteristics: the size of the available workforce, the unemployment rate of the workforce, the age profile of the workforce, its skills and education, the prevailing wage rates, and the extent to which the workforce is, or might be, unionized. These and other labor characteristics should be viewed as interrelated

---

[6]"Call for Alternatives to Rigid Eco Regulations," *Bahrain Tribune,* October 30, 2001, no pages listed.

[7]William Atkinson, "DC Siting—What Makes the Most Sense?" *Logistics Management & Distribution Report,* May 2002, S63–S66.

[8]"Interim State Population Projections, 2005," *www.census.gov.*

rather than as distinct attributes. For example, there may be a positive relationship between the age of the workforce and the prevailing wage rates (i.e., higher wage rates may be associated with an older workforce). Alternatively, there may be an inverse relationship between unemployment and wages (i.e., higher unemployment rates may be associated with lower relative wage rates).

Labor wage rates appear to be a key locational determinant as supply chains become more global in nature. For example, hourly compensation data (including benefits) among manufacturing firms in 2004 indicate average compensation of $23.17 in the United States, $21.90 in Japan, and $34.05 in Germany. By contrast, hourly compensation rates in Taiwan were $5.97, and they were $2.50 in Mexico.[9]

Thus, in relative terms, a company could have approximately similar compensation costs by hiring either nine Mexican workers or one U.S. worker. This wage differential at least partly explains the popularity of the **maquiladora** assembly plants located just south of the U.S.–Mexican border. These plants, which began in the mid-1960s, provided much needed jobs to Mexican workers and allowed for low-cost, duty-free production so long as all the goods were exported from Mexico. In the first few years of the twenty-first century, many maquiladoras went out of business, in part because companies established production plants in even lower-wage countries such as China and Guatemala. Since 2004, however, there has been a resurgence of maquiladoras that focuses on manufacturing products that depend on fast time to market, such as high-tech products.[10]

Companies interested in locating in countries with low-cost labor should recognize that there are sometimes limits to the number of supervisory personnel that can be brought in from other countries. The host-country's government may also insist that its own nationals be trained for and employed in many supervisory posts. In addition, countries with low-cost labor often have a multitude of **sweatshops,** which can be viewed as organizations that exploit workers and that do not comply with fiscal and legal obligations toward employees. Although many companies recognize that they have social responsibilities, which would include fair labor practices, to date only slightly more than 10 percent have formal requirements that address sweatshop labor.[11]

A workforce's union status is also a key locational determinant for some organizations. From management's perspective, unions tend to result in increased labor costs, due to higher wages, and less flexibility in terms of job assignments, which often forces companies to hire additional workers. As a result, some organizations prefer geographic areas in which unions are not strong; in the United States, for example, some states have **right-to-work laws,** which mean that an individual cannot be compelled to join a union as a condition of employment. Indeed, since the mid-1990s most non–U.S. automakers have chosen to locate new production plants in right-to-work states such as Alabama, Georgia, and Texas. However, the mere presence of a union doesn't necessarily mean that the union is strong, as illustrated by the case of an apparel sweatshop in Shanghai, China; although 70 percent of the workers belonged to the factory's union, the union was run by the factory's management![12]

Declining union membership (as measured by the percentage of workers who belong to unions) in industrialized nations such as the United States and Australia has resulted in efforts to unionize workers in "nontraditional" areas such as government agencies and service organizations. Such

---

[9]*www.bls.gov.*

[10]Bill Mongelluzzo, "Maquiladoras Rebound," *The Journal of Commerce,* February 20, 2006, 28–30.

[11]Garrett Brown, "Why Sweatshops Won't Go Away," *Industrial Safety and Hygiene News* 40, no. 6 (2006): 70–71.

[12]Dara O'Rourke, "Sweatshops 101," *Dollars & Sense,* September/October 2001, 14–18.

unionization efforts may cause new types of supply-chain disruptions and add new considerations to facility location decisions. For example, toll takers on the Ohio Turnpike are represented by the Teamsters Union, and if these toll takers were to strike the turnpike's management, Teamster truck drivers would honor the strike by refusing to drive the Ohio Turnpike. Alternate routes would need to be found for the freight, a situation that would likely increase transit times and shipment costs.

Racial, ethnic, and cultural considerations may also be important population characteristics. Many organizations, particularly those with a national or international presence, have workforces comprised of different races, ethnicities, and cultures. There may be a hesitancy to establish facilities in areas that are not racially, ethnically, or culturally diverse because it may be difficult to transfer workers to such locations. Moreover, an emerging issue involves managing so-called **expatriate workers,** or those employees who are sent to other countries for extended periods of time. Expatriate assignments can be costly, ranging up to $1 million per assignment, and turnover rates currently run between 20 and 40 percent. What makes the expatriate situation relevant to the current discussion is that the turnover tends to be caused by socialization, rather than technical (i.e., employee knowledge and skills), factors. As such, organizations must ensure that the expatriates (and their families, if relevant) are comfortable with the social and cultural factors of the country where they will be employed.[13]

Taxes and Subsidies

Although labor considerations are important for location decisions, taxes can also be important, particularly with respect to warehousing facilities. Warehousing facilities, and the inventories they contain, are often viewed as a prime source of tax revenues by the relevant taxing organizations. From a community's standpoint, warehousing facilities are desirable operations to attract because they add to the tax base while requiring relatively little in the way of municipal services.

Tax policies differ by location, and organizations should enlist the expertise of knowledgeable parties to determine the actual tax requirements of a particular site. Even when areas have what appear to be identical taxes, there may be significant differences in the manner in which assessments are made or in which collections are enforced. Some localities are so anxious to attract new business that they either formally or informally agree to go easy on the new operation for its first several years. No list of taxes is complete; a partial list includes sales taxes, real estate taxes, corporate income taxes, corporate franchising taxes, fuel taxes, unemployment compensation taxes, social security taxes, and severance taxes (for the removal of natural resources).

Of particular interest to logisticians and supply chain managers is the **inventory tax,** analogous to personal property taxes paid by individuals. As a general rule, the inventory tax is based on the value of inventory that is held on the assessment date(s). Not surprisingly, many logistics managers attempt to have their inventories as low as possible on the assessment date(s), and businesses may offer sales to reduce their inventory prior to the assessment date.

Although between 10 and 15 U.S. states currently assess inventory taxes, there are suggestions that inventory taxes may be obsolete by 2010. Inventory taxes have become increasingly difficult to collect, in part because of a lack of agreement on what is meant by inventory. Some states, for example, classify intellectual property as inventory.[14] Compounding matters are exemptions for items of political or economic importance. For instance, Virginia, a state noted for tobacco production, exempts tobacco that is in the possession of its producer. Other inventory exemptions deal more

---

[13]Sarah B. Lueke and Daniel J. Svyantek, "Organizational Socialization in the Host Country: The Missing Link in Reducing Expatriate Turnover," *International Journal of Organizational Analysis* 8, no. 4 (2000): 380–400.

[14]Kathleen Hickey, "Taxing Logistics," *Traffic World,* May 10, 2004, 15–16.

explicitly with distribution activities or functions. Some states exempt goods that are stored in public warehouses; some states exempt goods passing through the state on a storage-in-transit bill of lading.

As if business taxes are not difficult enough to understand, they represent only one side of the coin; the other side is to know the value of services being received in exchange for the taxes. A general rule of thumb is that the services received represent only about 50 percent of the taxes paid, and this imbalance may cause businesses to invest more money to receive the required level of service. For example, inadequate police services might cause a warehousing facility to hire its own security force.

To further complicate matters, governments may offer subsidies and/or incentive packages as an inducement for firms to locate in a particular area. For example, some localities subsidize new businesses by issuing tax-free bonds to prepare plant sites and construct buildings. Although this can be very attractive for enticing new businesses, this arrangement often places a burden on existing taxpayers. With respect to incentive packages, Dole Fresh Vegetables received approximately $22 million in incentives, such as tax credits and donated land, for locating a salad processing plant in Gastonia, North Carolina, that is scheduled to open by early 2007.[15]

Furthermore, the U.S. Department of Housing and Urban Development created **empowerment zones** in several cities beginning in the mid-1990s and has expanded the number of empowerment zones several times since then. The purpose of these zones is to encourage business development—through various tax credits—in economically depressed portions of cities. For example, organizations that hire and retain residents of empowerment zones earn wage credits of up to $3,000 per worker that can be applied against the organization's tax liabilities.[16]

Transportation Considerations

Transportation considerations in the form of transportation *availability* and *costs* are a key aspect of facility location decisions because transportation often represents such a large portion of total logistics costs. Moreover, it has been suggested that all things (such as space cost, labor availability, and so on) being equal, "the best locations are generally those where the best transportation services are located."[17]

Transportation availability refers to the number of transportation modes (**intermodal competition**) as well as the number of carriers within each mode (**intramodal competition**) that could serve a proposed facility. The evaluation of transportation availability is likely to depend on the type of facility that is being looked at. For instance, a manufacturing plant might need both rail service (to bring in raw materials) and truck service (to carry the finished goods), whereas a distribution center might need just truck service.

As a general rule, the existence of competition, whether intermodal, intramodal, or both, tends to have both cost and service benefits for potential users. Limited competition generally leads to higher transportation costs and means that users have to accept whatever service they receive. Thus, a poor location can significantly increase transportation costs as well as negatively affect customer service.

Geographically central facility locations are often the result of transportation costs and service considerations. With respect to transportation costs, centralized facilities tend to minimize the total transit distances, which likely results in minimum transportation costs. Centralized facilities can also maximize a facility's service area, as shown in Figure 8-4, which illustrates

---

[15]Peter Cleaveland, "Set Your Sites on Incentives," *Food Engineering,* June 2006, 64–70.

[16]Michael Keating, "Empowerment Zones Offer Major Tax Breaks," *Expansion Management,* January 2003, 41–45.

[17]William Atkinson, "Finding the Right Space in the Right Place," *Logistics Management,* May 2004, S76–S79.

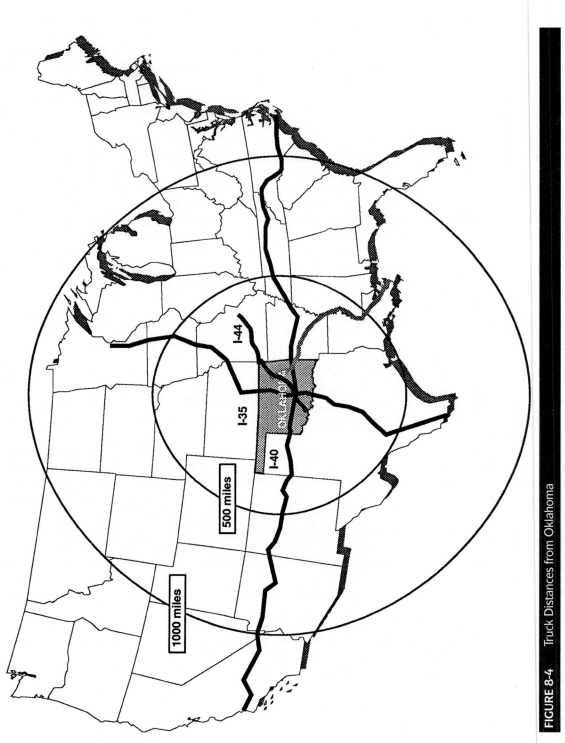

FIGURE 8-4 Truck Distances from Oklahoma

Source: Oklahoma Department of Commerce.

truck distances from the state of Oklahoma. Note how many states are located within 1,000 miles (generally considered two-day service by truck) of Oklahoma.

Proximity to Key Suppliers

Over the past two decades, many organizations have identified proximity to key suppliers as an important determinant when locating a facility. As a general rule, proximity allows for faster and more consistent deliveries, key considerations among organizations that operate based on a just-in-time philosophy that emphasizes little or no excess inventory. For example, in 2006 Honda announced plans to build a new manufacturing facility in Indiana, in large part because many of Honda's existing automotive suppliers are located within one-half day's transit time from the new facility.

Proximity to key suppliers has been the catalyst in the development of **supplier parks,** a concept that developed around automakers and their suppliers in Europe and has spread to other continents, including North America. With supplier parks, key suppliers locate on, or adjacent to, automobile assembly plants, which helps to reduce shipping costs and inventory carrying costs. As an example, the supplier park serving Ford Motor Company's Chicago assembly plant is generating transportation cost savings of $50 per vehicle.[18]

Trade Patterns

Firms producing consumer goods follow changes in population to better orient their distribution systems, and there are shifts in the markets for industrial goods as well. General sources of data regarding *commodity flows* can be studied, much like population figures, to determine changes occurring in the movement of raw materials and semiprocessed goods. The availability and quality of such data often vary from country to country, and it may be difficult to compare data across countries because of different methodologies used to collect the data.

With respect to commodity flows, logisticians are especially interested in (1) how much is being produced and (2) where it is being shipped. If a firm is concerned with a distribution system for its industrial products, this information would tell how the market is functioning and, in many instances, how to identify both the manufacturers and their major customers. At this point, the researcher would understand the existing situation and would try to find a lower-cost production–distribution arrangement. Should the firm join the existing patterns of trade (which is easier to do in an expanding market), or should it produce at a point where no manufacturers of similar products are located?

The development and implementation of multicountry trade agreements have generated profound impacts on trade patterns. For example, the United States, Canada, and Mexico are part of the North American Free Trade Agreement (NAFTA). Although Canada has long been the largest trading partner of the United States, since NAFTA's passage, Mexico has become the United States' third-largest trading partner. From a logistics perspective, this has increased the north–south movement of product, and the Interstate 35 corridor (which runs north–south between Mexico and Canada) has become a hotbed for distribution activity. Oklahoma City, Oklahoma, and Dallas, Texas, are two locations along Interstate 35 that have seen a dramatic increase in the construction of distribution facilities in recent years.

Trade patterns have also been influenced among those countries that are members of the European Union (EU). The virtual elimination of trade barriers among EU member countries has allowed companies to move from having distribution facilities in many countries toward

---

[18]Amy Wilson, "2 More Supplier Parks on Ford Radar," *Automotive News,* August 16, 2004, 30.

having only one or two facilities. When the EU consisted of 14 countries, the central location and strong transportation infrastructures of the so-called "Benelux" countries (Belgium, the Netherlands, and Luxembourg) were a favored location for distribution facilities to serve EU countries. However, since the EU's expansion into 10 Central and Eastern European countries in 2004, the Czech Republic has become a favored production and distribution site because of its relatively central geographic location.[19]

Quality-of-Life Considerations

An increasingly important locational factor is what can broadly be called **quality-of-life considerations.** Although it may be difficult to develop a standardized list of quality-of-life factors, their intent is to incorporate nonbusiness factors into the business decision of where to locate a plant or distribution facility. For instance, *Expansion Management* magazine has developed a Quality of Life Quotient that measures approximately 50 different quality-of-life factors that compare the attractiveness of various U.S. metropolitan areas. The factors include access to commercial air travel, an area's cost of living, crime rates, and educational opportunities, among others.[20]

There are a number of reasons for including quality-of-life considerations as a factor in facility location. For one, employees who are able to live a reasonable lifestyle tend to be happier and more loyal, thus reducing employee turnover and potentially dissatisfied customers. Second, because many organizations now compete nationally and internationally for talent, less-than-desirable geographic locations hinder the recruiting process. Third, the increasing emphasis on business relationships means that suppliers and customers may be visiting an organization's facilities. Attractive locations serve as a greater incentive for such visits than do unattractive locations.[21]

Locating in Other Countries

Quality-of-life considerations can be especially important when companies are thinking of facility locations in nondomestic countries. For example, despite temperatures that can reach 120 degrees for six months of the year, Dubai is viewed as a premier city in the Persian Gulf region—at least for prospective employers from Western Europe and North America. From a quality-of-life perspective, Dubai has a number of excellent hotels, a world-class airport, plentiful and affordable housing, low taxes and crime rates, shopping malls, and outstanding schools.[22]

Besides quality-of-life considerations, many other factors are to be considered if a firm is looking for a plant, office, or distribution site outside its home country. Many of these considerations are governmental in nature and deal with the relevant legal system, political stability, bureaucratic red tape, corruption, protectionism, nationalism, privatization, and expropriation (confiscation), as well as treaties and trade agreements.

Social unrest and crime are concerns in many parts of the world and increase the risks associated with conducting business. Some of the world's more dangerous places, in terms of crime, include Washington, DC; Mexico City, Mexico; Sao Paolo, Brazil; and Moscow, Russia. In terms of social unrest, Israel, Pakistan, and India are areas of concern.

Other differences to be noted include culture, customs, holidays, language and language diversity, level of education, and religion. Currency fluctuations and devaluations can result in

---

[19]Dagmar Trepins, "Logistics Finds Its Center in Eastern Europe," *Logistics Management,* February 2006, E67–E70.

[20]Bill King and Michael Keating, "2005 Quality of Life Quotient™," *Expansion Management,* May 2005, 8–16.

[21]Bill King, "Four Reasons Why Quality of Life is a Site Selection Consideration," *Expansion Management,* May 2004, 80.

[22]"Dubai Gets Hot," *Export Today's Global Business,* August 2000, 20.

frequent cost changes for expatriate workers. Tax laws in the host country, and the ability to repatriate profits, limit one's ability to use profits that operations in the host country might generate.

On an international scale, some workforces are considered mobile (migrants) and will move from one nation to another in search of work. Because of poor economic conditions in their home countries, migrant workers are quite willing to do menial jobs for very low pay. These workers travel from country to country, following jobs and sending part of their earnings back home. As this book is being revised, the United States is engaged in a rather contentious discussion involving the potential reform of immigration laws—legislation that could certainly affect the use of migrant workers.

SPECIALIZED LOCATION CHARACTERISTICS

The preceding discussion focused on some of the more common general considerations in selecting the site of a manufacturing, distributing, or assembling facility. This section deals with more specialized, or site-specific, considerations that should be taken into account in the facility location decision. Most of these considerations are invisible boundaries that can be of great significance in the location decision.

Land may be zoned, which means that there are limits on how the land can be used. For example, a warehouse might be allowed only in areas set aside for wholesale or other specified commercial operations. Restrictions on manufacturing sites may be even more severe, especially if the operation might be viewed as an undesirable neighbor because of the fumes, noise, dust, smoke, or congestion it may create. Distribution facilities are often considered to be more desirable because the primary complaints tend to involve only traffic volume and congestion caused by the trucks that serve the facilities. If a community is attempting to encourage, or discourage, business activity, zoning classifications can be changed, although the process may be time consuming.

Union locals have areas of jurisdiction, and a firm's labor relations manager may have distinct preferences with which locals he or she is willing to deal. Even though an individual union may ratify national labor agreements, local supplemental agreements often reflect the unique characteristics of a particular area. The different supplemental agreements provide companies with differing levels of managerial flexibility (or inflexibility).

Once a precise site is under consideration, many other issues should be dealt with before beginning construction or operations. For example, a title search may be needed to make sure that a particular parcel of land can be sold and that there are no liens against it. Engineers should examine the site to ensure that it has proper drainage and to ascertain the load-bearing characteristics of the soil.

Environmental regulations may require that due diligence be carried out with respect to who previously owned a prospective site and how it was used. One key environmental issue in some economically developed countries involves the use of **brownfields,** or locations that contain chemicals or other types of industrial waste. Brownfields are an important locational issue because many are found in urban areas that are often desirable from a locational point of view. In recent years, legislation in the United States has made it easier and less costly to redevelop brownfield sites.[23]

[23]Bennett Volyes, "Will the Brownfields Bloom?" *National Real Estate Investor,* June 2006, 31–34.

Another specialized characteristic involves the weather, and location decisions can be influenced by the potential for tornadoes, floods, and hurricanes, among others. Indeed, an increase in both the number and intensity of hurricanes affecting the United States since 2003 has led one company to reject any facility locations that are within 200 miles of the Gulf Coast, in part because just the *threat of a hurricane* resulted in increased employee absenteeism.[24]

Free Trade Zones

A highly specialized site in which to locate is a **free trade zone,** also known as *foreign trade zones* and *special economic zones.* Free trade zones have become extremely popular in recent years, with over 600 such zones worldwide, about 230 of which are located in the United States. Nondomestic merchandise may be stored, exhibited, processed, or used in manufacturing operations without being subjected to duties and quotas until the goods or their products enter the customs territory of the zone country. Free trade zones are often located at, or near, water ports, although they can also be located at, or near, airports.

Free trade subzones refer to specific locations at an existing free trade zone—such as an individual company—where goods can be stored, exhibited, processed, or manufactured on a duty-free basis. There are approximately 400 free trade subzones in the United States, and they are particularly popular among automotive manufacturers. For example, 17 of the 20 subzones in Detroit, Michigan, involve automobile manufacturers.[25]

FINDING THE LOWEST-COST LOCATION

Many products are a combination of several material inputs and labor. Traditional site location theory can be used to show that one or several locations will minimize transportation costs. Figure 8-5 shows a laboratory-like piece of equipment that could be used to find the lowest-cost location, in terms of transportation, for assembling a product consisting of inputs from two sources and a market in a third area.

Although most solutions to locational problems currently involve computer analysis, such analysis may not be needed if the relevant parameters are not too complex. Thus, grid systems can be used to determine an optimal location (defined as the lowest cost) for one additional facility.

GRID SYSTEMS

Grid systems are important to locational analysis because they allow one to analyze spatial relationships with relatively simple mathematical tools. **Grid systems** are checkerboard patterns that are placed on a map, as in Figure 8-6, and the grid is numbered in two directions: horizontal and vertical. Recall from geometry that the length of the hypotenuse of a right triangle is the square root of the sum of the squared values of the right triangle's two legs. Grid systems are placed so that they coincide with north–south and east–west lines on a map (although minor distortion is caused by the fact that east–west lines are parallel, whereas north–south lines converge at both poles).

---

[24]Peter Cleaveland, June 2006.

[25]See *www.foreign-trade-zone.com.*

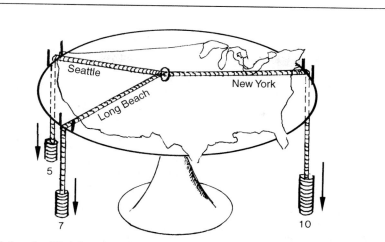

This is a simplified demonstration showing the various "pulls" which exist to determine the industrial location which minimizes the total ton miles of transportation used to transport both inputs and output. This method can be used for situations where there are "pulls" in three directions—either two sources of supply and one market, or one source of supply and two separate markets.

Assume we have two inputs, one produced in Long Beach and one produced in Seattle. The two inputs are combined to make a product which is sold in New York City. Assume further that to produce ten tons of the product consumed in New York, we must combine seven tons of the product which comes from Long Beach with five tons of the product which comes from Seattle. Assume finally that a transportation system is available anywhere and that the transport costs per ton mile are the same for either input or for the final product.

We take a circular table, placing a map of the U.S. on it and pairs of pegs on the table edge in the vicinity of Long Beach, Seattle, and New York as they are on the tabletop map. The pairs of pegs are so that a piece of string can pass between them.

We knot together three pieces of string, with all of them ending in one knot. To one of the pieces of string, which we pass through the pegs near Seattle on our map, we attach five identical metal washers (each one representing one ton). We attach seven washers to a second piece of string and pass it through the pegs in the vicinity of Long Beach on our tabletop map. To the third piece of string we attach ten washers and place it through the pegs in the vicinity of New York.

Then we take the knot and gently lift it to a point above the center of the table, with the washers on all three strings pulling down. We then drop the knot and it comes to rest at the spot on the map which represents the point in the U.S. where the manufacturing operation (for combining these two inputs into the single product) should locate. No other point will require less transportation effort—measured in ton-miles of freight moved.

(If transportation costs, or rates, differ on a per ton mile for each of the commodities or products involved, this can be taken into account by having the number of washers "weighted" to take into account the varying rates as well as the differences in weight being shippped. If for example in the situation described above carriers charged twice as much per ton mile to carry the finished product as they charged for carrying inputs, one would attach 20 washers (2 × 10) on the string reaching toward New York.)

Adapted from: Alfred Weber, *Theory of the Location of Industries,* translated by Carl J. Friedrich (Chicago: Univ. of Chicago Press, 1929).

FIGURE 8-5   Example of Transportation Forces Dictating Plant Location

Adapted from: Alfred Weber, *Theory of the Location of Industries,* translated by Carl J. Friedrich (Chicago: Univ. of Chicago Press, 1929).

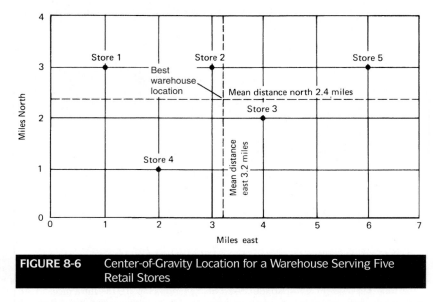

FIGURE 8-6   Center-of-Gravity Location for a Warehouse Serving Five Retail Stores

A **center-of-gravity approach** can be used for locating a single facility so that the distance to existing facilities is minimized. Figure 8-6 shows a grid system placed over a map of five existing retail stores. At issue is where a warehousing facility to serve these stores should be located. Assuming that each store receives the same volume and that straight-line distances are used, the best (lowest-cost) location for a warehousing facility to serve the five stores is determined by taking the average north–south coordinates and the average east–west coordinates of the retail stores.

In Figure 8-6, the grid system has its lower left (southwest) corner labeled as point zero, zero (0,0). The vertical (north–south) axis shows distances north of point 0,0. The horizontal (east–west) axis shows distances to the east. In this example, the average distance north is (3 + 1 + 3 + 2 + 3) or 12. This figure is divided by the number of stores (5), resulting in a north location of 12/5 or 2.4 miles. The average distance east is (1 + 2 + 3 + 4 + 6) or 16; 16 divided by 5 equals 3.2 miles. Thus, the best (lowest-cost) location is one with coordinates 2.4 miles north and 3.2 miles east of point zero.

Because it's not likely that each store will place equal demands on a prospective warehousing facility, the center-of-gravity approach can be easily modified to take volume into account—the *weighted center-of-gravity approach*. The idea behind the weighted center-of-gravity approach is that a prospective warehousing facility will be located closer to the existing sites with the greatest current demand.

To illustrate the weighted center-of-gravity approach, consider the preceding five-store example, but modify the assumption that each store receives the same volume. Assume that store 1 receives 3 tons of shipments per month, store 2 receives 5 tons, store 3 receives 4 tons, store 4 receives 2 tons, and store 5 receives 6 tons. To calculate the north weighted center-of-gravity location, each north coordinate is multiplied by the corresponding volume, and these values are summed; this total is then divided by the sum of the monthly volume. This procedure is repeated to calculate the east weighted center-of-gravity location.

The new data (see Table 8-1) indicate that the monthly volume for the five locations is 20 tons (3 + 5 + 4 + 2 + 6) and that the weighted center-of-gravity location is 2.6 miles north and 3.7 miles east. Thus, the weighted approach locates a warehousing facility slightly more north and more east than what was determined in the basic center-of-gravity approach (2.4 miles north; 3.2 miles east).

TABLE 8-1	Weighted Center-of-Gravity Example				
Store	*North Location*	*East Location*	*Monthly Volume (tons)*	*North × Volume*	*East × Volume*
1	3	1	3	$(3 \times 3) = 9$	$(1 \times 3) = 3$
2	3	3	5	$(3 \times 5) = 15$	$(3 \times 5) = 15$
3	2	4	4	$(2 \times 4) = 8$	$(4 \times 4) = 16$
4	1	2	2	$(1 \times 2) = 2$	$(2 \times 2) = 4$
5	3	6	6	$(3 \times 6) = 18$	$(6 \times 6) = 36$
Total			20	52	74
Weighted average				2.6	3.7

The two approaches just described are relatively simple and straightforward, and the calculations can be done relatively quickly to provide approximate locations of centralized facilities, at least in a transportation sense. Because neither the center-of-gravity nor the weighted center-of-gravity approach is very sophisticated, adjustments may have to be made to take into account real-world considerations such as taxes, wage rates in particular locations, volume discounts, the cost and quality of transport services, and the fact that transport rates taper with increased distances. These considerations increase the complexity, as well as the time, to do the necessary calculations and partially explain why some companies have turned to specialized software packages to help them with facility location decisions.

LOCATING INSIDE ANOTHER FIRM'S EXISTING CHANNELS

It is also possible to attempt to locate within another firm's existing channel structure. As pointed out in Chapter 1, a popular contemporary retail strategy involves *co-branding,* which refers to companies collaborating at one location where customers can purchase products from two or more name-brand companies. For example, the Starbucks Coffee Company has outlets located in select upscale department stores and lodging chains.

Dreyer's Ice Cream and Starbucks have a partnership for making several brands of coffee-flavored ice cream. Starbucks was able to utilize the Dreyer's direct-delivery-to-store system involving established transport routes and frozen-food carrying capability. Dreyer's also already had shelf space. It would have been prohibitively expensive for Starbucks to duplicate such a frozen-food distribution network.

It is generally believed that location within another firm's channel is feasible, assuming that the products involved are complementary. Many shopping malls, for example, have food courts that cater to the hungry and thirsty shopper—and increasingly, the food courts are populated by name-brand companies such as McDonald's, Pizza Hut, and Subway. Locating within another firm's channels can be an excellent way of entering nondomestic markets. For example, when Starbucks initially expanded into Japan, it formed a joint venture with a Japanese restauranteur.

FACILITY RELOCATION AND FACILITY CLOSING

Two specialized cases conclude this discussion of location choice, one involving facility relocation and the other involving facility closing. They are distinguished as follows: Facility relocation is associated with business growth, whereas facility closing is associated with business contraction.

More specifically, **facility relocation** occurs when a firm decides that it can no longer continue operations in its present facility and must move operations to another facility to better serve suppliers or customers. **Facility closing,** by contrast, occurs when a company decides to discontinue operations at a current site because the operations may no longer be needed or can be absorbed by other facilities.

A common reason for facility relocation involves a lack of room for expansion at a current site, often because of a substantial increase in business. In the United States, this has involved the relocation of industrial plants and warehousing facilities from aging and congested central cities to more attractive sites in suburban locations. Land costs and congestion in the central cities often make expansion difficult (or impossible), and transportation companies generally prefer the suburban sites because there is less traffic congestion to disrupt pickups and deliveries.

In theory, the relocation decision involves a comparison of the advantages and disadvantages of a new site to the advantages and disadvantages of an existing location. Although this inevitably involves quantitative comparisons, companies should also consider the potential consequences of relocation on their human resources—consequences that may not be easily quantified.

For example, plant relocations inevitably result in a plethora of employee-related questions, including: How many current employees will be offered positions at the new facility? Will the company use years of service, employee productivity, or other factors to decide who gets offered positions at the new facility? What happens to employee seniority? What percentage, if any, of relocation expenses will be paid by the employer? Will older employees be offered incentives to retire rather than relocate? Will employees who decide not to relocate be offered severance benefits?

Employers should keep current employees informed of planned relocations and how such relocations might affect them. Relocation information from other sources could lead to confusion, anger, and lower morale and could easily affect the productivity of the existing facility at a time when hiring replacements is likely to be very difficult. It's also important for employers to be cognizant of relevant legislation at the federal and state levels. For example, U.S. federal legislation in the form of the Worker Adjustment and Retraining Notification (WARN) Act mandates that employers give 60 days notice about plant closings and mass layoffs. Many individual states have additional requirements concerning large-scale employee layoffs.

Companies should also recognize that, no matter how well planned beforehand, a relocation from one facility to another is rarely trouble free; at a minimum, relocation glitches can add to logistics costs and detract from customer service. For example, transferring equipment, furniture, and supplies from an old facility to a new one may take longer than expected. Also, a newly constructed plant or warehousing facility is likely to have flaws or shortcomings that are only discovered after occupancy.

Facility closings can occur for various reasons, such as eliminating redundant capacity in mergers and acquisitions, improving supply chain efficiency, poor planning, or an insufficient volume of business. Whatever the reason(s), it is imperative for an organization to clearly specify why a plant is being closed. As an example, Michelin closed a tire manufacturing plant in Kitchener, Ontario (Canada) in mid-2006 and shifted production to other tire plants in the United States. Michelin cited several reasons for the plant closing, to include that the Kitchener facility had the lowest capacity among the company's North American tire plants.[26]

Although facility closings are largely a business-oriented decision, substantial obstacles can be part of closing individual facilities. Union contracts, for example, may prohibit (or limit) certain

---

[26]Brad Dawson, "Michelin Won't Budge on Canadian Plant Closing," *Rubber and Plastic News,* March 2006, 1, 22.

facilities from being closed. The human impact of facility closings should be considered as well; individuals are not only losing their jobs and pay, but some individuals may suffer a loss of self-esteem as well. Unpleasant as it may be, employees should be kept informed by their employers throughout the closing process. Poorly handled facility closings can result in tremendous amounts of unwanted negative publicity for a company, which does little more than exacerbate an already unpleasant situation. The bankruptcy of LTV Steel in the early twenty-first century provides one such example; unfortunately, many LTV workers first learned about key pieces of bankruptcy information from various media, including television and the Internet, before being notified by the company.[27]

Summary

This chapter discussed several issues associated with the location of warehousing, manufacturing, and assembly facilities. General factors in facility location were looked at, including population and trade patterns. Population characteristics are a double-edged sword in facility location in the sense that a population serves both as a market for goods as well as a source of labor. Changing trade patterns, spurred in part by multicountry trade alliances, have had a profound influence with respect to the location of distribution facilities.

This chapter also discussed specialized location characteristics, and it presented several examples of how grid systems can be useful for determining the lowest-cost location for a facility. The chapter concluded with a look at facility relocation and facility closing; companies should be cognizant of the human dimension associated with both relocation and closing.

Questions For Discussion And Review

1. How can advances in technology and communication influence the facility location decision?
2. Discuss the factors that influence the number of facilities that a firm chooses to operate.
3. Briefly describe the general factors influencing facility location.
4. How does a raw material's status as pure, weight-losing, or weight-gaining influence the facility location decision?
5. Discuss how environmental considerations might influence the facility location decision.
6. Discuss how population can be viewed as both a market for goods and a source of labor.
7. How might the factors considered important for locating a manufacturing facility differ from the factors considered important for locating a distribution facility?
8. Discuss the advantages and disadvantages to locating manufacturing, assembly, or distribution facilities in countries with relatively low wages.
9. What are right-to-work laws? How do they influence locational decisions?
10. What are expatriate workers? What challenges do they face?
11. Do you think inventories should be taxed? Why or why not?
12. What are empowerment zones? What is their relevance to locational decisions?
13. What mode of transportation do you think is the most important to firms when evaluating new sites? Why?
14. What are supplier parks? Give some examples.
15. Discuss how multicountry trade agreements have influenced the location of production or distribution facilities.
16. What quality-of-life considerations do you think are the most important for locational decisions? Why?
17. Beyond the general factors discussed in this chapter, what additional considerations are important when a firm is thinking of locating a facility (facilities) in other countries?
18. What is a free trade zone? What functions might be performed in it?

---

[27]Jennifer Scott Cimperman and Sandra Livingston, "Stumbling LTV Losing Support, Critics Say; Poor Handling of Crisis Has Angered Public, Union and Politicians," *The Plain Dealer*, April 15, 2001, 1A +.

19. Discuss advantages and disadvantages to grid systems, such as the center-of-gravity and weighted center-of-gravity approaches.
20. Distinguish between facility relocation and facility closing. How should companies deal with their human resources (workers) in both situations?

Suggested Readings

Cooke, Donna K. "African-American Business Ownership: Strength in Numbers, But Where?" *Journal of Applied Business Research* 21, no. 1 (2005): 37–43.

Garretson, Sara P. "Successful Site Selection: A Case Study." *IIE Solutions* 32, no. 4 (2000): 33–37.

Korpela, Jukka, Kalevi Kylaheiko, Antti Lehmusvaara, and Markku Tuominen. "The Effect of Ecological Factors on Distribution Network Evaluation." *International Journal of Logistics: Research & Applications* 4, no. 2 (2001): 257–269.

Morphy, Erika. "Sweatshops in the Supply Chain." *Export Today's Global Business* 16, no. 10 (2000): 22–29.

Mueller, Glenn R. "Brownfields Capital—Unlocking Value in Environmental Redevelopment." *Journal of Real Estate Portfolio Management* 11, no. 1 (2005): 81–92.

Norris, Lachelle. "The Human Face of Globalization: Plant Closings and Life Transitions." *Journal of Fashion Marketing and Management* 7, no. 2 (2003): 163–181.

Pfohl, Hans-Christian, and Karin Gareis. "Supplier Parks in the German Automotive Industry:

A Critical Comparison with Similar Concepts." *International Journal of Physical Distribution & Logistics Management* 35, no. 5 (2005): 302–317.

Salin, Victoria, and Rodolfo M. Nayga, Jr. "A Cold Chain Network for Food Exports to Developing Countries." *International Journal of Physical Distribution & Logistics Management* 33, no. 10 (2003): 918–932.

Vlachopoulou, Maro, George Silleos, and Vassiliki Manthou. "Geographic Information Systems in Warehouse Site Selection Decisions." *International Journal of Production Economics* 71, no. 3 (2001): 205–212.

Walter, Clyde Kenneth, and Richard F. Poist. "North American Inland Port Development: International vs Domestic Shipper Preferences." *International Journal of Physical Distribution & Logistics Management* 34, no. 7 (2004): 579–597.

Wu, Lifang, Xiaohang Yue, and Thaddeus Sim. "Supply Clusters: A Key to China's Success." *Supply Chain Management Review* 10, no. 2 (2006): 46–51.

C A S E S

CASE 8-1   AERO MARINE LOGISTICS

Aero Marine Logistics (AML) was incorporated as a Private Limited Company in South Delhi in the year 1996. The promoters of AML are two professionals who had gathered 15 years of experience working for Tata Steel (one of the biggest and oldest companies in India) in the field of shipping, customs clearance, forwarding, and transportation. Over the last five years, AML has been successful in building an infra-structure and pool of experienced personnel to handle the entire gamut of logistics. In fact, it was one of the first companies to offer door-to-

door delivery. It considers itself the specialists in customized solutions and services—a concept that is still unheard of in the transportation industry in the rural belts of northern India. AML handles the entire package of logistics for all its customers. Some of the services they offer include the following:

- *Import consolidation.* AML has a well-spread network of offices and trade connections in the United States, Europe, the Far East, and the Middle East to render import consolidation by both air and sea to any part of India. It promises a personalized prompt service with value for cost.

- *Door-to-door services.* AML is fully equipped to deliver door to door, which includes cargo pickup from the supplier's warehouse, warehousing prior to customs clearance, complete customs clearance of exports from overseas, and freight booking with airlines/shipping lines to receive cargo in India. It also undertakes local customs clearance and transportation to deliver to the door of the customer.

- *Exports.* AML has expertise in handling exports of various kinds of cargo by ocean and by air freight. It ensures the timely movement of cargo at the most competitive rates. It takes care of both the complete export documentation formalities and the physical movement of cargo.

- *Consultancy on customs and logistics.* AML is well equipped with professionals to guide customers regarding various modes of transportation and to help customers to optimize utilization of space and save on freight. It acts as liaison with different authorities like the RBI (Reserve Bank of India), Port Authority of India, India Civil Aviation Regulatory Body, TEXPROCIL (The Cotton Textiles Export Promotion Council of India), DGFT (Directorate General of Foreign Trade), etc., on behalf of clients for various permissions and quotas related to import and export of cargo. This could perhaps be classified as its most valuable service, which it hopes will build up its brand image. The red tape, bureaucracy, lack of work ethic, and corruption preclude anyone lacking either clout or established relationship channels (with *babus* or permanent government employees notorious for their apathy toward fulfilling job duties and with a penchant for bribe taking) to do business in India.

To enable it to offer these services, AML has partnered with various associates all over the globe to render forwarding services to all its customers. It has covered warehouse space of 1,000 square meters and has the ability to arrange for additional space. It has its own two 407 Tata trucks for pickup and delivery of small consignments. It has dedicated a fleet of five low-bed trailers for pickup and delivery of containers. All the field personnel have been provided with two-wheelers for faster conveyance between various points of work.

AML has grown rapidly and recently established an online presence whereby clients can place orders online and check the status of their cargo. So far the increase in sales from the online presence has not been much. Most of AML's clients are spread out in rural areas, and except for customers in Delhi, most do not have access to the Internet.

Today AML is handling an average of 200-plus TEUs (20-foot container equivalents) of imports and exports every month between Delhi and Mumbai (Bombay), which is the nearest big port (a distance of 1,407 kilometers). (See Exhibit 8-A.) Luckily, most containers are used for traffic in both directions; moving empties is unproductive. Main items for export are bathroom fittings and spares, machine spares and agricultural equipment, machine spares and chemicals, scientific equipment, medical equipment spares and chemicals, food processing machinery, furniture and kitchen equipment, and interiors. Main items for import are automobile engines and spares, cotton yarn, food products, electronics, televisions and components, rice, stone for stone crafting, etc.

Recently, one of the AML partners, Mr. S. Singh, was approached by the chairman of Freshfoods, Mr. R. Maan, with a promise of a huge potential volume (150,000 kilograms per month) for importing frozen mushrooms from Europe if AML would build up its Indian infrastructure to handle such volumes. Freshfoods is the biggest regional exporter/importer of food products in North India. It was founded 20 years ago by a collective of farmers wanting to find markets for their surplus produce of exotic and nonnative foods (like avocados and strawberries) that did not have much local demand except for five-star hotels catering to mostly foreign tourists.

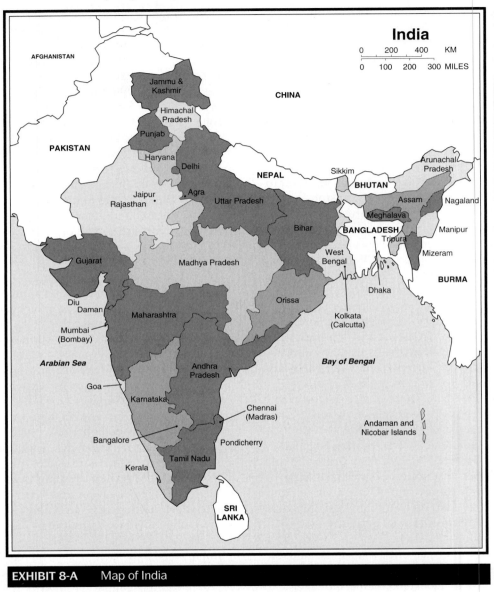

EXHIBIT 8-A   Map of India

The shift in eating habits in recent years had prompted Mr. Maan to promote mushrooms as a daily food item in a major way. To keep the price of imported mushrooms comparable with locally grown food items, huge quantities would have to be transacted to make use of economies of scale.

Mr. Singh realized that the first order from Mr. Maan was an experiment and that further orders would depend on whether the product caught on or not. AML needed to bet on a huge surge in demand for frozen mushrooms in the region if it wanted to be part of this new trend from the very beginning. Singh's partner—Mr. Kumar—is wary of investing heavily on the basis of this one order. After some bargaining, Mr. Mann agreed that Freshfoods would ship approximately 150,000 kilograms of mushrooms per month for 12 months and will pay $.20US per kilogram of mushrooms.

If AML decided to handle this product, it would need to add some equipment to its flatbed trailers to provide power to the refrigeration units on the containers. This is a one-time cost of 9 lakhs (one lakh = $2,222US). With temperatures soaring to 50 degrees Celsius (and the hot wind called *loo*—notorious for deaths associated with heat waves), for most of the long hot summer the energy costs of meeting special conditions could be prohibitive. AML expects them to total about 3 lakhs on an annual basis.

Mr. Singh then made inquiries to his rail carrier about the costs of leasing refrigerated containers. He was disappointed to learn that leasing was almost impossible. The container leasing companies wanted exorbitant rates because there was no backhaul traffic requiring refrigerated equipment and because some areas in North India were too isolated if they needed to send a worker to service malfunctioning equipment. The container leasing company did, however, offer to sell used refrigerated 20-foot containers for 7 lakhs apiece and would agree to service them for one year at an additional cost of 1 lakh per container. The used containers could be expected to last another 5 years. In a meeting involving Mr. Singh, Mr. Maan, and Mr. Veejay, a carrier representative, it was decided that ten 20-foot containers would be sufficient to handle the projected volume of mushrooms. Each container would make one round-trip each month. The cost of ocean freight expense from Amsterdam to Mumbai is $1700US for a single 20-foot container. The cost of land transportation per single 20-foot container from Mumbai to Delhi is $300US. Return costs for empty containers from Delhi to Mumba to Amsterdam are half as much, although about 10 percent of the time another cargo can be found that will cover the costs of return transport.

As the meeting broke up, Mr. Veejay said that the mushrooms were not a very dense cargo and that Mr. Singh could be using 40-foot refrigerated containers, which held twice as much as a 20-foot container, though handling costs were less than twice as much. The cost of ocean freight from Amsterdam to Mumbai is $2600US for a single 40-foot container. The cost of transportation per single 40-foot container from Mumbai to Delhi is $500US. Return costs from Delhi to Mumbai to Amsterdam are half as much, although about 10 percent of the time another cargo can be found that will cover the costs of return transport. Mr. Veejay felt that the 40-foot containers would need to be purchased. Five would be needed, with each making one round-trip per month. Containers were only available new, and the cost would be 15 lakhs apiece. Maintenance anywhere was guaranteed for the first year, and the containers had an estimated life of 10 years. ■

QUESTIONS

1. What would the first-year costs be to AML if it purchased the 10 used 20-foot containers? How long would it take to recoup the investment, assuming that the mushroom traffic continued?
2. What would the first-year costs be to AML if it purchased five new 40-foot containers? How long would it take to recoup the investment, assuming that the mushroom traffic continued?
3. Is one of the alternatives in questions 1 and 2 riskier? Why?
4. Mr. Singh has read about the supply-chain concept that attempts to identify and link all the participants from suppliers' suppliers to customers' customers. Who are all the participants in the supply chain, a part of which has been discussed in the case?
5. Logistics partnerships involve sharing costs and risks. What are *all* the costs and risks that this venture entails? How might they be shared?
6. With some help from your instructor, divide into groups representing most or all of the supply-chain members identified in question 4, and negotiate an agreement or agreements that share the costs, risks, and possible profits and losses from the venture being considered.

CASE 8-2　ALBERTA HIGHWAY DEPARTMENT, REGION VI

The Alberta Highway Department, Region VI, is headquartered in an area west of Lethbridge, Calgary, and Red Deer. One of its most important responsibilities, in the public's mind, is to keep open Canadian Route 1, which travels across all of Canada. At the very west of Region VI are the Rocky Mountains, and in a six-mile stretch between Lake Louise and the British Columbia border, the highway climbs from 3,000 to 6,000 feet. The climb in this stretch is uniform; the road's elevation increases 500 feet each mile as it moves to the west (see Exhibit 8-B).

A highway maintenance station is near Lake Louise, one mile to the east of the six-mile section. At this station are based several heavy-duty dump trucks that in the winter are mounted with snowplows in the front and sand-spreading devices in the rear.

Sanding is used after frost or freezing rains and in the spring when melting snows refreeze at night. The higher elevations require more sanding because they are subject to more freezing temperatures. For more than 10 years, since the highway was opened, records have been kept for the amount of maintenance required by each mile of highway. In terms of sanding, the average number of days per year that each mile requires sanding are as follows:

Mile 1　3000'–3500' elevation 40 days
Mile 2　3500'–4000' elevation 48 days
Mile 3　4000'–4500' elevation 53 days
Mile 4　4500'–5000' elevation 58 days
Mile 5　5000'–5500' elevation 65 days
Mile 6　5500'–6000' elevation 70 days

The dump trucks can carry 10 tons of sand, which is enough to spread over one mile of highway in both the eastbound and westbound lanes. Spreading sand is a slow process because, under slippery conditions, highway traffic moves slowly. Several trucks are required because when sanding is needed, it is needed quickly.

At the Lake Louise maintenance station are large silos for holding the salt-treated sand. At present, the silos can hold nearly 6,000 tons of

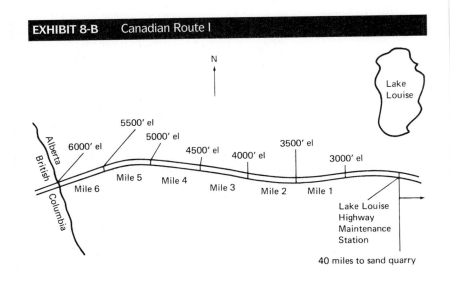

EXHIBIT 8-B　Canadian Route I

sand, some of which is used for lower stretches of highway. During the summer months, the silos are filled by special trailer dump trucks that carry the sand up from a quarry near Bow Valley, 40 miles to the east of the Lake Louise maintenance station. The silo is designed so that it can be split into two. Split segments of the silo can hold different capacities or equal capacities of sand. However, their total capacity is 6,000 tons.

Through a departmental program for encouraging employee suggestions, a proposal had been received from a sander truck driver that a portion of the Lake Louise sand silos be moved west toward the higher elevations, where more frequent sandings are needed.

The highway was constructed so that at one-mile distances (in this case, at elevations of 3,000, 3,500, 4,000, 4,500, 5,000, 5,500, and 6,000 feet) it is possible for maintenance trucks to turn around. The shoulders are also wide enough at these points so that the silos can be placed alongside. The silo relocation can be performed during summer months using regular maintenance crews and equipment, with no additional costs.

The principal reason for splitting and relocating a portion of the silos is to place sand closer to where it is needed and to reduce the travel time of maintenance trucks to and from the silos. The work crews are paid a constant rate for a fixed number of hours; if they are not sanding, they are performing other tasks. Hence, the only relevant costs are those of truck operation.

The facts and assumptions to be used in the analysis follow:

1. Costs of trucking sand from the quarry to the Lake Louise silos or to the relocated silos are three cents per ton-mile for the length of the full haul in one direction. (Empty backhaul costs are taken into account by these calculations.)

2. Some sand silo capacity must be kept at the Lake Louise maintenance station.

3. Spreader dump trucks are more costly to operate for carrying sand between silos and to where it is needed. The cost is 10 cents per ton-mile (which also takes empty backhauls into account).

4. No costs are assigned for spreader trucks to reach silos initially. The reason for this is that they are randomly located on the highway at the time the decision is made to spread sand. Truck crews are then dispatched by radio.

5. If a new silo is located, it must be at one of the turnaround sites between each of the miles.

6. If a new silo is located an even number of miles from the Lake Louise station, a midpoint will be established halfway between the two silos, and sanders will load at the silo nearest the mile of road needing sand.

7. If a new silo is located an odd number of miles from the Lake Louise maintenance station, a determination must be made as to which silo will provide sand for the middle one. (This is because maintenance trucks cannot turn at the middle of mile sections.)

8. No costs are assigned to operating the spreaders within a mile on either side of the silo. This is because they start spreading sand immediately upon leaving the silo. However, for sanding a stretch that is, say, between two and three miles from the silo, the cost of reaching the area would be $2 (10 tons × 10 cents × 2 miles). ∎

QUESTIONS

1. Should one portion of sand silos at the Lake Louise maintenance station be relocated to a point to the west at a higher elevation? If yes, where should it be relocated, how much capacity should it have, and what are the projected annual savings in truck operating costs? Show your work.

2. Assume that it is discovered that it would be impossible to split the silo into sections. However, it would be feasible to move the entire silo to a site farther up the slope. The section of highway from the Lake Louise maintenance station stretching west 1 mile to where it reaches the 3,000-foot elevation point must be sanded for 30 days per year. All points east of the Lake Louise maintenance station can be serviced from other points. Should the entire silo be moved to another point? If so, to where? What will the savings be? Show your work.

3. Ignore all statements made in question 2 and assume, instead, that the silo can be divided into three sections: one remaining at Lake Louise and the other two located somewhere along the 6-mile stretch. If two sections are to be located within the 6-mile section, where should they be placed? What will the savings be over the present system? Show your work.

4. This case was written some time ago, when fuel costs were very low. Assume now that the spreader dump truck costs 35 cents per ton-mile to operate (compared to 10 cents) and that the trailer dump truck used to move sand from the quarry costs 20 cents per ton-mile to operate (up from 3 cents). Answer question 1 again, but this time take into account the new truck operating costs.

5. Answer question 2 again but using the new trucking costs outlined in question 4.

6. Answer question 3 again, taking into account the new trucking costs outlined in question 4.

9

INVENTORY MANAGEMENT

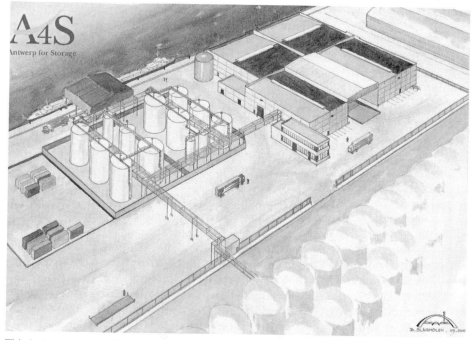

This facility, located in the Port of Antwerp, is designed for the storage and handling of hazardous materials. The facility serves deep-sea ships, barges, rail, and trucks. Some of the value-added services the operator offers are bagging, drumming, container stacking; filtration, heating, and sampling. Each tank is served by a separate, dedicated route of pumps and piping. The facility is operated as a 50/50 joint venture between a terminal company and a chemicals distributor.

Source: A4S N. V. (Antwerp for Storage).

Key Terms

- ABC analysis
- Complementary products
- Cycle (base) stock
- Dead inventory
- Economic order quantity (EOQ)
- Fixed order interval system
- Fixed order quantity system
- Inventory
- Inventory carrying (holding) costs
- Inventory flow diagram
- Inventory shrinkage

- Inventory turnover
- Just-in-time (JIT) approach
- Nodes
- Pipeline (in-transit) stock
- Reorder (trigger) point (ROP)
- Safety (buffer) stock
- Speculative stock
- Stockout costs
- Substitute products
- Vendor-managed inventory (VMI)

Learning Objectives

- To determine the costs of holding inventory
- To identify the costs associated with a stockout
- To understand the EOQ concept
- To differentiate the various inventory flow patterns
- To identify several contemporary approaches to managing inventory
- To discuss special concerns with inventory management

Inventory refers to stocks of goods and materials that are maintained for many purposes, the most common being to satisfy normal demand patterns. In production and selling processes, inventories serve as cushions to accommodate the fact that items arrive in one pattern and are used in another pattern. For example, if you eat one egg a day and buy eggs by the dozen, every 12 days you would buy a new container of eggs, and the inventory of eggs remaining in your refrigerator would decline at the rate of one egg per day. Figure 9-1 shows a bulk handling operation where a bin is between a vessel being discharged and a truck being loaded.

Inventory management is a key component of supply chain management, in part because inventory decisions are often a starting point, or driver, for other business activities, such as warehousing, transportation, and materials handling. Moreover, different organizational functions can have different inventory management objectives. Marketing, for example, tends to want to ensure that sufficient inventory is available for customer demand to avoid potential stockout situations—which translate into higher inventory levels. Alternatively, the finance group generally seeks to minimize the costs associated with holding inventory, which translates into lower inventory levels. As if managing these seemingly conflicting objectives within one organization isn't challenging enough, supply chains are made up of multiple organizations—each of which may have its own distinct inventory management philosophy. Indeed, each link in the supply chain may prefer having other links maintain the inventory.

One of the most prominent concerns about inventory is its cost, which is presented in greater detail later in this chapter. It is important to note here, however, that because inventory costs money, increases in inventory are not always desirable. For example, a firm may manufacture much more than it can reasonably sell, or a firm may manufacture products so that its warehousing facilities look full.

FIGURE 9-1   Coal Is Being Unloaded at Longview, Washington

Coal from the ship is dumped into the bin, where it is fed by a conveyor belt
to the waiting trucks. The inventory of coal in the bin acts as a cushion
between the differing rates of loading and unloading.
Source: Port of Longview, Washington.

It is also important to recognize that inventory carries its greatest cost after value has been
added through manufacturing and processing. Finished goods inventories are, therefore, much
more expensive to hold than raw materials or work in progress. Carrying costs for inventories
can be significant, and the return on investment to a firm for the funds it has tied up in inventory
should be as high as the return it can obtain from other, equally risky uses of the same funds.

The focus on inventory costs has intensified in recent years because of concern with **inventory turnover,** or the number of times that inventory is sold in a one-year period. Inventory turnover can be calculated by dividing the cost of goods sold for a particular period by the average inventory for that period. For example, if the cost of goods sold annually is $200,000 and average inventory on hand is $50,000, inventory turnover equals four.

Although there is no optimal inventory turnover ratio, inventory turnover figures can provide important insights about an organization's competitiveness and efficiency. Thus, a particular organization can compare its turnover figures to those of direct competitors or other organizations with "desirable" turnover ratios. With respect to efficiency, low turnover indicates that a company is taking longer to sell its inventory, perhaps because of product obsolescence or pricing problems.[1] By contrast, high turnover may signal a low level of inventories, which can increase the chance of product stockouts. The fact that stockouts can be quite costly to an organization is explored later in this chapter.

It's easy to say that organizations should strive for a proper balance of inventory; actually achieving it can be quite difficult because of the trade-offs that are involved. On the one hand, low inventory turnover results in high inventory carrying costs and low (or no) stockout costs. On the other hand, higher inventory turnover results in low inventory carrying costs and some (high) stockout costs.

This chapter begins with a look at various classifications of inventory and a discussion of inventory-related costs, followed by discussion of when to order and how much to order. This chapter also looks at several contemporary approaches to managing inventory. It concludes with a discussion of special concerns related to inventory management.

INVENTORY CLASSIFICATIONS

It's important to know the key classifications of inventory because the classification influences the way that inventory is managed. Although inventory generally exists to service demand, in some situations inventory is carried to stimulate demand, also known as *psychic stock*. This type of inventory is associated with retail stores, and the general idea is that customer purchases are stimulated by inventory that they can see.[2] This concept helps to explain, in part, why some retailers stock huge amounts of certain merchandise.

Inventory that services demand is most frequently classified as cycle (base) stock, safety (buffer) stock, pipeline (in-transit) stock, or speculative stock. Each type is explained in the following paragraphs.

Cycle, *or base,* **stock** refers to inventory that is needed to satisfy normal demand during the course of an order cycle. With respect to the egg example at the beginning of this chapter, one dozen (12) eggs represents the cycle stock—we use one egg per day, and we buy eggs every 12 days.

Safety, *or buffer,* **stock** refers to inventory that is held in addition to cycle stock to guard against uncertainty in demand or lead time. For example, uncertainty in demand could come from the fact that you occasionally decide to make a three-egg omelet as opposed to eating one egg per day. As an example of lead-time uncertainty, you may sometimes buy eggs every 14 days, rather than every 12 days. In both cases, a few extra eggs would ensure that you won't run out of eggs.

Pipeline, *or in-transit,* **stock** is inventory that is en route between various **nodes** (i.e., fixed facilities such as a plant, warehouse, or store) in a logistics system. Pipeline inventory is

---

[1]"'Turns' for the Better—Inventory Turns Impact Profits and Stock Prices," *Dow Theory Forecasts* 58, no. 4 (2002), 1, 4.
[2]Paul D. Larson and Robert A. DeMaris, "Psychic Stock: An Independent Variable Category of Inventory," *International Journal of Physical Distribution & Logistics Management* 20, no. 7 (1990): 27–37.

represented here by eggs that are in transit between a chicken farm and, say, a food wholesaler's distribution center or between the retail store and your kitchen.

Speculative stock refers to inventory that is held for several reasons, including seasonal demand, projected price increases, and potential shortages of product. For example, the fact that eggs are associated with Easter (e.g., Easter egg rolls, colored eggs) tends to cause an increase in demand for them prior to the Easter holiday.

INVENTORY-RELATED COSTS

Inventory Carrying Costs

As noted, a prominent concern involves the costs associated with holding inventory, which are referred to as **inventory carrying (holding) costs.** In general, inventory carrying costs are expressed in percentage terms, and this percentage is multiplied by the inventory's value. The resulting number represents the dollar value associated with holding the particular inventory. So, if the value of a particular item is $100 and the inventory carrying costs are 18 percent, the relevant annual inventory expense is $18.

Not surprisingly, an increase or decrease in the carrying cost percentage will affect the relevant inventory expense. Generally speaking, companies prefer to carry lower inventory as the carrying cost percentage increases, in part because there is greater risk (e.g., obsolescence) to holding the inventory. As a result, the determination of a carrying cost percentage should be quite important for many companies. However, the reality is that a recent study showed that slightly more than 50 percent of the surveyed companies had an established inventory carrying cost. Moreover, approximately 20 percent of the study respondents either did not know, or did not have access to, their organization's inventory carrying cost.[3] The lack of knowledge about inventory carrying costs is reflected by the fact that a commonly used estimate today for inventory carrying costs is 25 percent—a figure that dates from the mid-1950s.[4]

Inventory carrying costs consist of a number of different factors or categories, and the importance of these factors can vary from product to product. For example, perishable items such as dairy products, meat, and poultry are often sold with expiration dates, causing them to have little or no value after a certain date. By contrast, a box of lead pencils loses its value much more slowly through time. These two examples illustrate the obsolescence category of inventory carrying costs and refer to the fact that products lose value through time. Note that some products lose their value much more quickly than others.

Inventory shrinkage is another component of inventory carrying cost and refers to the fact that more items are recorded entering than leaving warehousing facilities. Shrinkage is generally caused by damage, loss, or theft, and although shrinkage costs can be reduced, such efforts often generate other costs. For example, although better packaging may reduce damage, loss, or theft costs, better packaging likely translates into increased packaging costs.

Another component of inventory carrying costs, storage costs, refers to those costs associated with occupying space in a plant, storeroom, or warehousing facility. Some products have very specialized storage requirements; ice cream, for example, must be stored at a temperature below –20 degrees Fahrenheit. Handling costs involve the costs of employing staff to receive, store, retrieve, and move inventory. There may also be inventory *insurance costs,* which insure

---

[3]"What's Your Inventory Carrying Cost, and Why Don't You Know It?" *Ioma's Inventory Management Report,* January 2005, 2–4.
[4]See L. P. Alford and John R. Bangs (eds.), *Production Handbook* (New York: Ronald, 1955).

inventory against fire, flood, theft, and other perils. Insurance costs are not uniform across products; diamonds, for example, are more costly to insure than shampoo.

Taxes represent yet another component of inventory carrying costs, and they are calculated on the basis of the inventory on hand on a particular date; considerable effort is made to have that day's inventory be as low as possible. Furthermore, *interest costs* take into account the money that is required to maintain the investment in inventory. In the United States, the prime rate of interest has traditionally provided a convenient starting point when estimating the interest charges associated with maintaining inventory.

Some inventory items have other types of carrying costs because of their specialized nature. Pets and livestock, for example, must be watered and fed. Tropical fish must be fed and have oxygen added to the water in which they are kept. Another cost, although it is generally excluded from carrying cost, is opportunity cost—the cost of taking a position in the wrong materials. This can be an issue for those companies that engage in speculative inventory. Opportunity costs are also incurred by firms that hold too much inventory in reserve for customer demand.

Stockout Costs

If avoiding an oversupply were the only problem associated with inventories, the solution would be relatively simple: Store fewer items. However, not having enough items can be as bad as, and sometimes worse than, having too many items. Such costs can accrue during stockouts, when customers demand items that aren't immediately available.

Although calculation of stockout costs can be difficult and inexact, it is important for organizations to do so because such knowledge can be beneficial when determining how much inventory to hold, while remembering that a trade-off must be balanced between inventory carrying costs and stockout costs. **Stockout costs,** or estimating the costs or penalties for a stockout, involve an understanding of a customer's reaction to a company being out of stock when a customer wants to buy an item.

Consider the following customer responses to a particular stockout situation. How should they be evaluated?

1. The customer says, "I'll be back," and this proves to be so.
2. The customer says, "Call me when it's in."
3. The customer buys a substitute product that yields a higher profit for the seller.
4. The customer buys a substitute product that yields a lower profit for the seller.
5. The customer places an order for the item that is out of stock (a *back order*) and asks to have the item delivered when it arrives.
6. The customer goes to a competitor only for this purchase.
7. The customer goes to a competitor for this and all future purchases.

Clearly, each of these situations has a different cost to the company experiencing a stockout. For example, the loss in situation 1 is negligible because the sale is only slightly delayed. The outcome from situation 2 is more problematic in that the company doesn't know whether the customer will, in fact, return. Situation 7 is clearly the most damaging, because the customer has been lost for good, and it's necessary to know the cost of developing a new customer to replace the lost customer. A commonly used guideline is that it costs five times as much to acquire a new customer as it does to retain an existing one.

To illustrate the calculation of stockout costs, assume for simplicity's sake that customer responses to a stockout can be placed into three categories: delayed sale (brand loyalty), lost sale (switches and comes back), and lost customer. Assume further that, over time, of 300 customers who experienced a stockout, 10 percent delayed the sale, 65 percent switched and came back, but the remaining 25 percent were lost for good (see Table 9-1).

TABLE 9-1   Determination of the Average Cost of a Stockout

Alternative	Loss	Probability	Average Cost
1. Brand-loyal customer	$ 00.00	.10	$ 00.00
2. Switches and comes back	37.00	.65	24.05
3. Lost customer	1,200.00	.25	300.00
Average cost of a stockout		1.00	$324.05

These are hypothetical figures for illustration.

The probability of each event taking place can be used to determine the average cost of a stockout. More specifically, as illustrated in Table 9-1, each probability is multiplied by the respective loss to yield an average cost per event. These average costs are then summed, and the result is the average cost per stockout. A delayed sale is virtually costless because the customer is brand loyal and will purchase the product when it becomes available. The lost sale alternative results in a loss of the profit that would have been made on the customer's purchase. In the lost customer situation, the customer buys a competitor's product and decides to make all future purchases from that competitor; the relevant cost involved is that of developing a new customer.

Although the example presented in Table 9-1 is quite simplified, several important points bear highlighting. As a general rule, the higher the average cost of a stockout, the better it is for the company to hold some amount of inventory (safety stock) to protect against stockouts. Second, the higher the probability of a delayed sale, the lower the average stockout costs—and the lower the inventory that needs to be held by a company. Table 9-1 provides strong evidence for the importance of a company's developing brand-loyal customers.

Trade-Offs Exist Between Carrying and Stockout Costs

As mentioned earlier, higher levels of inventory can lessen the occurrence of stockouts. Marginal analysis, which focuses on the trade-off between carrying and stockout costs, allows a company to determine an optimum level of safety stocks. Marginal analysis helps define the point at which the costs of holding additional safety stock are equal to the savings in stockout costs avoided.

An example of marginal analysis is presented in Table 9-2. In this example, we assume that inventory can only be ordered in multiples of 10 and that each unit of inventory is valued at $480 with carrying costs of 25 percent. As a result, the incremental carrying costs of moving from 0 units of safety stock to 10 units of safety stock are (10 × $480) × .25, or $1,200. Likewise, the incremental carrying costs of moving from 10 to 20 units of safety stock are $1,200.

TABLE 9-2   Determination of Safety Stock Level

Number of Units of Safety Stock	Additional Safety Stock ($480 per Unit)	Number of 25% Annual Carrying Cost	Total Value of of Incremental Safety Stock	Additional Orders Filled	Carrying Cost Stockout Costs Avoided
10	$ 4,800	$1,200	$1,200	20	$6,481.00
20	9,600	2,400	1,200	16	5,184.80
30	14,400	3,600	1,200	12	3,888.60
40	19,200	4,800	1,200	8	2,592.40
50	24,000	6,000	1,200	6	1,944.30
60	28,800	7,200	1,200	4	1,296.20
70	33,600	8,400	1,200	3	972.15

This example also assumes that the various levels of safety stock prevent a certain number of stockouts. For example, holding 10 units of safety stock for an entire year allows the firm to prevent 20 stockouts; moving from 10 units to 20 units of safety stock allows 16 additional orders to be filled. Using the average cost of a stockout ($324.05) from Table 9-1, a safety stock of 10 units allows the firm to prevent 20 stockouts, which saves the firm $6,481 ($324.05 × 20). The savings of $6,481 is much greater than the additional carrying costs of $1,200, so the firm wants to hold at least 10 units of safety stock. Twenty units of safety stock result in $1,200 of additional carrying costs, whereas the additional stockout costs avoided are $5,184.80 (16 × $324.05).

According to the data in Table 9-2, the optimum quantity of safety stock is 60 units. At this point, the cost of 10 additional units of inventory is $1,200, and $1,296.20 is saved in stockout costs. If the safety stocks are increased from 60 to 70 units, the additional carrying costs are again $1,200, and the savings are only $972.15. Therefore, the firm is best served by planning for about three stockouts to occur each year.

WHEN TO ORDER

A key issue with respect to inventory management involves when product should be ordered; one could order a fixed amount of inventory (**fixed order quantity system**), or orders can be placed at fixed time intervals (**fixed order interval system**). In a fixed order quantity system, the time interval may fluctuate while the order size stays constant; for example, a store might always order 200 cases of soft drinks. Its first order might be placed on January 3, a second order placed on January 6 (three-day interval), with a third order placed on January 11 (five-day interval). By contrast, in a fixed order interval system, the time interval is constant, but the order size may fluctuate. For example, a man goes grocery shopping with his wife every Sunday. Although the time interval for shopping is constant at seven days, the shopping list (inventory requirements) differs from week to week.

There needs to be a **reorder (trigger) point** (i.e., the level of inventory at which a replenishment order is placed) for there to be an efficient fixed order quantity system. Reorder points (ROPs) are relatively easy to calculate, particularly under conditions of certainty; a reorder point is equal to the average daily demand (DD) in units times the length of the replenishment cycle (RC):

$$ROP = DD \times RC$$

Suppose, for example, that average daily demand is 40 units, and the replenishment cycle is 4 days. The reorder point in this example is 40 × 4, or 160 units; in other words, when the inventory level reaches 160 units, a reorder is placed.

The reorder point under conditions of uncertainty can be calculated in a similar manner; the only modification involves including a safety stock (SS) factor:

$$ROP = (DD \times RC) + SS$$

Continuing with the previous example, suppose that the company decides to hold 40 units of safety stock. The reorder point becomes (40 × 4) + 40, or 200 units.

The fact that a fixed order quantity system works best when there is a predetermined reorder point indicates that this system requires relatively frequent, if not constant, monitoring of inventory levels. Under a fixed order quantity system, if sales start to increase, the reorder point will be reached more quickly, and a new order will automatically be placed. In most fixed order interval systems, by contrast, inventory levels are monitored much less frequently—often just before the scheduled order time. The infrequency of inventory monitoring makes the fixed interval system much more susceptible to stockout situations, and one is more likely to see higher levels of safety stock in a fixed interval system. It's entirely possible that a company could have some of its inventory under a fixed order quantity system, whereas other inventory uses a fixed order interval system.

HOW MUCH TO REORDER

Economic Order Quantity

A long-standing issue in inventory management concerns how much inventory should be ordered at a particular time. The typical inventory order size problem, referred to as the **economic order quantity (EOQ),** deals with calculating the proper order size with respect to two costs: the costs of carrying the inventory and the costs of ordering the inventory.

If there were no inventory carrying costs, customers would hold an immense inventory and avoid the vagaries of reordering. Alternatively, if there were no costs to ordering, one would continually place orders and maintain virtually no inventory at all, aside from safety stocks. There are, however, costs of carrying inventory and costs of ordering inventory. Inventory carrying costs are in direct proportion to order size; that is, the larger the order, the greater the inventory carrying costs. Ordering costs, by contrast, tend to decline with the size of the order, but not in a linear relationship. The nature of carrying costs and ordering costs are presented in Figure 9-2.

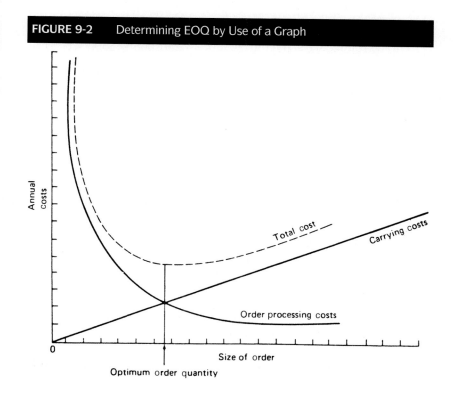

FIGURE 9-2   Determining EOQ by Use of a Graph

Although some view the EOQ as an outdated technique, others suggest that the EOQ allows "senior management to determine the money required to finance inventories, the length of time those funds are required, the source of that finance and the impact of its cost on the firm's profitability."[5]

The EOQ determines the point at which the sum of carrying costs and ordering costs is minimized, or the point at which carrying costs equal ordering costs (see Figure 9-2). Assuming that carrying costs and ordering costs are accurate, the EOQ "is absolutely the most cost-effective quantity to order based on current operational costs."[6]

Mathematically, the EOQ can be calculated in two ways; one presents the answer in dollars, the other in units. In terms of dollars, suppose that $1,000 of a particular item is used each year, the order costs are $25 per order submitted, and inventory carrying costs are 20 percent. The EOQ can be calculated using this formula:

$$EOQ = \sqrt{2AB / C}$$

Where

EOQ = the most economic order size, in dollars

    A = annual usage, in dollars

    B = administrative costs per order of placing the order

    C = carrying costs of the inventory (expressed as an annual percentage of the inventory dollar value)

Thus:

$$EOQ = \sqrt{2 \times 1000 \times 25 / .20} = \sqrt{250,000} = \$500 \text{ order size}$$

Alternatively, the EOQ can be calculated in terms of the number of units that should be ordered. Using the same information as in the previous example, and assuming that the product has a cost of $5 per unit, the relevant formula is:

$$EOQ = \sqrt{2DB / IC}$$

Where

EOQ = the most economic order size, in units

    D = annual demand, in units (200 units; $1,000 value of inventory/$5 value per unit)

    B = administrative costs per order of placing the order

    C = carrying costs of the inventory (expressed as an annual percentage of the inventory's dollar value)

    I = dollar value of the inventory, per unit

Thus:

$$EOQ = \sqrt{2 \times 200 \times 25 / .20 \times 5} = \sqrt{10,000 / 1} = 100 \text{ units}$$

---

[5]Bill Lee and Bruce Bowhill, "EOQ, EBS for Higher Management," *Engineering Management* 14, no. 5 (2004): 44–47.

[6]Dave Piasecki, "Optimizing Economic Order Quantity," *IIE Solutions* 33, no. 1 (2002): 30–33, 39.

TABLE 9-3	EOQ Cost Calculations			
Number of Orders Per Year	**Order Size ($)**	**Ordering Cost ($)**	**Carrying Cost ($)**	**Total Cost (sum of Ordering and Carrying Cost) ($)**
1	1,000	25	100	125
2	500	50	50	100
3	333	75	33	108
4	250	100	25	125
5	200	125	20	145

Although we've calculated EOQs, how do we know that the answers are correct? Because the EOQ is the point where carrying costs equal ordering costs, we need to calculate both of these costs (see Table 9-3). Ordering cost can be calculated by multiplying the number of orders per year times the ordering cost per order. For example, because an order size of $1,000 means that we're ordering once a year, the ordering cost would be 1 × $25, or $25.

Because of the assumption of even outward flow of goods, inventory carrying costs are applied to one-half of the order size, a figure that represents the average inventory. Average inventory is multiplied by the carrying costs of the inventory (expressed as a percentage of the dollar value). Thus, when ordering once per year, the order size of $1,000 is divided by 2, yielding $500. This, in turn, is multiplied by .20, resulting in a carrying cost of $100. The $25 ordering cost and $100 carrying cost are not equal, thus indicating that we haven't found the EOQ.

Recall that we calculated $500 (100 units) to be the EOQ. As shown in Table 9-3, a $500 order size means that we'll be ordering twice per year; the corresponding ordering costs are $50. Average inventory for a $500 order size is $250, meaning that our carrying costs are $50. Thus, we've proven that at an order size of $500, our ordering costs and carrying costs are equal. Table 9-3 presents the total cost calculations for several other order sizes. Note that ordering costs equal carrying costs at the EOQ and that the total cost is minimized as well.

Several caveats bear mention. First, EOQs, once calculated, may not be the same as the lot sizes in which a product is commonly bought and sold. Second, the simple EOQ formulation does not take into account the special discounts given to encourage larger orders or increased volumes of business. Third, there is an implicit assumption of demand certainty; that is, demand is continuous and constant over time. The inclusion of one, or more, of these caveats will alter EOQ calculations.

INVENTORY FLOWS

The figures from the fixed order quantity (e.g., EOQ) and the safety stock calculations can be used to develop an **inventory flow diagram,** which graphically depicts the demand for, and replenishment of, inventory. Figure 9-3 presents an illustration of inventory flow, based on the following assumptions: an EOQ of 120 units, safety stock of 60 units, average demand of 30 units per day, and a replenishment or order cycle of 2 days. Further, the beginning inventory is equal to the safety stock plus the EOQ (60 + 120 = 180). Recall from earlier in this chapter that the reorder point can be calculated as (daily demand × replenishment cycle) + (safety stock), or (30 × 2) + (60) = 120 units.

As shown in Figure 9-3, 180 units of inventory are available for sale at the beginning of day 1 (point A). The daily demand of 30 means that 150 units are available for sale at the beginning

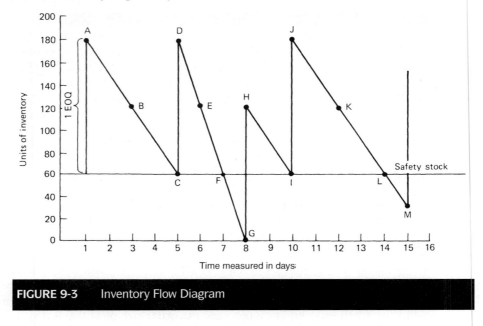

FIGURE 9-3   Inventory Flow Diagram

of day 2, and 120 units are available at the beginning of day 3. Because 120 units represent the reorder point (point B), an order is placed at the beginning of day 3. Because safety stock is not to be used under normal circumstances, reordering at 120 units means that 60 units (safety stock) will be on hand 2 days later when the EOQ arrives. The EOQ of 120 units arrives at point C, and then total inventory increases to 180 units at point D.

The rate of sales doubles to 60 beginning on day 5, the reorder point is hit at 120 units at the beginning of day 6 (point E), and another order is placed. Demand continues at 60 units on day 6, meaning that the regular inventory is exhausted, and at point F the safety stock is starting to be used. Demand is also 60 on day 7, leaving us with no inventory (point G) at the end of day 7. The EOQ arrives before opening on day 8, boosting the inventory to 120 units (point H), which is also the reorder point. Beginning on day 8, the demand settles back to 30 units per day.

Continuing with Figure 9-3, from point H, inventory is depleted 30 units on day 8 and 30 more on day 9, leaving the inventory at 60 (point I). The inventory ordered on day 8 arrives prior to opening on day 10, meaning that we have 180 units in stock at the beginning of day 10 (point J). Thirty units are demanded on days 10 and 11; inventory is thus 120 units (point K), and another reorder is placed at the beginning of day 12. Demand is 30 units on days 12 and 13, and inventory has reached 60 units (point L). However, because of a transportation delay, the replenishment cycle is 3 days instead of 2, and instead of arriving at the beginning of day 14, it arrives at the beginning of day 15. Day 14's demand of 30 units will be satisfied from safety stock (point M), and the EOQ arrives shortly thereafter.

The inventory flow example presented in Figure 9-3 illustrates that safety stock can prevent against two problem areas: an increased rate of demand and a longer-than-normal replenishment. This example also illustrates that when a fixed order quantity system such as an EOQ is used, the time between orders may vary. As long as demand was normal at 30 units and the replenishment cycle took 2 days, the time between orders was 4 days. However, when sales doubled to 60 units per day, the time between orders fell to 2 days.

As noted earlier in this chapter, one requirement for the utilization of a fixed order quantity system is that the level of inventory must constantly be monitored; when the reorder point is hit, the fixed order quantity is ordered. With continuing advances in computer hardware and software, many firms have the capability to constantly monitor their inventory and hence have the option of using a fixed order quantity system such as the EOQ. A reorder point for each item can be established electronically so it can indicate when the stock has been depleted to the point where a new order should be placed. Increasingly, these orders can be transmitted electronically.

CONTEMPORARY APPROACHES TO MANAGING INVENTORY

What has been described represents basic thinking about inventory management. Although such thinking continues to be relevant, additional approaches have evolved. Several of the more prominent approaches are presented in this section.

ABC Analysis

ABC analysis of inventory, which can be applied in several different ways, recognizes that inventories are not of equal value to a firm and that, as a result, all inventory should not be managed in the same way. An individual firm may stock hundreds or thousands of items, and it is a real challenge to determine the relative importance of each item. One commonly used rule of thumb, the *80/20 rule,* is that 80 percent of a company's sales come from 20 percent of its products (conversely, 20 percent of sales come from 80 percent of products). From a managerial perspective, this indicates that the primary focus should be on the 20 percent of products that generate the 80 percent of sales. For example, it might not be in a company's best interests to store very slow moving inventories in all its warehousing facilities; doing so increases inventory carrying costs and likely reduces its inventory turnover ratio.

Measures that can be used to determine ABC status include sales volume in dollars, sales volume in units, the fastest-selling items, item profitability, or item importance. For instance, with respect to item importance, one consideration with repair parts inventory would be how critical a part might be to customers. Likewise, a firm supplying medicine to hospitals might need to stock certain items because they are critically important. Thus, in terms of item importance, ABC might be operationalized as follows: A items could be the ones with the highest criticality, B items could be those with moderate criticality, and C items could have low criticality. Similar approaches could be applied to other measures of ABC status.

One issue with ABC analysis involves a determination of what percentage of items should be classified as A, B, and C, respectively. Although no right or wrong answers characterize this issue, it's important to recognize that either too high or too low a percentage of A items may reduce the potential efficiencies to be gained from the classification technique.

A second issue with ABC analysis involves how it can be used by managers. One use, as suggested earlier, is that ABC analysis can determine stocking patterns in warehousing facilities. For example, one company achieved a 25 percent space reduction in its logistics network by locating safety stock at only one warehousing facility.[7] In addition, as was pointed out earlier in this chapter, ABC analysis could be used to determine how frequently inventory gets monitored. Thus, A items might be checked daily (or, increasingly, hourly), B items weekly, and C items monthly.

---

[7]Mary Aichlmayr, "The Quick, the Dead, and the Slow Movers," *Transportation & Distribution,* February 2002, 38–42.

Before proceeding further, it should be noted that some companies are adding a fourth classification, D, to ABC analysis. *D* stands for either "dogs" or **dead inventory,** which refers to inventory for which there is no remaining demand. Note that such inventory serves to increase inventory carrying costs, as well as to reduce inventory turnover. Dead inventory is discussed in more detail later in this chapter.

Just-in-Time (JIT) Approach

One of the most popular contemporary approaches to managing inventories is the **just-in-time (JIT) approach.** Many believe that JIT originated with Japanese manufacturers, but the concept actually started in the United States in the 1920s with Henry Ford's integrated production and assembly plants. Japanese manufacturers, in particular Toyota Motor Company, refined the JIT approach to the point where JIT gave organizations that used it distinct advantages over their competitors.

From an inventory perspective, the JIT approach seeks to minimize inventory by reducing (if not eliminating) safety stock, as well as by having the required amount of materials arrive at the production location at the exact time that they are needed. The JIT approach views inventory as waste, whereas the so-called JIC (just-in-case) approach requires additional levels of inventory just-in-case something unexpected occurs.

Although the just-in-time approach is generally associated with inventory management because of its focus on minimizing inventory, the consequences of JIT actually go far beyond inventory management. The JIT approach has a number of important implications for logistics and supply chain efficiency. One implication is that suppliers must deliver high-quality materials to the production line; because of JIT's emphasis on low (no) safety stock, defective materials result in a production line shutdown. Improved product quality from suppliers can be facilitated by looking at suppliers as partners, as opposed to adversaries, in the production process. Chapter 2 noted that relational exchanges are one of the cornerstones of supply chain management.

This chapter has explored the trade-off between ordering costs and carrying costs: As ordering costs go up, carrying costs go down, and vice versa. Because JIT emphasizes minimal inventory levels, customers tend to place smaller, more frequent orders. As such, it is imperative that suppliers' order systems be capable of handling an increased number of orders in an error-free fashion. In addition, because the transit-time reliability tends to decrease with distance, suppliers need to be located relatively close to their customers. The supplier park concept that was discussed in Chapter 8 is an excellent example of locational proximity.

The combination of smaller, more frequent shipments and close supplier location suggests that trucking is an important mode of transportation in the JIT approach. As such, production and distribution facilities should be designed to support truck shipments—that is, there should be truck docks to facilitate product loading and unloading. Although this may appear to be the proverbial "no-brainer," consider the case of a U.S. manufacturer that designed a state-of-the-art distribution facility to be served by rail, only to switch to a JIT approach, thus making the new facility totally worthless. In fact, some companies involved in JIT have designed their production facilities so that trucks can drive inside them, thus bringing the product that much closer to the actual production point. Figure 9-4 shows a truck trailer that opens on its side for rapid discharge of parts for JIT inventory management.

Other inventory minimization (lean inventory) philosophies include Efficient Consumer Response (ECR), which is associated with the grocery and beverage industries, and Quick Response (QR), which is associated with the apparel industry. Where JIT tends to encompass

---

[8]Karl Edmunds, "ECR: Ready for Action," *Beverage World,* March 15, 2001, 76–78.

FIGURE 9-4   Trailer That Opens on the Side and Is Used for Rapid Discharge of Parts

It was designed for use by carriers serving manufacturers with just-in-time inventory management systems.

Source: Photo courtesy Fruehauf Corporation.

movement of materials and component parts from supplier to producer, lean inventory philosophies such as ECR and QR tend to focus on product movement from manufacturer to retailer. Just as collaboration among supply chain participants is key to successful JIT initiatives, collaboration among supply chain participants is also essential for ECR and QR to be successful.[8]

Although JIT continues to be a key concept in contemporary logistics, a confluence of events suggests that organizations should give careful consideration before adopting a JIT philosophy. More specifically, the JIT philosophy was conceived and nurtured in an environment—low fuel prices, minimal transportation congestion, excess transportation capacity, limited terrorism—far different than today. For instance, skyrocketing fuel prices, and the attendant fuel surcharges, along with congested transportation networks, serve to undermine JIT's focus on smaller, more frequent shipments that arrive exactly when needed.[9]

[9]Wendy Leavitt, "Beyond JIT," *Fleet Owner,* November 2005, 78.

Vendor-Managed Inventory (VMI)

In traditional inventory management, the size and timing of replenishment orders are the responsibility of the party using the inventory, such as a distributor or a retailer. Under **vendor-managed inventory (VMI)**, by contrast, the size and timing of replenishment orders are the responsibility of the manufacturer. Operationally, VMI allows manufacturers to have access to a distributor's or retailer's sales and inventory data, and this access is accomplished electronically by electronic data interchange (EDI) or the Internet. Although VMI is often associated with consumer products, it also has been applied to industrial products such as airplanes, construction equipment, fasteners (e.g., bolts, screws), and heating and cooling systems, among others.

VMI represents a huge philosophical shift for some organizations in the sense that they are allowing another party to have control over their inventories. This is a situation that necessitates tremendous trust on the part of distributors and retailers because of the potential for unscrupulous manufacturers to abuse the system by pushing unneeded inventories onto downstream parties.

VMI's benefits for distributors and retailers tend to involve reduced inventories, fewer stockouts, and higher revenues, whereas manufacturer benefits include improved demand forecasting because of earlier access to data. One potential drawback to VMI is inadequate data sharing between the relevant parties, in part because of trust and control concerns.[10]

Inventory Tracking

Advances in technology are making it easier (and less costly) to keep track of inventory, which can translate into marked improvements in supply-chain efficiency. Although the ubiquitous bar code is perhaps the most familiar tracking technology, radio-frequency identification (RFID) chips are growing in popularity. Unlike bar codes, RFID chips are able to transmit data through packaging, which offers the ability to monitor inventory without opening sealed boxes. As pointed out in Chapter 3, a major drawback to widespread RFID adoption has been cost related, to include the cost of the RFID tags and the necessary equipment to read the tags. In addition, RFID for the most part has tended to be long on potential but short in actual results. However, during the latter part of 2006, Wal-Mart, one of the major proponents of RFID technology, reported some of the first empirical results from an RFID initiative. More specifically, Wal-Mart's RFID initiative has generated nearly a 20 percent increase in sales of promotional items as well as a 60 percent reduction in stockouts for selected fast-moving items.[11]

INVENTORY MANAGEMENT: SPECIAL CONCERNS

Generalizations concerning inventory management are often hard to make. Each commodity has its own handling characteristics, and the framework through which each product is marketed may vary as well. What follows, then, is a discussion of different factors that might affect the management of inventories.

Complementary Products

This book takes a rather narrow view of **complementary products** and defines them as inventories that can be used or distributed together, such as razor blades and razors. These products may only intensify the pressures on retailers or wholesalers concerned with inventory maintenance. For example, consider the following dilemma: "So many complementary items exist for

---

[10]"VMI Gains Elusive for Some, But Not for Volvo Powertrain," *MSI*, March 2004, 38.

[11]William Hoffman, "Wal-Mart Tags up," *Traffic World*, August 14, 2006, 10–12.

cooking meat and fish that you'll never be able to display them in the same section (of the store)." Possible complementary products for the meat and fish section include cheeses, seasonings, skewers, skillets, and wines, among others.[12]

Another issue associated with complementary products involves the amount of inventory to be carried. Purchasing a canister vacuum cleaner, for example, generally means that a customer will periodically need to buy replacement bags for the canister. As such, the canister bags might be slow sellers, and some might argue that the bags should be dropped in favor of faster-moving products. Others, however, would point out that the sale and display of these bags is necessary to support the sale of canister vacuums.

Dead Inventory

As mentioned previously, **dead inventory** refers to product for which there is no demand—at least under current marketing practices. Because dead inventory increases inventory carrying costs, reduces inventory turnover, and takes up space in warehousing facilities, a structured process should be in place for managing it. For example, because dead inventory has often been associated with overproduction of items that customers don't want (or need), one suggestion would be to make to order, as opposed to make to stock. However, an increasing source of dead inventory in recent years involves special, highly customized orders that never end up with the customer, perhaps because the customer no longer wants or needs the product. Suggestions for dealing with this situation include partial (or full) prepayment by the customer as well as a no-return policy.[13]

Companies might also market their dead stock more aggressively, perhaps through drastic price reductions or bunching it with more attractive merchandise. Companies might also attempt to auction their dead inventory, and Internet sites are available that specialize in auctioning off dead stock. Some dead items can be donated to charitable causes, usually resulting in a partial tax write-off. Figure 9-5 is an ad from a service that helps firms find recipients for inventory donations.

Companies can also throw away dead stock, if for no other reason than to free up space in a warehousing facility. However, this "solution" should only be a last resort, because in so doing a company is, in effect, throwing away money.

Deals

Sometimes a manufacturer or wholesaler has an unbalanced inventory with too many slow-moving items. In order to clear its warehouses, the manufacturer or wholesaler may offer retailers a deal that involves a combination of desirable and less-desirable items. The price is set so that the retailer is likely to buy despite the fact that some of the less-desirable items may be difficult to sell, except at a very low price. This is offset by the fact that the deal includes some popular, fast-moving items and that its total price is relatively low. One challenge for the retailer is that the deal may increase its inventory levels of some unpopular, slow-moving items. This potential problem can be addressed in several ways, such as by selling the less-desirable items to discount retailers, whose competitive advantage is low-priced products (e.g., Big Lots). A number of Internet sites, such as Overstock.com, allow companies to sell excess or surplus inventories.

The terms *carload sale* and *truckload sale* mean that a retailer has purchased an entire railcar load or truck trailer load of a product and wishes to pass the quantity savings on to its cus-

---

[12]James Mellgren, "Category Complements: Increasing Specialty Food Sales," *Gourmet Retailer*, June 2006, 38–44.

[13]Scott Stratman, "Special Orders," *Electrical Wholesaling*, May 2006, 52–53.

Turn your
excess inventory
into a substantial tax break
and help send needy
kids to college.

Call for your
free guide
to learn how donating your
slow moving inventory
can mean a generous
tax write off
for your company.

Call (708) 690-0010
Peter Roskam
Executive Director

EAL

P.O. Box 3021, Glen Ellyn, IL 60138
FAX (708) 690-0565

Excess inventory today...
student opportunity tomorrow

"Something's got to go, Fenton. You, me or this inventory—and it's not going to be me."

FIGURE 9-5   Advertisement from a Service That Helps Firms Donate Excess Inventories to Charitable Causes

Source: Courtesy of Educational Assistance, Ltd., Glen Ellyn, IL 60137.

FIGURE 9-6   Gearing up for a Carload Tire Sale

This photo was taken in Miami in 1921. Note that the trucks in the center and on the left of the photo have solid rubber tires.
Source: Courtesy of the Florida Photographic Collection, Florida State Archives.

tomers. (Figure 9-6 shows the delivery of a carload of tires to a Miami retailer in the early 1920s.) Moving larger-than-usual quantities may have certain advantages from a retailing perspective, but it is almost totally dichotomous to current thinking that tends to focus on orderly on-time replenishment. Such deals occur less frequently because more buyers and sellers are entering into long-term agreements, such as VMI, whereby the seller agrees to replenish and maintain the buyer's inventory stocks.

Defining Stock-Keeping Units (SKUs)

Organizations should classify their materials as stock-keeping units (SKUs) or line items. Each SKU represents a type of individual item or product for which separate records are maintained. In addition to designating each product and product variation or size as an SKU, the inventory manager must designate the quantity—or minimum lot size—with which the inventory records will deal. As a result, the definition of an SKU may vary, depending on a party's position in the supply chain. Let's assume, for example, that we're concerned with managing 12-ounce cans of regular-flavored tomato sauce. A retailer typically keeps records in terms of individual items or case lots (with a case holding 12, 24, or some other number of individual items). As such, an SKU for a retailer might be the number of 12-ounce cans of regular-flavored tomato sauce.

The warehouse that supplies the retail store may deal only with case lots or pallet loads of product; pallet loads might contain between 24 and 50 cases, depending on the product. An SKU for the warehouse might be the number of 24-can cases of 12-ounce cans of regular tomato sauce. In turn, the distributor that sells to warehouses may deal with only pallet loads or vehicle loads, and it may accept orders only for pallet loads or vehicle loads of product. The distributor might view an SKU as the number of 42-case pallets containing 24-can cases of 12-ounce cans of regular tomato sauce.

Informal Arrangements Outside the Distribution Channel

The increasing quest for customer service and customer satisfaction is leading many companies to engage in what we'll broadly refer to as informal arrangements outside the distribution channel. It's fairly common, for example, for all dealers of a specific brand of automobile in a particular area (e.g., northeast Ohio) to have easy access to data about the new car inventories in that area. If one dealer has a ready buyer for a specific model and color of auto that it does not have in stock, the dealer can check the inventory list to see if any other area dealers have the desired car in stock. If so, the dealers will trade cars so that the initial dealer will have the exact auto that the buyer wants.

Franchised fast-food restaurants may also borrow or trade with each other, particularly among locations that are owned or controlled by the same franchisee. The transfer is often done by having an employee load the product in his or her own car for transport to where it's needed. These informal arrangements benefit all parties concerned, especially the customer—and without customers, businesses aren't going to be very successful. These examples indicate the hazards in blindly applying formal inventory analysis to certain situations and overlooking various informal relationships that can facilitate customer satisfaction.

Repair and Replacement Parts

Repair and replacement part inventories create a variety of potential challenges for logisticians. These items can be essential to customer service and satisfaction, yet it can be extremely difficult to forecast the demand for repair and replacement parts. For example, although companies might have some knowledge about the repair and replacement parts needed for routine or preventive maintenance of products, it is virtually impossible to forecast when the product might break down or fail. The difficulties in forecasting demand lead to challenges with respect to which parts to carry, the appropriate stocking levels for the parts that are carried, and higher inventory levels, among others.[14]

A second challenge involves the number of warehousing facilities that should be used for repair and replacement parts. One possibility is to locate the parts at numerous warehousing facilities in that this allows the parts to be fairly close to potential customers, and in emergency situations, where time is of the essence, this can be critical to customer satisfaction. Alternatively, the parts could be located at one centralized facility; although this would require use of premium transportation for some shipments, this cost is more than offset by the inventory cost savings that result from inventory being held in only one facility.

These and other challenges have led some organizations to outsource their repair and replacement parts business. For example, FedEx Express, an airline specializing in rapid delivery of parcels throughout the world, maintains a repair parts warehouse that is located right next to its main airline hub in Memphis, Tennessee. Various customers maintain their inventories of repair and replacement parts at this warehouse and use FedEx Express to fill and ship orders to where they are needed. Several other companies also offer so-called parts bank services (see Figure 9-7).

This discussion of repair and replacement parts inventories offers another opportunity to reinforce the importance of informal considerations when managing inventories and making business decisions. Several years ago, the owner of an automotive parts distributor became concerned with the amount of inventory his company was holding. A visit to the distributor's storage facility revealed that it was literally overrun with oil filters from one particular manufacturer. Indeed, it turned out that this one brand of oil filters accounted for approximately 20 percent of the facility's total inventory, a figure far higher than its actual demand.

The solution seemed pretty clear: Reduce the inventory of oil filters to a level more in line with demand. However, there was a reason for the high inventory of oil filters: The oil filter manufacturer sponsored annual contests that offered all-expenses-paid trips for two to desirable vacation locations such as Hawaii, and the trips were awarded based on the amount of oil filters purchased in a particular time frame. Because the distributor's spouse had become quite fond of these annual trips, the owner placed very large orders for the particular brand of oil filters, despite that fact that they weren't needed. The obvious solution to the problem—reducing the inventory of oil filters—wasn't feasible because the owner wanted to please his spouse. In this situation, personal considerations were more important than professional ones. It is important to remember that personal considerations often play a very important role in family-run businesses.

Reverse Logistics

For the most part, products flow toward the ultimate consumer in channels of distribution. However, as pointed out in previous chapters, an increasingly important contemporary issue in logistics management is *reverse logistics,* which involves products that flow from the ultimate consumer to other parties in a distribution channel. Examples of reverse logistics include returned items, as well as refurbished and recycled materials, and each has key inventory-related challenges.

---

[14]Lisa Harrington, "Getting Service Parts Logistics Up to Speed," *Inbound Logistics,* November 2006, 72–79.

UNFORTUNATELY, IN TODAY'S BUSINESS WORLD IT ISN'T ENOUGH TO HAVE ALL THE PARTS. YOU'VE GOT TO HAVE THEM IN ALL THE RIGHT PLACES!

LET PARTSTOCK® HANDLE YOUR SPARE PARTS INVENTORY AT 400 DEPOTS NATIONWIDE.

WHEN IT COMES TO PROVIDING EFFICIENT, COST-EFFECTIVE SERVICE IN THE FIELD, IT ISN'T EASY TO KEEP IT ALL TOGETHER. BUT NOW ASSOCIATED PARTSTOCK OFFERS A UNIQUE SOLUTION THAT ALSO HELPS YOU REDUCE YOUR SPARE PARTS INVENTORY. ☐ WHEN YOU'RE A PARTSTOCK CUSTOMER, YOUR SPARE PARTS ARE WAREHOUSED IN ANY OR ALL OF THE 400 PARTSTOCK DEPOTS LOCATED AROUND THE COUNTRY — READY TO BE DELIVERED IN AS LITTLE AS 60 MINUTES, WHEREVER YOUR FIELD SERVICE TECHNICIANS NEED THEM. ☐ YOU CAN TURN OVER YOUR SPARE PARTS TO PARTSTOCK QUICKLY AND EASILY, WITHOUT SETUP OR OVERHEAD EXPENSES. AND PARTSTOCK PUTS TOGETHER A COMPUTER-CONTROLLED DISTRIBUTION SYSTEM THAT'S CUSTOM-DESIGNED TO MEET YOUR SPECIFIC BUSINESS NEEDS. ☐ TO GET THE COMPLETE PICTURE ON PARTSTOCK, CALL 1-800-443-3443 AND REQUEST OUR FREE BOOKLET ON INVENTORY AND LOGISTICS. FIND OUT HOW PARTSTOCK CAN HELP YOU SAVE MONEY, KEEP YOUR CUSTOMERS HAPPY, AND ACHIEVE "PIECE" OF MIND ABOUT YOUR SPARE PARTS INVENTORY IN THE FIELD! ☐

ASSOCIATED PARTSTOCK
A Service of Associated Distribution Logistics

1-800-443-3443

FIGURE 9-7 Advertisement from a Parts Bank Service

Source: Courtesy of Associated Distribution Logistics (ADL).

Because return rates tend to vary across industries, returns management should be more important for some industries than for others. In fact, return rates in online commerce can approach 50 percent, compared to 20 percent in catalog retailing and about 5 percent in the auto parts industry. In addition, whereas forward distribution strives for predictability of product flow, product returns tend to be much less predictable.[15] This unpredictability of product flow can make it difficult for companies to achieve proper staffing levels at warehousing facilities.

Furthermore, forward distribution generally is characterized by relatively predictable product content in the sense that a carton labeled as "potato chips" most likely contains potato chips. There can be less predictability of product content with returned products; indeed one third-party returns specialist has discovered bricks and shirts stuffed in DVD-player boxes. The predictability of product content in forward distribution allows shipments to be monitored and recorded by computers (e.g., scanners or wands). Alternatively, the unpredictability of product content with returned goods means that every returned item needs to be physically inspected.[16] At a minimum, such physical inspections increase the processing time for returned items.

Refurbished and recycled materials present other types of inventory challenges; although both involve reverse logistics, refurbishing refers to upgrading an existing product, whereas recycling involves dismantling an existing product to collect component parts. Unlike returned items, refurbishing and recycling are predicated on sufficient product volumes, which means that there needs to be adequate storage space. A lack of storage space can lead to products being stored outdoors, which can reduce the ability to refurbish or recycle the product.[17]

Substitute Products

Substitute products refer to products that customers view as being able to fill the same need or want as another product. The substitutability can occur at a specific product level (e.g., one brand of cola is viewed as a substitute for another brand of cola), or it can occur across product classes (e.g., potatoes may be viewed as a substitute for rice). As pointed out previously in this chapter, knowledge of substitutability has important implications with respect to stockout costs and the sizes of safety stocks to be maintained. Thus, if a consumer has little hesitation in making substitutions, there would appear to be minimal penalties for a stockout. However, a point may be reached where customers become sufficiently annoyed at having to make substitutions that they decide to take their business elsewhere. Because of the many possibilities for substitutability, many grocery chains target in-stock rates of 95 percent for individual stores so that sufficient substitutes exist for a customer to purchase a substitute item rather than go to a competing store.

It's also important that companies have a thorough understanding of substitution patterns. For example, in many cases, substitutions are two-way, meaning that if brand A is substitutable for brand B, then brand B is substitutable for brand A. In some situations, however, one-way relationships exist; a bolt 7/16 inch in diameter could be used in place of a bolt that is 1/2 inch in diameter, but the reverse may not hold.

---

[15]Bob Trebilcock, "Return to Sender," *Warehousing Management,* May 2002, 24–27.

[16]Ibid.

[17]A. Michael Knemeyer, Thomas G. Ponzurick, and Cyril M. Logar, "A Qualitative Examination of Factors Affecting Reverse Logistics Systems for End-of-Life Computers," *International Journal of Physical Distribution & Logistics Management* 32, no. 6 (2002): 455–479.

Summary

This chapter addressed inventories and inventory management. Because many challenges are associated with holding inventories, some companies try to shift this burden to other parties in the supply chain. Many companies seek to improve their inventory turnover levels, or the number of times that inventory is sold in a one-year period.

When deciding what levels of inventories to maintain, companies try to minimize the costs associated with both too much and too little inventory. Too much inventory leads to high inventory carrying costs; too little inventory can lead to stockouts and the associated stockout costs. The worst outcome of a stockout is to lose both a sale and all future business from the customer.

The chapter also addressed when to order, as well as how much to order; reorder points signify stock levels at which a new order should be placed. With respect to how much to order, the economic order quantity (EOQ) minimizes ordering costs and inventory carrying costs.

Several contemporary approaches to managing inventory such as VMI and inventory tracking were discussed. The chapter concluded with a look at special concerns associated with inventory management, such as dead inventory and substitute products. This final section offered several examples of informal considerations that might affect inventory management.

Questions for Discussion and Review

1. What is inventory turnover? How can a high inventory turnover ratio be detrimental to a firm?
2. Distinguish among cycle, safety, pipeline, and speculative stock.
3. Define what is meant by inventory carrying costs. What are some of its main components?
4. Discuss the concept of stockout costs. How can a stockout cost be calculated?
5. Distinguish between a fixed order quantity and fixed order interval system. Which one generally requires more safety stock? Why?
6. Explain the logic of the EOQ model.
7. How can inventory flow diagrams be useful to a logistics manager?
8. Discuss what is meant by ABC analysis of inventory. What are several measures that can be used to determine ABC status?
9. What are implications of the JIT approach for supply chain management?
10. How does vendor-managed inventory differ from traditional inventory management?
11. Do complementary products or substitute products present the greater managerial challenge? Support your answer.
12. Define what is meant by dead inventory. What are several ways to manage it?
13. Explain how an SKU might have different meanings, depending on one's position in the supply chain.
14. Why is it important for a manager to understand informal considerations with respect to inventory management?
15. Discuss some of the challenges that are associated with managing repair and replacement parts.
16. Which presents the greater reverse logistics challenge: (1) returned items or (2) refurbished and recycled products? Support your answer.
17. What are substitute items, and how might they affect safety stock policies?
18. Which supply chain participant(s) should be responsible for managing inventory levels? Why?
19. Should inventories be considered investments? Why?
20. Since the mid-1990s, many beer and soft-drink cans and bottles have contained a *freshness date* stamped on them to indicate the latest date that the product should be consumed. What problems might such a system cause for the people responsible for managing such inventories? Discuss.

Suggested Readings

Davis, Don, Jim Buckler, Adam Mussomeli, and Dan Kinzler. "Inventory Transformation Revlon Style." *Supply Chain Management Review.* 9, no. 5 (2005): 53–59.

Dorling, Kim, John Scott, and Eric Deakins. "Determinants of Successful Vendor Managed Inventory Relationships in Oligopoly Industries." *International Journal of Physical Distribution & Logistics Management* 36, no. 3 (2006): 176–191.

Fitzsimons, Gavin J. "Consumer Response to Stockouts." *Journal of Consumer Research* 27 (September 2000): 249–266.

Guinipero, Larry C., Kishore G. Pillai, Stephen N. Chapman, and Ronald A. Clark. "A Longitudinal Examination of JIT Purchasing Practices." *International Journal of Logistics Management* 16, no. 1 (2005): 51–70.

Hadley, Scott W. "A Modern View of Inventory." *Strategic Finance* 86, no. 1 (2004): 31–35.

Herrin, Richard. "How to Calculate Safety Stocks for Highly Seasonal Products," *Journal of Business Forecasting* 24, no. 2 (2004): 6–10.

Metersky, Jeff, and J. Michael Kilgore. "How to Improve Your Inventory Deployment." *Supply Chain Management Review* 8, no. 7 (2004): 26–32.

Norek, Christopher D. "Returns Management: Making Order Out of Chaos." *Supply Chain Management Review,* May/June 2002, 34–43.

Piasecki, Dave. "Optimizing Economic Order Quantity." *IIE Transactions* 33, no. 1 (2001): 30–33, 39.

Stassen, Robert E., and Matthew E. Waller. "Logistics and Assortment Depth in the Retail Supply Chain: Evidence from Grocery Categories." *Journal of Business Logistics* 23, no. 1 (2002): 125–143.

Taylor, John C., Stanley E. Fawcett, and George C. Jackson. "Catalog Retailer In-Stock Performance: An Assessment of Customer Service Levels." *Journal of Business Logistics* 25, no. 2 (2004): 119–137.

White, Richard E., and John N. Pearson. "JIT, System Integration and Customer Service." *International Journal of Physical Distribution & Logistics Management* 31, no. 5 (2001): 313–333.

C A S E S

CASE 9-1 LOW NAIL COMPANY

After making some wise short-term investments at a race track, Chris Low had some additional cash to invest in a business. The most promising opportunity at the time was in building supplies, so Low bought a business that specialized in sales of one size of nail. The annual volume of nails was 2,000 kegs, and they were sold to retail customers in an even flow. Low was uncertain how many nails to order at any time. Initially, only two costs concerned him: order-processing costs, which were $60 per order without regard to size, and warehousing costs, which were $1 per year per keg space. This meant that Low had to rent a constant amount of warehouse space for the year, and it had to be large enough to accommodate an entire order when it arrived. Low was not worried about maintaining safety stocks, mainly because the outward flow of goods was so even. Low bought his nails on a delivered basis. ∎

QUESTIONS

1. Using the EOQ methods outlined in Chapter 9, how many kegs of nails should Low order at one time?
2. Assume all conditions in question 1 hold, except that Low's supplier now offers a quantity discount in the form of absorbing all or part of Low's order-processing costs. For orders of 750 or more kegs of nails, the supplier will absorb all the order-processing costs; for orders between 249 and 749 kegs, the supplier will absorb half. What is Low's new EOQ? (It might be useful to lay out all costs in tabular form for this and later questions.)
3. Temporarily, ignore your work on question 2. Assume that Low's warehouse offers to rent Low space on the basis of the *average* number of kegs Low will have in stock, rather than on the maximum number of kegs Low would need room for whenever a new shipment arrived. The storage charge per keg remains the same. Does this change the answer to question 1? If so, what is the new answer?
4. Take into account the answer to question 1 *and* the supplier's new policy outlined in question 2 *and* the warehouse's new policy in question 3. Then determine Low's new EOQ.
5. Temporarily, ignore your work on questions 2, 3, and 4. Low's luck at the race track is over; he now must borrow money to finance his inventory of nails. Looking at the situation outlined in question 1, assume that the wholesale cost of nails is $40 per keg and that Low must pay interest at the rate of 1.5 percent per month on unsold inventory. What is his new EOQ?
6. Taking into account all the factors listed in questions 1, 2, 3, and 5, calculate Low's EOQ for kegs of nails.

CASE 9-2   JACKSON'S WAREHOUSE

This case can best be assessed only by those familiar with STORM software, although other general business analysis software programs might be used. The terminology and approach are not exactly the same as used here, especially the use of Sigma lead times, which are measured in units and can be explained as measuring the "dipping" into safety stocks. Also, some of the topics will be new to readers of this text.

Located in Memphis, Tennessee, Jackson's Warehouse stores only 12 different items, which are sold to a select number of customers. Each item is known only by its stock-keeping unit (SKU) number. Table 9-A shows each SKU number, the annual demand for each, the unit cost to Jackson's warehouse, the lead time (the lapse of time between Jackson's ordering from its supplier and receiving the goods), and the standard deviation of lead time demand (sigma lead time), expressed as the number of units by which safety stocks are drawn down in times of heavy demand.

For SKUs with a unit cost of less than $500, it costs Jackson's $30 to process an order for any number of units of that single SKU, and for SKUs with a unit cost of $500 or above, it costs Jackson's $75 to process an order for any number of units of that single SKU.

Carrying costs are calculated as 30 percent of the average inventory of each SKU. The average inventory is the safety stock plus one-half the size of each order. (It is assumed that goods move outward in a fairly even flow so, at any one time, the amount in stock is halfway between the size of a full order and zero, plus safety stock.)

Assume that the warehouse wants to stock enough of each SKU to fill orders 95 percent of the time. ■

TABLE 9-A	Jackson's Warehouse Needs			
SKU Number	*Demand (Weekly)*	*Unit Cost to Jackson's*	*Lead Time (in weeks)*	*Standard Deviations of Demand Per Week (in units of product)*
402	4	$1,500	2	40
940	20	720	1	50
660	12	500	2	60
829	30	65	1	80
301	35	250	1	90
447	48	190	1	100
799	8	200	1	30
597	12	40	2	35
27	4	210	1	50
196	20	35	1	60
258	42	250	1	115
62	180	8	1	700

QUESTIONS

1. Perform an ABC analysis. Is it of much use if the firm maintains only 12 SKUs? Why or why not?
2. Find the reorder point for each of the SKUs expressed as the point to which existing inventory must drop to trigger a replenishment order.
3. How large a safety stock should be maintained for each SKU?
4. How much money will Jackson's have as its average investment in inventory?

5. Interest rates drop, and Jackson's now assumes that its carrying costs are 20 percent, rather than 30 percent. How will this change your answers to questions 2, 3, and 4, if at all? Explain.
6. Disregard your answers to questions 4 and 5. Answer question 3 again, this time assuming that Jackson's wants to keep enough of each SKU to fill orders 90 percent of the time.

10

WAREHOUSING MANAGEMENT

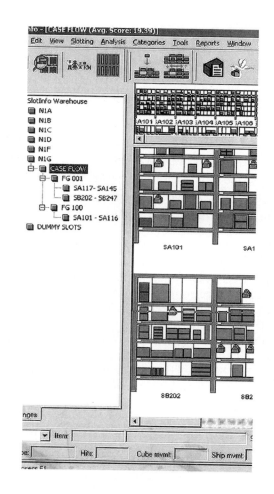

Key Terms

- Accumulating (bulk-making)
- Allocating (bulk-breaking)
- Assorting
- Bonded storage
- Contract (third-party) warehousing
- Cross-docking
- Distribution center
- Dunnage
- Field warehousing
- Fixed slot location
- Multiclient warehousing
- Occupational Safety and Health Administration (OSHA)

- Paperless warehousing
- Private warehousing
- Public warehousing
- Regrouping function
- Sorting out
- Throughput
- Variable slot location
- Warehouse
- Warehouse management system (WMS)
- Warehousing

Learning Objectives

- To understand the role of warehouses and distribution centers in a logistics system
- To identify the various types and functions of warehouses
- To distinguish the various alternatives available in warehouse design
- To examine the different types of handling equipment available
- To analyze the issue of employee safety in warehousing

A recurring theme in previous chapters has been the changing nature of the logistics discipline and the individual functions that comprise it. In the systems approach of logistics, changes to one function affect other functions as well. Indeed, many of the changes described in previous chapters—such as electronic ordering, facility consolidation, lean inventories, and transportation deregulation—have especially affected warehousing management. Although some experts have speculated that these changes would diminish warehousing's relevance in logistics systems, warehousing has adapted by expanding offerings of value-added activities that support increasingly demanding customer requirements.

Warehousing has been defined as "that part of a firm's logistics system that stores products (raw materials, parts, goods-in-process, finished goods) at and between points of origin and point of consumption."[1] Warehousing can be provided by either warehouses or distribution centers. **Warehouses** emphasize the storage of products, and their primary purpose is to maximize the usage of available storage space. In contrast, **distribution centers** emphasize the rapid movement of products through a facility, and thus they attempt to maximize **throughput** (the amount of product entering and leaving a facility in a given time period).

Warehousing and transportation are substitutes for each other, with warehousing having been referred to as "transportation at zero miles per hour." Figure 10-1, which presents an example of the trade-off between warehousing and transportation, indicates that placing a warehousing facility between the producer and customers adds a new layer of costs (those associated with

---

[1]Douglas M. Lambert, James R. Stock, and Lisa M. Ellram, *Fundamentals of Logistics Management* (New York: Irwin McGraw-Hill, 1998).

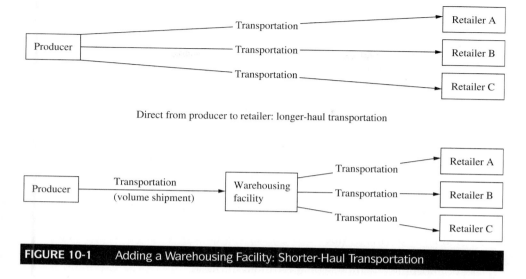

Direct from producer to retailer: longer-haul transportation

FIGURE 10-1   Adding a Warehousing Facility: Shorter-Haul Transportation

warehousing) into the system. Moreover, the warehousing facility generates shorter-haul transportation routes (from the producer to the facility; from the facility to the customers); as a general rule, short-haul transportation tends to be more costly per mile than long-haul transportation. However, the increased costs of short-haul transportation may be offset by lower transportation costs per unit of weight associated with volume shipments.

If the introduction of warehousing into a supply chain appears to result in a net increase in the total costs of conducting business, then why is warehousing desirable? A key reason for warehousing is because patterns of production and consumption do not coincide, and warehousing serves to match different rates or volumes of flow. Canned fruits and vegetables are examples of one extreme in which production occurs during a relatively short period, but sales are spread throughout the year. Because of changes in logistics thinking in recent years, the other extreme—sales concentrated in a relatively short time period, steady production rates throughout the year—is more likely to be addressed by having the production occur closer to the demand period.

Sometimes, larger quantities of goods are purchased than can be consumed in a short period of time, and warehousing space is needed to store the surplus product. This can occur for several reasons, such as guarding against anticipated scarcity or to benefit from a seller's advantageously priced deal.

Much of the preceding discussion could be viewed as a market-oriented approach to warehousing. However, warehousing management can also be relevant to production and raw materials considerations. For example, an automobile manufacturer might purchase extra amounts of steel in response to anticipated steel shortages.

Moreover, warehouses and distribution centers facilitate the **regrouping function** in a supply chain. This function involves rearranging the quantities and assortment of products as they move through the supply chain and can take four forms—accumulating (also referred to as bulk-making), allocating (also referred to as bulk-breaking), assorting, and sorting out. Accumulating and allocating refer to adjustments associated with the *quantity of product,* whereas assorting and sorting out refer to adjustments associated with *product assortment.*

Thus, **accumulating** involves bringing together similar stocks from different sources, as might be done by a department store that buys large quantities of men's suits from several different producers. **Allocating,** by contrast, involves breaking larger quantities into smaller quantities; continuing with our suit example, whereas the department store might buy 500 suits in size 42 short, an individual store might only carry one or two suits in this size.

Assorting refers to building up a variety of different products for resale to particular customers; our department store example might want to supply individual stores with a number of different suit sizes and styles. **Sorting out** refers to "separating products into grades and qualities desired by different target markets."[2] For example, the Dillard's department store chain carries upscale suit brands in stores located in high-income areas, whereas some Dillard's located in less-affluent areas may not carry any men's suits at all.

As previously mentioned, contemporary warehousing is characterized by a greater degree of value-adding activities than in the past. These include assembly, custom labeling, light manufacturing, product testing, repackaging, and reverse logistics considerations, among others.

In addition, the increased emphasis on time reduction in supply chains has led to the growth of **cross-docking,** which can be defined as "a process where a product is received in a facility, occasionally married with product going to the same destination, then shipped at the earliest opportunity, without going into long-term storage."[3] The experiences of Saks Inc., an upscale retail department store, illustrate some of the potential benefits from cross-docking. For example, it takes just *seven minutes* to move a carton from the inbound dock to an outbound trailer at the Saks cross-dock facility. Moreover, on a daily basis the Saks cross-dock can handle four times as much product, with one-half the labor, of its predecessor facility; in other words, the cross-dock facility is approximately *eight times* as productive as its predecessor![4]

Although there is some disagreement on how long a product can sit at a facility before it's no longer considered to be cross-docked (e.g., some experts argue for one day, others for three days), there is general agreement that the time products are at rest in a cross-dock facility should be as short as possible. There is also some disagreement with respect to the design of a cross-dock facility. Figure 10-2 shows a cross-dock design that resembles a motor carrier terminal—rectangular, long, and as narrow as possible.[5] Indeed, this is the design used by Saks for its cross-dock facility. Alternatively, some have characterized the cross-dock design presented in Figure 10-2 as "dumb," suggesting instead that all cross-dock doors should be on one wall, or placed at 90 degrees to one another.[6]

PUBLIC, PRIVATE, CONTRACT, AND MULTICLIENT WAREHOUSING

Businesses must decide the proper mix of public, private, and contract warehousing to use. Because companies have different strategies, goals, and objectives, there is no correct mix of these three types of warehousing. Thus, one organization might only use public warehousing, another organization might use only private warehousing, and a third organization might use a

---

[2]William D. Perreault, Jr., and E. Jerome McCarthy, *Basic Marketing,* 14th ed. (New York: Irwin McGraw-Hill, 2002), Chapter 11.

[3]Maida Napolitano, *Making the Move to Cross Docking* (Oak Brook, IL: Warehousing Education and Research Council, 2000).

[4]Connie Robbins Gentry, "Distribution Utopia," *Chain Store Age,* November 2005, 70–72.

[5]Napolitano, *Making the Move to Cross-Docking.*

[6]David Drickhamer, "It's Flow Time," *Material Handling Management,* June 2006, 36–41.

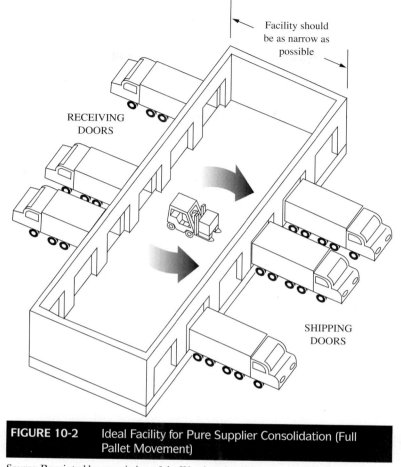

Facility should be as narrow as possible

RECEIVING DOORS

SHIPPING DOORS

FIGURE 10-2   Ideal Facility for Pure Supplier Consolidation (Full Pallet Movement)

Source: Reprinted by permission of the Warehousing Education and Research Council.

mix of all three types. Each of these three types of warehousing has distinct characteristics that might be either attractive or unattractive to potential users. These characteristics are discussed in the following sections.

Public Warehousing

Public warehousing is similar to common carriers in that they serve (are supposed to serve) all legitimate users and have certain responsibilities to those users. Public warehousing requires no capital investment on the user's part, which can certainly be an important consideration when borrowing (interest) rates are high. With public warehousing, the user rents space as needed, thus avoiding the costs of unneeded space. A related advantage is that users receive regularly scheduled bills for the space used, thus allowing them a fairly exact determination of their warehousing costs.

Public warehousing can also be attractive to prospective users because other parties have responsibilities for personnel decisions and regulatory knowledge. Warehousing is one of two major sources of labor in logistics (the other is transportation), and warehousing employees are often unionized, thus adding to the managerial challenges. With respect to regulatory knowledge, warehousing labor safety practices in the United States are monitored by the **Occupational Safety and Health Administration (OSHA).** From a managerial perspective, because OSHA standards are complex and lengthy, it can be quite costly and challenging to comply with OSHA regulations.

Public warehousing offers more locational flexibility than do company-owned facilities, and this can be important when a company is entering new markets. For example, an organization may want to start off slowly in new markets or may be uncertain how well its products will be received in these markets, and public warehousing can provide storage services in these markets without an overwhelming capital commitment.

Public warehousing may provide a number of specialized services that aren't available from other sources. For example, public warehousing is heavily involved in such value-added services as repackaging larger shipments into retail-size quantities and then shrink-wrapping them, assisting in product recalls, and doing price marking, product assembly, and product testing.

Two other notable public warehouse services are **bonded storage** and **field warehousing.** Although there are several types of bonded storage, they all refer to situations where goods are not released until applicable fees are paid. For example, U.S. Customs-bonded warehouses hold goods until import duties are collected. Internal Revenue Service-bonded warehouses hold goods until other federal taxes and fees are collected. In addition, certain federal laws related to storing agricultural products and some state laws require warehouses to be bonded in the sense that they must carry insurance to protect their customers.

A field warehouse is a facility temporarily established at the site of an inventory of goods, often the premises of the goods' owner. The warehouser assumes custody of the goods and issues a receipt for them, which can then be used as collateral for a loan. Using one's inventory of goods as loan collateral can be helpful, although the goods are temporarily frozen in the distribution channel.

Perhaps the biggest drawback to public warehousing is the potential lack of control by the user. For example, sometimes public warehousing doesn't have the space availability required by a particular user. And even if space is available, users may have little say in where their goods are stored—they may be placed wherever space is available, which may result in part of a user's inventory being stored in one area and the remainder in another. Moreover, some public warehousing is not open 24 hours a day, meaning that prospective users may not be able to access their products as needed or that users may need to tailor their operations to fit those of the public warehouse.

Private Warehousing

Private warehousing is owned or occupied on a long-term lease by the firm using the facility. As such, they generate high fixed costs and thus should only be considered by companies dealing with large volumes of inventory. In so doing, the high fixed costs can be spread out over more units of inventory, thus reducing the cost per unit of storage. The largest users of private warehousing are retail chain stores; they handle large volumes of merchandise on a regular basis. Manufacturing firms also utilize private warehousing. Figure 10-3 shows a distribution center built by a toy manufacturer.

In addition to large volumes, private warehousing also tends to be feasible when demand patterns are relatively stable. Fluctuating demand patterns could at times lead to insufficient

FIGURE 10-3   LEGO Distribution Center

LEGO Systems, Inc. built this 225,000-square-foot distribution center about one-quarter mile from its factory in Enfield, Connecticut. There was actually an area next to the factory, but if this facility had been built on that site, natural wetlands would have been destroyed. This facility is designed to handle 66,000 cases per day. Note that its design makes the building look like it had been built with giant Legos.
Source: Permission granted by LEGO Systems, Inc.

storage space for product, in which case the company might need to use public warehousing as a supplement, thus increasing total warehousing costs. At other times, by contrast, there could be too much space (excess capacity), which costs money as well.

Assuming both sufficient demand volume and stability of demand, private warehousing offers potential users a great deal of control over their storage needs. For example, the storage facility can be constructed to the user's specifications, which is a particularly attractive feature when a company has unique storage or handling requirements, as is the case with steel beams and gasoline. Moreover, in private warehousing, companies can control product placement with a facility; some products, for instance, should not be stored on the floor. Another aspect of control is that private warehousing offers access to products when an organization needs (or wants) them, as opposed to an organization having to tailor its activities to match a public facility's operating hours.

Private warehousing is also characterized by several important drawbacks, including the high fixed cost of private storage and the necessity of having high and steady demand volumes. In addition, a high-fixed-cost alternative, such as private warehousing, becomes less attractive in times of high interest rates because it is more costly to secure the necessary financing to build or lease the facility (to be fair, interest rates in some nations, such as the United States, have been relatively low in recent years).

Private warehousing may also reduce an organization's flexibility in responding to changes in the external environment. For example, companies that utilize private warehousing are suscepti-ble to changing demand patterns, such as those experienced with the passage of multicountry trade alliances. Likewise, organizational flexibility can be affected by mergers with, or acquisitions of, other companies, as illustrated by the case of a multibillion-dollar company that acquired a competitor's production and private warehousing facilities. Although the production facilities added much-needed manufacturing capacity, the warehousing facilities were largely redundant in nature. Yet the acquiring company had little choice but to continue operating them because of substantial penalties for premature lease terminations.

Contract Warehousing

For many years, organizations had two choices with respect to warehousing—public and private—but more recently, **contract warehousing** (also referred to as *third-party warehousing*) has emerged as another viable warehousing alternative. Although contract warehousing has been defined in a number of different ways, in this text it refers to "a long term, mutually beneficial arrangement which provides unique and specially tailored warehousing and logistics services exclusively to one client, where the vendor and client share the risks associated with the operation."[7] Contract warehousing thus provides another example of supply chain partnerships. Because contract warehousing is a relatively new alternative for logisticians, our understanding of it is not as thorough as it is for public or private warehousing.

Contract warehousing expenditures in the United States appear to be in excess of $25 billion annually and are expected to grow at an annual rate of about 10 percent over the next few years. This growth in contract warehousing appears to have come largely at the expense of public warehousing. More specifically, contract warehousing has embraced value-adding activities such as customization, reverse logistics, and repair and refurbishment to a greater degree than has public warehousing.[8]

Contract warehousing is becoming a preferred alternative for many organizations because it simultaneously mitigates the negative aspects and accentuates the positive aspects of public and private warehousing. With respect to the former, contract warehousing allows a company to focus on its core competencies (what it does best), with warehousing management provided by experts—experts who solely focus on the client's needs and wants.[9] Contract warehousing also tends to be more cost effective than private warehousing, with potentially the same degree of control because key specifications can be included in the contract.

Contract warehousing tends to be less costly than private warehousing and more costly than public warehousing. With respect to changes in the external environment, contract warehousing is viewed as more flexible than private warehousing but less so than public warehousing. This flexibility depends in part on the length of the contract; as the contract length increases, the flexibility to respond to change decreases. Although a consensus has yet to develop with respect to a preferred contract length, three- to five-year contracts appear to allow sufficient time for the warehousing provider to learn the client's business while allowing clients some flexibility in case the agreement fails to produce acceptable results.

Multiclient Warehousing

Another warehousing alternative, multiclient warehousing, has begun to emerge in the first part of the twenty-first century. In essence, **multiclient warehousing** mixes attributes of contract

---

[7]Warehousing Education and Research Council, *Contract Warehousing: How It Works and How to Make It Work Effectively* (Oak Brook, IL: Author, 1993).

[8]William Hoffman, "Contract Warehousing Evolves," *Traffic World,* January 31, 2005, 16.

[9]John R. Johnson, "Bigger and Better," *Warehousing Management,* October 2000, 22–25.

and public warehousing. For example, where contract warehousing is generally dedicated to just one customer and public warehousing may be used by any number of customers, a *limited number of customers* utilize a multiclient facility. In a similar fashion, the services in a multiclient facility are more differentiated than those in a public facility, but less customized than would be found in contract warehousing. Indeed, Pacer Distribution Services, a leading provider of multiclient warehousing, indicates that potential customers "have more complexity, require higher service and quality standards, and have a higher velocity when compared to a typical public warehouse client."[10]

DESIGN CONSIDERATIONS IN WAREHOUSING

Figure 10-4 shows the top and end views of a distribution center. In this example, the replenishment and order-picking functions are completely separated. Order pickers work in the center aisle, while stock replenishers work in the outer aisles, moving goods from reserve to live (active) storage. As order pickers empty cartons, they place them and other wrapping materials on the trash conveyor. The trash is carried to another room, where it can be separated into different types of materials, and each type is baled and then sold to a paper-products recycling plant.

Figure 10-5 illustrates a much more complex, high-rise distribution center that receives pallet loads, breaks them down into carton lots, and then reassembles the carton lots into new, outgoing pallet loads. Pallet loads are received at point 2, where a computer-controlled stacker takes each pallet and stores it in one of the openings in the 10-aisle, 65-foot-high storage area (point 1). As goods are needed to replenish stocks on the lane loaders (point 4), they are retrieved from one of the openings in point 1 and taken by the pallet carrier to one of several depalletizing stations (point 3).

At point 3, the pallets are manually unloaded and the cartons placed aboard a conveyor system, which takes them to the lane loaders (point 4). At the lane loaders, at least one lane is assigned to each product, and cartons are loaded onto the top of each lane. The bottom of the lane feeds onto a moving conveyor belt, which is at a right angle to the lanes. The lanes slope downward toward the belt, and at the bottom of each lane (near the conveyor belt) an electrically triggered device releases one case at a time onto the conveyor belt. The lane is of sufficient slope that gravity forces the case out and onto the conveyor belt.

As orders are assembled on the conveyor belt, they move toward point 5, where they are routed to one of four loading stations and are placed aboard pallets for outgoing shipments. This is also done manually. Hence, loading and unloading pallets are the only two manual operations; the other operations are by machine, and all operations are computer controlled.

General Considerations

One of the best pieces of advice with respect to the design of warehousing facilities is to use common sense, as illustrated by the following anecdote. Several years ago, a businessperson was convinced that warehouses were bland, boring, and visually unappealing, and thus decided to build a more aesthetically pleasing facility. To this end, he designed a warehouse with black floors, reasoning that the facility would stand out compared to other warehouses. Although the black floor was certainly eye-catching, it was an unmitigated disaster: The floor showed more dirt than comparable facilities, and the floor was extremely slippery—meaning that forklifts

[10]David Biederman, "A Different Warehouse," *Traffic World*, October 18, 2004, 19–21.

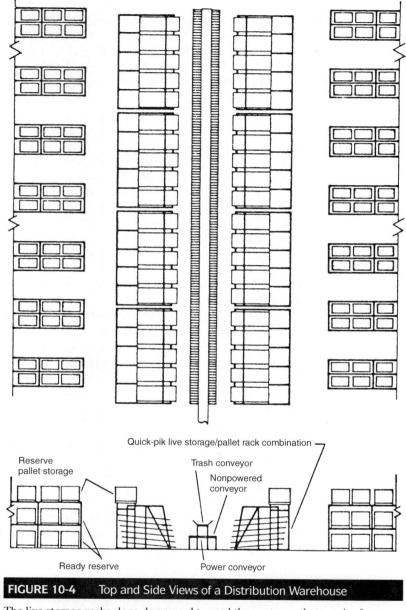

Quick-pik live storage/pallet rack combination

Reserve
pallet storage

Trash conveyor

Nonpowered
conveyor

Ready reserve

Power conveyor

FIGURE 10-4   Top and Side Views of a Distribution Warehouse

The live storage racks slope downward toward the center so that gravity forces
cartons to move toward the center.

Source: Courtesy of North American Equipment Corporation.

had a harder time stopping (some actually crashed into the walls!), and warehouse workers
were more prone to falling. This anecdote provides an excellent example of form triumphing
over function or style triumphing over substance. From a commonsense perspective, the primary design consideration should be the warehouse's function—be it long-term storage or
product movement—in the relevant logistics system, with aesthetics a secondary consideration.

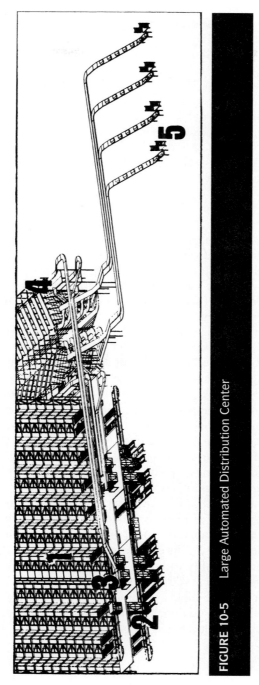

FIGURE 10-5 Large Automated Distribution Center

Source: Courtesy of SI Handling Systems, Inc.

251

One commonsense piece of advice is that prior to designing a warehousing facility, the quantity and character of goods to be handled must be known. Indeed, one of the challenges of online commerce for bricks-and-mortar organizations has been that many of them have attempted to fulfill online orders through warehousing facilities largely designed to supply retail store locations. Online orders tend to be much smaller than those going to retail stores; as a consequence, picking and assembling one or two items is much different from picking and assembling a pallet load of items.[11]

A second commonsense piece of advice is that it's important for an organization to know the purpose to be served by a particular facility because the relative emphasis placed on the storage and distribution functions affects space layout. A storage facility with low rates of product turnover should be laid out in a manner that maximizes utilization of the cubic capacity of the storage facility. Alternatively, because a distribution-oriented facility attempts to maximize throughput rather than storage, the facility should be configured to facilitate the flow of product into and out of it.

Trade-offs

Trade-offs must be made among space, labor, and mechanization with respect to warehousing design. Spaciousness may not always be advantageous because the distances that an individual or machine must travel in the storing and retrieving functions are increased. Moreover, unused space is excess capacity, and we know that excess capacity costs money. Alternatively, cramped conditions can lead to such inefficiencies as the product damage that can be caused by forklift puncture and movement bottlenecks caused by insufficient aisle width, to name but two.

Before layout plans are made, each item that will be handled should be studied in terms of its specific physical handling properties, the volume and regularity of movement, the frequency with which it is picked, and whether it is fast or slow moving compared to other items. This so-called product profiling might suggest, for example, that fast-moving items "be placed close to where order selectors go to pick them, in an effort to reduce walking time."[12]

Many trade-offs are inevitable when designing the structure as well as the arrangement of the relevant storage and handling equipment. Several of these trade-offs are discussed in this section; the trade-offs are often more complex than they appear because individual trade-offs are not independent from one another. Although there may not to be "right" or "wrong" answers with respect to warehousing design, an understanding of the various trade-offs might help managers make more efficient, as opposed to less efficient, decisions.

The experiences of PDI Logistics, a pharmaceutical distributor and third-party logistics provider, provide an excellent example of trade-offs among various warehousing design factors. PDI was experiencing dramatic annual growth in its business—so much growth that it quickly approached the capacity of its existing storage facility. Rather than build a new facility, PDI redesigned its existing facility with very narrow aisles (less than 5 feet wide), thus permitting better storage density. PDI saved money by not having to build a new facility, but because the very narrow aisles require highly specialized lift trucks, its equipment costs increased. However, because of this new equipment, PDI uses approximately one-third the number of employees as in the past, thus decreasing its labor costs.[13]

---

[11]James A. Cooke, "The Physical Challenges of the Virtual Sale," *Logistics Management & Distribution*, October 2000, 67–73.

[12]Cooke, "The Physical Challenges of the Virtual Sale."

[13]Mary Aichlmayr, "Before Building, Cube Out with Narrow Aisles," *Transportation & Distribution*, June 2002, 42–43.

Fixed versus Variable Slot Locations for Merchandise

With a **fixed slot location,** each SKU has one or more permanent slots assigned to it. This provides stability in the sense that the company should always know where a specific SKU is located. However, this may result in low space utilization, particularly with seasonal products. A **variable slot location** involves empty slots being assigned to incoming products based on space availability. Although this alternative results in more efficient space utilization, it requires a near-perfect information system because there must be flawless knowledge of each product's location.

Build Out (Horizontal) versus Build Up (Vertical)

A general rule of thumb is that it's cheaper to build up than build out; building out requires more land, which can be quite expensive, particularly in certain geographic locations. Alternatively, although building costs decline on a cubic-foot basis as one builds higher, warehousing equipment costs tends to increase. Figure 10-6 shows what might happen to labor when a company decides to build up, rather than out. Moreover, the build up versus build out issue illustrates the importance of understanding interfunctional trade-offs when thinking about warehousing design. For example, the Midlands section of Britain, located between London and Birmingham, is a popular site for distribution centers—there is available land for development, and the land is reasonably priced. Having said this, Midlands' locational popularity is dependent on a highway system offering speedy, reliable, and cost-efficient transportation service.[14]

Order-Picking versus Stock-Replenishing Functions

Organizations must decide whether workers who pick outgoing orders and those who are restocking storage facilities should work at the same time or in the same area. Although the latter scenario may result in fewer managerial personnel being needed, it may also lead to congestion

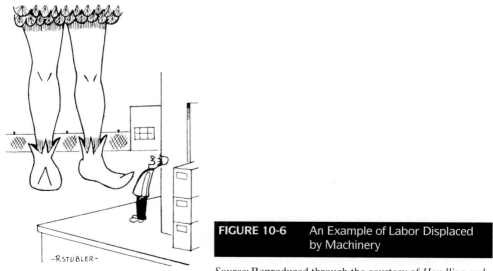

−R.STUBLER−

Sorry to let you go, but we've automated our high-rise order picking.

FIGURE 10-6   An Example of Labor Displaced by Machinery

Source: Reproduced through the courtesy of *Handling and Shipping Management* magazine and of Richard Stubler, the artist.

---

[14]Stan Luxenberg, "Warehouses for Warsaw," *NREI*, October 2004, 28–30.

within the facility due to the number of workers. One suggestion to reduce congestion is for order pickers and stock replenishers to use different aisles for their respective activities—again, this requires a very good information system to identify where a given employee is at any time.

Two-Dock versus Single-Dock Layout

A two-dock layout has receiving docks on one side of a facility and shipping docks on the other side, with goods moving between them. In a one-dock system, each and every dock can be used for both shipping and receiving, typically receiving product at one time of the day and shipping it at another time. Viewed from overhead, the goods move in a U-shaped rather than a straight configuration. This alternative reduces the space needed for storage docks, but it requires carriers to pick up and deliver at specific times. This alternative may also result in an occasional mix-up in that received product is sometimes reloaded into the vehicle that delivered it.

Space Devoted to Aisles versus Space Devoted to Storage

As aisle space increases, storage capacity decreases. Wider aisles make it easier to operate mechanical equipment and reduce the chances of accidents and product damage—but they increase the travel distances within a facility. Narrower aisles can increase the space utilization of a facility, but often require specialized equipment, such as a narrow-aisle lift truck, to do so. Indeed, narrow-aisle forklifts can operate in an aisle width of approximately six feet, compared to the 11-foot width that is needed by the standard forklift. However, narrow-aisle forklifts are generally more expensive to buy or lease than are standard forklifts.

Paperless Warehousing versus Traditional Paper-Oriented Warehousing Operations

A **paperless warehousing** facility generates and uses few or no paper documents and instead relies on some type of technology, such as bar codes or radio-frequency identification (RFID), to accomplish many of the relevant tasks. Because paperless warehousing requires more sophisticated technology than paper-intensive systems, paperless systems are not inexpensive. It's possible, however, for paperless systems to have payback periods of approximately 18 months. Several important benefits are seen with paperless warehousing, such as reduced clerical work, improved order picking efficiency, and a decrease in picking and shipping errors. For example, most paper-based systems require picked orders to be manually entered into a computer system. This information is often verified at the order staging area, a process that can delay shipping, add to order processing costs, and doesn't catch all errors.[15]

Retail Storerooms

The design of warehousing facilities is not an end in itself but rather one link in the distribution process. A retail store is often the next link, and some retail stores no longer have storerooms, causing products to go directly from a warehousing facility to the retailer's display shelves. To successfully execute such a process, retail chains often own two or three times as many truck trailers as they do tractors. Each time a tractor makes a delivery to a retail location, it leaves a trailer for the store to unload within a specified time period and picks up the previous trailer that was left to be unloaded. Hence, the parked trailer serves as a storeroom and reduces the truck-to-storeroom and storeroom-to-shelves movements to only one because the goods go directly from the parked trailer to the shelves.

---

[15]Mickey Jaffe, "Winning the War Against Paper," *Aftermarket Business,* October 2005, 64–65.

Other Space Needs

Although many would assume that the primary role of warehousing involves the storage of product, recent estimates suggest that only approximately *10 percent* of a facility's cubic capacity is actually occupied by product.[16] Because every warehousing facility sets aside areas for nonstorage activities, it's important to know about them. These nonstorage activities include, but are not limited to, the following:

1. An area where transport drivers and operators can wait while their equipment is loaded or unloaded
2. Staging, or temporary storage, areas for both incoming and outgoing merchandise
3. Employee washrooms, lunchrooms, and the like
4. Pallet storage and repair facilities (Facilities that receive unpalletized materials but ship on pallets may require a pallet-assembly operation.)
5. Office space, including an area for the necessary computer systems
6. An area designed to store damaged merchandise that is awaiting inspection by claim representatives
7. An area to salvage or repair damaged merchandise
8. An area for repacking, labeling, price marking, and so on
9. An area for accumulating and baling waste and scrap
10. An area for equipment storage and maintenance (For example, battery-powered lift trucks need to be recharged on a regular basis.)
11. Specialized storage for hazardous items, high-value items, warehousing supplies, or items needing other specialized handling (such as a freezer or refrigerated space)
12. A returned or recycled goods processing area

When designing warehousing facilities, it's also important to keep in mind external space-related needs, which unfortunately are sometimes overlooked. These include areas for vehicles waiting to be loaded and unloaded, space for vehicle maneuvering (e.g., turning, backing up), and employee parking.

WAREHOUSING OPERATIONS

Because operating a warehousing facility has many facets, efficient and effective warehousing management can be an exacting task. Workforce motivation can be difficult because of the somewhat repetitive nature of the work. It can also be strenuous and physically demanding, and on occasion warehousing facilities can be dangerous places. Some of the more prominent operational issues are discussed in the following sections.

Storage and Handling Equipment

Although it is possible to store palletized material on top of other palletized material, this can be inconsistent with the distribution center concept of fast throughput. The oldest pallet would always be on the bottom, and the pallet loads above it would have to be removed to get at the oldest pallet load (assuming a first-in, first-out philosophy). Hence, steel shelving or pallet racks are used, and each pallet sits on an individual shelf and can be stacked or removed without disturbing other pallet loads. Before installing storage equipment, companies should be familiar

---

[16]"Warehouses Must Balance Space and Time," *Modern Materials Handling,* June 2006, 21.

with applicable regulations; for example, building codes in earthquake-prone areas often limit the height of storage shelves and racks.

The use of racks may improve space utilization by allowing for narrower aisles. As previously mentioned, narrow aisles require specialized equipment capable of simultaneously moving both vertically and horizontally. Because of this, the most efficient layout of goods along any one aisle may be a path of upward and downward undulations. This would consume less time than a route that takes the equipment along a horizontal path and stops, then moves up or down and stops, then continues along the horizontal path and stops, and so on.

Goods can be moved by a combination of manual, mechanized, and automated methods, and the storage and handling equipment should be matched to the particular method. Although seemingly obvious, the fact that forklifts tend be to the standard workhorse in many warehousing facilities can lead to companies purchasing (or leasing) forklifts, even though they may not be needed.

Warehouse Management Systems

Increasingly, warehousing operations are being influenced by **warehouse management systems** (WMSs), which are software packages that "control the movement and storage of materials within an operation."[17] Activities that can be controlled by a WMS include inventory management, product receiving, determination of storage locations, order selection processes, and order shipping. Presently, about 30 percent of warehousing facilities in the United States have installed a WMS. Companies may be leery about WMS because the software alone costs between $100,000 and $500,000, and implementation costs can easily be several million dollars. In addition, only 40 percent of WMS installations are completed within budget, and 30 percent of the installations are considered failures.[18]

Despite these potential drawbacks, there are many potential benefits to warehouse management systems. Data entry errors can be dramatically reduced, and the travel distances for order picking can be reduced by nearly 50 percent. Other benefits to WMS include reduced operating expenses, fewer stockouts, increased inventory accuracy, and improved service to customers.[19] Figure 10-7 shows what might happen to a company that doesn't use a WMS.

Because there are over 200 WMS vendors and because the software's capabilities can vary from vendor to vendor, organizations should choose those that best fit what they're hoping to achieve. In the words of one warehousing consultant, "Don't assume all WMS are alike. They all perform the warehousing functions differently."[20] Moreover, the installation of a WMS can cause organizational upheaval in the sense that warehousing space may need to be reconfigured, and current employees will need varying degrees of training to become proficient with the new system.[21]

Employee Safety

Warehouses, distribution centers, and cross-docking facilities can be dangerous places to work; in 2004 alone, there were approximately 20 fatalities and over 14,000 injuries and illnesses in the U.S. warehousing industry.[22] Forklift drivers occasionally operate equipment in a reckless

---

[17]Dave Piasecki, "Warehouse Management Systems," *www.inventoryops.com.*
[18]René Jones, "WMS by the Numbers," *Electrical Wholesaling,* May 2006, 48–51.
[19]Ibid.
[20]Steve Salkin, "Avoiding the Pitfalls of WMS," *Warehousing Management,* April 2000, 36–40.
[21]Ibid.
[22]Lisa H. Harrington, "The Safety Zone," *Inbound Logistics,* May 2006, 44–54.

"SO *THAT'S* WHERE THE PAPAYAS ARE. MAYBE YOU'D BETTER CALL *LOGISTICON.*"

FIGURE 10-7 Stock Controls Are Necessary

If papayas (a tropical fruit) are kept too long, they attract insects. This cartoon accompanied the text of an advertisement for a computerized warehouse inventory control system.
Source: Courtesy of Logisticon Inc., Flexible Material Management Systems, Santa Clara, CA.

The 2005 Liberty Mutual Workplace Safety Index Findings

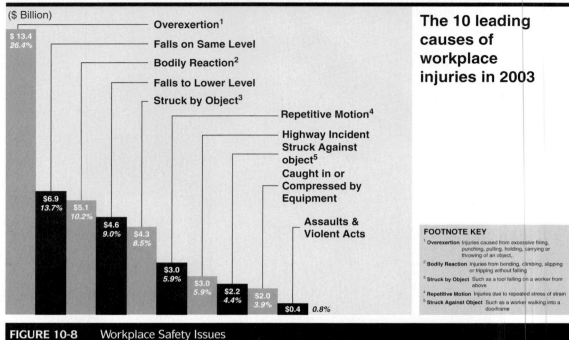

($ Billion)

Overexertion[1]
Falls on Same Level
Bodily Reaction[2]
Falls to Lower Level
Struck by Object[3]
Repetitive Motion[4]
Highway Incident
Struck Against object[5]
Caught in or Compressed by Equipment
Assaults & Violent Acts

$ 13.4
26.4%

$6.9
13.7%

$5.1
10.2%

$4.6
9.0%

$4.3
8.5%

$3.0
5.9%

$3.0
5.9%

$2.2
4.4%

$2.0
3.9%

$0.4   0.8%

The 10 leading causes of workplace injuries in 2003

FOOTNOTE KEY

[1] **Overexertion** Injuries caused from excessive firing, punching, pulling, holding, carrying or throwing of an object,.

[2] **Bodily Reaction** Injuries from bending, climbing, slipping or tripping without falling

[3] **Struck by Object** Such as a tool falling on a worker from above

[4] **Repetitive Motion** Injuries due to repeated stress of strain

[5] **Struck Against Object** Such as a worker walking into a doorframe

FIGURE 10-8   Workplace Safety Issues

Source: This information obtained from the Liberty Mutual Web site. For more information: *www.libertymutual.com/researchinstitute.*

matter, which can lead to bodily injury and even death. Workers can be injured due to improper lifting procedures, trying to carry too heavy a load, failing to observe proper hand clearances, and the like. Back and shoulder injuries are the most frequent among warehousing personnel; back support belts and braces are becoming more widely used, but they are only of value if workers also receive adequate training in how to safely lift various loads. Figure 10-8 provides a listing of workplace safety issues; many of these safety issues are associated with warehousing facilities.

When discussing employee safety, consider one warehousing professional's advice: "It costs more to recruit, train, and replace a worker than to provide a safe environment."[23] Indeed, many suggestions for dealing with warehousing safety are commonsense—and low cost—in nature. For example, suppose that a worker slips on a puddle of fluid. Rather than assigning blame for the slip, an organization could ask the simple question, "Where did the fluid come from?" Likewise, an organization that is truly committed to warehousing safety would explicitly measure it and incorporate safety metrics as part each employee's performance review.[24]

The management of employee safety can be influenced by governmental regulations. In the United States, for example, OSHA is responsible for industrial safety practices. Standards have been set for equipment and operations, and OSHA inspectors make frequent visits to industrial

[23]Ed Engel, "Getting a Lift from Safety," *Warehousing Management,* January–February 2001, 54–57.
[24]Susan Lacefield, "12 Steps to Better Warehouse Safety," *Logistics Management,* May 2004, 59–63.

workplaces to ensure regulatory compliance. In cases of noncompliance, citations can be issued, and fines can be levied. An important warehousing-related OSHA initiative in recent years has involved the training of forklift drivers. This initiative mandates that forklift workers actually have to drive forklifts as part of the training process; furthermore, driver performance must be evaluated every three years.[25]

Warehousing facilities generate large volumes of waste materials, such as empty cartons, steel strapping, and broken pallets, as well as wood and nails used for crating and dunnage. (**Dunnage** is material that is used to block and brace products inside carrier equipment to prevent the shipment from shifting in transit and becoming damaged.) The various waste materials must be properly handled because they pose threats to employee safety and may also be fire hazards.

Moreover, even with the best of practices, some goods that are received, stored, and shipped will be damaged. Special procedures must be established for handling broken or damaged items, if only from the standpoint of employee safety. A broken bottle of household ammonia, for example, results in three hazards: noxious fumes, broken glass, and a slippery floor. Aerosol cans pose hazards that are affected by the product in the cans. For example, cans of shaving cream cause little problem in fires because if they explode, the shaving cream serves to extinguish the fire; that is not the case with aerosol cans containing paints or lacquers, and such cans are often kept in special cages because in a fire they might become burning projectiles.

Indeed, fires are a constant threat in warehousing, in part because many materials used for packaging are highly flammable. In addition, although plastic pallets last longer, are cleaner, and are less likely to splinter than wooden pallets, plastic pallets tend to be a greater fire risk. High-rise facilities are more susceptible to fires because the vertical spaces between stored materials serve as flues and help fires burn.

More than 20,000 warehouse fires occur each year in the United States, most of which result only in property damage but some of which result in injury and death. The six most common causes of warehousing fires are arson, tobacco smoking, improper use of forklifts, electrical malfunctions, poor product disposal practices, and storage of incompatible materials.[26] Quite frankly, many warehousing fires can be prevented by common sense. Flammable products, for example, should not be stored near heat sources (such as space heaters).

Hazardous Materials

Hazardous materials (hazmat) must receive extra attention because of the injuries and property damage they can cause (see Figure 10-9). Indeed, hazmat-caused warehousing fires have caused over $75 million in property damage, not to mention the toll in terms of bodily injury and even loss of life.

Government regulations often require that shipping documents indicate the hazardous nature of the materials being transported. Warehouse employees should note these warnings when receiving materials and similarly should include such warnings on outbound shipping documents when materials leave warehouses. Government regulations also require organizations to create a materials safety data sheet (MSDS) for each hazardous product to be stored in a facility. The MSDS should contain explicit storage and handling information as well as what to do in case of an emergency.[27]

---

[25]Jim Truesdell, "OSHA Enacts Fork Lift Rules," *Supply House Times,* July 1999, 93–94.

[26]Jim Whalen, "Sounding the Alarm," *Warehousing Management,* April 2001, 26–30.

[27]David Maloney, "HAZMAT: Handle with Care," *Modern Materials Handling,* March 2004, 61–65.

Yes, sir, I know freezing will not hurt your product, but what will it do to my floor when it thaws?

FIGURE 10-9	Materials Stored in a Warehouse Can Damage Other Materials or the Warehouse Structure

Source: Warehousing Review 6, Nos. 2–7 (1977). Drawn by Art Stenholm; courtesy of International Warehouse Logistics Association.

Hazmat experts generally agree that the applicable regulations should only provide a starting point for proper storage of hazardous materials, in part because for some situations no regulations exist. These experts further suggest that hazmat storage can be managed effectively by answering four questions: *What* material is being stored? *Why* is it being stored? *Where* is it being stored? *How* is it being stored?[28]

A number of design elements must also be considered with the storage of hazardous materials. Buildings that store hazmat often have specially constructed areas so that materials can be contained in the case of an accident. Likewise, these facilities often have walls and doors that can withstand several hours of intense fire. It's also important for a hazmat storage facility to have proper sprinkling systems as well as excellent ventilation. These and other considerations have caused some organizations to use third-party logistics companies to manage hazmat storage.[29]

Warehousing Security

It is estimated that the theft and pilferage of products stored in warehousing facilities cause losses in the range of four to five times the products' value. Theft and pilferage can result in lost sales opportunities (both present and in the future), customer dissatisfaction, additional costs to prevent theft and pilferage, and the administrative time and costs associated with filing claims, and more.[30]

The terrorist attacks of September 11, 2001, have profoundly affected warehousing security. Cold-storage facilities, for instance, have enacted more stringent security procedures because these facilities often contain large quantities of ammonia, a key ingredient for making a bomb.[31] In addition, food distributors have experienced a dramatic increase in theft because, in an age of terrorism, food theft is not a high priority for local, state, or federal law enforcement.[32]

---

[28]Todd Nighswonger, "Are You Storing Hazardous Materials Safely?" *Occupational Hazards,* June 2000, 45–47.
[29]Ibid.
[30]Roger Morton, "Keep Product from Wandering Off," *Transportation & Distribution,* June 1999, 84–87.
[31]Kristi Labetti, "Designing for Security," *Frozen Food Age,* June 2002, 38–39.
[32]"Controlling Workplace Security," *Refrigerated Transporter,* January 2004, 18–20.

In general, warehousing security can be enhanced by focusing on people, facilities, and processes. In terms of people, one area of focus should be the hiring process for warehousing workers; a starting point might be determining whether an individual facility even has a formal hiring process. In terms of a facilities focus, a number of different low-tech (e.g., fences) and high-tech (e.g., closed-circuit video cameras) devices can help to enhance warehousing security; an obvious trade-off is the cost of the various devices. In terms of processes to improve warehousing security, the more times a shipment is handled, the greater the opportunities for loss or damage. Thus, logisticians would do well to reduce the number of times an individual shipment is handled. Table 10-1 highlights some possible shortcomings in warehousing security.

Cleanliness and Sanitation Issues

At first glance, cleanliness and sanitation might seem like issues that are more relevant to, say, restaurants than to warehousing operations. However, unclean and unsanitary warehousing facilities aren't likely to attract many new customers and could cause existing customers to take their business elsewhere. Moreover, clean and sanitary facilities have a positive impact on employee safety, morale, and productivity while also reducing employee turnover.[33]

Fortunately, warehouse cleanliness and sanitation are not predicated on complex theories or costly technology, but rather on common sense and diligence. For example, one prominent warehousing consultant suggests that cleanliness and sanitation can be facilitated by putting the "junk and old stuff" at the back of a facility where it is out of the way (and often out of sight). Another suggestion is to purchase a powered sweeper and use it at least once a day.[34]

Summary

This chapter focused on warehousing—the sites where inventories are stored for varying periods of time. Warehousing facilitates the regrouping function, which involves rearranging the quantities and assortment of products as they move through the supply chain. Warehousing is also needed because production and consumption may not coincide, and warehousing can help smooth out imbalances between them.

TABLE 10-1	Possible Shortcomings in Warehousing Security
Shortcoming	**Comment**
Making it too easy for dock personnel to work in collusion with truck drivers	Fewer than 5% who commit crimes are prosecuted
Relying on safeguards that simply don't work	Security cameras aren't always turned on
Approach to theft is too reactive	Don't wait until theft reaches an "unacceptable" level
Not weeding out on-the-job substance abusers or dealers	Approximately 90% of drug users either steal or deal to support their habit
Not checking your checkers on a frequent basis	They may become complacent
Not making it easy to report theft and substance abuse	Outsourcing the reporting may be more effective
Hiring high-risk employees	An ounce of prevention is worth a pound of cure

Source: Julia Kuzeljevich, "The SEVEN DEADLY SINS in Warehouse Security," *Canadian Transportation & Logistics,* April 2006, 44.

---

[33]Jim Apple, "Have You Done Your Housekeeping Chores?" *Modern Materials Handling,* April 2004, 64.
[34]Ibid.

This chapter also discussed public, private, contract, and multiclient warehousing. Public warehousing has a number of established duties regarding the care of goods, and customers pay only for the space that is actually used to store their products. Private warehousing is owned or occupied on a long-term basis by the firm using such facilities, and it is best used when an organization has large and steady demand patterns. Contract warehousing involves specially tailored warehousing services that are provided to one client on a long-term basis. Multiclient warehousing, a relatively new alternative, is a mixture of public and contract warehousing.

Various design considerations are relevant to warehousing, with trade-offs among them. For example, a decision to build up or out can affect a facility's utilization of labor, mechanization, and automation. Similarly, organizations that prefer a fixed slot location for merchandise may have to build larger facilities to have a sufficient number of storage slots.

The chapter concluded with an examination of some of the more prominent issues in warehousing operations. The discussion of warehouse management systems illustrated how technology can be used to improve warehousing operations. By contrast, effective management of warehousing cleanliness and sanitation, which involves common sense and diligence, tends to be low tech in nature.

Questions for Discussion and Review

1. Distinguish between warehouses and distribution centers.
2. Explain the four ways that warehousing facilitates the regrouping function.
3. Discuss some of the value-added activities that can be performed by warehouses and distribution centers.
4. What is cross-docking? How might it affect warehousing design?
5. Distinguish between bonded storage and field warehousing.
6. What are the advantages and disadvantages of private warehousing?
7. Discuss why contract warehousing is becoming a preferred alternative for many organizations.
8. Explain how common sense can be helpful in terms of warehousing design and operations.
9. In terms of warehousing design, give examples of trade-offs involving space, labor, and mechanization.
10. Distinguish between fixed and variable slot locations. How might they affect warehousing design?
11. Discuss the trade-offs associated with order-picking versus stock-replenishing functions.
12. Distinguish between a two-dock and a single-dock warehousing layout. Which one requires more space? Why?
13. What are some potential advantages to paperless warehousing operations?
14. Discuss how storage and handling equipment can influence warehousing operations.
15. What is a warehouse management system (WMS)? How can it benefit warehousing operations?
16. What is OSHA's role in warehousing safety?
17. What are the most common causes of warehousing fires? Which do you think is the easiest for managers to control? Justify your answer.
18. How might the storage of hazardous materials affect the design of a warehousing facility?
19. Discuss how warehousing security can be enhanced by focusing on people, facilities, and processes.
20. Why are cleanliness and sanitation issues relevant to warehousing operations?

Suggested Readings

Ackerman, Kenneth B. *Warehousing Tips.* Columbus, OH: Kenneth B. Ackerman Publishing, 2001.

Apte, Uday M., and S. Viswanathan. "Effective Cross Docking for Improving Distribution Efficiencies." *International Journal of Logistics: Research and Applications* 3, no. 3 (2000): 291–302.

Armstrong, Richard D. "An Overview of Warehousing in North America." *Journal of Transportation Law, Logistics & Policy* 73, no. 1 (2006): 48–53.

Brockman, Thompson. "21 Warehousing Trends in the 21st Century." *IIE Solutions,* January 2000, 31–36.

Cook, Robert L., Brian Gibson, and Douglas MacCurdy. "A Lean Approach to Cross Docking." *Supply Chain Management Review* 9, no. 2 (2005): 54–59.

de Koster, M. B. M. and P. M. J. Warffemius. "American, Asian, and Third-Party International Warehouse Operations in Europe." *International Journal of Operations and Production Management* 25, no. 8 (2005): 762–780.

Hales, H. Lee. "Put Your Warehouse in Order." *Industrial Engineer*, February 2006, 34–36.

Making the Move to Cross Docking. Oak Brook, IL: Warehousing Education and Research Council, 2000.

Min, Hokey. "The Applications of Warehouse Management Systems: An Exploratory Study." *International Journal of Logistics: Research & Applications* 9, no. 2 (2006): 111–126.

Moberg, Christopher R., and Thomas W. Speh. "Third-party Warehousing Selection: A Comparison of National and Regional Firms." *Mid-American Journal of Business* 19, no. 2 (2004): 71–76.

Saenz, Norman. "It's in the Pick." *IIE Solutions,* July 2000, 36–38.

C A S E S

CASE 10-1   SANDY'S CANDY

Sandy Nykerk was an operations analyst for Mannix Model Markets, a food-store chain headquartered in Omaha, Nebraska, with 55 stores in an area that extended east to Des Moines, Iowa; north to Sioux Falls, South Dakota; west to North Platte, Nebraska; and south to Emporia, Kansas. All the stores were served by daily deliveries five days a week from a large complex of Mannix warehouses in Omaha, with two exceptions. First, each store's produce department could buy some produce locally, which it usually did during the summer and autumn months. Second, some goods were delivered to the stores by vendors, usually operating through drivers–salespeople who would stock the goods on the shelves. Examples of these goods were dairy products, soft drinks, bakery items, name-brand snacks, beer, pantyhose, candy, and yogurt. Vendors delivered ice cream directly to the stores west of Grand Island, Nebraska, in part because Mannix was short of trucks with freezer capacity, especially during the summer months.

Mannix Model Markets was a member of a buying cooperative. The buying cooperative had forced many name-brand manufacturers to make their goods available to its members, in which case goods would be delivered first to each chain's warehouse and then via chain trucks to individual retail chain stores, where store personnel placed them on the shelves and treated them like any other product. The only good that could not be purchased through the cooperative was beer because some states had stricter regulations regarding the wholesaling of beer (and other alcoholic beverages), initially to ensure that they received all beverage tax receipts (although beer wholesalers opposed legislation to relax these regulations).

Sandy knew that most of the vendor-delivered goods were ones that Mannix Model Markets did not want to handle through its own distribution system. Milk, for example, would be very expensive to handle because it was costly to ship and had a short shelf life. Bakery products had similar characteristics, although Mannix did buy some bread from a private bakery and sold it in Omaha stores under its own label. Snack foods were also best handled by drivers–salespeople working for vendors because they were handled roughly in the Mannix distribution system; by the time pretzels or potato chips reached the shelves, they were mostly broken and filled only the bottom one-third of the bag.

The buying cooperative had recently entered into an agreement with Schoenecker's Candies, a well-known regional firm that produced eight different types of candies and caramels packaged and sold in cellophane bags. Mannix's experience was that Schoenecker's candies sold much better than any competing brand, almost irrespective of price, so Schoenecker's was the only brand that Mannix would carry. Sandy had received a note from her supervisor saying that Schoenecker's candies could now be purchased directly through the buying cooperative and handled through Mannix's regular distribution system. The supervisor wanted Sandy to calculate whether Mannix should stop having Schoenecker's candies delivered by drivers–salespeople and instead purchase the candy through the buying cooperative.

If the cost comparisons were fairly close, Mannix would prefer using its own system for several reasons, including some generalities regarding drivers–salespeople and some not specifically referring to the Schoenecker drivers–salespeople. The three objections to deliveries by drivers–salespeople were the following:

1. Their deliveries could not be scheduled, and sometimes their trucks would tie up an unloading dock, which could delay a Mannix truck waiting to discharge 10 or 20 tons of groceries.
2. Some drivers–salespeople needed space in the stockroom, and this meant that unknown people were wandering in an area where pilferage was sometimes a problem.
3. When a driver–salesperson appeared, this interrupted the store manager or assistant manager, who routinely would have to approve the next order and also would have to check in the new merchandise and agree on the amount of returned merchandise the driver–salesperson was removing from the store.

Store clerks disliked some drivers–salespeople, claiming that they took shelf-stocking work away from store personnel. Store management discounted this argument because they thought that many store clerks did not like to see how quickly the drivers–salespeople worked. (The drivers–salespeople were mostly nonunion and worked on a commission basis.) Also, the shelves stocked by drivers–salespeople were always neater than those stocked by ordinary store personnel. On occasion, when store clerks disliked a particular driver–salesperson, they would sabotage him or her by rearranging the shelves after he or she had left, hiding all the products behind those of a competitor.

Sandy started working on her assignment and found that she was comparing the efficiency of Mannix's distribution system, which handled 10,000 line items, with that of the Schoenecker Candy Company, which handled only eight types of candy in several different-size packages. Soon, Sandy's project became known among her fellow workers as the "Sandy Candy Puzzle." Finally, to organize her thoughts and provide a basis for comparison, Sandy took a sheet of paper, drew a line down the middle, and listed as many comparisons as possible. Her analysis is shown in Exhibits 10-A and 10-B.

Sandy completed her tally sheets and wondered why sales per store should be higher when drivers–salespeople serviced the merchandise. She was told that this was because they did a better job of arranging the goods on the shelves, they kept abreast of changes in demand, and they sometimes placed posters and other small displays on the candy shelves. ∎

QUESTIONS

1. Using those items of comparison for which costs can be calculated, determine the cost difference between the two delivery systems.
2. List and compare those factors for which it is difficult to assign precise costs.
3. Given the data that Sandy has, do you believe that Mannix Model Markets should get its Schoenecker candy through the buying cooperative or continue to rely on direct deliveries by Schoenecker's drivers–salespeople? Give your reasons.

Present System	Alternate System
Schoenecker Candy Co. has driver/salespeople deliver and stock shelves.	Purchase Schoenecker's Candies through buying cooperative and distribute to stores through Mannix Markets' own distribution system.

Buying Terms	
Every Friday, the d/s tallies sales for past seven days and store manager approves. Then three days later a bill comes from Schoenecker with 2% discount if paid within ten days (i.e., 13 days after the d/s makes the tally). The entire amount is due within 30 days (or 33 days of d/s tally).	Schoenecker must be paid within seven days after candy is received at Mannix warehouse. No discounts.

Wholesale and Retail Prices of Candy					
Package Size	Wholesale Price Paid to Schoenecker	Retail Price	Package Size	Wholesale Price Paid to Schoenecker	Retail Price
3½ oz.	13¢	19¢	4 oz.	10¢	19¢
8 oz.	28¢	39¢	9 oz.	20¢	39¢
12 oz.	42¢	57¢	13 oz.	30¢	57¢

Average Time in Inventory	
Goods are on consignment, meaning that Schoenecker owns them and only collects for those that are sold.	Candy would be in the Mannix warehouse for an average of two weeks and on a retail store shelf for an average of one week.

Average Sales per Store per Week	
110 3½-oz. pkgs., 70 8-oz. pkgs., and 40 12-oz. pkgs.	100 4-oz. pkgs., 60 9-oz. pkgs., and 30 13-oz. pkgs. (Sales were somewhat lower because store personnel do not take as good care of merchandise on shelves.)

Shrinkage on Store Shelf	
Unaccounted-for loss: 2 percent per week, paid for by Mannix Markets.	2 percent per week, paid for by Mannix Markets.

EXHIBIT 10-A   Sandy's Worksheet

4. If you were Sandy, what additional information would you like to have before being asked to make such a recommendation?
5. Candy sales increase during holiday seasons. Which of the two candy distribution systems do you think would do a better job of anticipating and supplying these seasonal increases? Why?
6. Assume you are in charge of labor relations for Mannix Model Markets. Would you like to see continued reliance on drivers–salespeople to supply the chain's candy needs? Why or why not?

Present System	Alternate System
Spoilage	
(Package torn open on shelf which cannot be sold): 1 percent a week, absorbed by Schoenecker Candy.	Same rate, paid for by Mannix Markets.
Ordering Costs	
Absorbed by Schoenecker Candy Co. However, store manager or assistant must approve order, twice a week, taking a total of 10 minutes time. Assistant manager makes $16,000 per year plus 15% fringe.	1½¢ per day, 4 days a week, for each of 24 items (8 types of candy in three sizes of package).
Shelf Stocking	
Absorbed by Schoenecker Candy Co.	20 minutes of clerk's time per week. (Clerk's hourly rate is $3.75 plus 10% fringe.) For every 10 stock clerks there is one supervisor paid $13,000 per year plus 15% fringe.
Warehousing Costs	
Absorbed by Schoenecker Candy Co.	The Mannix warehouse costs $10,000 per day to operate. Its throughput is 750 tons per day, five days a week.
Delivery to Store Costs	
Absorbed by Schoenecker Candy Co.	Only available cost figure is 3¢ per ton-mile, and the average distance from Mannix warehouse to a retail store is 50 miles.
Checking in Goods at Store	
Takes 10 minutes per of manager's or assistant manager's time.	No check-in necessary; controls are at warehouse, and truck is sealed in between warehouse and store.
Billing and Bill-Paying Costs	
Mannix Markets pays $1.00 per week to process and pay the Schoenecker Candy Co. invoice.	Believed to be less since, rather than spot-checking forms from each store, only the Mannix warehouse receipt form need be checked.

EXHIBIT 10-B   Sandy's Worksheet

CASE 10-2 MINNETONKA WAREHOUSE

Wayne Schuller managed a warehouse in Minnetonka, Minnesota. His major concern was the number of workers to assign to his single unloading dock. After he began contracting with motor carriers for deliveries, he found that they were assessing him stiff penalties if their trucks had to wait to be unloaded. Wayne started adding larger crews at the unloading dock, but often they seemed idle because there were no trucks to unload. Wayne recalled from college that queueing theory might be applicable to such a problem.

The theory of queueing is an analysis of the probabilities associated with waiting in line, assuming that orders, customers, and so on arrive in some pattern (often a random pattern) to stand in line. A common situation is that on the average a facility may have excess capacity, but often it is more than full, with a backlog of work to be done. Often, this backlog has costs associated with it, including penalties to be paid or customers who walk away rather than wait. If a firm expands its capacity to reduce waiting times, then its costs go up and must be paid even when the facility is idle. Queueing theory is used to find the best level of capacity, the one that minimizes the costs of providing a service and the costs of those waiting to use the service.

After some further research specific to his firm, Wayne determined the following facts:

1. Trucks arrive randomly at the average rate of four per hour, with a deviation of plus or minus one.

2. A team of two warehouse workers can unload trucks at the rate of five per hour, or one every 12 minutes.
3. A team of three warehouse workers can unload trucks at the rate of eight per hour, or one every 7.5 minutes.
4. A team of four warehouse workers can unload trucks at the rate of 10 per hour, or one every 6 minutes.
5. A team of five warehouse workers can unload trucks at the rate of 11 per hour, or one every 4.45 minutes.
6. The unloading times given in the preceding items (1–5) are average figures.
7. Each warehouse worker receives $14 per hour, must be paid for an entire shift, and—because of union work rules—cannot be assigned to other tasks within the warehouse.
8. Because of its contract with the carriers, the Minnetonka warehouse must pay the motor carriers that own idle trucks at the rate of $60 per hour while the trucks stand idle, waiting to be unloaded.

Use a software package that enables you to perform queueing operations. Note that the variable defined as number of servers (# servers) denotes number of teams of workers and accompanying equipment working as a complete server. In the situation described, the number of teams or servers is always 1, although the number varies in terms of costs and output. ■

QUESTIONS

1. For each of the four work team sizes, calculate the expected number of trucks waiting in the queue to be unloaded.
2. For each of the four work team sizes, calculate the expected time in the queue—that is, the expected time a truck has to wait in line to be unloaded.
3. For each of the four work team sizes, what is the probability that a truck cannot be unloaded immediately?
4. Which of the four work team sizes results in the lowest cost to Wayne?
5. Wayne is also considering rental of a forklift to use in truck unloading. A team of only two

would be needed, but the hourly cost would be $38 per hour ($28 for the workers and $10 for the forklift). The two workers could unload a truck in 5 minutes. Should Wayne rent the forklift?

6. Disregard your answer to question 5. Labor negotiations are coming up, and Wayne thinks he can get the union to give way on the work rule that prohibits warehouse workers on the unloading dock from being given other assignments when they are not unloading trucks. How much would Schuller save in unloading dock costs if he could reassign warehouse workers to other tasks when they are not unloading trucks, assuming that he has picked a good team of workers and each worker works 8 hours a day?

11 | PROCUREMENT

Key Terms

- Bribes
- Electronic procurement (e-procurement)
- Excess (surplus) materials
- Global procurement (sourcing)
- Investment recovery
- ISO 9000
- Kickbacks
- Malcolm Baldrige National Quality Award
- Maverick spending
- Obsolete materials

- Procurement
- Procurement card (p-card)
- Purchasing
- Quality
- Reverse auctions
- Scrap materials
- Six Sigma
- Socially responsible procurement
- Supplier development (reverse marketing)
- Supply management
- Waste materials

Learning Objectives

- To understand the distinction between procurement, purchasing, and supply management
- To learn about supplier selection and evaluation
- To understand quality issues in procurement
- To learn about electronic procurement
- To appreciate socially responsible procurement

Procurement, which refers to the raw materials, component parts, and supplies bought from outside organizations to support a company's operations, is an important activity and closely related to logistics because acquired goods and services must be entered into the supply chain in the exact quantities and at the precise time they are needed. Procurement is also important because its costs often range between 60 and 80 percent of an organization's revenues.

The magnitude of procurement expenditures meant that procurement's historical focus in many organizations was to achieve the lowest possible cost from potential suppliers; oftentimes these suppliers were pitted against each other in "cutthroat" competition involving three- or six-month arm's-length contracts awarded to the lowest bidder. Once this lowest bidder was chosen, the bidding cycle would almost immediately start again, and another low bidder would get the contract for the next several months. Today, by contrast, procurement has a much more strategic orientation in many organizations, and a contemporary procurement manager might have responsibility for reducing cycle times, playing an integral role in product development, or generating additional revenues by collaborating with the marketing department.[1]

The previous edition of this text indicated that procurement, **purchasing,** and **supply management** were terms that could be used almost interchangeably, but this is no longer the case. Although procurement and purchasing are viewed as synonymous terms, supply management is now viewed as a relational exchange approach involving a limited number of suppliers. You might recall from Chapter 2 that relational exchanges adopt a long-term orientation that can be characterized by attributes such as trust, commitment, dependence, and shared benefits.

---

[1]Carlos Niezen and Wulf Weller, "Procurement as Strategy," *Harvard Business Review* 84, no. 9 (2006): 22–24.

Keep in mind that because entire textbooks are devoted to procurement, it's really not possible for us to do justice to this topic in just one chapter. We'll begin our discussion with a brief overview of possible objectives for procurement, and this will be followed by a discussion of supplier selection and evaluation. We'll also look at quality issues in procurement, global procurement, electronic procurement, investment recovery, and socially responsible purchasing.

PROCUREMENT OBJECTIVES[2]

Because procurement has become more strategic in nature, its primary objective is no longer to achieve the lowest possible cost of supply. Potential procurement objectives include, but are not limited to, (1) supporting organizational goals and objectives, (2) managing the purchasing process effectively and efficiently, (3) managing the supply base, (4) developing strong relationships with other functional groups, and (5) supporting operational requirements. Each objective will be briefly discussed in the following paragraphs.

First and foremost, procurement's objectives must *support organizational goals and objectives.* If, for example, minimal inventory is an organizational objective, then procurement probably should not be attempting to minimize total procurement costs. With respect to *managing the purchase process effectively and efficiently,* effectively is concerned with how well procurement keeps its promises, whereas efficiently refers to how well (or poorly) procurement uses company resources in keeping its promises. A third procurement objective, *managing the supply base,* refers to the selection, development, and maintenance of supply sources.

Developing strong relationships with other functional groups recognizes that the interfunctional consequences of procurement decisions require more cooperation and coordination than has traditionally existed between procurement and areas such as logistics, manufacturing, and marketing. *Supporting operational requirements* means that procurement's focus is on satisfying internal customers and can be summarized by buying the right products, at the right price, from the right source, at the right specifications, in the right quantity, for delivery at the right time to the right internal customer.

SUPPLIER SELECTION AND EVALUATION

One of procurement's most important responsibilities involves supplier (vendor) selection and evaluation. The selection and evaluation of suppliers is a process that involves stating an organization's needs and then determining how well various potential suppliers can fulfill these needs (see Figure 11-1). The first step in this process, *identify need for supply,* can arise from a number of considerations, such as the end of an existing supply agreement or the development of a new product. *Situation analysis,* the second step, looks at both the internal and external environment within which the supply decision is to be made. Internal considerations include identification of the relevant stakeholders, where the supply is needed, and the appropriate quantity and quality of the supply, as well as applicable supply policies (e.g., minority supplier initiatives). The external environment includes economic considerations, the legal and regulatory frameworks controlling the purchase, and the marketplace within which potential suppliers operate.

Identify and evaluate possible suppliers is the third step. Myriad sources can be used to identify possible suppliers, such as salespeople, trade shows, trade publications, and the

---

[2]The material in this section is drawn from Robert Monczka, Robert Trent, and Robert Handfield, *Purchasing and Supply Chain Management,* 3rd ed. (Mason, OH: Thomson/South-Western, 2005).

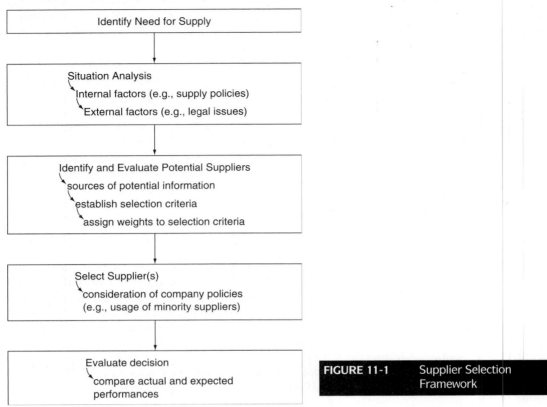

FIGURE 11-1   Supplier Selection Framework

Internet. It's important to recognize and understand the potential advantages and disadvantages to each source. For example, although trade shows might highlight offerings from several different supply sources (which could facilitate supplier comparisons), the costs to attend or exhibit at trade shows have skyrocketed in recent years; moreover, trade shows are often held only once a year. Evaluating suppliers can be facilitated if an organization (1) delineates relevant selection criteria and (2) assigns weights to these criteria. With respect to the latter, if an organization uses four relevant selection criteria, should all four be assigned equal weight (that is, 25 percent per criteria), or should certain criteria be weighted more heavily than others (e.g., two criteria weighted at 30 percent apiece and two others weighted at 20 percent each)?

This weighting technique serves as a foundation for generating a rating (score) for each possible supplier, and these ratings are instrumental in the fourth step of the supplier selection process, *select supplier(s),* which is where an organization chooses one or more companies to supply the relevant product. Internal considerations, which were mentioned in step 2, could influence the actual selection of a supplier or suppliers; for example, if an organization is leery of using only one supplier, then perhaps it would select the two suppliers with the highest scores. The final step of the supplier selection process, *evaluate decision,* involves a comparison of expected supplier performance to actual supplier performance. This evaluation can be facilitated if an organization has explicitly defined selection criteria, as mentioned in step 4.

The preceding paragraphs have presented supplier selection and evaluation as a seemingly straightforward and easy-to-follow process, but supplier selection and evaluation can actually be quite complex. First off, supplier selection and evaluation generally involve multiple criteria, and these criteria can vary both in number and importance, depending on the particular situation. As an example, a study involving the procurement of electronic components[3] looked at 10 possible selection criteria, whereas 16 selection criteria were investigated in a study of overseas vendors by Canadian apparel buyers.[4] Second, because some vendor selection criteria may be contradictory, it is important to understand potential trade-offs between them. For instance, it may be difficult for a supplier to achieve both competitive pricing and high-quality supply. Third, the evolution of business practices and philosophies, such as just-in-time and supply chain management, may require new selection criteria or the reprioritization of existing criteria. As an example, whereas EDI capabilities might have been an important supplier selection criteria in the early 1990s, in the contemporary environment Internet-related capabilities (e.g., tracking, pricing) have assumed increased relevance and importance.[5]

Supplier Development (Reverse Marketing)

Our discussion of supplier selection and evaluation has taken a "traditional" approach in the sense that there has been underlying assumptions that (1) suppliers initiate marketing efforts toward purchasers and (2) potential suppliers are available and willing to serve prospective purchasers. However, because increasingly potential suppliers are not available and willing to serve prospective purchasers, some purchasers are taking a more proactive role in the procurement process. To this end, **supplier development (reverse marketing)** refers to "a degree of aggressive procurement involvement not normally encountered in supplier selection" and can include a purchaser initiating contact with a supplier or a purchaser establishing prices, terms, and conditions, among other behaviors.[6]

There are several key reasons for why purchasers are adopting a more proactive and aggressive role in the procurement process. One is the myriad inefficiencies associated with suppliers initiating marketing efforts toward purchasers, such as suppliers possessing inadequate, insufficient, or untimely information. A second reason for more proactive and aggressive procurement is that the purchaser may be aware of important benefits, such as reduced inventory and improved forecasting accuracy, which are unknown to the supplier. Yet another reason is that achieving competitive advantage in the supply chain is predicated on purchasers adopting a more aggressive approach so as to compel suppliers to meet the necessary requirements.[7]

QUALITY ISSUES IN PROCUREMENT

It's important that we operationalize "quality" before beginning our discussion of quality issues in procurement. Consider that the American Society of Quality, which bills itself as the world's leading membership organization focused on quality, defines quality as "a subjective term for which each person has his or her own definition."[8] Although there are somewhat stringent

---

[3]Neeraj Bharadway, "Investigating the Decision Criteria Used in Electronic Components Procurement," *Industrial Marketing Management* 33, no. 4 (2004): 317–323.

[4]Ismat Thaver and Anne Wilcock, "Identification of Overseas Vendor Selection Criteria Used by Canadian Apparel Buyers," *Journal of Fashion Marketing and Management* 10, no. 1 (2006): 56–70.

[5]Birsen Karpak, Rammohan R. Kasuganti, and Erdooan Kumcu, "Are You Using Costly Outmoded Techniques to Purchase Materials?" *Business Forum* 27, no. 1 (2005): 14–19.

[6]Michiel Leenders, Harold E. Fearon, Anna Flynn, and P. Fraser Johnson, *Purchasing & Supply Management,* 12th ed. (McGraw-Hill/Irwin, 2002), Chapter 8.

[7]Leenders et al., *Purchasing & Supply Management.*

[8]*www.asq.org.*

definitions of quality, such as a product that is free from defects, deficiencies, or errors, we will take a more flexible approach and define **quality** as conformance to mutually agreed upon requirements.

The issue of quality in procurement often represents a delicate balancing act for the involved organizations. That is, if an organization buys an input of inferior quality, it runs the risk of lowering the quality of the final product. If an organization buys an input of higher quality than one's final product, it may be paying for something that is not needed. In short, in the buy–sell relationship, both parties must understand issues of quality and strive to match the quality levels of buyers and sellers in the supply chain.

Today, vendors are expected to have quality programs, and many have worked for years to achieve a good reputation for quality. One way for vendors to convince potential buyers that they are committed to quality is through a program known as ISO (International Standards Organization) 9000 certification. **ISO 9000** is a set of generic standards used to document, implement, and demonstrate quality management and assurance systems. Applicable to manufacturing and service industries, these standards are intended to help companies build quality into every core process in each department. Firms demonstrating a commitment to quality through training, reviews, and continuous improvement can receive ISO 9000 certification. After achieving ISO 9000 certification, organizations are audited each year and can be recertified every three years. Although ISO 9000 certification continues to become more commonplace throughout the world, it can still be a source of competitive advantage for certain companies. For example, the Web site for Bil-Jax, a North American manufacturer of scaffolds and other construction-related equipment, emphasizes that it is the only full-service manufacturer of scaffolds to have achieved both ISO 9000 certification and ISO 9000 recertification.[9]

Another quality-related concept or practice is known as **Six Sigma,** which emphasizes the virtual elimination of business errors. Those who remember the normal distribution (curve) from their statistics class will recall that Sigmas are related to standard deviations from the mean. The larger the number deviations, the more area under the normal curve that is covered. In the case of Six Sigma, or six standard deviations, the area covered is 99.99966 percent, leaving a tiny area, .00034, uncovered. More specifically, the Six Sigma approach suggests that there will be 3.4 defects, deficiencies, or errors per one million opportunities—obviously a very high standard.

From a North American perspective, Six Sigma is a relatively new approach in the sense that it really didn't begin to achieve widespread acceptance—and adoption—until the mid 1990s. Indeed, a recent worldwide Six Sigma study indicated that only about 10 percent of the responding organizations had established a structured performance improvement program prior to 1995. This same study also found that the most significant benefits from Six Sigma have been reduced costs, reduced errors and waste, and reduced cycle time, whereas the key drawbacks have involved overcoming business cultural barriers, investing the required resources (both human and money), and gaining top management commitment.[10]

Another quality-related initiative is the **Malcolm Baldrige National Quality Award,** which was established in the late 1980s to recognize U.S. organizations for their achievements in quality and performance. Initially only manufacturers, services, and small businesses were eligible for this award, but eligibility was expanded to include health care and educational institutions in the late 1990s.

The Baldrige Quality Awards, which are restricted to organizations headquartered in the United States, require interested parties to submit a formal application that is evaluated by a

---

[9]*www.biljax.com.*
[10]"Exclusive Worldwide Six Sigma Survey Reveals…" *Business Credit,* October 2005, 48–51.

committee largely made up of private-sector experts in business and quality. Applications are evaluated for achievement and improvement across seven categories: business results; customer and market focus; human resource focus; leadership; measurement, analysis, and knowledge management; process management; and strategic planning.[11] Importantly, organizations that choose not to apply for a Baldrige Award can use these seven categories as a template for evaluating the quality of current and prospective suppliers.

There are substantive differences between ISO 9000 and the Baldrige Award; ISO 9000 essentially allows an organization to determine if it complies with its specific quality system. In contrast, the Baldrige Award is more heavily focused on the actual results from a quality system as well as on continuous improvement.[12] The Baldrige Award also tends to be more externally focused in the sense that organizations benchmark themselves against organizations from outside their particular industry.

GLOBAL PROCUREMENT (SOURCING)[13]

Chapter 1 pointed out that world trade is expected to experience dramatic growth in the early years of the twenty-first century, and this increased globalization means that many organizations, rather than relying on local and domestic suppliers, will cast out a much wider net in search of supply sources. Indeed, a survey of approximately 300 senior-level business executives found that the percentage of supply sources outside one's domestic market is projected to increase from 22 to 38 percent in a six-year time span.[14]

Global procurement (sourcing), which refers to buying components and inputs anywhere in the world, is driven by two primary reasons, namely, the factor-input strategy and the market-access strategy. With the factor-input strategy, an organization is seeking low-cost or high-quality sources of supply, whereas the market-access strategy involves sourcing in markets where an organizations plans to do significant business.

A global sourcing development model would include the following components: planning, specification, evaluation, relationship management, transportation and holding costs, implementation, and monitoring and improving. Each of these will be briefly discussed next. *Planning* is the first step in global procurement and involves an honest assessment of global sourcing opportunities and challenges. The outcome of this stage should be a set of global procurement policies and procedures that are consistent with an organization's overall objectives. *Specification* involves quantifying and qualifying current sources across a variety of dimensions such as quality, costs, reliability, and standardization, among others.

An earlier section in this chapter discussed supplier selection and evaluation, and although the *evaluation* process associated with global procurement has similarities, there are potential differences as well. For example, should an organization use the same standards to evaluate international sources as are used to evaluate domestic sources? Another component in a global sourcing development framework, *relationship management,* has been discussed in previous chapters. Relationship management in global procurement is exacerbated by potential difficulties in cross-cultural communication such as language and time considerations.

---

[11]*www.quality.NIST.gov.*

[12]Ibid.

[13]This material in this section is drawn from Donald F. Wood, Anthony Barone, Paul R. Murphy, and Daniel L. Wardlow, *International Logistics,* 2nd ed. (New York: Amacom, 2002), Chapter 14.

[14]Patrick Byrne, "Supply Chain Trends Span the Globe," *Logistics Management,* March 2006, 26–27.

Because global sourcing increases the distance that components and inputs must be moved, managers must consider trade-offs between *transportation and holding costs.* The choice of a faster transportation alternative (e.g., air) will likely create higher transportation costs and lower inventory holding costs; alternatively, a slower transportation alternative (e.g., water) will create lower transportation costs and higher holding costs. *Implementation,* or carrying out, is often a major shortcoming to many global procurement plans; indeed, some organizations fail to specify an implementation plan. Moreover, the greater uncertainty associated with global sourcing means that implementation plans must be flexible and provide guidance for decision making when confronted with the unexpected.

Finally, *monitoring and improving* means that performance measures must be established for global procurement systems and that these measures should be reviewed on a regular basis. Comparisons can be made between actual and expected performance, and the results of these comparisons can be used to improve the global sourcing process. Commonly used performance measures for monitoring global sourcing systems include the percentage of early and late shipments, completeness of orders, and percentage of orders accepted or rejected on delivery.

ELECTRONIC PROCUREMENT

Electronic commerce is bringing many changes to the procurement discipline. **Electronic procurement** (also known as **e-procurement**) uses the Internet to make it easier, faster, and less expensive for an organization to purchase goods and services. One way of evaluating electronic procurement is by categorizing benefits as hard, soft, or intangible. *Hard benefits* refer to those that are directly measurable (e.g., a lower price), whereas *soft benefits* are more difficult to accurately quantify (e.g., time savings that can be shifted to value-adding activities). *Intangible benefits* are not directly measurable in financial terms (e.g., recognizing e-procurement as a potential market differentiation factor).[15]

The types of benefits that come from electronic procurement include transactional benefits, compliance benefits, management information benefits, and price benefits. *Transactional benefits* measure the transactional benefits (e.g., a reduced invoice-to-payment time) associated with e-procurement. *Compliance benefits* focus on the savings that come from adherence to established procurement policies. One example would be a reduction in **maverick spending,** which refers to employees who do not follow company guidelines about which suppliers to use in particular situations. *Management information benefits* encompass those that result from management information, customer satisfaction, and supplier satisfaction levels after implementation of electronic procurement. *Price benefits* are those that are given as the result of adopting e-procurement. For example, the electronic processing of invoices can save a great deal of money in terms of postage and stationery, and these savings can be passed on to the buyer.[16]

Just as there are benefits to electronic procurement, there are important drawbacks as well. One concern with electronic commerce in general and e-procurement in particular, involves the security of information that is being transmitted; there is a risk that sensitive or proprietary information could end up in the wrong hands. Another concern is that electronic procurement can be impersonal in the sense that human interaction is replaced by computer transactions. Moreover, despite substantial hype about the potential benefits of e-procurement, a recent survey discovered that only about 25 percent of the responding companies mandate the use of

---

[15]David Eakin, "Measuring E-Procurement Benefits," *Government Procurement,* August 2002, 6–12.
[16]Ibid.

electronic procurement. This survey also found a dramatic drop in user confidence with respect to having the required skills and knowledge to use e-procurement tools.[17]

One activity that has been greatly facilitated by electronic procurement is online reverse auctions. You might be familiar with traditional auctions in which multiple buyers bid on a particular product, with the product being sold to the highest bidder. By contrast, in a **reverse auction,** a buyer invites bids from multiple sellers, and the seller with the lowest bid is generally awarded the business. As reverse auctions have evolved, so too have their parameters; in some situations a buyer is exempted from accepting the lowest bid, whereas in other situations a buyer does not have to accept any of the bids.[18]

Buyers tend to like reverse auctions because they aim to generate low procurement prices, and the online nature of reverse auctions allows buyers to drill down to a seller's low price very quickly. Alternatively, sellers are critical of reverse auctions because their primary emphasis is low price. However, reverse auctions can provide sellers with valuable information such as the number of other bidders. This can be important in the sense that a large number of bidders will likely lead to a great deal of price competition.[19]

Utilization of **procurement cards** (also referred to as **p-cards**) has also grown dramatically with the evolution of electronic procurement. P-cards are similar to charge cards such as Visa and MasterCard that emphasize personal use. Organizations generally restrict the number of employees authorized to use procurement cards, and each month, an organization receives a detailed statement listing employees, details of their purchases, and purchase prices. Unlike personal credit cards, with p-cards an organization will make one payment for the total amount of purchases during one month, as opposed to making individual payments for each p-card holder.

P-cards can benefit organizations in several ways, one of which is a reduction in the number of invoices. In addition, these cards allow employees to make purchases in a matter of minutes, as opposed to days, and procurement cards generally allow suppliers to be paid in a more timely fashion. Having said this, p-cards may require control processes that measure usage and identify procurement trends, limit spending during the appropriate procurement cycle, and block unauthorized expenditures at gaming casinos or massage parlors.[20]

INVESTMENT RECOVERY[21]

Investment recovery, which identifies opportunities to recover revenues or reduce costs associated with scrap, surplus, obsolete, and waste materials, is often the responsibility of the procurement manager. Investment recovery can provide an organization with the opportunity to simultaneously do well and do good in the sense that investment recovery increases a seller's revenues (reduces a seller's costs) while addressing selected environmental considerations. For example, although aluminum recycling can provide revenues to an organization, the recycling conserves raw materials, uses less energy, and reduces various types of pollution. Figure 11-2 shows an example of how aluminum cans might be recycled.

[17]Maria Varmazis, "Buyers Become More Selective in Online Tools," *Purchasing,* September 15, 2005, 43–45.

[18]Bridget McCrea, "Going Once, Going Twice..." *Industrial Distribution,* July 2005, 30–32.

[19]Ibid.

[20]Bob Martinson, "The Power of the P-Card," *Strategic Finance,* February 2002, 30–35.

[21]Much of the material in this section is drawn from Michiel Leenders, P. Fraser Johnson, Anna Flynn, and Harold E. Fearon, *Purchasing & Supply Management,* 13th ed. (McGraw-Hill/Irwin, 2006), Chapter 11.

FIGURE 11-2   The Recycling of Aluminum Cans

Source: Courtesy of Aluminum Company of America.

Because even the best managed organizations will generate excess, obsolete, scrap, and waste materials, it's important to distinguish among these different categories of material. **Excess (surplus) materials** refer to stock that exceeds the reasonable requirements of an organization, perhaps because of an overly optimistic demand forecast. If an organization has several production facilities, excess materials might be transferred to the other facilities. Unlike excess materials, **obsolete materials** are not likely to ever be used by the organization that purchased it. Having said this, materials that are obsolete to one organization might not be obsolete to other users; as such, it might be possible to sell obsolete materials to other organizations.

Scrap materials refer to materials that are no longer serviceable, have been discarded, or are a by-product of the production process (e.g., scrap steel when producing an automobile or washing machine). Certain scrap materials, such as copper and nickel, have such economic value that procurement contracts sometimes include a price at which the scrap will be repurchased by the supplier. **Waste materials** refer to those that have been spoiled, broken, or otherwise rendered unfit for further use or reclamation. Unlike scrap materials, waste materials have no economic value.

The ways that organizations manage the investment recovery of excess, obsolete, scrap, and waste materials should be influenced by the materials' classification. Waste materials have limited investment recovery options because they are unfit for further use and have no economic value. As a result, it wouldn't be realistic to search for ways to reuse waste materials elsewhere in an organization or to find prospective buyers for the waste products. On the other hand, there are more expansive investment recovery options for excess materials, to include using them elsewhere within an organization, selling to another organization, returning to the supplier, and selling through a surplus dealer.

SOCIALLY RESPONSIBLE PROCUREMENT

The social responsibility concept suggests that an organization's responsibilities transcend economic considerations, such as the maximization of shareholder's wealth, and should incorporate societal objectives and values. There are social responsibility concerns at the corporate level (e.g., what are the behaviors of a socially responsible organization?), as well as social responsibility issues associated with organizational functions such as procurement. For purposes of this discussion, **socially responsible procurement** refers to "procurement activities that meet the ethical and discretionary responsibilities expected by society."[22]

Research suggests that socially responsible procurement consists of five dimensions, namely, diversity, the environment, human rights, philanthropy, and safety. Diversity is concerned with procurement activities associated with minority or women-owned organizations, whereas the environment includes considerations such as waste reduction and the design of products for reuse or recycling. Human rights issues include child labor laws as well as sweatshop labor. Philanthropy focuses on employee volunteer efforts and philanthropic contributions, and safety is concerned with the safe transportation of purchased products, as well as the safe operation of relevant facilities.[23]

We believe that ethical considerations (i.e., standards of conduct and moral principles) are also a part of socially responsible procurement. Indeed, research on procurement ethics dates back to the mid-1960s, and the competitiveness of the contemporary business environment creates—for some companies—a "win at all costs" philosophy that can exacerbate unethical behavior. Areas of ethical concern in procurement include gift giving and gift receiving; **bribes** (money paid before an exchange) and **kickbacks** (money paid after an exchange); misuse of information; improper methods of knowledge acquisition; lying or misrepresentation of the truth; product quality (lack thereof); misuse of company assets, to include abuse of expense accounts; and conflicts of interest, or activity that creates a potential conflict between one's personal interests and the employer's interests.

The topic of socially responsible procurement is much broader than the space devoted to it here indicates. Moreover, it's important to understand that the relevance, importance, and challenges associated with socially responsible procurement are likely to increase in the coming years.

Summary

Procurement is closely related to logistics because nearly anything purchased must be moved to wherever it is needed—in the right quantity and at the precise time. Procurement, an important activity because its costs often range between 60 and 80 percent of an organization's revenues, has assumed greater strategic orientation in many contemporary firms.

The chapter began with a discussion of procurement objectives and the importance for these objectives to be aligned with, and supportive of, those of the organization. One of procurement's most important responsibilities is supplier selection and evaluation, and this can be quite challenging, in part because of the multiple, and sometime conflicting, selection and evaluation criteria. Supplier development (reverse marketing) is becoming a more important part of the procurement process.

---

[22]Craig R. Carter and Marianne M. Jennings, "The Role of Purchasing in Corporate Social Responsibility: A Structural Equation Analysis," *Journal of Business Logistics* 25, no. 1 (2004): 145–186.
[23]Ibid.

Quality issues were discussed, with a particular emphasis on ISO 9000, Six Sigma, and the Malcolm Baldrige National Quality Award. Global sourcing, which refers to buying components and inputs anywhere in the world, continues to grow in scope. Because of the tremendous distances that can be involved in global sourcing, managers must understand the trade-offs between transportation and holding costs.

Electronic procurement is having a profound impact on organizational purchasing, and two such impacts, online reverse auctions and procurement cards, were discussed. Investment recovery was discussed, with a particular emphasis on managing excess, obsolete, scrap, and waste materials. The chapter concluded with a discussion of socially responsible procurement, and we learned that a number of ethical issues are associated with procurement.

Questions for Discussion and Review

1. What is procurement? What is its relevance to logistics?
2. Contrast procurement's historical focus to its more strategic orientation today.
3. Discuss three potential procurement objectives.
4. Name and describe the steps in the supplier selection and evaluation process.
5. Discuss the factors that make supplier selection and evaluation difficult.
6. Define supplier development, and explain why it is becoming more prominent in some organizations.
7. Why does the issue of quality in procurement represent a delicate balancing act for organizations?
8. What is the role of ISO certification in quality management programs?
9. Describe significant benefits and drawbacks to Six Sigma programs.
10. Discuss the Malcolm Baldrige National Quality Award.
11. How do ISO 9000 and the Baldrige Quality Award differ?
12. What are the components of the global sourcing development model presented in this chapter?
13. Pick, and discuss, two components of the global sourcing development model presented in this chapter.
14. Discuss the benefits and drawbacks to electronic procurement.
15. What is an online reverse auction? Why do buyers like them?
16. Discuss the benefits of electronic procurement cards.
17. Distinguish between excess, obsolete, scrap, and waste materials.
18. Should investment recovery be the responsibility of the procurement manager? If yes, why? If not, which party (parties) should be responsible for investment recovery?
19. Name, and give an example of, the five dimensions of socially responsible purchasing.
20. Discuss some of the ethical issues that are associated with procurement.

Suggested Readings

Cheraghi, S. Hossein, Mohammed Dadashzadeh, and Mutho Subramanian. "Critical Success Factors for Supplier Selection: An Update." *Journal of Applied Business Research* 20, no. 2 (2004): 91–108.

Emiliani, M. L. "Regulating B2B Online Reverse Auctions Through Voluntary Codes of Conduct." *Industrial Marketing Management* 34, no. 5 (2005): 526–534.

Essig, Michael, and Ulli Arnold. "Electronic Procurement in Supply Chain Management: Information Economics-Based Analysis of Electronic Markets." *The Journal of Supply Chain Management* 37, no. 4 (2001): 43–49.

Faes, Wouter, Paul Matthyssens, and Koen Vandenbempt. "The Pursuit of Global Purchasing Synergy." *Industrial Marketing Management* 29 (2000): 539–553.

Handfield, Robert B., and David L. Baumer. "Managing Conflict of Interest Issues in Purchasing." *Journal of Supply Chain Management* 42, no. 3 (2006): 41–50.

Handfield, Robert B., and Samuel L. Straight. "What Sourcing Channel is Right for You?" *Supply Chain Management Review* 7, no. 4 (2003): 62–68.

Houghton, Tim, Bill Markham, and Bob Tevelson. "Thinking Strategically About Supply

Management." *Supply Chain Management Review* 6, no. 5 (2002): 32–38.

Johnson, P. Frazier, Michiel R. Leenders, and Harold E. Fearon. "Supply's Growing Status and Influence: A Sixteen-Year Perspective." *Journal of Supply Chain Management* 42, no. 2 (2006): 33–43.

Lawrence, F. Barry, Daniel F. Jennings, and Brian E. Reynolds. *EDistribution* (Mason, OH: Thomson/Southwestern, 2003).

Martinson, Bob. "The Power of the P-Card." *Strategic Finance* 83, no. 8 (2002): 30–36.

Minahan, Tim A. "Strategies for High-Performance Procurement." *Supply Chain Management Review* 9, no. 6 (2005): 46–54.

Sanchez-Rodriguez, Christobal, and Angel R. Martinez-Lorente. "Quality Management Practices in the Purchasing Function: An Empirical Study." *International Journal of Operations & Production Management* 24, no. 7 (2004): 666–687.

Trent, Robert J., and Robert M. Monczka. "Achieving Excellence in Global Sourcing." *MIT Sloan Management Review* 47, no. 1 (2005): 24–32.

Wood, Donald F., Anthony Barone, Paul Murphy, and Daniel L. Wardlow. *International Logistics.* 2nd ed. (New York: Amacom, 2002).

C A S E S

CASE 11-1   EASING IRA'S IRE

Ira Pollack was difficult to work for. A self-made millionaire, he paid extremely high salaries but demanded much from his subordinates, including being on call 24 hours per day. In his Las Vegas penthouse, he would study and restudy each detail of his conglomerate's performance and then call some unlucky underling—at any hour—to vent his anger and demand that something or other be improved. His tantrums were legendary.

One of Pollack's underlings, Tamara Wood, was driving her new red Mercedes convertible along Rodeo Drive in Beverly Hills, looking for a parking space. Her college class from Northern Illinois University at DeKalb was holding its fifth reunion in Chicago, which she planned to attend. She wanted to buy a new outfit for the event, to show her former classmates that she had "arrived." A chauffeur-driven Rolls pulled away from the curb, leaving an empty space right in front of her favorite couturier. She swung her Mercedes expertly into the empty space, looked up, and was pleased to see that there was still nearly an hour left on the meter. "Daddy was right," she thought to herself, "Clean living does pay off."

As she turned off the ignition, Tamara's cell phone started buzzing. Wood hesitated. Would it be John, calling to thank her for that wonderful evening? Would it be Matt, seeing if she were free to spend next weekend on Catalina Island? Or maybe it was Jason, who was always wanting her to accompany him to Waikiki. She finally picked up the phone and sweetly said, "Hello."

"Dammit! Don't 'hello' me!" shouted a man's voice at the other end.

Wood's stomach churned, her muscles tightened, and she said, weakly, "Sorry, Mr. Pollack, I was expecting somebody else."

"That's obvious," he retorted. "At this hour of the day, you're on *my* time and *should* be thinking of business. How come you're not in the office?"

"I'm just making a customer-service follow-up," responded Wood, hoping that Mr. Pollack would not ask for too many details.

"Well, you *should* be worried about customer service," said Pollack. "That's why I've called. I've been studying performance records for all my operations dealing with the amount of time that elapses between our receipt of an order and when our customer receives a shipment. The performance of your distribution center in West Hollywood *stinks!* Drop what you're doing and *get back to your office* and figure out what's wrong! Then tell me what's needed to speed up your operation. Call me at any hour."

Wood heard the phone click. She forgot about DeKalb. She forgot about Chicago and the new outfit. She forgot about her night with John, about Catalina Island, and about Waikiki. She heard a faint beep to her left. She saw a maroon Jaguar, with a Beverly Hills matron motioning with one of her white-gloved hands as if to say, "If you're leaving, may I have your parking spot?"

"Dammit," thought Wood as she pulled away. "If it weren't for a hundred thou a year, I'd tell Pollack what he could do with his order-processing system."

Still muttering, she pulled into her reserved slot next to the West Hollywood distribution center. "Aloha!" chirped Ellen Scott, her assistant, as she walked in. "Jason has called three times about wanting you to fly to Hawaii. Also, you have two calls from John, one from Matt, one from your mother, who asked why you never phone her, and one from some fellow who wouldn't leave his name but said it was very personal. Tell me about the outfit you bought. I'll bet it's stunning."

"Forget about them, and hold all my calls," said Wood, crisply. "I'm not going anywhere. Pollack called me and is mad because our order-processing and delivery times are out of whack."

Two days passed. Wood had put her social life on hold and had not even phoned her mother. All her time was spent trying to figure out how to speed up her order-processing system. But she didn't know how to start. The accuracy of the system was not an issue, although additional costs could be. When Pollack paid his bonuses last year, he had told Wood that if her operation had cost one cent

EXHIBIT 11-A	Order-Processing and Shipment Tasks in Approximate Order of Completion		
Task	*Description*	*Duration (in days)*	*Precedence Relationships (tasks on right of < cannot commence until tasks on left are completed)*
A	Order received and entered into computer	0.25	A < D
B	Determine whether to fill from warehouse or ship direct from factory	0.50	B < C
C	Print picking order	0.30	C < H
D	Verify customer's credit	0.35	D < G, E
E	Check and determine buyer's eligibility for discounts	0.15	E < F
F	Prepare invoice and enter in accounts receivable file	1.00	F < K
G	Determine mode of transport and select carrier	1.65	G < J
H	Pick order at warehouse	0.75	H < I
I	Pack and label shipment	1.20	I < L
J	Notify carrier and prepare shipping documents	2.25	J < L
K	Transmit copy of invoice to shipping dock	1.20	K < L
L	Transport order to customer	3.50	

more to run, she would not have received a bonus. Because her bonus had paid for her new Mercedes, Wood was cost conscious, to say the least.

Wood's assistant helped her, too—at least through late Friday afternoon. Scott explained that she couldn't work on Saturday and Sunday because she'd accepted an invitation to spend the weekend at Catalina Island with an unnamed friend. Before Scott left, she and Wood had decided that there were 12 distinct operations involved in processing and shipping orders. Some could be performed at the same time, whereas others had to be performed in sequence—that is, one could not be started until the other was completed. (These tasks, the amount of time it takes to complete each, and the sequential relationships, if any, are shown in Exhibit 11-A.)

After compiling the information shown in Exhibit 11-A, Scott left. Wood was left with the task of trying to relate all those tasks to each other. She recalled a college textbook that she had never much cared for but that she had come across a few weeks earlier as she was searching for her Northern Illinois University yearbook. Wood looked at a PERT chart in that book and knew that she would have to construct something similar to analyze the distribution center's order-processing and shipping operations. She studied the text accompanying the chart, sighed, and thought to herself, "Where was I—or at least where was my mind—the day the professor explained all of this in class?" ■

QUESTIONS

1. Arrange the tasks shown in Exhibit 11-A in a network or PERT chart.
2. Determine the critical path. What is the least amount of time it takes between receipt of an order and its delivery to a customer?
3. Considering your answers to questions 1 and 2, what areas of activity do you think Wood should look at first, assuming she wants to reduce order-processing and delivery times? Why?
4. Now that she's a Californian ready for the race down the information superhighway, Wood wants to be able to impress Pollack with her knowledge of current technology. Recently, a sales representative from a warehouse equipment company called, trying to interest her in installing a "Star Wars—Robotic" order picker for the warehouse.

Controlled by lasers and powered by magnetic levitation, the device can pick orders (task H) in 15 minutes, rather than 6 hours (0.75 day), the current time needed. How valuable would such a device be to Wood? Why?
5. Another alternative is to use faster transportation. How should Wood choose between paying more for faster transportation and paying more for other improvements? Assume that her only goal is speed.
6. To offset some of the costs of speeding up the system, does the PERT chart indicate where there might be some potential savings from assigning fewer people to some tasks, thereby increasing the amount of time needed to complete these tasks? If so, which tasks are likely candidates? Why?

CASE 11-2   TEMPO LTD.

Fatih Terim was in his small office in Antalya, a Mediterranean port in southwestern Turkey. He looked at the clock on the wall and realized he had spent the entire afternoon thinking about one thing and one thing only—the most recent meeting with his Romanian business "connection." Terim had just completed a trip to the Balkans and was in his office evaluating his firm's progress in the region. This was necessary because he was thinking of going to Syria for the same reasons that had taken him to the Balkans: finding goods at cheap prices and selling them with handsome markups at home in Turkey or in other neighboring countries.

Terim had established Tempo Ltd. in 1989 in Antalya. Terim, then fresh out of Akdeniz University, quickly became an entrepreneur. The focus of his business was to buy goods from nearby foreign sources and then find buyers for those products in the domestic Turkish market. The first couple of years were easy for Terim because he was working very hard, and the Turkish economy was soaring. With the fall of communism, Terim saw even more opportunities. He started marketing Turkish-made goods to former communist countries around Turkey and in central Asia.

However, the Turkish economy took a major hit in April 1994. The sudden death of the country's president added to the nation's political instability. The value of Turkish lira (TL) plummeted against the U.S. dollar ($USD). In the following years, the Turkish economy took many more hits, including the financial crisis in the Asian markets, the Russian market crash, and most recently, the Argentinean crisis. In 1999, two major earthquakes hit the northwestern part of Turkey, where one-third of the nation's 67 million persons reside and which is the heartland of Turkish industry. Although Turkey recovered quickly from the earthquakes, political instability continued and pushed the entire economy into a slowdown. In 1993, one U.S. dollar could buy 7,000 Turkish liras. In 2003, that same one U.S. dollar could buy 1,567,000 TL. Despite these discouraging events,

the Turkish economy still has opportunities for growth. One reason such a major potential still exists is the simple fact that hard-working, sharp-trading people like Fatih Terim never stood still and kept putting together the best deals they could.

Today Terim's company has some connections in almost every European country and is working very hard to maintain these connections by generating steady flows of commerce. Terim's latest trip was to the Balkan nations of Bulgaria, Romania, and Greece. Terim held meetings with key businesspeople in all three nations. In both Bulgaria and Greece, Terim had entered into modest sales agreements that extend into the middle of next year.

In Romania, matters did not move as quickly. Terim's Romanian connection, George Hagi, was not interested in any of the small transactions that Terim was suggesting. Hagi, in an almost mysterious manner, did tell Terim that he looking for a Turkish partner willing to participate in a substantial, although not exactly legitimate, deal. The first aspect was that the customer wanted to buy Turkish chemicals to be used for fertilizers in agriculture. However, the terms of payment from the prospective customers would be in the form of barter rather than cash, and the goods bartered for the chemicals would be *kereste* (lumber). Although *barter* was a term and practice with which Terim was familiar, he had no idea what to do with *kereste*. Over the years, Tempo Ltd. had concentrated its business on small consumer products. However, he wasn't going to let a detail like this get in the way of new markets. He knew he could find a market in Turkey for lumber because little was produced domestically, and both new construction and earthquake reconstruction were underway.

What worried Terim was his new customers. He learned from Hagi that these new customers were either a large state-owned company in North Korea or the North Korean government itself, which is why Terim spent that entire afternoon thinking about just one thing. All day he tried to justify his possible decisions to himself. The problem was that North Korea was a communist regime, and beyond that, North Korea, according to NATO and the United Nations, was a country that provided support to certain terrorist activities all over the world. In early 2002, U.S. President George W. Bush had described Iran, Iraq, and North Korea as an "axis of evil." North Korea and those with whom it traded were under tight scrutiny from both the United Nations and the United States (which still stationed troops in South Korea).

Terim came up with the excuse that if he didn't sell to the North Koreans, someone else would eventually, so why should he give up this money? However, the solution was not that easy. Hagi said in his e-mail to Terim that if the negotiations went well, a party of North Korean bureaucrats would wish to visit Antalya for "inspection" purposes and that Terim would have to cover the costs of entertainment and accommodations. Those accommodations would range from luxurious hotel rooms to young attractive companions, of both sexes, for business-related dinners and receptions. Terim knew exactly what those inspection purposes were. They were pleasure trips for certain bureaucrats in North Korea. Unfortunately, he was also aware that this was the way things worked in Third World governments. Over the years, he had learned the tricks of the trade, and one thing he knew well was that without the *rusvet* (bribe: the grease money or large amounts of payments specifically for one-time transactions), such risky situations would end up as a "no sale." He wondered whether he should ask the Turkish agricultural chemical manufacturers to help with the entertainment costs. Also, should he and the chemical manufacturers touch base with each other with respect to the *rusvet* that would undoubtedly be expected by the North Koreans? Terim's position regarding *rusvet* was unclear. Indeed, the chemical manufactures should be expected to give him, or Hagi, a kickback for facilitating the sale of chemicals.

"Talk about core competency," Terim mumbled to himself. To get his mind off these sticky issues, he looked into the logistics costs to move the bartered lumber from North Korea. He would need to know those costs before proceeding. He had a couple of options.

The first option would be to ship the lumber by sea from Wonsan, North Korea, through the Sea of Japan, across the Indian Ocean, through the Suez Canal, and into the liman (port) of Antalya, Turkey. (See Exhibits 11-B and 11-C.) This would be the perfect solution, except, he suddenly realized, he would not be able to bring the lumber into Turkey legally because of trade sanctions against North Korea. Hence, this option was dropped.

His second option would be to send the lumber to a country where its entry would be legal. The country to which the kereste could be shipped legally was none other than Romania, one of Turkey's neighbors on the Black Sea. The reason was hidden in history. Since their communist years, Romania and North Korea had had strong ties that remained nearly intact after the fall of communism in Romania. So lumber could be loaded on to a *gemi* (ship) and could be shipped to Romania via the Dardanelles and the Bosphorus (the two straits that make up the gateway to the Black Sea) and finally to the port of Constantza, Romania, in the Black Sea. Once there, the lumber could be covered by new documents, and eventually the origin of the goods could be stated as "Romania," not "North Korea." The lumber could then move by *tir* (truck) to Turkey. This sounded like a feasible solution, but how much would such an operation cost? Terim recalled that Hagi had said that redoing documents in situations like this cost about 16,000,000,000 TL, including *rusvets*.

Terim's mind then shifted to a third option. From Wonsan, the lumber could be shipped to a port in Syria, in this case Latakia. From there, *tirs* could haul the lumber to Iskenderun at the southeastern border of Turkey. Because the border at Iskenderun is the most laxly guarded border in Turkey, small *rusvets* to low-ranking officers at the gates would allow the *kereste* to enter Turkey without any problems. The *rusvets* would be about 10 percent of the kereste shipment's value.

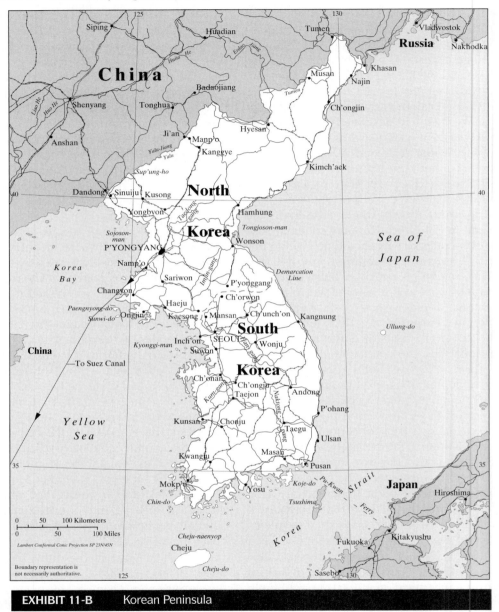

EXHIBIT 11-B   Korean Peninsula

The same could be done at the Liman of Antalya. However, the chances of getting caught were much higher. If Tempo Ltd. were caught red-handed, it would be fined a sum of double the total value of goods entering the country. Thus, this was a fourth, but discarded, option.

Only two options were feasible, and each came with certain risks. One was to ship the *kereste* to Romania, have new documents drawn, falsify the shipment's origin, and then send it to Turkey by *tir*. The other was to send the *kereste* by ship to Syria, truck it to Turkey, and bribe customs inspectors at the Turkish border. Terim was initially concerned with the logistics costs of getting the *kereste* inside the Turkish border. The *kereste* would be of various dimensions, bound together

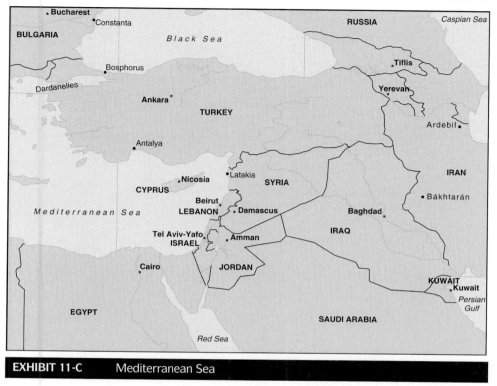

EXHIBIT 11-C   Mediterranean Sea

by metal straps into bundles measuring 1 meter by 1 meter by 5 meters, and the North Koreans would deliver and load the *kereste* aboard a break-bulk vessel in a North Korean port.

If Terim could get the *kereste* inside Turkey, it should sell for 783,500,000,000 TL. The Turkish chemical manufacturers expect to be paid 60 days after the chemicals leave the Turkish port, which will be same date as the *kereste* leaves North Korea.

Terim gazed at his notes, which were full of numbers and currency exchange rates.

Ocean transportation costs for Gemi (Shipping lines require payment in U.S. dollars):

Wonsan to Constantza	$42,000 USD
Wonsan to Latakia	$33,000 USD
Suez Canal charges	$ 3,100 USD
Tir:	
Constantza into Turkey	$15,000 USD
Latakia into Turkey	$12,000 USD
Handling fees at the Liman (Syria or Romania)	1.25% of the total value of goods

Generating false Romania-origin documents	16,000,000,000 TL
Projected amount of *rusvet* at Syrian–Turkish border	10 percent of shipment's value
Currency exchange rates	$1USD = 1,567,000 TL
Option 1: Wonsan/ Constantza/ Turkey would take 43 days ∎	Option 2: Wonsan/ Latakia/Turkey would take 22 days

QUESTIONS

1. Should Terim let somebody else complete the transaction because he knows that if he doesn't sell to the North Koreans, someone else will?
2. What are the total costs given in the case for the option of moving via Romania?
3. What are the total costs given in the case for the option of moving via Syria?
4. Which option should Terim recommend? Why?
5. What other costs and risks are involved in these proposed transactions, including some not mentioned in the case?
6. Regarding the supply chain, how—if at all—should bribes be included? What functions do they serve?
7. If Terim puts together this transaction, is he acting ethically? Discuss.
8. What do you suggest should be done to bring moral values into the situation so that the developing countries are somewhat in accordance with Western standards? Keep in mind that the risks involved in such environments are much higher than the risks of conducting business in Western markets. Also note that some cultures see bribery as a way to better distribute the wealth among their citizens.

CHAPTER
12
INTERNATIONAL LOGISTICS

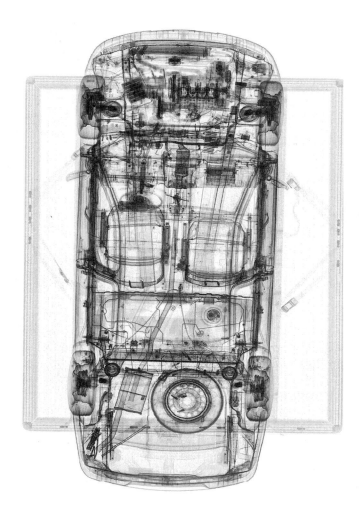

Key Terms

- Cargo preference
- Certificate of origin
- Commercial invoice
- Customshouse brokers
- Embargoes
- Export management company
- Export packers
- Import quotas
- Incoterms 2000
- International Air Transport Association (IATA)
- International freight forwarders
- International logistics

- Letter of credit
- Load center
- Nontariff barrier
- Nonvessel-operating common carrier (NVOCC)
- Ocean carrier alliances
- Shipper's export declaration (SED)
- Shipper's letter of instruction (SLI)
- Shipping conferences
- Short sea shipping
- Tariffs
- Terms of payment
- Terms of sale

Learning Objectives

- To identify the reasons for governmental intervention in the area of international trade
- To examine international documentation as well as terms of sale and payment
- To distinguish among the unique activities of international trade specialists
- To examine transportation and inventory considerations in international distribution

Many aspects of international logistics have been explored in earlier chapters. It is increasingly difficult to separate the practices of domestic and international logistics. **International logistics**—logistics activities associated with goods that are sold across national boundaries—occurs in the following situations:

1. A firm exports a portion of a product made or grown—for example, paper-making machinery to Sweden, wheat to Russia, or coal to Japan.
2. A firm imports raw materials—such as pulpwood from Canada—or manufactured products—such as motorcycles from Italy or Japan.
3. Goods are partially assembled in one country and then shipped to another, where they are further assembled or processed. For example, a firm stamps electronic components in the United States. It ships them to a free trade zone in the Far East, where low-cost labor assembles them, and then the assembled components are returned to the United States to become part of the finished product.
4. The firm is *global* in outlook and sees almost all nations as being markets, sources of supply, or sites for markets or for assembly operations.
5. Because of geography, a nation's domestic commerce crosses foreign borders, often in bond. For example, goods moving by truck between Detroit and Buffalo or between the Lower 48 states and Alaska, through Canada, travel in bond, which means that the carrier handling them has a special legal obligation to keep them sealed and to make certain that they are not released for sale or use within the country through which they are traveling. Products shipped in bond are not subject to normal duties of the country through which they are passing.

Until World War II, the concepts of international trade were simple. Industrialized powers maintained political and economic colonies that were sources of raw materials, cheap labor, and markets for manufactured products. When dealing with those colonies, manufacturers in the parent country bought low and sold high. World War II brought an end to the colonial system; since then, emerging nations have attempted to develop their own political and economic systems with varying degrees of success. As emerging nations attempt to flex their political and economic muscles, they cause changes in the traditional ways of conducting international business.

Developing nations often insist that an increasing proportion of assembling and manufacturing be conducted within their own borders. Because the national governments of these countries play a substantial role in expanding their economies, these governments are able to exert considerable influence over outside firms desiring to do business within their borders. National governments want their share of the supply chain's activity, and these governments are becoming more insistent that much of their foreign trade be carried on vessels or planes owned by companies headquartered within their boundaries. Governments want local firms to have at least a fair share of revenues from the sale of freight forwarding services, marine insurance, and other distribution functions.

Traditionally, the United States has been a major exporter of manufactured goods and agricultural products. Because of its wealth, the United States has also imported many consumer goods. Over the past 25 years, the United States has seen increasing annual trade deficits, which signifies that the dollar value of imports exceeds the dollar value of exports. Some of the key contributors to the U.S. trade deficit involve heavy importation of clothing, crude oil, office equipment, televisions and related electronic equipment, as well as automotive vehicles. Moreover, the United States currently runs trade deficits with the majority of its key trading partners; for example, during 2006, the U.S. trade deficit with China was approximately *$230 billion.*

It's important to recognize that international logistics is both more costly and more challenging than domestic logistics. One reason for the increased cost is that the relevant documentation requirements for international shipments are more substantial (i.e., a greater number of documents) and more complex than those associated with domestic shipments. In addition, as was pointed out in Chapter 11, international logistics is characterized by greater distances between origin and destination points, which means that managers must consider trade-offs between transportation and inventory holding costs. Although faster transportation between origin and destination will lead to lower inventory holding costs, faster transportation is generally associated with higher transportation costs, and the converse is true for slower transportation options.

The challenges associated with international logistics come from a number of sources. Economic conditions, such as changes in the relative value of currencies, have a profound affect on international trade patterns. When one country's currency is weak relative to other currencies, it becomes more costly to import products, but exports often surge; when one country's currency is strong relative to other currencies, the reverse occurs. Differences between countries in regulations, laws, and legal systems also add to the challenges of international logistics, and the degree of enforcement of existing regulations and laws is not uniform from country to country.

Cultural considerations, such as differences in language, also contribute to international logistics challenges. For instance, a mainland Chinese company exporting to the United States should recognize that shipments labeled in the Mandarin Chinese language aren't likely to be

TABLE 12-1	Beginning Dates for the Chinese New Year 2007–2014
Year	**Beginning Date**
2007	February 18
2008	February 7
2009	January 26
2010	February 14
2011	February 3
2012	January 23
2013	February 10
2014	January 31

Source: www.infoplease.com.

understood by U.S. workers. National holidays are another cultural aspect that can affect the effectiveness and efficiency of international logistics. Consider, for example, the Chinese New Year that, unlike the New Year that many of you are familiar with, does not take place on January 1. Rather, because the Chinese New Year is based on the lunar calendar, it has a different starting date each year (see Table 12-1). Moreover, the Chinese New Year is characterized by a 15-day celebration period when many businesses shut down—a situation that affects shipments within, into, and out of China during that time period.

For goods moving in cross-border trade, it is not safe to assume that handlers can read English, and it would not be unusual for some cargo handlers to even be illiterate. Hence, cautionary symbols must be used (see Figure 12-1). Cargo moving aboard ocean vessels has distinct markings that identify the shipper, consignee, destination point, and piece number (in

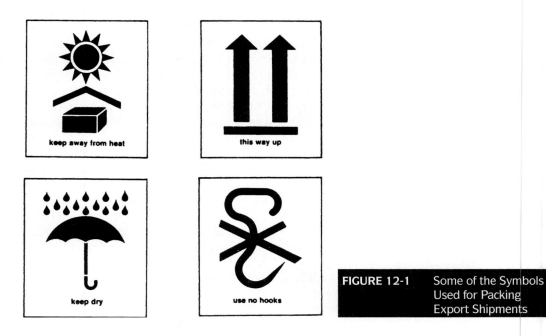

FIGURE 12-1	Some of the Symbols Used for Packing Export Shipments

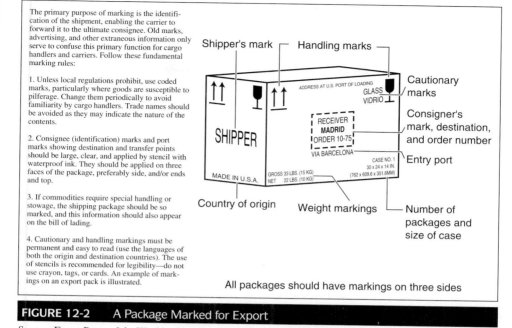

The primary purpose of marking is the identification of the shipment, enabling the carrier to forward it to the ultimate consignee. Old marks, advertising, and other extraneous information only serve to confuse this primary function for cargo handlers and carriers. Follow these fundamental marking rules:

1. Unless local regulations prohibit, use coded marks, particularly where goods are susceptible to pilferage. Change them periodically to avoid familiarity by cargo handlers. Trade names should be avoided as they may indicate the nature of the contents.

2. Consignee (identification) marks and port marks showing destination and transfer points should be large, clear, and applied by stencil with waterproof ink. They should be applied on three faces of the package, preferably side, and/or ends and top.

3. If commodities require special handling or stowage, the shipping package should be so marked, and this information should also appear on the bill of lading.

4. Cautionary and handling markings must be permanent and easy to read (use the languages of both the origin and destination countries). The use of stencils is recommended for legibility—do not use crayon, tags, or cards. An example of markings on an export pack is illustrated.

Shipper's mark

Handling marks

Cautionary marks

Consigner's mark, destination, and order number

Entry port

Number of packages and size of case

Country of origin

Weight markings

All packages should have markings on three sides

FIGURE 12-2   A Package Marked for Export

Source: From *Ports of the World,* 15th ed., a publication of CIGNA Property & Casualty.

multipiece shipments). Some cartons and crates moving internationally are marked with what looks like a cattle brand. This is a shipper's mark, and a drawing of the mark also appears on the documentation. This is for use in areas in which dockworkers cannot read but need a method to keep documents and shipments together. As with domestic cargo, care must be taken so that pilferable items are not identified. This may include changing the symbols every few months. Figure 12-2 shows a package with the various markings required for movement in cross-border commerce. The markings should be applied with a stencil, using waterproof ink. The bill of lading, packing list, letter of credit, and other documents pertaining to a shipment must contain similar markings. Note that markings on the box are in both inches and meters. Both weight and dimensions are given because density is a factor in determining international transportation charges.

GOVERNMENT INFLUENCES ON FOREIGN TRADE

Businesses involved in foreign trade find that a government's role is more significant than in domestic transactions, and as a result the buying and selling parties are not always free to contract the terms to suit their needs. In part, this is because most firms are first developed in domestic markets and take all existing governmental controls as a given factor. As a firm expands beyond its domestic markets, it finds requirements that differ for each nation with which the firm wishes to trade.

Figure 12-3 is from a guidebook prepared by an international airline that outlines, in general terms, the various restrictions that apply when shipping to two African nations. From the example of the two nations listed, it is easy to see that exporting involves complications. Note that both

SENEGAL

GOVERNMENT REPRESENTATION

The Republic of Senegal is represented in the United States by an Embassy at 2112 Wyoming Ave., N.W., Washington, D.C. and a United Nations Mission at 51 East 42nd St., New York. Both also act for Canadian affairs.

GENERAL INFORMATION

Customs Airports: Dakar, Saint Louis and Ziguinchor.
Collect Service acceptable to Dakar and Saint Louis only.
COD Service not acceptable.
Free House Delivery not acceptable.

DOCUMENTATION

Commercial consignments—2 commercial invoices containing the following declaration: "Nous certifions que les marchandises denommees dans cette facture sont de fabrication et d'origine (country of origin) et que les prix indiques ci-dessus s'accordent avec les prix courants sur le marche d'exportation."

Sample consignments—Without commercial value: No documents. With commercial value: same as for commercial consignments.

Gift consignments—no documentary requirements.

RESTRICTIONS

Live animals: Health certificate.

Dogs and other domestic animals: Health certificates issued not later than 3 days before shipment and stating that the animals originate from an area free from contagious diseases of the species for the preceding 6 weeks, and in case of cats and dogs, that no rabies has been detected for the same period.

PROHIBITED: Hares and rabbits.

Live plants and plant material: Health certificate.

Arms and ammunition: Special import permit.

PROHIBITIONS

All goods of Portuguese or South African origin; skins of hares and rabbits; beetroot sugar; blankets; cloth of textile fibers; cotton cloth; fibres; flower pots, stoneware, pottery, clay products, matches, ornamental bricks and other clay products for building purposes; outwear, shirts, except shirts over CFA 1700. value; shoes, except fashionable shoes over CFA 400. value; trousers under CFA 1900. value; sisal carpets and rugs; sugar cane, yarn and thread; cotton, apéritifs of alcohol or wine basis; digestives.

IMPORT AND EXCHANGE REGULATIONS

Liberalized items may be imported without quantitative restrictions on the basis of an import certificate, which is made out by the importer, endorsed by the Customs on clearance of the merchandise and delivered to an authorized bank for visa by the Exchange Control Office.

Non-liberalized goods require an import license, issued by the Director General for Economic Services and visaed by the Exchange Control Office. Validity of certificate and license is 6 months.

The currency exchange is obtained through the authorized banks on strength of import certificate or import license. No tolerance in value or quantity shown on import certificate or import license is permitted.

The importation of goods competitive with locally produced items may be prohibited from time to time.

Rate of exchange: 247 C.F.A. Francs = $1.00

SIERRA LEONE

GOVERNMENT REPRESENTATION

Sierra Leone is represented in the United States by an Embassy at 1701 19th Street, N.W., Washington, D.C. and a United Nations Mission at 30 East 42nd St., New York. Both also act for Canadian affairs.

GENERAL INFORMATION

Customs Airport: Freetown.

Collect Service acceptable.

COD Service not acceptable.

Free House Delivery not acceptable.

DOCUMENTATION

Commercial consignments—4 combined certificates of value and origin in English bearing the supplier's letterhead and his seal or stamp against his signature or that of his representative. In case of occasional shipment, when overprinting of the letterhead is prohibitive, the combined certificate must be accompanied with the supplier's own invoice duly signed against his seal or stamp, and containing the certification: "We hereby declare that this commercial invoice is in support of the attached certificate invoice No. . . . and that the particulars shown on the certified invoice are true and correct in every detail."

RESTRICTIONS

Live animals: Import authorization from Veterinary Dept.

Dogs: Additional health and rabies vaccination certificate in English.

Live plants and plant material: Import authorization from Agricultural Department.

PROHIBITED: Aniseed and Indian hemp.

Medicines and narcotics: Import license from Director of Medical services.

PROHIBITIONS

Arms and ammunition from Liberia, obscene photographs, shaving brushes from Japan, traps for night hunting.

IMPORT AND EXCHANGE REGULATIONS

Most goods may be freely imported under "Open General License." Specific import license required for a short list of specified items only . . . issued by the Import Licensing Authority of the Ministry of Commerce and Industry; the validity is generally 12 months.

Exporters should avoid overshipment of goods covered by specific import licenses. No tolerances are permitted.

The currency exchange is obtained through authorized banks. No exchange permit is required. An import license, whether specific or open, automatically entitles the importer to buy the relative foreign exchange.

Rate of exchange: 1 Leone = $1.20

FIGURE 12-3   Examples of Restrictions of Exporting to Other Nations

Source: Courtesy of Sabena Belgian World Airlines.

countries' embassy locations in the United States are listed. Consular offices are current sources of information regarding their nations' import and currency exchange regulations. Most nations maintain consular offices in major U.S. port cities, and these offices, for a fee, prepare a consular invoice, a document that contains approximately the same information as a commercial invoice. The importing nation uses it as the basis for levying applicable import duties.

Political Restrictions on Trade

Political restrictions on trade can take a variety of forms. Many nations ban certain types of shipments that might jeopardize their national security; for example, the United States does not ship military equipment or strategic materials to certain nations. Likewise, individual nations may band together to pressure another country to not be an active supplier of materials that could be used to build nuclear weapons. Some nations restrict the outflow of currency because a nation's economy will suffer if it imports more than it exports over a long term. These regulations are not concerned with specific commodities; rather, they are concerned with restricting the outflow of money. All imports require advance approval, and goods that arrive without prior approval are not allowed to enter.

A relatively common political restriction on trade involves **tariffs,** or taxes that governments place on the importation of certain items. Tariffs are often established to protect local manufacturers, producers, or growers, and once tariff barriers are built, they are not easily torn down. Sometimes, the tariff the importing nation charges differs according to the nation from which the good is coming. From an international sourcing standpoint, this influences the choice of production site.

Another group of political restrictions on trade can be classified as **nontariff barriers,** which refer to restrictions other than tariffs that are placed on imported products.[1] One type of nontariff barrier is an **import quota,** which limits the amount or product (either in units or by value) that may be imported from any one country during a period of time. The health and safety of a country's population often provides "convenient" reasons for applying nontariff barriers. Many nations are concerned with stopping the spread of plant and animal diseases and therefore inspect various commodities or products to make certain that they do not contain these problems. If material is found to be infested, it cannot enter the country until it is cleaned. Entry of other products may be prohibited because they do not meet safety standards. For example, because of the danger of earthquakes in Japan, upright refrigerators must be built so that they will remain upright, even when tilted as much as 10 degrees.

Another political restriction on trade, due to political tensions, involves **embargoes,** or the prohibition of trade between particular countries. For example, U.S. trade with Cuba has been banned since the late 1950s (corresponding to Fidel Castro's rise to Cuban prime minister and installation of a communistic government). In a similar fashion, because of long-standing political tensions, Israel and several Arab nations do not trade with each other, and this embargo has been extended to include nations that are sympathetic, or provide support, to Israel.

Government's Role in International Transport

As in other aspects of international business, governments are more involved in international transportation than they are in domestic transportation. One reason for this is that ocean carriers and international airlines can operate as extensions of a nation's economy, and most of the revenue they receive flows into that nation's economy. To that nation, international carriage functions as an export with favorable effects on the nation's balance of payments. However, to the nation on the other end of the shipment, the effect is opposite because it must import the transport service, and this has an adverse impact on its balance-of-payments position. Some nations with very weak balance-of-payments positions issue an import license, or permit, on the condition that the goods move on a vessel or plane flying that nation's flag, which means it is importing only the goods, not the transportation service required to carry them.[2] Situations such as this dictate carrier choice.

---

[1] Philip R. Cateora and John L. Graham, *International Marketing,* 13th ed. (New York: McGraw-Hill Irwin, 2007).

[2] As used here, flying a nation's flag is synonymous with being owned by private or public entities in that nation.

With respect to water transportation, many nations provide subsidies, train their own merchant marine officers, absorb portions of the costs of building commercial vessels, and engage in other activities to promote their own merchant fleets. Governments also support their own carriers through **cargo preference** rules, which require a certain percentage of traffic to move on a nation's flag vessels.

Historically, many international airlines were owned and operated by their national government; examples include Air India, Air China, and Alitalia (owned by the Italian government). However, over the past 20 years some government-owned international carriers have moved to the private sector, a process called privatization. A successful example of this process is British Airways (formerly British Overseas Airways Corporation, or BOAC), which was privatized by the British government in the late 1980s.

DOCUMENTATION[3]

You might recall that documentation, or the documents associated with a transportation shipment, was discussed as part of Transportation Management in Chapter 7. International logistics involves a system in which documentation flows are as much a part of the main logistical flow as the flow of the product. Companies that export products from their home country for sale in other countries soon find that preparing the requisite documentation, assembling them, and ensuring that they arrive where and when they are needed is quite a challenge. Although domestic shipments might only require several pieces of documentation, export shipments typically require approximately 10 documents, and for some cross-border trades, more than 100 separate documents can be required!

Documentation can act as a nontariff barrier in the sense that all the necessary documents are required at the point of importation. Failure to do this can cause delays or, in some cases, result in the shipment being seized by the customs authority of the importing country. Moreover, simply having all required documentation is often just a starting point; the exporting organization may be given specific instructions, such as the relevant languages as well as appropriate font types and sizes, for completing the documentation.

Given the vast array of documents that can be used for international shipments, it's only possible to discuss several of the most commonly used, and we'll look at certificates of origin, commercial invoices, shipper's export declaration, and shipper's letter of instruction. A **certificate of origin** specifies the country(ies) in which a product is manufactured and can be required by governments for control purposes or by an exporter to verify the location of manufacture. A **commercial invoice** is similar in nature to a domestic bill of lading in the sense that a commercial invoice summarizes the entire transaction and contains (should contain) key information to include a description of the goods, the terms of sale and payment (to be discussed in the next section), the shipment quantity, the method of shipment, and so on.

A **shipper's export declaration** (SED) contains relevant export transaction data such as the transportation mode(s), transaction participants, and description of what is being exported. SEDs often serve as the basis for a country's official export statistics. A **shipper's letter of instruction** (SLI) often accompanies an SED and provides explicit shipment instructions. For example, an SLI might indicate which parties should receive which documents, the method or route of shipment, what types of insurance to purchase, and which insurance company(ies) to use.

---

[3]This material in this section is drawn from Donald F. Wood, Anthony Barone, Paul R. Murphy, and Daniel L. Wardlow, *International Logistics,* 2nd ed. (New York: Amacom, 2002), Chapter 12.

Before concluding our discussion of the documentation requirements associated with international shipments, mention should be made about free trade agreements. Although some free trade agreements have led to a decrease in documentation requirements, others actually result in an *increase* in documentation, which could defeat the primary purpose of these agreements, namely, facilitating trade between participating countries.

Consider, for example, the U.S. and Central America Free Trade Agreement (CAFTA), which went into effect in 2005. To receive the favorable tariffs specified in this agreement, organizations will have to provide extensive documentation, beginning with a detailed certificate of origin that is supported by sworn affidavits from various supply chain participants such as suppliers and producers. By contrast, there is much less documentation required for products imported from China.[4]

TERMS OF SALE AND PAYMENT[5]

Choosing the **terms of sale** involves parties working within the negotiations channel, looking at the possible logistics channels, and determining when and where to transfer the following between buyer and seller:

1. The physical goods (the logistics channel)
2. Payment for the goods, freight charges, and insurance for the in-transit goods (the financing channel)
3. Legal title to the goods (the ownership channel)
4. Required documentation (the documentation channel)
5. Responsibility for controlling or caring for the goods in transit, say, in the case of live-stock (the logistics channel).

Transfer can be specified in terms of calendar time, geographic location, or completion of some task. One must think in terms of both time and location.

For many years a variety of selling terms evolved that were translated as terms of a seller's cost quotation. Each started with the product and added some additional service. The product and added services are listed in the following paragraphs, and from the seller's viewpoint, they are the different locations, or stages, for quoting a price to an overseas buyer. They are referred to as **Incoterms 2000** because they were developed and published by the International Chamber of Commerce in the year 2000. Use of the terms is not mandatory, although one would need a very good reason to insist on some other terms.[6] For each of the terms, the respective responsibilities of the seller's and the buyer's logistics managers change. Note that all Incoterms begin with the letters C, D, E, or F.

EX-Works (EXW)

In this most basic transaction, the seller transfers all risk of loss and all responsibility for expenses to the buyer at the seller's loading dock. In an EX-Works transaction, goods are made available for pickup at the seller's factory or warehouse. *Example:* EXW Toledo Incoterms 2000.

FCA (Free Carrier)

In this type of transaction, the seller is responsible for arranging transportation to a specific carrier at a named place. For example, a shipper (seller) located in Milwaukee may sell FCA

---

[4]Alan M. Field, "Too Complex?" *Journal of Commerce,* May 16, 2005, 16–18.

[5]This material in this section is drawn from Donald F. Wood, Anthony Barone, Paul R. Murphy, and Daniel L. Wardlow, *International Logistics,* 2nd ed. (New York: Amacom, 2002), Chapter 11.

[6]See Lauri Railas, "Incoterms for the New Millennium," *European Transport Law,* 2000, 9–22.

Chicago. In this transaction, the seller arranges to deliver goods to an agreed-upon carrier in Chicago. The goods are "delivered" when they are receipted by the buyer's carrier, and all risk of loss transfers to seller at that point. *Example:* FCA Chicago Incoterms 2000.

FAS (Free Alongside Ship)

In this transaction, the seller must arrange for delivery, and assume all risks, up to the ocean carrier at a port. Unofficial usage understands delivery to be "within reach of the ship's tackle." Freight costs up to alongside vessel, risk of loss, and costs of export clearance are borne by the seller. *Example:* FAS Savannah Incoterms 2000.

FOB (Free on Board)

Incoterms limit the use of FOB to carriage by water and define the point of title transfer as occurring when the goods have passed over the ship's rail. In other words, freight to a vessel, loading aboard, and export clearance are the seller's responsibilities. Once the goods are loaded, the risk of loss and costs of transport revert to the buyer. (This term is also used in domestic trade, meaning the price at a specified location.) *Example:* FOB Rotterdam Incoterms 2000.

CFR (Cost and Freight)

The "cost" portion of CFR refers to the merchandise. The "freight" portion refers to all the freight, including export clearance, up to the foreign port of unloading. What is not included is cargo insurance from the port of loading. Indeed, risks are shared in a CFR transaction. The seller must deliver over the ship's rail, so any loss up to that point is the seller's responsibility. Once loaded, the risk transfers to the buyer. This term is only used on waterborne shipments. *Example:* CFR Hong Kong Incoterms 2000.

CPT (Carriage Paid To)

This term is similar to CFR, but it can be used for any mode of transport, including air. CPT means that the seller will pay all freight costs all the way to the foreign port and that the buyer assumes all risk of loss beyond the loading port. *Example:* CPT Paris Incoterms 2000.

CIF (Cost, Insurance, and Freight)

A CIF transaction includes the costs of freight and the costs of insurance. The seller retains the risk of loss up to the foreign port of unloading. This term is used on waterborne shipments. *Example:* CIF Miami Incoterms 2000.

CIP (Carriage and Insurance Paid To)

This term is similar to CIF except that it is primarily used in multimodal transactions where the place of receipt and place of delivery may be different from the port of loading or place of unloading. *Example:* CIP Zurich Incoterms 2000.

DES (Delivered Ex Ship)

In this type of transaction, the seller must pay all the costs and bear all the risks of transport up to the foreign port of unloading, except the cost or risk of unloading the cargo from the ship. In the case of large pieces of equipment, or bulk cargoes, the costs of unloading can exceed the cost of the main freight. *Example:* DES Long Beach Incoterms 2000.

DEQ (Delivered Ex Quay)

This is the same as DES except that the terms provide for the seller to pay the costs of unloading the cargo from the vessel and the cost of import clearance. *Example:* DES New York Incoterms 2000.

DAF (Delivered at Frontier)

In DAF the seller's responsibility is to deliver goods to a named frontier, which usually means a border crossing point, and to clear the transaction for export. The buyer's responsibility is to arrange for pickup of the goods after they are cleared for export, to carry them across the border, to clear them for importation, and to pay any duties. *Example:* DAF Laredo Incoterms 2000.

DDP (Delivered Duty Paid)

This is a new term mainly used in intermodal transactions whereby the seller undertakes all the risks and costs from origin to the buyer's warehouse door, including export and import clearance and import customs duties. Essentially, the seller pays everything in a DDP transaction and passes on all related costs in the merchandise price. *Example:* DDP Baltimore Incoterms 2000.

DDU (Delivered Duty Unpaid)

This is the same as DDP except that duty is not paid. Because the importer is generally better informed about local customs, a DDU transaction is used when the buyer wants to avoid transportation and insurance issues. *Example:* DDU Milan Incoterms 2000.

Terms of payment refer to the manner by which a seller will be paid by a buyer and are much more challenging in international logistics than in domestic logistics. The goals of international buyers and sellers are pretty much the same as those for domestic buyers and sellers—buyers want to receive the product that was paid for, and sellers want to get paid. However, the vagaries of international trade, such as delayed transportation, reduce the likelihood of successfully achieving these goals.

Similar to terms of sale, different international terms of payment offer varying amounts of risk to the involved parties. For example, although payment in advance is of minimal risk to the seller, it is extremely risky to the buyer—what if the paid-for product is never received? A very popular payment alternative that spreads risk across both buyers and sellers is the letter of credit. A **letter of credit** is issued by a bank and guarantees payment to a seller provided that the seller has complied with the applicable terms and conditions of the particular transaction. A sample letter of credit appears in Figure 12-4; note the specific terms such as duplicate certificates of origin and duplicate packing lists, among others.

INTERNATIONAL TRADE AND SUPPLY CHAIN SPECIALISTS

Few companies involved in international logistics rely solely on in-house personnel to manage all shipping operations. Specialist firms have developed, and most companies involved in international trade eventually use one or more services that these specialists provide; these specialists are also intermediaries in the marketing channels and in the supply chain. Several of the more visible international trade and supply chain specialists will be discussed in this section.

International Freight Forwarders

International freight forwarders specialize in handling either vessel shipments or air shipments, yet their functions are generally the same. Some of their principal functions are discussed in the following paragraphs.

IRREVOCABLE COMMERCIAL LETTER OF CREDIT

Since 1852

WELLS FARGO BANK, N.A.

FORMERLY WELLS FARGO BANK AMERICAN TRUST COMPANY
HEAD OFFICE: 464 CALIFORNIA STREET, SAN FRANCISCO, CALIFORNIA 94104

INTERNATIONAL DIVISION — COMMERCIAL L/C DEPARTMENT — CABLE ADDRESS WELLS

OUR LETTER OF CREDIT NO. 27724 (THIS NUMBER MUST BE MENTIONED ON ALL DRAFTS AND CORRESPONDENCE) — AMOUNT US$12,288.00 — DATE April 1, 19

- The Japan Co.
- Box X 25
- Tokyo, Japan

S P E C I M E N

- Wells Fargo Bank N.A.
- Fuji Bldg., 2-3, 3-chome
- Marunouchi, Chiyoda-ku
- Tokyo, Japan

GENTLEMEN:

BY ORDER OF Wards, Oakland, California

AND FOR ACCOUNT OF same

WE HEREBY AUTHORIZE YOU TO DRAW ON us

UP TO AN AGGREGATE AMOUNT OF Twelve Thousand Two Hundred Eighty Eight and No/100 U.S. Dollars

AVAILABLE BY YOUR DRAFTS AT sight

ACCOMPANIED BY
Commercial Invoice and two copies certifying merchandise is in accordance with Purchase Order No. 08142.
Signed Special Customs Invoice in duplicate.
Certificate of Origin in duplicate.
Packing List in duplicate.
Full set clean ocean bills of lading to order shipper, blank endorsed, freight collect, notify Wards, Oakland, California, dated on board not later than May 25, 19 .

Relating to: Transistor Radios from FOB vessel Japanese Port to San Francisco Bay Port.

Partial shipments permitted. Insurance to be effected by buyers
Transhipment is not permitted.

Negotiating bank is to forward all documents attached to the original draft in one airmail envelope.

Courtesy Wells Fargo Bank

DRAFTS MUST BE DRAWN AND NEGOTIATED NOT LATER THAN June 5, 19
ALL DRAFTS DRAWN UNDER THIS CREDIT MUST BEAR ITS DATE AND NUMBER AND THE AMOUNTS MUST BE ENDORSED ON THE REVERSE SIDE OF THIS LETTER OF CREDIT BY THE NEGOTIATING BANK.
WE HEREBY AGREE WITH THE DRAWERS, ENDORSERS AND BONA FIDE HOLDERS OF ALL DRAFTS DRAWN UNDER AND IN COMPLIANCE WITH THE TERMS OF THIS CREDIT, THAT SUCH DRAFTS WILL BE DULY HONORED UPON PRESENTATION TO THE DRAWEE.
THIS CREDIT IS SUBJECT TO THE UNIFORM CUSTOMS AND PRACTICE FOR DOCUMENTARY CREDITS (1962 REVISION), INTERNATIONAL CHAMBER OF COMMERCE BROCHURE NO. 222.

W/ SPECIMEN
AUTHORIZED SIGNATURE

FIGURE 12-4 Letter of Credit

Source: Courtesy of Wells Fargo Bank.

Advising on Acceptance of Letters of Credit

When a client receives a letter of credit, the document contains many conditions that the seller must meet. The forwarder determines whether the client can meet these conditions and, if it cannot, will advise the client that the letter of credit must be amended. The buyer and buyer's bank must be notified before the order can be processed further.

Booking Space on Carriers

Space is frequently more difficult to obtain on international carriers than on domestic carriers for several reasons. Vessel or aircraft departures are less frequent, and the capacities of planes or ships are strictly limited. Connections with other carriers are more difficult to arrange, and the relative bargaining strength of any one shipper with an international carrier is usually weaker than it is with respect to domestic carriers. Forwarders are experienced at keeping tabs on available carrier space, and because they represent more business to the carrier than an individual shipper does, they have more success when finding space is difficult.

Preparing an Export Declaration

An export declaration is required by the U.S. government for statistical and control purposes and must be prepared and filed for nearly every shipment.

Preparing an Air Waybill or Bill of Lading

The international air waybill is a fairly standardized document; the ocean bill of lading is not. The latter may differ between ocean lines, coastal areas through which the shipments are moving, and for a variety of other circumstances. Ocean bills of lading are frequently negotiable, which means that whoever legally holds the document may take delivery of the shipment. Because nearly every ocean vessel line has its own bill of lading, a forwarder's expertise is necessary to fill it out accurately.

Obtaining Consular Documents

Consular documents involve obtaining permission from the importing country for the goods to enter. Documents are prepared that the importing country uses to determine duties to be levied on the shipment as it passes through customs.

Arranging for Insurance

Unlike domestic shipments, international shipments must be insured. Either the individual shipment must be insured or the shipper (or forwarder) must have a blanket policy covering all shipments. International airlines offer insurance at nominal rates. Rates on vessel shipments are higher, and the entire process is complex because of certain practices that are acceptable at sea. For example, if the vessel is in peril of sinking, the captain may have some cargo jettisoned (thrown overboard) to keep the vessel afloat. The owners of the surviving cargo and the vessel owner must then share the costs of reimbursing the shippers whose cargo was thrown overboard.

Preparing and Sending Shipping Notices and Documents

The financial transaction involving the sale of goods is carefully coordinated with their physical movement, and rather elaborate customs and procedures have evolved to ensure that the seller is paid when the goods are delivered. The export forwarder handles the shipper's role in the document preparation and exchange stages. It is necessary to have certain documents available as the shipment crosses international boundaries. (The forwarder serves to coordinate the logistics, documentation, ownership, and payment channels.)

Serving as General Consultant on Export Matters

Questions continually arise when dealing with new products, terms of sale, new markets, or new regulations. The forwarder knows the answers or how to find them. A conscientious forwarder also advises a shipper as to when certain procedures, such as similar shipments to the same market, become so repetitive that the shipper can handle the procedures in its own export department at a cost lower than the fees charged by the forwarder.

EXPORT QUOTATION WORKSHEET

DATE_____   REF/PRO FORMA INVOICE NO._____
COMMODITY_____   EXPECTED SHIP DATE_____
CUSTOMER_____   PACKED DIMENSIONS_____
COUNTRY_____   PACKED WEIGHT_____
PAYMENT TERMS_____   PACKED CUBE_____

PRODUCTS TO BE SHIPPED FROM_____
                TO_____

SELLING PRICE OF GOODS: $_____

SPECIAL EXPORT PACKING:
   $_____   quoted by_____
   $_____   quoted by_____
   $_____   quoted by_____ $_____

INLAND FREIGHT:
   $_____   quoted by_____
   $_____   quoted by_____
   $_____   quoted by_____ $_____

Inland freight includes the following charges:
☐ unloading   ☐ pier delivery   ☐ terminal   ☐ _____

OCEAN FREIGHT			AIR FREIGHT		
quoted by		tariff item	quoted by		spec code
$_____	_____	#_____	$_____	_____	#_____
$_____	_____	#_____	$_____	_____	#_____
$_____	_____	#_____	$_____	_____	#_____

Ocean freight includes the following surcharges: Air freight includes the following surcharges:

☐ Port congestion   ☐ Heavy lift   ☐ Fuel adjustment
☐ Currency adjustment   ☐ Bunker   ☐ Container stuffing
☐ Container rental   ☐ Wharfage   ☐ _____
☐ _____   ☐ _____

INSURANCE   ☐ includes war risk   ☐ INSURANCE   ☐ includes war risk
rate:_____ per $100 or $_____   rate:_____ per $100 or $_____

TOTAL OCEAN CHARGES $_____   **TOTAL AIR CHARGES** $_____ $_____
notes: notes:

FORWARDING FEES: $_____
Includes: ☐ Courier Fees ☐ Certification Fees ☐ Banking Fees ☐ _____

CONSULAR LEGALIZATION FEES: $_____

INSPECTION FEES: $_____

DIRECT BANK CHARGES: $_____

OTHER CHARGES: _____ $_____
              _____ $_____

TOTAL: ☐ FOB_____   ☐ C & F_____
       ☐ FAS_____   ☐ CIF_____ $_____

Form 10-020 Printed and Sold by *UNZ&CO* 190 Baldwin Ave., Jersey City, NJ 07306 • (800) 631-3098

FIGURE 12-5   A Forwarder's Export Quotation Sheet Showing Factors to Include When Determining the Price to Quote a Potential Buyer of a Product

Source: Reprinted with permission of Unz & Co., 190 Baldwin Ave., Jersey City, NJ.

CONSIGNEE:				INVOICE NO. DATE YOUR REF. NO.	

FROM:
TO: ☐ AIR   ☐ OCEAN   CARRIER:
B/L OR AWB NO.

	$
INLAND FREIGHT/LOCAL CARTAGE	
EXPORT PACKING	
AIR FREIGHT CHARGES	
OCEAN FREIGHT/TERMINAL CHARGES	
CONSULAR FEES	
INSURANCE/CERTIFICATE OF INSURANCE	
CHAMBER OF COMMERCE	
BROKERAGE FEES	
FORWARDING	
HANDLING AND EXPEDITING	
DOCUMENT PREPARATION	
MESSENGER FEES	
POSTAGE	
TELEPHONE	
CABLES	
CERTIFICATE OF ORIGIN	
BANKING: (LETTER OF CREDIT/SIGHT DRAFT)	
MISCELLANEOUS	
TOTAL	$

As amended by the United States Shipping Act of 1984.

_____ has a policy against payment, solicitation,
or receipt of any rebate, directly or indirectly, which would be unlawful under the United States Shipping
Act, 1916, as amended

FIGURE 12-6   Invoice Form Used by a Freight Forwarder to Bill Client for Handling an Export Shipment

Source: Reprinted with permission of Unz & Co., 190 Baldwin Ave., Jersey City, NJ.

Export forwarders' income comes from three sources. Similar to domestic forwarders, they buy space wholesale and sell it retail. By consolidating shipments, they benefit from a lower rate per pound. In addition, most carriers allow the forwarders a commission on shipping revenues they generate for the carriers. Also, forwarders charge fees for preparing documents, performing research, and the like. Figures 12-5 and 12-6 show forms used by forwarders. Figure 12-5 is used to prepare cost estimates for the client to use when quoting a price to a potential overseas buyer. Figure 12-6 is the form that a forwarder uses to bill a client for handling a shipment.

Customshouse Brokers
A function opposite of, but similar to, that of international freight forwarders is performed by **customshouse brokers,** who oversee the efficient movement of importers' goods (and accompanying paperwork) through customs and other inspection points and stand ready to argue for a lower rate in case one or two commodity descriptions apply.

Nonvessel-Operating Common Carriers

Another international logistics service provider, the **nonvessel-operating common carrier** (NVOCC), is often confused with the international freight forwarder. Although both forwarders and NVOCCs must be licensed by the Federal Maritime Commission (FMC), NVOCCs are common carriers and thus have common carrier obligations to serve and deliver, among others. NVOCCs consolidate freight from different shippers and leverage this volume to negotiate favorable transportation rates from ocean carriers. From the shipper's perspective, an NVOCC is a carrier; from an ocean carrier's perspective, an NVOCC is a shipper.

There has been an important modification in NVOCC rate regulations since publication of the previous edition of this book. Historically, NVOCCs were required to file their rates with the Federal Maritime Commission; these rates (1) were readily available to this public and (2) were applicable to *similarly situated shippers* or those shippers that sought transportation services under the same or similar circumstances (e.g., same or similar commodity; same or similar length of haul; same or similar origin and destination, among others). However, in early 2005, the FMC permitted NVOCCs to enter into contract arrangements with individual shippers, and although these contracts must still be filed at the FMC, their provisions are confidential.[7]

Export Management Companies

Sometimes the manufacturer seeking to export retains the services of an **export management company,** a firm that specializes in handling overseas transactions. Such companies represent U.S. manufacturers and help them find overseas firms that can be licensed to manufacture their products. They also handle sales correspondence in foreign languages, ensure that foreign labeling requirements are met, and perform other specialized functions. When handling the overseas sales for a U.S. firm, the export management firm either buys and sells on its own account or provides credit information regarding each potential buyer to the U.S. manufacturer, which can judge whether to take the risk.

Export management companies and international freight forwarders are closely related because, together, they can offer a complete overseas sales and distribution service to the domestic manufacturer that wants to export but does not know how. Sometimes, international freight forwarders and export management firms work out of the same office, the only apparent distinction being which phone line they answer. Export management companies are also retained by large firms that have exported for many years because they can perform their very specialized service less expensively than could the client.

Export Packers

As is true for the export functions discussed previously, a specialized service of export packing is performed by firms that are typically located in port cities. **Export packers** custom pack shipments when the exporter lacks the equipment or the expertise to do so itself. However, when exporters have repeat business, they usually perform their own export packing.

Export packaging involves packaging for two distinct purposes, in addition to the sales function of some packaging. The first is to allow goods to move easily through customs. For a country assessing duties on the weight of both the item and its container, this means selecting lightweight packing materials. For items moving through the mail, it might mean construction of an envelope with an additional small flap that a customs inspector could

---

[7]James Calderwood, "FMC Grants NVOCCs the Right to Negotiate Shipper Contracts," *Logistics Today,* February 2005, 13.

open and look inside without having to open the entire envelope. For crated machinery, this might involve using open slats rather than completely closed construction (the customs inspectors would likely satisfy their curiosity by peering and probing through the openings between the slats).

The second purpose of export packing is to protect products in what almost always is a more difficult journey than they would experience if they were destined for domestic consignees. For many firms, the traditional ocean packaging method is to take the product in its domestic pack and enclose it in a wooden container. Ocean shipments are subject to more moisture damage than are domestic shipments. Variations in temperature are also more extreme. Canned goods moving through hot areas sweat, causing the cans to rust and the labels to become unglued. Campbell's Soup adds desiccants to its cartons of soup, otherwise specks of rust will appear on the cans during their sea voyage.[8]

Transportation Considerations in International Distribution

Previous discussion has indicated that the distances associated with international shipments are often much greater than those associated with domestic shipments. Because these increased distances often mean that the buyer or seller must choose water or air transportation, we'll take a closer look at ocean shipping and international air transportation in this section. This section will also discuss surface transportation issues in nondomestic markets.

Before beginning our discussion, you should recognize the rather commonsense notion that international transportation can't be effective or efficient without fairly identical handling equipment being in place at each end of the trip. For example, containerization isn't feasible unless both the origin and destination ports are equipped with the appropriate container handling equipment. Having said this, even today there are countries where grain and sugar are still stowed or unloaded by stevedores carrying individual bags on their shoulders and walking up and down gangplanks. Although this manual loading and unloading is inefficient because of the increased loading or unloading times, the nations in which this practice occurs are often very poor, and manual cargo handling can be a means for providing jobs (and thus income) to many people.

The incidence (or burden) of costs can also be significant. For example, *roll on–roll off (RO–RO) vessels,* such as the one in Figure 12-7, have large doors in their sterns or on their sides. Ramps are stretched to the shore, and cargo is moved off RO–RO vessels in trailers. Once loaded, there is considerable wasted space—essentially the height of each trailer box above the deck floor. Thus, a vessel cannot carry as much cargo within a given amount of space. Yet the required port facilities are relatively inexpensive; only a ramp for driving trailers on or off a ship is needed. The trailers can be hitched to tractors and hauled directly to or from their landward destination. So, although more is spent per ton of cargo on vessel operations, less is spent for port operations.

Ocean Shipping

If you don't live near a seaport, you might not have an appreciation for the importance of water transportation in international trade; a frequently cited statistic is that approximately 60 percent of cross-border shipments moves by water transportation. Much of the world's shipping tonnage is used for carrying petroleum, and the associated tankers are either owned by oil companies or leased (chartered) by them from individuals who invest in ships. The leased vessels are chartered for specific voyages or for large blocks of time.

---

[8]*American Shipper,* September 2001, 26.

FIGURE 12-7   Loading a Travel Trailer Aboard a RO–RO (Roll On–Roll Off) Vessel at the Port of Seattle

Source: Don Wilson, Port of Seattle.

The charter market fluctuates widely, especially after events such as the closing and opening of the Suez Canal and the announcement of large U.S. wheat sales overseas. International commodity traders follow the vessel charter market closely because they know the differences in commodity prices in various world markets. When the charter rate between these two markets drops to the point that it is less than the spread in the commodity prices, a vessel is chartered to carry the commodity.

Dry-bulk cargoes, such as grain, ores, sulfur, sugar, scrap iron, coal, lumber, and logs, usually move in complete vessel-load lots on chartered vessels. A bulk carrier is shown in Figure 12-8. There are also large, specialized dry cargo ships that are often owned by shippers. Nissan Motor Company of Japan, for example, owns auto-carrying ships, some of which can carry 1,200 autos apiece, with the remainder carrying 1,900 vehicles. Most of these vessels carry autos to the United States and can then load with soybeans for the return voyages.

If a single shipper's needs do not fill the vessel completely, the vessel is topped off with compatible bulk cargo, such as grain, that can be loaded into an unused hold. This helps defray the total voyage costs for the party using the ship. Agents specialize in chartering fractional spaces (often individual holds) in vessels.

Another type of vessel that combines aspects of several vessel types is the parcel tanker, which has over 50 different tanks, ranging from 350 to 2,200 cubic meters. Each can carry a different liquid and is loaded and unloaded through a separate piping system. The tanks have

FIGURE 12-8 An Ocean Bulk Carrier Being Loaded with Export Coal Carried by a Mechanical Device at Far Left

Source: Photo courtesy of Electro-Coal Transfer Corp., Davant, LA.

different types of coating; some are temperature controlled. Some of the vessels go on round-the-world voyages and carry palm oil, coconut oil, chemicals, and refined petroleum products.

Today, operators of general cargo vessels might never handle, or even see, cargo on a piece-by-piece basis. Their ships are fully containerized, which means the only way they can load or unload cargo is to have the cargo stowed inside containers. Containers dominate the traffic between Europe and the United States, Europe and Asia, and the United States and Asia. Shippers or forwarders tender full containers, and if a shipper tenders a less-than-container lot, the vessel operator must load all the less-than-container lots into containers so that the cargo can be loaded aboard the containership. In large containerships, some of the containers are carried above the level of the deck; this increases the vessel's cubic carrying capacity.

We pointed out in an earlier chapter that the carrying capacity of containerships continues to increase, and this increased vessel size is one contributor to the growth of **load centers,** or major ports where thousands of containers arrive and depart each week. As vessel sizes increase, it becomes more costly to stop (call) at multiple ports in a geographic area, and as a result operators of larger containerships prefer to call at only one port in a geographic area. Load centers might affect the dynamics of international transportation in the sense that some ports will be relegated to providing feeder service to the load centers. In addition, load centers might affect supplemental transportation providers, such as truck and rail, particularly if the existing road and rail infrastructure is insufficient to accommodate the higher volumes that will be associated with the megaports.

Shipping Conferences and Alliances

Not surprisingly, different users of ocean liner (container) shipping have different service requirements. Some companies require daily sailings; for some other cargoes, such as wastepaper, time savings are of little significance. Shipping lines rely on steady volumes of wastepaper to keep their ships full. Vessel lines bump wastepaper cargoes at the last minute if they can find a load of higher-paying cargo, a practice known as *rolling.* In turn, wastepaper exporters require stability in freight rates because they account for 60 to 95 percent of their landed costs. Wastepaper accounts for 18 percent of the cargo carried from the United States to Asia, and because it originates in all 50 states, it can be used to fill containers that must be repositioned in Asia.

How do carriers take into account these varying demands for service? In the United States, service contracts were permitted under the Shipping Act of 1984; they were drawn up between shipping conferences (liner companies serving the same market) and specific shippers or shippers' associations (representing related shippers). A service contract consists of a commitment by the shipper to the conference or carrier of a minimum volume of cargo, usually expressed in TEUs with rate levels indicated as intermodal, point to point, or port to port. The carrier or conference must guarantee regular service. Contracts also include clauses for damages in case the shipper does not live up to its commitment—a typical shipper's problem is loss of overseas sales.

In terms of necessary contract provisions, shippers—by far—view predictable, stable rates as the most important factor. Other important contract provisions include all-inclusive freight rates (no adjustment factors) as well as guaranteed ship space and container availability. Discounts on service contracts are given if the carrier can operate from door to door without specifying the ports through which cargo must be routed. Discounts are also given for quicker releases of containers, and off-peak discounts are also offered for moving traffic when business is slow.

Until the mid-1990s, ocean general cargo (or break-bulk) liner rates affecting U.S. ports were set by **shipping conferences,** which are cartels of all ocean vessel operators operating between certain trade areas. Historically, shipping conferences provided both rate stability as well as guaranteed space availability due in large part to the ability of member carriers to collectively set rates and service levels without fear of antitrust prosecution. Since the mid-1990s there has been a general decline in the influence of shipping conferences; as an example, the Trans-Atlantic Conference Agreement (TACA) controlled approximately 60 percent of the Atlantic shipments in the mid-1990s versus about 40 percent of these shipments today.[9]

In the mid-1990s, another type of alliance began forming in the container trades in which carriers retain their individual identities but cooperate in the area of operations. There are presently three major **ocean carrier alliances:** the Grand Alliance (consisting of five carriers), the New World Alliance (three carriers), and CYKH Alliance (three carriers). These alliances provide two primary benefits to participating members, namely, the sharing of vessel space and the ability to offer shippers a broader service network. Whereas an individual carrier might only be able to provide weekly service on a particular route, an alliance might be able to offer daily service.[10] Although alliances are not conferences, their size allows them to exercise considerable clout in their dealings with shippers, port terminal operators, and connecting land carriers.

The relationship between buyers (shippers) and sellers (carriers) and groups of sellers (conferences or alliances) has changed dramatically over the last 20 years. In routes serving U.S. ports, this commercial relationship has moved from a tightly regulated environment to a largely

---

[9]R. G. Edmonson, "TACA's Reprieve," *Traffic World,* October 13, 2003, 33.
[10]Peter T. Leach, "Hanging Together," *Journal of Commerce,* September 26, 2005, 10–12.

unregulated environment wherein shippers and carriers are free to work out whatever commercial relationship best suits them in confidential contractual agreements. The U.S. policies toward liner pricing differ from those in much of the remainder of the world. A European journal said of the remainder of the world, "Liner shipping stands out in the world economy in being almost completely cartelized as far as pricing is concerned. Practically every trade route is covered by a separate coalition of liner conferences which fixes the freight rates."[11] Today, major U.S. shippers use contracts with alliances for most traffic between the United States and either Asia or Europe. In other markets, shippers may deal with vessel conferences or rate agreements. Memberships in alliances, rate agreements, and conferences are very fluid.

International Airfreight

Airfreight has had a very profound effect on international distribution because the airplane has reduced worldwide time distances. Although transit times between the East and West Coasts of the United States have shrunk from 5 days to less than 1, some international transit times have shrunk from as many as 30 days to 1 or 2.

The three types of international airfreight operations are chartered aircraft, scheduled air carriers, and integrated air carriers, specializing in carrying parcels. Chartering an entire aircraft is, of course, expensive, but sometimes the expense can be justified. Chartered aircraft have been used in the transport of livestock sold for breeding purposes. One charter airline carried 7,000 cattle from Texas to southern Chile. Nineteen flights were involved, each lasting 15 hours. The comparable time by sea was 20 days, and past experience showed that the sea journey was hard on the cattle, causing either lung damage or long delays before the animals could be bred. The U.S. military also charters aircraft to move freight, and commercial U.S. airlines have agreed to make available portions of their fleet when requested to do so by the Department of Defense.

The schedules and routes of international air carriers are established by negotiations between the nations involved. Rates are established by the **International Air Transport Association (IATA),** a cartel consisting of nearly all the world's scheduled international airlines. As a general rule, the principal function of international airlines is to carry passengers, and freight is a secondary consideration. Having said this, some scheduled airlines use all-freight aircraft in certain markets; Lufthansa, the German airline, was the first airline in the world to use an all-cargo Boeing 747. It was used in trans-Atlantic service and connected Germany with the Northeastern United States, replacing several smaller planes. Compared with earlier jets, the 747 has enormous capacity, as shown in Figure 12-9. As pointed out in an earlier chapter, Airbus is building the A380, an airplane that will dwarf the 747 in size. Although the A380 is intended mainly for passengers, it will also carry some freight and, eventually, be available in all-freight configurations.

For shippers of large quantities, international airlines offer a unit-load incentive in conjunction with some FAK (freight-all-kinds) rates. The airline supplies large pallets and, if necessary, igloos (a fiberglass pallet cover placed over the load to protect it and ensure that it does not exceed the allowable dimensions). To obtain the lower rates from IATA carriers, the shipper must tender the pallet loaded to airline specifications; at the other end of the journey, the entire pallet must be destined to one consignee. A special charge is made if it is necessary to unload or partially unload the pallet for customs inspection. Both the shipper and consignee may have the pallet for 48 hours each before demurrage charges are assessed.

---

[11]*European Transport Law,* XXXIV, no. 6 (1999): 761.

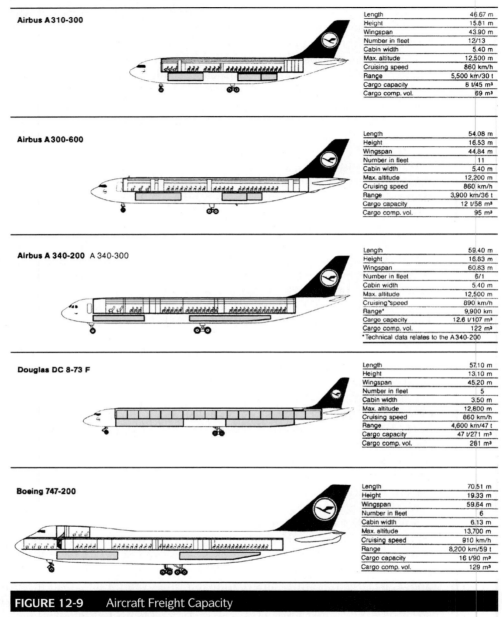

Airbus A310-300

Length	46.67 m
Height	15.81 m
Wingspan	43.90 m
Number in fleet	12/13
Cabin width	5.40 m
Max. altitude	12,500 m
Cruising speed	860 km/h
Range	5,500 km/30 t
Cargo capacity	8 t/45 m³
Cargo comp. vol.	69 m³

Airbus A300-600

Length	54.08 m
Height	16.53 m
Wingspan	44.84 m
Number in fleet	11
Cabin width	5.40 m
Max. altitude	12,200 m
Cruising speed	860 km/h
Range	3,900 km/36 t
Cargo capacity	12 t/58 m³
Cargo comp. vol.	95 m³

Airbus A 340-200 A 340-300

Length	59.40 m
Height	16.83 m
Wingspan	60.83 m
Number in fleet	6/1
Cabin width	5.40 m
Max. altitude	12,500 m
Cruising speed	890 km/h
Range*	9,900 km
Cargo capacity	12.6 t/107 m³
Cargo comp. vol.	122 m³
*Technical data relates to the A340-200	

Douglas DC 8-73 F

Length	57.10 m
Height	13.10 m
Wingspan	45.20 m
Number in fleet	5
Cabin width	3.50 m
Max. altitude	12,800 m
Cruising speed	860 km/h
Range	4,600 km/47 t
Cargo capacity	47 t/271 m³
Cargo comp. vol.	261 m³

Boeing 747-200

Length	70.51 m
Height	19.33 m
Wingspan	59.64 m
Number in fleet	6
Cabin width	6.13 m
Max. altitude	13,700 m
Cruising speed	910 km/h
Range	8,200 km/59 t
Cargo capacity	16 t/90 m³
Cargo comp. vol.	129 m³

FIGURE 12-9   Aircraft Freight Capacity

Source: Courtesy of Lufthansa Cargo.

The result of the IATA incentives to use containers and unit loads has been to increase the average size of shipments handled by the airlines. This has reduced the number of individual packages each airline terminal must handle. Airfreight forwarders have benefited because they are frequently in a better position than individual shippers to take advantage of incentives offered for larger shipments or consolidated shipments.

International air cargo rates are published in tariffs available from the airlines. There are both general cargo rates and lower specific commodity rates. Rate breaks encourage heavier shipments. Excerpts from a tariff with freight rates from Houston to some Latin American destinations are given in Figure 12-10.

A newer development in international airfreight is international parcel services offered by well-known carriers such as UPS, FedEx, and DHL International. Each provides land pickup and delivery services for documents and small parcels and are called *integrated carriers* because they own all their vehicles and the facilities that fall in between. These parcel services are of special significance to international logistics because they often provide the fastest service between many major points. They are also often employed to carry the documentation that is generated by—and is very much a part of—the international movement of materials, although many foreign trade documents can now be transferred electronically. These carriers also handle documentation services for their clients.

Surface Transport in Other Countries

You might recall from Chapter 6 that transport infrastructure varies from country to country. Having said this, some infrastructures are as well developed as those in the United States, with two notable differences. First, few nations have as wide a range of modes to choose from because the United States has traditionally encouraged development across all modes of transportation. Second, the degree of nationalization of transportation is often higher in many countries than in the United States.

The widespread use of seaborne containers has brought about hopes of standardizing land vehicles for carrying containers on the landward legs of their journeys. For example, the European Union (EU) has been making progress in its attempt to standardize truck dimensions within its member countries. At the same time, there is opposition to truck transportation in several European nations, such as Switzerland and Austria. These nations have been trying to force the use of containers on rail, but their efforts to date have not been widely successful. This lack of success is partially due to the fact that truck-rail intermodal is best suited for moving large volumes over long distances; by contrast, a majority of shipments within the EU tend to be small volumes moving relatively short distances.[12]

Rail equipment sizes, as well as bridge and tunnel clearances, vary throughout the world, and most nations use equipment that is much smaller than that used in the United States. Containers that can be loaded two to a railcar in the United States are frequently carried on individual railcars elsewhere. And, as pointed out in Chapter 6, different rail gauges can complicate the exchange of traffic between nations.

An alternative to surface transport in some nations is **short sea shipping** (SSS), which refers to waterborne transportation that utilizes inland and coastal waterways to move shipments from domestic ports to their destination.[13] Although SSS is more widely accepted and practiced in Europe (see Figure 12-11), there have been successful applications in the United States, perhaps most notably involving shipments between Alaska and Washington state. Short sea shipping is viewed as an excellent method for reducing highway congestion that is contributed to by trucks, as well as for reducing the corresponding truck-related noise and air pollution. However, SSS is unlikely to become a more common transportation option in the United States until highway driving speeds decrease to about 20 miles per hour.[14]

---

[12]Fredrik Barthel and Johan Woxenius, "Developing Intermodal Transport for Small Flows over Short Distances," *Transport Planning & Technology* 27, no. 5 (2004): 403–424.

[13]www.marad.dot.gov.

[14]Roger Morton, "Short Circuit," *Logistics Today,* April, 2005, 1, 10–11.

BULK GENERAL & SPECIFIC COMMODITY CARGO RATES FROM THE U.S. AND CANADA

2

From: HOUSTON (HOU)

Airline	Item	Commodity Description	Minimum Charge($)	1	100	220	440	660	880	1100	2200	4400	Flight Days
To: COZUMEL (CZM)													
AMERICAN AIRLINES (AA)	GEN	General Commodity	37.00	68	59	57	57	53	53	50	50	50	
To: CURACAO (CUR)													
EASTERN AIRLINES (EA)	GEN	General Commodity	40.00	144	108	108	108	102	102	83	83	83	
VIASA AIRLINES (VA)	GEN	General Commodity	50.00	146	108	108	108	102	102	88	88	88	3
To: DOMINICA (DOM)													
CARICARGO (DC)	GEN	General Commodity	50.00	121	97	97	97	97	97	79	79	79	
To: FORT DE FRANCE (FDF)													
CARICARGO (DC)	GEN	General Commodity	40.00	115	94	94	94	94	94	79	79	79	
EASTERN AIRLINES (EA)	GEN	General Commodity	40.00	155	108	108	108	108	108	97	97	97	
To: FREEPORT (FPO)													
EASTERN AIRLINES (EA)	GEN	General Commodity	35.00	90	69	69	69	69	69	57	57	57	4
To: GEORGETOWN (GEO)													
CARICARGO (DC)	GEN	General Commodity	50.00	125	112	112	112	112	112	95	95	95	
To: GRAND CAYMAN (GCM)													
CAYMAN AIRWAYS (KX)	GEN	General Commodity	39.00	80	66	66	66	66	66	55	55	55	
EASTERN AIRLINES (EA)	GEN	General Commodity	39.00	80	66	66	66	66	66	55	55	55	
CAYMAN AIRWAYS (KX)	0006	Foodstuffs, Spices, Beverages								35	35	35	
To: GRENADA (GND)													
CARICARGO (DC)	GEN	General Commodity	50.00	116	94	94	94	94	94	78	78	78	1
To: GUADALAJARA (GDL)													
AMERICAN AIRLINES (AA)	GEN	General Commodity	37.00	44	34	34	34	34	34	31	31	31	
To: GUATEMALA CITY (GUA)													
AVIATECA AIRLINES (GU)	GEN	General Commodity	45.00	81	81	59	59	56	56	50	50	50	1,3,5
EASTERN AIRLINES (EA)	GEN	General Commodity	45.00	137	104	104	104	92	92	78	78	78	1,3,5,6
TACA INTERNATIONAL (TA)	GEN	General Commodity	45.00	78	78	56	56	56	56	50	50	50	
AVIATECA AIRLINES (GU)	1081	Baby Poultry						44	44	44	44	44	
	2199	Textiles, Clothing or Footwear						45	45	38	38	38	
	4206	Surface Vehicle Parts						45	45	38	38	38	
TACA INTERNATIONAL (TA)	4742	Oil Drill Machines/Parts						50	50	42	42	42	
AVIATECA AIRLINES (GU)	6001	Chemicals,Drugs,Pharm.Medicine						50	50	42	42	42	
To: GUAYAQUIL (GYE)													
AECA AIRLINES (2A)	GEN	General Commodity	50.00	117	89	89	89	68	68	68	68	54 ag	
AEROPERU (PL)	GEN	General Commodity	50.00	131	98	98	98	80	80	69	69	69	
AIR PANAMA (OP)	GEN	General Commodity	40.00	131	98	98	98	80	80	69	69	69	
EASTERN AIRLINES (EA)	GEN	General Commodity	50.00	228	171	171	171	145	145	120	120	120	2,3,5,6,7
ECUATORIANA (EU)	GEN	General Commodity	50.00	224	168	168	168	142	142	117	117	117	
LADECO AIRLINES (UC)	GEN	General Commodity	50.00	166	125	125	125	101	101	88	88,	88	
To: IQUIQUE (IQQ)													
FAST AIR (UD)	GEN	General Commodity	50.00	370	279	279	279	279	279	198	198	198	
LAN-CHILE (LA)	GEN	General Commodity	50.00	375	283	283	283	283	283	211	211	211	Daily
To: IQUITOS (IQT)													
FAUCETT AIRLINES (CF)	GEN	General Commodity	45.00	193	138	138	138	116	116	110	110	110	
LAN-CHILE (LA)	GEN	General Commodity	50.00	256	200	200	200	161	161	140	140	140	3,6,7

Rates in Cents per Pound

FIGURE 12-10   Excerpts from an Airfreight Tariff Showing Rates from Houston to Several Latin American Points

Source: Courtesy of CRS Publishing Division, Miami, FL.

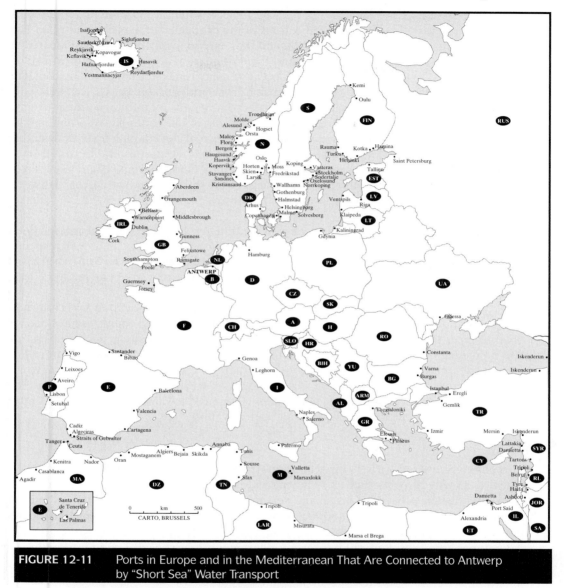

FIGURE 12-11   Ports in Europe and in the Mediterranean That Are Connected to Antwerp by "Short Sea" Water Transport

Source: Drawing copyright PUBLITRA, Belgium. Reprinted with permission.

INTERNATIONAL TRADE INVENTORIES

Even under the best conditions, the movement of products in an international supply chain is never as smooth as a comparable domestic movement. Because greater uncertainties, misunderstandings, and delays often arise in international movements, safety stocks must be larger.

Firms involved in international trade must give careful thought to their inventory policies. Most nations represent smaller potential marketing areas than the United States; thus, the inventory necessary to serve any one of them will be smaller. An inventory held in one nation may not necessarily serve the needs of markets in nearby nations because there may be minor, but significant, variations in the specifications of the product sold in each country. In Thailand and the Philippines, for example, it is hot, and there are many traffic jams, so General Motors builds cars with larger cooling systems, and the dashboard material is made to withstand prolonged exposure to the sun. Alternatively, because many roads in China are unpaved, General Motors equips vehicles with stronger suspensions and more durable tires.

Return items are virtually impossible to accommodate in an international distribution operation, especially if the return involves movements of the goods across a national boundary. This has important implications for a firm trying to achieve a high level of customer service standards on an international basis because it may be unreasonable to tell buyers to return a defective item to the factory where it was built. One U.S. retail chain tells its stores to contact domestic producers directly with questions regarding product defects. However, for imported products, no recourse is available. The stores are told to destroy the products or sell them at salvage prices.

Inventory valuation is difficult because of continually changing exchange rates. If goods are valued in the currency of where they are produced, that value can fluctuate with respect to the currency value of where the product is being stored. Moreover, when a nation's (or the world's) currency is unstable, investments in inventories rise because they are believed to be less risky than holding cash or securities.

Warehousing is another inventory-related consideration associated with international logistics. Whereas warehousing facilities in economically developed countries have been developed to meet the requirements of contemporary logistics systems (e.g., high ceilings, loading and unloading docks, sufficient lighting), the warehousing facilities in other countries can be more problematic. Inefficient warehousing practices can affect inventory carrying costs through increased storage, handling, obsolescence, or shrinkage costs. In China, for example, the combination of poor warehousing facilities and unskilled warehousing management has led to high levels of inventory loss, damage, and deterioration.[15]

Summary

This chapter covered various aspects of international logistics, which differs from domestic logistics in many respects, such as by having a requirement for numerous documents as well as by greater distances between origin and destination points. Governments attempt to influence foreign trade, in part because export sales help their economies, balance of payments, and currency values. They also may discourage imports by imposing tariffs or other restrictions (sometimes known as nontariff barriers). Governments may subsidize their international shipping and airlines.

Documentation, along with terms of sale and payment, are key issues in cross-border transactions, and they were discussed in this chapter. And because international logistics is complex, many firms rely on specialists to help with export and import transactions. These foreign trade specialists include freight forwarders, NVOCCs, customshouse brokers, export packers, and others.

The chapter also examined several transportation considerations in international distribution. We looked at ocean shipping, shipping conferences and alliances, international air freight, and surface transport in other countries. The chapter concluded with a discussion of international trade inventories.

---

[15]John Kerr, "10 Key Challenges for the Chinese Logistics Industry," *Logistics Management,* February 2005, S64–S68.

Questions for Discussion and Review

1. Explain how developing nations ensure that an increasing proportion of supply chain activities are conducted within their borders.
2. Discuss some of the challenges associated with international logistics.
3. What are some key political restrictions on cross-border trade?
4. Discuss the roles that a particular country's government might play in international transport.
5. What is a certificate of origin, a commercial invoice, and a shipper's export declaration?
6. What are determined by the terms of sale?
7. Pick, and describe, one C Incoterm, one D Incoterm, one E Incoterm, and one F Incoterm.
8. Discuss the role of the letter of credit with respect to international shipments.
9. Discuss four possible functions that might be performed by international freight forwarders.
10. What is an NVOCC?
11. What services do export management firms perform?
12. What are the two primary purposes of export packing?
13. What are RO–RO vessels?
14. What is a parcel tanker?
15. Explain the load center concept. How might load centers affect the dynamics of international transportation?
16. Discuss service contracts as applied to international water transportation.
17. Discuss the role of alliances in the container trades.
18. How do the rates established by the International Air Transport Association influence international airfreight?
19. Discuss some of the challenges to surface transport in other countries.
20. What are some challenges associated with inventory management in cross-border trade?

Suggested Readings

Barthel, Fredrik, and Johan Woxenius. "Developing Intermodal Transport for Small Flows over Short Distances." *Transportation Planning & Technology* 27, no. 5 (2004): 403–424.

Fung, Michael Ka-Yiu, Anming Zhang, Lawrence Chi-Kin Leung, and Japhet Sebastian Law. "The Air Cargo Industry in China: Implications of Globalization and WTO Accession." *Transportation Journal* 44, no. 4 (2005): 44–62.

Gourevitch, Peter, Roger Bohn, and David McKendrick. "Globalization of Production: Insights from the Hard Disk Drive Industry." *World Development* 28, no. 2 (2000): 301–317.

Huang, Yuelu, Charlotte Rayner, and Lee Zhaung. "Does Intercultural Competence Matter in Intercultural Business Relationship Development?" *International Journal of Logistics: Research & Applications* 6, no. 4 (2003): 277–288.

Lu, Yizhi, and John Dinwoodie. "Comparative Perspectives of International Freight Forwarder Services in China." *Transportation Journal* 42, no. 2 (2002): 17–27.

McNaughton, Rod B., and Jim Bell. "Channel Switching Between Domestic and Foreign Markets." *Journal of International Marketing* 9, no. 1 (2001): 24–39.

Maloni, Michael, and Eric C. Jackson. "North American Container Port Capacity: An Exploratory Analysis." *Transportation Journal* 44, no. 3 (2005): 1–22.

Paixao, Ana Cristina, and Peter Bernard Marlow. "Fourth Generation Ports: A Question of Agility?" *International Journal of Physical Distribution & Logistics Management* 33, no. 4 (2003): 355–376.

Railas, Lauri. "Incoterms for the New Millennium." *European Transport Law,* 2000, 9–22.

Sahay, B. S., and Ramneesh Mohan. "Supply Chain Management Practices in Indian Industry." *International Journal of Physical Distribution & Logistics Management* 33, no. 7 (2003): 582–606.

Vidal, Carlos, and Marc Goetschalckx. "Modeling the Effect of Uncertainties on Global Logistics Systems." *Journal of Business Logistics* 21, no. 1 (2000): 95–115.

Wood, Donald F., Anthony Barone, Paul Murphy, and Daniel L. Wardlow. *International Logistics.* 2nd ed. (New York: Amacom, 2002).

CASES

CASE 12-1 HDT TRUCK COMPANY

HDT Truck Company has been located in Crown Point, Indiana, since 1910. Its only products—large trucks—are built to individual customer specifications. The firm once produced automobiles but dropped out of the auto business in 1924. The firm nearly went out of business in the late 1930s, but by 1940 its fortunes were buoyed by receipt of several military contracts for tank retrievers—large-wheeled vehicles that can pull a disabled tank onto a low trailer and haul it to a location where it can be repaired.

Since World War II, HDT had manufactured only large off-road vehicles, including airport snowplows, airport crash trucks, oil-field drilling equipment, and the like. HDT purchased all components from small manufacturers that were still clustered in the Milwaukee–Detroit–Toledo–Cleveland area. Essentially, all HDT did was assemble components into specialized vehicles containing the combinations of frame, power plant, transmission, axles, cab, and other equipment necessary to do the job. The assembly line was relatively slow. After wheels were attached to the frame and axles, the night shift labor force would push the chassis along to its next station on the line so it would be in place for the next day's shift. By using one shift, two trucks could be assembled each day. If large orders for identical trucks were involved, it was possible to assemble three trucks per day. Quality declined whenever the pace became quicker. HDT officials had decided they could not grow and became satisfied with their niche in the very-heavy-truck market. With only two exceptions, since 1970, HDT had always had at least a four-month backlog of orders. In the 1960s, its best market had been airports, but since 1980 its best market had been for oil-field equipment, first for the North Slope in Alaska and then for the Middle East. The U.S. military was also a regular customer.

In late 2002, HDT received an order for 50 heavy trucks to be used in the oil fields of Saudi Arabia. The terms of sale were delivery on or before July 1, 2003, at the Port of Doha, Saudi Arabia. Specifically, HDT would receive $172,000 per truck in U.S. funds FAS (free alongside ship) at the discharging vessel in Doha, which meant that HDT was responsible for all transportation costs up until the time and point the trucks were discharged from the ship's tackle at Doha. Once each truck was unloaded, HDT would be paid for it.

Chris Reynolds, production manager at HDT, estimated that production could start approximately April 1, 2003, and the order would take 18 working days to complete. Because weekends were involved, all 50 trucks would be completed by April 20 to 25. Reynolds thought that May 1, 2003, was a more realistic completion date because he had always found it difficult to restrict the assembly line to constructing trucks for only one account. The reason for this was that Vic Guillou, HDT's sales manager, liked to have trucks being built for as many accounts as possible on the assembly line at any one time. Prospective buyers frequently visited the plant and were always more impressed when they could see a diverse collection of models being built for a wide range of uses.

Norman Pon, HDT's treasurer, wanted to give priority to building trucks that were being sold on an FOB plant basis because that would improve his cash flow position. At the time the $172,000 price had been set on the truck sale to Saudi Arabia, Pon had argued (unsuccessfully) that the price was too low. Guillou, on the other hand, argued that the sale was necessary because the Arab world represented a growth market by anyone's definition, and he wanted HDT trucks there. HDT's president, Gordon Robertson, had sided with Guillou. Robertson thought that Pon was a good treasurer but too much of a worrier when it came to making important decisions. Pon, in turn, thought that Robertson had yet to shed the image he had acquired in the 1980s when his late father was president of HDT. Pon had lost count of the number of times the elder Robertson had needed cash to buy his son's way out of some embarrassing situation. Guillou was young Robertson's fraternity roommate in college, and Pon thought the two of them shared a similar love of life in the fast lane. At the time the order was signed in 2002, Guillou argued that the FAS destination port represented the best terms of sale because ocean charter rates were declining as a result of an oversupply of tonnage. Guillou predicted that by mid-2003 charter rates would be so low that the cheapest method of transport would be to load all 50 trucks on one vessel. Pon countered that HDT should try to make a profit only from the manufacture of trucks because nobody in the firm knew much about ocean shipping. Robertson, who was a gambler at heart, disagreed.

In March 2003, Reynolds had the 50-truck order scheduled to be on the line from April 2 to 29, which represented 2.5 trucks per working day. Other work was scheduled for the assembly line at the same time, so the production schedule was considered firm. Component parts for the oil-field trucks and for the other trucks were already arriving. Orders were backlogged for over seven months, the highest figure since 1989. This was due, almost in total, to Guillou's additional sales of oil-field equipment to Arab producers. Three separate orders were involved and totaled 115 trucks.

Robertson and Guillou left Crown Point for an industry convention in San Diego. Robertson phoned from San Diego that he and Guillou had decided to vacation in Mexico for a while before returning to Crown Point. Robertson knew that HDT could function in his absence and knew that with Pon overseeing operations, the company's assets would be safe. Several days later, a Mexican postcard postmarked in Tijuana arrived, saying that both were enjoying Mexico and would stay longer than initially planned.

Pon was relieved to learn that Guillou and Robertson would be gone for a longer time and immediately began wondering what types of bills they were accumulating in Mexico and for which ones they would want company

reimbursement. Both had several credit cards belonging to the company. Based on experience, Pon also expected Robertson to phone on his cell phone for a cash advance or transfer about once a week. (Robertson did not want charge records generated for some of his expenses.) As usual, Pon started wondering how paying for the Robertson and Guillou vacation venture would affect HDT's cash flow. Pon looked at his cash flow projections, which were always made up for six weeks in advance, in this case through the first of April, when some of the bills for components of the oil-field trucks would come due. In fact, if Reynolds's schedule were adhered to, all the components would be on hand by April 10 and, if HDT were to receive the customary discounts, all of the components would have to be paid for in the period between April 8 and April 20 (HDT received a 1 percent discount for goods paid for within 10 days of actual or requested receipt, whichever came later). For a moment, Pon thought that the worst might happen: The component bills would be due at the same time as Robertson's and Guillou's request for a hefty cash advance. He called the Crown Point Bank and Trust Company, where HDT had a line of credit, and learned that the current rate was 8 percent per annum. He then asked Bob Vanderpool, who was HDT's traffic manager, when the oil-field trucks would arrive in Saudi Arabia.

"I don't know," was Vanderpool's reply. "I assumed that Guillou had arranged for transportation at the time you decided to charge $172,000 per truck, but I'll check further." He did and phoned back to tell Pon that Guillou's secretary could find nothing in the files to indicate that Guillou had checked out charter rates. "That figures," muttered Pon. "Would you mind doing some checking?" Vanderpool said he *would* mind doing some checking. Pon then suggested to him that there were several other newer orders also destined for the Arab countries so Vanderpool should start thinking about widening his area of expertise. Vanderpool reluctantly agreed, and Pon heard nothing until Vanderpool passed him in the hall a few days later and said the assignment was much more time-consuming than he had imagined. One week later, Vanderpool said he had done as much as he could and would turn the figures over to Pon. Vanderpool also said that he did not have the authority to charter a ship and suggested that Pon determine who could do so in Robertson's absence. Later that day, Vanderpool came to Pon's office with a thick file.

"It looks like you've been doing a lot of figuring," said Pon.

"No, not me," said Vanderpool, "but two outsiders. One is Bob Guider, an international freight forwarder in Chicago whom we use for our export parts shipments. And he put me in touch with Eddie Quan, a New York ship broker who is on top of the charter market. We have two alternatives."

"What are they?" asked Pon.

"Well," answered Vanderpool, "the St. Lawrence Seaway will open in mid-April, so we could use it. The problem is that the Seaway route is circuitous, especially to reach the Arab countries. Also, there aren't many scheduled Seaway sailings to that area, and because the Seaway will just be opening again, cargo space is hard to come by. Therefore, if we're not going to charter a ship, the best bet is to use Baltimore."

"What about chartering a ship?" asked Pon. "Why not use Baltimore for that?"

"In theory, we could," answered Vanderpool. "But Quan says the size of ship we want is rather small and not likely to be sailing into Baltimore. We could arrange to share a ship with another party, but many bulk cargoes are pretty dusty and might not be compatible with our vehicles. Quan says there is one foreign vessel entering the Great Lakes in April that is still looking for an outbound charter. Seaway vessels, you know, are smaller because of the lock size restrictions. If we want to charter that vessel, we'll have to move quickly, because if somebody else charters her, she's gone."

"What kind of vessel is it?" asked Pon.

"The vessel's name is the *Nola Pino,* the same name as a French movie actress of the 1960s. You may recall that some Greek shipping magnate named the vessel after her, but his wife made him give up both Nola Pino the actress and *Nola Pino* the ship. At present, it's scheduled to be in Chicago the last week in April with a load of cocoa beans and ready for outbound loading May 1. Quan thinks we could charter it for $2,400 per day for 30 days, which would be enough time for it to load, transit the Seaway, reach Doha, and discharge the trucks by May 29 or 30."

"Tell me about the alternative," said Pon.

"Baltimore has fairly frequent sailings to the area we want to reach," said Vanderpool. "We could load two trucks per day on railcars here and send them to Baltimore. Two ships a week are scheduled from Baltimore to Doha. It would take the trucks an average of 4 days to reach Baltimore, where they would wait an average of 3 days to be loaded aboard ship. The figure should be 3.5 days, but the railroad will hustle if it knows we're trying to connect with an outgoing sailing. Sailing time to Doha averages 15 days—a little more, a little less, depending on the amount of cargo to be handled at ports in between."

"That averages 22 days per truck," stated Pon, who had been putting the figures in his calculator. What are the charges?"

Vanderpool answered, "It costs $120 to load and block two trucks on a flatcar, which is, of course, $60 apiece as long as they move in pairs. Sticking to pairs, the rail rate for two on a flatcar totals $1,792 to Baltimore. Handling at Baltimore is $200 per truck, and ocean freight rate from Baltimore to Doha is $1,440 per truck. We also have to buy insurance, which is about $150 per truck."

"That totals $2,790," said Pon, after consulting his calculator. "What are the costs if we charter the *Nola Pino?* You said it could be $72,000 for the vessel. What else is involved?"

"There are two ways of getting the trucks to port," said Vanderpool. "The loading and blocking would be only $40 per truck because we'd be doing all 50 at one time. The rail rate per truck would average out to $180 each, and it would take 1 day for them to reach Chicago and another day to be loaded. We'd be tying up a wharf for 1 day, and the wharfage charge runs $2 per foot, and the *Nola Pino* is 535 feet long. We'd be responsible for loading and stowing the cargo, and this would cost $4,000 for all 50 trucks. The Seaway tolls are $1.80 cents per ton or, in our case, $54 per truck. At Doha, the unloading costs will be $4,200 for the entire vessel. Marine insurance will be $210 per truck."

"Are there any other alternatives?" asked Pon.

"The only other one that comes close is to drive the trucks from here to Chicago," answered Vanderpool. "We would need temporary licenses and a convoy permit and pay to have the fuel tank on each truck drained before it is loaded. The problem is that the convoy would cross state lines, and we would need temporary licenses and permits in Illinois as well. We'd also need 50 drivers and have to pay for their time and for their trips back home."

"Do me one favor," said Pon. "Please call Frank Wood, our outside counsel, and ask him what steps we have to go through to charter a ship. Tell him I'm especially concerned about the liability. Give him Quan's phone number. I want to make sure there are no more costs involved. If Robertson's fooling around is on schedule, he'll be phoning me asking that I cable cash. I'd really appreciate it if you would summarize what you've told me in two columns, with the charter costs on the left and the overland Baltimore cost column on the right. Then when Robertson calls, I can ask him to decide."

"One question," asked Vanderpool.

"Shoot," responded Pon.

"Why should the charter figures be on the left?"

"Because on a map (see Exhibit 12-A), Chicago is to the left of Baltimore and that's the only way I'll keep them straight when I'm talking on the phone." ■

EXHIBIT 12-A   Map of the Northeastern United States

QUESTIONS

1. Assume you are Vanderpool. Draft the comparison Pon just requested.
2. Which of the two routing alternatives would you recommend? Why?
3. Assume that the buyer in Saudi Arabia has made other large purchases in the United States and is considering consolidating all its purchases and loading them onto one large ship, which the buyer will charter. The buyer contacts HDT and, although acknowledging its commitment to buy FAS Doha, asks how much HDT would subtract from the $172,000 per truck price if the selling terms were changed to FOB HDT's Crown Point plant. How much of a cost reduction do you think HDT should offer the buyer? Under what terms and conditions?
4. Answer question 3 with regard to changing the terms of sale to delivery at port in Baltimore. The buyer would unload the trucks from the railcars.
5. Is there an interest rate that would make HDT change from one routing to another? If so, what is it?
6. Assume that it is the year 2005, and the cost to HDT of borrowing money is 12 percent per year. Because the buyer will pay for trucks as they are delivered, would it be advantageous for HDT to pay overtime to speed up production, ship the trucks as they are finished via the Port of Baltimore, and collect its payment earlier? Why or why not?

CASE 12-2 BELLE TZELL CELL COMPANY

Headquartered in Tucson, Arizona, the Belle Tzell Cell Company manufactured one standard-size battery for use in portable power tools and in military weapons. Nell Tzell was the company's current president. Her mother, Belle, had retired from active management 10 years earlier, although she and several of Nell's aunts still owned a controlling interest in the company. Belle and her late husband, Del, had founded the firm in 1945, and it had prospered by selling batteries and dry cells to a number of electronics firms that had sprung up in the Arizona–New Mexico area after World War II.

Toward the end of her presidency, in the late 1960s, Belle had taken one action that increased the capacity of the firm. In response to a bid by the Mexican government, she had moved part of her operations south of the border into Nogales to take advantage of low-cost Mexican labor and to quell Belle's fears that both the U.S. and Arizona governments would increase their controls on pollution and require safer working conditions for employees. The Mexican government provided a low-cost loan and required Belle to enter into a partnership with a Mexican citizen, who would own 51 percent of the Belle Tzell Cell Company's Mexican operation. The operation that Belle moved to Nogales was the facility for making lead panels. This operation involved combining strong acids with lead and was considered hazardous to employee health. Noxious vapors damaged the workers' lungs, and the acidic wastes left over from the curing processes were dumped into a nearby streambed, killing aquatic life for at least 10 miles downstream.

Belle retired a few months after the Nogales plant went into production and told Nell that it would take "only a few more months to get the bugs out." That was well over 25 years ago, and if anything, the bugs had increased. Although actual production costs remained low and the Mexican plant was still nonunion, its production was very undependable. Because it was under Mexican ownership, the Mexican who owned 51 percent of the stock insisted that most of the plant's management be Mexican also. However, neither the Mexican who owned the 51 percent of the stock nor most Mexicans capable of managing the operation cared to live in Nogales. They preferred the bright lights of Mexico City. The plant's workforce was continually changing. Despite the fact that wages were high by Mexican standards, new workers soon suffered either burns from acid splashes or lung irritation because of the fumes and would leave. Because Nogales was just south of the U.S.–Mexican border, Mexican workers preferred to cross the border illegally and work at higher-paying jobs in the United States until they were found by U.S. immigration authorities and deported. Also, maquiladoras were also developing in the area just south of the border, and they offered other employment opportunities.

Although Nell would have preferred to close her Nogales lead panel plant, the cost of establishing such a facility in the United States made such a move impossible. This was because of the new worker safety requirements of the federal government, operating through the Occupational Safety and Health Administration (OSHA), and new controls on air and water pollution and toxic waste disposal administered by the U.S. Environmental Protection Agency (EPA).

Transportation costs for delivering acids to the plant would also be very high because carriers considered them to be an extremely hazardous material requiring specialized, expensive trailer tanks to avoid acid spills.

Although the Mexicans were capable of turning out high-quality products, lax supervision resulted in wide variations in the quality of the final product. Sometimes, this would not be noticed until the workers in the Tucson plant attempted to install the lead plates that had been received from Nogales.

Relatively little of the Tzell Company's operations were in Tucson. Their offices were on the second floor of a building, cramped on a narrow lot with little room for expansion. Downstairs, the lead plates from Nogales were combined with printed circuits from Taiwan and placed inside plastic cases purchased from one of several suppliers in Tucson. Each day's production filled two 35-foot trailers parked at the north end of the building. At night, the two trailer loads would be delivered to various major buyers. The Tucson plant was operating at capacity and rarely ever caught up with sales. Several times Nell had wanted to increase the number of production lines, but she was unable

to expand the building at its present site. In addition, Nell's aunts, who still controlled the company, were unwilling to allow her to relocate to a new site or larger plant because the financial resources required for the move would cut into their current incomes.

The present Tucson plant was a long, narrow building set in a north–south direction between two parallel streets. The south side fronted on 17th Street and contained a receiving dock that was built to accommodate only one trailer. Street parking was not allowed on 17th Street, and neighbors would complain to the Tucson Police Department if a truck parked on the street for even a few minutes. The building stretched north, with the east and west sides within a foot of their respective lot lines. The north end of the building was on 16th Street. Here was a large parking lot used by employees and the loading dock that could accommodate three trailers. Prior to the opening of the Nogales plant, the employee parking lot was filled every day, with all 32 slots occupied. Today, only about 10 slots were used because employees were using carpools and local buses. Even Nell was in a carpool, sharing rides with David Kupferman, her operations manager, who lived several homes away on the same street.

Kupferman had worked for the Tzell Company for only a few weeks, and as he and Nell were driving from work one day, she said, "Dave, you know I'm caught between two rocks and two hard places. My mother and aunts won't let me expand here in Tucson, and our Nogales plant produces more ulcers than anything else. Your predecessor left because the strain of coordinating the two plants was too great. Believe it or not, the majority of our operations take place in Nogales. You'd better visit there, soon, to see what it's like."

"I can hardly wait," responded Kupferman. "After my last argument with them over poor quality, I'm afraid they'll dunk my head in an acid vat if I ever set foot inside that plant. How come you became so dependent on Mexico for your operations?"

Nell explained the reasons, and added, "For many years the savings gave us a competitive edge. In cost or money terms, two-thirds of our operation is now down in Nogales."

"Two-thirds?" asked Kupferman. "That seems high. How do you figure it?"

"Look at it this way," said Nell. "We take in a little over $4 million per year, or about $16,000 per working day. We spend about $15,000 per working day. Of that, about $10,000 is spent at Nogales for labor, raw materials, and overhead. We spend just over $1,000 a day moving the lead plates from Nogales here, although $800 of that is import duties on the lead plates. Here in Tucson, our manufacturing operation takes only about $3,000 per day, about two-thirds for labor and one-third for the printed circuits and plastic battery cases. The remainder of the money goes for companywide overhead and for profit."

"I see," said Kupferman. "How, then, do you see the problems?"

Nell answered, "First of all, our problems are caused by our success in selling. Right now we have a backlog of orders, but I am unable to expand capacity either here or in Nogales. Mother and my aunts won't allow major capital improvements, and although I might be able to build a small addition to the north of the Tucson plant, the cost would be prohibitive, especially when one considers the small increase in capacity that would result."

"It's too bad your family won't let you expand more," offered Kupferman.

"Actually, I don't blame them," said Nell. "Our business is really volatile, and I've also been unable to interest serious outside investors in helping me expand. Several bankers told me that I'd have to get my production act together before I should think about either expanding or borrowing much outside money. Right now, the banks will loan me any working capital I want at 12 percent, if it's secured by inventories or equipment. However, I'm unable to assemble enough funds for any type of expansion."

"I still don't understand your coordination problem," said Kupferman. "Your Nogales plant produces one trailer load of battery plates per day, which is exactly the input you need for a day's output at Tucson. The battery plates can be trucked at night, and if you can get your quality control act together at Nogales, you'd have a smooth, continuous operation."

"I hate to say this," said Nell, "but your predecessor said just about the same thing eight months ago. And like you, he thought that quality control at Nogales was the key to solving my problem."

"So what did he do wrong?" asked Kupferman.

"He was going to use a two-pronged approach, which I'll tell you about in the office," said Nell as she wheeled her Porsche from 16th Street into the company parking lot. "Get a cup of coffee, and we'll continue this conversation in my office," she said as they climbed the stairs to the second floor offices.

Kupferman got two cups of coffee, walked into her office, and sat down. Nell was looking through her messages and exclaimed, "Damn it, it happened again! We just got penalized $3,000 because of a late delivery to Jedson Electronic Tools. They were late on delivering a government order and decided we were responsible because our delivery was late, which it was. The purchase order to us had a penalty clause in it, and now they're going to collect. This is exactly the problem we have to lick! The Nogales plant either misses making a shipment or sends a load of such poor quality that we can't use it right away. We then assign our people here to other tasks for the day, such as inserting only the printed circuits into the plastic cases. They do this until the battery plates arrive, and then they add all the battery plates. At the end of 2 days we're caught up, except that yesterday we made no deliveries and yesterday's promised output is 1 day late. That's why we lose customers. To them, we're just another tardy supplier. Right now the industry practice is to specify a delivery date, with cost penalties included for either early or late deliveries. Indeed, some of our customers are adopting JIT inventory systems and are trying to specify a 60-minute window during which they'll accept our daily deliveries. They won't accept deliveries earlier, and late ones will be penalized. Our major competitors are already dancing to this tune, and we will have no choice but to follow."

"How often do we have this kind of problem—when we can't make deliveries because of some foul-up in our quality?" asked Kupferman.

"For a long time, it was only once a month or so," responded Nell, "but as we reached our plants' capacity and there was less slack, the problem has been happening almost weekly. One week, about two months ago, we hit the jackpot and had three days in a row of bad production. That threw us out of kilter for nearly two weeks, even after paying overtime both here and at Nogales. That's when your predecessor's ulcer started bleeding, and he left. Too bad, too, because I think he was just about ready to solve our problem."

"What changes had he intended to make?" asked Kupferman.

"Well," responded Nell, "your predecessor had studied probability in college and had computed the chances of foul-ups in Nogales occurring one right after the other. He calculated that we should close down our Tucson plant for five days or have the Nogales plant run five days of overtime so that it could produce a five-day supply of lead battery plates. He said that if we kept the Nogales plant scheduled so that there was always five days' worth of plates between Nogales and Tucson, we would never have to be out of usable lead battery plates here in Tucson."

"If his calculations are accurate, why haven't you implemented his plan?" asked Kupferman.

"We couldn't figure out where to store the approximately five loads of battery plates," responded Nell. "It's more complicated than you think. Here, let me read to you your predecessor's memo, written while he was recovering from surgery, no less. It says, and I quote, 'There are three alternatives: warehousing in Nogales, warehousing here in Tucson, or leasing five truck trailers and parking them either outside the Nogales plant or in the 16th Street parking lot here in Tucson.'" Nell looked at Kupferman

directly and continued, "David, what I want you to do is to figure out the costs of these three alternatives and get back to me with a recommendation."

Kupferman took his empty coffee cup, walked back to his office, and started gathering the cost figures Nell had asked for. He discovered that to warehouse the five loads of lead battery plates in Nogales would cost $300 per week, plus $120 per week for local drayage in Nogales (i.e., trucking the plates from the plant to the warehouse). To truck the plates directly from the Nogales plant to a Tucson warehouse rather than to the Tzell Tucson plant was the second alternative. Few Tucson warehouses wanted to touch the business for fear that the plates would contaminate other merchandise they were storing. The best quote Kupferman could get was for $350 per week plus a requirement that the Tzell Cell Company provide a bond to protect the warehouseman from damages the plates might cause. Local drayage costs within Tucson from the warehouse to Tzell's 17th Street receiving dock would be $150 per week.

The trailer idea involved leasing five trailers, loading them with battery plates, and parking them at either the Nogales plant or at the 16th Street parking lot. Trailers could be leased and licensed for use in both Mexico and Arizona for $7,000 per year each. In addition, a used truck–tractor, costing approximately $15,000, would have to be purchased and used for shifting trailers around the plants where they were stored. The truck–tractor would have a useful life of five years.

The advantage of storing the trailers at Nogales was to delay the payment of import duties of about $800 per trailer load of battery plates. However, a problem with the current system was that Mexican border agents, sensing the urgency in the Tzell shipments, attempted to shake down the Tzell drivers to let the trailers exit from Mexico. Trailers were subject to delays and sometimes would be searched thoroughly to make certain that they were carrying no works of art or Mexican national treasures. One Mexican agent—nicknamed "Pancho Villa"—inspected trailers ever so slowly, complaining aloud that the reason he moved slowly was that he was depressed by the fact that Christmas was coming (no matter what month it happened to be) and that he lacked sufficient money to buy gifts for all of his very extended family.

Kupferman had yet to visit the Nogales plant, but before presenting his findings to Tzell, he wanted to make certain that the parking lot at the Nogales plant was fenced. He phoned Juan Perez, the plant manager, who said very little until he realized that Kupferman was not calling to complain about something. Perez answered Kupferman's query by saying that the yard was not fenced but that it would be possible to park the loaded trailers with their closed rear doors against a solid masonry wall, making entry impossible. "Besides," he added, "this plant has such a bad reputation for causing illness and injury that no local thief would come within a mile of it."

Kupferman was trying to think of a witty response and the Nogales manager continued, "But you said 'up to five trailers.' Why so many?"

Kupferman told him of his predecessor's calculations that the Nogales plant should produce five days of output in advance of that needed by the Tucson plant.

"Why so many?" repeated Perez.

"To make sure that Tucson never has to shut down or be late with orders," answered Kupferman. "The only reason we have problems here is because of delayed or poor-quality shipments from you. When Tucson falls behind, we can't make deliveries, and that costs us money."

"Nonsense!" responded Perez. "You blame all your problems on us. Let me tell you two things. First, not all production delays are caused down here. It's just that we're not in the same building as the home office, and we tend to get blamed for everything. Second, because the Tucson plant makes a single standard product, it would be cheaper to have it produce a day or two's inventory in advance, ready to use in case either the Tucson plant or my operation fouls up. You'll have to excuse me now. We've just had another acid spill."

Kupferman heard a click and then a humming sound. He hung up. He decided to walk to Nell's office and tell her what Perez had said.

She admitted that Perez was correct, "just a little bit," about some of the delays being at the Tucson plant. In fact, she conceded that Kupferman's predecessor had overlooked the problems at the Tucson assembly line when he made his calculations that the Nogales plant produce a five-day advance supply of battery plates as a cushion. She told Kupferman to start over and assume that delays could occur by conditions in either plant or both. She felt that Kupferman would find that sales should be cut back for a few days so that either or both plants could turn out some advance production that would serve as a continual cushion of safety stock. She wanted enough inventory in reserve that the Tzell Cell Company could fill 99 percent of all orders on time. Kupferman would have six months to set up the system and another six months to test and debug it. After that, he would be expected to maintain a 99 percent performance level of filling orders on time.

During the next few days of ride sharing, Nell and Kupferman talked about everything except work. Nell commented that she missed seeing him at the community swimming pool. Kupferman responded that he had been spending his time indoors, studying probability.

After several weeks, Kupferman had finally calculated the probabilities that would allow Tzell Cell Company to maintain Nell's required 99 percent level of on-time deliveries. First of all, his predecessor had been correct, insofar as he had calculated. One solution was to have the Nogales plant produce five days' worth of battery cell plates in advance of the Tucson plant. This was because the Tucson plant was responsible for only two of the delivery delays in a year of 250 working days. However, Kupferman also made calculations about the sizes of completed stocks for the Tucson plant to manufacture in advance and keep as a safety stock cushion. If the Tucson plant produced and maintained as safety stock one day's output of completed batteries, the Nogales plant would only have to maintain a four-day lead in production of lead battery plates ahead of their use in Tucson. If the Tucson plant produced in advance and maintained as safety stock two days' output of completed batteries, the Nogales plant would have to produce only two days' worth of battery plates in advance of their use in the Tucson plant. And if the Tucson plant made three days' output in advance and held it as safety stock, the Nogales plant would not have to produce a surplus of plates in advance of what was required each day in Tucson. That is, each night the truck would leave with the Nogales output and drive to Tucson, where the plates would be used the next day. Even if there were problems with the shipment from Nogales, there would be a three-day safety stock of finished batteries in Tucson.

Kupferman intended to determine warehousing costs for the safety stocks of completed batteries in Tucson, but Nell told him to plan on using the trailer idea instead. The trailers would be parked in the 16th Street lot. At night they would be parked so that no doors were exposed. For $3,000, the lot's fence could be made more secure and a gate would be added. Nell told Kupferman to use carrying costs of 25 percent per year on both the work-in-process (plates) and finished goods (batteries).

Kupferman took a clipboard with a pad of paper and made four columns, one for each of the alternatives:

1. Five days' worth of plates in Nogales; no extra batteries in Tucson
2. Four days' worth of plates in Nogales; one day's worth of batteries in Tucson
3. Two days' worth of plates in Nogales; two days' worth of batteries in Tucson
4. No extra plates in Nogales; three days' worth of batteries in Tucson

Each alternative would give the firm the ability to provide a 99 percent or better level of on-time order filling. ∎

QUESTIONS

1. What are the total inventory carrying costs of alternative 1?
2. What are the total inventory carrying costs of alternative 2?
3. What are the total inventory carrying costs of alternative 3?
4. What are the total inventory carrying costs of alternative 4?
5. Which alternative do you think Kupferman should recommend? Why?
6. Tzell "wanted enough inventory in reserve that the Tzell Cell Company could fill 99 percent of all orders on time." This is, as you may recall, a customer service standard. How reasonable is a 99 percent level? Why not, say, a 95 percent level? How would Nell and Kupferman determine the relative advantages and disadvantages of the 95 percent and the 99 percent service levels? What kind of cost calculations would they have to make?
7. Jedson Electronic Tools invoked a penalty clause on a purchase order that Tzell Cell Company had accepted, and the Tzell Cell Company had to forfeit $3,000. Draft, for Nell Tzell's signature, a memo indicating when and under what conditions the Belle Tzell Cell Company should accept penalty clauses in purchase orders covering missed delivery times or "windows."
8. In your opinion, is it ethical for a U.S.-based firm to relocate some of its operations in Mexico to avoid the stricter U.S. pollution and worker-safety laws? Why or why not?
9. Should the firm be willing to pay bribes at the Mexican border to get its shipments cleared more promptly? Why or why not?

III

ORGANIZING, ANALYZING, AND CONTROLLING LOGISTICS SYSTEMS

Parts 1 and 2 presented an overview of logistics and focused on the individual components of the logistics portions of the supply chain. Part 3 examines methods of organizing, analyzing, and controlling logistics as used by a firm and those firms with which it is linked.

Chapter 13 examines the various control systems that must be implemented to ensure that the logistics system operates efficiently. Controls are also needed to minimize losses from pilferage and theft. Since September 11, 2001, concern has increased regarding the vulnerability of the logistics channel.

Chapter 14 focuses on the techniques of organizing and analyzing logistics systems. These techniques are designed to isolate and reduce inefficiencies in logistics operations.

CHAPTER

13

LOGISTICS SYSTEMS CONTROLS

"Write a letter to Santa? It's easier just to break into his computer distribution system."

Even the most traditional supply chains are vulnerable.

Source: Cartoon copyright © 1992 Harley Schwadron. Distributed by Sandhill Arts. Reprinted with permission.

Key Terms

- Activity-based costing
- Batch number
- Container Security Initiative (CSI)
- Control
- Customs Trade Partnership Against Terrorism (C-TPAT)
- Graphical information systems (GIS)
- Pilferage
- Product recall
- Productivity
- Short-interval scheduling
- System security
- Theft (stealing)
- Transponders
- Transportation Worker Identification Credential (TWIC)

Learning Objectives

- To examine accounting control in a logistics system
- To learn about worker productivity
- To discuss issues associated with returned goods management
- To learn about theft and ways to manage it
- To examine the impact of terrorism on logistics systems

Logistics management would be relatively easy if it entailed only establishing a logistics system and then putting it into operation. However, well-run organizations recognize that logistics systems, once operational, need to be controlled. Indeed, control mechanisms should be built into a logistics system as it is being designed, and the controls should be continually monitored. **Control** refers to measurement that ensures conformity with an organization's policies, procedures, or standards. For example, budgets are a form of accounting control. In the early stages, budgets are planning mechanisms and a means of fulfilling corporate goals. After being approved, budgets become a control mechanism.

This chapter focuses on logistics systems controls and is of special importance to those training for an entry-level position in supply chain management. Much of one's initial performance with a new employer is evaluated on the basis of how well the employee exercises control responsibilities. This chapter focuses primarily on controlling functions that are somewhat protective in nature and must be employed to keep a firm's position from worsening. In a competitive world with small and shrinking profit margins, application of tight controls may enable a firm to maintain its position while competitors fall behind.

Special attention is paid to logistics and supply chain security issues, in part because the terrorist attacks of September 11, 2001, have caused many organizations to look at security issues from a much broader perspective. As an example, tank trucks carrying gasoline or corrosive chemicals could be used as moving bombs. Figure 13-1 shows a device fitted onto a Kenworth truck that reads fingerprints; the driver's prints would need to be on file for the vehicle to be started.

The word *control* is chosen deliberately. The topics discussed in this chapter cannot be eliminated; they can only be controlled. Persons involved in logistics management will confront the issues and problems presented in this chapter on a regular basis during the course of their careers.

FIGURE 13-1 Device in a Kenworth Truck for Reading and Matching Fingerprints

According to a Kenworth press release "When the driver's fingerprint is verified . . . the vehicle can be operated at normal traffic speeds. If the fingerprint doesn't match, the vehicle can still be started but at a severely restricted horsepower, thus limiting operation to well below normal speeds." The fleet dispatcher also receives a wireless message saying that an unauthorized driver is moving the truck. The dispatcher also has the ability to use a wireless system to disable the truck. *Source:* Kenworth Truck Company.

ACCOUNTING CONTROLS

One challenge with respect to accounting controls is that accountants often view control mechanisms in terms of monetary costs (or value), whereas logisticians can view control mechanisms from either a monetary or a nonmonetary perspective. For example, accountants measure inventory in terms of its dollar value, whereas logisticians measure inventory in terms of the number of stock-keeping units (SKUs), and these different measurements can result in managerial disconnects. If one has an inventory of grain, its monetary value fluctuates based on the appropriate commodity exchange rates, even though the actual quantity and quality remain unchanged.

In addition, in times of inflation, identical items added to inventory at different times means that each unit has a different cost, and even though inventory levels are not affected, it makes a difference whether an organization uses historic cost or current value as an indicator of the inventory's total value. Or, consider the concept of depreciation, which reduces the monetary value of inventory by a certain amount per period of time, even though the actual quantity of inventory may be unchanged. Both authors have consulting experiences with companies that showed a particular SKU to be fully depreciated, with an accounting value of $0—while the companies' warehousing facilities contained several hundred units of physical inventory of the particular SKU.

One approach to accounting controls involves the use of standard costs and flexible budgets. With standard costs, an organization must establish standard or acceptable costs for each activity, and then the organization must determine acceptable deviations from these standard costs. Suppose, for example, that the established standard cost for handling pallets is $3.00 per pallet and that the actual per pallet handling cost in a given time period is $3.10. Although some organizations might tolerate the $.10 per pallet cost overrun, others might not.

The standard costs should be applied to activities to determine their reasonable budget; if the standard cost of handling a pallet is $3, and 10,000 pallets are handled in a particular time period, then $30,000 should be budgeted for handling pallets. If the standard costs per unit change as the volume handled changes, this also should be reflected in the budget. The budget is flexible in the sense that it is tied to actual activity.

Another approach to accounting controls that has become popular in logistics in recent years is activity-based costing. **Activity-based costing (ABC)** is focused on better understanding the cost of a product by identifying what activities drive particular costs. Unlike traditional accounting techniques, activity-based costing attempts to trace an expense category to a particular cost object. With activity-based costing, cost objects consume activities, and activities consume resources.[1]

Activity-based costing consists of five steps:

- Identify activities
- Determine cost for each activity
- Determine cost drivers
- Collect activity data
- Calculate product cost[2]

This five-step ABC process will be illustrated by the following hypothetical example. Suppose that a company is interested in applying the ABC process to its order cycle process for two products that it sells. You might recall that the order cycle consists of four primary activities—order transmittal, order processing, order picking and assembly, order delivery. So, we've identified the relevant activities (step 1); next comes a determination of cost for each activity, as shown in Table 13-1. Step 3 requires us to determine cost drivers, and in this example they are order transmittal → number of orders; order processing → number of

TABLE 13-1   Cost for Each Activity

Activity	Cost
Order transmittal	$ 1,000
Order processing	$ 3,000
Order picking and assembly	$12,000
Order delivery	$ 6,000

[1] www.pitt.edu/~roztocki.
[2] Ibid.

TABLE 13-2	Activity Data and Product Cost Calculation				
Activity	**Cost**	**Product 1 data**	**Product 1 cost**	**Product 2 data**	**Product 2 cost**
Order transmittal	$ 1,000	3 orders	$ 300	7 orders	$ 700
Order processing	$ 3,000	4 activities	$ 1,200	6 activities	$1,800
Order picking and assembly	$12,000	110 boxes	$ 6,600	90 boxes	$5,400
Order delivery	$ 6,000	30 locations	$ 4,500	10 locations	$1,500
Total	$22,000		$12,600		$9,400

processing activities; order picking and assembly → number of boxes; order delivery → number of delivery locations.

The two remaining steps, activity data and product cost calculation, appear in Table 13-2. With respect to order transmittal, three orders were received for Product 1 and seven orders for Product 2, for a total of 10 orders. Because Product 1 accounts for 30 percent of the total orders (3/10), the relevant transmittal cost is $300, which represents 30 percent of the $1,000 total order transmittal cost. Likewise, because Product 2 accounts for 70 percent (7/10) of the total orders, its relevant transmittal costs are $700. The product costs for the three other activities are calculated in a similar fashion. Note that the data in Table 13-2 indicate that the total order cycle cost is $22,000; according to the ABC process, Product 1 is responsible for $12,600 in costs, and Product 2 is responsible for $9,400.

Before concluding this brief discussion of ABC, it's important to recognize that the cost drivers can vary from organization to organization and should be driven by company-specific considerations such as organizational structure, operational structure, and products.[3] For example, in our hypothetical example the number of delivery locations was the cost driver associated with order delivery. Another potential cost driver for order delivery could be the number of customers receiving deliveries.

WORKER PRODUCTIVITY

Productivity is important because it provides insight into the efficiency (or inefficiency) with which corporate resources are being utilized. Improved productivity can reduce an organization's costs, and this could result in stable product prices as well as improved organizational profitability. For example, suppose that one company's truck tractors currently travel 100,000 miles per year, their fuel consumption is five miles per gallon (MPG), and a gallon of fuel costs $2.50. If this company could improve fuel consumption from 5.0 to 5.5 MPG, its annual fuel consumption per tractor would be reduced from 20,000 gallons (100,000 miles per year divided by 5 MPG) to 18,182 gallons (100,000 divided by 5.5). Likewise, the annual fuel bill per tractor would be reduced from $50,000 (20,000 gallons times $2.50 per gallon) to $45,455 (18,182 times $2.50)—a savings of $4,545 per tractor. Although this might not seem like a very impressive number, consider that a company with 1,000 tractors could save $4,545,000 in fuel costs, whereas a carrier with 10,000 tractors could save over $45,000,000 in fuel costs.

At a basic level, **productivity** can be defined as the amount of output divided by the amount of input. An understanding of this relationship leads to the recognition that there are but three ways to improve productivity—reduce the amount of input while holding output constant, increase the amount of output while holding input constant, or increase output while

---

[3]John Karolefski, "Time is Money," *Food Logistics*, June 2004, 18–22.

at the same time decreasing input. Understanding the three ways to improve productivity is important to the logistics manager because several logistics activities, particularly warehousing and transportation, are heavily dependent on human labor. For productivity purposes, human labor is considered an input (i.e., workers receive wages or salaries), and most humans are resistant to productivity suggestions that focus on reducing their wages or salaries (i.e., input). Moreover, in many areas, warehouse workers, drivers, and helpers are unionized, and union contracts make it difficult, if not impossible, to reduce the number of employees or to adjust employee compensation and benefit packages. As such, productivity improvement efforts in logistics are often directed toward *increasing the amount of output while holding input constant.*

Labor productivity can be made more efficient by scheduling work in advance. Industrial engineering techniques can establish acceptable times for performing each task (such as opening a truck door, stacking a pallet, or picking a case of outgoing goods), with the acceptable times varying according to the particular situation. For example, a pallet's location in a warehouse or its height above the floor can affect the acceptable performance times. In addition, picking and assembling an order comprised of cases of different dimensions requires more time than if the cases are of the same size.

The industrial engineering data can be used in at least two ways to improve productivity. First, the goods within a warehousing facility can be arranged so that the more popular or faster-moving items are located in places where they will require less time for storage and retrieval. Second, an order picker's travel sequence can be arranged in a way that minimizes the time that the person (and whatever equipment is being used) will require.

Short-Interval Scheduling

One useful method of analysis, **short-interval scheduling,** involves looking at each worker's activity in small time segments. An amount of time is assigned to each unit of work, and then the individual's work is scheduled in a manner that utilizes as much of each worker's time as possible and maximizes output for each worker.

Short-interval scheduling is useful to supervisory personnel in part because each day's work for the operation is plotted out and is, in essence, a summation of each worker's tasks. For a warehouse, the scheduling may also be tied to departure times for delivery trucks and arrival of trucks with incoming freight. Because an operation's entire workday can be prescheduled, the supervisor can tell as the day progresses how the actual progress compares to the schedule. If at the end of the first hour of an eight-hour shift less than one-eighth of the work has been completed (or at the end of two hours less than one-fourth of the work has been completed, and so on), the supervisor can take steps to catch up by the end of the day.

Short-interval scheduling can also be used by intermediate management to assess the effectiveness of supervision. One firm uses a Lost Time Review report that is filled out by the immediate supervisor on a daily basis. In case the immediate supervisor fails to note or explain the lost time, the information appears on an Unexplained Lost Time form, which intermediate management prepares to cover instances when more time was spent on a job than had been assigned and the immediate supervisor failed to report it.

Managing the Warehouse Worker

Knowledge of supervisory techniques is important to students of logistics because fairly early in their career, they are likely to receive an assignment that includes supervision of others. Some workers are more obviously in need of supervision than others (see Figure 13-2). In addition, the skills of workers assigned to the same task also may vary (see Figure 13-3).

"That new man may bear watching."

FIGURE 13-2 The Objective of Supervision Is to Improve Performance

Source: Reproduced by permission of the artist and the Masters Agency.

FIGURE 13-3 Employees Have Varying Degrees of Skills

Source: Reproduced by permission of the artist and the Masters Agency.

Many supervisors use a three-part approach consisting of performance audit, feedback, and positive reinforcement to manage employees. After a worker's performance is measured, it is important that this information be fed back to the worker so that he or she is aware of it. Once performance information is made available to workers, the next step is to reinforce their good performance with some form of reward—from an approving nod to a year-end bonus.

Many warehousing facilities have clearly articulated work rules that serve a number of purposes, the most important of which is to keep the workforce in general, and individual employees in particular, from engaging in unproductive and potentially destructive activities. Figure 13-4 shows one warehouse's set of work rules, but it's simply not enough to have a set of clearly articulated work rules—to be effective, the work rules must be enforced.

As mentioned earlier in the chapter, the unionization of warehouse workforces can provide a substantial challenge to improving warehousing productivity. This is because union work rules are often very specific in the sense that job descriptions spell out in exacting detail the responsibilities associated with a particular job. Thus, if an order picker's forklift were to malfunction, the order picker might be prohibited from remedying the situation because forklift repairs are the responsibility of another group of workers. Although detailed specifications help create additional jobs, the relative lack of worker flexibility can potentially hinder productivity by increasing inputs (e.g., additional workers, hence additional labor costs) while also decreasing output. For example, the order picker with the malfunctioning forklift may have to delay order picking until the forklift is repaired or another forklift becomes available for use.

In an effort to improve productivity, the contracts that are negotiated with unionized warehousing workers increasingly contain performance-related standards. These performance standards frequently require a great deal of give-and-take between union and management negotiators. There might be give-and-take with respect to the number of performance standards that will be used, as well give-and take in terms of acceptable performance levels for each applicable standard. Union negotiators are looking out for the interests of their members, whereas management may be concerned with the interests of several stakeholder groups, such as customers and investors.

Managing Drivers

A distinction needs to be made between warehousing and trucking when discussing the management of logistics labor. This distinction is important from a productivity perspective, as will become evident in this section. In warehousing, supervisors can be physically present and are expected to be on top of nearly any situation. When a worker in a warehouse falls behind schedule, it is usually noticed relatively quickly, and corrective action can be taken in a timely fashion.

However, once on the road, truck drivers are removed from immediate supervision, and their work becomes more difficult to evaluate. Truck drivers can fall behind schedule or be delayed for a variety of reasons such as traffic conditions, a bottleneck at a loading dock, or perhaps too much time socializing with fellow drivers at a particular truck stop. Initially, a manager has little choice but to accept the driver's explanation for the delay. As such, it is necessary to have a control mechanism so that drivers who often encounter uncontrollable delays (e.g., traffic conditions) can be distinguished from those who encounter controllable delays (e.g., socializing with fellow drivers).

Ours is a company that has been built on service to its customers. Our business has grown both in the number of customers and in the area which we serve. We are constantly striving to improve our service, because it is only through growth and progress that a company can give to its employees the good wages, increased benefits, and job security that everyone wants.

In order to meet these aims it is necessary to adhere to a set of rules. Whenever people work together they have certain rights and privileges. Along with these rights they have certain obligations and responsibilities. So that each employee will know what is expected of him we have drawn up a list of work rules which are necessary for the orderly and efficient operation of our business. By following these rules you contribute to the progress of the company and therefore to the stability of your own job. These rules therefore benefit you rather than hinder you. They are fair rules and to keep them fair to everyone they will be enforced in every required situation.

These rules are listed in two groups, by type of violation, and are as follows:
- Violations subject to discharge on the first offense.
- Violations subject to constructive discipline.

Violations Subject to Discharge on the First Offense

(1) The possession of, drinking of, or use of any alcoholic beverages or narcotic drugs on company property; or being on company premises at any time under the influence of alcohol, or drugs, or while suffering from an alcoholic hangover which materially affects work performance.

(2) The transportation of, or failure to notify the company of, unauthorized persons on company equipment or its property.

(3) Theft or misappropriation of company property or the property of any of its customers or employees.

(4) Deliberate or malicious damage to the company's equipment and warehouse facilities or to the merchandise and property of its customers.

(5) Intentional falsification of records in any form, including ringing another employee's time card, or falsifying employment application.

(6) Fighting while on duty or on company premises or provoking others to fight.

(7) Smoking in a building or van, or any restricted area, or while loading or unloading merchandise and other items.

(8) Immoral or indecent conduct which affects work performance or makes the employee unsuited for the work required.

(9) Unauthorized possession of, or carrying of, firearms or other weapons.

(10) Insubordination — refusal to perform assigned work or to obey a supervisor's order, or encouraging others to disobey such an order.

Violations Subject to Constructive Discipline

The rules printed below are subject to constructive discipline. This means that for the first offense you will be given a constructive reprimand. For a second offense you will receive a disciplinary layoff without pay, the length of which will depend upon the seriousness of the offense; subject to the terms of the collective bargaining agreement which may exist between employee and union. For a third offense you will be discharged, subject to the collective bargaining agreement.

If you have had a violation, followed by a record of no violations for a nine (9) month period, the original violation will be withdrawn from your record.

(1) Excessive tardiness regardless of cause. (Being tardy and not ready to perform work at the designated starting time may at the company's option result in the employee being sent home without pay.)

(2) Absenteeism without just cause and excessive absenteeism regardless of cause. If you must be absent for a justifiable reason notify the company in advance. Justified absence will be

FIGURE 13-4   Sample Warehouse Work Rules

Source: Courtesy of American Warehouse Association.

excused if the company is notified as soon as possible before the beginning of the shift; however, too many justified and excused absences may be grounds for constructive discipline as well as unjustified, unexcused absence. If you are absent from work for three consecutive work days without notification followed by failure to report for work on the fourth day you will automatically be removed from the payroll with the notification "quit without notice."

(3) Failure to work reasonable overtime.

(4) Unauthorized absence from assigned work location.

(5) Failure to observe proper break periods, lunch periods, and quitting times, unless otherwise directed by your supervisor.

(6) Disregard for common rules of safety, safe practices, good housekeeping and sanitation.

(7) Unauthorized or negligent operation or use of machines, tools, vehicles, equipment and materials.

(8) Loss or damage to the property of the company or its customers which could have been reasonably avoided.

(9) Failure to complete work assignments within a reasonable length of time or loafing on such assignments.

(10) Garnishments not satisfied prior to the hearing before the court issuing same.

(11) Gambling on company premises.

(12) Use of immoral, obscene or indecent language on company premises.

(13) Trying to persuade or organize other employees to disobey any of these rules and regulations. ∎

FIGURE 13-4   (Continued)

For example, Figure 13-5 provides the monthly delivery performance of drivers in terms of the number of cases, the weight handled, and the amount of time spent waiting and unloading. "P" indicates that pallets are utilized and that the receiver uses a forklift truck to unload the trailer. "C" means specialized wheeled carts are used instead of pallets. Various comparisons are made, including the average cost per ton and the average cost per case. "ADJ CS/HR" (Adjusted Cases per Hour) takes into account both waiting and unloading time.

The arrangement of data shown in Figure 13-5 can be used, for example, to support a driver's contention that his or her relatively poor performance is caused by delays at the customer's receiving dock. The contention could be verified by having a different driver make deliveries to determine whether the delays still happen. If they do, the supplier could approach the customer with the relevant data and indicate that improvements are needed in the receiving dock procedures.

Technological considerations play an increasingly important role in managing truck drivers and their productivity. For example, some firms photograph or videotape drivers making pickups at their loading docks. Moreover, Figure 13-6 shows the printout of the activity recorded by a *tachograph,* a recording instrument that is installed inside a truck and produces a continuous, timed record of the truck, its speed, and its engine speed. From the information on the tachograph chart, one can tell how efficiently the truck and driver are being used. If the driver works on a regular route, it may be possible to rearrange the stops so that the driver can avoid areas of traffic congestion. Bad driving habits, such as high highway speeds and excessive engine idling, can also be detected. In case of an accident, the

AMALGAMATED FOOD STORE SERVICES INC.   PAGE NO. 2

DELIVERY PERFORMANCE ANALYSIS
WEEK ENDING 11/01/

REPORT NO. 2 —STORE—

DRIVER	P	STORE	CASES	WEIGHT	WAIT	UNLD	CS/HR	ADJ CS/HR
B ,D.	P	AMES MARKET # 7	467	30,699	.1	.3	1,556	1,167
D ,P.	P	AMES MARKET # 7	1,055	6,000	.1	.5	2,110	1,758
F ,J.	P	AMES MARKET # 7	242		.1	.4	605	484
M ,J.	P	AMES MARKET # 7	120		.2	.3	400	240
		TOTAL	1,884	36,699	.5	1.5	1,256	942
F ,J.	C	FORD'S MARKET # 1	1,038	24,525	.1	1.1	943	865
F ,J.	C	FORD'S MARKET # 1	446	14,306	.1	.9	495	446
F ,J.	P	FORD'S MARKET # 1	50	2,000	.1	.2	250	166
		TOTAL	1,534	40,831	.3	2.2	697	613
F ,J.	C	FORD'S MARKET # 2	300	12,000	.1	.7	428	375
M	C	FORD'S MARKET # 2	729		1.2	1.5	486	270
M	C	FORD'S MARKET # 2	1,242	30,420	.1	1.8	690	653
V ,B.		FORD'S MARKET # 2	1		.1	.1	10	5
		TOTAL	2,272	42,420	1.5	4.1	554	405
G A.	C	FORD'S MARKET # 3	913	23,049	.2	1.0	913	760
M	C	FORD'S MARKET # 3	1,200	30,601	.3	1.0	1,200	923
		TOTAL	2,113	53,650	.5	2.0	1,056	845
M	C	FORD'S MARKET # 4	408	10,392	.2	.9	453	370
M J.	C	FORD'S MARKET # 4	671	15,109	.2	.9	745	610
		TOTAL	1,079	25,501	.4	1.8	599	490

FIGURE 13-5   Delivery Performance of Truck Drivers

tachograph chart is invaluable in reporting and explaining what occurred just prior to impact.

The interfaces involving wireless communications, global positioning systems (GPS), and graphical information systems (GIS) offer tremendous technology-related opportunities to improve driver productivity. Global positioning systems use satellites that allow companies to compute vehicle position, velocity, and time, whereas **graphical information systems** allow companies to produce digital maps that can drill down to site-specific qualities such as bridge heights and customer locations. GPS and GIS are evolving toward a situation in which instant updates can be provided to GIS databases—data that can be leveraged to provide real-time route planning that can direct drivers away from accidents and other traffic bottlenecks.[4]

---

[4]Aaron Huff, "Location Isn't Everything," *Commercial Carrier Journal,* October 2002, 62–65.

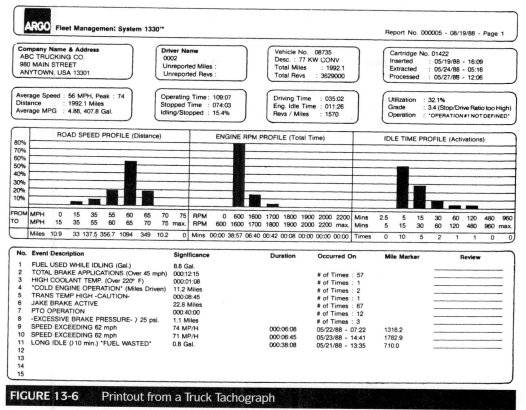

FIGURE 13-6 Printout from a Truck Tachograph

Source: Argo Instruments, Inc., Fleet Management Systems.

ENERGY CONTROLS

The large increases in energy costs that have taken place in recent years mean that logistics managers must look for ways to reduce energy consumption and costs. Consider that in late 2003 the price per barrel of oil was about $25, and by mid-2006 the price per barrel was approaching $80. Although oil prices have been declining from the $80 level, as this book is being prepared per barrel costs of oil are still around $65.

Warehousing and transportation represent two logistics activities where most energy costs occur and where energy-saving measures should be focused. For instance, design, lighting, and color represent three possible energy control areas in warehousing. With respect to design, facilities might be positioned so that dock doors aren't placed on the north side of a building (most cold winds blow from the north). Lighting provides a variety of opportunities for managing energy consumption; skylights and large windows that incorporate solar energy can reduce electricity usage between 40 and 60 percent. In addition, fluorescent lights provide for better lighting quality as well as reduced energy consumption.[5]

Roof color is often overlooked as an area for warehousing energy control. The roof is a focal point because it tends to be the largest exposed surface of a warehouse facility. Research that

---

[5]Mary Aichlmayr, "Smart Energy Management Pays Off," *Transportation & Distribution*, July 2002, 38–42.

compared black and white roofing for a 100,000-square-foot, air-conditioned facility indicated electricity savings, over a 10-year period, of approximately $40,000 in the Chicago area and nearly $300,000 in the Miami area.[6]

Transportation is a second logistics activity where considerable energy savings can take place, particularly because transportation is a primary consumer of energy. Indeed, transportation accounts for approximately two-thirds of all petroleum consumption in the United States. We've also pointed out on several occasions that transportation is often the highest-cost logistics activity in many companies, and so higher fuel prices quickly translate into increased logistics costs. Given that $60 per barrel oil prices are projected to be the norm at least through 2012, a number of companies are likely to reconfigure their modal allocations in the sense that airfreight and expedited transportation will be de-emphasized in favor of rail and truck intermodal service.[7] Keep in mind that a shift from faster (e.g., air, expedited) to slower transportation (e.g., rail and truck intermodal) will require adjustments in a company's inventory and warehousing practices as well.

Although many transportation companies impose fuel surcharges to be reimbursed for higher fuel costs, shippers are increasingly balking at surcharges. As a result, transportation providers are actively searching for ways to reduce their fuel consumption, hence, fuel costs. One such approach involves companies closely examining their current operations. For example, UPS Air Freight has long prided itself on cargo flights that arrived earlier than scheduled—until learning that each early arrival results in several thousand dollars in additional fuel costs.[8] Motor carriers are currently pursuing a variety of fuel reduction options, to include reducing vehicle idling times, joining fuel purchasing networks, implementing route optimizations systems, and implementing fuel purchase optimization systems.[9]

MAINTAINING CHANNEL INTEGRITY

As channel relationships evolve into supply chains, a continual matter of concern is maintaining the integrity of the product and the product flow. Although one must trust his or her partners, one cannot assume that the partners will be able to detect everything that goes wrong. One must continually monitor the quality of materials shipped and received, as well as performance in some of the other channels.

Outside threats to supply chain integrity also occur. One such threat is product tampering, and although tampering usually occurs at the retail level, several parties—the retail store, the product, and the product's manufacturer—may all suffer from bad publicity. Sometimes, no actual tampering takes place; a person need only announce to the media that he or she has tampered with some product, and the ensuing publicity will have a similar effect.

An example of breached channel integrity involved the alleged sale of fake Similac, a baby formula, in Safeway grocery stores. An individual purchased some powdered baby formula destined for export, packaged it in cans that were nearly identical copies of the Similac can, and sold it to a food broker that regularly supplied Safeway. The broker then sold it to Safeway, and the fake Similac ended up on Safeway's shelves. When the authorities moved in, over 6,000 cans of the fake Similac were recovered from wholesale and retail

[6]Ibid.

[7]Clay Risen, "What High Energy Prices Mean for Supply Chain Transportation," *World Trade,* April 2006, 36–39.

[8]Aaron Karp, "Fueling Savings," *Air Cargo World,* December 2005, 10–11.

[9]Wendy Leavitt, "Not a Penny More," *Fleet Owner,* June 2006, 90–95.

stocks. The purpose of mentioning this incident here is to show how an existing channel can be compromised.

In the remainder of this chapter, we will look at managing three selected channel and supply chain integrity topics—returned goods, theft, and terrorism.

MANAGING RETURNED GOODS

You might be surprised to learn that the annual cost of returned goods in the United States alone exceeds $100 billion. The process of managing returned goods, sometimes referred to as reverse logistics, focuses on three critical factors: (1) why products are returned, (2) how to optimize returned goods management, and (3) whether returned goods should be managed internally or outsourced to a third party.[10] Importantly, returned goods necessitate a reversal in the usual forward (i.e., producer toward consumer) flow of merchandise.

With respect to the first factor (why goods are returned), goods and materials are returned for a variety of reasons, such as the customer making an error in ordering, perhaps by writing down an incorrect part number. Alternatively, the shipper can make an error when filling an order, such as sending an incorrect product or an incorrect quantity of product. Another reason for returned products involves damage in transit. Moreover, in an age of increasingly sophisticated consumer products, customers sometimes cannot get whatever they bought to work. Goods may also be returned because of a **product recall,** which occurs when a hazard or defect is discovered in a manufactured or processed item, and its return is mandated by a government agency.

The second factor in managing returned goods, optimizing returned goods management, involves a number of strategic and tactical considerations. One basic decision concerns the design of the returned goods–reverse logistics system, such as whether return operations should be incorporated into existing warehousing and production facilities. If so, how will returned products be segregated from other products in an effort to reduce loss of returned product, to prevent mixing returned and nonreturned goods, and to prevent returned products from mistakenly being shipped out of the particular facility?[11]

Optimizing returned goods management is incumbent on goods being carefully counted and the appropriate records (e.g., accounting, inventory) being adjusted accordingly. After a returned item has been counted and recorded, it is important to evaluate the item in terms of a series of questions:

- Is the product damaged and unsalable, or can it be refurbished and resold?
- Was it returned as part of an overstock arrangement with a retailer?
- Is it a product that is being recalled?
- Is the item in an unopened package that can go into inventory for immediate resale?
- Does the item need to undergo special testing?
- What is the item's worth?
- How do the company's returned goods policies apply to this item?[12]

The scope of the preceding questions indicates that returned goods should not be managed as an afterthought. This leads directly to the third critical factor in managing returned goods—whether returned goods should be managed internally or outsourced to a third party. If a company

---

[10]John Paul Quinn, "Are There Ever Any Happy Returns?" *Logistics Management,* June 2005, 63–66.
[11]Ibid.
[12]Ibid.

decides to internally manage returned goods, there must be recognition that one or more employees will have returned goods as their primary, if not only, job responsibility. Outsourcing of returns management to a third party is also an option; although many companies have recognized the importance of returns management, they don't view it as a core competency. There are several third-party logistics companies, such as GENCO, whose primary expertise involves returns management.[13]

Product Recalls

We'll spend some time looking at one specific type of returned product situation—that involving product recalls. Since 2005, well-publicized product recalls in the United States have involved automobiles, batteries for laptop computers, ice cream, infant (baby) formula, and packaged spinach, to name a few. Product recalls are deserving of additional attention because the scope and costs of product recalls often dwarf those of other returned goods scenarios.

The scope and costs of a product recall are well illustrated in a 2006 recall involving batteries used to power laptop computers; these batteries could potentially overheat and catch on fire. With respect to the scope, Dell Computer was forced to recall approximately *4.1 million* laptop computers, and Apple recalled approximately *1.1 million* laptops. As for costs, Sony Corporation, manufacturer of the defective batteries, announced a write-off of over *$400 million* to cover the costs associated with the battery recall.

Once a product recall campaign is completed (or underway, depending on how it is conducted), the manufacturer and its distributors must take immediate steps to refill the retailer's shelves with either defect-free batches of the same product or a substitute product. Although this step is not as important as the recall, it must be undertaken to minimize losses. Otherwise, competitors will take the opportunity to suggest that a retailer use their product lines to fill empty shelf space.

Sometimes, products are recalled through channels different from those through which they are distributed. Goods are returned to the manufacturer even though it may simply destroy them after they are received. In theory, it seems easier to authorize retailers or wholesalers to destroy recalled products. However, if the goods are hazardous, it may be desirable for the manufacturer to supervise their destruction. The risk that the defective goods will not be properly disposed of and that individuals will be injured is always present. Accounting controls are necessary to ensure that individuals returning recalled materials are reimbursed only for the goods they return. Sometimes, merchandise will be returned in addition to that which was being recalled, and a decision must be made on how to handle those additional goods.

Product recall takes many forms, depending on the type of product. The responsible government agencies (including state and local as well as foreign governments) each have their own procedures. Often, a manufacturer will initiate the recall before being forced to do so by the regulatory agency. The degree of danger posed by the defect also differs, with the most serious danger being those products that are discovered to be directly life threatening. Less serious are the defects that are possible threats to life, such as those linked to causes of cancer if exposure is over a long period of time. An even less-serious problem is posed by products that are mislabeled (such as a label that reads "contents 16 ounces," when the package contains only 12 ounces). Sometimes, the problem can be overcome by merely changing the product's label or adding a warning label. A lamp manufacturer might be required to add a sticker to each lamp, saying, "Do not use lightbulbs larger than 60 watts in this lamp." In this instance,

---

[13]Ibid.

the manufacturer could have the stickers attached at some intermediate point between the place of manufacture and the retail outlet.

In the United States several federal agencies are involved with product recalls. For example, the Food Safety and Inspection Service of the U.S. Department of Agriculture inspects meat, poultry, and eggs and relies on voluntary recalls. It is also concerned with processed meat and poultry products as well as pizzas and frozen dinners containing a certain percentage of meat. It also supervises standards of state agencies that regulate the cleanliness of meat sold within that state.

The National Highway Traffic Safety Administration is concerned with motor vehicles and their accessory parts. It does not engage in recalls; it is responsible only for causing the manufacturer to notify purchasers that a defect has been discovered. Buyers are instructed to take their vehicles to the nearest dealer to have the defect corrected at no cost. The method of notification is by registered mail to the first purchaser of record. Sometimes, it is not necessary for the owner to take the vehicle back to the dealer. In one instance, the manufacturer issued a corrected sticker showing different tire pressures; the owners were instructed to place the decal over the original one (or to see a dealer if they had difficulty following the instructions).

The Food and Drug Administration (FDA) is concerned with food, drugs, and cosmetics. In what it considers a Class I Recall (i.e., the most serious of hazards, such as botulism toxin in foods), the FDA will issue a public warning. Moreover, the FDA will insist that the product be recalled at the consumer level and all intermediate levels and that 100 percent effectiveness checks be made of all distribution points. Yet another federal agency involved in product recalls is the Consumer Product Safety Commission (CPSC). Its main objective is to ban the sale of products deemed hazardous, thereby making it an offense for a retailer, wholesaler, or other distributor to sell a banned product. If the CPSC bans the sale of a specific item, the product becomes frozen in all distribution channels because it cannot be sold. Manufacturers and distributors may be forced to repurchase the banned items.

From a distribution control standpoint, the FDA has procedures for recalls that result in a reverse flow of the defective products from the consumer back to the manufacturer. The CPSC merely bans the sale of the product and halts it in its place in the distribution network.

In addition to these federal agencies, state and municipal agencies can also inspect products and force them to be withdrawn from commerce. Individual firms may also recall products on their own, in advance of government agency involvement.

The possibility of defective products and product recalls increases the need for positively identifying each product or batch of products processed, manufactured, or assembled by a company. Items such as laptop computers, home appliances, and automobiles contain serial numbers, and all their movements through a distribution system are recorded by that number. Items that do not have serial numbers, such as canned vegetables and soft drinks, commonly use **batch numbers,** which refer to an alphanumeric identification that specifies where a product was processed or manufactured. For example, the batch number 33 C 7 B 2 5 would indicate the following information:

33: Day of the year (February 2)
C: Plant
7: Year 2007
B: Production line B
2: Second shift
5: Fifth hour of that shift

Serial numbers can be advantageous in the sense that they can be matched with a specific purchaser of a product. If a recall is necessary, the affected company can individually contact all customers that purchased the product in question. Although batch numbers may be able to trace a product as far as a particular retailer, there is generally no way to know who bought the product in question. In a recall situation, this means that information will need to be communicated through mass media such as newspapers, radio, television, and increasingly, the Internet.

Whatever form it takes, product recall is an extremely serious matter for the manufacturer and all parties in the distribution network. Well-managed firms have practice recalls (sometimes called fire drills) to determine the speed, degree of coverage, and effectiveness they can effect. All actions that a firm takes to prepare for a hypothetical recall are important for two reasons: First, they allow better performance when a real emergency arises. Second, in case the recall is not completely successful and lawsuits result, a portion of the firm's defense might be the precautionary actions it had undertaken.

Before concluding our discussion of product recalls, it's important to recognize that recalls can generate adverse publicity as well as large lawsuits. Top management, to include the CEO, must be actively involved in any recall activity. Other involved personnel could include members of a firm's legal, controller, public relations, quality control, product engineering, logistics, and marketing staffs. Management, who may never have known how the firm's logistics system functioned, will be anxiously examining its effectiveness in handling a product recall.

Organizations should also recognize that product recalls may offer an excellent opportunity for service recovery—a topic previously mentioned in Chapter 4—as illustrated by two very different recall situations. One situation involved the recall of cyanide-laced capsules of Tylenol. This situation, which occurred in the early 1980s, is still recognized as a textbook example of a well-managed product recall. Johnson & Johnson, the manufacturer of Tylenol, had an established recall plan in place that allowed it to respond effectively and efficiently to the emergency. All Tylenol capsules were removed from the marketplace, and Tylenol was reintroduced with tamperproof packaging. Within one year of the initial recall, Tylenol had regained nearly all the market share it commanded prior to the recall.

The other recall, which occurred in 2000, involved 6.5 million Firestone/Bridgestone tires that were mostly mounted on the Ford Explorer sports utility vehicle and were linked to fatal accidents seemingly caused by tread separation. Unlike the Tylenol case, the Ford–Firestone situation degenerated into finger-pointing between the two companies in terms of which party was responsible for the accidents. Besides appearing somewhat childish with their finger-pointing, the recall caused irreparable damage to a business partnership that spanned nearly 100 years—not to mention the long-term alienation of current, as well as prospective, customers.

CONTROLLING THEFT

An ongoing problem facing nearly all businesses is **theft** (stealing), which can be defined as the taking and removing of personal property with the intent to deprive the rightful owner of it.[14] Unfortunately, it is difficult to accurately quantify the impact of theft, in part because some companies are hesitant to report this data—a reported theft serves as direct evidence of a logistics system shortcoming. Moreover, accurate quantification of cargo theft is difficult in the United States because the current Uniform Crime Reporting system does not have a separate designation for cargo theft.

---

[14]www.m-w.com/dictionary.

You might be wondering why logisticians would be concerned about theft, particularly because many organizations carry insurance to compensate themselves in cases of theft. However, even though insurance will reimburse an organization for the market value of the stolen items, the time and costs (e.g., documentation) associated with theft tend not to be covered by insurance. A second logistical concern is that theft results in the planned flow of goods being interrupted and can lead to stockouts in the distribution channel.

In addition, theft can factor into the facility location decision in the sense that many organizations will avoid locating their facilities in areas characterized by high crime rates.[15] It's also possible for the stolen products to reappear in the market at a lower price to compete with products that have moved through traditional channels. Indeed, there are suggestions that approximately 2 percent of the products available on Internet auction sites are actually stolen goods.[16]

Pilferage, which refers to employee theft, cannot be eliminated, and both warehousing and transportation operations are especially vulnerable to pilferage. Controlling pilferage can be challenging for the logistics manager, and the control begins with the hiring process. In fact, one of the best ways to manage pilferage is to avoid hiring people who are predisposed to steal, such as people with credit, alcohol, or drug problems. Some organizations utilize psychological tests as part of the hiring process in an effort to identify prospective employees who might pilfer.

Organizations can better control pilferage if they have clearly articulated and enforced pilferage-related policies. To this end, experts recommend that the best pilferage policy should be based on zero tolerance because problems inevitably arise for those companies that tolerate a "small amount" of pilferage. For example, there may be disagreement in terms of how to operationalize "amount"—are we concerned with the number of units or the dollar value of items? Once this has been established, then what is meant by "small"—does, say, five units or $75 qualify as "small"? Quite simply, a zero-tolerance policy means that pilferage exceeding zero units or zero dollars is unacceptable.

The discussion to this point has been primarily focused on domestic theft. When goods move in international commerce, particularly by ship, they are much more vulnerable to theft. For example, *rust bucket fraud* involves chartering an aged ship that is loaded with goods worth more than the ship. After setting sail, it makes an unscheduled stop, sells off the cargo to the highest bidder, and exchanges its regular crew for a scuttling crew that takes it out to sea, where it runs into "bad" weather. The crew manages to escape, and the hulk lies too deep for divers to examine. Alternatively, some ships vanish, only to reappear under a new name and a new flag. Yet others are diverted to a different port, where the cargo is sold to the highest bidder while the original purchaser waits in vain for delivery.

Moreover, pirate attacks on ships are also a threat, even in the early part of the twenty-first century. Unlike the somewhat romanticized pirates of movies and literature who wore eye patches and carried swords, contemporary pirates use speedboats, cell phones, and automatic weapons. The International Maritime Bureau, an arm of the International Chamber of Commerce, compiles weekly and annual reports of worldwide pirate attacks. Although 2005 saw the lowest number of pirate attacks since 1999, there were still over 275 such attacks, with approximately 30 percent occurring in Indonesia.[17] Over 20 percent of all pirate

[15]Perry A. Trunick, "To Catch a Thief," *Logistics Today,* July 2005, 35–40.

[16]Julia Kuzeljevich, "The Seven Deadly Sins in Warehouse Security," *Canadian Transportation & Logistics,* April 2006, 44.

[17]www.icc-ccs.org/main/news.php?newsid=63.

attacks in recent years have involved tankers, which is of concern because of the potential for an environmental accident as well as the fact that some tankers could be used as floating bombs.

System Security

One of the most effective methods of protecting goods is to keep them moving through the system. Goods waiting in warehouses, in terminals, or to clear customs are more vulnerable to theft than goods that are moving. No list of methods of improving **system security** (that is, security throughout the entire supply chain) is complete; determined thieves are likely to overcome almost any hindrance or barrier placed in their way. However, a few suggestions are offered here, mainly to reflect the breadth of measures that might be taken:

- Decals are required for autos in employee parking lots, and nonemployees may be required to park in designated areas as well as to register with a company receptionist. This makes it more difficult for outsiders to access an organization's facilities.
- Forklifts in warehouses are locked at night, making it difficult to reach high items or to move heavy items.
- Seals (small wirelike devices that once closed cannot be reopened without breaking) are used more and more, with dispatchers, drivers, and receiving personnel all responsible for recording the seal number and inspecting its condition. Figure 13-7 shows a seal device used for pallet loads, and Figure 13-8 shows a seal used for truck trailer or container doors.

FIGURE 13-7   This Device Seals Pallets. It Has Four Clips That Fasten Together and Is Used in Conjunction with Strapping

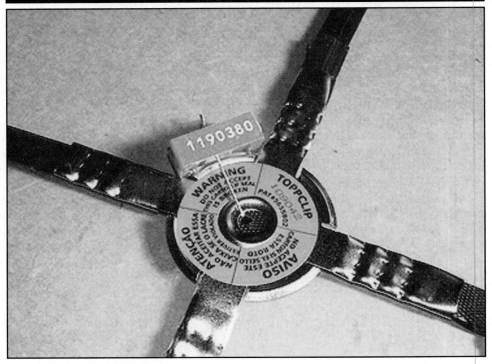

Source: CGM Security Solutions, Inc.

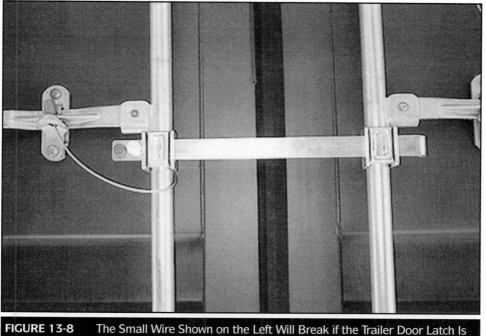

FIGURE 13-8   The Small Wire Shown on the Left Will Break if the Trailer Door Latch Is Opened. The Plug At its Upper End Is Marked with a Unique Number

Source: CGM Security Solutions, Inc.

- Electronic tags or strips are embedded in products at the time of their manufacture, and they can activate alarms at warehouse or retail store doors.
- Organizations should take a proactive approach to theft; waiting until theft reaches "unacceptable" levels might mean that certain dysfunctional behavior has been permitted for so long that it has come to be viewed as typical or acceptable.
- Experts suggest that companies should facilitate an employee's ability to report theft and other aberrant behavior, such as through a hotline that guarantees anonymity as well as retribution from potential retaliation or retribution.

Note that many of the preceding suggestions are common sense in nature (e.g., decals, locked forklifts); indeed, common sense is viewed as a basic foundation for controlling theft. Importantly, commonsense approaches to system security are often no cost, or low cost, in nature.[18]

Building Security

Because product at rest is particularly susceptible to theft, interest in providing building security for warehouses and other distribution facilities has increased in recent years. Figure 13-9 shows some of the security measures that can be built into a warehouse. Note that the design presented in Figure 13-9 limits access to parking, offices, warehousing space, and dock space.

Electronic devices can be used to provide various building-related security functions. For example, closed-circuit television cameras can be used to view different areas of a particular

[18]Michael Imlay, "Off-Highway Robbery," *Off-Road Business,* November 2005, 55–57.

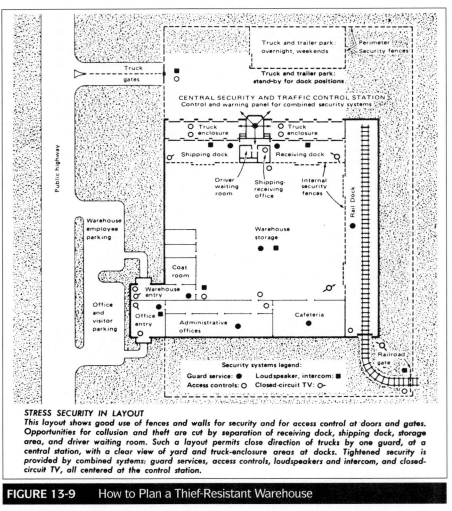

STRESS SECURITY IN LAYOUT
This layout shows good use of fences and walls for security and for access control at doors and gates. Opportunities for collusion and theft are cut by separation of receiving dock, shipping dock, storage area, and driver waiting room. Such a layout permits close direction of trucks by one guard, at a central station, with a clear view of yard and truck-enclosure areas at docks. Tightened security is provided by combined systems: guard services, access controls, loudspeakers and intercom, and closed-circuit TV, all centered at the control station.

FIGURE 13-9 How to Plan a Thief-Resistant Warehouse

Source: Courtesy of Modern Materials Handling.

facility. For areas where there should be no movements, it is possible to have monitoring devices store the image that contains no movement in digital memory and, when a change in the image occurs—such as would be caused by intruders in a freight storage area—initiate an alarm. Unfortunately, organizations sometimes fail to activate or monitor their closed-circuit cameras, which defeats their purpose. Moreover, security experts suggest that closed-circuit television and alarms are relatively ineffective in controlling pilferage.[19]

A second type of electronic device is used to control access to particular facilities. An example is a magnetically encoded tag that each employee must insert into a sensing device that records the event and determines whether the door or gate should be unlocked. A third category of electronic devices is invisible photoelectric beams and many types of listening devices that can record unauthorized movements. Within a warehouse, heavier security may be

---

[19]Kuzeljevich, "The Seven Deadly Sins in Warehouse Security."

placed around areas where higher-value material is kept. There is virtually no limit to the sophistication or cost of the security devices that can be employed. Having said this, the more sophisticated security devices also tend to be more expensive, and organizations are faced with the trade-off of whether the additional protection is worth the additional cost.

Vehicle Security

Ironically, if building security makes it difficult, if not impossible, to steal goods, then thieves may turn their attention to stealing goods while they are in transit. As such, vehicle security becomes an important consideration for many companies. As pointed out earlier, common sense can be an important aspect in managing vehicle security. For instance, one of the authors once worked for a less-than-truckload motor carrier, and there were several instances where trucks were stolen because drivers had stopped to make a delivery—*and left the key in the ignition, with the motor running!*

Vehicle security is a particularly acute issue in the trucking industry because theft tends to be two-pronged—theft of a vehicle's contents and theft of a vehicle itself. Attributes that make trucks an attractive modal option, such as geographic flexibility, also serve to make trucks potentially attractive to thieves. For example, the geographic flexibility that allows trucks to serve many different places also provides the ability to take a stolen vehicle—and its contents—to many different places.

Vehicle security in the early part of the twenty-first century is a mixture of relatively low- and high-technology alternatives. With respect to low-technology alternatives, numbers are painted on the top of truck trailers to make them easier to spot from the air if they are stolen. In addition, some truck-leasing companies attempt to thwart truck theft by etching a vehicle identification number (VIN) in up to 40 different locations on each vehicle—glass, frame, drive-line components, various engine parts, and virtually any other part with resale value. Altering or destroying all the VINs can be extremely time consuming—each vehicle would need to be almost totally deconstructed—and thus not worth the potential "rewards."

A somewhat more high-technology approach to vehicle security involves the use of cameras and video screens. For example, because thieves have been known to climb onto the rear of a truck waiting at a traffic signal and then force their way inside the vehicle, some companies have equipped their tractors and trailers with multiple cameras that can provide nearly 360 degrees of coverage and real-time data to drivers. Figure 13-10 shows a four-section video screen in a truck driver's cab in which one can view activities behind and on both sides of a tractor–trailer.

Discussion earlier in this chapter indicated that high-technology alternatives such as global positioning systems and geographic information systems can be helpful in improving driver productivity. Global positioning systems can also be valuable for managing vehicle security; if an organization knows the location of its drivers, then it likely knows the location of its vehicles as well. Moreover, radio frequency identification (RFID) is emerging as a valuable technology for managing vehicle security; **transponders** (a small device that responds to radio signals from an outside source) can be placed (generally hidden, so that thieves can't easily find them) on vehicles, and global positioning systems can be used to monitor the location of the transponder.

Computer and Data Security

As technology continues to evolve, computer and data security become a bigger and bigger issue for many companies. Indeed, a 2006 study indicated that information security is the most important technology issue that companies face today.[20] Moreover, the theft of

---

[20]Paul Demery, "Safe Driving? Is Your Lap Strapped in?" *Accounting Technology,* September 2006, 45–49.

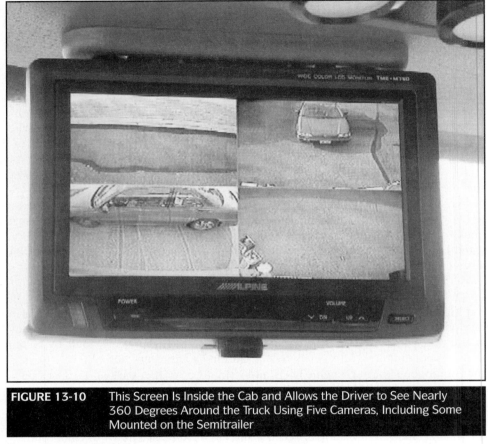

FIGURE 13-10   This Screen Is Inside the Cab and Allows the Driver to See Nearly 360 Degrees Around the Truck Using Five Cameras, Including Some Mounted on the Semitrailer

Source: Kenworth Truck Company.

proprietary information for an "average" company is estimated to cost approximately $300,000 annually.[21]

One of the challenges associated with computer and data security is that whereas laptop computers provide portability to users, laptops are also much more susceptible to loss or theft than are desktop computers. The loss or theft of a laptop not only involves the equipment itself, but also potentially compromises the data stored in it. As such, managers are faced with two control issues with respect to computer and data security; the first involves developing business practices that reduce the likelihood of employees losing critical data files (e.g., what a company can do to decrease the chance of a laptop being lost or stolen), whereas the second seeks to protect the data files that are stored on, or can be accessed through, the laptop (e.g., the use of firewalls and data encryption).[22]

---

[21]Ray Zambroski, "Think Before You Send," *Communication World,* May-June 2006, pp. 38–40.
[22]Demery, "Safe Driving? Is Your Lap Strapped in?"

PROTECTION AGAINST TERRORISM

The terrorist attacks in the United States on September 11, 2001, have had a profound impact in terms of managing logistics systems. Processes, procedures, and activities that might have been given minimal attention prior to September 11 are now viewed from an entirely different perspective. For example, prior to September 11, 2001, the storage and transport of hazardous materials was primarily managed from a safety perspective. Although safety remains an important perspective, the storage and transport of hazardous materials in today's world is managed with an eye to potential terrorist considerations. We mentioned in a previous chapter that several major U.S. cities are attempting to reroute rail shipments of hazardous materials, in part because of terror concerns. We've indicated in this chapter that petroleum tank trucks and ocean tankers have the potential to be mobile bombs.

In a similar vein, inbound containers are receiving much greater scrutiny today than prior to September 11. One of the things learned after the terrorist attacks was that a relatively small percentage of containers that arrived at U.S. ports was scanned to learn about their actual contents. This alarmed some U.S. legislators, and the result has been a series of legislative proposals in recent years focused on increasing the inspection of inbound containers. For example, one proposal would require all containers bound for the United States to be electronically inspected prior to sailing from a nondomestic port as well as each container to be secured with a tamper-proof seal. This proposal, and others like it, has the potential to be quite disruptive to international trade because a number of nondomestic ports currently do not have the technology required to inspect containers. These ports would either have to acquire and install the relevant technology (which is quite expensive) or perhaps stop sending containers to the United States.

One response to the September 11th attacks involved the creation of a new federal agency in the United States, the Department of Homeland Security (DHS); two of its major aims are to prevent terrorist attacks in the United States as well as to reduce the vulnerability of the United States to terrorism. A total of 22 separate U.S. government entities were incorporated into the DHS, with the Transportation Security Agency (TSA) and Customs and Border Protection (CBP) being two of the most important from a logistics perspective.

The Transportation Security Administration is responsible for the security of the U.S. transportation system. You might be familiar with the TSA because it is the agency that conducts the passenger screening at U.S. commercial airports. The TSA also plays a number of roles with respect to freight security, such as using dogs to screen airfreight. In addition, the TSA is in the process of developing a **Transportation Worker Identification Credential** (TWIC) that is meant to be a common credential to identify workers across all modes of transportation. One of the key attributes of TWIC is that the corresponding card would contain both personal and biometric data, with the biometric data being used to exclude certain workers from secure areas at ports and terminals. Although there is general support for the TWIC concept, it is yet to be fully operational because of disagreements about how it should be implemented.[23]

Customs and Border Protection is responsible for securing U.S. borders to protect the American people and the U.S. economy. One key CBP function is inspecting cargo, and a number of high-profile CBP initiatives have affected the management of logistics systems. The Trade Act of 2002, which required submission of advanced electronic data on all shipments entering and leaving the United States, is aimed at identifying high-risk shipments that might threaten U.S. safety and security. Table 13-3 summarizes the manifest times for inbound and outbound shipments involving air, rail, water, and truck.

---

[23]R. G. Edmondson, "Plugging Away on TWIC," *Journal of Commerce,* September 4, 2006, 30–31.

TABLE 13-3	Timeline for Presenting Electronic Advance Manifest Information

Inbound to U.S.

Mode	Timeline
Air and courier	Four hours prior to arrival in U.S., or "wheels up" from certain nearby airports
Rail	Two hours prior to arrival at a U.S. port of entry
Ocean vessel	24 hours prior to lading at foreign port
Truck	Free and Secure Trade (FAST): 30 minutes prior to arrival in U.S.; non-FAST: one hour prior to arrival in U.S.

Outbound from U.S.

Mode	Timeline
Air and courier	Two hours prior to scheduled departure from U.S.
Rail	Two hours prior to the arrival of the train at the border
Ocean vessel	24 hours prior to departure from U.S. port where cargo is laden
Truck	One hour prior to the arrival of the truck at the border

Source: Erlinda Byrd, "Rules for Improving Cargo Security," *Customs and Border Protection Today,* March 2004.

CBP is also involved in the **Container Security Initiative** (CSI), an agreement in which the world's ports agree to allow U.S. customs agents to identify and inspect high-risk containers bound for the United States before they are loaded onto ships. Key international ports such as Hong Kong, Singapore, Shanghai, and Rotterdam are currently participating in the CSI.

One of the best-known CBP programs enacted since September 11 is the **Customs Trade Partnership Against Terrorism** (C-TPAT), in which public (CBP) and private (e.g., retailers and manufacturers) organizations work together to prevent terrorism against the United States through imports and transportation. Private organizations apply to CBP for C-TPAT certification, and the process involves demonstrating that organizations have improved the physical security of their containerized shipments as well as the ability to track people who have access to the containerized shipments. Although the government-provided benefits to C-TPAT certification include fewer security inspections of inbound containers along with faster processing time through Customs, many companies have discovered that the C-TPAT process has also led to a reduction in cargo theft.[24]

Summary

This chapter discussed logistics systems controls, and it's important to recognize that managers cannot eliminate, but rather must control, many issues. The chapter first examined accounting controls, with a particular focus on activity-based costing.

Worker productivity was a second issue that was discussed, with a closer look at managing warehouse workers as well as transportation drivers. The latter are usually more difficult to manage than the former because drivers are often out of their supervisors' immediate sight.

The large increases in energy costs in recent years mean that logistics managers must look for ways to reduce energy consumption and costs. Warehousing and transportation are two logistics activities in which considerable energy savings can take place.

---

[24]Christine Blank, "Cruise through Customs," *Multichannel Merchant,* August 2006, 46–47.

There was a discussion of managing returned goods, with a particular emphasis on product recalls. The chapter also looked at controlling theft, and we examined building security and vehicle security, as well as computer and data security.

The terrorist activities of September 11, 2001, have profoundly affected the management of logistics systems. Select initiatives of the Transportation Security Administration and Customs and Border Protection were discussed.

Questions for Discussion and Review

1. Discuss how accountants and logisticians differ in terms of their approach to accounting controls.
2. What is activity-based costing (ABC)? What are the five steps of the ABC process?
3. Define what is meant by productivity. Discuss how productivity can be improved.
4. What is short-interval scheduling? How can it be useful to managers?
5. In what ways can unionized workforces be a challenge to improving worker productivity?
6. Why does driver supervision tend to be more difficult than supervision of warehouse workers?
7. Discuss how driver productivity can be improved with global positioning systems and geographic information systems.
8. Describe some ways in which transportation companies might reduce their fuel consumption.
9. Describe the three critical factors in managing returned goods.
10. What U.S. federal agencies are involved in product recalls, and what are their respective jurisdictions?
11. Discuss practice recalls (fire drills).
12. What are the reasons why logisticians might be concerned with theft?
13. Explain how logistics managers can attempt to control pilferage.
14. In what ways are goods moving in international commerce more vulnerable to theft than goods moving in domestic commerce?
15. Discuss three electronic devices that can be used to provide building-related security functions.
16. How is vehicle security in the early twenty-first century a mixture of relatively low- and high-technology alternatives?
17. Describe the two issues that managers face with respect to computer and data security.
18. What are two examples of how the terrorist attacks of September 11, 2001, have affected the management of logistics systems?
19. What are some ways in which the Transportation Security Administration is attempting to improve the security of the U.S. transportation system?
20. Discuss the Customs Trade Partnership Against Terrorism (C-TPAT).

Suggested Readings

Brandman, Barry. *Security Best Practices.* Oak Brook, IL: Warehousing Education and Research Council, 2002.

Felcher, E. Maria. "Product Recalls: Gaping Holes in the Nation's Product Safety Net." *Journal of Consumer Affairs* 37, no. 1 (2003): 170–179.

Helferich, Omar Keith, and Robert L. Cook. *Securing the Supply Chain.* Oak Brook, IL: Council of Logistics Management, 2002.

Kerpoe, Lisa. *Using Competencies in the Warehouse.* Oak Brook, IL: Warehousing Education and Research Council, 2001.

Lin, Binshan, James Collins, and Robert K. Su. "Supply Chain Costing: An Activity-Based Perspective." *International Journal of Physical Distribution & Logistics Management* 31, nos. 9/10 (2001): 702–713.

Luft, Gal, and Anil Korin. "Terrorism Goes to Sea." *Foreign Affairs* 83, no. 6 (2004): 61–71.

Martha, Joseph, and Sunil Subbakrishna. "Targeting a Just-in-Case Supply Chain for the Inevitable Next Disaster." *Supply Chain Management Review* 6, no. 5 (2002): 18–23.

Min, Hokey. "An Examination of Warehouse Employee Recruitment and Retention Practices in the USA." *International Journal of Logistics: Research & Applications* 7, no. 4 (2004): 354–359.

Schwarz-Miller, Ann, and Wayne K. Talley. "Technology and Labor Relations: Railroads and

Ports." *Journal of Labor Research* 23, no. 4 (2002): 512–533.

Sheffi, Yossi. "Supply Chain Management under the Threat of Terrorism." *International Journal of Logistics Management* 12, no. 2 (2001): 1–11.

Thibault, Marc, Mary R. Brooks, and Kenneth J. Button. "The Response of the U.S. Maritime

Industry to the New Container Security Initiative." *Transportation Journal* 45, no. 1 (2006): 5–15.

Warren, Matthew, and William Hutchinson. "Cyber Attacks against Supply Chain Management Systems: A Short Note." *International Journal of Physical Distribution & Logistics Management* 30, nos. 7/8 (2000): 710–716.

CASES

CASE 13-1   BRANT FREEZER COMPANY

Located in Fargo, North Dakota, the Brant Freezer Company manufactured industrial freezers. They came in one size and were distributed through public warehouses in Atlanta, Boston, Chicago, Denver, Los Angeles, Portland, and St. Louis. In addition, some space was used in the company's Fargo warehouse. Young Joaquin (J. Q.) Brant, with a fresh M.B.A. degree from the University of South Alabama, returned to the family firm, where he had once worked during summers. On his first day of work, J. Q. met with his father. His

father complained that they were being "eaten alive" by warehousing costs. The firm's controller drew up a budget each year, and each warehouse's monthly activity (units shipped) and costs were tallied.

Exhibit 13-A shows actual 2003 figures for all warehouses, plus actual figures for the first five months of 2004. Projected 12-month 2004 budgets and shipments are also included. If you are familiar with Excel or other spreadsheet software, you might try using it to answer the following questions. ■

QUESTIONS

1. When comparing performance during the first five months of 2004 with performance in 2003, which warehouse shows the most improvement?

2. When comparing performance during the first five months of 2004 with performance in 2003, which warehouse shows the poorest change in performance?

3. When comparisons are made among all eight warehouses, which one do you think does the best job for the Brant Company? What criteria did you use? Why?

4. J. Q. is aggressive and is going to recommend that his father cancel the contract with one of the warehouses and give that business to a competing warehouse in the same city. J. Q. feels that when word of this gets around, the other warehouses they use will "shape up." Which of the seven should J. Q. recommend be dropped? Why?

5. The year 2004 is nearly half over. J. Q. is told to determine how much the firm is likely to spend for warehousing at each of the eight warehouses for the last six months in 2004. Do his work for him.

6. When comparing the 2003 figures with the 2004 figures shown in the table, the amount budgeted for each warehouse in 2004 was greater than actual 2003 costs. How much of the increase is caused by increased volume of business (units shipped) and how much by inflation?

7. Prepare the firm's 2005 warehouse budget, showing for each warehouse the anticipated number of units to be shipped and the costs.

8. While attending classes at the university, J. Q. had learned of logistics partnerships. Should Brant Freezer Company attempt to enter into a partnership relationship with these warehouses? If so, what approach should it use?

EXHIBIT 13-A Warehouse Performance

	2003 Figures				2004 Figures			
	Units Shipped		Warehouse Costs		Units Shipped		Warehouse Costs	
	12 Months Jan.–Dec.	*5 Months through May 31*	*12 Months Jan.–Dec.*	*5 Months through May 31*	*Projected 12 Months Jan.–Dec.*	*Actual 5 Months May 31*	*Budgeted 12 Months Jan.–Dec.*	*Actual Costs through May 31*
Atlanta	17,431	4,080	156,830	35,890	18,000	4,035	178,000	40,228
Boston	6,920	3,061	63,417	27,915	7,200	3,119	73,000	29,416
Chicago	28,104	14,621	246,315	131,618	30,000	15,230	285,000	141,222
Denver	3,021	1,005[a]	28,019	8,600*	3,100	1,421	31,000	14,900
Fargo (company warehouse)	2,016	980	16,411	8,883	2,000	804	17,000	9,605
Los Angeles	16,491	11,431	151,975	109,690	17,000	9,444	176,000	93,280
Portland	8,333	4,028	73,015	36,021	9,000	4,600	85,000	42,616
St. Louis	5,921	2,331	51,819	23,232	8,000	2,116	56,000	19,191

[a]Denver warehouse closed by strike March 4–19, 2003.

CASE 13-2   RED SPOT MARKETS COMPANY

The Red Spot Markets Company operates a chain of grocery stores in New England. It has a grocery distribution center in Providence, Rhode Island, from which deliveries are made to stores as far north as Lowell, Massachusetts, as far west as Waterbury, Connecticut, and as far northwest as Springfield, Massachusetts. No stores are located beyond the two northernmost points in Massachusetts. Stores to the west are supplied by a grocery warehouse located in Newburgh, New York. The Providence grocery distribution center supplies 42 Red Spot retail stores.

Robert Easter, Red Spot's distribution manager, is responsible for operations at the Newburgh and Providence distribution centers. By industry standards, both centers were fairly efficient. However, of the two, the Providence center lagged in two important areas of control: worker productivity and shrinkage. Warehouse equipment and work rules were the same for both the Newburgh and Providence centers, yet the throughput per worker hour was 4 percent higher for the Newburgh facility. Shrinkage, expressed as a percentage of the wholesale value of goods handled annually, was 3.6 percent for the Newburgh center and 5.9 percent for the Providence center. Jarvis Jason had been manager of the Providence distribution center for the past three years and, at great effort, managed to narrow the gap between the performance rankings of the two Red Spot facilities. Last week he requested an immediate reassignment, and Easter arranged for him to become the marketing manager for the Boston area, which would involve supervising the operations of 11 Red Spot markets. The transfer involved no increase in pay.

Easter needed a new manager for the Providence distribution center, and he picked Fred Fosdick for the task. Fosdick graduated from a lesser Ivy League college, where he majored in business with a concentration in logistics. He had been with Red Spot for two years and had rearranged the entire delivery route structure so that two fewer trucks were needed. As part of this assignment, he also converted the entire system to one of unit loads, which meant everything loaded on or unloaded from a Red Spot truck was on a pallet. Fosdick was familiar with the operations of both the Providence and Newburgh centers. He has been in each facility at least 50 different times. In addition, he spent two weeks at the Providence center when the loading docks were redesigned to accommodate pallet loading. Fosdick was surprised that Jason had requested his reassignment to a slot that did not involve an upward promotion. That was his first question to Easter after Easter asked whether he was interested in the Providence assignment.

"I'm sorry you started with that question," said Easter to Fosdick. "Now we'll have to talk about the troublesome aspects of the assignment first, rather than the positive ones. To be frank, Fred, one of the union employees there made so much trouble for Jason, he couldn't stand it."

"Who's the troublemaker?" asked Fosdick.

"Tom Bigelow," was Easter's answer.

Fosdick remembered Bigelow from the times he had been at the Providence center. Thomas D. Bigelow was nicknamed T. D. since his days as a local Providence high school football star. Fosdick recalled that during work breaks on the loading dock, Bigelow and some of the other workers would toss around melons as though they were footballs. Only once did they drop a melon. Fosdick recalled hearing the story that Bigelow had received several offers of athletic scholarships when he graduated from high school. His best offer was from a southern school, and he accepted it. Despite the fact that the college provided a special tutor for each class, Bigelow flunked out at the end of his first semester and came back to Providence, where he got a job in the Red Spot warehouse.

In the warehouse, Bigelow was a natural leader. He would have been a supervisor except for his inability to count and his spotty attendance record on Monday mornings. On Mondays, the day that the warehouse was the busiest because it had to replenish the stores' weekend sales, Bigelow was groggy, tired, and irritable. On Mondays, he would sometimes hide by loading a forklift with three pallets, backing into any empty bay, and lowering the pallets in position (which hid the lift truck from view), and he would fall asleep. The rest of the week Bigelow was happy, enthusiastic, and hardworking. Indeed, it was he who set the pace of work in the warehouse. When he felt good, things hummed; when he was not feeling well or was absent, work dragged.

"What did Bigelow do to Jason?" Fosdick asked Easter.

"Well, as I understand it," responded Easter, "about two weeks ago Jason decided that he had had it with Bigelow and so he suspended him on a Monday morning after Bigelow showed up late, still badly hung over. It was nearly noon, and he told Bigelow to stay off the premises and to file a grievance with his union shop steward. He also told Bigelow that he had been documenting Bigelow's Monday performance—or nonperformance—for the past six months and that Red Spot had grounds enough to fire Bigelow if it so chose. He told Bigelow to go home, sober up, and come back on Tuesday when they would discuss the length of his suspension. Bigelow walked through the distribution center on his way out, and I'm sure Jason felt he had control of the matter.

"However," continued Easter, "by about one o'clock, Jason realized he had a work slowdown on his hands. Pallet loads of bottled goods were being dropped, two forklifts collided, and one lift truck pulled over the corner of a tubular steel rack. At 4:00 P.M. quitting time, there were still three trucks to be loaded; usually they would have departed by 3:30. Rather than pay overtime, Jason let the workforce go home, and he and the supervisor loaded the last three trucks.

"On Tuesday, Bigelow did not show up, and the slowdown got worse. In addition, retail stores were phoning with complaints about all the errors in their orders. To top it off, at the Roxbury store, when the trailer door was opened, the trailer contained nothing but empty pallets.

Tuesday night somebody turned off the switches on the battery chargers for all the lift trucks, so on Wednesday, the lift-truck batteries were dying all day. I got involved because of all the complaints from the stores. On Wednesday, Jason got my permission to pay overtime, and the last outgoing truck did not leave until 7:00 P.M. In addition we had to pay overtime at some of our retail stores because the workers there were waiting for the trucks to arrive. While I was talking to Jason that afternoon, he indicated that he had fired Bigelow."

Easter lit his cigar and continued. "On Wednesday, I decided to go to Providence myself, mainly to talk to Jason and to determine whether we should close down the Providence center and try to serve all our stores out of Newburgh. This would have been expensive, but Providence was becoming too unreliable. In addition, we had a big weekend coming up. When I showed up in Providence, Jason and I had breakfast together in my hotel room Thursday morning, and he told me pretty much the same thing I've been telling you. He said he knew Bigelow was behind all the disruption and that today, Thursday, would be crucial. I've never seen Jason looking so nervous. Then we drove to the distribution center. Even from a distance, I could tell things were moving slowly. The first echelon of outgoing trucks, which should have been on the road, was still there. Another 20 of our trucks were waiting to be loaded. On the other end of the building, you could see a long line of arriving trucks waiting to be unloaded; usually there was no line at all. I knew that our suppliers would start complaining because we had established scheduled unloading times. However, I decided not to ask Jason whether he had begun receiving phone calls from them."

"Inside the center, the slowdown was in effect. Lift-truck operators who usually zipped by each other would now stop, turn off their engines, dismount, and carefully walk around each other's trucks to ensure there was proper clearance. Satisfied of this, they would then mount, start their engines, and spend an inordinate amount of time motioning to each other to pass. This was only one example. When we got to

Jason's office, he had a message to phone Ed Meyers, our local attorney in Providence, who handles much of our labor relations work there. He called Meyers and was upset by the discussion. After he hung up, he told me that Meyers had been served papers by the union's attorney, charging that Wednesday's firing of Bigelow was unjustified, mainly because no provable grounds existed that Bigelow was behind the slowdown. Meyers was angry because, in firing Bigelow on Wednesday, Jason may have also blown the suspension of Bigelow on Monday. Jason and I started talking, even arguing. I talked so much that my cigar went out," said Easter, "so I asked Jason, who was sitting behind his desk, for a match. He didn't carry matches but looked inside his center desk drawer for one. He gasped, and I didn't know what was the matter. He got up, looking sick, and walked away from his desk. He said that a dead rat had been left in his desk drawer, and he wanted a transfer. He was in bad shape and the distribution center was in bad shape, so I had the opening in the Boston area and I let him have it. Actually, right now he and his family are vacationing somewhere in Eastern Canada. He needs the rest."

Fosdick was beginning to feel sorry that he knew all the details, but he persisted. "Then what?" he asked Easter.

"Well, I took over running the distribution center. I phoned Meyers again, and he and I had lunch. He thought that Jason had blown the case against Bigelow and that we should take him back. So on Friday, Meyers, Bigelow, the union attorney, the shop steward, Bigelow's supervisor, and I met. Jason, of course, was not there. It was a pleasant meeting. Everything got blamed on poor Jason. I did tell Bigelow that we would be documenting his performance and wanted him to know that Jason's successor, meaning you, was under my instructions to tolerate no nonsense. Bigelow was so pleasant that day that I could not imagine him in the role of a troublemaker. The amazing thing was that, when he went out into the center to resume work, a loud cheer went up and all the drivers started blowing their lift-truck horns. For a moment, I was afraid all the batteries would run down again. But I was wrong. They were plain happy to see Bigelow back. You know, the slowdown was still in effect when Bigelow walked onto the floor. I'd say it was 10:00 A.M. and they were an hour behind. Well, let me tell you what happened. They went to work! By noon we were back on schedule, and by the end of the shift we were a half-hour ahead of schedule. In fact, the last half-hour was spent straightening up many of the bins that had been deliberately disarranged during the slowdown. I tell you, Tom Bigelow does set the work pace in that warehouse!"

"So what do you suggest I do at the center?" asked Fosdick.

"Well, the key is getting along with Bigelow. Talk to Meyers about the kind of records you should keep in case you decide to move against Bigelow. Be sure to consult with Meyers before you do anything irreversible. Frankly, I don't know whether Bigelow will be a problem. We never had trouble with him that I knew about before Jason was there. According to Bigelow and the union attorney, Jason had it in for Bigelow. If I were you, I'd take it easy with Bigelow and other labor problems. See what you can do instead about the inventory shrinkage."

On the next Monday morning, Fosdick showed up at the Providence distribution center. After gingerly looking in all his desk drawers, he had a brief meeting with his supervisors and then walked out to meet the entire workforce on a one-to-one basis. Many remembered Fosdick from his earlier visits to the facility. Because it was a Monday morning, he had not expected to encounter Bigelow, who was present, clear-eyed, alert, and enthusiastic. Bigelow was happy to see Fosdick and shook his hand warmly. Bigelow then excused himself, saying he had to return to work. The truck dispatcher said that the workforce was ahead of schedule again: It was 11:00 A.M., and they were about 15 minutes ahead. Fosdick returned to his office, and there was a phone message from Ed Meyers. Meyers asked to postpone their luncheon for that day until Tuesday noon. Then Robert Easter called to ask how things were going on Fosdick's first day.

Easter was pleased that things were going smoothly.

It was lunchtime. Fosdick decided to walk to a small café where he had eaten at other times. It was two blocks from the distribution center and on the side away from the office. So he walked through the center, which was quiet since it was closed down for lunch. He walked by the employees' lunchroom and heard the normal sounds of 50 people eating and talking. Just outside the lunchroom was one lift truck with an empty wooden pallet on it. As Fosdick watched, one of the stock clerks came out of the lunchroom with an opened case of sweet pickles from which three jars had been taken. Next came another stock clerk with an opened carton of mustard from which two bottles had been removed. One of the clerks suddenly saw Fosdick and said weakly, "We take these opened cases to the damaged merchandise room." Fosdick went into the lunchroom. There, on the center table were cases of cold meat, cheese, soft drinks, mayonnaise, and bread. All had been opened and partially emptied to provide the workers' lunches.

Bigelow was making himself a large sandwich when he saw Fosdick approach. "Don't get uptight," he said to Fosdick. "You've just come across one of the noncontract fringe benefits of working at the Red Spot Providence distribution center. May I make you a sandwich?" ∎

QUESTIONS

1. How should Fosdick respond to the immediate situation?
2. What controls, of the types discussed in this chapter, might have been used by Red Spot Markets to reduce or eliminate the problems discussed in the case?
3. What longer-range steps should Fosdick take to control the operations of the Providence distribution center?
4. What longer-range steps should Fosdick take to improve the Providence distribution center's productivity?
5. What longer-range steps can Fosdick take to reduce the distribution center's high rate of shrinkage?
6. Assume that Fosdick decides that the practice of free lunches from the opened cases of goods must be stopped. Develop and present the arguments he should give in a meeting with the union shop steward.
7. (This is a continuation of question 6.) Assume, instead, that you are the union shop steward. Develop and present your argument that the free lunches represent a long-standing employee benefit enjoyed by the distribution center's employees and that management's attempt to stop them is a breach of an unwritten contract and will be resisted.
8. Much of the situation described in the case seems to evolve around the personality of T. D. Bigelow. How should he be treated? Why?

14

ORGANIZING AND ANALYZING LOGISTICS SYSTEMS

Automatic Guided Vehicle

Key Terms

- "C-level" position
- Centralized logistics organization
- Comprehensive systems analysis
- Customer profitability analysis
- Decentralized logistics organization
- Disintermediation
- Flexibility
- Fragmented logistics structure
- Industry systems analysis
- Information (channel) strategy
- Market strategy
- Partial systems analysis
- Process strategy
- Relevancy
- Responsiveness
- Systems analysis
- Systems constraints
- Unified logistics structure

Learning Objectives

- To examine organization structure for logistics
- To learn about traditional and contemporary organizational design for logistics
- To discuss problems and opportunities in systems analysis
- To investigate select examples of partial systems analysis
- To learn about the various audits associated with comprehensive systems analysis

This chapter continues Chapter 13's managerial theme and focuses on organizing and analyzing logistics systems. The degree to which logistics activities are fragmented or unified plays a key role in determining an organization's logistical effectiveness and efficiency, in part because a unified structure increases the likelihood of coordination across the various logistical activities. Moreover, today's dynamic business environment requires an organizational design that is more flexible and responsive than traditional command-and-control frameworks.

This chapter also discusses logistics systems analysis, both from a small-picture (partial systems analysis) and big-picture (comprehensive systems analysis) perspective. Both partial and comprehensive systems analysis aim to improve an organization's logistical effectiveness and efficiency.

ORGANIZING LOGISTICS WITHIN THE FIRM

The organization of logistics activities within a firm depends on a number of factors, including the number and location of customers, as well as an organization's size, among others.[1] For example, the number and location of customers might influence whether a firm adopts a centralized or decentralized logistics organization (to be more fully discussed in the Organization Structure section that follows). An organization's size might influence the organizing of logistics activities in the sense that there are limitations in the degree of specialization of managerial talents in small firms. In such situations, one consideration in organizing might be to even out the workloads of each manager. Thus, one manager might have transportation-related responsibilities, another manager might be responsible for ordering and inventory management, and a third manager might be assigned warehousing responsibilities.

---

[1] David J. Bloomberg, Stephan LeMay, and Joe B. Hanna, *Logistics* (Upper Saddle River, NJ: Prentice Hall, 2002).

It's not possible to present a comprehensive discussion of the many organizational topics associated with logistics. As a result, we'll focus on three key organizational topics, namely, organizational structure for logistics, logistics strategy, and organizational design for logistics.

Organizational Structure for Logistics

Two basic organizational structures are associated with logistics, namely, fragmented and unified. In a **fragmented logistics structure,** logistics activities are managed in multiple departments throughout an organization. For example, outbound transportation, demand forecasting, warehousing management, and customer service might be assigned to the marketing department, whereas procurement, inbound transportation, packaging, and materials handling might be assigned to the manufacturing department. A fragmented logistics structure might also see order management under the control of the accounting department, and inventory management might be under the auspices of the finance department.

Although the example in the previous paragraph suggests logistics activities that are spread across four separate departments, a fragmented logistics structure comes in all shapes and sizes. In a fragmented structure, it's possible for the various logistics activities to be managed in two, three, four, or more departments. Likewise, although our example assigns particular logistics activities to certain departments, there is no established template for which logistics activities should be assigned to which departments. For example, an organization might divide inventory management into three categories—raw materials, work-in-process, and finished goods; raw materials and work-in-process might be managed by the manufacturing department, whereas finished goods might be the purview of the marketing department.

One problem with a fragmented logistics structure is that because logistics activities are scattered throughout the firm, they likely remain subservient to the objectives of the department (e.g., marketing, manufacturing) in which they are housed. Moreover, because effective and efficient logistics is predicated on a high degree of coordination among logistics activities, such coordination can become difficult when the logistics activities are spread throughout an organization.

In a **unified logistics structure,** multiple logistics activities are combined into, and managed as, a single department. The unified structure can be further classified based on the number and type of activities assigned to the department. A basic unified logistics structure might have responsibility for transportation, inventory management, and warehousing. A more progressive unified structure would include these basic activities plus several additional logistics activities such as order management and customer service. An advanced unified structure would include both the basic and progressive activities, along with several other logistics activities such as demand forecasting and procurement.

Regardless of how many, or what type, of logistics activities are managed, the unified logistics structure should be better positioned than the fragmented structure to achieve coordination across the various activities. For example, efficient and accurate communication among inbound and outbound transportation, warehousing, inventory management, procurement, and so on should be facilitated when they are combined into one department. Indeed, so-called leading-edge logistics companies—firms with demonstrably superior logistical capabilities—exhibit different logistics organizational structures than do other organizations. For example, leading-edge organizations are more likely to use a unified, as opposed to fragmented, logistics organizational structure. In addition, leading-edge companies tend to manage more types of logistics activities than do other companies, including less-traditional logistics activities such as demand forecasting and procurement.[2]

----

[2]Donald J. Bowersox, Patricia J. Daugherty, Cornelia Dröge, Dale B. Rogers, and Daniel Wardlow, *Leading Edge Logistics: Competitive Positioning for the 1990s* (Oak Brook, IL: Council of Logistics Management, 1989).

An important issue in logistics organization structure is whether the logistics department should be centralized or decentralized. A **centralized logistics organization** implies that the corporation maintains a single logistics department that administers the related activities for the entire company from the home office. A **decentralized logistics organization,** in contrast, means that logistics-related decisions are made separately at the divisional or product group level and often in different geographic regions.

There are advantages to both approaches, with a primary advantage of centralization being its relative efficiency, whereas a primary advantage of decentralization is its customer responsiveness. Centralization allows an organization to take advantage of the cost savings that can arise from volume-creating opportunities. Suppose, for example, that an organization has four distribution facilities that annually generate 125,000 pounds of outbound freight, for a total outbound volume of 500,000 pounds. A centralized logistics organization should be able to achieve lower transportation rates for 500,000 pounds of volume than the individual facilities could each achieve for 125,000 pounds of volume.

Advocates of decentralization question the ability of a centralized logistics unit to provide the required levels of customer responsiveness. Indeed, this text has regularly emphasized that today's marketplace is made up of heterogeneous customers who aren't necessarily well served by centralized logistics practices. For instance, an organization with a mixture of consumer and business-to-business product lines might benefit from decentralization because of differing logistical requirements of consumer and business-to-business segments. Likewise, many global firms need to decentralize operations because of geographic and time distances from the home office. As an example, the time difference between the United States and China (at least 12 hours depending on one's location in the United States) doesn't readily lend itself to timely resolution of issues if managed under a centralized approach. Figure 14-1 illustrates the decentralized organization of a multinational medical supply firm.

Another important issue in logistics organization structure is the job title or corporate rank (e.g., manager, director, vice president, chief) of the top logistics person; indeed, one attribute of leading-edge organizations is that logistics tends to be headed by senior-level (vice president, chief) personnel.[3] Although in recent years logistics has assumed greater importance in many organizations in the sense that the top logistics person holds a vice president title, to date logistics has generally been excluded from holding a **"C-level" position,** which refers to corporate officers such as a chief executive officer (CEO), a chief operating officer (COO), or a chief financial officer (CFO). In other words, there are few companies in which logistics is led by a chief logistics officer.

Organizational Strategy

A discussion of logistics organization structure would not be complete without mention of logistics strategy, particularly given that the organizational management discipline has long been interested in the relationship between strategy and structure. A longstanding management tenet is that organizations can best achieve competitive advantage when there is a match (fit) between organizational structure and strategy.

One of the more popular frameworks suggests that logistics is characterized by three strategic orientations—process, market, and information (also referred to as channel).[4] In a **process strategy,** traditional logistics activities are managed as a value-added system. Emphasis is on achieving maximum efficiency, the primary goal is to cut costs, and the focus is on rationalizing

---

[3]Bowersox et al., *Leading Edge Logistics.*

[4]Donald J. Bowersox and Patricia J. Daugherty, "Emerging Patterns of Logistical Organizations," *Journal of Business Logistics* 8, no. 1 (1987): 46–60.

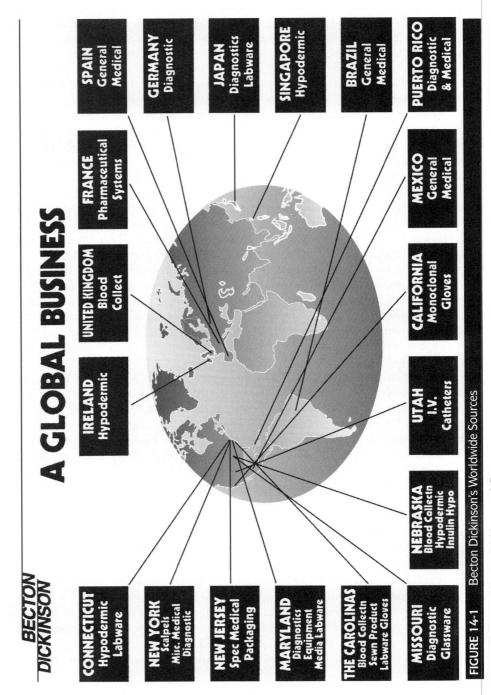

BECTON
DICKINSON

A GLOBAL BUSINESS

SPAIN
General
Medical

GERMANY
Diagnostic

JAPAN
Diagnostics
Labware

SINGAPORE
Hypodermic

BRAZIL
General
Medical

PUERTO RICO
Diagnostic
& Medical

FRANCE
Pharmaceutical
Systems

UNITED KINGDOM
Blood
Collect

IRELAND
Hypodermic

MEXICO
General
Medical

CALIFORNIA
Monoclonal
Gloves

UTAH
I.V.
Catheters

NEBRASKA
Blood Collectn
Hypodermic
Insulin Hypo

CONNECTICUT
Hypodermic
Labware

NEW YORK
Scalpels
Misc. Medical
Diagnostic

NEW JERSEY
Spec Medical
Packaging

MARYLAND
Diagnostics
Equipment
Media Labware

THE CAROLINAS
Blood Collectn
Sewn Product
Labware Gloves

MISSOURI
Diagnostic
Glassware

FIGURE 14-1   Becton Dickinson's Worldwide Sources

Source: Courtesy of Becton Dickinson and Company.

complex activities into an efficient value-added system. With a **market strategy,** a limited number of traditional logistics activities are managed across business units. Emphasis is on achieving synergy from coordinated physical distribution, the primary goal is to serve common customers from various business units, and the focus is on reducing the complexity faced by customers. In an **information (channel) strategy,** a diverse group of logistics activities, together with other activities, are managed as a channel system. Emphasis is on the coordination and control of dealer and distributor networks, and the focus is on achieving interorganizational coordination and collaboration through logistics and information management.[5]

Recent empirical research suggests that although the dominant contemporary emphasis involves maximizing efficiency, the two other dimensions (market and information) cannot be ignored. Rather, an organization's logistics strategy tends to be a blend of the three dimensions, as opposed to acting as three distinct entities.[6]

Organizational Design for Logistics[7]

Organizational design is much broader than the familiar series of boxes and lines (an example of organizational boxes and lines appears in Exhibit 14-A) that detail who reports to whom in an organization. Organizational design is also concerned with issues such as who makes work-related decisions and the appropriate communication channels between workers and managers, among others. Broadly speaking, three primary types of organizational design are used, hierarchical (also called functional), matrix, and network.

Hierarchical, or functional, organizational design has its foundations in the command and control military organization, where decision making and communication often follow a top-down flow. One advantage to hierarchical design is flexibility in exercising command in the sense that no one manager commands more than a "limited" number (e.g., 10, 20, 25) of employees. In addition, each employee reports to one, and only one, supervisor. One disadvantage of hierarchical design is that societal changes, such as individuality and questioning authority, are not easily accommodated in a command and control philosophy.

In a matrix design, one employee might have cross-functional responsibilities. For example, the manager of small appliances at a particular organization might report to logistics, marketing, and production executives, and the small appliance manager would have responsibility for the production, marketing, and logistics of small appliances. One advantage of this design is that the multifunction manager (such as the small appliance manager in our example) can be very responsive to customer requirements. One disadvantage is that a matrix organization tends to be more costly because more managerial-level employees are necessary in comparison to a hierarchical organization.

Both the hierarchical and matrix forms of organization are well suited for environments dominated by costly information and restricted communication—constraints that have been lessened by the Internet. Moreover, hierarchical and matrix organizations flourish when there are a limited number of decision alternatives as well as limited time constraints on making a decision. However, the contemporary environment is increasingly characterized by myriad decision alternatives and a shorter time window for making decisions. To this end, a network organization design attempts to create an organization that is responsive to the parameters of the contemporary business environment.

---

[5]Michael A. McGinnis and Jonathan W. Kohn, "Logistics Strategy—Revisited," *Journal of Business Logistics* 23, no. 2 (2002): 1–18, at page 2.

[6]ibid.

[7]Much of the material in this section is drawn from G. Bruce Friesen, "Organization Design for the 21st Century," *Consulting to Management* 14, no. 3 (2005): 32–51.

A key attribute of a network organizational design is a shift from function to process. In a functional–hierarchical philosophy, products and processes were divided into easy-to-complete tasks. A process philosophy, by contrast, focuses on combining tasks into *value-creating products and activities.* For example, effective and efficient order management is a process designed to produce satisfied and loyal customers, and as we discovered in Chapter 4, order management consists of a number of different tasks such as order receipt, order entry, credit check, order triage, order picking, and so on. It's only when these tasks work in concert that value is created.

The network organization's emphasis on process and value creation has important implications for organization design. Because processes and value creation tend to be customer focused, organizational design should facilitate an organization's interaction with its customers. For example, one way to facilitate customer interaction is to move decisions as close as possible to the point at which action is required, which requires empowering lower-level employees and managers with the authority to make decisions. You should recognize that the concept of worker empowerment is antithetical to the specifications of hierarchical organizational design.

Moreover, from a logistics perspective, a network organizational design is manifested in terms of relevancy, responsiveness, and flexibility. **Relevancy,** which refers to satisfying current and emerging customer needs, can be facilitated by developing mutually beneficial relationships with key customers; at a minimum, these relationships should provide an understanding of customer needs and wants. **Responsiveness** reflects the degree to which an organization can accommodate unique or unplanned customer requests; responsiveness can be achieved when the appropriate decision makers are provided with both relevant information and the authority to address unique or unplanned requests. **Flexibility,** which can be defined as an organization's ability to address unexpected operational situations, is predicated on avoiding early commitment to an irreversible course of action. One example of logistics flexibility would be the postponement of assembly, labeling, and so on until exact customer requirements are known.[8]

WHAT IS SYSTEMS ANALYSIS?

As used in this text, the term **systems analysis** refers to the orderly and planned observation of one or more segments in the logistics network or supply chain to determine how well each segment or the entire system functions. On the one hand, systems analysis can be rather narrow in scope, with the focus on looking at a single aspect of logistics (what we'll call **partial systems analysis**), such as a time-and-motion study of individuals who handle incoming freight at a receiving dock. Alternatively, systems analysis can be relatively broad in scope, with the objective of comprehensively analyzing a firm's entire logistics system (what we'll call **comprehensive systems analysis**), including its relationships with many longtime suppliers and customers.

Friction is inherent when performing systems analysis, in part because different constituencies have different viewpoints and perspectives. For example, top management might view systems analysis (either comprehensive or partial) as an opportunity to identify policies and practices that could improve logistical effectiveness and efficiency. Alternatively, operating personnel might view systems analysis as an excuse to modify existing work rules, to reduce the hours or number of workers needed, or to close production or warehousing facilities.

The types of analyses that might be performed are limited only by an organization's imagination and the availability of resources to conduct the analysis. Figure 14-2 shows a checklist

---

[8]Donald J. Bowersox, David J. Closs, and Theodore P. Stank, *21st Century Logistics: Making Supply Chain Integration a Reality* (Oak Brook, IL: Council of Logistics Management, 1999), Chapter 3.

To analyze your business, answer the following Key Logistics Strategy Questions........

Circle the appropriate number next to the question.

	Significant	Moderate	Somewhat	Not Applicable

COMPANY MARKETS

1) Has your company recently opened (or closed) new market areas generating need for additional logistics and customer service capability? — 6 4 2 0

2) Has there been a shift in the shipments to the types of customers within your company? (wholesalers, distributors, retailers, etc.) — 9 6 3 0

COMPANY PRODUCTS

3) Have there been additions and/or deletions to your company's product lines? — 6 4 2 0

4) Has a recent ABC analysis produced a difference in major and minor volume products? — 4 3 2 0

CUSTOMER SERVICE

5) Has a survey of representative customers indicated service problems? — 4 3 2 0

6) Has the customer service complaint level increased recently? — 4 3 2 0

7) Have there been any changes in EDP systems or order processing which have resulted in modifications to order cycle times? — 6 4 2 0

8) Have other system changes altered inventory reporting, resulting in increased stock outs? — 6 4 2 0

LOGISTICS OPERATIONS

9) Have internal distribution center operating factors such as labor or facility costs caused changes in location and/or operations? — 6 4 2 0

10) Has purchasing, engineering, or marketing made changes to type, quality, pack, unit, or size of product packaging? — 6 4 2 0

11) Has marketing or sales altered the characteristics (size, cycle, timing, etc.) of product promotions? — 6 4 2 0

12) Have you reached capacity in terms of volume or inventory of existing distribution facilities? — 9 6 3 0

13) Do you shuttle amounts of product between distribution locations? — 6 4 2 0

TRANSPORTATION OPERATIONS

14) Has the profile of product shipments changed in terms of TL, LTL, UPS, etc.? — 6 4 2 0

15) Does the company move inbound and outbound products across common shipping lanes? — 6 4 2 0

PRODUCT OPERATIONS

16) Has the company changed or introduced new production source points for products? — 9 6 3 0

17) Has product capacity been changed at existing production locations? — 6 4 2 0

18) Do frequent changes occur in production schedules and between product source points? — 4 3 2 0

OTHER

19) Have distribution and transportation costs increased as a percent of sales? — 9 6 3 0

20) Have there been internal structural changes within the company resulting in integration or segregation of primary business operating units? — 9 6 3 0

TOTAL POINTS

If your total points are:

* **Less than 40** - you have outlined minor issues which should be addressed as a part of your overall planning process

* **Between 40 and 70** - you should prioritize these issues and structure an analysis effort to resolve them as a part of a specific plan

* **Over 70** - you should conduct a strategy study to redirect the logistics functions to more closely correlate to the business strategy of the company.

FIGURE 14-2   A Scoring Checklist Used to Determine Logistics Planning or Strategy Study

Source: Courtesy of Robert E. Murray of REM Associates.

prepared by a consultant; it lists some of the questions that a firm should address in determining whether systems analysis is needed. Firms with high scores (i.e., more needs) are advised to conduct a strategy study to redirect the logistics functions to more closely correlate to the business strategy of the company.

Many firms have personnel who conduct systems analysis projects throughout the firm, whereas other firms prefer to use outside consultants. Although consultants can be quite expensive, they bring outside viewpoints and broader perspectives to bear on most problems and are generally viewed as bringing a neutral, objective viewpoint to the situation.

Industry Systems Analysis

Before discussing firm-specific systems analysis, mention should be made of **industry systems analysis,** which is an analysis that is performed by a trade association, professional organization, or other entity, on an industrywide basis. Individual firms cooperate by supplying data about their operations to the relevant research body. The research body then compiles data for the entire industry and reports the data in a manner that maintains each participating firm's anonymity. The participating firms can use the findings to determine how their performance compares to that of the industry as a whole or to various other industry segments (e.g., comparison to leading-edge companies). Two examples of industry systems analysis are presented next.

The Retail Industry Leaders Association (RILA) is a trade association consisting of the largest and fastest-growing companies in the retail industry. An example of RILA-related industry systems analysis is a National Shopping Behavior Study, conducted for RILA by a consulting firm, which discussed shopping patterns during the 2005 holiday season and the implications of these patterns for inventory and in-store services during 2006.[9] Alternatively, the Warehousing Education and Research Council (WERC) is a professional organization devoted to warehouse management and its role in the supply chain. An example of WERC-sponsored industry analysis is its annual publication on metrics that are used in warehousing operations.[10]

PARTIAL SYSTEMS ANALYSIS

Partial analysis is one of the building blocks of total systems analysis, and sometimes for the purposes intended, partial analysis is sufficient. It is difficult to measure a system's overall performance without measuring and understanding the performance of the various components that make up the entire system. Partial analysis contributes toward an understanding of how an entire system functions.

One danger posed by making decisions based on partial analysis of a system is that one might inadvertently commit the entire system without having tested whether the entire system would benefit. In addition, its confined focus is also a limitation because whatever findings are developed is also narrow. They cannot be used to improve an entire system, nor do partial systems analyses work well within the context of an overall reengineering effort. We'll discuss several types of partial systems analysis in this section.

Customer Profitability Analysis

Customer profitability analysis (CPA) refers to the allocation of revenues and costs to customer segments or individual customers to calculate the profitability of the segments or customers.

---

[9]*www.retail-leaders.org.*
[10]*www.werc.org.*

CPA has been facilitated by the acceptance of Activity-based costing in the sense that Activity-based costing suggests that different products are characterized by differences in the amount and types of resources consumed. In a similar vein, customer profitability analysis suggests that different customers (segments) consume differing amounts and types of resources; for example, some customers might require telephone-based communication with an organization, whereas other customers are able to communicate electronically with an organization. Customer profitability analysis is also facilitated by the sophistication of contemporary information management systems that allow both revenue and cost activities to be directly assigned to specific customers or segments.[11]

Customer profitability analysis explicitly recognizes that all customers are not the same, and some customers are more valuable than others to an organization. CPA can be used to identify different groups of customers from a profitability perspective, and such a grouping can better help in allocating an organization's resources. One grouping classification, for example, mirrors the ABC classification for inventory, and "A" customers could represent those that make a positive contribution to the bottom line. Although "B" customers might not be profitable, they allow for volume purchasing; "C" customers are highly unprofitable and might be candidates for elimination.[12] Similar to the ABC classification for inventory, the ABC customer profitability classification suggests different logistical approaches for different customer classifications. With respect to product availability, for example, organizations might attempt to minimize or avoid stockout situations for A customers, while limiting product availability for C customers.

Warehousing Productivity Analysis

Recall from Chapter 13 that productivity is a measure of output divided by input, and although a number of different productivity metrics can be used to assess warehousing productivity, not all are relevant to all kinds of facilities. Representative measures of warehousing productivity include cases shipped per person, product lines shipped per person, pallets shipped per person, average warehouse capacity used, and forklift capacity used, among others. These and other productivity metrics can be utilized to provide comparisons within an organization through time. In addition, external data may be available that can be used for benchmarking purposes depending on the relevant metrics being analyzed. Suppose, for example, that the cases shipped per hour at a particular warehouse have risen from 72 to 84 between 2004 and 2006. Although this represents a 16.7 percent ([84–72]/72) productivity improvement between 2004 and 2006, the 84 cases per hour might be viewed much differently when compared to 2006 warehousing industry data that shows a median of 99 cases shipped per hour and a best practice metric of more than 250 cases per hour.[13]

It's important to recognize that increases in warehousing productivity do not always require significant investment in technology or mechanized or automated equipment. For example, one suggestion for improving warehousing productivity involves a review of existing procedures and practices to identify the tasks that are creating the largest inefficiencies and then developing methods to reduce or eliminate the inefficiencies without adding to or upgrading present technology or equipment. Organizations can also examine their facility layouts; long horizontal runs and frequent backtracking could be symptoms of layout problems. Something as basic as adding

---

[11]Erik M. van Raaij, Maarten J.A. Vernooij, and Sander van Triest, "The Implementation of Customer Profitability Analysis: A Case Study," *Industrial Marketing Management* 32, no. 7 (2003): 573–583.

[12]Jason Bader, "How to Grade Customer Profitability," *Electrical Wholesaling,* October 2006, 36–39.

[13]Karl B. Manrodt and Kate L. Vitasek, "DC Measures 2006," *WERC Watch,* Spring 2006.

cross aisles could reduce the length of horizontal runs as well as the length of backtracking. Furthermore, although research suggests that worker incentives such as monetary awards can improve warehousing productivity, some worker incentive programs have been counterproductive because they ended up costing more than they were saving.[14]

Transportation Cost Analysis

Another example of partial systems analysis involves transportation cost analysis, and although transportation cost analysis often focuses on outbound shipments, inbound shipments should not be neglected. Indeed, simultaneous consideration of inbound and outbound freight shipments might identify opportunities to simultaneously reduce transportation expenditures while also improving customer service, as illustrated by one of the author's consulting experiences. The client in question used the same trucking company for some of its inbound and outbound shipments, but this wasn't common knowledge because inbound shipments were controlled by the procurement department, whereas outbound shipments were controlled by the production department—and the two departments rarely communicated with each other, even though they were located in the same building.

Because these two departments had little interaction, the procurement department telephoned the trucking company to schedule inbound deliveries and the production department telephoned the same trucking company to schedule outbound shipments. The lack of coordination between procurement and production meant that the trucking company routinely sent one truck to deliver inbound shipments and another truck to pick up outbound shipments. In other words, higher than necessary transportation costs were incurred because two phone calls were needed and two trucks were supplied when it would have been possible to have one truck deliver the inbound shipments and then pick up the outbound shipments.

Transportation cost analysis can provide important input into the shipment consolidation decision. Because transportation costs tend to be lower per unit of weight for larger shipments, there is a natural motivation to consolidate smaller shipments into larger ones. Wal-Mart, for example, is pursuing a "Remix" distribution strategy that strongly encourages its vendors to work with logistics service providers to consolidate less-than-truckload shipments into truckload shipments before being delivered to a Wal-Mart store.[15] It's important to recognize that shipment consolidation decisions, such as Wal-Mart's "Remix" strategy, will likely affect other logistical activities such as warehousing and inventory management.

Transportation cost analysis continues to be facilitated by advances in information technology. Some trucking companies, for example, can examine inbound or outbound deliveries for a representative period of time using data gathered from a customer's paid freight bills. This can allow both the carrier and the customer to determine whether individual shipments or shipment patterns can be improved. Moreover, it's also possible to conduct sensitivity analysis to determine the transportation costs for varying levels of transportation service. Although sensitivity analysis can provide insights about potential transportation cost savings if shifting from one service level to another, the sensitivity analysis does not estimate other relevant costs (e.g., unhappy customers because of slower transportation service).

Identifying Packaging Inefficiencies

The final partial systems analysis that we'll discuss involves packaging inefficiencies. Indeed, packaging inefficiency can have a number of undesirable logistics consequences, to

---

[14]Maida Napolitano, "Low Cost Ways to Boost Warehouse Efficiency," *Logistics Management,* August 2003, 59–64.

[15]William Hoffman, "Wal-Mart Remixes Its Inbound Delivery System," *Pacific Shipper,* May 22, 2006, 28–29.

TABLE 14-1	A Hypothetical Example of Packaging Inefficiency
Product:	One (1) Desktop tape dispenser (cube = 30 inches) 12 dispensers per carton
Product cube per carton:	30 cubic inches times 12 dispensers = **360 cubic inches**
Carton dimensions:	1,140 cubic inches
Carton efficiency:	Product cube per carton divided by carton cube **360 / 1,140 = 31.6%**
60 cartons can be put on a pallet	
Pallet capacity:	90,720 cubic inches
Carton cube per pallet:	1,140 cubic inches per carton times 60 cartons = **68,400 cubic inches**
Pallet load efficiency:	Carton cube per pallet divided by pallet capacity **68,400 / 90, 720 = 75.4%**

Carton efficiency times pallet load efficiency = the amount of pallet cube that is actually product:

31.6% times 75.4% = 23.8%

include increased loss, increased damage, slower materials handling, higher storage costs, and higher transportation costs. Chapter 5 introduced the building-blocks concept of packaging, and to refresh your memory, this means that a very small unit is placed into a slightly larger unit, which is then placed into a larger unit, and so on. This building-blocks concept is also useful for analyzing packaging inefficiency in the sense that packaging inefficiency tends to be compounded as one moves from a very small unit to a smaller unit, to a small unit, and so on.

The compounding nature of packaging inefficiency is illustrated in the hypothetical example involving desktop tape dispensers that is presented in Table 14-1. According to Table 14-1, less than one-third of the available case cube is occupied by actual product, while approximately three-quarters of available pallet space is occupied by cases. Multiplying the case efficiency (31.6 percent) by the pallet load efficiency (75.4 percent) means that less than 25 percent (23.8 percent) of available pallet space is occupied by actual product. One implication of this level of inefficiency is that an increased number of pallets will be needed, which in turn leads to higher storage and transportation costs.

The identification of packaging inefficiencies is important because these inefficiencies have been described as the "last frontier" of logistics savings opportunities. Moreover, there can be impressive cost savings as well as service improvements from improved packaging efficiency. For example, R. G. Barry, a footwear manufacturer, has reduced transportation spending by 25 percent and warehousing costs by 35 percent through improved packaging. Similar to the example presented in Table 14-1, R. G. Barry's savings resulted from optimizing "the box inside the carton, and then the carton on the pallet, and then the pallet in the warehouse." The improved packaging efficiency has also led to a substantial reduction in damaged product for R. G. Barry.[16]

---

[16]William Hoffman, "Thinking Inside the Box," *Traffic World,* December 11, 2006, 17.

COMPREHENSIVE SYSTEMS ANALYSIS

Comprehensive systems analysis looks at the entire logistics system to determine how well all its components function together. Because of the interactions among the various functional areas of logistics, logistics system analysis can be a complex and time-consuming undertaking.

Establishing Goals, Objectives, and Systems Constraints

Before beginning a comprehensive systems analysis, it is imperative that the system goals and the system objectives of the analysis be delineated, and there must be agreement about the relevant goals and objectives. As a reminder, goals tend to be broader in nature than objectives; examples of goals would be increased market share, cost minimization, or profit minimization, among others. Examples of objectives might be a customer order transmittal time of less than 24 hours or a one-hour electronic notification to customers if an ordered product is out of stock. System goals must be realistic, and systems objectives must be achievable within the context of a firm's operational scope.

System constraints—factors in the system that cannot be changed for various reasons—must also be specified. In one sense, each system constraint simplifies the situation because it tends to reduce the number of alternatives to be analyzed. Figure 14-3 shows a system constraint in which the bridge opening limits the width of what can pass through.

FIGURE 14-3   A Floating Dry Dock Passing Through a Bridge in Portland, Oregon

Source: Courtesy of Port of Portland, and Ackroyd Photography, Inc.

An example of a system constraint involves the Disneyland theme park in Anaheim, California, where only nighttime (11:15 P.M. to 7:15 A.M.) deliveries are allowed from a central warehouse to 110 vending locations throughout Disneyland. When the Disney World theme park in Florida was built, this constraint was overcome by constructing a network of tunnels and distribution, storage, and preparation facilities *beneath the new park* so that shops and restaurants can be serviced, invisibly to park guests, at any time. Vendors in Disney World, freed from the physical constraints of Disneyland, operate with lower inventory and warehousing costs.

Conducting a Comprehensive Systems Analysis

Establishing goals, objectives, and constraints should facilitate decisions about how to conduct a comprehensive systems analysis. For example, monetary resource constraints might mitigate against the use of outside consultants (because of the expense), whereas time constraints might argue for a small (in terms of number of people) analysis team. Trade-offs are also associated with conducting a comprehensive systems analysis. For example, although a systems analysis team made up of transportation, warehousing, inventory management, order management, and procurement personnel could provide a balanced and holistic perspective, it might be difficult to schedule times when all these participants are available for face-to-face meetings.

A comprehensive systems analysis consists of several different audits—channels, competition, customer, facilities, product, social responsibility, and supplier. Although each audit will be discussed individually, keep in mind that there are interactions between and among the various entities. For example, an organization's competitive environment likely affects its channel design, and an organization's social responsibility philosophy could influence channel, facility, product, or supplier considerations.

Channels Audit

Because current logistics thought includes the development of long-term relationships with other firms in one's distribution and supply channels, a logistics system design study should include some contact with these parties in the logistics channel to determine whether mutually beneficial agreements might be negotiated or, if in place, continued. This is the *channels audit*. At the very least, one wants to keep these options open and remain flexible in terms of being available for future partnerships (see Figure 14-4). When looking at suppliers and customers, one should also examine the possibilities of leveraging the assets of both. Although leveraging is often thought of in monetary terms, it could be in other terms also, say, customer service.

Channels audits can also be used to determine whether some channels can be shortened. Because each channel participant adds costs to the overall system, each participant should be retained only so long as its benefits or value added exceeds its costs. Indeed, the Internet's influence has led to an increase in **disintermediation,** or the removal of channel levels, in part because an intermediary's former value-adding capabilities might now be provided through the Internet.

Moreover, the channels audit might identify the need for distribution or channel rearrangement. With respect to distribution rearrangement, consider the recorded music industry, where customers historically bought physical products such as record albums, cassettes, or compact discs that were distributed through retail outlets such as music stores or mass merchandisers, among others. Today, by contrast, technological advances allow for digital distribution of songs, meaning that there is less demand for prerecorded cassettes or compact discs. The decreased demand for cassettes and compact discs has resulted in the failure of many longstanding music retailers, such as Tower Records, which closed in 2006.

They're a heck of a nice outfit to do business with!

| **FIGURE 14-4** | Flexibility Makes It Easier to Work Together |

Source: Copyright © Seaway Review, *Harbor House Publishers,* Boyne City, MI 49712. Reproduced with permission.

As for channel rearrangement, the Internet offers some organizations the option of a direct distribution channel (i.e., from producer to consumer with no intermediaries in between). Although this can provide potential customers flexibility in terms of purchasing products, it can also cause friction among existing channel participants, such as retailers, that risk losing sales revenues to online purchases. In addition, the logistics associated with direct distribution are different from the logistics associated with indirect distribution (e.g., smaller, less-predictable orders with direct distribution).

Competition Audit

The *competition audit* outlines the competitive environment facing an individual company, and unlike most other audits, the information required for the competition audit is generally not available within a company's own database or records. The competition audit should begin with an identification of current, as well as potential, competitors, in part because potential competitors may present more formidable challenges than do current competitors. For example, Wal-Mart's superior logistical capability often causes tremendous upheaval when it expands into product lines that have been dominated by certain retailers. Indeed, Wal-Mart is now the world's largest toy retailer, and Wal-Mart's dominance in toy retailing has led to bankruptcies and restructurings among venerable toy retailers such as FAO Schwarz and Toys "R" Us.

Moreover, an "ideal" competition audit would provide information about competitors' logistical activities, practices, and capabilities. Such information could include, but is not limited to, competitors' order transmittal methods, the accuracy and speed of their order management process, competitors' fill rates, their loss and damage records, and competitors' inventory turnover ratios. However, such logistics-specific information tends not to be readily available, and although there are ways of collecting it (e.g., industrywide questionnaires that disguise the true purpose or ultimate recipient of the data), many of these methods could be ethically questionable.

Customer Audit

The *customer audit* focuses on current as well as potential customers and provides a key input for system analysis because, in the end, the system is designed to satisfy the needs and requirements of a firm's customers. An organization's internal database can be a valuable source for conducting a customer audit in the sense that it provides information about the geographic location of customers, the number and quantity of products ordered by customers, the regularity or irregularity of customer orders, and so on.

A thorough customer audit should look beyond historical data to identify potential customers that might be served by an organization. Moreover, a thorough customer audit should also identify relevant customer-related trends that create logistics-related opportunities or challenges to an organization. Because customer expectations continue to increase through time, it becomes imperative for organizations to identify and meet or exceed relevant expectations. For example, near real-time notification of order status, which was virtually unheard of as recently as 10 years ago, has become the norm across a wide spectrum of industries.

Facilities Audit

The *facilities audit,* which focuses on an organization's various facilities, provides important data for evaluating the system. At a minimum, the facilities audit should consider the age, location, capacity, and configuration of production plants and storage facilities. A facilities audit might also include evaluations of work crews, job descriptions, and performance ratings of managers and supervisors.

A facility's age can be important to know because older facilities tend to reflect the prevailing engineering and technological wisdom at the time they were constructed—and it's safe to say that there are advances in engineering and technological knowledge through time. Moreover, older facilities may not be in compliance with contemporary health, safety, and environmental regulations; the Americans with Disabilities Act (ADA), which took effect in the 1990s, has detailed requirements with respect to design considerations (e.g., aisle width, signage placement and size). Changing trade patterns, both within and across countries, necessitate periodic analysis of the location of an organization's production plants and storage facilities. The relocation of a great deal production from the United States to China has caused a dramatic reconfiguration of many logistical systems.

A facility's capacity can be evaluated across dimensions such as its total capacity and the percent of capacity being used, among others. The percent of capacity being used provides insights into the efficiency or inefficiency of capacity utilization in the sense that excessive unused capacity can be quite costly to an organization. Configuration considerations include, but are not limited to, a facility's shape, layout, and placement of dock doors. One of the authors once toured a distribution center in the shape of a trapezoid, in which inbound and outbound operations were conducted through two dock doors located on the shortest "leg" of the trapezoid. Not surprisingly, this facility was plagued by lengthy loading and unloading times as well as high labor costs (two shifts, rather than one, were needed to do the necessary work).

Product Audit

The *product audit* evaluates the existing product line, and most of the relevant information should be available in a firm's existing records. The product-related information includes, but is not limited to, (1) annual sales volume, (2) seasonality, (3) packaging (including size, weight, and special handling needs), (4) transportation and warehouse information, (5) present manufacturing or assembly facilities, (6) ease with which manufacturing of product can be scheduled, (7) warehouse stocking locations, (8) present transport modes utilized, (9) sales by region, (10) complementary products that are often sold at the same time as the product under consideration, (11) relationship to other products in the firm's total product line, and (12) product profitability.

The product audit can also be helpful in terms of evaluating decisions about adding new products or new product lines to an existing product mix. As an example, Procter and Gamble's (P&G) acquisition of Gillette has allowed P&G to broaden its product mix by adding a number of personal care products that are targeted to males (historically, P&G's personal care products were largely targeted to females). In addition, there appears to be a great deal of synergy between the two companies because Gillette's personal care products are distributed in the same channels as P&G products, they have similar production requirements as P&G personal care items, and the Gillette products have similar packaging, handling, transportation, and warehousing requirements.

Social Responsibility Audit

The social responsibility concept suggests that an organization's obligations transcend purely economic considerations such as profit maximization. To this end, the *social responsibility audit* identifies the relevant social responsibility dimensions in the supply chain and then assesses current activities or practices along the supply chain regarding these dimensions. Because supply chains differ across industries, the relevant social responsibility dimensions may also differ. For example, animal welfare—the idea that animals should not endure unnecessary suffering—is likely to be a relevant social responsibility issue in the food supply chain as opposed to, say, the automotive supply chain.[17]

Potential social responsibility dimensions include the environment, ethics, diversity, safety, philanthropy, and human rights, among others, and myriad activities or practices can be used to assess each of these dimensions. In terms of the environment, for example, organizations might focus on reusing and recycling products, reducing the amount of packaging, improving fuel efficiency, and reducing various types of pollution. Ethical considerations include improperly sharing information, as well as bribes and gift giving, whereas diversity might evaluate the use of minority and female suppliers. Safety-related activities or practices include the safe movement and storage of products, particularly those of a hazardous nature, preventive vehicle maintenance, and proper workplace equipment (e.g., hardhats, goggles). Philanthropic logistics activities might include the donation of excess or obsolete inventory to charitable organizations, and sweatshop labor continues to be a preeminent human rights consideration.

Supplier Audit

The supplier audit evaluates an organization's suppliers of raw materials, component parts, and professional services such as third-party logistics providers. A variety of aspects can be relevant to this audit, including the number of suppliers, the type(s) of suppliers, supplier costs, the cost

---

[17]Michael J. Maloni and Michael E. Brown, "Corporate Social Responsibility in the Supply Chain: An Application in the Food Industry," *Journal of Business Ethics* 68, no. 1 (2006): 35–52.

effectiveness and efficiency of suppliers, an assessment of supplier quality, and other performance criteria that are specified in the supplier evaluation process that was discussed in Chapter 11.

Supplier audits can also have a diagnostic purpose in the sense that current supplier practices and activities can be evaluated for their compliance or noncompliance with relevant corporate policies. If there are discrepancies between the current practices and corporate policies, the supplier audit can further indicate if the appropriate penalties for noncompliance are being provided. For example, one of the authors provided consulting services for a company that had a core carrier policy that specified the 10 trucking companies that were to be used for any shipments moving by truck. In reality, the company used well over *100 different trucking companies* each year, in part because the specified penalties for noncompliance were rarely applied.

Acting on the Audit Data

Once the various audits have been completed, the next step is to examine and analyze the collected data. The data should be examined and analyzed for each individual audit, and analyses should also be conducted between and among the different audits. Contemporary software packages make it much faster and easier to simultaneously analyze data from multiple audits.

Although comprehensive systems analysis is concerned with improving logistical effectiveness and efficiency, it is rare that a logistics system is completely redesigned at one time. A one-time, across-the-board redesign can be quite expensive to implement and can also be traumatic for many firms because of a natural resistance to change. Again, contemporary software packages can be useful for identifying the biggest bottlenecks to logistical efficiency—and thus the areas in need of immediate change. Having said this, the proliferation of logistics-related software packages could actually be counterproductive (see Figure 14-5).

"Fred's targeting our systems options as we speak."

FIGURE 14-5 There May Be an Overabundance of Logistics-Related Software Packages

Source: Used with the permission of Material Handling Management, copyright Penton Media, Inc.

Summary

This chapter covered two primary topics, namely, organizing and analyzing logistics systems. With respect to the former, the chapter looked at organizational structure for logistics and discussed the fragmented and unified structures as well as centralized and decentralized logistics organizations. Organizational design for logistics was also discussed, with a particular emphasis on network organizational design and its implications for logistics.

As for analyzing logistics systems, the chapter looked at systems analysis, both from an industrywide (industry systems analysis) and firm-specific (partial systems analysis, comprehensive systems analysis) perspective. Several representative examples of partial systems analysis were presented, including customer profitability analysis, warehousing productivity analysis, transportation cost analysis, along with identifying packaging inefficiencies.

This chapter also covered comprehensive systems analysis. Prior to beginning a comprehensive systems analysis, the relevant goals, objectives, and systems constraints must be established. The various audits associated with comprehensive systems analysis were examined, and the chapter concluded with a brief discussion of acting on the data collected in the various audits.

Questions for Discussion and Review

1. Discuss several issues that influence the organization of logistics activities within a firm.
2. Compare and contrast the fragmented and unified logistics organizational structures.
3. What are the differences between a centralized and a decentralized logistics department?
4. Discuss the process, market, and information logistics strategies.
5. Describe the hierarchical and matrix organizational design.
6. From a logistics perspective, how is network organizational design manifested in terms of relevancy, responsiveness, and flexibility?
7. Define logistics systems analysis. Why is friction inherent when performing logistics systems analysis?
8. What is industry systems analysis? What is its value?
9. What is partial systems analysis? Why is it used?
10. Discuss customer profitability analysis.
11. Explain how warehousing productivity can be improved without significant investment in technology or mechanized, or automated equipment.
12. How have advances in information technology facilitated transportation cost analysis?
13. Explain the compounding nature of packaging inefficiency. What cost savings and service improvements can occur with better packaging efficiency?
14. How might goals, objectives, and constraints facilitate decisions about how to conduct a comprehensive systems analysis?
15. Discuss how the channels audit might identify the need for distribution or channel rearrangement.
16. Why should the competition audit identify both current and potential competitors?
17. Explain why the facilities audit should consider the age and capacity of production plants and storage facilities.
18. How can the product audit be helpful in evaluating decisions about adding new products or new product lines?
19. Describe several dimensions of the social responsibility audit.
20. Name the seven types of comprehensive logistics systems audits that should be performed. Which do you view as the most important? The least important? Why?

Suggested Readings

Bhatnagar, Rohit, and S. Viswanathan. "Re-engineering Global Supply Chains." *International Journal of Physical Distribution & Logistics Management* 30, no. 1 (2000): 13–34.

Elmuti, Dean. "The Perceived Impact of Supply Chain Management on Organizational Effectiveness." *Journal of Supply Chain Management* 38, no. 3 (2002): 49–57.

Fawcett, Stanley E., and Gregory M. Mandan. "The Rhetoric and Reality of Supply Chain Integration." *International Journal of Physical Distribution & Logistics Management* 32, no. 5 (2002): 339–362.

Lowson, Robert. "The Implementation and Impact of Operations Strategies in Fast-Moving Supply Systems." *Supply Chain Management: An International Journal* 7, no. 3 (2002): 146–163.

Maloni, Michael J., and Michael E. Brown. "Corporate Social Responsibility in the Supply Chain: An Application in the Food Industry." *Journal of Business Ethics* 68, no. 1 (2006): 35–52.

McGinnis, Michael A., and Jonathan W. Kohn. "Logistics Strategy Revisited." *Journal of Business Logistics* 23, no. 2 (2002): 1–17.

Minis, Ioannis, Marion Paraschi, and Apostolos Tzimourtas. "The Design of Logistics Operations for the Olympic Games." *International Journal of Physical Distribution & Logistics Management* 36, no. 8 (2006): 621–641.

Mollenkopf, Diane, and G. Peter Dapiran. "World-Class Logistics: Australia and New Zealand." *International Journal of Physical Distribution & Logistics Management* 35, no. 1 (2005): 63–74.

Poirer, Charles C. "Achieving Supply Chain Connectivity." *Supply Chain Management Review* 6, no. 6 (2002): 16–22.

Ross, David F. "The Intimate Supply Chain" *Supply Chain Management Review* 10, no. 5 (2006): 50–57.

Smeltzer, Larry R. "Integration Means Everybody: Big and Small." *Supply Chain Management Review* 5, no. 5 (2001): 36–44.

Towill, Denis, and Martin Christopher. "The Supply Chain Strategy Conundrum: To be Lean or Agile or To be Lean and Agile?" *International Journal of Logistics: Research & Applications* 5, no. 3 (2002): 299–310.

Van Raaij, Erik M., Maarten J. A. Vernooij, and Sander van Triest. "The Implementation of Customer Profitability Analysis: A Case Study." *Industrial Marketing Management* 32, no. 7 (2003): 573–583.

Whitfield, Gwendolyn, and Robert Landeros. "Supplier Diversity Effectiveness: Does Organizational Culture Really Matter?" *Journal of Supply Chain Management* 42, no. 4 (2006): 17–29.

CASES

CASE 14-1 COLUMBIA LUMBER PRODUCTS COMPANY

The Columbia Lumber Products Company (CLPC) was headquartered in Portland, Oregon, where it had been founded in 1899. For many years, its principal product had been only lumber; in the 1940s it began producing plywood, and in 1960, particleboard. The first two products, lumber and plywood, were produced at various sites in Oregon and marketed on the West Coast and as far east as Chicago.

Particle board was produced in Duluth, Minnesota, at a plant built in 1962 with a U.S. Area Redevelopment Administration Loan. Initially, the input to the plant was trimmings and other scrap from CLPC's Oregon operations. Particleboard sales increased so quickly that the Duluth operation consumed not only all of the former waste from CLPC's Oregon plant but also waste purchased from various lumber and wood products operations in Minnesota and northern Wisconsin.

In terms of product volume, CLPC's sales doubled between 1960 and 1990. However, nearly all the growth had been in particleboard; lumber and plywood sales remained relatively constant (although varying with changes in the home construction industry). In 1996, exports accounted for 9 percent of CLPC's sales. Nearly all of this was plywood sold to Japan. Fifteen percent of CLPC's 1996 purchases were from foreign sources, 5 percent was mahogany from the Philippines used for plywood veneer, and 10 percent was wood scrap purchased from Ontario, Canada, for use in CLPC's Duluth plant. Particleboard produced in Duluth was marketed in all states east of the Rocky Mountains, although sales in the southern United States were somewhat less than spectacular.

The slowdown in home production, which started in the late 1970s and, in the Midwest, really never ended, resulted in many years of little or no growth in CLPC's sales. Common stock dividends had been cut several times. In 1996, they were 37 cents per share, down considerably from their peak—in 1976—of $2.21.

Stockholders, the outside directors, and various lending institutions were becoming increasingly unhappy. After a long, tense board of directors meeting, agreement was reached only with respect to what some of the organizational problems were. A partial list follows:

1. The corporation headquarters was in Portland, although any growth occurred in the Midwest. Possibly the headquarters, or at least more functions, should be shifted to an office in Duluth, where the plant was, or to Chicago, where the largest sales office was. A major relocation away from Portland would be difficult. Many employees would choose to remain on the West Coast. Even for those willing to relocate, there was a split between those willing to relocate to Duluth and those willing to relocate to Chicago.

2. There were too many vice presidents (see Exhibit 14-A). Because four vice presidents (engineering, finance, human resources, and purchasing) would reach mandatory retirement age by 1997, the number of vice presidents should be reduced from nine to no more than six (plus one executive vice president).

3. Logistics and distribution costs were higher than industry averages. The majority of customer complaints dealt with poor deliveries. In Exhibit 14-A, a T shows where a traffic management function was located. Geographically, the traffic manager for overseas operations was located in Seattle, which was a foreign trade center for the Pacific Northwest. The Chicago sales office had a traffic manager who handled all fiberboard distribution, and lumber and plywood distribution east of the Rockies. Production and purchasing shared a traffic manager who was headquartered in Portland and whose principal duty was overseeing shipments of waste products from Oregon to Minnesota. Another traffic manager (in Portland), who reported to the sales vice president, was acknowledged to be the firm's senior traffic manager and more or less coordinated the efforts of the other three. Recently Irwin Buchanan III had been promoted to that post. He was the only one authorized to initiate action before regulatory bodies, and he also handled the negotiations with carrier rate-making bodies and with carriers. (CLPC used contract truckers and rail for most of its shipping.)

4. The purchasing department handled the details of fleet management, which included about a hundred autos on long-term lease for use by management and by the sales force. Several light trucks were leased for use around the plants.

5. CLPC also owned two small aircraft, which often were the target of questions during stockholders' meetings. One plane was based at Portland, the other at Duluth.

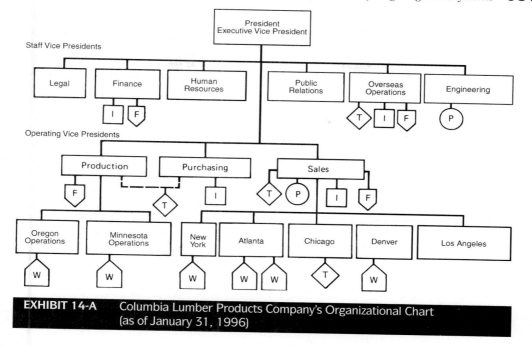

EXHIBIT 14-A   Columbia Lumber Products Company's Organizational Chart (as of January 31, 1996)

Each was used in its respective region for trips to sites without scheduled airline service. Both planes were under control of the production department. Other departments, especially sales, complained that the planes were being used for the benefit of the production department, rather than for the benefit of the entire firm.

6. P in the exhibit shows two packaging engineering functions. The one under engineering was located in Portland and dealt with plywood products. The one under sales was located in Chicago and handled particleboard products. The two packaging engineering functions saw their roles differently. The one in Portland was concerned mainly with safe packing and packaging of products moving between CLPC plants or from CLPC plants to customers. The Chicago packaging engineers were interested in finding new markets for particleboard and lumber as packaging materials to be sold to others. w in the exhibit shows where there are company-owned

warehouses. Numerous public warehouses were also used, although not continually. I shows locations of individuals concerned with inventory levels. All four individuals were located in Portland. F indicates where sales forecasting took place. Only sales and production devoted much staff to forecasting. Each quarter, however, the financial vice president's office coordinated all forecasts to ensure comparability. Computer operations were under control of the engineering division. CLPC's executive vice president determined priorities for computer access and use.

7. The human resources department handled employee moves, although only a few had taken place since 1980. An outside director, who was familiar with current federal legislation, suggested that CLPC negotiate a contract with a household goods carrier to handle all CLPC employee moves. This action would be especially significant if a major reorganization resulted in numerous employee transfers. ■

QUESTIONS

1. Draw a new organization chart for Columbia Lumber Products Company that you feel best overcomes the directors' criticisms of CLPC's present (January 31, 1996) organization. Indicate the geographic location of all operations shown on the new chart. Explain why you established the organization chart the way you did.

2. Assume that the firm should be reorganized in a manner that emphasizes sales and marketing. This would include a physical distribution system, which would support the marketing effort. Draw an organization chart that you think would accomplish this aim. Indicate the geographic location of all operations on the new chart and explain why you drew the chart as you did.

3. Assume that the firm wants to reorganize into a highly centralized form, closely managed from a single home office. Draw a new chart that takes this into account. Indicate the geographic location of all operations on the chart and explain why you organized it as you did.

4. Assume, instead, that the firm wants to reorganize into a highly decentralized form, where many important decisions can be made out in the field. Draw up a new chart, including the geographic location of all activities. Explain why you drew it up as you did.

5. Young Irwin Buchanan III, the firm's senior traffic manager, heard rumors that the number of vice presidents was to be reduced. He felt that this would reduce his chances of ever achieving vice presidential—or presidential—status. Luckily, he had access to some money in a family trust fund. He wondered whether he should propose to form a separate, third-party firm to contract with CLPC to perform CLPC's logistical operations. What functions should it offer to perform?

6. (This is a continuation of the situation in question 5.) Assume that young Buchanan does decide to form an outside firm to handle CLPC's logistics operations. Draft his letter to CLPC's management containing such a proposal.

CASE 14-2   TRIGO EXPORT CO., LTD.

The Trigo Export Company, Ltd., of Montreal, was appointed to be the manufacturer's export agent for the Ziola Tractor Company, Ltd., of Winnipeg. The tractor company was best known for its snow blowers, but the same 4 1/2-horsepower engine and frame were modified to become a garden tractor. The Trigo Company specialized in agricultural implements sold in Central and South America, and its agreement with Ziola covered only sales to that area.

Trigo's sales force was aggressive and, after only two weeks, got the chance to bid on a large shipment of garden tractors to be delivered to Belem (a Brazilian port near the mouth of the Amazon). The customer was a charitable organization, and the only quantities mentioned were "somewhere between 40 and 100 units" of the Ziola Speedwagon model. After the shipment arrived in Belem, the tractors would be distributed by the charity to various settlements in the Amazon basin. Trigo's sales representative advised his home office that he thought price per unit would be an important criterion that the buyer would use in evaluating bids. He also said that two U.S. firms and a Korean firm were submitting bids. All bids would be FAS (free alongside) vessel in Belem.

He said that Trigo should quote prices for (a) 40 units, (b) 100 units, and (c) whatever quantity between 40 and 100 that had the lowest cost per tractor. In case either 40 units or 100 units happened to have the lowest cost per unit, quotes would be needed for only (a) and (b).

Trigo's staff, with some help from people working for Ziola, began gathering facts. Following are some of them:

1. No import duties, permits, or licenses are required.
2. Documentation costs would be CAN$250 per shipment.
3. Ziola would sell to Trigo any quantity of tractors up to 500 at CAN$700 each, FOB

(free on board) plant (at Winnipeg). This price would include packaging for export and a separate, related bar code for each carton in the shipment. The packaging materials consisted of at least 40 percent recycled contents. Ziola would load the packaged tractors into 20-foot intermodal containers and deliver the loaded containers to the railroad's Winnipeg container station.

4. Trigo had to select a port. Canada has two major East Coast ports, Montreal and Halifax. Montreal is positioned better to handle traffic to and from Europe, whereas Halifax is the northerly stop used by vessel lines calling along the Atlantic Coast. Trigo decided to use the port of Halifax. Combined rail and ocean costs through this port were the lowest. Sailing services were less frequent than at some U.S. North Atlantic ports, but time saving did not appear to be an issue. Three scheduled liner operators—Frota Amazonica, S.A.; Ivaran Lines; and Hanjin Shipping Co.—all quoted similar rates. Their rates included port charges in Halifax and unloading in Belem. Port charges in Belem would be separate (but would be assumed by the buyer of the tractors).

5. Rail charges from Winnipeg to the container terminal at Halifax were CAN$400 per 20-foot container. This was cheaper than using a truck.

6. The exterior dimensions of each packaged tractor were 1 meter by 1 meter by 1 meter. The weight of each tractor was 200 kilos, and the package weighed 20 kilos for a total of 220 kilos per tractor. (Shipping charges by weight include both the tractor and its package.)

7. The interior dimensions of the 20-foot containers are 2.35 meters wide, 6.12 meters long, and 2.50 meters high.

8. Ocean rates from Halifax to Belem for loaded containers carrying cargo of this type are CAN$110 per ton (of 2,200 pounds). However, the ocean lines also use the rule of the measurement ton, which means that if a cubic meter weighs less than 1,000 kilograms, the cubic meter shall be considered as weighing 1,000 kilograms. Freight charges would have to be paid just before the cargo was loaded aboard ship. Rail transit time from Winnipeg to Halifax was five days.

9. Insurance charges were 1 percent of the shipment's value while the goods were in Canada and 2 percent while they were at sea.

10. Ziola expected to be paid the day the loaded containers were delivered to the railroad in Winnipeg. The Brazilian buyer would pay for the tractors as they were unloaded from the ship in Belem. Trigo would own the tractors for an estimated 25 days: 5 from Winnipeg to Halifax, 2 in Halifax, 17 at sea, and 1 in Belem. Trigo's line of credit at the Bank of Montreal was currently costing 12 percent interest annually.

11. Trigo wanted to mark up all costs by 10 percent to cover its overhead and profit. ■

QUESTIONS

1. Ziola's export packaging materials consisted of at least 40 percent recycled contents. Should this be mentioned in the quotation given to the potential Brazilian buyer?

2. Each package in this shipment will be bar coded. Is this an example of supply chain integration? Why or why not?

3. What price should be quoted for 40 tractors?

4. What price should be quoted for 100 tractors?

5. Is there another quantity between 40 and 100 where the costs per tractor are lower? If so, what is it? What are its costs per tractor?

6. For how long into the future should the price quote be made (i.e., for how long should

Trigo agree to deliver at a certain price?)? Why?

7. In what currency should Trigo ask to be paid? Why?

8. After preparing the bid, Ziola calls Trigo and says that they are thinking of redesigning the tractor frame so that it can be disassembled, taking up half the space. A Ziola Speedwagon could fit into an export package measuring 1 meter by 1 meter by 0.5 meter. The weight of the packaged tractor would continue to be 220 kilos. By how much, if at all, would this new package size reduce the answers for questions 3 and 4?

Glossary

ABC analysis Concept that recognizes that because inventories are not of equal value to a firm, they should not be managed in the same way.

Accumulating (bulk-making) Bringing together inventory from different sources.

Activity-based costing (ABC) A technique that seeks to better understand the cost of a product by identifying what activities drive particular costs.

Accessorial service Transportation service that is supplemental to line-haul transportation.

Agile supply chain Focuses on an organization's ability to respond to changes in demand with respect to volume and variety.

Allocating (bulk-breaking) Breaking larger quantities into smaller quantities.

Amodal shipper A transportation manager who purchases a prespecified level of transportation service and is indifferent to the mode(s) or carrier(s) used to provide the actual transportation service.

Application-specific software Refers to software that has been developed for managers to deal with specific logistics functions or activities (e.g., transportation management systems).

Artificial intelligence (AI) Sophisticated use of the computer in which it is programmed to "think" as a trained, skilled human in specific situations.

Assorting Building up a variety of different products for resale to a particular customer.

Backhaul A return trip or movement in a direction of secondary importance or purpose.

Back order Materials requested by a customer that are unavailable for shipment at the same time as the remainder of the order. They are usually shipped when available.

Bar-code scanners Electronic devices that read bar codes and can be used to keep track of inventory, reorder inventory, and analyze inventory patterns.

Barge Flatboard boat used to transport heavy products.

Batch number Refers to alphanumeric identification that specifies where a product was processed or manufactured.

Benchmarking Using measures of another organization's performance to judge one's own performance.

Bill of lading The most important single transportation document that is the basic operating document in the industry.

Bonded storage Refers to warehousing situations where goods are not released until applicable fees are paid. As an example, Internal Revenue Service–bonded warehouses hold goods until other federal taxes and fees are collected.

Bribes Money paid before an exchange.

Broker A company that helps both shipper and carrier achieve lower freight rates and more efficient utilization of carrier equipment. Brokers also help match carriers to loads.

Brownfields Locations that contain chemicals or other types of industrial wastes.

Building-blocks concept Combining smaller packages into larger units that can be more efficiently handled at one time.

Bulk cargo Refers to cargo stowed loose, without specific packing, and generally handled with a pump, scoop, or shovel.

Bullwhip effect Characterized by variability in demand orders among supply chain participants.

"C-level" position Refers to corporate officers such as a chief executive officer (CEO), chief operating officer (COO), or chief financial officer (CFO).

Cargo preference Requires a certain percentage of traffic to move on a nation's flag vessels.

Carrier An individual or firm in the business of carrying cargo or passengers.

Cause and effect (associative) forecasting Assumes that one or more factors are related to demand, and the relationship between cause and effect can be used to estimate future demand.

Center-of-gravity approach An approach for locating a single facility that minimizes the distance to existing facilities.

Centralized logistics organization An organization maintains a single logistics department that administers the related activities for the entire company from the home office.

Certificate of origin Specifies the country(ies) in which a product is manufactured.

Channel intermediaries Facilitators that make the channel function better.

Class rate system A system that simplifies each of the three primary rate factors—product, weight, and distance.

Classification Numbers assigned to various types of freight, based mainly on the carrier's costs of handling that type of product, and, along with weight and distance, used as a basis for determining the costs of shipment.

Closed-loop systems Refers to systems that consider the return flow of products, their reuse, and the marketing and distribution of recovered products.

Co-branding One location where customers can purchase products from two or more name-brand retailers.

Collaborative planning, forecasting, and replenishment (CPFR) Retail industry initiative where trading partners share planning and forecasting data to better match supply and demand.

Commercial invoice A document used in cross-border trade that summarizes the entire transaction and contains key information such as a description of the goods, the terms of sale and payment, and so on.

Commodity rate A specific rate for every possible combination of product, weight, and distance.

Common carrier Transportation carrier that has agreed to serve the general public and assumes four legal obligations: service, delivery, reasonable rates, and avoidance of discrimination.

Communication system These help various stakeholders to work together by interacting and sharing information in many different forms.

Complementary products Inventories that are used or distributed together (e.g., razor blades and razors).

Comprehensive systems analysis Looks at the entire logistics systems to see how well all of its components function together.

Concealed damage Damage that is not initially apparent but is discovered after a package is opened.

Consignee The receiver of a shipment.

Consignor The shipper of goods.

Consolidate Assemble small shipments into a single, larger shipment.

Containers A uniform sealed reusable metal "box" in which goods are shipped.

Container Security Initiative (CSI) An agreement in which the world's ports agree to allow U.S. customs agents to identify and inspect high-risk containers bound for the United States before they are loaded onto ships.

Contract carrier A contract carrier provides specialized service to each customer based on a contractual arrangement.

Contract logistics A long-term arrangement between a shipper and another party to provide logistics services.

Contract (third-party) warehousing A type of contract logistics that focuses on providing unique and specially tailored warehousing services to particular clients.

Control Measurement that ensures conformity with an organization's policies, procedures, or standards.

Cost trade-offs Changes to one logistics activity cause some costs to increase and others to decrease.

Cross-docking A process where product is received in a facility, occasionally married with product going to the same destination, then shipped at the earliest opportunity, without going into long-term storage.

Cube out Occurs when a cargo takes up a vehicle's or a container's cubic capacity before reaching its weight capacity.

Customer profitability analysis (CPA) Refers to the allocation of revenues and costs to customer segments or individual customers to calculate the profitability of the segments or customers.

Customer satisfaction Compares actual experience to the expected experience, and if the actual experience equals or exceeds the expected experience, then the customer is satisfied.

Customer service Strives to keep customers happy and creates in the customer's mind the perception of an organization that is easy to do business with.

Customshouse brokers An intermediary that oversees the efficient movement of importers' goods (and accompanying paperwork) through customs and other inspection points.

Customs Trade Partnership Against Terrorism (C-TPAT) A program in which public and private organizations work together to prevent terrorism against the United States through imports and transportation.

Cycle (base) stock Inventory needed to satisfy demand during an order cycle.

Data Facts or recorded measures of certain phenomena.

Data mining Utilizes sophisticated quantitative techniques to find hidden patterns in large volumes of data.

Dead inventory (stock) Product for which there is no demand.

Decentralized logistics organization Logistics-related decisions are made separately at the divisional or product group level and often in different geographic regions.

Decision support system (DSS) Helps managers make decisions by providing information, models, or analysis tools.

Delivery window The time span within which a scheduled delivery must be made.

Demand management The creation across the supply chain and its markets of a coordinated flow of demand.

Demurrage A charge assessed by rail carriers to users that fail to unload and return vehicles or containers promptly.

Density A measure of how heavy a product is in relation to its size.

Detention A payment from a shipper or consignee to a truck carrier for having kept the carrier's equipment too long.

Department of Transportation (DOT) U.S. federal government body with primary responsibility for transportation safety regulation.

Dimensional (dim) weight Considers a shipment's density (the amount of space occupied relative to weight) to determine a shipment's billable weight.

Disintermediation The removal of levels (layers) from a channel of distribution.

Distribution center A warehouse with an emphasis on quick throughput, such as is needed in supporting marketing efforts.

Diversion Occurs when the shipper notifies the carrier, prior to the shipment's arrival in the destination city, of a change in destination.

Documentation The documents associated with transportation shipments.

Draft The depth in the water to which a vessel can be loaded.

Dunnage Material that is used to block and brace products inside carrier equipment to prevent the shipment from shifting in transit and becoming damaged.

Economic order quantity (EOQ) An order size that minimizes the sum of carrying and ordering costs.

Economic utility Refers to the value or usefulness of a product in fulfilling customer needs and wants.

Electronic commerce Economic activity that can be conducted via electronic connections such as EDI and the Internet.

Electronic data interchange (EDI) Computer-to-computer transmission of business data in a structured format.

Electronic procurement (e-procurement) Uses the Internet to make it easier, faster, and less expensive for an organization to purchase goods and services.

Embargoes Prohibition of trade between particular countries.

Empowerment zone Created by the U.S. Department of Housing and Urban Development to encourage business development—through various tax credits—in economically depressed portions of cities.

Enterprise resource planning (ERP) system System that attempts enterprisewide coordination of relevant business processes by allowing (conceptually, at least) all functional areas within a firm to access and analyze a common database.

Ergonomics The science that seeks to adapt work or working conditions to suit the abilities of the worker.

Excess capacity Unused available space.

Excess (surplus) materials Stock that exceeds the reasonable requirements of an organization.

Expatriate workers Employees who are sent to other countries for extended periods of time.

Exempt carrier For-hire carriers that have been exempted from economic regulation through provisions in various pieces of legislation.

Expediting The need to rapidly move a shipment to its final destination.

Export management company Firm that helps a domestic company become involved in foreign sales. They often locate foreign firms that can be licensed to manufacture the product in the foreign country.

Export packers An international logistics specialist that custom packs shipments when the exporter lacks the equipment or expertise to do so itself.

Facility closing A company discontinues operations at a current site because the operations are no longer needed or can be absorbed by other facilities.

Facility location Refers to choosing the locations for distribution centers, warehouses, and production facilities to facilitate logistical effectiveness and efficiency.

Facility relocation A firm must move operations to another facility to better serve suppliers or customers.

Fast supply chain Emphasizes a speed or time component.

Field warehousing A facility temporarily established at the site of inventory; the warehouser assumes custody of the inventory and issues a receipt for it, which can then be used as collateral for a loan.

Fixed order interval system Inventory is replenished on a constant, set schedule and is always ordered at a specific time; the quantity ordered varies depending on forecasted sales before the next order date.

Fixed order quantity system Inventory is replenished with a set quantity every time it is ordered; the time interval between orders may vary.

Fixed slot location Each product is assigned a specific location in a warehouse and is always stored there.

Flags of convenience Refers to ships that register in nations that have lax maritime registration rules, particularly with respect to safety requirements.

Flexibility An organization's ability to address unexpected operational situations.

FOB destination (delivered) pricing Price that includes both the price of the product and the transportation cost of the product to the purchaser's receiving dock.

FOB origin pricing Price of the product at seller's place of business. Buyer must arrange for transportation of the product from the seller's place of business.

Form utility Refers to a product's being in a form that (1) can be used by the customer and (2) is of value to the customer.

Fourth-party logistics (lead logistics provider) General contractor that ensures that third-party logistics companies are working toward relevant supply chain goals and objectives.

Fragmented logistics structure Logistics activities are managed in multiple departments throughout an organization.

Free (foreign) trade zone An area, usually near a port or an airport, where goods can be stored or processed before entering through the importing nation's customs inspections.

Freight absorption Buyer pays a lower freight charge than the shipper incurs in shipping the product.

Freight bill An invoice submitted by a transportation carrier requesting to be paid.

Freight claims A document that notifies a transportation carrier of wrong or defective deliveries, delay, or other delivery shortcoming.

Freight forwarder Consolidates freight shipments and buys transportation services in volume rates.

Global positioning systems (GPS) Use satellites that allow companies to compute vehicle positions, velocity, and time.

Global procurement (sourcing) Refers to buying components and inputs anywhere in the world.

Goods in transit Goods moving between two points, often accompanied by a live bill of lading.

Graphical information systems (GIS) Allow companies to produce digital maps that can drill down to site-specific qualities such as bridge heights.

Grid system A location technique utilizing a map or grid, with specific locations marked on the north–south and east–west axes. Its purpose is to find a location that minimizes transportation costs.

GSCF model A framework that identifies eight relevant processes, such as customer relationship management, demand management, and order fulfillment, associated with supply chain management.

Hazardous materials A substance or material in a quantity and form that may pose an unreasonable risk to health and safety or property when transported in commerce.

Import quotas Absolute limits to the quantity of a product that can be imported into a country during a particular time period.

In bond Cargo on which taxes or duties have yet to be paid. The owner must post a bond or use a bonded carrier or warehouse to guarantee that the materials will not be sold until the taxes or duties are paid.

Inbound logistics The movement and storage of materials into a firm.

Incoterms 2000 Terms of sale for international transactions that represent, from the seller's viewpoint, the different locations, or stages, for quoting a price to an overseas buyer.

Industry systems analysis Analysis that is performed by a trade association, professional organization, or other entity, on an industrywide basis.

Information A body of facts in a format suitable for decision making.

Information (channel) strategy A strategic orientation where a diverse group of logistics activities, together with other activities, are managed as a channel system.

Intermodal competition Refers to the number of transportation modes available to prospective users.

Intermodal transportation Using a container that can be transferred from the vehicle of one mode to a vehicle of another, and with the movement covered under a single bill of lading.

International Air Transport Association (IATA) A cartel consisting of nearly all the world's scheduled international airlines.

International freight forwarders An international trade specialist that can handle either vessel shipments or air shipments and that offers a number of different functions such as booking space on carriers, obtaining consular documents, and arranging for insurance, among others.

International logistics Refers to logistical activities associated with goods that move across national boundaries.

Intramodal competition Refers to the number of carriers within each mode.

Inventory Stocks of goods and materials that are maintained for many purposes.

Inventory carrying (holding) costs The costs of holding an inventory, such as interest on investment, insurance, deterioration, and so on.

Inventory flow diagram Depicts the demand for, and replenishment of, inventory.

Inventory shrinkage Refers to the fact that more items are recorded entering than leaving warehousing facilities.

Inventory tax Analogous to personal property taxes paid by individuals, an inventory tax is based on the value of inventory that is held by an organization on the assessment date.

Inventory turnover The number of times an inventory is used or replaced each year.

Investment recovery Identifies opportunities to recover revenues or reduce costs associated with scrap, surplus, obsolete, and waste materials.

ISO 9000 A set of generic standards used to document, implement, and demonstrate quality management and assurance systems.

Just-in-time (JIT) approach Seeks to minimize inventory by reducing (if not eliminating) safety stock, as well as having the required amount of materials arrive at the production location at the exact time they are needed.

Judgmental forecasting Refers to forecasting that involves judgment or intuition and is preferred in situations where there is limited, or no, historical data.

Kickbacks Money paid after an exchange.

Land bridge Refers to a combination of water transportation and surface transportation between an origin and destination port.

Landed costs Price of the product at its source plus transportation costs to its destination.

Letter of credit An international payment option that is issued by a bank and guarantees payment to a seller provided that the seller has complied with the applicable terms and conditions of the particular transaction.

Line-haul Terminal-to-terminal movement of freight or passengers.

Load center A major port where thousands of containers arrive and depart per week. These ports specialize in the efficient handling of containers.

Logistics According to the Council of Supply Chain Management Professionals, that part of supply chain management that plans, implements, and controls the efficient, effective forward and reverse flow and storage of goods, services, and related information between the point of origin and the point of consumption to meet customers' requirements.

Logistics information system (LIS) People, equipment, and procedures to gather, sort, analyze, evaluate, and distribute needed, timely, and accurate information to logistics decision makers.

Logistics service provider (LSP) Companies that specialize in providing various types of logistics services.

Make-to-order Products are produced after receiving a customer order.

Make-to-stock Products are produced prior to receiving a customer order.

Malcolm Baldrige National Quality Award Established in the late 1980s to recognize U.S. organizations for their achievements in quality and performance.

Maquiladora Manufacturing plants that exist just south of the U.S.–Mexican border.

Marginal analysis Analyzing the impacts of small changes, such as adding or subtracting one unit of input.

Market strategy A strategic orientation in which a limited number of traditional logistics activities are managed across business units.

Mass logistics A one-size-fits-all approach in which every customer gets the same type and levels of logistics service.

Materials handling The short-distance movement of material between two or more points.

Materials management   Movement and storage of raw materials, parts, and components within a firm.

Maverick spending   Refers to employees who do not follow company guidelines about which suppliers to use in particular situations.

Multiclient warehousing   Mixes attributes of public and contract warehousing; services are more differentiated than a public facility but less customized than in a contract facility.

Nesting   Packaging tapered articles inside each other to reduce the cubic volume of the entire shipment.

Nodes   Fixed facilities, such as a plant, warehouse, or store, in a logistics system.

Nontariff barriers   Restrictions other than tariffs that are placed on imported products.

Nonvessel-operating common carrier (NVOCC)   In international trade, a firm that provides carrier services to shippers but owns no vessels itself.

Obsolete materials   Refer to materials that are not likely to ever be used by the organization that purchased it.

Occupational Safety and Health Administration (OSHA)   A U.S. federal agency that regulates workplaces to ensure the safety of workers.

Ocean carrier alliances   Refers to an alliance in the container trades in which ocean carriers retain their individual identities but cooperate in the area of operations.

Office automation systems   Provide effective ways to process personal and organizational business data, to perform calculations, and to create documents.

On-demand software   Refers to software that users access on a per-use basis instead of software they own or license for installation.

Opportunity costs   The cost of giving up an alternative opportunity.

Order cycle   Elapsed time between when a customer places an order and when the goods are received.

Order delivery   The time from when a transportation carrier picks up the shipment until it is received by the customer.

Order fill rate   The percentage of orders that can be completely and immediately filled from existing stock.

Order management   The management of the various activities associated with the order cycle.

Order picking and assembly   Includes all activities from when an appropriate location is authorized to fill an order until goods are loaded aboard an outbound carrier.

Order processing   The time from when the seller receives an order until an appropriate location is authorized to fill the order.

Order transmittal   The time from when the customer places or sends the order to when the seller receives it.

Order triage   Classifying orders according to preestablished guidelines so that a company can prioritize how orders should be filled.

Package testing   Simulation of the types of problems that the package will be exposed to in warehouses and in transit.

Packaging   Materials used for the containment, protection, handling, delivery, and presentation of goods.

Pallet (skid)   A small platform (made of plastic, steel, or wood) on which goods are placed for handling by mechanical means.

Paperless warehousing   Generates and uses few or no paper documents and relies on technology to accomplish the relevant tasks.

Parcel   In transportation, a small quantity or small package.

Parcel carriers   Companies that specialize in transporting parcels.

Part-to-picker system   The pick location is brought to the picker (e.g., carousels).

Partial systems analysis   Looks at a single aspect of logistics, such as a time-and-motion study of individuals who handle incoming freight at a receiving dock.

Partnerships   Positive, long-term relationships between supply chain participants.

Perfect order   An order that simultaneously achieves relevant customer metrics.

Phantom freight   Occurs in delivered pricing when a buyer pays an excessive freight charge calculated into the price of the goods.

Physical distribution   Storage of finished product and movement to the customers.

Picker-to-part system   An order picker goes to where the product is located (e.g., a forklift).

Pick-to-light technology   The orders to be picked are identified by lights placed on shelves or racks.

Piggyback transportation   Truck trailers on flatcars, also referred to as TOFC.

Pilferage   Employee theft.

Pipeline (in-transit) stock   Inventory that is in route between various nodes in a logistics system.

Place utility   Having products available where they are needed by customers.

Possession utility Refers to the value or usefulness that comes from a customer being able to take possession of a product.

Postponement The delay of value-added activities such as assembly, production, and packaging to the latest possible time.

Power retailer Retailers that are characterized by large market share and low prices.

Private carrier Companies whose primary business is other than transportation provide their own transportation service by operating truck, railcars, barges, ships, or airplanes.

Private warehousing A warehousing facility that is owned or occupied on a long-term lease by the firm using it.

Process strategy A strategic orientation in which traditional logistics activities are managed as a value-added system.

Procurement (purchasing) Raw materials, component parts, and supplies brought from outside organizations to support a company's operations.

Procurement cards (p-cards) Are similar to credit cards for personal use, only p-cards are used for organizational purchases.

Product recall Refers to a situation in which a hazard or defect is discovered in a manufactured or processed item, and its return is mandated by a government agency.

Productivity The amount of output divided by the amount of input.

Public warehousing Similar to common carriers in that public warehousing serves all legitimate users and has certain responsibilities to those users.

Pull inventory system An inventory system that responds to actual (rather than forecasted) customer demand.

Pure materials Materials that lose no weight in processing.

Push inventory system An inventory system that responds to forecasted (rather than actual) customer demand.

Quality Conformance to mutually agreed upon requirements.

Quality-of-life considerations Their intent is to incorporate nonbusiness factors (e.g., cost of living, crime rate, educational opportunities) into the decision of where to locate a plant or distribution facility.

Radio-frequency identification (RFID) The use of radio frequency to identify objects that have been implanted with an RFID tag.

Rail gauge The distance between the inner sides of two parallel rail tracks.

Reconsignment Similar to diversion, but it occurs after the shipment has arrived in the destination city.

Regrouping function Involves rearranging the quantities and assortment of products as they move through the supply chain.

Relationship management Creating, maintaining, and enhancing strong relationships with customers and other stakeholders.

Relevancy Satisfying current and emerging customer needs.

Reorder point (ROP) The level of inventory at which a replenishment order is placed.

Responsiveness The degree to which an organization can accommodate unique or unplanned customer requests.

Reverse auctions A buyer invites bids from multiple sellers, and the seller with the lowest bid is often awarded the business.

Reverse logistics Goods that flow from the consumer to the manufacturer (e.g., product recalls and product recycling).

Right-to-work laws State laws that specify that a worker does not have to join the union to work permanently at a facility.

Routing The process of determining how a shipment will be moved between consignor and consignee or between place of acceptance by the carrier and place of delivery to the consignee.

Routing guide Provides guidance in terms of a preferred list of carriers for shipments moving between two points.

Safety (buffer) stock Inventory that is held in addition to cycle stock to guard against uncertainties in supply and/or lead time.

SCOR model A framework that identifies five key processes—plan, source, make, deliver, return—associated with supply chain management.

Scrap materials These are materials that are no longer serviceable, have been discarded, or are a by-product of the production process.

Seamless distribution Refers to removing impediments to the flow of information and goods.

Service recovery A process for returning a customer to a state of satisfaction after a service or product has failed to live up to expectations.

Shippers' associations Nonprofit membership cooperatives that perform basically the same function as freight forwarders.

Shipper's export declaration (SED)   Contains relevant export transaction data such as the transportation mode(s), transaction participants, and description of what is being exported.

Shipper's letter of instruction (SLI)   Often accompanies an SED and provides explicit shipment instructions.

Shipping conferences   Cartels of all ocean vessel operators operating between certain trade areas.

Short-interval scheduling   An analysis of workers' productivity over short periods of time. Each worker is assigned specific duties that he or she should be able to complete during the time period provided.

Short sea shipping   Refers to waterborne transportation that utilizes inland and coastal waterways to move shipments from domestic ports to their destination.

Shrink-wrap   Plastic wrapping that when heated shrinks in size to form a cover over the product.

Simulation   A technique used to model the systems under study, typically using mathematical equations to represent relationships among components of a logistics system.

Six Sigma   A practice that emphasizes the virtual elimination of business errors that strives to achieve 3.4 defects, deficiencies, or errors per one million opportunities.

Slip sheet   A flat sheet of either fiberboard material or plastic that is placed under the unit load.

Slurry systems   Transport products that are ground into a powder, mixed with water, and then shipped in slurry form through a pipeline.

Socially responsible procurement   Procurement activities that meet the ethical and discretionary responsibilities expected by society.

Sorting   Separating products into grades and qualities desired by different target markets.

Speculative stock   Inventory that is held for several reasons such as seasonal demand, projected price increases, and potential product shortages.

Stock-keeping unit (SKU)   Each separate type of item that is accounted for in an inventory.

Stockout   Being out of an item at the same time there is a willing buyer for it.

Stockout cost   Costs to seller when it is unable to supply an item to a customer ready to buy.

Stowability   Refers to how easy a commodity is to pack into a load.

Substitute products   Products that customers view as being able to fill the same need or want as another product.

Supplier development (reverse marketing)   A degree of aggressive procurement involvement not normally encountered in supplier selection.

Supplier parks   Key suppliers locate on, or adjacent to, automobile plants, which helps reduce shipping costs and inventory carrying costs.

Supply chain   All activities associated with the flow and transformation of goods from the raw material stage, through to the end user, as well as the associated information flows.

Supply chain collaboration   Cooperative, formal or informal supply chain relationships between manufacturing companies and their suppliers, business partners, or customers, developed to enhance the overall business performance of both sides.

Supply chain management (SCM)   According to the Council of Supply Chain Management Professionals, SCM encompasses the planning and management of all activities involved in sourcing and procurement, conversion, and all logistics management activities. Importantly, it also includes coordination and collaboration with channel partners, which can be suppliers, intermediaries, third-party service providers, and customers. In essence, supply chain management integrates supply and demand management within and across companies.

Supply management   A relational exchange approach involving a limited number of suppliers.

Surface Transportation Board (STB)   A U.S. government agency with primary responsibility for regulating railroad pricing and service.

Sweatshops   Organizations that exploit workers and that do not comply with fiscal and legal obligations toward employees.

Systems analysis   The orderly and planned observation of one or more segments in the logistics network or supply chain.

Systems approach   A company's objectives can be realized by recognizing the mutual interdependence of the major functional areas of the firm, such as marketing, production, finance, and logistics.

System constraints   Factors in the system that cannot be changed for various reasons.

System security   Refers to security throughout the entire supply chain.

Tailored logistics   Groups of customers with similar logistical needs and wants are provided with logistics service appropriate to those needs and wants.

Tariffs   Taxes that governments place on the importation of certain items.

TEU   Twenty-foot equivalent unit; a measure of the number of 20-foot containers that are used or handled.

Terminal   A carrier or public facility where freight (or passengers) is shifted between vehicles or modes.

Terms of payment   Refer to the manner by which a seller will be paid by a buyer for an international transaction.

Terms of sale   For international transactions, refers to determining when and where to transfer between buyer and seller, the physical goods, the payment for goods, legal title, required documentation as well as responsibility for controlling and caring for goods while in transit.

Theft (stealing)   Taking and removing personal property with the intent to deprive the rightful owner of it.

Third-party logistics (logistics outsourcing)   A long-term arrangement between a shipper and another party to provide logistics services that is characterized by a relational focus, a focus on mutual benefits, and the availability of customized offerings.

Throughput   Refers to the amount of product entering and leaving a facility in a given time period.

Time series forecasting   A group of forecasting techniques that is based on the idea that future demand is solely dependent on past demand.

Time utility   Having products available when they are needed by customers.

TOFC (trailer on flatcar)   Piggyback traffic, or loading truck trailers onto rail flatcars.

Ton miles   The number of tons times the number of miles.

Total cost approach   Concept that suggests that all relevant activities in moving and storing products should be considered as a whole (i.e., their total cost), not individually.

Tracing   A carrier's attempt to determine a shipment's location during the course of its move.

Transaction processing system   Collects and stores information about transactions and may also control some aspects of transactions.

Transit time   The elapsed time from when an order is picked up by a transportation carrier until it is received by the customer.

Transponders   A small device that responds to radio signals from an outside source.

Transportation   Actual physical movement of goods and people between two points.

Transportation management   The buying and controlling of transportation services by either a shipper or consignee.

Transportation Worker Identification Credential (TWIC)   A common credential that will be used to identify workers across all modes of transportation.

Unified logistics structure   Multiple logistics activities are combined into, and managed as, a single department.

Unitization   The term associated with the handling of unit loads.

Unit load   Boxes or other containers secured to a pallet or slip sheet.

Unit load devices   An alternative name for airfreight containers.

Variable slot location   A system in which products are stored wherever there is empty space available in a warehouse.

Vendor-managed inventory (VMI)   A system in which the size and timing of replenishment orders into a retailer's system are the manufacturer's responsibility.

Voice-based order picking   The use of speech to guide order-picking activities.

Warehouse   Emphasize the storage of products and their primary purpose is to maximize usage of available storage space.

Warehouse management systems (WMS)   Software packages that control the movement and storage of materials within a warehousing facility.

Warehousing   That part of a firm's logistics system that stores products at and between points of origin and point of consumption.

Waste materials   These are materials that have been spoiled, broken, or otherwise rendered unfit for further use or reclamation.

Weighing out   Cargo reaches a vehicle's or a container's weight capacity without filling its cubic capacity.

Weight break   The shipment size that equates transportation charges for different rates and weight groups.

Weighted center-of-gravity approach   Similar to the center-of-gravity locational approach, excepting that shipping volumes are also taken into account.

Weight-gaining product characteristics   A product that gains weight in processing; the processing point should be close to the market.

Weight-losing product characteristics   A product that loses weight during the production process; the processing point as near to its origin as possible.

Wireless communication   Refers to communication without cables and cords, and includes infrared, microwave, and radio transmissions.

Subject Index

Name Index